THE PAPERS OF ULYSSES S. GRANT

THE PAPERS OF

ULYSSES S. GRANT

Volume 4: January 8 – March 31, 1862

Edited by John Y. Simon

ASSISTANT EDITOR

Roger D. Bridges

SOUTHERN ILLINOIS UNIVERSITY PRESS

CARBONDALE AND EDWARDSVILLE

FEFFER & SIMONS, INC.

LONDON AND AMSTERDAM

77017

To Lloyd Lewis (1891–1949)

Contents

Maps and Illustrations

===

MAPS

ILLUSTRATIONS

Frontispiece

Introduction

═══

ON JANUARY 8, 1862, Brigadier General Ulysses S. Grant, at Cairo, Illinois, received instructions from his commanding officer, Major General Henry W. Halleck, to demonstrate with his army in Kentucky. "Make a great fuss," wrote Halleck; "be very careful however to avoid a battle." Although the object of the subsequent demonstration was to keep the Confederates so wary of attack by Grant's forces that they would neglect to detach additional men for central Kentucky, reconnaissance developed evidence of the weak link in the Confederate line at Fort Henry on the Tennessee River.

On his return from Kentucky, Grant lost no time in leaving for St. Louis to ask Halleck for permission to move against Fort Henry. After some hesitation, Halleck gave permission, and Grant immediately mounted his expedition. Fort Henry fell easily to a gunboat attack when the Confederates decided to concentrate their forces eleven miles east at Fort Donelson, commanding the Cumberland River. As soon as Fort Henry surrendered, Grant began to plan his move toward Fort Donelson. Of all the messages between Grant and Halleck in this period, none is more intriguing than one never sent. "General Halleck did not approve or disapprove of my going to Fort Donelson," Grant recalled. "He said nothing whatever to me on the subject."

With the capture of an entire Confederate army at Fort Donelson after three days of battle, Grant won the first major Union victory of the Civil War. His demand for "unconditional surrender" gave him national acclaim and a promotion to major general. The victory had resounding impact as the Confederate line cracked, putting virtually half of Tennessee in U.S. possession.

Yet Grant's sudden rise to fame was nearly fatal to his military career. Both Halleck and Major General George B. McClellan,

xiii

general-in-chief, doubted that Grant could be entrusted with command of an important army. As soon as Charles F. Smith was nominated as major general, Halleck gave him command of the forces advancing on the Tennessee River, while Grant was ordered to remain at Fort Henry. "It may be all right but I dont now see it," wrote Grant. In order to justify the shift of commanders Halleck thought it necessary to send a flurry of charges to Washington concerning alleged misconduct by Grant after the victory at Fort Donelson.

The completeness of the victory had brought problems as well as glory. "I fear they will prove an Elephant," wrote Grant as he sent an entire captured army northward. Meanwhile, discipline deteriorated in the victorious army as soldiers appropriated spoils as trophies of battle. Government policy at that time neither fully protected nor condemned slavery, and this placed military commanders in awkward positions—none more so than Grant, who had plunged deep into the heartland of slavery. Thus Grant was tested both as commander and as military administrator. His close attention to the details of his district is nowhere more apparent than in the fact that he continued to draft personally many of the orders signed by his adjutant.

Perhaps some of the charges Halleck made were rooted in honest misunderstanding and communications failure; yet there is also evidence that Halleck only pretended friendship with Grant. Actually, Grant's command was threatened on three levels, with the displeasure of his superior officer representing only one danger. Ambitious officers close to Grant in rank, especially Brigadier General John A. McClernand, looked forward to leading victorious armies southward. Thirdly, some junior officers were bent on vengeance, especially two quartermaster captains, Reuben B. Hatch, arrested on suspicion of corruption, and William J. Kountz, arrested for disobedience of orders. Kountz filed charges of misconduct involving drinking against Grant which followed him for many years. Because of the importance of this theme in the Grant story, considerable documentation has been gathered to supplement the note to Grant's endorsement to Kountz, January 29, 1862.

By the middle of March, Grant had cleared up most of his difficulties with Halleck, left his detractors in Cairo behind him, recovered from several weeks of poor health, and had taken command of a large army on the Tennessee River poised to strike at the lower South. With confidence restored, Grant planned to link his army with the Army of the

Ohio under Major General Don Carlos Buell and to lead the combined force against the main Confederate army at Corinth, a major railroad center in northern Mississippi. Grant moved to Savannah, Tennessee, a convenient point for meeting Buell, nine miles upriver from the main body of his troops at Pittsburg Landing. With plans for an offensive uppermost in his mind, he gave little thought to any possible attack by the enemy. When a Confederate army smashed through U.S. lines at Shiloh early in April, driving the troops back upon Pittsburg Landing, Grant was put to the greatest test yet of his generalship and personal resiliency.

We are indebted to C. Percy Powell and Karl L. Trever for searching the National Archives; to Barbara Long for maps; to Kathryn Overturf and Harriet Simon for typing; to Stephen L. Bell and Marcia Swider, graduate students at Southern Illinois University, for research assistance; and to Thomas G. Alexander, holder of a fellowship in advanced historical editing from the National Historical Publications Commission, for editorial assistance.

In addition to renewing our thanks to those people whose assistance has been acknowledged in previous volumes, we wish to express our gratitude to: Leona T. Alig, Indiana Historical Society; James R. Bentley, The Filson Club; Dr. John T. Bickmore, Dayton, Ohio; Roger Bruns, National Historical Publications Commission; H. Bartholomew Cox, National Historical Publications Commission; Caroline Dunn, Indiana Historical Society; Chad J. Flake, Brigham Young University; John D. Kilbourne, Historical Society of Pennsylvania; Lynda Lasswell, The Papers of Jefferson Davis; Kermit J. Pike, Western Reserve Historical Society; James S. Schoff, New York City; John Barr Tompkins, Bancroft Library; Frank E. Vandiver, Rice University; and Maxwell Whiteman, Philadelphia, Pa. Financial support for the Ulysses S. Grant Association for the period during which this volume was prepared came from Southern Illinois University and the National Historical Publications Commission.

JOHN Y. SIMON

January 18, 1971

Editorial Procedure

1. Editorial Insertions

A. Words or letters in roman type within brackets represent editorial reconstruction of parts of manuscripts torn, mutiliated, or illegible.

B. [...] or [— — —] within brackets represent lost material which cannot be reconstructed. The number of dots represents the approximate number of lost letters; dashes represent lost words.

C. Words in *italic* type within brackets represent material such as dates which were not part of the original manuscript.

D. Other material crossed out is indicated by ~~cancelled type~~.

E. Material raised in manuscript, as "4th," has been brought in line, as "4th."

2. Symbols Used to Describe Manuscripts

AD	Autograph Document
ADS	Autograph Document Signed
ADf	Autograph Draft
ADfS	Autograph Draft Signed
AES	Autograph Endorsement Signed
AL	Autograph Letter
ALS	Autograph Letter Signed
D	Document
DS	Document Signed
Df	Draft
DfS	Draft Signed

ES	Endorsement Signed
LS	Letter Signed

3. *Military Terms and Abbreviations*

Act.	Acting
Adjt.	Adjutant
AG	Adjutant General
AGO	Adjutant General's Office
Art.	Artillery
Asst.	Assistant
Bvt.	Brevet
Brig.	Brigadier
Capt.	Captain
Cav.	Cavalry
Col.	Colonel
Co.	Company
C.S.A.	Confederate States of America
Dept.	Department
Gen.	General
Hd. Qrs.	Headquarters
Inf.	Infantry
Lt.	Lieutenant
Maj.	Major
Q. M.	Quartermaster
Regt.	Regiment or regimental
Sgt.	Sergeant
USMA	United States Military Academy, West Point, N. Y.
Vols.	Volunteers

4. *Short Titles and Abbreviations*

ABPC	*American Book-Prices Current* (New York, 1895–)
CG	*Congressional Globe* Numbers following represent the Congress, session, and page.
J. G. Cramer	Jesse Grant Cramer, ed., *Letters of Ulysses S. Grant to his Father and his Youngest Sister, 1857–78* (New York and London, 1912)
DAB	*Dictionary of American Biography* (New York, 1928–36)

Garland	Hamlin Garland, *Ulysses S. Grant: His Life and Character* (New York, 1898)
HED	*House Executive Documents*
HMD	*House Miscellaneous Documents*
HRC	*House Reports of Committees* Numbers following *HED, HMD,* or *HRC* represent the number of the Congress, the session, and the document.
Ill. AG Report	J. N. Reece, ed., *Report of the Adjutant General of the State of Illinois* (Springfield, 1900)
Lewis	Lloyd Lewis, *Captain Sam Grant* (Boston, 1950)
Lincoln, Works	Roy P. Basler, Marion Dolores Pratt, and Lloyd A. Dunlap, eds., *The Collected Works of Abraham Lincoln* (New Brunswick, 1953–55)
Memoirs	*Personal Memoirs of U. S. Grant* (New York, 1885–86)
O.R.	*The War of the Rebellion: A Compilation of the Official Records of the Union and Confederate Armies* (Washington, 1880–1901)
O.R. (Navy)	*Official Records of the Union and Confederate Navies in the War of the Rebellion* (Washington, 1894–1927) Roman numerals following *O. R.* or *O. R.* (Navy) represent the series and the volume.
PUSG	John Y. Simon, ed., *The Papers of Ulysses S. Grant* (Carbondale and Edwardsville, 1967—)
Richardson	Albert D. Richardson, *A Personal History of Ulysses S. Grant* (Hartford, Conn., 1868)
SED	*Senate Executive Documents*
SMD	*Senate Miscellaneous Documents*
SRC	*Senate Reports of Committees* Numbers following *SED, SMD,* or *SRC* represent the number of the Congress, the session, and the document.
USGA Newsletter	*Ulysses S. Grant Association Newsletter*
Young	John Russell Young, *Around the World with General Grant* (New York, 1879)

5. Location Symbols

CSmH	Henry E. Huntington Library, San Marino, Calif.
CU-B	Bancroft Library, University of California, Berkeley, Calif.

DLC	Library of Congress, Washington, D.C. Numbers following DLC-USG represent the series and volume of military records in the USG papers.
DNA	National Archives, Washington, D.C. Additional numbers identify record groups.
IaHA	Iowa State Department of History and Archives, Des Moines, Iowa
I-ar	Illinois State Archives, Springfield, Ill.
IC	Chicago Public Library, Chicago, Ill.
ICarbS	Southern Illinois University, Carbondale, Ill.
ICHi	Chicago Historical Society, Chicago, Ill.
ICN	Newberry Library, Chicago, Ill.
IHi	Illinois State Historical Library, Springfield, Ill.
InHi	Indiana Historical Society, Indianapolis, Ind.
InNd	University of Notre Dame, Notre Dame, Ind.
InU	Indiana University, Bloomington, Ind.
KHi	Kansas State Historical Society, Topeka, Kan.
MH	Harvard University, Cambridge, Mass.
MHi	Massachusetts Historical Society, Boston, Mass.
MiD	Detroit Public Library, Detroit, Mich.
MiU-C	William L. Clements Library, University of Michigan, Ann Arbor, Mich.
MoSHi	Missouri Historical Society, St. Louis, Mo.
NHi	New-York Historical Society, New York, N.Y.
NjP	Princeton University, Princeton, N.J.
NjR	Rutgers University, New Brunswick, N.J.
NN	New York Public Library, New York, N.Y.
OClWHi	Western Reserve Historical Society, Cleveland, Ohio.
OFH	Rutherford B. Hayes Library, Fremont, Ohio.
OHi	Ohio Historical Society, Columbus, Ohio.
OrHi	Oregon Historical Society, Portland, Ore.
PHi	Historical Society of Pennsylvania, Philadelphia, Pa.
PPRF	Rosenbach Foundation, Philadelphia, Pa.
RPB	Brown University, Providence, R.I.
TxHR	Rice University, Houston, Tex.
USG 3	Maj. Gen. Ulysses S. Grant 3rd, Clinton, N.Y.

USMA	United States Military Academy Library, West Point, N.Y.
ViU	University of Virginia, Charlottesville, Va.
WHi	State Historical Society of Wisconsin, Madison, Wis.

Chronology

═══

JAN. 8.   USG received orders from Maj. Gen. Henry W. Halleck to prepare a reconnaissance into Ky.

JAN. 8.   USG ordered Brig. Gen. John A. McClernand at Cairo, Ill., Brig. Gen. Eleazer A. Paine at Bird's Point, Mo., and Col. John Cook at Fort Holt, Ky., to advance to Fort Jefferson, Ky., on the following day. USG also ordered Brig. Gen. Charles F. Smith at Paducah, Ky., to advance on Mayfield, Ky., starting Jan. 10.

JAN. 9.   Dense fog and a stranded steamboat delayed the start of USG's reconnaissance.

JAN. 10.   USG's forces occupied Fort Jefferson.

JAN. 11.   After four of his pickets were shot near Bird's Point, USG ordered all citizens within six miles of the post put under guard at Bird's Point.

JAN. 11.   Three C.S.A. gunboats reconnoitering close to Fort Jefferson were chased back to Columbus, Ky., by two U.S. gunboats.

JAN. 12.   USG ordered the arrest of his former q.m., Capt. Reuben B. Hatch, who was suspected of fraud.

JAN. 13.   USG's forces reconnoitered within three miles of Columbus.

JAN. 14.   On board a gunboat, USG reconnoitered close to Columbus.

JAN. 14. USG ordered the arrest of Capt. William J. Kountz, in charge of water transportation at Cairo, for disobeying orders.

JAN. 14. USG's forces advanced from Fort Jefferson to Blandville, Ky.

JAN. 15. USG joined his forces in Ky.

JAN. 18. USG ordered his forces in Ky. to return to Cairo and vicinity. All were back on Jan. 21.

JAN. 19. U.S. victory at Logan's Cross-Roads, near Mill Springs, Ky., cracked the C.S.A. defense line.

JAN. 22. Smith reported to USG that his reconnaissance convinced him that two gunboats could capture Fort Henry, Tenn.

JAN. 23. USG left Cairo for St. Louis to ask Halleck for permission for a Tennessee River campaign.

JAN. 28. USG returned to Cairo and telegraphed to Halleck for permission to attack Fort Henry.

JAN. 30. Halleck gave USG permission to attack Fort Henry.

FEB. 2. USG's expedition left Cairo.

FEB. 4. USG's advance forces landed near Fort Henry.

FEB. 4. On board the gunboat *Essex*, USG steamed within a mile of Fort Henry "to ascertain the range of the rebel guns."

FEB. 5. USG brought additional troops from Paducah to near Fort Henry.

FEB. 6. C.S.A. Brig. Gen. Lloyd Tilghman, at nearly evacuated Fort Henry, surrendered to Flag Officer Andrew H. Foote before USG's troops arrived.

FEB. 6. USG occupied Fort Henry and prepared to advance to Fort Donelson, Tenn.

FEB. 7. USG sent a gunboat to destroy a railroad bridge eleven miles upriver from Fort Henry. USG inspected the site on the following day.

FEB. 7. USG's cav. reconnoitered within a mile of Fort Donelson.

FEB. 8. A U.S. gunboat fleet on the Tennessee River reached Florence, Ala.

FEB. 9. USG accompanied a cav. reconnaissance toward Fort Donelson.

FEB. 9. C.S.A. Brig. Gen. Gideon J. Pillow assumed command of Fort Donelson.

FEB. 10. USG held a council of war which reached the unanimous decision to move on Fort Donelson at once.

FEB. 12. USG marched most of his army from Fort Henry to begin the siege of Fort Donelson.

FEB. 13. C.S.A. Brig. Gen. John Floyd assumed command at Fort Donelson.

FEB. 13. USG began to attack Fort Donelson.

FEB. 14. Five U.S. gunboats arrived to join the attack on Fort Donelson.

FEB. 14. USG was assigned command of the District of West Tenn. Brig. Gen. William T. Sherman replaced USG in command of the District of Cairo.

FEB. 14. U.S. gunboats attacked Fort Donelson unsuccessfully.

FEB. 15. While USG conferred with Foote, C.S.A. forces attacked the U.S. right at Fort Donelson with some success, but then retired. USG launched a counterattack on the left which convinced C.S.A. commanders that their position was hopeless.

FEB. 16. In the early morning hours Floyd relinquished command of Fort Donelson to Pillow, who passed it on to Brig. Gen. Simon B. Buckner. As Floyd and Pillow fled, Buckner asked USG for "terms of capitulation." USG demanded and received the "unconditional and immediate surrender" of Fort Donelson.

FEB. 19. Clarksville, Tenn., surrendered to two U.S. gunboats.

F EB. 19. USG was promoted to maj. gen. to rank from Feb. 16.

F EB. 20. USG visited Clarksville.

F EB. 23. USG again visited Clarksville, returning to Fort Donelson the following day.

F EB. 24. Brig. Gen. William Nelson with a division of troops arrived at Clarksville by boat. USG immediately sent him on to Nashville, Tenn.

F EB. 25. Nashville was occupied by U.S. forces.

F EB. 27. USG spent the day at Nashville, returning to Fort Donelson the following morning.

M AR. 1. Halleck ordered USG to advance on the Tennessee River to destroy a railroad bridge near Eastport, Miss., and railroad connections at Corinth, Miss., Jackson and Humboldt, Tenn.

M AR. 2. C.S.A. forces evacuated Columbus.

M AR. 3. President Abraham Lincoln nominated McClernand, Smith, and Lewis Wallace as maj. gens.; John Cook, Richard J. Oglesby, William H. L. Wallace, John McArthur, Jacob G. Lauman, and John A. Logan as brig. gens. The appointments were confirmed on March 21.

M AR. 3. Maj. Gen. George B. McClellan responded to Halleck's complaints against USG by authorizing his arrest.

M AR. 4. Halleck ordered USG to remain at Fort Henry and to place Smith in charge of the Tennessee River advance. He accused USG of disobeying orders by failing to report regularly.

M AR. 5. C.S.A. Gen. P. G. T. Beauregard assumed command of the Army of the Miss.

M AR. 6–8. U.S. forces won a victory at the battle of Pea Ridge or Elkhorn Tavern, Ark.

M AR. 7. USG asked Halleck to be relieved from further duty in his dept.

MAR. 9. USG again asked to be relieved.

MAR. 9. The *Monitor* and *Merrimack* fought at Hampton Roads, Va.

MAR. 10. Halleck informed USG that he could take general direction of the Tennessee River expedition.

MAR. 11. The Dept. of the Miss. was created by merging the Dept. of the Mo. and part of the Dept. of the Ohio. Halleck assumed command on March 13.

MAR. 11. McClellan was relieved as general-in-chief while retaining command of the Army of the Potomac.

MAR. 11. Smith occupied Savannah, Tenn.

MAR. 12. One battalion of USG's cav. skirmished at Paris, Tenn.

MAR. 12. Smith sent Brig. Gen. Lewis Wallace's division to Crump's Landing, Tenn.

MAR. 13. For the third time USG asked to be relieved.

MAR. 13. Halleck asked USG to resume command.

MAR. 14. USG agreed to resume command.

MAR. 14. New Madrid, Mo., fell to U.S. forces.

MAR. 15. Sherman's division occupied Pittsburg Landing, Tenn.

MAR. 17. USG arrived at Savannah and began to move his troops forward to Pittsburg Landing.

MAR. 19. USG inspected encampments at Crump's Landing and Pittsburg Landing.

MAR. 21. USG inspected the encampment at Pittsburg Landing.

MAR. 29. C.S.A. armies of Ky. and Miss. were consolidated as Army of the Miss. with Gen. Albert Sidney Johnston in command, Beauregard second in command.

MAR. 31. Hd. qrs. of the District of West Tenn. were officially transferred from Savannah to Pittsburg Landing, although USG remained at Savannah to await the arrival of the Army of the Ohio under Maj. Gen. Don Carlos Buell.

The Papers of Ulysses S. Grant
January 8 – March 31, 1862

To Maj. Gen. Henry W. Halleck

———

Head Quarters, Dist. of Cairo,
Cairo, Jan.y 8th 1862.

MAJ. GEN. H. W. HALLECK
COMD.G DEPT. OF THE MO.
ST. LOUIS, MO.
GEN.

Your instructions of the 6th were received this morning and immediate preparations made for carrying them out. Commodore Foote will be able to coopperate here with three Gunboats. Two others will go up the Tennessee with a transport accompanying, having on board a battalion of Inf.y and one section of Artillery. Gen. Smith will move upon Mayfield, and the Cavalry from here, and probably two Regts. of Infantry, will effect a junction with him there. From this point I have instructed Gen. Smith to threaten Camp Beaurigard & Murray,[1] but in such a way as to make it appear that the latter, and probably Dover,[2] are the points in the greatest danger.—Gen. Smith is informed that reinforcements are to arrive from St. Louis, and that I will occupy the ground from Fort Jefferson to Blandville, and cut off all probability of an attempt to get on his flank, or in his rear, from Columbus. The continuous rains for the last week or more has rendered the roads extremely bad and will necessarily make our movements slow. This however will opperate worse upon the enemy, if they should he should he come out to meet us, than the enemy upon us.

I will probably send two steamers to a point below island No 1 where there is a bottom road leading directly to Columbus, and one leading into the back country, intersecting other roads leading to the same place. The troops on these steamers will be fully protected by the Gunboats and will not go far from their transports.

I have not prepared instructions for the troops moving from this place as I will be along and may have to vary from any plan that could now be drawn up.

This movement will commence to-morrow, and every effort will be made to carry out all your designs.

> I am Gen.
> Very respectfully
> Your Obt. Svt.
> U. S. Grant
> Brig. Gen.

ALS, DNA, RG 393, Dept. of the Mo., Letters Received. *O.R.*, I, vii, 537–38. On Jan. 6, 1862, Maj. Gen. Henry W. Halleck wrote to USG. "I wish you to make a demonstration in force on Mayfield, & in the direction of Murray—Forces from Paducah & Fort Holt should meet it at Mayfield & threa[ten] Camp Beauregard & Murray, letting it be understood that Dover is the object of your attack. But dont advance far enough to expose your flank or rear, to an attack from Columbus, & by all means avoid a serious engagement—Make a great fuss about moving *all* your forces towards Nashville, & let it be so reported by the newspapers. Take proper precautions to deceive your own men as well as the enemy—Let no one, not even a member of your own staff, know the real object—I will send you some forces from this place to increase the deception—Let it be understood that 20 or 30 thousand men are expected from Missouri & that your force is merely the advanced guard to the main column of attack—The object is to prevent reinforcements from being sent to Buckner—Having accomplished this, you will slowly retire to your former positions, but, if possible keep up the idea of a general advance. Be very careful however to avoid a battle. We are not ready for that—But cut off detached parties & give your men a little experience in skirmishing. If Com. Foote can make a gunboat demonstration at the same time, it will assist in carrying out the deception" LS, DNA, RG 393, Dept. of the Mo., Telegrams Received. *O.R.*, I, vii, 533–34.

In accordance with Halleck's instructions, misleading newspaper dispatches from Cairo soon appeared. On Jan. 18, correspondent Charles C. Coffin, Cairo, wrote to Mass. Senator Henry Wilson. "The despatches were dictated by General Grant himself." ALS, DNA, RG 107, Letters Received. On Jan. 12, Capt. William S. Hillyer wrote to Brig. Gen. John A. McClernand. "Gen Grant thin[ks] it would *do no harm* if the accompanying copy of the Chicago Tribune could fall into the hands of the enemy at Columbus—Can you manage to have it so disposed of" ALS, McClernand Papers, IHi.

1. Murray, Ky., about thirty-seven miles southeast of Paducah.
2. Dover, Tenn., on the Cumberland River near Fort Donelson. USG, following Halleck, was probably referring to Fort Donelson itself, about which U.S. Army officers had little information.

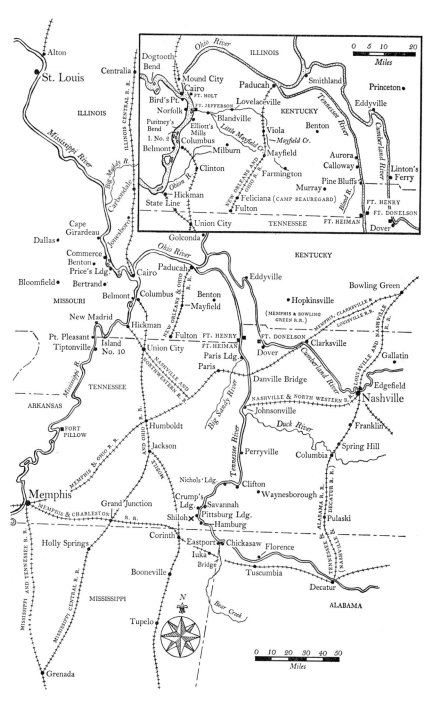

Grant's Area of Operations in early 1862

To Flag Officer Andrew H. Foote

———

Head Quarters, Dist of Cairo
Cairo, Jany 8th 1862.

COM. A. H. FOOTE
COMMDG "G" "B." FLOTILLA
CAIRO, ILLS.

Will you please cause the following names of your command to be detailed as attendants at Mound City Hospital: Wm May, J. L. Erickson, M. Demming of "G" "B" Lexington. These men are now at the Mound City Hospital.

I am, Sir, Very Respectfully
Your Obt Servant
U S GRANT
Brig. Genl. Commdg.

Copies, DLC-USG, V, 1, 2, 3, 85; DNA, RG 393, USG Letters Sent.

To Brig. Gen. John A. McClernand

———

Head Quarters, Dist. of Cairo,
Cairo, Jan.y 8th 1862.

GEN. J. A. MCCLERNAND
COMDG CAIRO, ILL.
GEN.

Will you please send by bearer the sketch of Columbus left by Mr. Stoufer at your Head Quarters.

I am anxious to have the map in the hands of the Engineer completed as early as possible.

Respectfully
Your Obt. Svt.
U. S. GRANT
Brig. Gen Com

ALS, McClernand Papers, IHi.

To Brig. Gen. John A. McClernand

Head Quarters, Dist of Cairo
Cairo, Ills. Jany 8th 1862.

GENL. J. A. MCCLERNAND
COMMDG. CAIRO, ILLS.
GENERAL:

You will hold your entire command, with the exception of one Company at Mound City, the Sick and disabled, unarmed Cavalry, and a small guard, say 300 men, in readiness to move tomorrow by 12 O'clock on Steamers.

Sufficient Tents, Camp and Garrison Equipage and transportation, with five days supplies will be taken along. I shall be very busy to-day, and night also, but will have a conference with you at early candle light, at your office if convenient for you.

Respectfully
Your Obt. Servant.
U. S. GRANT.
Brig. Genl. Commdg.

Copies, DLC-USG, V, 1, 2, 3, 85; DNA, RG 393, USG Letters Sent. On Jan. 8, 1862, Capt. John A. Rawlins wrote to Capt. William J. Kountz. "You will provide and have in readiness, at this place, by tomorrow morning, the 9th inst. at 9 O'clock, A. M. River Transportation for at least six thousand (6000) Infantry, and one thousand Cavalry (1000) with their Equipments and land transportation." Copies, *ibid.* On the same day, Rawlins wrote again to Kountz. "You will have Steamer, Coal, Co. after making one trip to Bird's Point and Fort Holt tomorrow evening.—Hold herself in readiness to take on Board the Baggage of two companies of Cavalry, and proceed to Mound City, after which he will take on board the Regiment of Infantry at that place, and bring them to this place." Copies, DLC-USG, V, 2, 85; DNA, RG 393, USG Letters Sent.

To Brig. Gen. John A. McClernand

———

Head Quarters, Dist. of Cairo
Cairo, Jan.y 8th 1862

GEN. J. A. McCLERNAND
COMD.G CAIRO ILL.
GEN.

As soon as ready for the move your Command will proceed to Fort Jefferson & encamp for the night.

The Cavalry, Artillery & transport Wagons, (empty) will land at Fort Holt and will proceed from that point to Fort Jefferson.

The Ammunition may be divided, if necessary, among the accompanying wagons sufficiently to lighten the pieces & Caissons to make their transportation practicable.

On the arrival of troops from Birds Point, at Fort Jefferson, to-morrow morning, the advance will be moved to Elliotts Mills.

The arrangement of Guards is left with the Commander of the advance.

By Order
U. S. GRANT
Brig. Gen. Com.

ALS, McClernand Papers, IHi. The date of this letter can be read as either Jan. 8 or 9, 1862. This letter is entered in the USG letterbooks as orders dated Jan. 9 issued by Capt. John A. Rawlins. Copies, DLC-USG, V, 1, 2, 3, 85; DNA, RG 393, USG Letters Sent. *O.R.*, I, vii, 541. The entry in the register of letters received by Brig. Gen. John A. McClernand indicates that the same message was received on Jan. 8 and 9. McClernand Papers, IHi.

On Jan. 9, McClernand wrote to USG. "Genl. McClernand desires to know of Genl. Grant, that as a matter of precaution, would it not be better to have a Gun boat to go as Convoy to the transports." *Ibid.* On Jan. 10, USG returned McClernand's letter with an endorsement. "The directions were given for Gun boats to keep below the transports all the time. Your moving will be the signal for them to start." *Ibid.*

Maj. Gen. John A. McClernand. McClernand, and the eight other officers whose pictures follow, received promotions in the U.S. Army for their services at Fort Donelson.
Courtesy Illinois State Historical Library.

Maj. Gen. Charles F. Smith.
Courtesy National Archives.

Maj. Gen. Lewis Wallace.
Courtesy Indiana Historical Society.

Brig. Gen. John Cook.
Courtesy Illinois State Historical Library.

Brig. Gen. Jacob G. Lauman.
Courtesy Illinois State Historical Library.

Brig. Gen. John A. Logan.
Courtesy Illinois State Historical Library.

Brig. Gen. John McArthur.
Courtesy Illinois State Historical Library.

Brig. Gen. Richard J. Oglesby.
Courtesy Illinois State Historical Library.

Brig. Gen. William H. L. Wallace.
Courtesy Illinois State Historical Library.

The gunboat attack on Fort Donelson. Sketched by Alexander Simplot. *Harper's Weekly, March 15, 1862.*

Batteries at Fort Donelson. Sketched by Alexander Simplot.
Harper's Weekly, March 22, 1862.

To Brig. Gen. Eleazer A. Paine

Head Quarters, Dist of Cairo
Cairo, Jany 8th, 1862

Gen. E. A. Paine
Commdg Bird's Point, Mo.
General:

Hold your Command, with the exception of the sick and disabled men, four companies of Cavalry, one Regiment of Infantry, Men for the siege Guns, two Sections of Artillery, and such others, as are not well armed, in readiness to move by 12 O'clock A. M. tomorrow.

Sufficient Tents, Camp and Garrison Equipage, transportation and rations will be taken for five days. If more rations should be required in your absence, an agreement will be made, for forwarding them from here.

Every man should have his Cartridge box filled, and a supply of at least twenty rounds, should also be carried in Wagons.

You will leave Bird's Point by Boat, and as all your force will be required, send immediately for such troops as you now have not.

Give no intimation of the direction you expect to move, to any one, not even your Staff.

Respectfully,
U. S. Grant.
Brig. Genl. Commdg.

Copies, DLC-USG, V, 1, 2, 3, 85; DNA, RG 393, USG Letters Sent.

To Brig. Gen. Charles F. Smith

———

Head Quarters, Dist. of Cairo,
Cairo, Jan.y 8th 1862.

GEN. C. F. SMITH
COMD.G U. S. FORCES
PADUCAH, KY.
GEN.

In pursuance of instructions from Head Quarters of the Department you will hold as much of your force in readiness to move by to-morrow night as, in your judgement, it will be safe to withdraw from Paducah, taking into account the fact that the force moving, as well as a very large one from here, will be between you and the enemy.

Five days rations will be taken, with every facility for drawing further supplies from the post if it should prove necessary.

I will detail to you the plan of Gen. Hallack to-morrow, and send such orders as may be necessary.

As troops are to be sent from St. Louis to carry out the design of Gen. Hallack it is not probable that the movement can be commenced before Friday morning.[1]

Respectfully
Your Obt. Svt.
U. S. GRANT
Brig. Gen. Com.

ALS, James S. Schoff, New York, N. Y. On Jan. 8, 1862, Brig. Gen. Charles F. Smith telegraphed to USG. "Lieut Goodell, thirteth Ill regiment commanding a camp opposite caseyville has expressed to me much alarm Lest a party of Rebel cavalry three hundred he says cross over & attack him   I have sent the conestoga I know nothing of this command   it is not under my orders   I recommended him to write to his commanding officer" Telegram received, DNA, RG 393, Dept. of the Mo., Telegrams Received. On Jan. 11, Lt. S. Ledyard Phelps wrote to Flag Officer Andrew H. Foote. "Last night I returned from a trip up the Ohio to Caseyville, Ky; having gone to look after a detachment of men, at Rock Quarry opposite Carrsville Ky. This detachment was threatened by attack from the Rebels. We were detained on the [. .] by fog and on the 10th returned. Before day on the 10th I found a steamer landing freight at an unusual landing in the shoot of Hurricane

Island Ky and also found another backing out from the landing at Ford's Ferry. While steamers are licensed to make such landings there is no hope of stopping smuggling and rebel lines of communications I have to day been up the Tennessee River in the Lexington as far as seven mile Island to ascertain about the stage of water. If not navigable it would have been useless to detach a force from this post with a view to a demonstration in that direction by water. There is a small rise since my last trip up and any of the Gun Boats can now navigate the river. The stage of the Cumberland is more important. On it lies Nashville" Copy, *ibid.*, District of Cairo, Letters Received. *O.R.* (Navy), I, xxii, 497. On Jan. 12, USG endorsed this letter. "Respectfully forwarded to Head Quarters Dept of the Mo" ES, DNA, RG 393, District of Cairo, Letters Received.

1. Jan. 10.

To Brig. Gen. Charles F. Smith

Head Quarters, Dist. of Cairo
Cairo, Jan.y 8th 1862.

GEN. C. F. SMITH
COMD.G U. S. FORCES
PADUCAH, KY.
GEN.

With the forces indicated in my communication of this morning, and to carry out the instructions of Maj. Gen. Halleck, you will move slowly upon Mayfield, leaving Paducah on Friday.[1] Some of the force from here will start on the same day and will reach Mayfield about the same time.

The force to join you there will be principally Cavalry. If the roads are not impracticable two Regiments of Infantry will be sent. From Mayfield threaten Camp Beaurigard & Murray, but so as to have it understood that Dover is the object of attack. But dont advance far enough to leave your flank & rear exposed to a force that might be thrown in by way of Union City from Columbus, or other points. I will have a Colum from Fort Jifferson, six or seven miles below here, extending to Blandville; also a force on the Ky. shore below island No 1 whilst the Gunboats will drop down as close to Columbus as practicable and throw in an occasional shell.

Gen. Halleck is sending me additional forces from Mo. to assist in carrying out the general plan, and is desirous that it should, apparently inadvetantly, be allowed to leak out that Nashville is the object of the attack, that 20 to 30 thousand reinforcements are coming from Mo. and that this is only the advance of a much more formidable movement.

I will send you another Gunboat. It seems to me that it would add to the deception, and further aid in preventing reinforcements being sent to Bowling Green, to send them up the Tennessee river. Let the transport steamer you have take one section of Artillery and say four companies of Infantry and accompany them.

Anything like a general engagement is to be avoided, but a little skirmishing with any troops now known to be at Beaurigard, will be of advantage to our troops and should rather be courted than avoided. In retiring again upon Paducah if possible keep up the appearance of a design to move towards Dover as long as it is practicable to do so.

The troops taken from here, unless it is known to be safe for them to return to their proper stations, by the way of Blandville, will retire with you to Paducah, and return here by steamer.

Very respectfully
Your Obt. Svt.
U. S. GRANT
Brig. Gen. Com.

ALS, James S. Schoff, New York, N.Y.

1. Jan. 10, 1862.

To Col. Thomas H. Cavanaugh

Head Quarters, Dist of Cairo,
Cairo, Jany 8th 1862.

COL. T. H. CAVANAUGH.
COMMDG. SHAWNEETOWN, ILLS.
COLONEL:

In addition to information contained in your letter handed me by Mr. Hunter, I was told yesterday by two citizens of Ky. loyal men, that quite a trade in Whiskey, Coffee, Tea and even Powder is Kept up between Shawneetown, and the rebel Army.

Small amounts are purchased by single individuals, and when once in Ky. they are collected, into one mass, and started for the Southern Army.

I want, your Command to add their might, in breaking up this traffic. If the Surveyor of the Port, will not cooperate with you in this, it may become necessary to do, what they now charge you with "i. e." "declare Martial law." I fully sustain your course as shadowed forth in your letter.

All men that you arrest with evidence against them, sufficient to warrant their detention, either as Spies, or aiding the Enemy in any other manner, send before the Provost Marshal there with all the evidence against them, names of witnesses, where to be found, and such goods, as you may capture intended for the Southern Army.

Yours Truly
U. S. GRANT
Brig. Genl Commdg.

Copies, DLC-USG, V, 1, 2, 3, 85; DNA, RG 393, USG Letters Sent. On Jan. 4, 1862, Col. Thomas H. Cavanaugh, Shawneetown, wrote to USG. "I beg leave to submit the following report, to date, viz:—According to your verbal instructions, I have had the Steamboat 'Stella Blanche,' belonging to two Kentucky rebels, brought to this Port, where she now lies. Have you any further orders, concerning her? I have caused the owners of the Steam Ferry boat, plying between the two shores, to be notified not to be carry freight or passengers, to and fro, without a permit. Dr. Colvard, one of the owners, complains of my proceedings, and will,

I apprehend, appeal from my order to Head Quarters, in which event, I had as
well apprise you, that Dr. Colvard's partner, living in Kentucky, is a good Union
man in Illinois, and just as hearty a Secessionist in Kentucky, as I am well informed;
while men here of the highest standing, give it as direct from Dr. Colvard himself,
that his object is to get his boat taken possession of by the Government, and then
claim exemplary damages. He said to me in person, he wished I would order him
to stop his boat, or tie her up, as my order would ruin him, in which lies a tacit
admission that his contraband trade, was a source of profit. As you direct, I will
proceed. I have no report of Col. Kirkham's trip into Kentucky. I was informed
however, he met with no opposition, accomplished nothing, brought a[way] no
records, but received considerable eclát from the rebels. He does not report to
me, or acknowledge me as commandant of the Post, and says you are to send
him four companies of Cavalry, to *assist him*, in any expedition he may undertake
into Kentucky. This he asserts every where. Is it so? I have obtained a large
amount of valuable information in regard to the illegal trafic between the sym-
pathizers in this section and the Rebels in Kentucky, of which I shall avail myself
shortly, as opportunity offers; but there should be a force at Ford's Ferry and
Cave in Rock, to stop this trafic altogether. The reason is:—Goods are bought at
Evansville and here, for towns in the interior, manifestly. They are taken in the
country twelve, fifteen, or twenty, miles, and are then hurried to the river below
and crossed over. The next lot, I shall have a spy on the track of. Large lots cross
at Mt. Vernon, Ind., I am told, into Kentucky, and quantities are bought in Evansville, and shipped to different points on the river in Ky. In whose jurisdiction is
Evansville? I am awaiting orders for directions in regard to the duties of Provost
Marshalls. I have only made a temporary appointment. Another matter I will
mention, although, perhaps, of minor importance, is:—That Col. Kirkham is in
the habit of granting passes upon the Steamboats, which, in my opinion, is contrary to orders. It is, however, for you to decide. The Deputy Port Surveyor, Mr.
McKedig, has this moment called upon me to say that Capt. Mellon, the Chief of
the Department, has instructed him not to recognise permits granted by Military
commanders; in which case, to prevent conflict, between us, I will await your
instructions in the premises. I think, however, there need be no conflict of action
here, but I will not say the same for those acting above here, if the same course is
pursued in the future, until you order otherwise." ALS, *ibid.*, District of Cairo,
Letters Received. On Jan. 7, Cavanaugh wrote to USG. "Knowing that a deputation of merchants, of doubtful loyalty, are to leave here to-night, to appeal to you
against my restrictions of Trade with Kentucky, it is my duty to you and myself,
as I conceive it, to apprise you of what I have done, as well as of some other
matters having a bearing upon the subject. I am given to understand, they will
represent to you, that I have declared Martial Law, in this city. I inclose Special
Order No. 2. You can judge for yourself. This place has had no trade with Kentucky, except in a retail way, until purchasing could no longer be done in larger
cities, as I am well informed. On last evening the Acting Provost Marshall, Capt
Isaac Elwood, stopped a quantity of whiskey and other merchandise, going to
Kentucky. Hence the trouble. Surveyor McCodig, came to their relief and permitted the goods to pass, as he has done in very many other cases. Is not this
wrong? The true Union men here, are determined to support me in breaking up
this traficing with the Rebels, and have sent the Mayor of their city to represent
the true State of the case to you. To him I refer you for answers to all questions
you may desire to ask. If my proceedings are correct, and you are satisfied to

acknowledge them as so, I am content, although I am apprehensive that the two men C. Carrall and Thomas Ridgway will be sent you soon, charged with sedition" ALS, *ibid*.

To Col. John Cook

———

Head Quarters, Dist. of Cairo
Cairo, Jan.y 8th 1862

COL. J. COOK
COMD.G FORT HOLT, KY.
COL.

Hold all the able bodied men of the 7th & 28th Regts. & Cavalry, of your command in readiness for a move to-morrow at any hour after 12 O'clock you may receive orders.

You will take five days rations and Camp & Garrison equipage sufficient for your command and of course the land transportation for it.

See that every man has his cartridge box filled & at least twenty rounds of ammunition more in wagons.

Let no inferrence drop, not even to your Staff, of any expected move, but simply that you are to be in readiness.

Respectfully
Your Obt. Svt.
U. S. GRANT
Brig. Gen. Com

ALS, IHi.

To Col. Leonard F. Ross

Cairo Jany 8th 1862

Col Ross,

Captain Carpenter[1] should go for money to Head Quarters, Department of Missouri, where he is said to be employed. I do not know as to his reliability.

U. S. Grant,
Brig Genl Com'dg.

Telegram, copy, DNA, RG 393, Post of Cape Girardeau, Telegrams. On Jan. 7, 1862, Col. Leonard F. Ross twice telegraphed to USG. "Maj Rawalt came in at 1 O'clock this Morning with seven of Thompsons Scouts—Maj Williams among the No. Is Capt Carpenter of the 'Jessie Scouts' a reliable 'Union Man'?" "Capt Carpenter of the 'Jessie Scouts' wants money. Shall I advance to him?—" Copies, *ibid.* On the same day, Ross wrote to USG. "In obedience to your orders by Telegraph I start the Steamer 'Illinois' for Cairo in charge of Lt Laird 11th Mo Vol's.—Capt Carpenter succeeded in identifying himself before the arrival of your dispatch and left on the Steamer 'Arago' for below—Stated that he would be in Cairo in three or four days—He had a pass from Capt Hillyer for 'Capt Carpenter and party' (two others)—" Copy, *ibid.*, Letters Sent.

On Jan. 10, Capt. William McMichael wrote to USG. "C. Carpenter of the 'Jessie Scouts' is not regularly under orders and pay from these Head Quarters. For information and services rendered some weeks since Carpenter received considerable pay; but his remuneration depends entirely upon the value of the information returned by him—He seems admirably adapted for the dangerous services in which he engages. During the times that General Fremont was in command, he several times performed such services as clearly indicated that he adds great shrewdness to the reckless courage which he undoubtedly possesses." LS, *ibid.*, Dept. of the Mo., Letters Sent (Press).

On Jan. 8, Capt. William S. Hillyer wrote to Ross. "I am directed by the General Commdg. to say to you that the Companies of Cavalry for which the Steamer 'Illinois,' was ordered to this place, will be sent up in a few days, on account of her non-arrival here, they will be necessarily delayed." Copies, DLC-USG, V, 2, 85; DNA, RG 393, USG Letters Sent. On the same day, 1st Lt. Clark B. Lagow wrote to the capt., steamer *Illinois.* "I am directed by the Gen. Commdg. to say to you, that you will immediately return to Cape Girardeau, and report to Col. Ross at that Post." Copies, *ibid.* On Jan. 10, Ross telegraphed to USG. "Has the 'Illinois' started up?—if So, when?—" Copy, *ibid.*, Post of Cape Girardeau, Telegrams. On Jan. 11, USG telegraphed to Ross. "The Steamer Illinois was sent back on Monday." Copy, *ibid.*

1. According to a newspaper account, Capt. Charles Carpenter, born in Ohio, a Jayhawker before the Civil War, had been employed as a scout and spy by Maj. Gen. John C. Frémont during his command of the Western Dept. Carpenter

commanded the Jessie Scouts, an irregular organization named for Frémont's wife. Special Correspondence of the *Philadelphia Inquirer*, June 16, 1862, in *Missouri Republican*, June 23, 1862. See letter to Brig. Gen. John A. McClernand, Feb. 5, 1862.

To Maj. Gen. Henry W. Halleck

———

Cairo, Jan. 9th 1862

To Maj. Genl. Halleck.
Saint Louis.

The fog is so dense that it is impossible to cross the river; this will defer any movement for one day. A steamer is now laying across the channel at Dogtooth bend,[1] which will prevent reinforcements arriving by river, until she is removed.[2] Have reinforcements started?

Genl. Grant.

Telegram, copy, DNA, RG 393, Dept. of the Mo., Telegrams Received. On Jan. 10, 1862, Maj. Gen. Henry W. Halleck telegraphed to USG. "Reinforcements are receiving arms. Delay your movement till I telegraph. Let me know when the channel is clear." Copies, DLC-USG, V, 4, 5, 7, 8; DNA, RG 94, Generals' Papers and Books, Telegrams Sent in Cipher by Gen. Halleck; *ibid.*, RG 393, USG Hd. Qrs. Correspondence; *ibid.*, Dept. of the Mo., Telegrams Sent. *O.R.*, I, vii, 543.

1. Dogtooth Bend on the Mississippi River about twenty-three miles above Cairo.
2. On Jan. 9, Capt. John A. Rawlins wrote to Capt. William J. Kountz. "You will immediately, or as soon as the Fog, has sufficiently dispersed, to admit of it, send a Boat and Barge, up the Mississippi River for the purpose of lightening the Steamer 'Arizonia,' lying grounded on a Bar, and assist her in getting off." Copies, DLC-USG, V, 1, 2, 3, 85; DNA, RG 393, USG Letters Sent.

To Flag Officer Andrew H. Foote

Head Quarters, Dist. of Cairo
Cairo, Jan.y 9th 1862.

COMMODORE A. H. FOOTE
COMD.G CAIRO FLOTILLA,
DEAR COMMODORE,

Full directions have now been given for the movement of troops on the expedition just fitting out. It will commence this evening by the advance, under Gen. McClernand, taking position at Fort Jefferson.

Will you be kind enough to direct such of the Gunboats as you may think it expedient to send to accompany the transports, and occupy a position for their protectin?

Very respectfully
Your Obt. Svt.
U. S. GRANT
Brig. Gen.

ALS, Northern Illinois University, De Kalb, Ill. *O.R.*, I, vii, 541; *O.R.* (Navy), I, xxii, 489–90. On Jan. 9, 1862, Flag Officer Andrew H. Foote wrote to Secretary of the Navy Gideon Welles. "I have received from Genl. Grant Comdg. this Post, confidential communications in relation to an Expedition of Troops, planned by Genl. Halleck. On consultation with Genl. Grant I have ordered two Gun Boats up the Tennessee river in charge of Lt. Comdg. Phelps—a judicious Officer. Also two Gun Boats will leave this place to day for the protection of the Transports which take troops a short distance down the river. I shall ~~resesve~~ reserve one Gun Boat to go down the river, with myself, to morrow or next day, in time to join the two other Boats when they move farther down. Our force being thus divided, the Department will infer that it will be rather of a demonstrative character than otherwise. I shall in person however accompany and take charge of the Gun Boats which go down the Mississippi—remaining here on account of the pressure of work till the latest moment." ALS, DLC-Robert T. Lincoln. *O.R.* (Navy), I, xxii, 489. Foote's instructions to Lt. S. Ledyard Phelps and Commander William D. Porter are *ibid.*, pp. 488, 490–91.

To Brig. Gen. John A. McClernand

———

Head Quarters, Dist. of Cairo
Cairo, Jan.y 9th 1862.

Gen. J. A. McClernand
Comd.g Cairo Ill.
Gen.

To-morrow you will proceed with your command to Fort Jefferson at as early an hour as practicable on the transports assigned. It may be necessary for one of the steamers to make two trips.

If possible your command might get up to the top of the bluff to encamp for the night, and make Elliott's Mills on Saturday,[1] and Blandville the next day should the programme not be changed by unforeseen circumstances.

Very respectfully
Your Obt. Svt.
U. S. Grant
Brig. Gen. Com

ALS, McClernand Papers, IHi. A copy of this letter misdated Jan. 7, 1862, is *ibid.*, and the letter is entered in misdated form in book records, *ibid.* On Jan. 9, Brig. Gen. John A. McClernand wrote to USG. "Your order for the preparation of my command, including the—

10th Regt.	(Col Morgan)	537 rank and file.	
18th ”	” Lawler	677 ”	” ”
27th ”	” Buford	689. ”	” ”
29th ”	” Rearden	554. ”	” ”
30th ”	Lt ” Dennis	575 ”	” ”
31st ”	” ” White	679. ”	” ”
48th ”	Col Haynie.	580. ”	” ”
4th ” Cavalry	Col Dickey	786 ”	” ”
4 Cos do.		275 ”	” ”
Schwartz's Artillery		80. ”	” ”
Dresser's do.		59 ”	” ”

for embarkation, reached me last night. Today at 10½ o'c. A. M all were ready for embarkation, but for want of adequate transportation could not be embarked. Waiting at the landing until 1 o'c. P. M. and still being unprovided with transportation, I informed you of the fact which, according to the explanation of Capt Kountz, Master of Transportation, ~~was~~ is attributable to an interfering fog. Pursuant to your further order based upon the state of case, I have since sent all the Cavalry with their trains across the river to Fort Holt, in such transports as I found available for that purpose. The Cavalry encamping there for the night, will await further orders. Tonight I will instruct Capt Kountz to provide sufficient transportation for the infantry and artillery of my command, designed for the expedition, with their trains. And with the view to insure an early embarkation, will obtain from him a list of transports and their landings, so that I may lose no time in marching the different portions of my command to the transports assigned to them respectively. I expect to be able to leave the landing with my whole remaining force by 9 o'c. in the morning, or at such time as you may direct. . . . P. S. The above force has been necessarily somewhat reduced by various details ordered for duty at this Post." LS, DNA, RG 393, District of Cairo, Letters Received.

On Jan. 9, Capt. John A. Rawlins issued Special Orders No. 11. "Capt. W. J. Kountz A. Q. M. & Master of transportation will see that all the transports required for immediate use, are properly manned. Should river men, who are not otherwise employed, refuse to serve, such number of them, as may be required, will be forced to serve, as prisoners, and without compensation. The Officer of the day will afford Capt. Kountz all necessary aid in enforcing this order." Copies, DLC-USG, V, 15, 16, 82, 87, 89; DNA, RG 393, USG Special Orders. On the same day, Rawlins wrote to Capt. William J. Kountz. "In loading the Artillery, Cavalry and transportation on Steamers, you will not have them pass over the Naval Wharf Boat, but find some other place to have them embark. The Infantry can be allowed to pass over said Wharf. Boat." Copies, DLC-USG, V, 1, 2, 85; DNA, RG 393, USG Letters Sent.

1. Jan. 11.

To Brig. Gen. Eleazer A. Paine

———

Head Quarters, Dist of Cairo
Cairo, Jany 9th 1862.

GEN. E. A. PAINE.
COMMDG 2ND BRIGADE,
BIRD'S POINT, MO.
GENL:

On the arrival of transports at Bird's Point you will cause the Artillery, Cavalry, and transport wagons, to be ferried to Fort. Holt and go into camp for the night immediately below there[.] Before having the wagons cross, move every thing aboard the transports that can be dispensed with, leaving sufficient guard from each company on board to look after the Company property.

In the morning every thing crossed to Fort. Holt, will proceed to Fort Jefferson. As the roads will be heavy it may be necessary for the Artillery to distribute their ammunition, among the wagons accompanying.

With the balance of your command now under orders, you will proceed by transports to the same place, and their await further orders.

By order
B͟f U. S. Grant, Brig Gen. Commdg

Copies, DLC-USG, V, 1, 2, 3, 85; DNA, RG 393, USG Letters Sent. *O.R.*, I, vii, 541.

To Brig. Gen. Charles F. Smith

——————

Head Quarters, Dist. of Cairo
Cairo, Jan.y 9th 1862.

Gen. C. F. Smith,
Comd.g U. S. Forces
Paducah Ky.
Gen.

Owing to the density of the fog it will be impossible to make any movement here to-day. This will delay your movement also, it being desirable to effect a junction at Mayfield.

As the matter now stands the column leaving Paducah need not start until Saturday.[1] If there should be further delay I will telegraph you.

Very respectfully
Your Obt. Svt.
U. S. Grant
Brig. Gen. Com.

ALS, James S. Schoff, New York, N. Y. *O.R.*, I, vii, 541–42. On Jan. 9, 1862, Capt. John A. Rawlins wrote to Capt. William J. Kountz. "You will have the Steamer 'W. H. B' return to Paducah, Ky. with all possible dispatch, and the

Captain will see that the Mail to Brig. Genl. Smith, is delivered to him, no matter where he may be." Copies, DLC-USG, V, 1, 2, 85; DNA, RG 393, USG Letters Sent. On the same day, Brig. Gen. Charles F. Smith telegraphed to USG. "I propose Leaving the fortieth Ills & the provost Marshalls guard two companies Shall I go naked or with tents" Telegram received, *ibid.*, Dept. of the Mo., Telegrams Received. On Jan. 10, Smith telegraphed to USG. "Your dispatches of 9th just recd by a Cavalry man   I shall leave here tomorrow at Eight a m" Telegram received, *ibid.* This USG letter and the following letter were sent together.

1. Jan. 11.

To Brig. Gen. Charles F. Smith

———

Cairo, Jan.y 9th 1862

GEN.

Knowing that Capt. Kountz had telegraphed for Steamer Wilson I sent you a dispatch yesterday to retain the Steamer. Although the Capt. may be a very good Steamboat man he knows but little of Military etiquette and I am affraid will never learn.

I was not aware that any leave had been granted Gen. Wallace[1] from here but learning that he was coming to Cairo, I supposed on leave regularly obtained, directed a telegraph to be sent him not to come. This was in consequence of the order from Gen. Halleck for an advance movement.

I had made application for a Quartermaster ~~here~~ to take at least a part of Capt. Hatches duties off his hands during Gen. Frémonts Administration, and also since Gen. Halleck took command. After an investigation of the lumber purchases in Chicago, and geting no Qr. Mr. from St. Louis, I ordered Capt. Baxter down and required him to make all purchases until such time as something ~~something~~ may be done at Head Quarters for our relief.

Capt. Kountz was sent here from St. Louis to take charge of the river transportation, and for no other duty. Having written to have some lumber sent down here, and hearing nothing in reply, I sent a verbal message by Capt. Kountz to make enquiries about it.

> respectfully
> Your Obt. Svt.
> U. S. Grant
> Brig. Gen.

ALS, James S. Schoff, New York, N. Y. This letter was attached to the preceding letter. On Jan. 8, 1862, Brig. Gen. Charles F. Smith telegraphed to USG. "I dont understand your Telegraph about retaining Steamer" "The Steamer Wilson Left here at three this P M" Telegrams received, DNA, RG 393, Dept. of the Mo., Telegrams Received. On the same day, Smith wrote to USG, "in reference to ordering steamer 'Wilson' from Paducah without his knowledge." DLC-USG, V, 10; DNA, RG 393, USG Register of Letters Received.

1. Brig. Gen. Lewis Wallace of Ind. served as 2nd lt. in the Mexican War, and on the eve of the Civil War was a Democratic lawyer-politician at Crawfordsville. Wallace served briefly as Ind. AG, then, on April 25, 1861, was appointed col., 11th Ind. He was promoted to brig. gen. as of Sept. 3 and assigned to Paducah. *Lew Wallace: An Autobiography* (New York and London, 1906).

To Col. John Cook

> Head Quarters, Dist of Cairo
> Cairo, Jany 9th 1862.

Col. John Cook.
Commdg 3rd Brigade
Fort Holt, Ky.
Colonel:

You will move with your command to Fort Jefferson tomorrow, and there, await further orders. As the roads will be heavy a transport will be furnished, to move ~~the heavy~~ baggage.

> U. S. Grant.
> Brig. Genl. Commdg.

Copies, DLC-USG, V, 1, 2, 3, 85; DNA, RG 393, USG Letters Sent. On Jan. 9, 1862, Col. John Cook telegraphed to Capt. John A. Rawlins. "Will the Genl indicate the hour we move tomorrow & will troops arriving at Fort Holt be under my command or some one else. Please Answer" Telegram received, *ibid.*, Dept. of the Mo., Telegrams Received. On Jan. 10, 1st Lt. Clark B. Lagow wrote to

Cook. "I am directed by the Commdg. General, to say to you, that you will not move your command forward until tomorrow, at which time you *will*." Copies, DLC-USG, V, 2, 85; DNA, RG 393, USG Letters Sent.

To Brig. Gen. Lorenzo Thomas

———

Head Quarters Dist of Cairo
Cairo Jany 10th 1862

Genl L Thomas
Adj. Genl. of the Army
Washington D. C.
Genl.

I have not yet, received all the returns from Regiments and Detachments of this command, from which to compile my returns for the month of December 1861

Respectfully
Your Obt. Sevt.
U. S. Grant
Brig. Genl. Comdg.

LS, DNA, RG 94, Letters Received. On Jan. 10, 1862, USG sent a similar letter to hd. qrs., Dept. of the Mo. *Ibid.*, RG 393, Dept. of the Mo., Register of Letters Received.

To Brig. Gen. John A. McClernand

———

Head Quarters, Dist. of Cairo,
Cairo, Jan.y 10th 1862

Gen. J. A. McClernand
Comd.g Advance Forces,
Fort Jefferson Ky.
Gen.

Direct regimental & detachment commanders to make out provision returns for two days, commencing from the end of the time they have already drawn for, and sent to Capt. McAlister.[1]

The rations will be issued and forwarded giving soft bread for the troops whilst laying still.

> Very respectfully
> Your Obt. Svt.
> U. S. Grant
> Brig. Gen. Com.

ALS, McClernand Papers, IHi. On Jan. 11, 1862, Brig. Gen. John A. McClernand replied to USG. "Your communication of last evening concerning provision returns, was this morning, received, and will receive prompt attention. I report to you in brief that the expedition under my command, arrived last night and disembarked in good order. Mounted Scouts were sent in large force in every direction, and Capt Dollins company of Cavalry posted at the ford of Mayfield Creek, at Elliotts Mills during the night. This Co. has been this morning relieved by Capt. O'Harnetts Co. From which Co. Scouts were also sent a short distance beyond The command was encamped at Fort Jefferson and notwithstanding the severity of the weather, the men passed the night comfortably, and are in good condition and spirits this morning. A few sick have been reported, who are being returned to the Hospital at Cairo this morning. A heavy guard was posted during the night and the country in all directions scoured by mounted parties. No enemy however appeared and the camp remained undisturbed. Two prisoners were captured this morning, by Capt. Dollins, who will be subjected to a preliminary examination, and if necessary reported to you at Cairo for your disposal. In a business communication sent to you this morning, I sollicited your attention to the supply of articles immediately needful for the safety and comfort of the command. I would again refer to the importance of having a full supply of engineering and intreching implements. The arrangement of the several Regts in Camp will be revised this morning, in order to perfect our means of defence, to secure compactness of organization and facilitate police and guard duties. My arrangements are made with equal reference to a defensive position here, or an advance movement at any moment. As soon as the Regimental reports are furnished, I will furnish you a more detailed return. The Enemies boats are menacing us on the river. The Gunboats at Cairo will be of service. This may be the prelude to an attack by land" LS, DNA, RG 393, District of Cairo, Letters Received. The letter was endorsed for USG by John Riggin, Jr. "Referred to Col. J. D. Webster, to be returned as soon as read." AES, *ibid*.

1. Capt. Richard McAllister of Iowa was appointed commissary of subsistence on Aug. 3, 1861. See *Calendar*, Dec. 28, 1861.

To Brig. Gen. Charles F. Smith

———

Head Quarters, Dist. of Cairo.
Cairo, Jan.y 10th 1862.

Gen. C. F. Smith
Comd.g U. S. Forces
Paducah, Ky.
Gen.

In reply to yours of to-day enquiring as to the probable time your command will be out is received.

A force sufficient to escort a train should be left to follow you, with two days rations in addition to the five you start with.

Should the transportation at hand be sufficient to carry this extra two days rations however it will be better to start with it. Should no directions reach you to remain longer retire so as to reach Paducah by the end of that time.

Circumstances, of which you alone can be judge may make it necessary to return before the end of the time indicated. Either to avoid an unequal contest, to prevent the enemy getting in your rear, or hearing of a decisive battle being fought at Bowling Green, however decided, will be sufficient grounds for retiring, at any time, in the absence of other instructions

Very respectfully
Your Obt. Svt.
U. S. Grant
Brig. Gen. Com.

ALS, James S. Schoff, New York, N. Y. On Jan. 10, 1862, Brig. Gen. Charles F. Smith wrote to Capt. John A. Rawlins. "Please say to the Commander of the District that the force here has been ready to move since 5 o'c p. m. yesterday. The force to remain will be the 40th. Ills. regt., 2 Cos. forming the Provost Marshal's gd. and one Co.y of foot Art.y to serve the heavy guns. A section of Art. & four Cos. of Inf.y will be sent up the Tennessee on the day after I march. I should like to be informed how long I am to remain out. Will I receive instructions on that point? I will take two days to get to Mayfield—25 miles. The roads will not admit of faster travel." ALS, DNA, RG 393, District of Cairo, Letters Received. Since this letter was not received at Cairo until Jan. 13, the substance was probably transmitted by telegraph.

To Brig. Gen. Charles F. Smith

———

Head Quarters, Dist of Cairo
Cairo, Jany 10th 1862.

GEN. C. F. SMITH
COMMDG U. S. FORCES.
PADUCAH, KY.
GENL:

A telegraph just received from Gen. Halleck notifies me of a delay in sending reinforcements from St Louis, and directs that no advance be made, until further notice from him

If the telegraph is in working order, when the notice is received, I will inform you by that uncertain means of communication, if not by express.

To add to our difficulties a Steamer has got aground about twenty miles above here, where the channel is very narrow, and swung round so as to entirely cut off navigation from here during the present low stage of water, or until removed. I have sent a Steamer to her relief.[1]

Very Respectfully,
Your Obt. Servant
U. S. GRANT
Brig. Genl. Commdg.

Copies, DLC-USG, V, 1, 2, 3, 85; DNA, RG 393, USG Letters Sent. *O.R.*, I, vii, 543.

1. See telegram to Maj. Gen. Henry W. Halleck, Jan. 9, 1862.

To Brig. Gen. Charles F. Smith

————

Head Quarters, Dist of Cairo
Cairo, Jany 10th 1862.

GEN. C. F. SMITH
COMMDG U. S. FORCES
PADUCAH KY.
GENERAL:

The immense amount of stores kept here for the troops here, and ~~prospective~~ those to come, and for the Navy make it almost impossible to find Storage room. If you can dispense with the Given's Wharf Boat, and allow her to be brought here, it will be a very great relief as well as a saving to Government.

Should you require more room, than you will then have left, there is a smaller Wharf Boat at Smithland, that can be brought down.

Very Respectfully
Your Obt Servant
U. S. GRANT
Brig. Gen. Commdg.

Copies, DLC-USG, V, 1, 2, 3, 85; DNA, RG 393, USG Letters Sent. On Jan. 8, 1862, Capt. William J. Kountz wrote to USG. "I wish to charter or purchase the large wharf Boat at Paducah belonging to Given and others. The terms on which they propose to charter the boat is ~~for~~ is $500 pr month giving the United States the priviledge of purchasing at any time without paying previous charter at a valuation of $8.000 The Government has been using the boat since the army first went to Paducah, between three and four months which amount I think can be included in the valuation of $8000. provided the U. S. should make the purchase. The boat in my opinion is not required at Paducah" LS, *ibid.*, District of Cairo, Letters Received.

To Col. Napoleon B. Buford

Head Quarters, Dist. of Cairo
Cairo, Jany 10th 1862.

Col. N. B. Buford.
Commdg Cairo, Ills.
Colonel:

In addition to instructions given this morning, the following, is for your guidance in the absence of the main force.

All troops arriving by rail or river will report to the Commdg Officer of this point. Such as may arrive by river you will assign, first, one Regiment at Fort Holt, to go into Camp, below the defences. After that at least two regiments should be placed at Bird's Point.

No new arrivals are to occupy any of the quarters vacated by troops leaving here, without further orders.

Should more than three Regiments arrive by water, you will dispose of them according to your judgment. I will be back here tomorrow, and shall any further instructions appear necessary, I will then give them. All mails for my Head Qrs. will be left with the clerk,[1] who will have directions.

Very Respectfully, Your Obt. Servt
U. S. Grant. Brig Gen. Commdg.

Copies, DLC-USG, V, 1, 2, 3, 85; DNA, RG 393, USG Letters Sent. On Jan. 10, 1862, 1st Lt. Clark B. Lagow wrote to Col. Napoleon B. Buford. "I am directed by the Genl. Commanding, to say to you that Special Guard, must be Kept in the Absence of the main column from here, upon the Wharf Boats and Commissary Stores, on the river, also the Magazine. There will be a regiment arrive here, during the Absence of the column, which will be assigned quarters in Barracks, here with you." Copies, *ibid.*

1. According to a "Roll of Non commissioned Officers and Privates employed on extra duty as Clerks and orderlies at Cairo Illinois during the month of January 1862," three clerks were employed by order of USG. Private Sidney A. Stockdale, Co. E, 8th Ill., served Jan. 1–Jan. 28; Private William Hoyt, Co. E, 48th Ill., served Jan. 1–Jan. 22; Corporal Dennison R. Town, Co. D, 11th Ill., served Jan. 1–Jan. 10. *Ibid.*, Dept. of the Tenn., Miscellaneous Letters Received. Stockdale was apparently the clerk meant by USG. See letter to Capt. John C. Kelton, Jan. 20, 1862.

To Maj. Gen. Henry W. Halleck

————

By Telegraph from Cairo Jan'y 11 *1862*

To Genl. Halleck

McClernand's Brigade had shipped to Fort Jefferson before the receipt of your despatch. Will not move further until further orders.

U. S. Grant
Brig. Genl.

Telegram received, DNA, RG 94, Generals' Papers and Books, Telegrams Received by Gen. Halleck; copy, *ibid.*, RG 393, Dept. of the Mo., Telegrams Received. On Jan. 11, 1862, USG again telegraphed to Maj. Gen. Henry W. Halleck. "The channel is clear." Telegram received, *ibid.*, RG 94, Generals' Papers and Books, Telegrams Received by Gen. Halleck; copy, *ibid.*, RG 393, Dept. of the Mo., Telegrams Received. On Jan. 11, Halleck telegraphed to USG. "I can here nothing from Buell, so fix your own time for the advance. Three regiments will go down on Monday." Copies, *ibid.*, RG 94, Generals' Papers and Books, Telegrams Sent by Gen. Halleck; *ibid.*, RG 393, Dept. of the Mo., Telegrams Sent. See telegram to Maj. Gen. Henry W. Halleck, Jan. 9, 1862.

To Brig. Gen. John A. McClernand

————

Head Quarters, Dist. of Cairo
Cairo, Jan.y 11th 1862

Gen. J. A. McClernand
Comd.g Advance Forces,
Fort Jefferson, Ky.
Gen.

Your despatches received. I have just sent Col. Webster to see Commodore Foote with a request to ~~return~~ go down with another Gun boat.

We have not got a single heavy gun on a siege carriage, consequently cannot move heavy artillery as suggested by you.

I will try and run down this after[noon] and see you.

Very respectfully

Your Obt. Svt.

U. S. GRANT

Brig. Gen.

ALS, McClernand Papers, IHi. On Jan. 11, 1862, Brig. Gen. John A. McClernand wrote four letters to USG. "Upon return from you to my quarters, I found Capt. Stewart Comg—the Cavalry reconnoissance of to day who reported to me that he had extended his reconnoissance not only to Blandville but six miles beyond there on the road to Columbus. He further reports that of the enemy were seen by him, and that from all he had learned, the enemy were ignora[nt] of my movement. He captured two men who had been conveying one or more rebels to Columbus. He learned that some days since reinforcements had been sent from Columbus to Bowling Green, and that the enemy were seizing all suitable horses, he could find for cavalry use—" Copy, *ibid*. "Among the supplies needed for immediate use on this expedition, 150 axes fixed and ready for use, 100 shovels and spades, 50 hatchets, 2 grind stones, fixed for use, for sharpening axes and spades. The Clerk of the Quarter Master and Commissary Department leaves for Cairo to procure articles of immediate necessity   The Str 'Alps' which had been reseved for the trip to Cairo this morning having departed without orders, the Keystone has been detailed for that purpose. Please direct her to return as soon as the supplies can be put on board. A supply of bread is needed. Capt. Stewarts Co. having none. A further and formal report will be made by next Steamer." Df, *ibid*. "Lieut. W. H Heath is despatched to explain to you verbally, information concerning threatening movements of the enemy, at the bar, foot of Island No. 2. It is thought they can be captured by dep by despatching batteries and boats, s fr with troops, to be debarked op say at Norfolk the point now of our landing." Df, *ibid*. "Since my despatch by Lt Heath the two Gun boats dropped down under cover of the fog, and heavy cannonading has been heard. I shall not be surprised if our boats got below those of the enemy before the latter were aware of it and have sunk or taken them. I have sent a steamer to learn and report. I will advise you from time to time of what may transpire." Copy, *ibid*.

On the same day, Maj. Mason Brayman wrote to USG. "Genl M'Clernand sends Dr. J A Parker a prisoner taken under circumstances, justifying his brief detention to you, for further explanation, asking kind treatment." ADfS, *ibid*. Again on the same day, Brayman wrote to USG. "General McClernand instructs that A Parker and John Adams, two persons arrested and brought into camp by mounted pickets, and whom it would probably be dangerous, from what is known of them, to allow to go at large, be sent to you for temporary detention. He also instructs me to say that he recommends that they be well cared for during their detention." DfS, *ibid*.

To Brig. Gen. Eleazer A. Paine

———

Head Quarters, Dist of Cairo
Cairo, Jany 11th 1862.

BRIG GEN. E. A. PAINE
COMMDG BIRD'S POINT, MO.
GENERAL:

I undestand that four of our pickets were shot this morning. If this is so, and appearances indicate that the assassins were citizens, not regularly organized in the rebel Army, the whole country should be cleaned out, for six miles around, and word given that all citizens making their appearance within those limits are liable to be shot. To execute this, patrols should be sent out, in all directions, and bring into camp at Bird's Point all citizens, together with their Subsistence, and require them to remain, under pain of death and destruction of their property until properly relieved.

Let no harm befall these people, if they quietly submit but bring them in, and place them in camp below the breastworks and have them properly guarded.

The intention is not to make political prisoners of these people, but to cut off a dangerous class of spies.

This applies to all classes and conditions, Age and Sex. If however, Woman and Children, prefer other protection than we can afford them, they may be allowed to retire, beyond the limits indicated, not to return until authorized.

Report to me as soon as possibe every important occurrence within your command.

Very Respectfully,
Your Obt. Servant,
U. S. GRANT.
Brig. Gen'l. Commdg.

Copies, DLC-USG, V, 1, 2, 3, 85; DNA, RG 393, USG Letters Sent. *O.R.*, I, viii, 494–95; *ibid.*, II, i, 255. See letter to Brig. Gen. Eleazer A. Paine, Jan. 12, 1862.

To Col. Leonard F. Ross

Cairo Jany 11th, 1862.

COL. ROSS,

Will give the Cavalry asked for immediately.

U. S. GRANT.

Telegram, copy, DNA, RG 393, Post of Cape Girardeau, Telegrams. On Jan. 11, 1862, Col. Leonard F. Ross telegraphed to USG. "Secession Companies are forming at Bloomfield and Dallas—I want armed Cavalry as soon as possible." Copy, *ibid.* On the same day, Capt. John A. Rawlins wrote to Brig. Gen. Eleazer A. Paine. "I am directed by Brig. Gen. Grant to say that you will order the balance of the Batt. of 7th Ills. Cavalry (a part of which are now at Cape Girardeau,) under orders of date the 6th inst to proceed to Cape Girardeau, immediately upon the arrival of Steamer to-day at Bird's Point landing where they will report to Col L. F. Ross, Commdg Post, for duty. Captain of the Steamer will report to you upon his arrival at the landing." Copies, DLC-USG, V, 1, 2, 3, 85; DNA, RG 393, USG Letters Sent. On the same day, 1st Lt. Clark B. Lagow wrote to Capt. William J. Kountz. "I am directed by the Genl. Commdg. to say to you, that you will furnish transportation for two companies of Cavalry from Bird's Point to Cape Girardeau, immediately   Capt of Steamer reporting to Brig. Gen. Paine, at Bird's Point for orders." Copies, *ibid.*

On Jan. 12, Ross wrote to USG. "Two additional Companies of the 7th Ill's Cavalry arrived to day—They are American but like the other two Companies here are unarmed. It is unnecessary General for me to State that these men are of no use whatever at this Post.—I regret very much the necessity of again calling your attention to our wants here but I am quite certain that you must have been unadvised of the true condition of the troops sent me. If the two German Companies were armed, they could not be used to advantage at this point. If you have any use for them at Cairo, I would suggest that they be returned there, and in their stead be sent *Americans well armed*—and I understand that some three or four Companies of that Regiment are well armed with Revolvers. I informed you in one of my dispatches that Secession Companies were being organized at Dallas, and Bloomfield. These organizations are still progressing. With a proper Cavalry force I think these forces of the enemy could be dispersed and broken up, and the presence of an efficient body of Cavalry here would have a salutary effect in preventing future organizations of the kind and would encourage & Strengthen the Union Sentiment of the people. Five or six Companies in my opinion could be used here to advantage, and if you have no immidiate use for them below, I would earnestly recommend that from four to six Companies be stationed here during the winter, or till such time as they may be be wanted in some other field—They can be as well, and as cheaply provided for, here as at Cairo. If you conclude to add to the Cavalry force here, I would like them to be from the 7th Ill. Cavalry, that they be *Americans, well armed*, and that the Companies be selected by Col Kellogg—I hope you may see proper to give our application a favorable hearing. . . . P. S. But few of Thompsons men are coming in now and taking the oath of allegiance   Those who have not already come in—will, I think, organize and fight us again in the Spring—I hope Major Rawalt, will be continued at this Post. He is becoming acquainted with the country and people, and is I think just the man for the place." Copy, *ibid.*, Post of Cape Girardeau, Letters Sent. See letter to Capt. John C. Kelton, Dec. 2, 1861, note 1, and *Calendar*, Jan. 1, 1862.

Concerning John Lellyett

Head Quarters, Dist. of Cairo
Cairo, Jan.y 11th 1862.

Mr. Lellyett[1] is the principle of the party employed by Gen. Buell to perform some secret servise in Tennessee and Ky. and I presume knows of what he speaks.

U. S. GRANT
Brig. Gen.

AES, MH. Written on a letter of Jan. 11, 1862, from John Lellyett, Paducah, to USG. "I trust you may not find so much annoyance as information in the letters I write you; or if otherwise, that you will excuse what is purely the result of a deep anxiety on my part for the success of the arms of our Government against a rebellion which I hate as it is causeless, wicked, and oppressive. What I have now to say is not intended even as a *suggestion* as to what ought to be the plans of our generals; but only to convey a peice of suggestive *information*, which may or may not be of use according to circumstances. If it should be the intention to advance a force to a point south of this—say to Mayfield, or farther—it occurs to me that the following fact should, as it may already, be known to our officers: From a point further west than where the Railroad from this place crosses the line of Tennessee, to within a few miles of Fort Henry, and to within a few miles of the point where the M. C. & L. RR crosses the Tennessee River, runs a good country road, right along the line of Kentucky and Tennessee. It is called the 'State Line Road.' It is ordinarily a very good road, and not easily obstructed, as it crosses few if any streams, of any size. It is not a macadamized turnpike, but the ground is not as soft and spongey as many other roads in that section. By referring to the map, you will observe that the creeks heading near this part of the state line, run *from* it in both directions. It is a sort of low ridge road. It occurred to me that you should be informed of this route, as it could be used for a purpose. If it were desired to menace Columbus in force, and then suddenly turn about and attack Fort Henry—that is, the new fortifications on this side the river opposite Fort Henry, which command it—this road can be easily gained either from Mayfield or a point south of it which might seem even more threatening to Columbus, or the rear of Columbus, than Mayfield. Or if Fort Henry were taken, troops can march thence by this road to the rear of Columbus, (so as to cut off its communications,) by a very eligible route. You can judge of the distances by the maps. I have no positive information about these distances—only that the road is straight, and higher and dryer than is common with roads in this section. My object, as I before said, is merely to convey information, not to make any suggestion, further than the information itself is suggestive." ALS, *ibid*. Lellyett had also written to USG on Jan. 7. "I open this letter to make a suggestion, and to impart a trifle of information, which however you have probably had before, about the Tennessee and Cumberland Rivers. If at any time it should be deemed advisable to undertake an expedition up one or the other or both those streams—which by the way would seem to me a good idea—I have this to suggest. The Cumberland is generally from December to April navigable to Gallatin landing, above Nashville, for boats drawing three feet water. It is very rarely during this perio[d] of the year, too l[ow] for that. Also during the same period, it is seld[om] too low to allow [bo]ats drawing five feet to reach Clarkesville. During a great portion of the year, but at uncertain seasons, boats of any size can go to Nashville and Gallatin Landing. But it is absolutely certain, that obstructions have been sunk in the channel of that river, at, near, or below Dover. If at any time Dover were taken, a day or two would be time enough to enable the enemy, if prepared, and in case of low water, to sink obstructions at other points above Dover. In view of these facts, I submit if it would not be wise to depend principally upon the little floating batteries and their tugs for the ascent of the Cumberland, should the thing ever be attempted. Steamers of some power should of course accompany such expedition, able to drag out obstructions. Some of them are trees, with large rocks attached. I submit, further, if it would not be wise to mount rifled cannon on a few of these batterie[s] for this service, instead of mortars. In case of *high* water, our iron gunboats can clean out the river batteries; otherwise, the little batteries can do much service, and if not sufficient, the batteries can be taken by land. All along the shore, outside the forts the floating batteries could clear the woods. The Tennessee River is much more navigable than the Cumberland; but with this qualification these remarks apply to that also." ALS, DNA, RG *393*, District of Cairo, Letters Received.

1. John Lellyett, a staunch Unionist of Tenn., was forced to leave his state in July, 1861. He then served the U. S. Army as an intelligence agent in Ky. Early allied with Senator Andrew Johnson, the two quarreled bitterly in May, 1862, when Johnson was military governor of Tenn. and Lellyett was postmaster at Nashville. Letters of Lellyett are in DLC-Andrew Johnson and DLC-Robert T. Lincoln. See also Lincoln, *Works*, VIII, 58–72; Clifton R. Hall, *Andrew Johnson: Military Governor of Tennessee* (Princeton, 1916), p. 70.

To Maj. Gen. Henry W. Halleck

By Telegraph from Cairo Jan'y 12 *1862*

To Maj Genl Halleck

Please direct that no Quarter Masters vouchers given here be allowed to go before the Committee until further notice. Every day developes further evidence of peculation.

U. S. Grant

Telegram received, DNA, RG 94, Generals' Papers and Books, Telegrams Received by Gen. Halleck; copies, *ibid.*, RG 393, USG Hd. Qrs. Correspondence; *ibid.*, Dept. of the Mo., Telegrams Received; DLC-USG, V, 4, 5, 7, 8. On Jan. 13, 1862, Maj. Gen. Henry W. Halleck wrote to David Davis of the Commission on War Claims at St. Louis. "Genl Grant has just telegraphed that Quarter master's accounts from Cairo before commission should not be acted on till further notice —as every day develops evidence of peculation" ALS, DNA, RG 217, Papers Relating to the Davis-Holt-Campbell Claims Commission. See letter to Brig. Gen. Montgomery C. Meigs, Jan. 13, 1862.

To Maj. Gen. Henry W. Halleck

———

Head Quarters, Dist. of Cairo,
Cairo, Jan.y 12th 1862.

MAJ. GEN. H. W. HALLECK
COMD.G DEPT. OF THE MISSOURI,
ST. LOUIS, MO.
GEN.

Before the receipt of your telegraph directing delay in the demonstration previously ordered, I had commenced by sending the portion of my command immediately under Gen. McClernand, to Fort Jefferson. As it would be attended with a goodeal of trouble to bring these troops back, and have a demoralizing effect upon them besides, I have left them there.—They occupy a good camp ground and have Mayfield creek, a stram not fordable, between them and the enemy. Yesterday three of the enemies gunboats come up to reconoiter but finding two of ours laying below the camp they did not venture near enough to see our position, or for our Gunboats to engage them effectively.

They placed themselvs across the stream, at very long range, and by the time Capt. Porter[1] & ~~Walke~~, Lieut. Paulding[2] Comd.g the Gunboats, weighed anchor and got under headway they were off.

Capt. Porter chased them under their guns at Columbus, one shot certainly, and he thinks two, taking effect upon one of their boats, disabling her to some extent if not entirely for present use.

Capt. Porter pulled up, and brought with him, one of their buoys intended to mark the location of their torpedoes, or the channel to navigate to avoid them.

~~The~~ Reinforcements starting from St. Louis on Monday,[3] as I am advised by your last telegram, I will commence the move again on ~~Wednesday~~ Teusday.

I have just learned through the Memphis Appeal, and also from a man who has just made his way from New Orleans, and who spent last Thursday & Friday in Columbus,[4] that seven regiments have left Columbus recently for Bowling Green. I am inclined to believe that the Garrison of Columbus is now weaker than it has been for several months back. It is also probable that the best armed and best drilled troops have been taken.

I have placed Capt. Hatch, A. Q. M. in arrest and directed him to turn over all public property to Capt. A S. Baxter. This was done on notice from Washington that charges would be prefered against the former, and if not already in arrest he should be so placed at once.[5]

Every day develops further evidence of corruption in the Quartermaster's Department, and that Mr. Dunton, Chief Clerk, if not chief conspirator is at least an accomplice. I have ordered his arrest and confinement.

I have telegraphed you requesting that no more vouchers given here, by the Quartermaster, be audited for the present. This was intended to mean those given by Capt. Hatch. As his conduct will probably be the subject of a legal investigation I forbear saying all that I fear is true.

I address the Comd.g Gen. in person deeming this matter which should only be known to such persons as he may desire should know it.

> I am Gen.
> Very respectfully
> Your Obt. Svt.
> U. S. Grant
> Brig. Gen. Com

P. S. I have directed the books and safe of Capt. Hatch to be taken possession of, and kept guarded, until orders are received disposing of this matter.

U. S. G.

ALS, DNA, RG 393, Dept. of the Mo., Letters Received. *O.R.*, I, vii, 545–46.

1. On Jan. 13, 1862, Commander William D. Porter, commanding gunboat *Essex*, reported this engagement to Flag Officer Andrew H. Foote. *O.R.* (Navy), I, xxii, 499–500.
    2. Lt. Leonard Paulding commanded the gunboat *St. Louis*.
    3. Jan. 13.
    4. See letter to Brig. Gen. Eleazer A. Paine, Jan. 12, 1862, note.
    5. See letter to Brig. Gen. Montgomery C. Meigs, Jan. 13, 1862.

To Brig. Gen. John A. McClernand

———

Head Quarters, Dist. of Cairo
Cairo, Jan.y 12th 1862.

GEN. J. A. MCCLERNAND,
COMD.G ADVANCE COLUMN
FORT JEFFERSON KY
GEN.

I have directed the Quartermaster and Commissary each to put supplies aboard of a Steamer and send it to Fort Jefferson.

Capt. Leland is directed to accompany the Com.y supplies and issue on proper returns.

There will also be an Agt. of the Qr. Mr. Dept. to issue the forage.

Respectfully
Your Obt. Svt.
U. S. GRANT
Brig. Gen. Com.

ALS, McClernand Papers, IHi. On Jan. 12, 1862, Brig. Gen. John A. McClernand wrote to USG. "In addition to what I said on the subject, in another communication of this date, I beg to add that increasing perplexities arising in regard to supplies, makes it in my opinion, of the first importance that a large boat with ample supplies of provisions and forage should be sent here at the earliest moment, from which necessary supplies for my command may be drawn. Any excess of supplies may be easily taken back on the same boat bringing them. A Brigade commissary to accompany seems to be an absolute necessity. Many of officers are absolutely destitute of provisions this morning. Cannot the paymaster visit this command? Many of them have received no pay whatever. A large wharf boat, moored to the shore with a Brigade commissary department on board, might afford the best means of supply." LS, DNA, RG 393, District of Cairo, Letters Received. On the same day, Capt. William S. Hillyer wrote to McClernand. "I am instructed by Gen Grant to say to you in reply to your communication of this date that it is the duty of the commanding General to see that proper supplies are furnished for the soldiers, and that as the officers receive commutations of rations they must provide for themselves. In this instance you are authorized to make such arrangement as you think proper for the supply of the officers under your command, but this permission is not to be regarded as a precedent for future action—There is no commissary here who can be assigned as Brigade Commissary, but if you think it necessary to have one you may appoint any Lieutenant of your command to act as Brigade Commissary during this expedition or until further orders—" ALS, McClernand Papers, IHi. On the same day, McClernand wrote to USG. "The order which prohibits the sale of provisions, prevents them from securing supplies here. They have not been able to draw pay, & many have no money. And as they left Cairo prepared for only a short expedition of five days, they are becoming destitute. The sutlers are either not here, or so poorly supplied as to afford no relief. It is not well to send a large number of men to Cairo for supplies, but desirable that some general arrangement be made." ADf, *ibid.*

Also on Jan. 12, McClernand wrote three additional letters to USG. "I avail myself of the departure of the Rob Roy, briefly to communicate with you. I have sent forward, an armed reconnaisance, consisting of the 10th & 18th and six companies of cavalry under command of Capt Stewart to Elliott's Mills—the cavalry, covered by the infantry, to advance as far as can be safely done towards Columbus. I have also suggested to Capt Porter of the Essex, the propriety of moving down and harassing the enemy on the river, to divert attention from the other movement and to weaken their means of river defence." LS, DNA, RG 393, District of Cairo, Letters Received. "I have just returned from a personal reconnoisance, advancing some three miles beyond Elliotts Mills on the way to Columbus. The cavalry force sent out this morning, and of which I advised you to-day, is reported to have driven in the pickets at Columbus. The cavalry is supported by the 10th & 18th, now at Elliotts Mills. Capt Porter at my suggestion went down with the two *Gun Boats*, and their firing is now heard near Columbus. I will again communicate with you when the Cavalry return." Copy, McClernand Papers, IHi. "The reconnoitring force, mentioned in my last dispatch, having returned, since dark, I have the honor to communicate to you the result of their operations. The 10th and 18th Cols Morgan and Lawler having halted at Elliotts Mill, the cavalry, consisting of six companies, Capt Stewart, Commanding pushed on within some two miles of the defences of Columbus, reconnoitring the roads and the country, and captured three prisoners and four horses. Capt Stewart further reports, that he learned that reinforcements were sent some days since from Columbus to Bowling Green, Ky. and that considerable dissatisfaction was expressed by inhabitants, along the road, at the frequent seizure of horses, belonging to individuals, for rebel service. Capt Stewart's advance is the nearest that has been made, by any Federal force, on the Kentucky shore, to Columbus. Both Infantry and Cavalry returned without meeting with any injury or accident, whatever. A prisoner brought in by the scouts this evening reports that the engagement between the Federal and Rebel Gun boats yesterday excited much alarm among the rebels at Columbus, and induced a general belief among them that they were to be immediately attacked by a land force." LS, DNA, RG 393, District of Cairo, Letters Received.

To Brig. Gen. Eleazer A. Paine

———

Head Quarters, Dist of Cairo
Cairo, Jany 12th 1862.

GEN. E. A. PAINE
COMMDG 2ND BRIGADE
BIRD'S POINT, MO.
GENERAL,

The citizens brought in, under directions of yesterday, may be put in tents, as suggested by you. They can use the tents of troops who do not go out with you, or such surplus tents, as may be in the hands of troops at Bird's Point.

If you have reason to believe, that the parties guilty of shooting our pickets, are discovered, inform me, and I will order a Court of Commission, that will act without delay.

Very Respectfully
Your Obt Servant
U. S. GRANT.
Brig Gen. Commdg

Copies, DLC-USG, V, 1, 2, 3, 85; DNA, RG 393, USG Letters Sent. *O.R.*, I, viii, 495. On Jan. 12, 1862, Brig. Gen. Eleazer A. Paine wrote to Capt. John A. Rawlins. "I have sent out patrols in obedience to Gen. Grants orders. I wish to ask Gen Grant if I can the persons arrested into tents. I shall probably have a hundred in to night. Will Gen. Grant give me more definite instructions. I think I shall find out who shot the picketts and when I do I shall shoot the guilty parties on very short notice. I send this by a Mr. Lartigue from New Orleans, and from Columbus on Friday morning. He appears very intelligent." ALS, DNA, RG 393, District of Cairo, Letters Received. See letters to Brig. Gen. Eleazer A. Paine, Jan. 11, 19, 1862.

To Brig. Gen. Charles F. Smith

———

Head Quarters, Dist. of Cairo
Cairo, Jan.y 12th 1862.

GEN. C. F. SMITH
COMD.G U. S. FORCES
PADUCAH, KY.
GEN.

Dispatches from Gen. Halleck says he can hear nothing from Gen. Buell; to set my own time. As the expected reinforcements will not leave St. Louis, and Camp Douglas, until to-morrow I will not move to Blandville until Teusday.[1] This will bring the force, which is to form a junction with you, into Mayfield on Thursday. This will regulate the time for the departure of your Column.

Three gun boats come up yesterday to near where Gen. McClernand is encamped. Our Gunboats engaged them chasing them under their batteries at Columbus. Our boats were not touched. Two shots hit one of the rebel boats and it is thought disabled her for present use.

Very respectfully
Your Obt. Svt.
U. S. GRANT
Brig. Gen.

ALS, James S. Schoff, New York, N. Y.

1. Jan. 14, 1862.

To Col. Thomas H. Cavanaugh

————

Head Quarters, Dist of Cairo,
Cairo, Jany 12th 1862

Col. T. H. Cavanaugh.
Commdg Shawneetown, Ills.
Col:

Your communication of the 9th inst is received. I am glad to learn that your Regiment is mustered into service, and expect ere long to give you active employment. I have directed the Chief Quartermaster here, to make arrangements for supplying your command with forage.[1] Your provisions will be supplied from here, and should be drawn for, half-monthly, always sending in your Returns, at least five days before the supply on hand has given out.

I have nothing to add to, or retract from, former instructions, as to the breaking up of the illicit trade, now being carried on with the opposite side of the river. Your jurisdiction in this respect will extend from the Wabash to Cave in Rock.

About the thirty guns you speak of, I know nothing. I cannot issue any orders in the matter whatever. I do not believe there is any authority from Government to accept them, nor the men to handle them. Make out a statement of all the facts, and submit it to Head Quarters of the Department, through these Head Quarters.

Very Respectfully,
Your Obt. Servant,
U. S. Grant.
Brig Genl. Commdg.

Copies, DLC-USG, V, 1, 2, 3, 85; DNA, RG 393, USG Letters Sent. On Jan. 20, 1862, Lt. Col. John Olney, 6th Ill. Cav., wrote to USG "in reference to refusal of Paymaster to pay the men of his command." DLC-USG, V, 10; DNA, RG 393, USG Register of Letters Received.

1. See following letter.

To Capt. Algernon S. Baxter

Head Quarters, Dist of Cairo
Cairo, Jany 12th 1862.

CAPT. A. S. BAXTER
A. Q. M.
CAIRO, ILLS.
SIR:

It will be necessary for you to make immediate arrangement to have hay delivered at Shawneetown. There is one entire Regiment of Cavalry there consuming about eight tons per days. They have now on hand about ten days supply.

As soon as possible I want you, or an efficient agent in your employ, to visit Shawneetown, and see how the affairs of your Department are conducted, and give such instructions, as may seem necessary to insure a full supply of all that is required there, and a proper accountability for the same.

Respectfully,
U. S. GRANT.
Brig. Genl. Commdg.

Copies, DLC-USG, V, 1, 2, 3, 85; DNA, RG 393, USG Letters Sent. On Jan. 12, 1862, Capt. John A. Rawlins issued USG General Orders No. 2. "Capt. A. S. Baxter A. Q. M. Vols. is hereby appointed District Quartermaster, for the District of Cairo He will make, or properly provide for making, all contracts, and purchases, within the District, including contracts for water Transport, and every thing pertaining to the Quartermasters Department. All contracts, estimates for funds, and requisitions, within this District, will be sent through the Chief of the Department, here, for approval, before passing to higher authority, and no contract, within the District, will be regarded as valid, without this, or higher authority. Hereafter, all demands from these Head Quarters for transportation, either by land or water, will be made directly upon the Chief Quartermaster. Capt. W. J. Kountz A. Q. M. will report to Capt. Baxter, as Master of Water Transportation, and will in future receive his orders from him." Copies, DLC-USG, V, 12, 13, 14, 95; DNA, RG 393, USG General Orders. See following letter.

To Capt. Reuben B. Hatch

Head Quarters, Dist of Cairo
Cairo, Jany 12th 1862.

CAPT. R. B. HATCH
A. Q. M.
CAPTAIN:

Orders having been received from Washington, calling for your arrest, I have ordered Capt. Baxter to relieve you in your duties as Quartermaster in this District. As you are responsible for a large amount of Public Property I do not feel it just to you, to make your confinement close. You have therefore the limits of Cairo, and should it be necessary in the course of your duties in turning over property, to go to either of the Posts, garrisoned by troops now using property for which you are accountable permission will be granted. Capt C. B. Lagow will deliver this, and receive your sword.

Respectfully
U. S. GRANT.
Brig. Gen. Commdg.

Copies, DLC-USG, V, 1, 2, 3, 85; DNA, RG 393, USG Letters Sent. See letters to Maj. Gen. Henry W. Halleck, Jan. 12, 1862, and to Brig. Gen. Montgomery C. Meigs, Jan. 13, 1862. On Jan. 12, 1862, Capt. John A. Rawlins issued Special Orders No. 13. "By directions from the Quarter master Gen. of the Army Capt. R. B. Hatch A. Q. M. Vols is hereby placed in arrest. . . . All moneys, Stores, and property, of every description, pertaining, to the Quarter masters Dept., in possession of Capt. Hatch will be turned over to Capt. A. S. Baxter, A Q. M. Vols forthwith, who will receipt for the same." Copies, DLC-USG, V, 15, 16, 82, 87, 89; DNA, RG 393, USG Special Orders. On the same day, Rawlins issued Special Orders No. 14. "Capt. R. B. Hatch, will forthwith, turn over to Capt. C B. Lagow all books pertaining to the Public businiss of his Dept. together with the public safe, and contents for safe keeping until such time, as they may be called for by legal authority. The books will be placed in the Safe if practicable, if not well secured with the Pay master or in some secure place." Copies, *ibid.* At some later time, not specified, USG added a postscript to these orders. "Capt Hatch can have such papers as are necessary to complete his reports. The remainder will be packed up in the Capt's presence and placed in a secure place, say in the Paymaster's vault. Mr. Dunton may be authorized to assist Capt. Hatch in getting up his reports. as soon as this change is made, a note will be delivered to you, addressed to Col. Buford, authorizing the partial release of Mr. Dunton delivered as soon as all papers are packed as directed." Copy, DLC-USG, V, 85.

General Orders No. 3

Head Quarters Dist of Cairo
Cairo Ill. January 13. 1862

GENERAL ORDER NO. 3

During the absence of the Expedition now starting upon soil hitherto occupied almost solely by the Rebel Army, and where it is a fair inference that every stranger met is our enemy, the following orders will be observed.

Troops, in marching, will be kept in the ranks, Company officers being held strictly accountable for all stragglers from their Companies.

No firing will be allowed in camp or on the march, not strictly required in the performance of duty.

Whilst in Camp, no permits will be granted to officers or soldiers to leave their regimental grounds, and all violations of this order must be promptly and summarily punished.

Disrepute having been brought upon our brave soldiers by the bad conduct of some of their numbers, showing on all occations, when marching through territory occupied by sympathisers of the enemy, a total disregard of rights of citizens, and being guilty of wanton destruction of private propety the Genl. commanding, desires and intends to enforce a change in this respect.

Interpreting Confiscation Acts by troops themselves, has a demoralizing effect, weakens them in exact proportion to the demoralization and makes open and armed enemies of many who, from opposite treatment would become friends or at worst non-combatants.

It is orded, therefore that the severest punishment, be inflicted upon every soldier, who is guilty of taking or dstroying private property, and any commissioned officer guilty of like conduct, or of countenancing it shall be deprived of his sword and expelled from the camp, not to be permitted to return.

On the march, Cavalry Advance guards will be well thrown

out, ~~baggage~~ also flank guards of Cavalry or Infantry when practicable.

A rear guard of Infantry will be required to see that no teams, baggage or disabled soldiers are left behind

It will be the duty of Compan~~ies~~y Commanders to see that rolls of their Companies are called immediatly upon going into camp each day and every member accounted for

By order

U. S. GRANT Brig. Gen'l Comdg.

Copies, DLC-USG, V, 12, 13, 14, 95; DNA, RG 94, 9th Ill., Letterbook; *ibid.*, 48th Ill., Letterbook; *ibid.*, RG 393, USG General Orders; (Printed) McClernand Papers, IHi. *O.R.*, I, vii, 551.

On Jan. 22, 1862, Capt. John A. Rawlins wrote to Lt. Col. Harrison E. Hart, 22nd Ill. "The sentence of forfeiture of pay of your Regiment, for violation of Genl. Order No 3, from these Head Qrs. and disobedience of orders, in not desisting from destroying property on the night of the 15th inst, when repeatedly ordered to do so, is remitted. Your regiment was not charged with stealing, but with illegally and improperly destroying property. The Genl. Commdg. however remits his sentence, in consequence of previous good conduct on the part of the 22nd, and his confidence in the Regiment, whenever called on for active duty. And because he has good reason to believe, that Genl. Orders No 3. were violated, by other troops equally with this Regt. and where it is not in his power to ascertain who the guilty parties were. An investigation into the matter cannot be had, without manifest injury to the service, in exposing a state of facts, contemplated, to be removed by Genl. Orders No 3." Copies, DLC-USG, V, 1, 2, 3, 85; DNA, RG 393, USG Letters Sent.

To Brig. Gen. Montgomery C. Meigs

———

Head Quarters Dist of Cairo

Cairo Jany 13, 1862

GEN M. C. MEIGS
QUARTER MASTER GENERAL
WASHINGTON D. C.
GENERAL.

I received your communication of the 6th inst. on yesterday.

I immediately caused Capt R. B. Hatch to be placed in arrest and upon what seemed to me probable evidence of guilt as an

accomplice I had his chief clerk arrested and put in confinement
—I also had all the books and papers of the Department seized
and locked up in the safe and the key kept in custody of a member
of my staff.

All of which is done and kept subject to further orders—

Very Respectfully

U. S. GRANT

Brig. Gen.

LS, DNA, RG 92, Consolidated Correspondence, Cairo Fraud Investigation. On
Jan. 6, 1862, Brig. Gen. Montgomery C. Meigs had written to USG. "I have to
day received and read the Report of Aide de Camp Hillyer on the charges against
Q. M. Capt R P. Hatch, of Volunteers. If you have not already placed Capt Hatch
under arrest, I have to request that you will do so—Charges will be preferred
against him so soon as they can be put into form, by the proper Officers" Copy,
ibid., Letters Sent. On Jan. 8, Meigs referred the report of Capt. William S.
Hillyer to the War Dept. and the arrest of Capt. Reuben B. Hatch was approved
by Secretary of War Simon Cameron. *Ibid.*, RG 107, Register of Letters Received.
The endorsements are on the copy of Hillyer's report *ibid.*, RG 92, Consolidated
Correspondence, Cairo Fraud Investigation. On Jan. 10, Meigs wrote to USG.
"Having referred the papers and testimony in the case of Capt J Hillyers investi-
gation of lumber purchased at Chicago for Cairo, to the Judge Advocate of the
Army, he has returned it with the opinion of which I enclose a copy   The charges
have been preferred by the Judge Advocate   As you have power to order a Ct.
Martial in the case, I respectfully request you to do so   The charges are signed
by the Qr M. Genl   I have directed Capt. Hatch to dismiss the clerk Wilcox"
Copy, *ibid.*, Letters Sent. A copy of the Jan. 2 letter of Bvt. Maj. John F. Lee,
Judge-Advocate of the Army, is *ibid.*

To Maj. Gen. Henry W. Halleck

BY TELEGRAPH FROM Cairo Jan'y 13 *1862*

To MAJ. GENL HALLECK

Will you please telegraph to Springfield Ill, and have carbines in hands of Express Co. forwarded? They are the same I
wrote about last week.

U. S. GRANT

Brig. Genl.

Telegram received, DNA, RG 94, Generals' Papers and Books, Telegrams
Received by Gen. Halleck; copy, *ibid.*, RG 393, Dept. of the Mo., Telegrams
Received. See letter to Capt. John C. Kelton, Jan. 3, 1862.

To Brig. Gen. John A. McClernand

———

Head Quarters, Dist. of Cairo,
Cairo, Jan.y 13th 1862.

Gen. J. A. McClernand
Comd.g Advance Forces,
Fort Jefferson Ky.
Gen.

Instruct your Guard at Elliotts Mills to move to Blandville as soon as relieved to-morrow, by forces sent from ~~here~~ Birds Point. If deemed safe the force from the Mills may move by the road West of Mayfield Creek.

I will start a force as early as possible in the morning for the purpose of relieving that Guard.

I would advise an early start to the top of the hill with the teams but no movement of troops, except advance Guard, until troops from Birds Point arrive.

Respectfully
Your Obt. Svt.
U. S. Grant
Brig. Gen. Com

ALS, McClernand Papers, IHi. On Jan. 13, 1862, Brig. Gen. John A. McClernand wrote to USG. "Your communication of this date brought by Capt. Kountz, is received. The guard at Eliotts Mills will be continued there, according to your instructions, until re-inforced by the forces from Birds Point. I have already determined on the plan of my movement to Blandville. Being sufficiently familiar with the different roads to be assured, I have decided to move a part of my command upon the *Hill* or upper Road to Blandville. Another portion, upon the lower road, running near the former, both uniting about half the way to Blandville. To-day, I have sent forward a Cavalry Company to Blandville, by the Hill road, which will return by the road south of Mayfield Creek, and Eliotts Mills. Lieut Freeman accompanies the detachment for the purpose of selecting a place for encampment at or near Blandville. I will conform to your instructions as to the time and manner of starting on the morrow—hoping that the re-inforcements from Bird's Point will arrive here in time to prevent delay. From what has been said you will learn that the country south of the creek, along the Eliotts Mills road has become quite familiar to us. The supplies of forage and provisions, upon which everything depends, have not arrived." LS, DNA, RG 393, District of Cairo, Letters Received; DfS, McClernand Papers, IHi.

On the same day, 1st Lt. Clark B. Lagow wrote to McClernand. "I am directed by the Genl. Commanding to say to you, that you will send at once to these Head Quarters, the number of men that will move forward of your command, tomorrow. Also names of Regiments and detachments and number of each" Copies, DLC-USG, V, 1, 2, 3, 85; DNA, RG 393, USG Letters Sent. McClernand's report, dated Jan. 13, listed 4,202 inf., 662 cav., and 139 art., for a total of 5,003 men. Copy, McClernand Papers, IHi.

Also on Jan. 13, McClernand wrote to USG. "James Johnson was arrested by the mounted reconnoitring party commanded by Capt Stewart under very strong suspicions of being a rebel. He was mounted on a horse newly shod. When Capt S. approached the house of Johnson, two men left their horses and fled leaving them which proved to be rebel cavalry horses. Albert Dickenson arrested at the same time, is sent to you for detention for safety. Thos J. Mason arrested at same time, is charged with tendering his services and being anxious to assist in conveying despatches to Genl Polk, having mistaken Capt Stewart and his force for confederate reconnoitring party. They are sent to you for such action as you may deem proper in the premises." DfS, *ibid.*

To Brig. Gen. John A. McClernand

Head Quarters, Dist. of Cairo,
Cairo, Jan.y 13th 1862.

Gen. J. A. McClernand
Comd.g Advance Forces
Fort Jefferson, Ky.
Gen.

Your communication of this date is just received.

I ordered yesterday a supply of forage, provisions and Coal. Supposed all had gone except the provisions. They will be down to-night. The order will be renewed for forage at once.

The cavalry and 28th Ill. are ordered to leave Fort Holt at 8 O'Clock a. m. for Elliotts Mills to relieve your guard there.

Respectfully
Your Obt. Svt.
U. S. Grant
Brig. Gen. Com

ALS, McClernand Papers, IHi. On Jan. 13, 1862, Brig. Gen. John A. McClernand wrote to USG. "Capt W. D. Porter of the Gunboat force stationed here, informs me that the supply of *coal* is nearly exhausted, and suggests that it is not safe for them to return to Cairo for coaling; but rather a barge be Sent down with a cargo for their use here at once. . . . P. S. There are carbines at Springfield which are very much needed by the cavalry. Col Dickey calls my attention to this matter" ADf, *ibid*. On Jan. 13, Capt. William S. Hillyer wrote to McClernand. "I am instructed by Gen Grant to inform you in reply to your communication of this date that the General ordered coal to be transported to Ft Jefferson yesterday but the state of the wind prevented the barges from going down—You will let the Gun boats use the coal now on the steamers there and coal will be sent down by steamers to day as soon as possible. The carbines will be got from Springfield if possible—" ALS, *ibid*. On the same day, McClernand wrote to USG. "Your despatch of this date by Lieut. Heath, is this moment received. I am pained to repeat that neither provisions nor forage have arrived, and it is now nearly 9 o'clock at night. Our forage, particularly *Hay*, is exhausted, and the supply of provisions must soon be so. What shall be done in this perplexing dilemma? Having completed the reconnoisance to Blandville, and selected ground for encampment in the vicinity of that place, I am prepared so far as I can make myself so, to take up the line of march by nine o'clock in the morning. Please direct me as quickly as possible, what shall be done?" LS, DNA, RG 393, District of Cairo, Letters Received; DfS, McClernand Papers, IHi.

On Jan. 13, Hillyer wrote to Capt. Algernon S. Baxter. "You will send as much of the Gun Boat Coal as possible by Steamers to Fort Jefferson as soon as you can. If the Gun Boats have a partially filled Flat Boat that you think can be safely towed send down in that way. Otherwise load the Steamboats. Make all possible dispatch. This coal is for use of the Gun Boats." Copies, DLC-USG, V, 1, 2, 3, 85; DNA, RG 393, USG Letters Sent. On the same day, Capt. John A. Rawlins wrote to Baxter. "I am informed, the troops are out of forage at Fort Jefferson. You will see that they are supplied at once. I have also just been informed that there is not at this time, one days supply of coal for transports. It will not do to allow them to be out of fuel." Copies, *ibid*. On the same day, Baxter replied to Rawlins. "A barge load of forage is on it's way to Fort Jefferson, and Capt Dunlap is attending to his Brigade there.—A large quantity was sent last night and it's not possible for them to be out—I have 20,000 Bush Coal here. the Gun boats have about 500 000 bush. and other parties have here 150 to 200,000 Bush" ALS, *ibid*., District of Southeast Mo., Letters Received.

To Brig. Gen. Charles F. Smith

———

Head Quarters, Dist of Cairo
Cairo, Jany 13th 1862.

GEN. C. F. SMITH
COMMDG U. S. FORCES
PADUCAH, KY.
GEN:

The 20th Regiment of Ky. Volunteers now being sworn into service, and Col. Bruce[1] necessarily becoming Commanding Officer of the Post, I advise the withdrawal of the Company of the 12th Ills. and Lt. Col. Chetlain from there. Make such orders in this matter as you deem most expedient for the good of the service.

> Very Respectfully
> Your Obt Servant
> U. S. GRANT.
> Brig Genl. Commdg.

Copies, DLC-USG, V, 2, 85; DNA, RG 393, USG Letters Sent. On Jan. 13, 1862, Brig. Gen. Charles F. Smith replied to USG. "I have yr letter of this date about the troops at Smith-land. If I had the time & the steamer I would gladly bring down the 5 cos. from there. The force at Camp Beauregard is represented by my latest advices so weak that I think I will run over them before morning in the direction of Murray. I want these men to say they have done something." ALS, *ibid.*, District of Cairo, Letters Received.

1. Col. Sanders D. Bruce, 20th Ky.

To Capt. Reuben B. Hatch

———

> Head Quarters, Dist of Cairo
> Cairo Jany 13th 1862.

CAPT. R. B. HATCH A. Q. M.
CAIRO, ILLS.
CAPTAIN:

To grant your request of this morning, would necessarily require the return of the Keys of your safe and all papers connected with your Department. This I cannot do until I hear from Head Quarters of the Department where every step that has been taken is reported.

I hope sincerely, that a hasty, or rather I should say, prompt investigation will take place, and that you may entirely clear yourself of every imputation.

> Respectfully,
> Your Obt. Servant.
> U. S. GRANT.
> Brig. Genl. Commdg.

Copies, DLC-USG, V, 2, 85; DNA, RG 393, USG Letters Sent. On Jan. 13, 1862, Capt. Reuben B. Hatch wrote to Capt. Algernon S. Baxter. "I cannot surender to you the room I have been occupying as an office unless I at the same time am ordered by the commander of the Disct to surrender and give up all my books and papers to you—they are now under Guard—it would have been very desireable to me to have finished my last quarters report immediately—but cannot do it and it may be as well for you to take possision of the papers and Books if ordered to take the office" ALS, *ibid.*, District of Cairo, Letters Received. On Jan. 14, Baxter wrote to Capt. John A. Rawlins. "In order to protect all parties, I suggest that Capt Hatch be allowed to take his *abstracts* and stationery sufficient to complete his reports, to another office—All other 'papers' and contents of safe in the office to be taken immediately and packed in a box in presence of Capt Hatch & some officer you may appoint, and delivered to Paymaster Cook for safe keeping, until further ordered—" ALS, *ibid.*, RG 94, Staff Papers, R. B. Hatch. On Jan. 14, Rawlins wrote to Baxter. "You will take immediate possession of all Offices and quarters heretofore appropriated to the Dist Quartermaster's Department. Capt. R. B. Hatch will remove to such quarters as you may designate for his occupancy. You will communicate this order to Capt. Hatch and if not immediately obeyed report the same to these Head Quarters." Copies, DLC-USG, V, 1, 2, 3, 85; DNA, RG 393, USG Letters Sent.

On Jan. 13, Capt. William S. Hillyer wrote to Hatch. "Genl Grant has just shown me a portion of your letter which states that you have been informed that I said that money was paid you by the lumbermen in my presence   I never said anything of the kind—for it is not true—I did not know that the lumbermen were in the hotel at all untill the next day after they were there   The room was assigned to us by the Hotel Keeper upon my suggestion that I desired a large and convenient room" Copy, Oglesby Papers, IHi. Hatch copied his undated reply on the same sheet. "Your name was not mentioned   I simply stated the rumor on the street I am under arest by direction from Washington   I know not what offense I have committed only that I have been a Republican" ALS, *ibid.* On Jan. 15, Hatch wrote to Rawlins enclosing a clipping of a newspaper letter from Cairo, Jan. 8, written by Frank G. Chapman to the *New York Herald*, accusing Hatch of fraud. ALS, DNA, RG 94, Staff Papers, R. B. Hatch. Also enclosed was an undated letter from Hatch to Chapman charging him with "malicious and wilfull falshood," and reminding him that he was "a brother mason." Copy, *ibid.*

In a letter from which the date has been torn away, probably dated Jan. 28, Hatch wrote to USG. "Enclosed with this you will please find an application for the extention of my limits on parole at least so I can visit my family—I understand from Washington that my case has been placed intirely in your hands and as you are about to leave here it may be prolonged some time therefore I ask your endorsement upon the request and confidently expect a response favourable" LS, Oglesby Papers, IHi. On Jan. 28, Hatch wrote to USG. "Having been placed under arrest under most trying circumstances—with boundaries by far too circumscribed to enable me to place myself before my country in the position I have ever occupied as an honest and upright man, I most earnestly solicit an extension of my limits under parole as will enable me in an honorable manner to prepare myself for any order that may in your judgment be deem[ed] necessary in my case" LS, *ibid.* In an undated letter, Hatch wrote to Col. Richard J. Oglesby. "I suppose I am to be Court Martialed for something   I fear it is because I have been a Republican   will you assist Jack Grimshaw as my council   you knowledge of what I have tried to do for the comfort of the army is more than any other commanding officer   Jack will see you when he comes   answer and Oblige Your Friend" LS, *ibid.*

To Capt. John C. Kelton

———

Head Quarters, Dist. of Cairo,
Cairo, Jan.y 14th 1862

Capt. J. C. Kelton
A. A. Gen. Dept. of the Mo.
St. Louis Mo.
Sir:

The troops from St. Louis, expected to-day, have not yet arrived.[1] I have commenced the move directed a few days since without them however, occupying to-night Blandville, Elliotts, Mills and Fort Jefferson.

Yesterday a reconnoitering party of Cavalry, supported by Infantry, went within three miles of Columbus, driving in the enemies Picketts.

To-day I accompanied Commodore Foote with the Gunboats Essex, St. Louis and Taylor to within one & a half miles of the batteries at Columbus. A few shells were thrown around the batteries by the Essex & St. Louis with what effect I cannot tell. The enemy replied with two or three shots without effect.[2] In making this move I found myself much embarrassed by deficiency in the Quarter-Masters Department. Capt. Kountz who was recently sent here as Master of transportation, from his great unpopularity with river men, and his wholesale denunciation of everybody connected with Government here as thieves and cheats was entirely unable to get crews for the necessary boats. for our transportation. I was compelled to order that boatmen, if they declined serving voluntarily, should be put aboard the boats and made to serve as prisoners. Many expressed a willingness to serve if I said so but would not work under the Captain, and others left the city, as I am informed, solely to avoid the possibility of having to serve under his direction. He seems to have desired to be placed on duty here for no other purpose than to wreak his revenge upon some river men who he dislikes, and to get into the service of Government a boat in which he has an interest, either as owner or a former proprietorship not yet settled for.

He has caused so much trouble and shown such a disregard for my orders that I have been compelled to order his arrest.[3]

I would respectfully ask that he be ordered to another field of duty. As I shall be off tomorrow morning charges cannot be prefered until my return and it is embarrassing to the service, just at this time, to have Courts Martials setting.

I respectfully submit this matter to the Gen. Comd.g the Dept. for his decission.

Col. Cavanaugh, commanding a regiment of Cavalry, now stationed at Shawneetown, has received a telegraphic orders from Springfield, Ill. to report himself there to organize a Brigade,[4] his regiment to form a part, to be reported for orders to Gen. Buell.

As his services can be spared for a few days I have given him leave to go to Springfield but informed him that his regiment cannot be moved without orders coming through Head Quarters of the Dept. The Col. desires me to say that he has a decided preference for remaining in this Department. This however I do not regard as it is his duty to go where ordered and where his services can be of the most value.

> Very respectfully
> Your Obt. Svt.
> U. S. Grant
> Brig. Gen. Com.

ALS, DNA, RG 393, Dept. of the Mo., Letters Received. *O.R.*, I, vii, 551–52.

1. On Jan. 13, 1862, Maj. Gen. Henry W. Halleck telegraphed to USG. "Three regiments of infantry leave this morning for Cairo in Steamers." Copies, DLC-USG, V, 4, 5, 7, 8; DNA, RG 94, Generals' Papers and Books, Telegrams Sent in Cipher by Gen. Halleck; *ibid.*, RG 393, USG Hd. Qrs. Correspondence;

ibid., Dept. of the Mo., Telegrams Sent. On Jan. 17, Halleck forwarded a copy of USG's letter to Maj. Gen. George B. McClellan. AES, *ibid.*, RG 94, Letters Received.

2. On Jan. 14, Flag Officer Andrew H. Foote telegraphed to Secretary of the Navy Gideon Welles. "In company with General Grant, Comd'g. the military forces, I have just made a reconnoissance with the Essex, St. Louis, and Taylor down the river within a mile and a half of Columbus. We fired several shots about the batteries which were returned by two or three guns. The object of this demonstration was in connection with the Army movements." Telegram received (punctuation added), DLC-Robert T. Lincoln.

3. On Jan. 19, Capt. John A. Rawlins issued Special Orders No. 18. "Capt. W. J. Kountz now in arrest, and having only the limits of the St Charles Hotel, is hereby given the limits of the City of Cairo Ill." Copies, DLC-USG, V, 15, 16, 82, 87, 89; DNA, RG 393, USG Special Orders.

4. On Jan. 21, Col. Thomas H. Cavanaugh, 6th Ill. Cav., Springfield, telegraphed to USG. "Brigade is formed: Three regiments infantry, Two cavalry (Mine included), Two batteries (thirty pieces) flying artillery, one battery James Cannon. Will report in person." Telegram received (punctuation added), *ibid.*, Dept. of the Mo., Telegrams Received.

To Brig. Gen. John A. McClernand

Head Quarters, Dist. of Cairo,
Cairo, Jan.y 14th 1862.

GEN. J. A. MCCLERNAND
COMD.G ADVANCE FORCES
FORT JEFFERSON, KY.
GEN.

In accordance with previous instructions encamp at or near Blandville tonight.

To-morrow ~~send~~ March with your entire command from seven to ten miles on the most practicab[le] route to Mayfield, probably through Lovelaceville.[1] ~~The~~ Next morning start two regiments of Infantry, and all the Cavalry but four companies, to join Gen. Smith at Mayfield. At the same time send out a good portion of the Cavalry you expect to retain on a reconnaisance towards Columbus and leave anything but an appearance of an intention to return this way, with a portion of your force, until you actually start on the return. In the afternoon, say starting at

12 m. return again to Blandville. You will there find additional forces and will receive directions for future movements.

Should I not be with you you may find it necessary to vary the above instructions.

It is not expected that the force thrown forward to Mayfield will be sent in the face of a large ~~force~~ Army, nor that you will remain off from the balance of the troops, and so remote from the base of our lines, to receive an attack from a superior force. The management in this respect will have ~~will have~~ to be left to your judgement knowing that you will be ~~the~~ better able to judge of the feasability of the plan indicated than any one, not present, could be.

> Very respectfully
> Your Obt. Svt.
> U. S. GRANT
> Brig. Gen. Cm.

ALS, McClernand Papers, IHi. *O.R.*, I, vii, 553. On Jan. 14, 1862, Brig. Gen. John A. McClernand wrote to USG. "I have broken up my camp. The forces and their trains are in marching orders. I only await the arrival of the forces to be sent to relieve me here, and the guard at Elliotts Mills as required in your order of the 13th Please advise me as to the movement to be made, and send the relief immediately" LS, DNA, RG 393, District of Cairo, Letters Received. On the same day, McClernand again wrote to USG. "My forces, notwithstanding the shortness of the time given, and the inexperience of the men, were in marching order awaiting the arrival of the forces sent to my relief, which occurred about noon. I immediately marched, and the advance columns are now preparing the camping ground previously selected, within a mile and a half of the village of Blandville. The different commands are coming forward in good order. No accidents have happened, and we expect to be in camp to-night. The weather is cold and invigorating—snow lying upon the ground. So far as has proceeded well" DfS, McClernand Papers, IHi.

1. Lovelaceville, Ky., on Mayfield Creek about twelve miles from the Mississippi River.

To Brig. Gen. Eleazer A. Paine

———

Head Quarters, Dist of Cairo
Cairo, Jany 14th 1862.

Brig. Genl. E. A. Paine
Commdg Forces,
Bird's Point, Mo.
Genl:

Tomorrow march your command to Blandville, leaving one Regiment of Infantry, and on[e] squadron of Cavalry at Fort Jefferson, and to guard the road at Elliotts Mill. Have all approaches from Columbus watched so as to avoid all chance of surprise. You will receive further instructions at Blandville.

Respectfully
Your Obt. Servant
U. S. Grant.
Brig. Genl. Commdg.

Copies, DLC-USG, V, 1, 2, 3, 85; DNA, RG 393, USG Letters Sent. *O.R.*, I, vii, 553. On Jan. 13, 1862, John Riggin, Jr., wrote to Brig. Gen. Eleazer A. Paine. "You will be in readiness to move your force, heretofore designated, to Fort Jefferson per transports tomorrow." Copies, DLC-USG, V, 2, 85; DNA, RG 393, USG Letters Sent. On the same day, Riggin wrote to Capt. Algernon S. Baxter. "You will provide Steamers at Bird's Point for transportation of forces there, for Fort Jefferson. To be in readiness tomorrow morning." Copies, *ibid.* Also on Jan. 13, Col. William H. L. Wallace, Bird's Point, wrote to his wife. "We are again under marching orders, to leave here tomorrow—We cross into Ky, where we go to I dont know—I was mistaken in writing to you yesterday that the troops which went down from Cairo had returned—They are still encamped at Fort Jefferson & we go there tomorrow—It is cold, very cold—It has snowed some today & the river is covered with floating ice—" ALS, ICarbS.

To Col. Napoleon B. Buford

———

Head Quarters, Dist of Cairo
Cairo, Jany 14th 1862

COL. N. B. BUFORD
COMMDG POST,
CAIRO, ILLS.
COLONEL:

Mr. Dunton, for the purpose of assisting Capt. Hatch in making out his quarterly report may be released from confinement, on his parole not to leave Cairo.

Respectfully,
U. S. GRANT
Brig. Genl. Commdg.

Copies, DLC-USG, V, 1, 2, 3, 85; DNA, RG 393, USG Letters Sent. On Jan. 14, 1862, Capt. Reuben B. Hatch wrote to USG. "It is to me very desireable to have my last quarters report completed and as I have trusted much of that to Mr Dunton would it be inconsistent and out of order for me to ask you to allow him to attend to it untill finished under any restrictions you may subject him too   you well know my duties have been varied and much more than an ordinary man like myself could attend to in detail—I hope nothing has been done intentionally wrong—yet there may have been and I may have too suffer for it—I only care for my little family at home—In finishing my report I wish to try to save myself and my securities—I have tried to do right   designing men may have ruined me" ALS, DNA, RG 109, Union Provost Marshals' File of Papers Relating to Individual Civilians.

On Jan. 20, G. B. Dunton wrote to U.S. Senator Orville H. Browning. "I wrote you a few days since concerning a 'lumber transaction' which was at that time being bruited in some of the newspapers and concerning which I made some explanations. I have no emendations to make now even with the results which have followed. It may not be known to you that like Major Hatch, I too am under arrest for what I do not know. There are of course no charges against me but having been the Chief Clerk I suppose it was considered a duty to arrest me. I am on parole and have the limits of Cairo assigned as the territory I may occupy. It can do no good to keep me under arrest for I have not been and am not a responsible party and can at any time be found. If the Major and myself could have our limits *extended* so that one or both of us could visit Washington and have the privilege of explaining matters, I have no doubt all could be made perfectly satisfactory. So far as I know nothing wrong has been done and Major H's desire is that we may both have our limits extended sufficiently to accomplish the above. I think it a specimen of the basest ingratitude on the part of the Govt toward Hatch who has striven for 9 months day and night, and always under the deepest embarrassments, to accomplish some good for the cause to now be put under arrest and thereby more or less disgraced on the testimony of idle newspaper correspondents or that of evil disposed or malicious persons. No man has worked harder or more continuously than he and to what end? If our Govt thus rewards her public servants God forbid that any man having a decent touch of self respect should throw himself away for it. I speak plainly to you for I know you are *his* friend and am proud to think that he is *mine* also. In conclusion allow me to ask you to use your influence to accomplish the extension of our boundary—Mrs Dunton joins me in sending our kind wishes to you" ALS, *ibid.*, RG 94, Letters Received. On Jan. 27, Browning wrote to Secretary of War Edwin M. Stanton. "You will remember that on saturday I had a very brief conversation with you in regard to Quarter Master R B Hatch of Cairo, and his clerk Mr Dunton, both of whom are under arrest. Mr Dunton is a civilian—a man of high character, a christian gentleman, and under arrest without being charged even with an indiscretion, much less a crime. This ought not to be. It injures our cause. If he is guilty of any offence let him be tried and punished. I will not attempt to screen him or any one else from punishment for crime; but it is an outrage for good men to be arrested and imprisoned without even a charge against them. Let him be set at liberty till charges are prefered. I will guaranty his forth coming to answer. I enclose a letter from Mr Dunton for your perusal. No man has heretofore maintained a higher charater for honor and integrity than Mr Hatch. He ought to be granted a speedy trial away from Cairo. This is all his friends ask, and this is reasonable and just. If he is guilty let him be punished, but he has a right to a fair, speedy trial. If you can, do give Mr Grimshaw of Illinois, who bears this, an interview." ALS, *ibid.*

To Col. John Cook

———

Head Quarters, Dist of Cairo
Cairo, Jany 14th 1862.

COL. JOHN COOK
COMMDG FORCES,
FORT, HOLT, KY.

Your command will march tomorrow to Blandville leaving Fort Jefferson at 10 O'clock, A. M.

Respectfully
Your Obt Servant
U. S. GRANT
Brig. Genl. Commdg

Copies, DLC-USG, V, 1, 2, 3, 85; DNA, RG 393, USG Letters Sent. *O.R.*, I, vii, 552. On Jan. 12, 1862, Capt. John A. Rawlins wrote to Col. John Cook. "You will have the men of your command, now under marching orders, supplied with five days complete rations from Wednesday morning the 15th inst. and ½ forage of grain, and half forage of hay for your cattle for same time. The requisite returns for rations, and requisitions for forage for the time above designated, you will have made out at once. Officers drawing pay for commutation of rations or forage will attend to providing their own supplies." Copies, DLC-USG, V, 1, 2, 3, 85; DNA, RG 393, USG Letters Sent. On Jan. 13, Cook telegraphed to USG. "There will march from This Post tomorrow as near as we can ascertain rank & file fifteen hundred 1500 viz 7th Ills Vol six hundred & fifty 28th Ills Vols seven hundred Delanos cavalry seventy Moores Co D 2d Ill cavalry seventy five" Telegram received, *ibid.*, Dept. of the Mo., Telegrams Received.

To Brig. Gen. James W. Ripley

————

Head Quarters, Dist. of Cairo
Cairo, Jan.y 15th 1862

SPECIAL REQUISITION
BRIG. GEN. RIPLEY,
CHIEF OF ORDNANCE
WASHINGTON D. C.
GEN.

Please send to address of Capt. Brinck, Act. Ord. Officer Cairo, Ill. for the use of the Army Five thousand (5000) of Ketchum's improved Hand Grenades[1] of following sizes, viz: One thousand of fives, two thousand of threes and two thousand of Ones

Recapitulation
2000 (Threes)
2000 (Ones)
1000 (Fives)

Respectfully
Your Obt. Svt.
U. S. GRANT
Brig. Gen. Cm

ALS, DNA, RG 156, OCO Document File.

1. An illustration of a Ketchum hand grenade is available in Francis A. Lord, *They Fought for the Union* (New York, 1960), p. 171.

To Col. C. Carroll Marsh

Head Quarters, Camp in Field
O'Neils, Mill, Jany 16th 1862.

COL. C. C. MARSH
20TH ILLS. VOLS.
FORT. JEFFERSON KY.
COLONEL:

You will send the accompanying dispatch to Col. Johnson at Elliott's Mills as soon as possible.[1]

Let six of your companies of your Regiments be got ready, and moved as soon as possible to join Col. Johnson's command at Elliott's Mill, when they will camp for the night, leaving the remaining force to garrison Fort Jefferson

Have three or four Cavalry men stationed at Fort Jefferson, to bring any dispatches, which may come there for me. If you have no Cavalry for the purpose, you can detain the Cavalry, which carry you this dispatch if you have no other.

By order of Brig. Gen. Grant.
WM S. HILLYER
Aid-de-Camp

Copies, DLC-USG, V, 1, 2, 3, 85; DNA, RG 393, USG Letters Sent. *O.R.*, I, vii, 555. On Jan. 16, 1862, Col. C. Carroll Marsh wrote to Capt. John A. Rawlins. "The messenger to Cairo has just returned with accompanying dispatches—Six Companies of the 20th sent to Elliott Mills as ordered left here at 12 M—Four deserters from Columbus came into my camp today—have sent them to Cairo— they report about forty thousand troops there—None have left there for sometime —All the rebel gun boats have gone below—Capt Porter has rec'd positive orders not to move his boats without direct orders from Com Foote—Troops at Columbus are engaged day and night on entrenchments   I sent you the late papers this morning." ALS, DNA, RG 393, District of Cairo, Letters Received.

1. On Jan. 16, Capt. William S. Hillyer wrote to Col. Amory K. Johnson, 28th Ill. "You will push out a strong party of Cavalry and Infantry for reconnoisance on Columbus road for four or five miles towards Columbus, or as far as can be done with security, taking no baggage, and return to Camp at your present position tonight. Six companies of Col. Marsh's, 20th Ills. Vols. will join you at Elliott's Mills tonight." Copies, DLC-USG, V, 1, 2, 3, 85; DNA, RG 393, USG Letters Sent. *O.R.*, I, vii, 555–56. On Jan. 17, Johnson wrote to USG. "[— — — —] received from you at 1 P M [— — — —] with six (6) companies

of [— — — —] Delano's Cavalry, proceeded in [— — —] Columbus, taking the bluff, on [— — —] as the middle road and continued [— — —] to within two (2) miles of Columbus with[out] seeing any thing, neither enemy or signs of any having been out during the day, and could only hear of (4) four scouts early in the morning having passed in the direction of Mayfield. Night overtook me at the above point, and owing to the crispness of the crust over the snow and the impractibility of moving with any degree of silence, I deemed it prudent to return to my camp, which I did by way of the lower or Putnys bend road arriving at my camp at 10 o clock P. M. of 1[7th] inst, without having seen an armed rebel, and give as my opinion that their outposts do not extend beyond their works or lines exceeding one and one half (1½) miles from Columbus. The middle or bluff road is quite practible for the movement of troops for all arms of the service"
ALS, DNA, RG 393, District of Cairo, Letters Received. The top right quarter of the first page is torn away.

To Capt. John C. Kelton

Head Quarters, Camp in the field
Jan.y 17th 1862.

CAPT. J. C. KELTON,
A. A. GEN. DEPT. OF THE MISSOURI,
ST. LOUIS, MO.
CAPT.

On Teusday[1] Gen. McClernand moved from Fort Jefferson to near Blandville with over six thousand men. On Wednsday his position was occupied by Gen. Paine with a force of about two thousand   Gen. McClernand moving with his Brigade towards Milburn,[2] Fort Jefferson a[n]d Elliotts Mills being occupied during this time by two Infantry regiments and some Cavalry & Artillery. The bridge at Coaths Mills was also guarded by one regiment.

On this day, Wednsday, I visited all the different commands, except the one at Elliotts Mills and returned for the night to Coaths Mills.

Written instructions were left with Gen. McClernand to move on to Milburn and from there to send a dispatch across to Gen. Smith, one already prepared, and to return to Blandville by a route East of Mayfield Creek. This would take two days, bringing him in to Blandville to-night. Reconnoisances were made by our troops to within one & a half miles of Columbus and to below the town along the railroad. All was quiet and as yet no skirmish has taken place unless it was with Gen. McC.s command, which I do not think likely, to-day. Yesterday having my forces between me and the enemy I made a reconnoisance of about thirty-five miles, taking my Staff and one company of Cavalry with me.

I find that the Mayfield Creek is fordable at but few points from its mouth up as far as I went, and at those points the water is up to the saddle skirts and the banks very steep.

To-day I have reconnoitired the roads South of the creek and to the Mississippi river at Puntney's bend.[3]

Having rode hard during the day and finding that I should be late returning I sent a note to Capt. Porter of the Navy requesting him to drop down to Puntneys and for a steamer to accompany him to bring myself and escort up to Fort Jefferson. On turning the point in sight a rebel gunboat was discovered and a Cavalry force of propably One hundred men on shore. I got in probably twenty minuets after the rebel Cavalry had fled.

To-morrow I shall visit all points occupied by the Cairo forces and the next day commence a movement back to old quarters, unless orders should be received requiring a change.

I heard from Columbus yesterday. No forces have left there for some days. They were strongly apprehensive a few days ago of an attack but thought most of the force threatning them had gone to Mayfield.

Very respectfully
Your Obt. Svt.
U. S. GRANT
Brig. Gen. Cm.

ALS, DNA, RG 393, Dept. of the Mo., Letters Received. *O.R.*, I, vii, 557–58.

1. Jan. 14, 1862.
2. Milburn, Ky., about fourteen miles east of Columbus.
3. Puntney's Bend, on the Mississippi River about ten miles south of Cairo by river.

To Brig. Gen. John A. McClernand

Head Quarters, Camp in the field,
Near Blandville Ky.
Jan.y 17th 1862.

GEN. J. A. MCCLERNAND,
COMD.G ADVANCE FORCES
GEN.

Encamp tonight at the bridge near Blandville and remain for further instructions.

Yesterday I made, with one company of Cavalry, a reconnaisance of probably thirty miles going on the West side of Mayfield Creek and returning by the East side. I was in hopes of coming up with your command, but finding so many different roads that might be taken by you, and still carry out the plan for your return to this place, I abandoned the idea of seeing you during the day.

I shall go to Elliotts Mills to-night but before going shall extend my reconnoisance over some of the road ~~south~~ West of the creek, possibly as far as Puntneys bend.

Respectfully
Your Obt. Svt.
U. S. GRANT
Brig. Gen.

ALS, McClernand Papers, IHi.

To Col. Leonard F. Ross

Fort Jefferson Ky Jan 17th [*1862*]

COL. ROSS.

Keep the 55th at Cape Girardeau until sent for.

U. S. GRANT.
Brig. Gen'l. Com'd'g.

Telegram, copy, DNA, RG 393, Post of Cape Girardeau, Telegrams. See telegram to Col. Leonard F. Ross, Jan. 19, 1862. On Jan. 16, 1862, Col. Leonard F. Ross telegraphed to USG. "Last night I started three Expeditions into Country, to Dallas, Bloomfield, & Benton. Will report on return. The Steamer January aground above, fifty-fifth (55th) Illinois aboard—Illinois can't go up for ice. I send land expedition with provisions." Telegram received (punctuation added), DNA, RG 393, Dept. of the Mo., Telegrams Received; copy, *ibid.*, Post of Cape Girardeau, Telegrams. On Jan. 17, Ross telegraphed to USG. "The Dallas and Bloomfield Expeditions have returned, bringing twenty three prisoners, among them Captain Day, Q. M. One Battalion Independent Rangers—all discharged men from Thompson's Army   Shall I release them by administering Oath. Dallas expedition not yet heard from." Copy, *ibid.* On Jan. 19, USG telegraphed to Ross. "You will release no more prisoners of war on parole but send them to St Louis." Copy, *ibid. O.R.*, II, i, 533.

On Jan. 18, Ross wrote to USG. "The three expeditions started from this post on the 15th Inst have returned—they were all successful   Capt Murdock returned from Bloomfield last evening with 40 prisoners—among them a Lieut Col. 3 Captains two Surgeons & the adjutant—will write more at length in the course of the day—" LS, DNA, RG 393, District of Cairo, Letters Received. On the same day, Ross telegraphed the same information to USG. Telegram received, *ibid.*, Dept. of the Mo., Telegrams Received. On Jan. 20, USG telegraphed to Ross. "Dispatch received. Write me full Report of the expedition." Copy, *ibid.*, Post of Cape Girardeau, Telegrams. On Jan. 19, Ross wrote to USG. "I have the Honor to submit the following report. Having learned from reliable sources that the citizens of Stoddard Scott & Bollinger Counties under the lead of Captains Bowles & Kitchen—of Genl. Thompsons division Confederate Army—were organizing for the purpose of joining the Rebel forces at New Madrid, On the 15 Inst. I ordered Major F M Smith of the 7 Ill Vol with five companies of Inty, one company of Cavalry under command of Captain Graham 7th Ill Cavalry and one piece of Artillery under command of Sergeant. *Dyer* Campbells Battery, light Artillery to proceeded to Benton Scott Co Mo. and there attack and disperse any organization that might be found capturing such persons as had been in the Rebel Army who had not subsequently surrendered themselves and taken the oath. At the same time I ordered Captain Murdock of Mo State Militia—to take charge of an expedition to Bloomfield Stoddard Co. Mo. consisting of Fifty of his own company (mounted) and a portion of Co—7th Ill. Cavalry Captain Webster commanding with similar instructions, also an expedition to Dallas Bollinger Co Mo. under command of Major Rawalt 7th Cavalry consisting of one hundred mounted men with the same instructions—designing to surprise and capture all persons in rebellion against the U. S. Government, as also their property which might be of use in conducting the ~~war~~ present rebellion—In accordance with such instructions the several expeditions moved simultaneously from this post, on the evening of the 15th inst—for their respective destinations. All of which resulted as satisfactorily as the circumstances & surroundings indicated   On the 17th inst the various expeditions returned bringing with them the following prisoners. From Dallas Major Rawalt with Eighteen prisoners formerly of Thompsons command, but who had been discharged from further service   The Expedition under Captain Murdock was the more successful inasmuch as many of the discharged officers of Thompsons command were attending a Ball in Bloomfield preparatory to their reenlisting—and were probably not anticipating an attack, until they found themselves surrounded. Thirty nine prisoners were captured—among them were Lt Col. Farmer 2nd Reg. Mo. State Guards, Captain Cole Co. A. 2nd Regt. M. S. G. & some ten other officers all of whom were discharged by virtue of expiration of term of enlistment. The Expedition to ~~Dallas~~ Benton arrested and brought in some Five persons charged with aiding and abetting the Rebels—as also having been in the service of the Confederate Government. A number of guns was also destroyed—the intensity of the cold making the carrying of the same very troublesome. Considerable property consisting of Stock, Horses saddles bridles &c. was brought in to the post by the Expeditions and by my Order was turned over to the Quarter Master of this post. I can not speak too highly of the promptness of both officers and men in the several expeditions above reported— The weather was cold and dissagreeable—and they were to a considerable extent unacquainted with the general character of the service upon which they were ordered—yet they responded with a promptness and alacrity that ultimately ensued the success of the same I desire further to state, that in this instance I have the satisfaction of knowing that the news of the expeditions did not as *usual* precede the march of the troops—but that on the contrary the knowledge of the same was kept within the limits of this post owing to the thorough~~ness~~ness of the officers in charge of the pickets. I have in accordance with my best judgment looking at the matter ~~from~~ in the light of all the facts that I can gather—released several of the prominent parties upon their parole of honor—a copy of which I enclose herewith. I regarded this as the best method ~~of~~ to pursue—hoping by so doing at least to establish a more perfect understanding of the object and aim of our Government among those whose enmity arises unquestionably from (as I have previously intimated) ~~a~~ perverted statements on the part of our enemies—These men have pledged their return (upon honor) at such time as you may indicate through this post, and I am fully satisfied ~~they~~ of their honesty of purpose—feeling as they expressed themselves a desire to be (after their observation & limited acquaintance here) permanently out of the service. I desire further to state in this connexion that much remains undone yet in those localities, which I hope to effect, as soon as I can procure arms for the cavalry now located at this point. Many are returning and will yet return from the 'Rebel Army' who fear to come voluntarily and take the oath ~~but who if taken~~—because of an expressed determination on the part of Gen Thompson to hang such persons—but who if taken by force will be I am satisfied hereafter loyal citizens. I do not desire to intrude my opinions but I am satisfied that the best policy to pursue towards the remainder of the prisoners is as pursued towards those above indicated I shall however await your approval before doing so." ALS, *ibid.*, RG 94, War Records Office, Union Battle Reports. *O.R.*, I, viii, 52–53; *ibid.*, II, i, 532–33. On Jan. 23, USG endorsed Ross's letter. "Respectfully forwarded to Head Quarters, Dept. of the Mo. I disapprove the plan of Paroling prisoners of Thompsons Army, as suggested by Col. Ross but refer the matter to the Gen. Comd.g Dept. for his orders in the matter." AES, DNA, RG 94, War Records Office, Union Battle Reports. *O.R.*, I, viii, 53; *ibid.*, II, i, 533.

On Jan. 21, Ross wrote to USG. "In addition to report of yesterday, I desire to add that the expedition to Bloomfield was originally assigned to Major Livingston 11th Mo Vol Inty designing to give a command to each of the Majors at this post; before the expedition started however Major L. was taken *sick*, and the comd was turned over to Capt Murdock. In order to properly arm the Cavalry that was sent I had to obtain the temporary loan of some rifles from the 11th Mo

Vol, leaving a portion of that regiment for the time unarmed. I earnestly hope that
the cavalry regiment at this post be armed as ~~soon~~ as early as practicable, as we
must rely wholly, (almost) upon them to hold in check the roving bands of robbers
and plunderers infesting S. E. Mo. I would like to take a regiment of Inty, some
Artillery & Cavalry and hold Bloomfield for a few days until those *men* could be
driven from state. The roads are so heavy below that there is any danger of
reinforcements being sent from New Madrid or Columbus   There are reports
of Price moving eastward near Arkansas line   I have heard nothing however
reliable—Have you any such Information(?)" ALS, DNA, RG 94, War Records
Office, Union Battle Reports. On Jan. 23, USG endorsed this letter. "Respectfully forwarded to Head Quarters, Dept. of the Mo." AES, *ibid.*

To Brig. Gen. John A. McClernand

Head Quarters, Camp in the Field
Near Blandville, Jan.y 18th/62

Gen. J. A. McClernand
Comd.g Advance Forces,
Gen.

The object of the expedition having been accomplished all
the forces will now be withdrawn to their former positions as
expeditiously as practicable. A guard will be left at this place,
O'Neal's Mills,[1] and at the bridge above until you have passed,
and none of the force will leave Fort Jefferson until your advance
has arrived there.

There are some supplies here for a portion of your command
and I should have been glad could you have made this point to-
night. If the state of the roads however makes it impracticable it
will make no material difference.

The country now has been reconnoitered from Puntney's
bend, to the railroad South of Columbus. The enemy has shown
himself in no place, unless to your command since I heard from
you, except yesterday at Puntney's bend. I went down there
yesterday with about 100 Cavalry and finding that I should be
in the night geting to Fort Jefferson sent a note to Capt. Porter
requesting him to drop down there with the gunboats to convoy
a steamer to take my Cavalry up. He found the place occupied by

a rebel gunboat and the land by about the same amount of Cavalry that I had with me. They left probably twenty minuets before my arrival.

> Respectfully &c.
>
> U. S. GRANT
>
> Brig. Gen. Cm

ALS, McClernand Papers, IHi. (Incomplete) *O.R.*, I, vii, 560. The final paragraph is omitted in copies in DLC-USG, V, 1, 2, 3, 85; DNA, RG 393, USG Letters Sent. On Jan. 18, 1862, Brig. Gen. John A. McClernand wrote to USG. "In order to hasten the delivery of the despatch this company in his charge marches without baggage or supplies   Please furnish them with rations and forage for immediate use, cause the men be refreshed when they will immediately return to Blandville by Lovelaceville Ky." Copy, McClernand Papers, IHi. On Jan. 19, Capt. John A. Rawlins wrote to McClernand. "Should this reach you before you have left O'Neill's Mills, I would be pleased if you would examine the character of lumber they are sawing there. I have been told since my return to this place, he is sawing square timber to be used in boat building, and for making casements over the batteries at Columbus. If you find this true destroy such lumber, and take out some portion of the machinery of the mill, the saws for instance, as will render it useless for the present. Owing to the intolerable state of the roads I would not direct you to turn back for this matter. An expedition can be sent out for the purpose before the roads get in a condition to send the lumber to Columbus." Copies, DLC-USG, V, 1, 2, 3, 85; DNA, RG 393, USG Letters Sent.

1. O'Neal's Mill, near Blandville, was the site of a bridge across Mayfield Creek.

To Brig. Gen. Eleazer A. Paine

> Head Quarters, Dist of Cairo
>
> Cairo, Jany 19th 1862.

GEN E. A. PAINE
COMMDG 2ND BRIGADE
FORT. JEFFERSON, KY.
GENL:

You will proceed to Bird's Point as soon as practicable with a portion of your command, as much as can be taken with their baggage with the transportation supplied.

On your arrival all citizen prisoners, against whom, you have no charge, will be released, and all Negroes who have flocked into camp, will be permitted to return to their masters.

I learn from Col. Perczel,[1] that there are many of this class, now in camp, who have flocked there through fear. Some discretion will have to be used in forcing these people out of camp, now that they are in. I would require all, however, who have masters in Camp, to take their negroes with them.

> Respectfully
> Your Obt. Servant
> U. S. Grant.
> Brig. Genl. Commdg.

Copies, DLC-USG, V, 1, 2, 3, 85; DNA, RG 393, USG Letters Sent. *O.R.*, I, vii, 560. See letters to Brig. Gen. Eleazer A. Paine, Jan. 12, 1862, and to Col. Nicholas Perczel, Jan. 19, 1862.

1. Nicholas Perczel, born in Hungary in 1812, served as a maj. in the Hungarian Revolution of 1848, and later settled at Davenport, Iowa, as a merchant. Edmund Vasvary, *Lincoln's Hungarian Heroes* (Washington, 1939), pp. 69–70. On Sept. 1, 1861, Perczel was commissioned col., 10th Iowa.

To Col. Nicholas Perczel

> Head Quarters, Dist of Cairo
> Cairo, Jany 19th 1862.

Col. N. Perczel
Commdg Bird's Point, Mo.

Yours of the 16th is just received. your course is approved. Gen. Paine will return to day with a portion of his command, and will have the necessary orders for his guidance, in the matters referred to you.

You will make no more arrests of Citizens.

> Respectfully,
> Your Obt Servant
> U. S. Grant.
> Brig. Genl. Commdg.

Copies, DLC-USG, V, 1, 2, 3, 85; DNA, RG 393, USG Letters Sent. On Jan. 15, 1862, Col. Nicholas Perczel wrote to USG. "Lt Colonel Prince of the 7th Illinois Cavalry has returned to day from an Expedition towards carrying out your Orders of the 12th instant for the clearing out the vicinity of this Post for six miles. While out on this Expedition he came to old John Birds house and found property consisting of about 40 negroes, horses, cattle—a great quantity of grain, provisions, and very valuable household goods, which in his opinion will fall the prey of some marauding party if there is nobody to care for it. The said Lt Colonel reports that the wife of John Bird is anxious to stay on the place and would be willing to give up every thing required for the use of our Army provided her personal property should be preserved under her own superintendence   I have the honor to inform you of Mrs Birds wishes, and I request you to give me instructions how to proceed in relation her case" LS, *ibid.*, District of Cairo, Letters Received. On Jan. 16, Capt. William S. Hillyer wrote to Perczel. "Your dispatch of the 15th is just received. You will permit Mrs Bird to stay on her place and retain her personal property under her own superintendence" ALS, *ibid.*, RG 109, Union Provost Marshals' File of Papers Relating to Individual Citizens. On Jan. 18, Capt. John A. Rawlins wrote to Perczel. "If the quarters of the 20th Ills. Vols. are occupied by the people brought in from the surrounding country, you will cause them to be vacated, at once, and the people quartered in some other appropriate place." Copies, DLC-USG, V, 1, 2, 3, 85; DNA, RG 393, USG Letters Sent. See letters to Brig. Gen. Eleazer A. Paine, Jan. 12, 19, 1862.

To Col. Leonard F. Ross

Cairo Jany 19th 1862.

COL. ROSS

The reinforcements will remain at Cape Girardeau and await transportation by River.

U. S. GRANT.

Telegram, copy, DNA, RG 393, Post of Cape Girardeau, Telegrams. See telegram to Col. Leonard F. Ross, Jan. 17, 1862. On Jan. 19, 1862, Col. Leonard F. Ross telegraphed to USG. "The fifty-fifth (55th) did not Come down here, but sent down last night for our ferry boat to Cross to Illinois shore & for transportation to Jonesboro. I sent the boat & mules this morning. Shall I order the troops here?" Telegram received (punctuation added), DNA, RG 393, Dept. of the Mo., Telegrams Received. On the same day, Capt. John A. Rawlins wrote to Ross. "The 55th Ills. Vols., and one of the regiments stationed at Cape Girardeau will hold themselves in readiness to move to this place by river. Transportation will be sent from here." Copies, DLC-USG, V, 1, 2, 3, 85; DNA, RG 393, USG Letters Sent.

To Commander William D. Porter

Head Quarters, Dist of Cairo.
Camp in Field, Jany 19th 1862.

CAPT. PORTER, U. S. A.
COMMDG GUN BOATS OFF FORT JEFFERSON, KY.
CAPTAIN:

Col. Cook being unable to cross Mayfield Creek, it will be necessary for him to march his command to Putney's Bend to embark. Will you please move down opposite that point for his protection? A Steamer will follow about 10 O'clock to take the command on board.

Respectfully,
Your Obt. Servant
U. S. GRANT.
Brig. Genl. Commdg.

Copies, DLC-USG, V, 1, 2, 3, 85; DNA, RG 393, USG Letters Sent. *O.R.*, I, vii, 561. On Jan. 18, 1862, Capt. William S. Hillyer wrote to Col. John Cook. "You will move your command, if possible across the creek and to Fort Jefferson, starting early tomorrow morning. If it is not practicable to cross the creek, then move down the bottom to Puntney's Bend, and a Steamboat protected by Gunboat will be sent to bring you off. Send dispatch, with information which route you will take." Copies, DLC-USG, V, 1, 2, 3, 85; DNA, RG 393, USG Letters Sent. *O.R.*, I, vii, 559–60.

To Capt. Algernon S. Baxter

———

Head Quarters, Dist of Cairo
Cairo, Jany 19th 1862.

CAPT. BAXTER
DIST QR. M.
CAIRO, ILLS.
CAPTAIN:

Assign the 7th Iowa Regiment to quarters in the vacant buildings, under the Mississippi Levee. It will be necessary to provide lumber to fit them up without delay.

Respectfully
Your Obt Servant
U. S. GRANT
Brig. Gen. Commdg.

Copies, DLC-USG, V, 1, 2, 3, 85; DNA, RG 393, USG Letters Sent. On Jan. 19, 1862, Capt. John A. Rawlins wrote to Capt. Algernon S. Baxter. "You will turn over to the 7th Iowa Vols. such land transportation, as you can spare." Copies, DLC-USG, V, 2, 85; DNA, RG 393, USG Letters Sent. On the same day, Rawlins wrote to Col. Jacob G. Lauman. "You will proceed with your command to Fort Holt, Ky, and there encamp for the present, reporting to the Commanding Officer at that Post." Copies, DLC-USG, V, 1, 2, 3, 85; DNA, RG 393, USG Letters Sent. On Jan. 21, Lauman, Fort Holt, wrote to his wife. "We arrived at Cairo on Saturday night and were ordered to Birds Point by the officer in authority the next day, but Genl. Grant returning before we got off changed our destination to this place so we landed here yesterday morning spending the first night on the cars, the 2nd on the 'Memphis City.' " *Fort Henry and Fort Donelson Campaigns* (Fort Leavenworth, 1923), p. 114.

To Brig. Gen. Montgomery C. Meigs

Head Quarters, Dist. of Cairo,
Cairo, Jan.y 20th 1862.

Gen. M. C. Meigs
QuarterMaster General U. S. A.
Washington D. C.
Gen.

I would respectfully call your attention to a claim now probably being pressed at Washington. It is the case of the Steamer Jas. Montgomery, lost in the Mississippi whilst in Government service. At the time she was lost she had gone up the river solely to aid in geting the Gunboat Benton, then aground, again afloat.

I understand that the contractor, Mr. Eads,[1] who I believe is also in Washington, was to deliver this vessel at Cairo. Should he not sustain this loss? Several other Government steamers were also sent up on the same mission at an expense of several thousand dollars.

I am very respectfully
Your Obt. Svt.
U. S. Grant
Brig. Gen. Com

ALS, DNA, RG 92, Consolidated Correspondence, Gunboats. See letter to Capt. John C. Kelton, Dec. 15, 1861.

1. James B. Eads, an engineer of St. Louis, inventor of a practical diving bell, had designed and constructed the ironclad gunboats of the Mississippi River fleet.

To Capt. John C. Kelton

Head Quarters, Dist. of Cairo,
Cairo, Jan.y 20th 1862.

CAPT. J. C. KELTON
A. A. GEN. DEPT. OF THE MISSOURI,
ST. LOUIS, MO.
CAPT.

I returned this evening to Cairo leaving the last of the troops from here at Fort Jefferson. They will be brought back to-morrow.

The effect of the demonstration made by the troops, upon the enemy, cannot be positively stated, but there is but little doubt that Columbus was reinforced, likely from Union City and Camp Beaurigard.[1]—Several persons come into our lines from Columbus whilst we were out, and two gentlemen are in to-day from New Orleans. All agree in saying that public confidance in ultimate success is fast on the wane in the South.

The expedition, if it had no other effect, served as a fine reconnoisance. I have nothing official from Gen. Smith but understand that Camp Beaurigard was destroyed. The detachment of troops from Paducah, that went up the Tennessee, landed two & a half miles from Fort Henry.

Gen. Smith will reach Paducah, with all his force, to-morrow. I will then prepare a report of the entire expedition unless the Gen. Comd.g Department should see fit to permit me to visit Head Quarters, as I have before desired.[2]

I have this evening issued a Circular calling upon Company & regimental Commanders for a list of river & seafaring men of their respective commands who are willing to transfer to the gunboat service.[3] Men are absolutely necessary before the gunboats, now nearly ready for ~~service~~ use, can be ~~of~~ used. I contemplated transfering such men as desire it to that service, subject to the approval of the Dept. Commander.

I would call the attention of the Comd.g Gen. to the conduct of an Association of Engineers, in the City of St. Louis, who are interfering with men of their calling entering the service of the United States. Capt. Porter U. S. N. reports a case in point. He says that he sent to St. Louis for an Engineer for the Tug Sampson. One was engaged but on being informed by the Association that they held a Mortgage upon his property and would foreclose it if he accepted such service was forced to decline.

> Respectfully
> Your Obt. Svt.
> U. S. Grant
> Brig. Gen.

ALS, DNA, RG 393, Dept. of the Mo., Letters Received. Misdated Jan. 25, 1862, in *O.R.*, I, vii, 565–66.

1. On Jan. 17, Maj. Gen. Leonidas Polk wrote to Capt. William W. Mackall that, since U. S. strength had been reported at 40,000, while his own effective force was just under 13,000, he had concluded not to be drawn out from Columbus, but to prepare for a siege. *Ibid.*, p. 837. On Jan. 25, Polk reported 14,132 men present at Columbus. *Ibid.*, p. 848. On Jan. 2, Brig. Gen. James L. Alcorn had taken his command from Camp Beauregard to Union City, Tenn. *Ibid.*, pp. 816–17.

2. On Jan. 22, Maj. Gen. Henry W. Halleck telegraphed to USG. "All additional forces sent to you will be stationed at Smithland, where preparations will be made for a large encampment. You have permission to visit Head Qrs." ALS (telegram sent), DLC-Henry W. Halleck. *O.R.*, I, vii, 561–62.

3. Copies, DNA, RG 45, Letterbooks of Officers at Sea, David D. Porter; *ibid.*, RG 94, 9th Ill., Letterbook. *O.R.* (Navy), I, xxiv, 233. On Feb. 1, Master Joshua Bishop wrote to USG, forwarding a "list of men shipped as seamen &c. on gunboats." DLC-USG, V, 10; DNA, RG 393, USG Register of Letters Received. Also on Feb. 1, Thomas Price of Eau Claire, Wis., 16th Wis., telegraphed to USG. "Will you accept Eight men from the 16th Wisconsin Reght to be transferred to the Gun boats under Commodore Foote" Telegram received, *ibid.*, Dept. of the Mo., Telegrams Received.

To Capt. John C. Kelton

Head Quarters, Dist. of Cairo
Cairo, Jan.y 20th 1862.

CAPT. J. C. KELTON
A. A. GEN. DEPT. OF THE MISSOURI
ST. LOUIS, MO.
CAPT.

During my absence the 7th Iowa,[1] 8th Wisconsin[2] & 45th Ill. Vols.[3] Cols. J. G. Lauman, Murphy, & J. E. Smith Commanding arrived here.

A portion of the 52d Ill.[4] is just in also. The balance of this regiment and all of the 46th[5] are expected to-night. The 55th Ill. is probably at Cape Girardeau,[6] and if so will be brought here in a few days.

It is my intention to establish a Camp at Fort Jefferson, Ky. for these troops, and all new arrivals hereafter, subject to the approval of the Department Commander.

Respectfully
U. S. GRANT
Brig. Gen. Com

ALS, DNA, RG 393, Dept. of the Mo., Letters Received. On Jan. 18, 1862, Col. Napoleon B. Buford wrote to USG. "I have the honour to report the 45th Regt Col J. E. Smith, arrived at 7 P. M. on the 16th and are quartered in barracks Also the 8th Wisconsin, Col R. C. Murphy arrived by R. R. at 8 P. M. on the 17th —As it was raining & dark & they could not be supplied with stoves, Wood, Water, and straw, I had them remain in the Cars all night. This morning it was raining and the troops vacated the Cars at 9.30. and are now marching to occupy the vacant barracks—I have unofficial notice that the 7th Iowa, is en route for this place via R. R. having left the river—On arrival I shall send them to Birds Point,— also that the 55th Illinois, is at Cape Girardeau, having been landed 20 miles above & marched to the Cape—I think the changes in the weather will allow them to get here by Boats—they will be sent to Fort Holt—Your official letters were brought to me on the 16th & 17th—I have attended to the discharges &c—I have sent you one package via Lieut Stevens, care of Col Marsh, at Fort Jefferson— This day I have delivered to your orderly, Hoyt, at the office, official reports &c— With this I send you a package, which will be forwarded by the first opportunity —Your orderly Hoyt has shown me a letter to him from S. A. Stockdale, sec: directing him to retain your official letters—I have broken the seals of some of them, before I had this communication" LS, *ibid.*, District of Cairo, Letters Received.

1. The 7th Iowa had been sent by USG to Benton Barracks in St. Louis after incurring heavy losses at the battle of Belmont. See letter to Col. Jacob G. Lauman, Nov. 11, 1861.

2. The 8th Wis. had been mustered in on Sept. 13, 1861. On Jan. 15, 1862, Col. Robert C. Murphy, Sulphur Springs, Mo., telegraphed to Capt. John C. Kelton. "I leave here by rail tomorrow at day-light with my command—Eighth Wis.—nine hundred & thirty-one men—via St Louis to Cairo. I have not received any orders when, where, or to whom I am to report." Telegram received, DNA, RG 107, Telegrams Collected (Unbound).

3. See letters to Capt. John C. Kelton, Dec. 18, 23, 1861. On Jan. 6, 1862, Capt. John A. Rawlins wrote to Col. John E. Smith. "Your communication of the 31st ult. received. In answer thereto, Brig. Gen. Grant instructs me to say there is no absolute necessity for your moving to this place before the 12th inst. You will make requisitions for Tents and every thing required, save transportations which will be furnished you here." Copies, DLC-USG, V, 1, 2, 3, 85; DNA, RG 393, USG Letters Sent. On Jan. 15, Smith telegraphed to USG from Chicago. "Forty fifth leaves at five p. m" Telegram received, *ibid.*, Dept. of the Mo., Telegrams Received. On Jan. 20, Rawlins wrote to Smith. "You will proceed with your command tomorrow the 21st inst to Fort Holt, Ky. where you will go into Camp for the present, reporting to Col. John Cook, Commdg Post. Transportation will be furnished by Capt. A. S. Baxter District Quartermaster." Copies, DLC-USG, V, 1, 2, 3, 85; DNA, RG 393, USG Letters Sent. On the same day, Rawlins wrote to Capt. Algernon S. Baxter. "You will provide transportation for the removal of the 45th Ills. Vols. to Fort. Holt, Ky. on tomorrow, the 21st inst. at as early an hour as possible, or as soon as the Regiment is ready." Copies, *ibid.*

4. See letter to Capt. Baldwin, Jan. 20, 1862.

5. The 46th Ill., mustered in Dec. 28, 1861, at Camp Butler, Springfield, apparently joined USG's command on Feb. 14, 1862, before Fort Donelson.

6. See telegrams to Col. Leonard F. Ross, Jan. 17, 19, 1862.

To Capt. Algernon S. Baxter

Head Quarters, Dist of Cairo
Cairo, Jany 20th 1862.

CAPT. A. S. BAXTER
A. Q. M. CAIRO, ILLS.

You will designate a Steamer of large Storage capacity, and in good running order, to report at once, to Capt. McAllister, C. S.

The Boat will be coaled for four days run, if practicable.
Respectfully &c
U. S. GRANT.
Brig. Genl. Commdg.

Copies, DLC-USG, V, 1, 2, 3, 85; DNA, RG 393, USG Letters Sent.

To Capt. Baldwin

———

Head Quarters, Dist of Cairo
Cairo, Jany 20th 1862.

CAPT BALDWIN
COMMDG STEAMER, "CITY OF MEMPHIS"
SIR:

Receive on board your Steamer the 52nd Regt. Ills. Vols., to quarter them for the night. You will not return to Fort Jefferson, until these troops are off your Boat in the morning.
Yours, &c.
U. S. GRANT,
Brig Gen Commdg

Copies, DLC-USG, V, 1, 2, 3, 85; DNA, RG 393, USG Letters Sent. On Jan. 20, 1862, Capt. John A. Rawlins wrote to Capt. Richard McAllister. "A portion of the 52nd Ills. Vols. have arrived without their Regimental Commissary, without rations, without knowing how many men they have, and without a Provision Return. It will be necessary to give them something to eat, and charge it on the first issue, after the arrival of the remainder of the Regiment." Copies, *ibid.* Special Orders No. 95, Dept. of the Mo., Jan. 30, directed Col. Thomas W. Sweeny, 52nd Ill., to join his regt. at Cairo.

To Brig. Gen. Montgomery C. Meigs

—

Head Quarters, Dist. of Cairo,
Cairo, Jan.y 22d 1862.

Gen. M. C. Meigs
Quartermaster U. S. A.
Washington D. C.
Gen.

Charges against Capt. Hatch, A. Q. M. were received two days ago. I have not yet ordered a Court, nor applied for one, for the reason that I feel that an investigation should be had, prior to trial, and see if additional charges should not be prefered.

Since my investigation into the lumber purchase many other irregularities have been disclosed, such as selling clothing and other property by the Quartermaster, hiring boats at one price and giving vouchers for a different price. These charges may not prove true, but are asserted. I fear also it has been praticed to some extent to receive grain in bulk, and sack it here when the price paid included good sound gunnies.

Capt. Hatch is in arrest, by my order, and his head clerk was placed in confinement. I have since however extended his limits to the city.

On placing Capt. Hatch in arrest I ordered him to turn over all public property in his possession to Capt. Baxter, and had all papers pertaining to the Department, that could be got hold of, placed under lock and key in the vault of the Paymaster. Since that a bundle has been picked up in the river which on being examined proved to be books pertaining to Quartermaster business.

I reported to Gen. Halleck the fact of the arrest of Capt. Hatch, confinement of his clerk and seizure of his papers, but have received no orders in the matter.

I would respectfully recommend that some suitable person be appointed to investigate all the charges of corruption that are made against the Agt. of your Department at this place. If they are true it is proper that the offences should be punished, if not true Capt. Hatch should be officially exhonerated.

> I am Gen. Very respectfully
> Your Obt. Svt.
> U. S. GRANT
> Brig. Gen.

ALS, DNA, RG 92, Consolidated Correspondence, Cairo Fraud Investigation. On Jan. 29, 1862, Brig. Gen. Montgomery C. Meigs endorsed this letter to Secretary of War Edwin M. Stanton. "Respectfully referred to the Secy of War. I recommend that this letter be referred to the comee on frauds—They can better than any officer investigate such a state of things. The officers of this Dept are too few & too fully occupied with more important matters to be detailed on this investigation" AES, *ibid.* On Feb. 16, Stanton endorsed the letter to Meigs. "The Qr Master General is directed to transmit this letter to the Congressional Committe on Frauds & Contracts" AES, *ibid.* On Jan. 29, Bvt. Col. Ebenezer S. Sibley, deputy q. m. gen., wrote to USG. "You are respectfully informed that your letter of the 22d inst. relative to charges against Capt. Hatch A Q. M has been submitted to the Secty. of War, with the recommendation that it be referred to the Comm of Congress 'To investigate 'Frauds in Contracts' '" Copy, *ibid.*, Letters Sent.

On Feb. 12, Asst. Secretary of War Thomas A. Scott wrote to Stanton. "I spent the whole of this day in examination of matters connected with the Quarter Master's Department at Cairo—the condition of affairs under Qr. M. Hatch was about as bad as could well be imagined. From the evidence we have been able to procure (herewith enclosed) you will perceive that a regular system of fraud appears to have been adopted. Many transactions, large & small, have been used by the Qr. Masr. and perhaps others under him, to promote his private interests. Hatch was placed under arrest in January & confined to the limits of Cairo, but he is now absent on parole of honor on a visit to his family in Illinois; in my judgment it is doubtful of his return Knowing as he must that the evidence against him is overwhelming. A few days after his arrest two of his Ledgers were found at the lower point of Cairo, in the water at a point where the Ohio and Mississippi meet. They were washed on shore, the intention evidently being to destroy them. One of these books is an Invoice Ledger of property purchased & prices to be paid: it is said that the vouchers for this property, now on record in Washington, will show increased amounts for the Govt. to pay—the original amount of course to be paid the seller, and the difference, it is supposed, was to belong to Quarter Master's Department *as perquisites.* The other book is a Property Ledger showing distribution. The books are not so seriously damaged but that they may be used for examination of accounts rendered to the Quarter Master General or Auditor's Department at Washington. I will have them put up carefully and forwarded to you by Express. The Quarter Master's Department, on arrest of Capt. Hatch, was placed in the hands of Capt. Baxter (Brigade Q. M. volunteer service) who by some means succeeded in obtaining funds directly from Washington for disbursement. It was soon found that he had not enough judgment or discretion, and was relieved to make place for Capt. Turnley—regular officer—who had previously been on duty at St Louis: The Commission at St Louis are of the opinion that a number of his (Capt. Turnley's) transactions while there were not clear of corruption. As I now know the position of matters I am prepared to recommend that an entire reorganisation be made at this post, in so far as it relates to chief officer (present commander wishes to go into the field) and to the Qr Master Department, and that an efficient Brigadier General—a regular officer and a good business man—be sent here. Also a reliable officer as Quarter Master with instructions to put this post under strict military discipline, and to discard all present contracts; this Q. M. to have to officers as assistants— one to take charge of forage and delivery of supplies to camps connected with the post—the other to take charge of steamboat interests and the transhipment of property from Rail Road to boats, also forwarding the same to destination, and in connection with those duties attend to receiving coal and supplies by river. With this arrangement the principal Q. Master could devote his time to arranging and contracting for supplies, & other matters connected with his department, all of which contracts should be subject to the approval of the General in command of post. The Q. Master should receive his funds at Cairo through Major Allen Chief Q. M. at St Louis & be responsible to him. With this organisation Cairo can soon be placed in respectable condition   The Commissary Department is now in good hands. also the Pay Department. The health of troops is good. Medical Dept. is in fair condition, and with the reorganisation of the Medical Bureau for the Department of the West, at St Louis, as recommended in previous report, all the deficiencies that now exist in Hospital Department here would soon be reme- died. Ordnance stores are light excepting amunition of which a good stock is on hand ready for service. There is but a 1000 stand of altered U. S. muskets on hand. This evening an Illinois Regiment, armed without muskets, will take 900 of these, thus leaving but 100 in store. I would recommend that 3000 stand of Austrian Rifles with accoutrements be sent here to replace unservicable arms and to provide for regiments or detachments that may arrive here without arms, from Illinois, Iowa or Wisconsin. The accounts of Capt. Hatch should be pressed to settlement immediately. I find that there is a large amount owing to people who hold certifi- cates, or due bills, in places of the regular vouchers which they signed—and a large number of vouchers for material furnished was signed by parties without receiving any certificate whatever. The whole subject of past liabilities and the accounts of Hatch should be placed in charge of some competent and reliable officer for audit & payment, who should be instructed to reduce all claims to fair prices. The new organisation should not be encumbered with past claims. The accounts of Capt. Baxter should also be adjusted without delay. I understand that he recd $150.000 from Washington—some of which he expended here, & he took with him to the field for expenses in connection with Army on Tennessee River $10.000. For the supposed balance he gave checks on N. York to Capt. Turnley, which Capt. Turnley had in his possession. I directed him immediately to send them forward by Express and secure the funds. Capt. Dunlap, another Asst. Q. M. here, has received about $250.000 for disbursement on account of purchases made by the Governor of Illinois: he has shown me his correspondence with Genl. Meigs & says he can & will account satisfactorily for all money received by him. A general settlement of all accounts previous to the date that new organi- sation may take hold (if authorised by you) should be made   As I am now within 40 miles of Paducah I will run up there tomorrow with a small freight tug and make such an examination as I can and report & will return to Cairo tomorrow night unless a battle comes off at Fort Donelson in which case I may borrow 48 hours to witness the fun. On my return to Cairo I expect to get from the Commanding officer a clean and full statement of the forces belonging to the post and of their condition—which their records would not give in the shape desired There is a general looseness in this respect which my visit may to a certain extent remedy. The advantage of coming in personal communication with our officers at important posts—in the manner you directed me to do—will prove useful If the Sec'y of War and Commanding General could pass around quietly every few months it would do great good. From Cairo I will go to Springfield, Illinois, & from there probably run down to St Louis to see General Halleck again unless I receive instructions from you at Springfield that will require movements in another direction." ALS, DLC-Edwin M. Stanton.

On Jan. 30, Brig. Gen. Lorenzo Thomas wrote to Maj. Gen. Henry W. Halleck. "Captain Reuben B. Hatch, Brigade Quarter Master is in arrest at Cairo —It is desired that he be brought to trial immediately—Acknowledge by telegraph." Copy, DNA, RG 94, Letters Sent. On Jan. 31, Halleck telegraphed to Thomas. "Court martial already ordered on Capt. Hatch. It is said that he kept two sets of books—public & private. After his arrest an attempt was made to destroy the latter by throwing them into the Missisip. Fortunately they were recovered. It will take some time to compare the books & prepare charges & specifications." ALS (telegram sent), *ibid.*, Staff Papers, R. B. Hatch. On Jan. 31, Meigs wrote to Stanton. "I enclose a statement written down from information given me by Mr. Chapman, a reporter for the press, who has just arrived from Cairo, and, who, I understand was directed by the President to call upon me and communicate this information. I sometime since requested that an Assistant Inspector General be sent to Cairo to investigate the affairs of the Quarter-Master's Department. There is no Quarter-Master of experience at my disposal. All the Officers are already overburdened with duties from which they cannot be detached without injuring the public service. Mr Chapman suggests the name of Mr J. C. Miller of Chicago, as a lawyer of acuteness and experience, and a fit person to investigate these charges. I advise that he or some other gentleman of legal knowledge, who has the confidence of the War Department be appointed Inspector of the Quarter-Master's Department, with authority to go to Cairo, investigate these allegations, and all other abuses in the Quarter-Master's Department at that place, and prepare charges against the Officers who may be involved. General Grant in a letter dated Jan. 22, 1862, informs me that the books of the Quarter Master, Capt. Hatch, have been found in the river Ohio, and he thinks that the charges already preferred against Capt. Hatch, ought not to be acted on, until further investigation is had, which he thinks will develope great frauds." LS, *ibid.*, RG 92, Consolidated Correspondence, Cairo Fraud Investigation.

On Jan. 31, Jackson Grimshaw of Quincy, Ill., attorney for Hatch, wrote to President Abraham Lincoln. "On behalf of Captain Reuben B. Hatch Quarter Master at Cairo Illinois I respectfully ask that under the Articles of War (see Article 92) you order a court of inquiry into the official conduct of Captain Hatch. A court martial has been ordered on one charge, but others have been insinuated and I respectfully ask you to call a court of inquiry under the Article of War above referred to as speedily as the good of the service will permit." ALS, DLC-Robert T. Lincoln. On Feb. 1, Lincoln endorsed this letter to Maj. John F. Lee, judge advocate gen. "Would it be proper for me to order a Court Martial, as within requested." AES, *ibid.* On the same day, Lee endorsed the letter. "Respectfully returned, with copy of report of quarter master general *on the facts.* Genl. Grant has authority to appoint a court. He can do so more conveniently than higher authority, because on the spot, he knows the state of the service, & what officers to put on the detail. The quarter master general has applied to him to appoint a court. He means to do it. He suggests sufficient and controlling reasons for some delay. Doubtless he will make no unnecessary delay. Under these circumstances I cannot advise the President to interpose at this time." AES, *ibid*. On Feb. 3, Meigs wrote to Lee. "Capt Hatch upon testimony taken by Capt Hillyer aide de camp to Gen Grant and upon report of Capt Hillyer was placed in arrest by order of Gen'l Grant on request from this office. The papers were referred to the Sec'y of War by this office for the Judge Advocates action. A charge was prepared by the Judge Advocate and sent to Gen'l Grant with request that he would order a Court Martial. He replies that there are other matters alleged which he thinks should be investigated before bringing Capt Hatch before a court on this single charge. He thinks that by such investigation great frauds will be developed. He states among other things that the books of the Quarter Master Capt Hatch or a portion of them had been found in the Ohio River. I have advised the Secretary of War to send out to Cairo some person qualified to investigate the whole matter and I understand he will do so   I understood also that the committee on frauds would send a subcommittee to look into these affairs in Illinois. Gen'l Grants letters were by this office referred to the Secretary of War for such action as might be proper. I return this letter of Mr Grimshaw endorsed by the President. With the above facts you will be able to advise the President whether it would be proper and efficient to order a Court of Inquiry or no. I fear that such a court would be long employed and that the services of the Officers upon it could be ill spared from their military duties." ALS, *ibid*.

On Feb. 24, Ill. Governor Richard Yates, Secretary of State Ozias M. Hatch, and Auditor Jesse K. Dubois wrote to Lincoln that the charges against Reuben B. Hatch were "*frivolous* and without the shadow of foundation in fact." LS, DNA, RG 94, Staff Papers, R. B. Hatch. On March 20, Lincoln endorsed this letter to Lee. "The within is signed by our Illinois Governor, Sec. of State & State Auditor —all good & true men—I also personally know Capt. R. B. Hatch, and never, before heard any thing against his character. If the Judge Advocate has the means of doing so I will thank him to give me his opinion of the case." AES, *ibid*. On March 21, Meigs endorsed the letter. "The investigation by the aid-de-camp of Gen. Grant sent to Chicago is very much against Capt. Hatch. Charges prepared by the Judge Advocate were preferred against him, and while he is certainly entitled to trial which the General Commanding should give him as soon as the interests of the service will permit, it would be in my opinion highly improper to pass over such charges, and restore an officer to duty until a trial cleared him. If convicted he ought to be dismissed the service. I recommend that the President call Gen Halleck's attention to the case, and thus procure the speediest possible trial. Some of Capt. Hatch's books have been received at this office, having been found *in* the Ohio river." ES, *ibid*. On March 27, Lincoln's secretary, John G. Nicolay, forwarded the letter to Halleck. ALS, *ibid*.

On March 26, Meigs wrote to Stanton that Lincoln wanted a commission to investigate the Hatch case. LS, DNA, RG 107, Letters Received from the President, Executive Dept., and War Dept. Bureaus. On April 2, Lincoln suggested members for the commission. Lincoln, *Works*, V, 177. In June, Stanton appointed a commission consisting of George S. Boutwell, Charles A. Dana, and Stephen T. Logan (soon replaced by Shelby M. Cullom), with Thomas Means as solicitor, to settle claims at Cairo. Between June 18 and July 31, the commission investi-

gated 1,696 claims, amounting to $599,219.36, approving claims amounting to
$451,105.80. Charles A. Dana, *Recollections of the Civil War* (New York, 1898),
pp. 11–14.

Before the commission met, Hatch had been released from arrest, assigned to
duty at Paducah, then arrested again. Letter of Jackson Grimshaw, *Chicago Tribune*, May 29, 1862. See also Nicolay to Lee, May 19, DLC-Robert T. Lincoln.
The commission report, delivered to Stanton on Aug. 5, was never printed and
has not been found in DNA. Kenneth W. Munden and Henry Putney Beers,
Guide to Federal Records Relating to the Civil War (Washington, 1962), p. 388.
On July 29, Means wrote to Hatch stating that the commission had acquitted him
of all blame. Copy, DNA, RG 107, Letters Received, Irregular Series. A copy of
this letter was sent to Lincoln Aug. 29 by U. S. Representative William A.
Richardson, who urged that Hatch be restored to duty. LS, *ibid*. Also enclosed
were letters of Grimshaw, Aug. 29, and U. S. Senator Orville H. Browning,
undated, to the same effect. *Ibid*. On Nov. 8, Meigs wrote to Thomas. "I respectfully request that Captain R. B. Hatch, Assistant Quarter Master of Volunteers,
may be ordered to report to Col. Robert Allen, Quarter Master, U. S. A. St.
Louis, Mo. for assignment to duty." LS, *ibid*., RG 94, Letters Received.

To Capt. John C. Kelton

Head Quarters, Dist. of Cairo;
Cairo, Jan.y 22d 1862.

Capt. J. C. Kelton
A. A. Gen. Dept. of the Missouri,
St. Louis, Mo.
Sir;

In view of the urgency to fill up the crews of the Gunboats at
this place I would respectfully suggest to the Gen. Comd.g
Department the propriety of transfering from the Fusilier regiment, now at Camp Douglas, such as are willing to go into that
service.

Such misrepresentations have been made to induce men to
enlist in that regiment that great dissatisfaction prevails and
many would hail any change with joy.

Respectfully
Your Obt. Svt.
U. S. Grant
Brig. Gen.

ALS, DNA, RG 393, Dept. of the Mo., Letters Received. See letter to Allen C. Fuller, Dec. 26, 1861. The Mechanics-Fusileers, originally slated to become the 56th Ill., were then in a state of disorder at Camp Douglas, Chicago. See *Chicago Tribune*, Jan. 1, 4, 14, 17, 1862. On Jan. 28, 1862, the regt. was mustered out of service, possibly as a result of a suit filed by a soldier charging that his enlistment was the result of fraudulent promises by officers. *Ibid.*, Jan. 26, 30, 1862.

To Capt. John C. Kelton

Head Quarters, Dist. of Cairo,
Cairo, Jan.y 22d 1862.

CAPT. J. C. KELTON,
A. A. GEN. DEPT. OF THE MISSOURI
ST. LOUIS, MO.
SIR;

The 55th Ill. Vols. Col. David Steward[1] Commanding, arrived this evening. I forwarded them to Paducah without landing. This I deemed advisable from the fact that the Ohio river is now much swolen and is raising at a rate that will overflow all the Ky. shore, and Illinois for miles, within the next four days.

I have given orders for the removal of the troops at Fort Holt to Norfolk.

Very respectfully
Your Obt. Svt.
U. S. GRANT
Brig. Gen.

ALS, DNA, RG 393, Dept. of the Mo., Letters Received. On Jan. 21, 1862, Col. Leonard F. Ross telegraphed to USG. "The fifty fifth Reached here on Steamer D A January today at Eight oclock a m" Telegram received, *ibid.*, Telegrams Received; copy, *ibid.*, Post of Cape Girardeau, Telegrams. On the same day, Ross telegraphed to USG. "Shall I have the January proceed to Cairo with her Govt Stores   if so had I not better send a Company as an Escort" Telegram received, *ibid.*, Dept. of the Mo., Telegrams Received. On the reverse of this telegram, John Riggin, Jr., drafted a telegram in the name of USG. "Steamer January will proceed to Cairo with troops & cargo aboard destined £here" Df (telegram sent), *ibid.*; copy (misdated Jan. 20), *ibid.*, Post of Cape Girardeau, Telegrams. On Jan. 22, Capt. John C. Kelton issued Special Orders No. 68, Dept. of the Mo.

"In pursuance of Special Order No. 4 from the Adjutant General's Office, Washington, of January 6th 1862, Brigadier General U. S. Grant, will detail an officer to muster out of Service the Band of the 55th Illinois Volunteers" Copies, *ibid.*, Dept. of the Mo., Special Orders; DLC-USG, V, 83.

1. David Stuart, born in Brooklyn, N. Y., graduated from Amherst College, practiced law in Detroit, and was elected U. S. Representative as a Democrat in 1852. After his defeat for re-election, he moved to Chicago. In 1861, he participated in recruiting two regts., known as the Douglas Brigade; on July 22, he was appointed lt. col. of the first of these, the 42nd Ill., but resigned on Oct. 31 when appointed col. of the other, the 55th Ill.

To Col. John Cook

Head Quarters, Dist of Cairo.
Cairo, January 22nd 1862.

Col. J. Cook
Commdg 3rd Brigade
Fort Holt, Ky.
Colonel:

In view of the rapid rise in the Ohio it will be necessary to move your command from its present position temporarily. You will therefore hold it in readiness to move to Norfolk tomorrow, leaving two companies to guard the heavy Guns until the last minute.

Respectfully
Your Obt. Servant.
U. S. Grant.
Brig. Gen. Commdg.

Copies, DLC-USG, V, 1, 2, 3, 85; DNA, RG 393, USG Letters Sent. On Jan. 22, 1862, Capt. John A. Rawlins wrote to Capt. Algernon S. Baxter. "You will send all the available water transportation to Fort. Holt, Ky. on tomorrow, the 23rd inst. at as early an hour as practicable to transport the troops now stationed there to Norfolk, Mo." Copies, DLC-USG, V, 1, 2, 85; DNA, RG 393, USG Letters Sent.

To Col. David Stuart

———

Head Quarters, Dist of Cairo
Cairo, Jany 22nd 1862.

COL. D. STEWART
COMMDG 55TH ILLS. VOLS.
COLONEL:

You will proceed with your Regiment to Paducah, Ky. and report to the Commanding Officer at that Post for Orders. The District Quartermaster will be instructed to provide you, the same transportation that brought you here.

Respectfully,
U. S. GRANT.
Brig. Gen. Commdg.

Copies, DLC-USG, V, 1, 2, 3, 85; DNA, RG 393, USG Letters Sent.

To Maj. Gen. Leonidas Polk

———

Head Quarters, Dist. of Cairo,
Cairo, Jan.y 23d 1862.

MAJ. GEN. L. POLK.
COMD.G FORCES
COLUMBUS, KY.
GEN.

I forward by *Flag of Truce*, in command of Col. Webster, Chief of Engineers and Chief of Staff, the prisoner Groves[1] whose release has been obtained at your special request.

Groves was taken sick on his way from Columbus Ohio and has been confined in hospital here ever since. Hence the delay in sending him.

I would request that Mr. Owens[2] be released on your side in exchange. I make this request understanding that objections were raised to exchanging Owens for prisoners who were arrested for political offences and did not belong to regularly mustered organizations.

I send also telegraphic dispatch of Mr. Flanders,[3] long a resident of New Orleans, which I trust you will have the kindness to permit to pass over the wires. I also forward a number of open letters to be mailed to parties in the South.

> I am Gen. Very respectfully
> Your Obt. Svt.
> U. S. GRANT
> Brig. Gen.

P. S. I will esteem it a personal favor to be reciprocated whenever it may be in my power if you will forward the family of Mr. Flanders to this place, under a *Flag of Truce*, when they arrive in Columbus.

> U. S. G.

ALS, DNA, RG 109, Documents Printed in *O.R.* *O.R.*, II, i, 533–34. On Feb. 2, 1862, Maj. Gen. Leonidas Polk wrote to USG. "On a former occasion I brought to your notice the fact, that you were in possession of certain prisoners taken by your command at Paducah, eight in number, who I pro[posed] to exchange for. They were taken while [under] the command of Capt Bowlin of the Ca[valry.] There are other prisoners taken by you at [Cheat] Mountain now at Camp Chase, belonging to the 1st Tenn Regt. and others, for whom I propose to exchange; The names of these men are found on the accompanying slip; I propose also to exchange for as many Surgeons of those taken at Mill Spring, as I have of yours; these will make in all about twenty. I propose in addition to these, to exchange all the rest of your prisoners in my hands, that were taken at Belmont, for an equal number of ours, rank for rank. I note what you say in your last communication with regard to the prisoner Owens; I beg leave to say, that this man's is no ordinary case, his character is such, that I prefer not to return him for the present: The arrangement for the delivery of young Groves, you will remember, was made more than a month before, you desired the release of Owens, and Groves' surrender not being conditioned on the surrender of Owens but the result of a disposition, to reciprocate former courtesies—for example—the paroling of Lieut. Smith, without a consideration—I do not feel I am called upon, to release him, on Groves' account. I beg leave respectfully to refer you to Inspector General, E D Blake, for the arrangement of the details, of the proposed [ex]change." LS, DNA, RG 393, District of Cairo, Letters Received; DfS, *ibid.*, RG 109, Documents Printed in *O.R.* *O.R.*, II, i, 537.

1. See letters to Capt. John C. Kelton, Nov. 29, 1861, and to Commanding Officer, Military Prison, Columbus, Ohio, Dec. 19, 1861.

2. According to a newspaper account, Elisha Owens, who lived about twenty-five miles south of Paducah, killed a C. S. A. recruiting agent in late 1861, then fled to Paducah. In early Jan., 1862, he was lured back to his home and captured by C. S. A. cav. Letter of "W. L. D.," Paducah, Jan. 8, 1862, in *Cincinnati Commercial*, Jan. 13, 1862.

3. Probably Benjamin F. Flanders, born in New Hampshire, graduated from Dartmouth College, who settled in New Orleans and became active in teaching, newspaper editing, and local politics, and was an official of the New Orleans, Opelousas & Great Western Railroad Co. at the start of the Civil War. His Unionist sentiments resulted in his exile from New Orleans until the city was occupied by U. S. troops; then he was appointed city treasurer, later elected U. S. Representative.

To Maj. Gen. Henry W. Halleck

BY TELEGRAPH FROM Cairo Jan'y 23 *1862*

TO MAJ. GEN HALLECK

Before receiving your despatch I had ordered troops from Ft Holt to Norfolk. The latter will not overflow. Shall I change this order?

U. S. GRANT

Telegram received, DNA, RG 94, Generals' Papers and Books, Telegrams Received by Gen. Halleck; copy, *ibid.*, RG 393, Dept. of the Mo., Telegrams Received. On Jan. 23, 1862, Maj. Gen. Henry W. Halleck telegraphed to USG. "It is reported that Fort Holt is likely to be overflowed; if so send the troops to Smithland." DfS, DLC-Henry W. Halleck; copies, DLC-USG, V, 4, 5; DNA, RG 94, Generals' Papers and Books, Telegrams Sent in Cipher by Gen. Halleck; *ibid.*, RG 393, Dept. of the Mo., Telegrams Sent; *ibid.*, USG Hd. Qrs. Correspondence. On Jan. 24, Halleck telegraphed to USG. "They can remain at Norfolk at present; but I think they had better go into camp at Smithland if Fort Holt cannot be reoccupied." DfS, DLC-Henry W. Halleck; copies, DLC-USG, V, 4, 5, 7, 8; DNA, RG 94, Generals' Papers and Books, Telegrams Sent in Cipher by Gen. Halleck; *ibid.*, RG 393, Dept. of the Mo., Telegrams Sent; *ibid.*, USG Hd. Qrs. Correspondence. On the same day, Capt. John A. Rawlins issued Special Orders No. 22. "The 7th Iowa, and 52nd Ill. Regts. Vols. with their camp and Garrison Equipage and transportation, will proceed to Smithland Ky. where they will go into camp, taking with them ten days rations and forage. Immediately on their arrival Col. J. G. Lauman 7th Ill. Vols will assume command of Smithland Ky. reporting to Brig. Genl. C. F. Smith Comdg. at Paducah Ky; and Lt. Col. Chetlain now in command at Smithland will with the five companies of Intfantry in his command return to Paducah in one of the Transports used in transporting forces to Smithland which will await his embarkation" Copies, DLC-USG, V, 15, 16, 82, 87, 89; DNA, RG 393, USG Special Orders.

On Jan. 23, Rawlins wrote to Col. William H. L. Wallace. "I am instructed by Brig. Genl. Grant to say, under orders from Head Quarters Dept. of the Mo. he will send several of the recently arrived Regiments to Smithland Ky. and if agreable to you, in place of one of them, will send yours, in order that you may be placed in command of the forces at that Post. You will communicate your wishes in this matter at once as the orders for the removal of the troops will be issued tomorrow the 24th inst. If you determine to go, the quarters you vacate, will be occupied by another Regiment." LS, *ibid.*, RG 94, War Records Office, Dept. of the Mo.

To Maj. Gen. Henry W. Halleck

———

Head Quarters, Dist. of Cairo
Cairo, Jan.y 23d 1862.
Respectfully forwarded to Head Quarters, Dept. of the Missouri.

U. S. Grant
Brig. Gen. Com.

AES, DNA, RG 393, District of Cairo, Letters Received. Written on a letter of Jan. 21, 1862, from Brig. Gen. Charles F. Smith to Capt. John A. Rawlins, datelined "Camp on the Tennessee, 20 miles below Fort Henry (Calloway,) Ky" "I arrived this morning with our seven days supply of provisions about exhausted. But found a steamer with stores for a week under convoy of the Lexington. Had the rain continued another day when the command was between Farmington & Murray, we must have ~~aband~~ abandoned many wagons. The result of this march has satisfied me that a larger force *accompanied by a train of supplies* cannot be moved south from ~~Mayf~~ Paducah during the season of rain, which is expected to commence in the latter part of this month. The roads were something horrible & new tracks had to be cut thro' the woods. It took an entire day for one brigade to move three miles. I heard nothing of the enemy, save rumors that Fort Henry had been abandoned, which I do not credit. I have just dispatched the Lexington to go up and draw the fire of the Fort to ascertain the truth of this rumor. When this vessel returns I shall resume my homeward march by easy stages. . . . P. S. The rebel gunboat 'Dunbar' has been down the river as far as Birmingham, say 18 or 20 miles ~~belo~~ from here, within a few days." ALS, *ibid.* On Jan. 22, Smith wrote to Rawlins. "Finding it would take the greater part of to day to distribute our stores I went up in the Lexington to have a look at Ft. Henry. As the river is now fourteen feet above its very low stage a week since we took the right hand (our right) channel of the island just below the Fort and got about two and one-half miles from it, drawing a single shot from the enemy which fell (say) half-a mile short; this in response to four several shots fired at them. There were evidently from two to three thousand men there. The appearance of the works corresponds, as far as could be discovered, with the rough sketch that Genl. Grant has seen in my quarters at Paducah. The hill on the west bank, which commands the fort some sixty feet or so, seems to be covered by a thick growth of timber. ~~Then~~ going by the number of roofs seen in the fort it must cover considerable space. I think two iron clad gun-boats would make short work of Ft. Henry. There is no masked battery at the foot of the island as was ~~sup~~ supposed or, if so, it is now under water. Two stern wheel steamers were at the fort but moved away rapidly at our first gun. The Dunbar, a fast side wheel steamer, plies up and down, and was chased last evening by the Lexington, without effect. She is said to be armed with two twelve pounder rifled guns. The Commander of the Lexington thinks she has not be altered in any way. I shall resume my march at 8 o'c tomorrow morning, at which time the Lexington and transport Wilson will start for Paducah, carrying some ~~broken down~~ sick men & the mail." ALS, *ibid. O.R.*, I, vii, 561. Both letters from Smith were forwarded to hd. qrs., Dept. of the Mo., and are now found in the records of the District of Cairo through the efforts of Rawlins in 1866–1867 to reclaim the letters. Rawlins' correspondence is in DLC-USG, VIA.

To Capt. John C. Kelton

Head Quarters Dist of Cairo
Cairo Jany 23rd 1862

Capt. J. C. Kelton
A. A. Genl.
Dept. of the Mo
St Louis Mo

I have the honor to send the following list of Officers available for a General Court Martial with one designated as Judge Advocate

1	Col. John. A. Logan	31st Ill	Vols. President
2	Lt. Col. Wm. E. Small	10th Iowa	"
3	Lt. Col. E. Dennis	30th Ill.	"
4	Lt. Col. J. A. Maltby	45th "	"
5	Major Wm. W. Sanford	48th "	"
6	Major Evan Richards	20th "	"
7	Capt. Thos. W. Smith	10th "	"
8	Capt. McHenry Brooks	27th "	"
9	Capt. John. S. Whiting	29th "	"
10	Capt. Michael Langton	30th "	"
11	Capt. Irving. C. Batson	31st "	"

12 Capt. Jackson. G. Young   48th Ill. Vols.
     Capt. J. B. Hawley   45th Ill Vols Judge Advocate
                              Respectfully
                              Your Obt. Svt.
                              U. S. GRANT
                              Brig. Genl. Comdg.

P. S. This is intended to relieve the Court already ordered by Special Order No   a portion of whom are also members of the Board for examining qualification of officers for retaining their commissions.

                              U. S. G.

LS, DNA, RG 393, Dept. of the Mo., Letters Received. The postscript is also in USG's hand. On Jan. 25, 1862, by Special Orders No. 77, Dept. of the Mo., Capt. John C. Kelton appointed a court-martial composed as USG requested, omitting only Capt. Jackson G. Young, 48th Ill. Copy, DLC-USG, V, 83. On Jan. 23, Brig. Gen. John A. McClernand wrote to Lt. Col. Thomas H. Burgess, 18th Ill. "Genl. McClernand, acknowledges the receipt of his application for a leave of absence—Genl. Grant was consulted, says the charges preferred against you, and forwarded to Genl. Halleck, have been returned and a court martial ordered for to morrow, your presence will be needed—declines." Register of Letters, McClernand Papers, IHi. See letter to Capt. John C. Kelton, Jan. 6, 1862. On Jan. 28, Harriet A. Eaton, Tamaroa, Ill., wrote to USG. "my Husband Major Samuel Eaton 18th Reg Ills Vols. is under arrest by the order of Gen Jno A McClernand and confined to his small room. he has asked the General for larger limits but his demands has not been acceded to. As he informes me and as I well know his close confinement injures his health. I respectfully ask you to allow him larger limits than his quarters." ALS, McClernand Papers, IHi. On Jan. 29, USG endorsed this letter. "Refered to Gen. J. A. McClernand Comd.g Post" AES, *ibid.*

On Feb. 28, McClernand wrote to USG. "Maj. Saml Eaton of the 18th Ill. Regt writes me a manly letter asking for a trial upon the charges preferred against him, or to be released so that he may join his regiment. Under the circumstances I recommend the latter, which I hope will meet with your approbation." Copy, *ibid.* A copy of the letter of Feb. 24 from Maj. Samuel Eaton to McClernand is *ibid.* An endorsement indicates that Eaton was released.

To Brig. Gen. John A. McClernand

                              Hd. Qrs. Dist of Cairo,
                              Cairo Jany 23, 1862.

By an arrangement by the Dist Quarter Master the labor of transfering freight has been materially reduced, and I have authorized the employment of three or four laborers to perform the duty so as to avoid generally making details. On the present occasion I have ordered the transfer of freight ~~of freight~~ from the Steamer Uncle Sam to a Wharf Boat, hence the necessity, of a detail

U S GRANT.
Brig. Genl.

Copy, Register of Letters, McClernand Papers, IHi.

To Brig. Gen. Eleazer A. Paine

Head Quarters, Dist of Cairo
Cairo, Jany 23rd 1862.

GEN. E. A. PAINE
COMMDG U. S. FORCES.
BIRD'S POINT, MO.
GENL:

All prisoners taken by my order prior to the late expedition into Ky. and since released, should have all the private property, taken from them, returned. I am well aware of the difficulty a Commanding Officer has in enforcing the rule that no property taken is to be conveyed to the use of Officers or Soldiers, but when cases are known the offending parties should be summarily punished. Persons from Missouri, have been in Cairo to day looking for their Stock, and I believe without success. I believe your notions of the impropriety of this conduct agree with mine, and I hope you will use rigorous means to break up this dangerous and disgraceful policy.

Respectfully
Your Obt Servant
U. S. GRANT.
Brig. Genl. Commdg.

Copies, DLC-USG, V, 1, 2, 3, 85; DNA, RG 393, USG Letters Sent. *O.R.*, II, iii, 211. See letters to Brig. Gen. Eleazer A. Paine, Jan. 12, 19, 1862.

To Col. Leonard F. Ross

Head Quarters, Dist of Cairo
Cairo, Jany 23rd 1862.

COL. L. F. ROSS.
COMMDG U. S. FORCES.
CAPE. GIRARDEAU, MO.
COLONEL:

Your letter of yesterday, asking for my construction of Genl. Orders No 16, present series from Head Quarters of the Department[1] is received.

The order referred to, is only ambiguous as to whether you are to consider Cape Girardeau, in the vicinity of the Enemy's forces.

In this matter, I would say that your construction would be right, taking the ground, either that you are, or are not, in such vicinity. As you have referred the matter to me however, I would say, abolish passports. This should not relax your efforts, to prevent improper persons from passing through your lines especially persons desirous of working their way South.

I leave tonight for St Louis, will be back on Sunday[2] morning. Immediately on my return, I will send five Companies of Cavalry to the Cape. One of the Infantry Regiments now there, will be ordered here, or to Smithland, Ky. and probably a Company of Artillery. Will use every effort to arm your Cavalry completely.

Respectfully
Your Obt Servant
U. S. GRANT
Brig. Genl. Commdg.

Copies, DLC-USG, V, 1, 2, 3, 85; DNA, RG 393, USG Letters Sent. On Jan. 22, 1862, Col. Leonard F. Ross wrote to USG. "Will you oblige me by giving your construction of Genl Order No 16. New Series—(As to passports)   1st—As to application to this post. 2d . . . As to the portion in reference to passes beyond the lines. And generally as to its bearing, Meaning and intent in reference to the gov't. of our local Provost Marshal." Copy, *ibid.*, Post of Cape Girardeau, Letters

Sent. On the same day, Ross drafted a telegram to USG asking the same question which was not sent. Copy, *ibid.*, Telegrams.

1. On Jan. 16, Capt. John C. Kelton issued General Orders No. 16, Dept. of the Mo. "The system of passports by local provost-marshals in this city and State is hereby abolished. No passports will be issued except in places in the vicinity of the enemy's forces, and then by the commanding officers of such places, and only for passing the lines. No passport will exempt suspected parties from arrest outside of the particular jurisdiction of the officer by whose authority it is issued, nor will persons without passports be arrested except on well-grounded suspicion." *O.R.*, I, viii, 495.

2. Jan. 26.

To Col. Leonard F. Ross

Cairo Jany 23rd 1862

COL. ROSS.

As the Senior you are in my opinion entitled to the Command. Col. Plummer can refer the matter to higher authority.

U. S. GRANT

Telegram, copy, DNA, RG 393, Post of Cape Girardeau, Telegrams. On Jan. 23, 1862, Col. Leonard F. Ross telegraphed to USG. "Col. Plummer arrived yesterday. to day he claims command of this post. I have refused to surrender the same —in as much as I certainly rank him. Do you direct me to surrender the Commad to him." Copy, *ibid.* On Jan. 24, Ross wrote to USG. "In reference to my despatch of yesterday I desire to submit a fuller statement. When Col. Plummer 11th Mo. Vol. reached here, or soon after, he came to me at Head Quarters and demanded the surrender of the Command at this Post to him, ranking him I refused to do so. He stated that he believed he would assume command any how, and so published it to the command. I stated to him that if he did I would arrest him. He then asked what I would do if he refused to obey arrest. I replied that I would put him in *Irons*. I did so regarding the course if so pursued by him as highly mutinous and having a tendency to liscense any officer who might desire to individually assert an assumed right. Unpon the question of rank, I have never been a stickler but in this instance I have thought advisable at least to refer the matter to my Commanding General knowing that justice will be done. If rank in Military parlance amounts to any thing, duty to my regiments requires that I should assert it. And I may further say, however, that if the question had been presented me at a time when the service would have suffered from the delay attending a settlement of the question by you, I would probably have yielded, as I have in one instance heretofore. In this matter I trust I may be understood as but insisting upon a right which I would cheerfully recognize in any officer my superior   The service can suffer no serious inconvenience from the delay if any occurs in its settlement, hence I made the inquiry I did by telegraph yesterday. I trust the matter will end without any harsh feelings on either part—as it will most certainly as far as I am concerned, in whatever way in accordance with military usage you may determine the question." Copy, *ibid.*, Letters Sent.

On Jan. 27, Ross telegraphed to USG. "I made application for a short leave of absence   Has it been granted"   Telegram received, *ibid.*, Dept. of the Mo., Telegrams Received. On Jan. 28, Ross telegraphed to USG. "My leave of absence is received   Is my Regt to be ordered from this place within two weeks"   Telegram received, *ibid.* On Jan. 23, Ross received fifteen days leave by Special Orders No. 70, Dept. of the Mo. Copy, *ibid.*, RG 94, Dept. of the Mo., Special Orders.

To Mary Grant

Cairo,
Jan. 23d, 1862.

DEAR SISTER:

You have seen through the papers notice of my return from the great expedition into Kentucky. My orders were such and the force with me also so small that no attack was allowable. I made good use of the time however, making a splendid reconnoissance of the country over which an army may have to move. I have now a larger force than General Scott ever commanded prior to our present difficulties. I do hope it will be my good fortune to retain so important a command for at least one battle. I believe there is no portion of our whole army better prepared to contest a battle than there is within my district, and I am very much mistaken if I have not got the confidence of officers and men. This is all important, especially so with new troops. I go tonight to St. Louis to see General Halleck; will be back on Sunday[1] morning. I expect but little quiet from this on and if you receive but short, unsatisfactory letters hereafter you need not be surprised.

Your letter asking me to intercede in behalf of Lieut. Jones[2] was received. I have no one of equal rank now to offer in exchange, unless it should be some one of Jeff Thompson's command, but if it should fall in my power to effect Lieutenant Jones' release, I shall be most happy to do so. Write to me giving the first name, where he now is, when taken and under what circumstances.

I think you may look for Julia and the children about the 1st of February.

As I said before the three oldest will be left to go to school. Jess is too small. You will like him the best of any of the children, although he is the worst. I expect he will whip his Aunt Mary the first day. Buck,[3] though never really sick, is very delicate. He is the best child I ever saw and is smart.

Give my love to all at home. I must close.

BROTHER ULYS.

J. G. Cramer, pp. 77–79.

1. Jan. 26, 1862.
2. Possibly 1st Lt. William G. Jones of Ohio, USMA 1860, taken prisoner at San Lucas Spring, Tex., on May 9, 1861, and exchanged on Feb. 20, 1862. USG was not involved in his exchange.
3. Ulysses S. Grant, Jr.

To Elihu B. Washburne

Head Quarters, Dist. of Cairo,
Cairo, Jan.y 23d 1862.

HON. E. B. WASHBURN
WASHINGTON D. C.
SIR:

The bearer, Capt. Baxter who goes to Washington, by my order,[1] in hopes of doing something for the relief of this much distressed portion of our Army is at present my District Quartermaster.

I am at last satisfied that I have an efficient and faithful servant of the Government in Capt. Baxter and anything that you can do to further the object of his mission will not only be regarded as a personal favor to myself but will serve to advance the cause you and I both have so much at heart.

Capt. Baxter can tell you of the great abuses in his Department, here and the efforts I have put forth to correct them, and consequently the number of secret enemies necessarily made.[2]

I am desirous of retaining Capt. Baxter in his present position and if promotion to a higher grade is necessary to enabl[e] me to do so I would very much desir[e] that the promotion be given.

Very respectfully
Your Obt. Svt.
U. S. GRANT
Brig. Gen.

ALS, IHi.

1. Special Orders No. 21, Jan. 23, 1862. "Capt A. S. Baxter A. Q. M. will proceed to Washington D. C. and transact such Public business as he has been instructed to attend to, and return to this place with as little delay as possible." Copies, DLC-USG, V, 15, 16, 82, 87, 89; DNA, RG 393, USG Special Orders. See letter to Maj. Gen. Henry W. Halleck, Feb. 14, 1862.

2. See letter to Elihu B. Washburne, Nov. 7, 1862. On Jan. 21, Capt. Algernon S. Baxter complained about the shortage of funds at Cairo to Capt. Lewis B. Parsons at St. Louis. This letter was forwarded by Parsons to Maj. Gen. Henry W. Halleck, by Halleck to Maj. Gen. George B. McClellan, and by McClellan to Secretary of War Edwin M. Stanton. ALS, DNA, RG 107, Letters Received from the President and Executive Depts., and War Dept. Bureaus. *O.R.*, I, viii, 512–13.

To Brig. Gen. Lorenzo Thomas

Head Quarters District of Cairo
Cairo Illinois Jany 28th/1862

ADJUTANT GENERAL
OF THE ARMY
WASHINGTON D C

I have the honor to transmit to you herewith the Monthly returns of that part of My Command orginally embraced within the District of South East Mo for the Month of December 1861.

My returns for the present Month will be sent you as soon as Sub-reports are in from which I can compile ~~the same~~ it

> I Am Sir Very Respectfully
> Your Obt. Serv't
> U S Grant
> Brig Gen'l Commanding

Copies, DLC-USG, V, 4, 5, 7, 8, 88; DNA, RG 393, USG Hd. Qrs. Correspondence. A notation in DLC-USG, V, 88, states that a copy of this letter was sent to Capt. John C. Kelton.

To Maj. Gen. Henry W. Halleck

By Telegraph from Cairo [*Jan.*] 28th *1862*
To Major Genl Halleck
With Permission I will take Fort McHenry on the Tennesee and hold & establish a large camp there

U. S. Grant

Telegram received, DNA, RG 94, Generals' Papers and Books, Telegrams Received by Gen. Halleck; copies, *ibid.*, RG 393, Dept. of the Mo., Telegrams Received; *ibid.*, USG Hd. Qrs. Correspondence; DLC-USG, V, 4, 5, 7, 8, 9, 88. *O.R.*, I, vii, 121. On Jan. 28, 1862, Flag Officer Andrew H. Foote telegraphed to Maj. Gen. Henry W. Halleck. "Grant and myself are of opinion that Fort Henry on the Tennessee can be carried with four Iron-clad Gun-boats and troops to be permanent-occupied. Have we your authority to move for that purpose?" Telegram received, DNA, RG 94, Generals' Papers and Books, Telegrams Received by Gen. Halleck; copies, *ibid.*, RG 45, Area 5; *ibid.*, RG 393, Dept. of the Mo., Telegrams Received; *ibid.*, USG Hd. Qrs. Correspondence; DLC-USG, V, 4, 5, 7, 8, 9, 88. *O.R.*, I, vii, 120; *O.R.* (Navy), I, xxii, 524. On Jan. 29, Halleck telegraphed to Foote. "I am waiting for Gen. Smith report on road from Smithland to Fort Henry—As soon as that is received will give order Meantime have everything ready" Telegram received, DNA, RG 45, Area 5. *O.R.* (Navy), I, xxii, 525. On Jan. 29, Foote wrote to Halleck. "I have this instant recd. your telegram in relation to Fort Henry and will be ready with four iron clad Gun Boats to leave here early on saturday. Lt. Comdg. Phelps of the 'Conestoga' has been here for a day or two, and in consultation with Genl. Grant we have come to the conclusion that the Tennessee will soon fall as the Ohio is falling above and therefore it is desirable to make the contemplated movement the latter part of this week. Four Mortars & Beds are 'en route' from Pittsburg and more will soon be forwarded. I send Lt. Pritchard, with orders to report to you, agreeable to your suggestion to Genl. Grant. It is said that the road from Paducah to Fort Henry, or opposite, is good even at this season." ALS, DNA, RG 393, Dept. of the Mo., Letters Received. *O.R.* (Navy), I, xxii, 525–26. See letter to Maj. Gen. Henry W. Halleck, Jan. 29, 1862.

USG sent his telegram after returning from a visit to St. Louis lasting approximately four days. On Jan. 23, USG datelined his letters from Cairo. On Jan. 24, Brig. Gen. John A. McClernand described himself as "in temporary command of this district" in reporting his expedition into Ky. to Halleck. *O.R.*, I, vii, 68–72. See also McClernand to President Abraham Lincoln, Jan. 28, 1862. ALS, DLC-Robert T. Lincoln. On Jan. 26, USG informed McClernand, probably by telegraph, that he "will not leave St Louis until monday evening [*Jan. 27*]" Register of Letters, McClernand Papers, IHi. On Jan. 28, Capt. John A. Rawlins wrote to McClernand. "I am directed to inform you that Gen. Grant arrived home this morning, and will again resume command." Copies, DLC-USG, V, 1, 2, 3, 85; DNA, RG 393, USG Letters Sent.

In St. Louis USG had requested Halleck to approve an attempt to capture Fort Henry. "I was received with so little cordiality that I perhaps stated the object of my visit with less clearness than I might have done, and I had not uttered many sentences before I was cut short as if my plan was preposterous. I returned to Cairo very much crestfallen." *Memoirs*, I, 287. In view of USG's renewed request immediately upon his return to Cairo, Halleck's quick assent, and the immediate assignment of troops to Smithland, USG's later recollection of the interview appears exaggerated. On Jan. 28, by Special Orders No. 24, USG sent the 12th Iowa and 28th Ill. to Smithland. Copies, DLC-USG, V, 15, 16, 82, 87, 89; DNA, RG 393, USG Special Orders. On Jan. 29, by Special Orders No. 25, USG sent the 15th Ill. to Smithland. Copies, *ibid.*

USG forwarded additional reports of Brig. Gen. Charles F. Smith to St. Louis. On Jan. 27, Smith wrote to Rawlins. "On the 25th. inst. I briefly reported my return on that day. The distance from Calloway to Aurora is by water about three miles, by land six; from the latter place to this it is forty miles, a good road even at this period of the year, but destitute of water except in the rainy season. We accomplished the march in forty six miles—in three days, an average of fifteen miles per day   This is the state road, but is not marked on any map I have seen; it is generally on a ridge of clay and gravel and is called the ridge road. Its course is nearly straight from Aurora to Paducah; at no point farther than ten miles from the river. My reports of the —— and —— inst.s will give all the necessary information about the march, except on one point: outrages committed by the Men in Killing hogs & poultry, this in despite every precaution taken by myself, and Brigade and regt.l commanders. Horses even were attempted to be carried off. Some men are in arrest for such offences, whom I shall bring before a proper tribunal for trial. The reason for this is, in my belief, that the comp.y officers have not done their duty; they will not see, if they do not in fact encourage, this misconduct. The General will pardon me if I venture to make a suggestion in reference to the future. I know nothing about the course of operations to be pursued, but if Union City (which I have always thought to be a strong strategic post is to be occupied, the most feasible means of supplying our troops there, at this period of the year, is from here by rail to the state line. Place good engines and wood cars on our road, repair the road as we go, & guard the whole line with a str a strong force. The distance from the end of the rail-way to the Columbus road is but eight miles to be marched, or we can march the thirty five miles to Union city from the terminus of the road. I speak of this on account of the extreme difficulty of sending wagon trains for a large force at this period of the year. I send herewith a rather meager itinerary of the march." ALS, *ibid.*, RG 94, War Records Office, Union Battle Reports. *O.R.*, I, vii, 72–73. On Jan. 28, Smith wrote to Rawlins. "I transmit herewith an Itinerary of the recent march of this command which ought to have accompanied my report of yesterday. I spoke of the march from Fulton, the terminus of the rail-way from this place to the state line, to Union City as thirty five miles; it is only eleven miles. From Fulton to the Mobile and Ohio Rail-way by the state line is eight miles; it is the same distance from Fulton to the Nashville and North Western railway. (See accompanying sketch.)" ALS, DNA, RG 94, War Records Office, Union Battle Reports. *O.R.*, I, vii, 73. The accompanying sketch is in DNA, RG 94, War Records Office, Union Battle Reports, as is the itinerary, parts of which are printed in *O.R.*, I, vii, 73–74. On Jan. 29, USG endorsed the itinerary. "Respectfully forwarded to Hd Qrs. Dept. of the Mo." AES, DNA, RG 94, War Records Office, Union Battle Reports.

To Capt. John C. Kelton

Head Quarters, Dist. of Cairo,
Cairo, Jan.y 28th 1862.

CAPT. J. C. KELTON,
A. A. GEN. DEPT. OF THE MO.
ST. LOUIS, MO.
SIR:

Col. Cavanaugh has just reported that Gov. Yates is now ready to increase his command to a Brigade if authorized to do so.

Col. C. commands the 6th Ill. Cavalry now at Shawneetown but I propose to move his command to Smithland if not otherwise directed. Their services are not required at Shawneetown and to remove these troops further from home would be of advantage to their discipline. There would still be an embryo regiment at Shawneetown not yet mustered into the service of the United States.[1]

I have understood that Capt. Eddy, Asst. Qr. Mr. at Springfield, has a supply of wagons, mules, harness and it may be, ambulances. I would respectfully suggest that he be directed to fit out with the above articles as completely as practicable all troops sent to this command.

As I understand from Col. Cavanaugh these troops will only be sent on notice being given from Head Quarters that they will be accepted.

> Very respectfully
> Your Obt. Svt.
> U. S. GRANT
> Brig. Gen.

ALS, DNA, RG 393, Dept. of the Mo., Letters Received. On Jan. 30, 1862, Maj. Gen. Henry W. Halleck wrote to USG. "Your letter of the 28th in relation to Col Cavanaugh's command is received. You will organise your command into brigades, & divisions or columns precisely as you may deem best for the public service, and will from time to time change such organizations as you may deem the public service requires, without the slightest regard to political influences or to the orders and instructions you may have heretofore received. In this matter the good of the service, & not the wishes of politico-military officers, is to be consulted. Get all the troops you can from Illinois, and organise & supply them the best you can when you get them. Dont let any political applications about brigades and divisions trouble you a particle. All such applications & arrangements are sheer nonsense, & will not be regarded." ALS, *ibid.*, RG 94, Generals' Papers and Books, Letters Sent by Gen. Halleck (Press). *O.R.*, I, vii, 572.

1. The 56th Ill., Col. Robert Kirkham.

To Capt. John C. Kelton

> Head Quarters Dist. of Cairo
> Cairo, Jan'y 28th 1862

CAPT. J. C. KELTON
A. A. GEN'L, DEPT. OF THE MISSOURI
SAINT LOUIS, MO:
CAPT:

I have the honor to inform you that the following List of Blanks are required for use in this District to wit:

1000 Non-Commissioned Officers Warrants.
1000 Final Statements of Deceased Soldiers.
500 Quarterly Returns   ”   ”
1000 Morning Guard Reports
10.000 Regimental Morning Reports

10.000 Muster and Pay Rolls attached
   5000 Regimental Monthly Returns
10000 Company Monthly Reports
   200 Company Morning Report Books
   500 Division Returns

A general assortment of Hospital and Medical Blanks Sufficient for this command

You will please send them as soon as practicable, as they are
much needed.

> I am, Sir, Respectfully
> Your Obt Sev't
> U. S. GRANT
> Brig'r Gen'l Com'd'g.

Copies, DLC-USG, V, 7, 88; DNA, RG 393, USG Hd. Qrs. Correspondence.

To Maj. Gen. Henry W. Halleck

Head Quarters, Dist. of Cairo
Cairo, Jan.y 29th 1862.

MAJ. GEN. H. W. HALLECK
COMD.G DEPT. OF THE MO.
ST. LOUIS MO.
GEN.

In view of the large force now concentrating in this District
and the present feasibility of the plan I would respectfully suggest
the propriety of subduing Fort Henry, near the Ky. & Tennessee
line, and holding the position. If this is not done soon there is
but little doubt but that the defences on both the Tennessee and
Cumberland rivers will be materially strengthened. From Fort
Henry it will be easy to operate either on the Cumberland, (only
twelve miles distant) ~~or~~ Memphis or Columbus. It will besides
have a moral effect upon our troops to advance them towards
the rebel states.

The advantages of this move are as perceptable to the Gen. Comd.g Dept. as to myself therefore further statements are unnecessary.

> I am Gen. Very respectfully
> Your Obt. Svt.
> U. S. Grant
> Brig. Gen.

ALS, DNA, RG 393, Dept. of the Mo., Letters Received. *O.R.*, I, vii, 121. See telegram to Maj. Gen. Henry W. Halleck, Jan. 28, 1862. On Jan. 30, 1862, Maj. Gen. Henry W. Halleck telegraphed to USG. "Make your preperations to take & hold Fort Henry. I will send you written instructions by mail." Copies, DLC-USG, V, 4, 5, 7, 8, 9, 81, 88; DNA, RG 94, Generals' Papers and Books, Telegrams Sent by Gen. Halleck in Cipher; *ibid.*, RG 393, Dept. of the Mo., Telegrams Sent; *ibid.*, USG Hd. Qrs. Correspondence. *O.R.*, I, vii, 121. On Jan. 30, Halleck wrote to USG. "You will immediately prepare to send forward to Fort Henry, on the Tennessee river, all your available forces from Smithland, Paducah, Cairo, Fort Holt, Birds Point, &c. Sufficient garrisons must be left to hold these places against an attack from Columbus. As the roads are now almost impassable for large forces, and, as your command is very deficient in transportation, the troops will be taken in steamers up the Tennessee river, as far as practicable: supplies will also be taken up in steamers as far as possible. Flag Officer Foote will protect the transports with his Gun-boats—The Benton & perhaps some others should be left for the defense of Cairo—Fort Henry should be taken & held at all hazards —I shall immediately send you three additional companies of artillery from this place. The river front of the fort is armed with 32 pdrs., & it may be necessary for you to take some Guns of large calibre, and establish a battery on the opposite side of the river—It is believed that the guns on the land side are of small calibre, & can be silenced by our field artillery. It is said that the north side of the river below the fort is favorable for landing—If so you land, & rapidly occupy the road to Dover, & fully invest the place, so as to cut off the retreat of the garrison. Lt Col. McPherson U. S. Engrs will immediately report to you, to act as chf. engineer of the expedition—It is very probable that an attempt will be made from Fort Columbus, to reinforce Fort Henry; also from Fort Donelson at Dover— If you can occupy the road to Dover you can prevent the latter. The steamers will give you the means of crossing from one side of the river to the other—It is said that there is a masked battery opposite the island below Fort Henry—If this cannot be avoided or turned, it must be taken—Having invested Fort Henry, a cavalry force will be sent forward to break up the rail-road from Paris to Dover— The bridges should be rendered impassible, but not destroyed. A telegram from Washington, says, that Beauregard left Manassas four days ago with fifteen regiments, for the line of Columbus & Bowling Green. It is therefore of the greatest importance that we cut that line before he arrives. You will move with the least delay possible   You will furnish Com. Foote with a copy of this letter—P. S. A telegraph line will be extended as rapidly as possible from Paducah east of the Tennessee river to Fort Henry. Wire & operatives will be sent from St Louis." LS, DNA, RG 393, Dept. of the Mo., Telegrams Received. *O.R.*, I, vii, 121–22.

To Maj. Gen. Henry W. Halleck

Head Quarters, Dist. of Cairo
Cairo, Jan.y 29th 1862.

Respectfully forwarded to Head Quarters, Dept. of the Mo. with the request that if consistent with the good of the service Lieut. Freeman be retained as an officer of the Engineer Corps and attached to Gen. McClernand's Comd. Lieut. Freeman I believe to be a worthy officer well qualified for the position he has been filling under an appointment from Gen. Frémont.

U. S. GRANT
Brig. Gen Com

AES, USMA. Written on a letter of Jan. 29, 1862, from Brig. Gen. John A. McClernand to USG. "You are not unaware of my persevering efforts, from the first, to obtain the assistance of efficient officers as members of my Staff, and that, hitherto, having been wholly unseconded by Federal authority contrary to what I deemed well founded expectation, I have had to perform not only the duties of General but of General's Staff. The wear of these multiplied duties is exhausting me. In order to obtain some mitigation of them—with the consent of Col J. D. Webster Chief Engineer of the District and of 2d Lieut. Henry C. Freeman (Civil Engineer) attached to the same corps, I ask that he may be assigned to duty as Engineer in my command. Bringing this subject to the attention of Genl Cullom, Chief of Maj. Genl. Halleck's Staff and of Engineers of the Department of the Mo, (to whom I am not wholly unknown and who I believe would respond to any reasonable request I might make,) I have confidence that it would be satisfactorily attended to, and Lieut Freeman accordingly assigned." LS, *ibid.*

On Feb. 1, Brig. Gen. George W. Cullum wrote to Col. Joseph D. Webster. "Brig Genl McClernand informs [*me*] that he has your consent to transfer Lieut. H. C. Freeman to his Staff, from which I infer that he has completed the temporary duty, for which I authorized his being retained. You will thefore discharge him, when Genl McClernand can make arrangements to secure his services as an aid de Camp under the law." Copies, DLC-USG, V, 7, 8, 9; DNA, RG 393, USG Hd. Qrs. Correspondence. Although 1st Lt. Henry C. Freeman subsequently served as act. engineer and aide to McClernand, his position remained irregular until he was confirmed on July 17, 1862, as aide-de-camp to Maj. Gen. Henry W. Halleck. See *Calendar*, Dec. 26, 1861.

To Flag Officer Andrew H. Foote

Head Quarters, Dist of Cairo.
Cairo, Jany 29th 1862.

FLAG OFFICER FOOTE
U. S. G. B. FLOTILLA.
CAIRO, ILLS.
SIR:

The final Discharge from the Army, of all Soldiers, who, with the consent of their Company and Regimental Commanders, become enrolled in the Gun Boat Service, will be procured immediately, upon notice of such enrollment being sent to these Head Quarters.

I am, Sir, Very Respectfully,
Your Obt. Servant
U. S. GRANT
Brig. Genl. Comdg.

Copies, DLC-USG, V, 1, 2, 3, 85; DNA, RG 393, USG Letters Sent. On Jan. 27, 1862, Maj. Gen. Henry W. Halleck wrote to USG. "Authority is just received from Washington to permit volunteers who desire it to be discharged & recruited by Com. Foote for navy service on the Gun boats; but this must be so distributed among the regiments as not to destroy the efficiency of any organised company. Please inform Com. Foote that if he can send a recruiting officer here, a considerable number of river-men can be obtained from the regiments here. Keep me informed of the progress made in thus supplying the Gunboats." ALS, *ibid.*, RG 94, Generals' Papers and Books, Letters Sent by Gen. Halleck (Press). On Jan. 31, Brig. Gen. Eleazer A. Paine wrote to Capt. John A. Rawlins. "Your letter, being an order as it purports, to Capt Swanwick of the 22nd Regt. Ill. Infty. permitting the discharge of a man named George Woolley private in said Swanwicks company, for the purpose of enlisting him in the Gun Boat service, was handed me to-day If any order for such purpose is to be enforced upon the officers of the Regiment or company it certainly should pass thro' the Comdg. Officer of this post. But the Regulations of 1861 and Major Genl. Hallecks order I believe forbid the transfers contemplated by your order. I may be mistaken but it is my recollection that the changing from one branch of the service to another is forbidden. If permitted it will nearly ruin the Regiments in this Brigade. Four of the men have already sent in their names, and think that they are now released from duty. Others find fault with their officers who do not at once consent to it, when in fact no official notice has ever been received here that such a step was to be taken so demoralizing to our men. I desire very much that Brig Genl. Grant Comdg. this District would at once publish an order forbidding any enlistments

among the soldiers for the Gun Boat Service." ALS, *ibid.*, RG 393, District of
Cairo, Letters Received.

On Jan. 27, Flag Officer Andrew H. Foote wrote to Asst. Secretary of the
Navy Gustavus V. Fox. "Genl Grant has issued a proclamation that soldiers may
be transferred to the Gun Boats. They are flocking to us, but their Colonels and
Captains refuse to let them go, and thus far the proclamation is a farce and the
Gun Boats suffer." Robert Means Thompson and Richard Wainwright, eds.,
Confidential Correspondence of Gustavus Vasa Fox (New York, 1918–19), II, 32.
See letter to Capt. John C. Kelton, Jan. 20, 1862, note 3.

To Brig. Gen. John A. McClernand

Head Quarters, Dist. of Cairo,
Cairo, Jan.y 29th 1862

GEN. J. A. McCLERNAND
COMD.G POST
CAIRO, ILL.
GEN.

Yours of this date enclosing correspondence with Capt.
Kountz is just received. As Capt. Kountz does not refer to me for
information as to the nature of the charges against him I have
no objection to leave the information where he can get it.

No charges have been prefered against him. When they are
a copy will be sent him. I have simply requested that he be relieved from duty here and sent to some other field of usefulness.

His arrest was for "Disobedience of Orders," "Disrespect to
his Superior Officer" and "Conduct wholly subversive of good
order and Military discipline."

As I believe the good of the service demands that as few
Courts Martials as practicable be had it was not my intention to
prefer charges and I now await the decission of Maj. Gen.
McClellan to whom the matter was refered.

Respectfully
Your Obt. Svt.
U. S. GRANT
Brig. Gen.

ALS, McClernand Papers, IHi. On Jan. 29, 1862, Brig. Gen. John A. McClernand wrote to USG. "It becomes my duty to enclose copies of correspondence between Capt W J Kountz Asst Qr Master, U. S. and myself, in which he asks to be informed touching the cause of his arrest and detention and for a speedy trial in relation to the same." Copy, *ibid*. There is no record of the reference of this matter to Maj. Gen. George B. McClellan. See endorsement to Capt. William J. Kountz, Jan. 29, 1862.

To Brig. Gen. John A. McClernand

Head Quarters, Dist. of Cairo
Cairo, Jan.y 29th 1862

GEN. J. A. MCCLERNAND
COMD.G POST
CAIRO, ILL.
GEN.

The prisoners Fraser & Polk, taken in Ky. by your order, have called upon me desiring their release and expressing a willingness to take the desired oath. I know nothing of the merits of these cases and refer the matter to you to be decided according to your judgement.

Respectfully
Your Obt. Svt.
U. S. GRANT
Brig. Gen.

ALS, McClernand Papers, IHi. On Jan. 11, 1862, Maj. Mason Brayman wrote to USG. "Genl. M'Clernand orders sent for your disposal, two prisoners named: Lou T. Polk   Daniel Frazer. They were taken by Capt. W. Stewart to-day, near Blandville, this afternoon returning from ~~to~~ Columbus whither they had been to convey recruits—not being themselves in the army, though undoubtedly rebels." ADfS, *ibid*. In an undated letter, Capt. Warren Stewart wrote to Brig. Gen. John A. McClernand. "The prisoners Polk & Frasier was taken Jan 11th 1862 at Westons—They were on their return from Columbus, having acted as escort to a rebel who was acting with rebel army, returning with the rebels horse, & armed, were arrested, as they were aiding and assisting rebels in the army, by their own confession were guilty"   ALS, *ibid*. On Jan. 29, Brayman wrote to USG. "Genl. McClernand instructs me to reply to yours of this date, that the prisoners Polk and Frazer, were captured by Capt Stewart, on the 11th Inst on their way from Columbus, having acted as escort to a rebel going to join the army at that place. They were bringing back his horse, and were armed. By their own confessions and statements they were clearly guilty of aiding in the operations of the rebels. He thinks their detention proper." Copy, *ibid*.

To Commanding Officer, Cape Girardeau

Head Quarters, Dist of Cairo,
Cairo, Jany 29th 1862.

COMMDG OFFICER
CAPE GIRARDEAU MO.
SIR:

Hereafter no more prisoners of war than those belonging to regularly organized companies, will be released on their parole, but will be forwarded to Saint Louis for the present and to Alton[1] as soon as that place is fitted up for their reception.

Arrangements will soon be effected for the exchange of prisoners, and as we have many in the South, it is important to retain all we have, or may get, to release ours with.

Prisoners who have been taken up for offences justifying their arrest, and who do not belong to organized Companies, if released, should take the prescribed oath, and give Bonds, with good and sufficient security for their faithful observance of the oath taken.

Respectfully,
U. S. GRANT
Brig. Genl. Commdg.

Copies, DLC-USG, V, 1, 2, 3, 85; DNA, RG 393, USG Letters Sent. *O.R.*, II, i, 535. On Jan. 25, 1862, Col. Leonard F. Ross wrote to USG. "I am frequently importuned by the prisoners—now held here in obedience to your order—for permission to take the oath of allegiance. They are those returned, Thompson's troops, and are very anxious to return to their homes and pursue their ordinary avocations. A release upon parole of honor, or discharge upon taking the oath of allegiance—would be gladly hailed by them, as from all I can gather they are heart sick of opposing the Federal Gov't. Will you do me the kindness to reply— as to course thought preferable by you—if either." Copy, DNA, RG 393, Post of Cape Girardeau, Letters Sent. *O.R.*, II, i, 534. On Jan. 29, Ross telegraphed to USG. "Capt Murdock came in yesterday with twenty five prisoners from Caster Creek. Major Herrla late of Jeff Thompsons command arrived last night with flag of truce from Thompson to arrange for exchange of Prisoners" Telegram received, DNA, RG 393, Dept. of the Mo., Telegrams Received. *O.R.*, II, i, 536. On Jan. 27, Brig. Gen. M. Jeff Thompson wrote to Ross. "I would be pleased to know in what light you regard the prisoners or persons your forces have lately captured at Bloomfield and other portions of my district—whether as citizens or soldiers? I allude to those who have been soldiers in the Missouri State Guard but who have been disbanded. Citizen Herr, formerly major of the Fifth Regiment of Infantry, bears this communication and will return with the answer. Major Herr will make any arrangement for exchange and can explain more fully my wishes in the case than I can express in a short business letter." *Ibid.*, p. 535. On Jan. 30, Ross replied to Thompson. "In reply to yours of the 27th instant I desire to say that all matters pertaining to exchange of prisoners and the light in which the parties lately captured at Bloomfield and Dallas are to be regarded will be referred to the district commandant, Brigadier-General Grant." *Ibid.*, p. 536.

1. A lengthy report on the number and condition of prisoners at Alton, Ill., prepared April 3, is *ibid.*, II, iii, 421–23.

To Capt. William J. Kountz

Head Quarters, Dist. of Cairo
Cairo, Jan.y 29th 1862.

Capt. Kountz was placed in arrest for disobedience of orders and disrespect to his superior officer, and application made for his removal. No charges have yet been prefered nor was it the intention to prefer them at present, at least not until Gen. McClellan to whom the matter has been refered is heard from.

U. S. GRANT
Brig. Gen

AES, DNA, RG 94, ACP K21, CB 1863. Written on a letter of Jan. 29, 1862, from Capt. William J. Kountz to Capt. John A. Rawlins. "On the 15th inst I was placed in arrest by Capt Hillyer aid-de-camp who stated to me at the time that he acted by order of Brig Genl U S Grant   I am still in arrest, but have not been furnished with any charge, or other statement as the grounds of my arrest   I have the honor to request to be informed on what grounds I was arrested and still held in arrest—to be furnished with a copy of the charge and specifications; also that a court may be ordered at the earliest date in my case"   LS, *ibid*. On Feb. 10, Kountz enclosed this letter in a letter to Secretary of War Edwin M. Stanton. "I regret that I am compelled to address you a letter in regard to my private matters, but as great injustice has been done me since my arrival at this place, I take the responsibility of writing you this letter, about one month ago I was placed in arrest by Brig Genl Grant, without any cause being assigned; and after several appeals that I should have a trial or know the cause of my arrest, I have received no information except that contained in the enclosed letter—now I appeal to you to know if I shall remain here and wait the pleasure of a man who has proved himself to be my personal enemy, and I believe a worse enemy of the country's

and if you will place me in a position where I can be heard I will prove it to you"
LS, *ibid.*

Although the official cause of Kountz's arrest appears to have developed during the reconnaissance into Ky., his personality and methods appear to have antagonized immediately both army officers and boatmen at Cairo. See letter to Capt. William J. Kountz, Dec. 21, 1861. On Jan. 14, 1862, Robert Forsyth, St. Louis, wrote to Maj. Gen. Henry W. Halleck. "In Sending you the enclosed petition I desire to say I was partialy instrumental in getting Capt Kountz appointed. as I gave him letters to Major Genl G B McClellan & other friends and am now anxious to reconsider same & make all amends in my power. I consider G W Graham Esq a loyal & good man & well fitted for the position of Comodore. Please Consider this petition." ALS, DNA, RG 393, Dept. of the Tenn., Miscellaneous Letters Received. Forsyth enclosed a petition to Halleck dated Jan. 4. "We, your humble petitioners would most respectfully represent that the removal of Captain G. W. Graham from the service of the United States at this point in the capacity of commander of the Transport fleet used for conveying troops and stores from this to other posts, has produced the greatest dissatisfaction among the men qualified to discharge the duties of Transport Officers, and other duties connected with the Naval forces for the suppression of Rebellion. We therefore do most earnestly recommend the appointment of said George W. Graham as Assistant Quartermaster of U. S. Vols. with the rank of Captain and that he be assigned to duty as Commander of the U. S. Chartered Steamboats and Transports at this post and in the 'District of Cairo' believing it to be for the best interests of the service. And we do further petition, that, during the interim necessary to obtain such appointment said G. W. Graham shall be reinstated in the command of the Transport Fleet with power to execute all duties pertaining thereto" DS, *ibid.* The petition was signed by Cols. Napoleon B. Buford, John Cook, Isham N. Haynie, Amory K. Johnson, John McArthur, C. Carroll Marsh, Richard J. Oglesby, James S. Rearden, Morgan L. Smith, William H. L. Wallace, and nine other officers.

At the same time, the St. Louis papers carried several items indicating a campaign against Kountz. "G. W. B." reported from Cairo, Jan. 7, that local boatmen preferred George W. Graham to Kountz. *Missouri Democrat,* Jan. 10, 1862. An anonymous letter questioned his loyalty. *Missouri Republican,* Jan. 11, 1862. Thirty-one Cairo boatmen drew up a petition. "*Resolved,* That in the appointment of W. J. Kountz, we believe that the interest of the Government has been jeopardized, that a more unpopular man with all classes of boatmen, could not have been selected; that his course heretofore, and especially since taking command of the transport service, is so very obnoxious that it would be difficult for him to procure the services of the best and most loyal boatmen. *Resolved,* That in giving this expression we do it with no animosity, but have the interest of our country in view. *Resolved,* That a copy of the above resolutions be forwarded to Brigadier General U. S. Grant, Commander of the forces at Cairo, Hon. F. P. Blair, Washington City; also to St. Louis, Louisville, Cincinnati, and Pittsburgh papers." Dispatch from Cairo, Jan. 12, 1862, *ibid.,* Jan. 13, 1862. See also letter of Chas. M. Scott, *Missouri Democrat,* Jan. 16, 1862; dispatch from Cairo, Jan. 22, 1862, *ibid.,* Jan. 24, 1862.

Kountz apparently retaliated for his arrest by preparing charges against USG. "Charges and specifications preferred against Ulysses S. Grant, Brigadier General Commanding District of South East Missouri [now District of Cairo]

Charge 1st

Drunkenness while on duty, in violation of the Forty-fifth Act of First Section of the Articles of War, regulating the United States Army.

Specification 1st

In this, that the said Ulysses S. Grant Brigadier General, and commanding at the post of Cairo, in the State of Illinois, the same being in the District of South East Missouri, heretofore to-wit: On the or about the sixth day of December 1861, and while on duty; accompanying a 'flag of truce' from Cairo Ill to Columbus, Ky the same being on a Government steamboat on the Mississippi river, between Cairo Ill and Columbus, Ky. did then and there while so on duty become, of his own voluntary act, beastly drunk, insomuch that the said Ulysses S. Grant, was then and there, from the said cause, incapacitated for any business Contrary to the rules and regulations for the Army of the United States.

Specification 2nd

In this, that the said Ulysses S. Grant Brigadier General commanding &c, on the day and year, and at the place last aforesaid, being on duty with a 'Flag of Truce' sent from the Union Government forces, at Cairo Ill, to the Rebel forces at Columbus Ky, did then and there, and while with men who were in rebellion against the Government of the United States, by the use of intoxicating liquors, drank in the presence of, and with said rebels, become beastly drunk, and by reason thereof, incapacitated for duty, contrary to the rules and articles of the Army of the United States.

Specification 3rd

In this, that the said Ulysses S. Grant at the time and place stated in first Specification, and while on duty as a United States officer, to wit, as Brigadier General in the United States army, become intoxicated contrary to the rules and articles for the government of the United States Army

Specification 4th

In this that on the 7th day of December 1861 and on divers days since said day, the S said Ulyssis S. Grant, Brigadier General &c, at the city of Cairo, Ill. and while on duty as Commanding General of the District of South East Missouri, the same including Cairo Ill. did become and was then and there intoxicated to drunkenness, and was then and there guilty of drunkenness, contrary to the rules and regulations of the United States Army

Charge 2nd

Conduct unbecoming an Officer and a Gentleman

Specification 1st

In this, that the said Ulysses S. Grant, heretofore, to wit: on the or about the 6th day of December 1861, at Cairo, Illinois and on divers days and times since said day, has been repeatedly and often openly drunk, and so much intoxicated as to be unfitted for any business, thereby setting an evil example to the officers and soldiers under his command.

I, William J. Kountz, prefer the above charges and specifications against Ulysses S. Grant, and ask that a Court Martial may be convened to try the same." DS, DLC-Edwin M. Stanton. This document had been received at hd. qrs., Dept. of the Mo., on Jan. 26 and on the same day was endorsed by Col. Joseph C. McKibbin. "Not sent through the proper channel—Respectfully referred to Brig Genl U S Grant"   AES, *ibid*. On Jan. 29, USG endorsed the charges. "Capt. Kountz will please furnish a copy of these charges for this office and one copy to be sent to Head Quarters of the Dept." AES, *ibid*. On Feb. 12, Kountz added his endorsement. "I complied with the above at the time and gave the with in to Maj Rawlins on the 30th of Jan 62"   AES, *ibid*. An undated copy of the charges was endorsed on Jan. 30 by USG. "Respectfully forwarded to Head Quarters, Dept. of the Mo." AES, DNA, RG 94, ACP 4754/1885.

The Kountz charges were followed on Feb. 8 by another series of charges. "Charges against Brigadier Genl U. S. Grant.

Charge First

Visiting Capt G. W. Graham Head Quarters on the Wharfboat at this place and drinking liquor publicly while the sale and use of liquor was prohibited by the Provost Martial by the order of the commanding General U. S. Grant thus setting a bad example to his officers and men

Charge Second

For drinking with traitors and enemies to the Federal Government, while under a Flag of Truce, becoming drunk and incapable of attending to business: to the disgrace of the United States Army

Charge Third

For occupying the cooks room on a Government Steamer while under a Flag of Truce, and vomiting all over the floor—(cause drunkeness) conduct unbecoming a gentleman or an Officer

Charge Fourth

For getting drunk at the St Charles Hotel and loosing his sword and uniform; and behaving in a manner disgraceful to the United States Army

Charge Fifth

For receiving on board of a Government Steamer bearing a Flag of Truce, a Harlot who had been sent to Capt G. W. Graham on a pretence of being passed South, said Harlot got drunk during the trip, drinking with the Officers and was not sent south, but returned to the Hotel where General U. S. Grant visited her private room: No 5 publicly, conduct disgraceful to an Officer in the United States Army.

Charge Sixth

Visiting a Negro Ball in company with his Aids, QuarterMaster, and Capt Graham, There drinking a large amount of Champaigne wine, and becoming drunk, conduct unbecoming a commanding General, to the injury and disgrace of the United States Army

Charge Seventh

For retaining men on his Staff who have been repeatedly drunk in his presence, disgraceful to his high position

Charge Eighth

Getting so drunk that he had to go up stairs on all fours, conduct not becoming a man

Charge Ninth

For playing Cards for money while he was a disbursing Agent, (disburseing secret service money)"

Copy, DLC-Edwin M. Stanton. Although these charges were unsigned, they appear to be connected to the Kountz charges. The lists of witnesses overlap, and Kountz is an overly conspicuous omission on the second list. The two sets of charges are copied in the same clerical hand in the Stanton Papers.

Another related document is a statement of Feb. 4 by Capt. George H. Myers and Capt. M. H. Burne. "We, the undersigned, having been called on to appraise the valuation of the Steamer (Steam Boat) 'Luella' Do certify that in our opinion the Cash valuation is Seven Thousand five hundred Dollars" This document has an unsigned endorsement. "Genl U. S. Grant, when called upon by the owner of the within named Boat, refused to pay any more than Eight Dollars per day for charter for the same: while he recognized the correctness of (45) Forty five Dollars per day charged by the Steamer 'Wilson' which was not worth in real valuation (1500) Fifteen Hundred Dollars. Strange that Genl Grant should know that a Ferry Boat at Cape Girardeau was only worth Eight Dollars per day, while he did not know that a Boat at Cairo, was not worth forty five (45) dollars per day." Copy, *ibid*.

On Jan. 17, Kountz wrote to Stanton. "Stealing from Govt is still going on here, and men who are deep in *Guilt* still hold position. Do for Heavens sake send an investigating committee here, and I will give them all the points nescessary to break up the greatest system of Swindling, in the west. I have been put under arrest, my limits is the Hotel; if in your power, which I believe it is, I would be most happy to be released from limits, and placed on duty, as I am sure the Govt is loosing more than Two hundred Dollars pr day by my being under arrest: I am willing to a Court Martial, if I have done anything wrong. I have heard two Stories about my arrest, one disobeying orders another, Speaking disrespectfully of the General in Command. So far as I know, both are false. You will confer a favor by an answer" LS, DNA, RG 107, Letters Received. On Jan. 16, Kountz had written to Joshua Hanna, Pittsburgh, Pa. "I have been ordered under arrest for I know not what neither have I the most distant Idea one thing sure I have done nothing wrong the act is a milicious one & I assure you that the whole thing has been done for the sake of spoil use such influences as you have to have me released with out limit my limits is the Hotel Please let me hear from you" ALS, *ibid*., RG 94, ACP K21, CB 1863. On Jan. 20, Hanna wrote to Stanton. "Having aided with a number of our prominent citizens in obtaining the appointment of Capt W J Kountz to the responsible position of buying, chartering, and employing Boats for the Goverment at St Louis Cairo and on the Ohio River— we learn with much regret of his *arrest* at *Cairo*. I now enclose you his letter to me on the subject, after a consultation with some of his friends we are fully perswaded his arrest is caused by persons who have found him in their way in speculating off the Goverment—of which I need now enlarge on the extent to which this has been carried at that and other points exceeds any thing in the history of our country—But I will say having known Capt Kountz from his infancy that he is honest to the last cent and would make a closer bargain and be more exacting for the Goverment than for himself—he may have been exited and abrupt in his manner, but I know he done his whole duty concientiously His friends request his immediate tryal or release—and we know of no man on our rivers who will fill his place better or with more economy to the Govermt" ALS, *ibid*. On Jan. 24, Kountz wrote to Maj. Mason Brayman. "As I am ignorant of the cause of my arrest, I have the honor to request that I be furnished with a copy of the Charges that may have been preferred against me, and ask an immediate investigation, having been ten days under arrest. Please communicate this, my request, to the General in Command" ALS, McClernand Papers, IHi. On Jan. 24, Brayman wrote to Kountz. "Your communication of this date is received. In reply to your request for a copy of the charges against you, and an immediate investigation, I have to advise you, that your arrest took place while Genl. McClernand was absent and not in command of the Post or District. I am not aware that Genl. Grant, on leaving him in command furnished the charges or indicated officialy his wishes respecting their investigation   I will submit your request to Genl. McClernand and shall be happy to communicate to you such information as he may direct. . . . P. S. Your two previous communications, received during the march in Kentucky, were submited to Genl. McClernand." DfS, *ibid.* On Jan. 26, Kountz wrote to James K. Moorhead, U. S. Representative from Pa. "I suppose you have learned before this of my being under arrest   this is my 13th day and no charges against me yet   a friend of mine went to one of genl. Grants aids who was an intimate acquaintance of his and asked what Capt Kountz was arrested for   he was told there was no charges against him but I was so verry unpoplar with the steam boat men that I was arested that another man might be put in my place and also said that the Genl liked me very will and so did his agetent   I am satisfied in my owne mind that the Genl has some interest in some of the speculations that has been going on here and my presents will not only ~~destroy~~ stop the present but brake up the future as there has been no money paid here but the most Rascally bill ever you herd off which I repudiateted by order Maj Allen Chief Qr Master St Louis   I have been well suported by him ~~I~~ My life has been Threatened   I have been advised by men who professed to be my friend to leave the place or I would be assasinated   one friend of the same kind wrote me a long letter adviseing me to leave as he knew of a plot that had been made to kill me befour the first of February   I find all of these friends is implicated in some way in the frauds connected with the steam boating business   I have discovered where a boat was chartered at 1200$ double what she was worth and returned to the Qr Master at St Louis at ~~at~~ 1800 per month   another at 900$ & returned at 1350$ Coal bought at 10 cts & put into the Gov at 12 cts —I could cover ten pages giveing you details of the reason why they do not want me at Cairo   There was a man by the name of G W Graham who was removed for these deshonest returns placed in my place as soon as I was removed   There is a ferry boat that was sold here over one year ago for 900$ is chartered to the Government at 1350$ per month and so it was when I came hear   I have Prefered charges againts Genl Grant for drunkenness and conduct unbecomeing ~~an officer or~~ a Gentleman or officer   he on Three different occations when visiting Columbus Drank with Trators until he became beastly drunt   on one Occation he got into the cook Room & vomited allover the floor   at an other time was so drunk at the Hotel for 3 day he was not fit to attind to business   at an other time went with his staff Capt Graham and others to an negro Ball and the report is that Grant got so drunk that a negro Girl refused to dace with him   This is the man who had me arested   This is only a few of the many evils that has been going on here   I have been supported by Genl. McClernand who is a very worthy indestryous & good man but his hands has been tied"   ALS, DNA, RG 92, Consolidated Correspondence, Gunboats. On Feb. 26, Kountz wrote to Stanton. "Feeling as I do that my acts during this rebellion entiles me to some consideration as you are aware I travelled from Cairo to Washington at my owne expense & through my efforts aided by your influence Succeeded in haveing the blockade ordered at

Cairo, at which time there was 4000 tons passing daily   At which time you recomended that I should apply for a position to take charge of River transportation of the west. which I did at once by Volunteering my services free of charge and served the Government and paid my owne Travelling & other expences until the 16th of november when by wish of Genl. Meigs I was appointed A. Q. M. of vol and sent west to take charge of river transportation   on my arival at St Louis I found that Col Blair had put a veto on my oporations there by telegraphing to Washington to have my oporations suspended until he would Get to washington in person (Maj Allen Chief Qr M at St Louis is my informant)   Col Blair is a very stanch friend of Capt Bart Able who I exposed for robbing the *Gov*   He Able was dismissed but another put in his place to obey his bidding   So Blair carried his point there   I feel that I have been badly sacrificed and my usefulness distroyed   If I had charge of the river business of the department I could save for the gov 2000$ per day and have the service better done   I do say most cincerly that I never would have been put under arrest if I had acted my part in the popular system of you tickle me and Ill Tickle you   I want to serve the country in a way that I can make myself the most useful & save the bleeding treasury   If you consider my case worthy of your favourable consideration please let me hear from you . . . P. S. There is a man in charge of river Transports at this place that is no Boatman nor does he know the value or fitness of boats"   LS, *ibid.*, RG 107, Letters Received. On March 13, Kountz wrote to Brig. Gen. Montgomery C. Meigs. "I most respectfully tender you my resignation of the office of Assistant Quartermaster U. S. A." LS, *ibid.*, RG 94, ACP K21, CB 1863. On March 24, Whitelaw Reid reported that charges of drunkenness made by Kountz against USG had "sprung from personal feelings." Letter of "Agate," March 24, 1862, in *Cincinnati Gazette*, March 28, 1862. On April 2, Kountz replied that he was prepared to prove his charges "by more than twenty respectable witnesses." *Ibid.*, April 10, 1862. Temporarily, at least, Kountz stopped here.

Charges made by Kountz are similar to other charges made against USG in late 1861. On Dec. 17, 1861, Benjamin H. Campbell of Galena, recently returned from St. Louis, wrote to Congressman Elihu B. Washburne. "I am sorry to hear from good authority, that Gnl Grant is drinking very hard, had you not better write to Rawlins to know the fact." ALS, DLC-Elihu B. Washburne. On Dec. 30, Rawlins wrote to Washburne. "Yours of the 21st is at hand. I was no less astounded at the contents of your note than you must have been at the information, reported to you. I thank you for the confidence manifested by you in the frank manner of your inquiry—I feel that you of all other men had the right, as you would feel it your duty to investigate the charge. I know how much you have done for Genl. Grant and how jealous you are of his good name, and assure you it is appreciated by not only Genl Grant but by all his friends. I will answer your inquiry fully and frankly, but first I would say unequivocally and emphatically that the statement, that 'Genl. Grant is drinking very hard['] is utterly untrue and could have originated only in malice. When I came to Cairo, Genl Grant was as he is today, a strictly total abstinence man, and I have been informed by those who knew him well, that such has been his habit for the last five or six years. A few days after I came here a gentleman made him a present of a box of champagne wine, on one or two occasions he drank a glass of this with his friends but on neither occasion did he drink enough to in any manner affect him. About this time General Grant was somewhat dispeptic and his Physician advised him to drink two glasses of ale or beer a day. He followed this prescription for about one or two (2) weeks (never exceeding the two glasses per day), and then being satisfied it did him no good he resumed his total abstinence habits, until some three or four weeks after the Battle of Belmont, while he was rooming at the St. Charles Hotel, Col. Taylor of Chicago, Mr Dubois Auditor of State and other friends were visiting Cairo, & he was induced out of compliment to them to drink with them on several occasions *but in no instance* did he drink enough to manifest it, to any one who did not see him drink. About this time Mr. Osborne President of the Ill C. R. R. Co. our mutual friend J. M. Douglas and several of their friends made a visit to Cairo and gave dinner (or lunch) on the cars, to which the General and I were invited with others; champagne, was part of the fare. Sitting near the Genl. I noticed he did not drink more than half a glass. The fact of his drinking at all was remarked, simply because of his usual total abstinence. But no man can say that at anytime since I have been with him has he drank liquor enough to in the slightest unfit him for business, or make it manifest in his words or action. At the times I have referred to he continuing probably a week or ten days, he may have taken an occasional drink with those gentlemen and others visiting Cairo at that time, but never in a single instance to excess and at the end of that period he voluntarily stated he should not during the continuance of the war again taste liquor of any kind, and for the past three or four weeks, though to my knowledge frequently importuned on visits of friends he has not tasted any kind of liquor. Ever since I have been with Genl. Grant he has sent his reports in his own hand writing to Saint Louis daily when there was matter to report, and never less than three times a week and during the period above referred to, he did not at all relax this habit. If there is any man in the service who has discharged his duties faithfully & fearlessly who has ever been at his post, and guarded the interest confided to him with the utmost vigilance, Genl. Grant has done it. Not only his reports, but all his orders of an important character are written by himself, and I venture here, the statement, 'there is not an officer in the Army who discharges the duties of his command, so nearly without the intervention of aides, or Assistants as does General Grant.['] Some ten or twelve days ago an article was published in the Chicago Tribune, charging frauds on the Quarter Masters Department here, in the purchase of lumber at Chicago. Genl. Grant immediately sent Capt. W. S. Hillyer a member of his staff to Chicago, with instructions to thoroughly investigate & report the facts. That report and a large mass of testimony, substantiating the charge had been forward to St. Louis when orders came from Washington to investigate the charge. The investigation had already been made. Thus time and again has he been able to send back the same answer when orders were received from St Louis in reference to the affairs of this District. I am satisfied from the confidence and consideration you have manifested in me that my statement is sufficient for you but should the subject be mooted by other parties you can refer them to Col. J. D. Webster colonel of the 1st Illinois artillery, General Grants Chief of Staff, a man who is well known in Chicago as a man of unquestionable habits, a man who has been a counsellor of the General through this campaigne, who was with him at and all through the Battle of Belmont, who has seen him daily and has every opportunity to know his habits. I would further refer them to Genl. Van Rensalear, who specially sent to inspect the troops, and investigate the condition of this District by Major Genl. McClellan, and Genl's. Sturgiss and Sweeny who were sent here by Major Genl. Halleck for the same purpose. These gentlemen after a full and thorough investigation returned to Saint Louis some two weeks ago. I know not what report they made; but this I do know; that a few days after their return an order arrived from St Louis creating the District of Cairo a District including SouthEast Missouri Southern Illinois and all of Kentucky west of the Cumberland, a District nearly twice as large as General Grants former command, and General Grant was assigned to the command. I would refer them to Flag Officer A. H. Foote, of the U. S. Mississippi Naval Fleet, a man whose actions and judgment are regulated by the strictest New England standard, a strict and faithful member of the Congregational Church; & who for months has had personal as well as official intercourse with the General. If you could look into Genl Grants countenance at this moment, you would want no other assurance of his sobriety. He is in perfect health, and his eye and intellect are as clear and active as can be. That General Grant has enemys no one could doubt, who knows how much effort he has made to guard against & ferret out frauds in his District, but I do not believe there is a single Colonel or Brig Genl. in his command who does not desire his promotion, or at least to see him the Commanding General of a large division of the Army, in its advance down the Mississippi when that movement is made. Some weeks ago one of those irresponsible rumors was set afloat, that Genl. Grant was to be removed from the command of the District and there was a universal protest expressed against it by both officers & men. I have one thing more to say and I have done, this already long letter. No one can feel a greater interest in General Grant than I do; I regard his interest as my interest, all that concerns his reputation concerns me; I love him ~~as I love~~ a father, I respect ~~respect~~ him because I have studied him well, and the more I know him the more I respect & love him. Knowing the truth, I am willing to trust my hopes of the future upon his bravery & temperate habits; Have no fears General Grant by bad habits or conduct will never disgrace himself or you, whom he knows & feels to be his best and warmest friend (& from conversations I have frequently had with him) whose unrequested kindness toward him he will never forget and hopes some time to be able to repay. But I say to you frankly and I pledge you my word for it, that should General Grant at any time become a intemperate man or an habitual drunkard, I will notify you immediately, will ask to be removed from duty on his staff (kind as he has been to me) or resign my commission. For while there are times when I would gladly ~~place~~ throw the mantle of charity over the faults of friends, at this time and from a man in his position I would rather tear the mantle off and expose the deformity. Having made a full statement of all the facts within my knowledge and being in a position to know them all & I trust done justice to the character of him whom you and I are equally interested in I remain your Friend" ALS, *ibid*.

On Dec. 30, William Bross of the *Chicago Tribune* wrote to Secretary of War Simon Cameron. "Evidence entirely satisfactory to myself and Associate Editors of the Tribune has become so convincing that Gen U. S. Grant commanding at Cairo is an inebriate, that I deem it my duty to call your attention to the matter. The inclosed anonymous letter would not deserve a moment's attention, were not facts abundant from other sources that what the writer says is true. His treatment to myself refered to in the first paragraph I care nothing about, but I was satisfied that he would not have acted as he did, had he been sober. The names on the second page of the letter may assist you to get at the facts. We think it best to call your attention to this painful matter, rather than to attack Gen. Grant in the Tribune. As you may not know me personally I refer to Dr Chas V. Dyer & His Excellency President Lincoln" ALS, *ibid*. On Jan. 4, 1862, Cameron forwarded the letter to President Abraham Lincoln. AES, *ibid*. The anonymous letter is no longer available, but was once the subject of a newspaper article which quoted excerpts. "Your Mr. Bross who was so badly treated here by General Grant and by Captain Lagow ought not to influence you against others of General Grant's staff officers." The writer went on to accuse Grant of frequently being too drunk to fill his station and of "being perfectly inebriate under a flag of truce with rebels." The letter continued: "All these things are facts which the world ought to know. Until we can secure pure men in habits and men without secesh wives with their own little slaves to wait upon them, which is a fact here in this camp with Mrs. Grant, our country is lost." Robert Anderson, "A New Lincoln Letter," *Chicago Sunday Tribune Magazine*, Jan. 14, 1962, p. 45. On Jan. 4, Lincoln endorsed the anonymous letter. "Bross would not knowingly misrepresent. Gen. Grant was appointed chiefly on the recommendation of Hon. E. B. Washburne—Perhaps we should consult him" AES (facsimile), *ibid.* On Jan. 6, Cameron added his endorsement. "Respectfully referred to Hon. E. B. Washburne, with the request that he will return these papers to the Dept." AES, *ibid.*

To *Allen C. Fuller*

Head Quarters, Dist. of Cairo
Cairo, Jan.y 29th 1862

COL. A. C. FULLER
ADJT. GEN. STATE OF ILLINOIS,
SPRINGFIELD ILL.
COL.

I would respectfully request that, if practicable, a complete company (with all its officers) and two detachment of about seventy men in all, with a Capt. and one Lieutenant be attached to the 10th Ill. Vols. Col. Morgan Comd.g. There is also a vacancy of one Field officer in this regiment. This is a very fine regiment and I am desirous of seeing it filled up.

I am Col. Very respectfully
Your Obt. Svt.
U. S. GRANT
Brig. Gen.

Through Hd Qrs.
Dept. of the Mo.
St. Louis, Mo.

ALS, Records of 10th Ill., I-ar. On Jan. 31, 1862, Capt. John C. Kelton endorsed this letter. "Respectfully referred to His Excellency the Governor of Illinois, with the request that if there is an unattached Company, he will assign it as requested." ES, *ibid.*

To Col. Silas D. Baldwin

————

Cairo 30 Jany 62

You had better stay where you are until you get tents and arms

Genl U S G

Df, DNA, RG 393, Dept. of the Mo., Telegrams Received. Written on a telegram of Jan. 30, 1862, from Col. Silas D. Baldwin, 57th Ill., Chicago, to USG. "I have been ordered to report to you. Our arms have not arrived from Washington. We have no tents. We have been four months in Camp without pay." Telegram received (punctuation added), *ibid.*

To Col. John Cook

————

Head Quarters, Dist. of Cairo,
Cairo, Jany 30th 1862.

Col. John Cook
Commdg Fort Holt Ky.
Colonel:

You will perceive by the closing paragraph of General Order No 73, from Head Quarters of the Army, Washington, that a minor cannot be discharged on account of Minority. Neither is the oath of Mr. Southwick (taken in Springfield Ills, whilst the Soldier is here) to the infirmities of his son, of any value towards obtaining his discharge on a Certificate of Disability, ~~upon~~.

Surgeons are regularly appointed in the Army who alone are competent to make Certificates of Disability upon which a Soldier can be discharged.

If private J. H. Southwick, is properly recommended for a discharge by the Surgeon of his Regiment, it will receive attention.

Respectfully
Your Obt. Servant
U. S. GRANT.
Brig. Genl. Commdg.

Copies, DLC-USG, V, 1, 2, 3, 85; DNA, RG 94, Letters Received; *ibid.*, RG 393, USG Letters Sent. On Feb. 6, 1862, Ninian W. Edwards, Springfield, Ill., wrote to President Abraham Lincoln at the request of William Southwick of Springfield, enclosing a copy of USG's letter and also a petition of Jan. 27 requesting the discharge of Southwick's son, John H. Southwick, sixteen years old, prepared by his father and signed by twelve prominent citizens of Springfield. On Feb. 11, Lincoln's secretary, John Hay, transmitted the papers to Secretary of War Edwin M. Stanton. *Ibid.*, RG 94, Letters Received. Southwick was discharged on April 25, 1862.

To Capt. Richard McAllister

———

Head Quarters, Dist of Cairo
Cairo, Jany 30th 1862.

CAPT. R. MCALLISTER
COM. OF SUB.
CAIRO ILLS.
CAPTAIN:

You will without delay have stored on board a Steamer, to be designated by the Qr. Master one hundred and fifty thousand (150,000) rations, complete with invoices, and receipts ready for the signature of such Officers of the Department as may be ordered to take charge of them

Respectfully &c
U. S. GRANT.
Brig. Gen. Commdg.

Copies, DLC-USG, V, 1, 2, 3, 85; DNA, RG 393, USG Letters Sent.

To Maj. Gen. Henry W. Halleck

Head Quarters, Dist. of Cairo
Cairo, Jan.y 31st 1862.

MAJ. GEN. H. W. HALLECK
COMD.G DEPT. OF THE MO.
ST. LOUIS, MO.
GEN.

Enclosed herewith I send you a communication from Gen.
Smith containing the latest and most reliable information I have
from the upper Tennessee.[1]

I am quietly making preparations for a move without as yet
having created a suspicion even that a move is to be made.
Awaiting your instructions which are expected in the morning
I have not made definite plans as to my movement, but expect
to start sunday[2] evening, taking 15.000 men. I would move by
steamers as far as practicable taking but little Cavalry and but little transportation (land) expecting to forward these afterwards.

I shall go in person and take with me either Gen. McClernand or Gen. Smith to command after my return.

I will report from this 'til starting by telegraph.

I am Gen. very respectfully
Your Obt. Svt.
U. S. GRANT
Brig. Gen.

ALS, DNA, RG 393, Dept. of the Mo., Letters Received. *O.R.*, I, vii, 575. On
Feb. 1, 1862, Maj. Gen. Henry W. Halleck wrote to USG. "You are authorised
to withdraw col Ross' regiment, 17th Ill. from Cape Giradeau for the Tennessee
expedition as soon as they are wanted. The remaining forces are sufficient for that
place. Your requisitions for horses mules, waggons, &c. cannot be filled immediately. By using steamers on the river, and as the troops will not move far from
their supplies and water transportation, much of the usual trains can be dispensed
with for several weeks. Dont cumber up the expedition with too large a train.
The object is to move *rapidly* & *promptly* by steamers, & to reduce the place before
any large reinforcements can arrive." ALS, DNA, RG 393, Dept. of Kan., Letters
Received. *O.R.*, I, vii, 577.

1. USG enclosed a letter of Jan. 30 from Brig. Gen. Charles F. Smith to Capt. John A. Rawlins. "Please say to the Com.g Genl. that within the last Forty eight hours a very intelligent person from Hickman (a resident), *Harding* by name, came to me with the following statement: That himself and 25 or 30 Union men for refusing to take the oath of allegiance to the Southern Confederacy were ordered to be arrested; he alone escaped, and by the aid of the rail-way conductor got to the bridge above Fort Henry. From conversations he overheard in the cars he says the force at Fort Henry is not less than 6000 men—at Bowling Green 70 to 80.000. The enemy believed our movement meant an attack on Fort Henry hence the re-inforcement. The steamers I saw at the fort no doubt brought the re-inforcements. Since writing the above I have information from Columbus fully confirming the re-inforcement of fort Henry and adding the enemy is prepared to throw in that direction at short notice a force of 15,000 altogether (including the garrison). The fort on the Cumberland is a weak concern; it is on the west bank, tho' they have a circular (half-moon) battery on the other side. Genl. *Wallace* is about leaving here for Smithland. . . . P. S. By direction of Genl. *Halleck* I have sent my Engr., Capt. *Rziha*, to make a reconnaissance of the country between the Tennessee & Cumberland rivers from Smithland to the two forts." ALS, DNA, RG 393, Dept. of the Mo., Letters Received. On Jan. 30, Smith telegraphed to USG. "Fort Henry has been reinforced   Its garrison is now Six thousand men. I have ordered Capt Rziha to make a reconnoisance between the Tenn & Cumberland." Telegram received, *ibid.*, Telegrams Received.

2. Feb. 2.

To Capt. John C. Kelton

Head Quarters Dist of Cairo
Cairo, Jany 31st 1862.

CAPT. J. C KELTON
A A GENL. DEPART OF THE MO.
SAINT LOUIS, MO.
SIR:

I have the honor to inform you that I have ordered Brig Genl Wallace to Smithland Kentucky, to take command of the Troops at that place.

I am, Sir, Respectfully
Your Obt Servt
U. S. GRANT
Brig. Genl Com'd'g.

LS, DNA, RG 94, Generals' Papers and Books, Lewis Wallace. On Jan. 28, 1862, Capt. John A. Rawlins issued Special Orders No. 24. "Brig. Genl. L. Wallace will proceed with as little delay as practicable to Smithland, Ky. and take command of that Post. He will take with him his Staff." Copies, DLC-USG, V, 15, 16, 82, 87; DNA, RG 393, USG Special Orders. See telegram to Elihu B. Washburne, Feb. 10, 1862.

To Brig. Gen. Charles F. Smith

Head Quarters, Dist. of Cairo,
Cairo, Jan.y 31st 1862.

Gen. C. F. Smith
Comd.g U. S. Forces
Paducah, Ky.
Gen.

On Monday[1] next I expect to start from Smithland, Paducah and this place some 15.000 men for Fort Henry to take and occupy that position.

Full instructions will be received from Gen. Halleck in the morning.[2] At the present I am only in possession of telegraphic orders to "take and hold.'

If my instructions contain nothing to change the plan I would adopt I will want a Brigade from Paducah and all the command from Smithland except the 52 Ill & one battalion to be designated by yourself. These troops will take with them all their baggage but no baggage train, these being left to take up afterwards. I do not regard over a Squadron of Cavalry as being necessary for the whole command in taking the position. All that might afterwards be required can be sent from here.

The troops going from your command may take such rations as they have on hand at the time of starting, not less than two days supply however, preparations being made here for issuing on arrival at place of debarcation.

A supply of Ammunition will also be taken from here but

every regiment should take all they have on hand and not less than forty rounds.

Should I not be able to write more definitely by to-morrows boat I will telegraph during the day if a change from the above is necessary.

But very little preparation is necessary for this move and if possible the troops and community should be kept from knowing anything of the design. I am well aware however this caution is entirely unnecessary to you.

It is impossible to spare a boat just now to run exclusively between Paducah & Smithland[3] but until one can be sent the Steamer from here can continue her trips to the latter place upon your order as often as necessary.

> Very respectfully
> your Obt. Svt.
> U. S. GRANT
> Brig. Gen.

ALS, James S. Schoff, New York, N. Y. *O.R.*, I, vii, 575. On Feb. 1, 1862, Capt. John A. Rawlins wrote to Brig. Gen. Charles F. Smith. "I am instructed by Brig. Genl. Grant to say that the preperations for reducing Fort Henry required of you, will be the same as stated in his communication of yesterday, with the exception that you will take all the available forces, including Cavalry, which can be spared from Paducah and Smithland, leaving only such forces as may be absolutely necesessary to hold these places against attack . . . P. S. I am further instructed by the General Commanding to say you will organize your forces at Paducah and Smithland into Brigades. He will send you the 7th Ills. Vols. from here, Col. John Cook, Commanding. Col. Cook will be the senior Colonel of the expedition, and entitled to the command of a Brigade, and he deems him qualified much better, perhaps, than many who from rank are forced to have such commands. Col. Cook may be relied upon implicity to carry out any instructions he may receive." Copies, DLC-USG, V, 1, 2, 3, 85; DNA, RG 393, USG Letters Sent. *O.R.*, I, vii, 578.

1. Feb. 3.
2. See letter to Maj. Gen. Henry W. Halleck, Jan. 29, 1862.
3. On Jan. 30, Capt. Gilbert A. Pierce, Paducah, wrote to USG. "The General Commanding at this Post, directs me to inform you that, a *Small Steamer* is very much needed to supply the wants of the Command at *Smithland*, and to respectfully ask that the proper officer at Cairo may be directed to send—immediately if possible—a boat to that place." ALS, DNA, RG 393, District of Cairo, Letters Received. On Jan. 31, Smith telegraphed to USG. "A Steamer much needed at Smith Land. Four thousand Pistols cartridges for Thielman's Cavalry

at Smith Land wanted imm.—navy Size. Requisitions by mail." Telegram received (punctuation added), *ibid.*, Dept. of the Mo., Telegrams Received. On Jan. 31, Rawlins wrote to Capt. Wilbur F. Brinck. "You will send to morrow, A. M. to Brig Genl. C. F. Smith, Paducah, Ky. Four thousand (4000) Pistol Cartridges. (Navy size). Requisition will be approved here." Copies, DLC-USG, V, 2, 85; DNA, RG 393, USG Letters Sent.

To Col. *Napoleon B. Buford*

Head Quarters, Dist of Cairo
Cairo, Jany 31st 1862.

COL. N. B. BUFORD
COMMDG POST, CAIRO, ILLS.
COLONEL:

You will please direct the casements in Fort Cairo to be opened to receive ammunition now here, and awaiting storage.

Very Respectfully
Your Obt. Servant
U. S. GRANT.
Brig. Genl. Commdg.

Copies, DLC-USG, V, 2, 85; DNA, RG 393, USG Letters Sent. The copy in Vol. 85 bears the notation: "Sent to Brig. Gen. McClernand and through him, to Col. N. B. Buford."

To Capt. *Algernon S. Baxter*

Head Quarters, Dist. of Cairo
Cairo, Jany 31st 1862

CAPT. A. S. BAXTER
A. Q. M. CAIRO, ILLS.
SIR:

Immediately upon the arrival tonight of the Cars, transporting Troops, (16th Ills. Vols.) you will have them transferred to the Steamer. "Aleck Scott" where they will remain until morning, when the Steamer will proceed with them to Fort. Holt, Ky.

You will please have this order promptly executed, that the Cars may at once return to Centralia, Ills.[1] for troops now waiting there.

Respectfully
U. S. GRANT.
Brig. Genl. Commdg.

Copies, DLC-USG, V, 1, 2, 3, 85; DNA, RG 393, USG Letters Sent. On Feb. 1, 1862, Capt. John A. Rawlins wrote to the commanding officer, 16th Ill. "You will proceed on the Steamer 'Aleck Scott' to Bird's Point, Mo. and there immediately debark, and report to Brig. Genl. E. A. Paine, Commdg, for position and orders. . . . P. S. Capt Reily of the Steamer 'Aleck Scott' will proceed to Bird's Point, Mo. under directions of Commanding Officer, of the 16th Illinois Regiment." Copies, *ibid*. On the same day, Rawlins wrote to Capt. Algernon S. Baxter. "You will provide immediate transportation for the 32nd Ills. Vols. just arrived, to Bird's Point, Mo, that the rail road Cars, may at once be vacated." Copies, DLC-USG, V, 2, 85; DNA, RG 393, USG Letters Sent.

Baxter had been ordered to Washington on Jan. 23. See letter to Elihu B. Washburne, Jan. 23, 1862. According to a newspaper account, Baxter left Cairo on Jan. 25; Capt. Parmenas T. Turnley arrived to replace him on Jan. 28. Letter from Cairo, Jan. 28, 1862, in *Chicago Tribune*, Jan. 30, 1862. USG and Rawlins continued to address correspondence to Baxter after his departure.

1. Centralia, Ill., 109 miles north of Cairo on the Illinois Central Railroad.

To Capt. Parmenas T. Turnley

Head Quarters, Dist of Cairo
Cairo, Jany 31st 1862.

CAPT. P. T. TURNLEY,
CHIEF Q. M. DIST OF CAIRO
CAIRO, ILLS.
CAPTAIN:

I will require steam transportation for say, ten thousand Infantry, and four companies of Artillery, with all their Camp Equipage, rations, &c as soon as practicable. The Steamers should be coaled for four days run, But little land transportation will be taken aboard the steamers.

> Respectfully &c
> U. S. GRANT
> Brig. Genl. Commdg.

Copies, DLC-USG, V, 1, 2, 3, 85; DNA, RG 393, USG Letters Sent.

To Capt. Parmenas T. Turnley

> Head Quarters, Dist of Cairo
> Cairo, Jany 31st 1862.

CAPT P. T. TURNLEY
CHIEF Q. M. DIST. OF CAIRO.
CAPTAIN:

You will please direct six thousand rations of grain, and half rations of hay for an equal number of animals, to be put aboard the Steamer, designated to day to receive Subsistence Stores.[1]

Invoices will be made out, and receipts ready for the signature of the Officer, who may be appointed to receive it.

> Respectfully &c
> U. S. GRANT.
> Brig. Gen. Commdg.

Copies, DLC-USG, V, 1, 2, 85; DNA, RG 393, USG Letters Sent.

1. On Feb. 1, 1862, USG wrote to Capt. Richard McAllister. "Increase the number of Rations on board Steamer 'Uncle Sam,' 100,000 rations as soon as possible." Copies, DLC-USG, V, 1, 2, 3, 85; DNA, RG 393, USG Letters Sent.

General Orders No. 5

Head Quarters Dist of Cairo,
Cairo, Feb'y. 1st 1862

GENERAL ORDERS NO. 5.

For the temporary government, the forces of this Military District will be divided and commanded as follows, to-wit:

The First Brigade will consist of the 8th, 18th, 18th 27th 29th 30th and 31st Regiments of Illinois Volunteers, Schwartzs and Dresser's Batteries, and Stewarts, Dollins' O'Harnett's and Carmichael's Cavalry Col R J Oglesby Senior Colonel of the Brigade, Commanding.

The Second Brigade will consist of the 11th 20th 45th and 48th Illinois Infantry, 4th Illinois Cavalry Taylors and McAlisters Artillery, (the latter with four seige guns, Col. W. H. L Wallace Commanding

The first and second Brigades will constitute the first Division of the District of Cairo, and will be commanded by Brig Gen John A. McClernand

The Third Brigade will consist of the 8th Wisconsin 49th Illinois, 25th Indiana, four Companies of Artillery, and such troops as are yet to arrive, Brig. Gen. E. A. Paine, Commanding.

The fourth Brigade will be composed of the 10th 16th 22nd and 32d Illinois, and 10th Iowa Infantry, Houghtalings Battery of Light Artillery, four Companies of the 7th and two Companies of the 1st Illinois Cavalry, Col. Morgan, Commanding

Gen E. A. Paine is assigned to the Command of Cairo and Mound City, and Col. Morgan to the Command of Birds point.

By order
U S GRANT Brig. Gen Comg

Copies, DLC-USG, V, 12, 13, 14, 95; DNA, RG 393, USG General Orders. *O.R.*, I, vii, 578.

To Maj. Gen. Leonidas Polk

Head Quarters, Dist. of Cairo,
Cairo, Feb.y 1st 1862.

MAJ. GEN. L. POLK,
COMD.G CONFEDERATE FORCES
COLUMBUS, KY
GEN.

The bearer, Capt. Elliott[1] of the United States Army has just arrived from Pilot Knob, Mo. bearer of a proposal to exchange prisoners of War held by us for those taken by Gen. Thompson at Big river bridge on the 15th of October last.

I also hold a number of prisoners belonging to Gen. Thompson's command, who I am willing to exchange on the same terms proposed by Col. Carlin,[2] for any prisoner of the United States Army held by the Confederacy.

I would respectfully request that, if inconsistent with your rules to permit Capt. Elliott to visit New Madrid, you forward the proposal of Col. Carlin to Gen. Thompson and return his reply to Cairo, by any means that may suit your pleasure.[3]

Very respectfully
your Obt. Svt.
U. S. GRANT
Brig. Gen.

ALS, DNA, RG 109, Documents Printed in *O.R. O.R.*, II, i, 537. On Feb. 4, 1862, Maj. Gen. Leonidas Polk wrote to USG. "I have the honor to acknowledge the receipt of your communication of the 1st inst in regard to the exchange of Capt. Elliott, and other prisoners taken by Genl. Jeff Thompson at Big River Bridge on the 15th October for an equal number of prisoners of war held by you. It was not thought advisable to permit Capt. Elliott to proceed to New Madrid, and my answer has been delayed, because I desired to consult with Genl Jeff Thompson. Up to this time he has not been heard from, but I will say, that I shall be pleased to accept your propositions in behalf of Colonel Carter [*Carlin*], upon the terms proposed in your note of the 2d inst." DfS, DNA, RG 109, Documents Printed in *O.R. O.R.*, II, i, 538. See letter to Maj. Gen. Leonidas Polk, Feb. 2, 1862. On Feb. 6, Capt. Nathaniel H. McLean, asst. adjt. gen. to Maj. Gen. Henry W. Halleck, wrote to USG. "I am instructed by the Major General Commanding to say that, he approves of the agreement made by you and Major Genl.

Polk, for the exchange of Capt Elliott 33d Ills Vols and other prisoners taken by Genl Jeff Thompson, at the Big River bridge on the 15th of Oct for an equal number of prisoners of war held by you. I herewith inclose a copy of Genl. Orders No. 30 current series from these Head Quarters, with the requirements of which you will please comply at your earliest convenience." ALS, DNA, RG 393, Dept. of the Mo., Letters Sent (Press). *O.R.*, II, i, 538–39. General Orders No. 30, Dept. of the Mo., Feb. 3, outlined procedures for the exchange of prisoners of war. *Ibid.*, p. 164.

1. Capt. Isaac H. Elliott of Princeton, Ill., 33rd Ill., taken prisoner by Brig. Gen. M. Jeff Thompson at the Big River Bridge, Mo., Oct. 15, 1861, was currently on parole. *Ibid.*, I, iii, 202; *ibid.*, II, i, 139, 539. *Missouri Republican*, Oct. 17, 1861.

2. William P. Carlin of Carrollton, Ill., was appointed col., 38th Ill., Aug. 15, and ordered to take command at Ironton, Mo., Sept. 20, 1861.

3. On Feb. 19, 1862, Thompson informed Carlin that the prisoners taken would be released. *O.R.*, II, i, 539.

To Maj. Gen. Henry W. Halleck

BY TELEGRAPH FROM Cairo Feby 1 *1862*

To MAJ. GENL. HALLECK

I will leave here tomorrow night. Force larger than Col McPherson[1] supposed could be taken, by three thousand.

U. S. GRANT

Telegram received, DNA, RG 94, Generals' Papers and Books, Telegrams Received by Gen. Halleck; copy, *ibid.*, RG 393, Dept. of the Mo., Telegrams Received. *O.R.*, I, vii, 577. On Jan. 31, 1862, Maj. Gen. Henry W. Halleck had telegraphed to USG. "The 25th Indiana Infantry, and three batteries leave here on Steamer to-morrow morning. The 32nd Ill leave Springfield to day & the 49th Ill & a battalion of artillery by Sunday or monday; all for Cairo. Keep me informed by telegram of all your movements." Copies, DNA, RG 94, Generals' Papers and Books, Telegrams Sent in Cipher by Gen. Halleck; *ibid.*, RG 393, Dept. of the Mo., Telegrams Sent; *ibid.*, USG Hd. Qrs. Correspondence; DLC-USG, V, 4, 5, 7, 8. *O.R.*, I, vii, 576.

1. Lt. Col. James B. McPherson of Ohio, USMA 1853, who ranked first in his class, was appointed an asst. instructor in practical engineering at USMA upon graduation, and later supervised the construction of Fort Delaware (1857) and the fortifications on Alcatraz Island, San Francisco (1857–1861). *DAB*, XII, 160–61; Whitelaw Reid, *Ohio in the War: Her Statesmen, Her Generals, and*

Soldiers (Cincinnati, 1868), I, 561–90. On Nov. 12, 1861, he was assigned to Halleck's staff as asst. to the chief engineer. On Jan. 31, 1862, by Special Orders No. 99, Dept. of the Mo., Halleck ordered McPherson to report to USG as chief engineer. See letter to Maj. Gen. Henry W. Halleck, Jan. 29, 1862.

To Brig. Gen. John A. McClernand

Head Quarters, Dist. of Cairo
Cairo, ~~Jan.y~~ Feb.y 1st 1862.

GEN. J. A. MCCLERNAND
COMD.G CAIRO, ILL.
GEN.

The troops of your Division will be held in readiness to move, by Steamer, to-morrow taking with them all their Camp & Garrison equipage, three days rations and forage, and not to exceed four teams to each regiment.

The necessary instructions, in this regard, have been given those troops not formerly of your Command.

One regiment of Infantry, and Dickey's[1] Cavalry for want of transportation, will be detached to garrison Cairo.

Respectfully
your Obt. Svt.
U. S. GRANT
Brig. Gen. Cm

ALS, McClernand Papers, IHi. *O.R.*, I, vii, 577. On Feb. 1, 1862, USG wrote to Brig. Gen. John A. McClernand. "The Steamers Chancellor Fanny Bullett ~~Illinois~~ & Key Stone will be going to Paducah and can take the 4th Cavalry, or so much of it as can go aboard of the~~sem~~ ~~boats~~ to-morrow morning." ALS, McClernand Papers, IHi.

1. Col. Theophilus Lyle Dickey of Ottawa, Ill., 4th Ill. Cav., was the father-in-law of Col. William H. L. Wallace, 11th Ill. A native of Ky., and a graduate of Miami University, Oxford, Ohio, Dickey was a prominent lawyer, judge, and politician. He was a delegate to the 1856 Ill. Republican state convention, but supported Stephen A. Douglas for the U. S. Senate in 1858, and for the presidency in 1860. Dickey, who had served briefly as a capt. in the Mexican War, raised

the 4th Ill. Cav., which was mustered in on Sept. 26, 1861, at Springfield, and was ordered to Cairo. *DAB*, V, 290–91; Isabel Wallace, *Life & Letters of General W. H. L. Wallace* (Chicago, 1909).

To Brig. Gen. John A. McClernand

Head Quarters, Dist. of Cairo
Cairo, Feb.y 1st 1862.

Subsistence stores can be sold to officers requiring them but forage never.

Such officers as are entitled to horses can draw forage from the Quartermaster on forage returns. This will require a suspension of eight dollars for each months forage drawn from their pay for the month forage is drawn in kind.

U. S. GRANT
Brig. Gen.

AES, McClernand Papers, IHi. Written on a letter of Feb. 1, 1862, from Brig. Gen. John A. McClernand to USG. "The nonpayment of many officers and their destitution of money will make it a military necessity that such officers should be allowed to draw rations and forage from their regimental Commissaries and Quarter Masters." LS, *ibid.* On the same day, Col. James S. Rearden wrote to McClernand. "My command has recieved no pay for services to include a later date than 31st Octr 1861. In consequence of this, my company officers as well as the Field and Staff, are without money. If it is possible, I would suggest that the officers of the command be paid previous to starting on the present Expedition, in order to enable them to supply themselves with the necessary provisions and suplies for a campaigne away from Barracks. If the officers are paid, they can to some extent relieve the wants of the men until they are regularly paid" ALS, DNA, RG 393, District of Cairo, Letters Received. On Feb. 1, McClernand endorsed the letter to USG. "I earnestly recommend, as a necessity of the public service, that an order be made not only for the payment of the ~~Company~~ Field, Staff & Comp. officers of the 29th Reg. but those of all other regiments, not paid, which may be immediately ordered to move." AES, *ibid.* Also on the same day, Capt. John A. Rawlins issued Special Orders No. 28. "Commissioned officers of regiments that have not been paid to include the month of December will be permitted to purchase subsistence stores from the regimental Commissaries and have the same charged to be paid for as soon as practicable." AD (in USG's hand), McClernand Papers, IHi.

To Brig. Gen. John A. McClernand

———

Head Quarters, Dist. of Cairo
Cairo, Feb.y 1st 1862

Make the detail asked from troops that are expected to remain at Cairo.

Maj. Brayman should address his correspondence to my Adj. Gen. and not to me as is his constant habit.

U. S. GRANT
Brig. Gen. C

AES, McClernand Papers, IHi. Written on a letter of Maj. Mason Brayman to USG, Feb. 1, 1862. "Genl McClernand instructs me to request that a detail of sixty men to report to Capt McAllister at one o Clock this P. M. for duty, in response to a call made yesterday.

> 60 are on duty there this forenoon,
> 100 ” ” ”   at Fort Col Webster
> 75 ” ” ”   ” naval mag.   ”
> 30 ” ” ”   ” upper mag
> 16 ” ” ”   ” Capt Brincks

and others are called during the day. The details are heavy, and aggravate the prevailing sickness among the men &c" LS, *ibid.* On the same day, Brayman wrote to Capt. John A. Rawlins. "Please make my apology to Genl. Grant for having addressed official communications to him instead of yourself. I was aware of its irregularity but finding such ~~that~~ to be the prevailing practice here, I, in past, adopted it, through inadvertence, not disrespect. I will take pleasure in conforming to the suggestion made in his note of to-day." ADfS, *ibid.*

To Brig. Gen. Eleazer A. Paine

———

Head Quarters, Dist of Cairo
Cairo, Febry 1st 1862.

GENL. E. A. PAINE
COMMDG BIRD'S POINT, MO.
GENL:

In the assignment of Commanders to Brigades, I have placed you in immediate command of Cairo, and dependencies.

You will assign all Troops that may arrive during my absence, to the best advantage for the protection of all the points under your command, Keeping an eye at the same time, to Paducah, Ky, and reinforce it, should an attack there be threatened. The two first Regiments arriving should be placed at Fort Holt, and can occupy the quarters already built.

You will consolidate the Returns of your command, and forward directly to Head Quarters of the Department. Advise me, however, as often as possible of the condition of things here, and keep me posted as to the movements of the enemy, so far as you may be informed.

The standing orders of the Post, you will receive from Brig. Genl. John. A. McClernand.

> Respectfully,
> Your Obt. Servant.
> U. S. GRANT.
> Brig'. Gen. Commdg.

Copies, DLC-USG, V, 1, 2, 3, 85; DNA, RG 393, USG Letters Sent. *O.R.*, I, vii, 577. See General Orders No. 5, Feb. 1, 1862.

To Brig. Gen. Eleazer A. Paine

———

> Head Quarters, Dist of Cairo.
> Cairo, Febry 1st 1862.

GEN. E. A. PAINE
COMMDG. U. S. FORCES.
BIRD'S POINT, MO.
GENL:

Hold the 11th and 22nd Regiments in readiness to move tomorrow morning by Steamers, with three days rations. They will take all their baggage, but only four teams to each Regiment.

Provisions have been made for rations and ammunition, but

these Troops should have at least 40 rounds of the latter with them.

I would like to see Col. Oglesby, immediately, and yourself to night, or in the morning.

If you have sent any Troops out, recall them at once.

> Respectfully
> Your Obt. Servant
> U. S. GRANT.
> Brig. Genl. Commdg

Copies, DLC-USG, V, 1, 2, 3, 85; DNA, RG 393, USG Letters Sent. On Feb. 1, 1862, Capt. John A. Rawlins wrote to Brig. Gen. Eleazer A. Paine. "I am instructed by Brig. Gen. Grant to inform you that in his order to you this morning, directing you to hold the 11th and 22nd Ills. Regiments in readiness to move tomorrow, he intended to say the 11th and 20th Regts. You will therefore please countermand the order to the 22nd and issue it to the 20th." Copies, *ibid*.

To Col. Joseph D. Webster

————

> Head Quarters, Dist of Cairo
> Cairo, Febry 1st 1862.

COL. WEBSTER
CHIEF OF ENGS. & CHIEF OF STAFF,
CAIRO, ILLS.
COL:

Please take immediate steps to get the four (4) Howitzers in Fort Cairo, including the 8 in. Gun ready to move.

> Respectfully,
> U. S. GRANT
> Brig. Genl. Commdg.

Copies, DLC-USG, V, 2, 85; DNA, RG 393, USG Letters Sent.

To Capt. Parmenas T. Turnley

Head Quarters, Dist of Cairo
Cairo, Febry 1st 1862.

CAPT. P. T. TURNLEY,
CHIEF Q. M. DIST. OF CAIRO
CAPTAIN:

Thribble the grain directed yesterday, to be put aboard Steamer. The amount of Hay may be increased, but so as not to embrace the boat in receiving troops, horses and land transportation.

Respectfully
Your Obt. Servant.
U. S. GRANT.
Brig. Genl. Commdg.

P. S. Assign to Capt Brinck, Ordnance Officer, a suitable boat on board of which to store ammunition, as I will direct him to ship.[1]
U. S. G.

Copies, DLC-USG, V, 1, 2, 3, 85; DNA, RG 393, USG Letters Sent.

1. On Feb. 1, 1862, USG wrote to Capt. Wilbur F. Brinck. "Have immediately placed aboard such Steamer, as Capt. Turnley may appoint, 600,000 rounds of Musket and Rifle Ammunition, assorted in about the proportions our different arms run." Copies, *ibid.*

To Capt. Parmenas T. Turnley

Head Quarters, Dist. of Cairo
Cairo, Febry 1st 1862.

CAPT. P. T. TURNLEY,
CHIEF Q. M. DIST OF CAIRO.
CAPTAIN:

Three Steamers will arrive today with Troops from St Louis.
I want them to proceed immediately to Paducah, and arrangements made to retain the Steamers for the present

Respectfully,
Your Obt. Servant.
U. S. GRANT.
Brig. Genl. Commdg.

Copies, DLC-USG, V, 1, 2, 85; DNA, RG 393, USG Letters Sent.

General Orders No. 7

Head Quarters District of Cairo
Cairo February 2d 1862

GENERAL ORDERS No. 7

On the expedition now about starting from Smithland, Paducah, Cairo, Bird's point, and Fort Holt, the following orders will be observed.

1   No firing, except when ordered by proper authority will be allowed.

2   Plundering and disturbing private property is positively prohibed

3   Company officers will see that all their men are kept within Camp, except when on duty.

4th Rolls will be called Evening and Morning, and every man accounted for, and absentees reported to Regimental Commanders.

5   Company Commanders will have special care that rations
     and amunition are not wasted or destroyed by carelessness—

6   Troops will take with them three days rations and forage,
     all Camp and garrison Equipage and not to exceed four
     teams to each Regiment.

7   Regimental commanders will be held strictly accountable for
     the acts of their Regiments, and will in turn hold Company
     Commanders accountable for the conduct of their Companies
     Capt. W. W. Leland, Com'y of Subsistance, is appointed
     Chief Commissary in the Field.

                 By Order—U. S. Grant, Brig. Genl. Comd.g
              Jno. A. Rawlins
              Ast. Ajt. Gen

Copies, DLC-USG, V, 12, 13, 14, 95; DNA, RG 94, 9th Ill., Letterbook; *ibid.*,
RG 393, USG General Orders; (Printed), Lawler Papers, ICarbS. *O.R.*, I, vii,
579–80.

To Maj. Gen. Leonidas Polk

                                        On board Flag of Truce
                                        Febry 2nd 1862.

Major Gen. L. Polk
Commdg Confederate Forces
Columbus, Ky.
Genl:

     Yours of this date, borne by Flag of Truce, is just received,
and contents noted.

     The exchange asked for ~~can~~ can be made on the following
terms; to-wit: Rank for rank—grade for grade. In case of Commissioned Officers, one of one grade will be considered worth
two of the next inferior grade; One Colonel being equal to two
Lieut. Colonels, four Majors or eight Captains, and so on down
to the lowest grade.

     A different rule may be agreed upon hereafter, but I am not
prepared to offer any other at present.

I will take the names of those asked for in your communication, and will forward the names of those I would like to have in return. ~~soon.~~ In case of exchanges, if agreeable to you, those released by us will be sent to your lines, and our prisoners, will be sent to the Federal lines at the most convenient point from where those prisoners may be.

I will take the earliest opportunity of informing you where the Prisoners, whose names are given, can be sent.

> I am, Very Respectfully,
> Your Obt Servant.
> U. S. GRANT.
> Brig. Genl. Commdg.

Copies, DLC-USG, V, 1, 2, 3, 85; DNA, RG 393, USG Letters Sent. *O.R.*, II, i, 538. See letter to Maj. Gen. Leonidas Polk, Feb. 1, 1862. On Jan. 31, 1862, Maj. Gen. Henry W. Halleck had written to USG. "You are authorized to exchange with the enemy any prisoners of war you may now have or may hereafter capture. You may also inform Genl Polk that on releasing any of our prisoners he may have, you will release an equal number, grade for grade, each party sending the released prisoners under a flag of truce to the lines of the other party. Where the same grade cannot be given it is proposed to give two of the grade next below, that is, for one colonel, give two Lieut colonels, or 4 majors, or 8 captains, &c. This is the basis proposed by Genl Sterling Price and will be followed till some other rule shall be adopted. Endeavour, if possible, to effect the exchange of Captain Prime and others at Nashville, Tenn. I have prisoners of war here to fill any cartel you may succeed in negociating. Where an exchange is made a full descriptive list must be forwarded to these Head quarters giving name, rank, company regiment & corps. All prisoners of war, not guilty of crimes against the laws of war, will be supplied, where necessary the same as our own soldiers & submitted to no more restraints than may be deemed necessary for their safe keeping. Where guilty of crime they will not be exchanged, but will be kept in custody." ALS, DNA, RG 393, District of Cairo, Letters Received. *O.R.*, II, i, 536. On Feb. 2, Capt. John C. Kelton directed 1st Lt. Orson Hewitt, 27th Ill., to return to Cairo "with the prisoners of war now in your charge, and turn them over to Brigdr. Genl. Grant, who will carry out the instructions he has rec'd from these Head Quarters, in reference to the exchange of these prisoners." ALS, DNA, RG 393, Dept. of the Mo., Letters Sent (Press).

To Maj. Gen. Henry W. Halleck

————

Cairo, Feb. 2d. 1862

To Maj. Gen. Halleck.

I leave at Cairo and depencies, eight (8) regiments of infantry, six companies of cavalry, two companies Artillery and the weak of the entire command. More troops should be here soon if a change of commander is expected at Columbus.

U. S. Grant.
Brig. Gen.

Telegram, copy, DNA, RG 393, Dept. of the Mo., Telegrams Received. *O.R.*, I, vii, 579. On Jan. 29, 1862, Maj. Gen. George B. McClellan had informed Maj. Gen. Henry W. Halleck and Brig. Gen. Don Carlos Buell that C. S. A. Gen. P. G. T. Beauregard had been ordered from Va. to Ky. with fifteen regts. *Ibid.*, p. 571. On Jan. 30, Halleck wrote to USG, giving him the information. See letter to Maj. Gen. Henry W. Halleck, Jan. 29, 1862. On Jan. 26, Secretary of War Judah P. Benjamin had ordered Beauregard to assume command at Columbus. *O.R.*, I, v, 1048. Beauregard did not bring any regts. with him, and Columbus was abandoned before he reached it. *Ibid.*, I, vii, 895–96; T. Harry Williams, *P. G. T. Beauregard: Napoleon in Gray* (Baton Rouge, 1954), pp. 113–20; Alfred Roman, *The Military Operations of General Beauregard in the War between the States* (New York, 1883), I, 210–34. See letter to Brig. Gen. George W. Cullum, Feb. 25, 1862, notes 7, 8.

To Brig. Gen. John A. McClernand

————

Head Quarters, Dist. of Cairo,
Cairo, Feb.y 2d 1862.

Gen. J. A. McClernand
Comd.g. Cairo Ill.
Gen.

I shall leave as soon as possible for Paducah to arrange there.

Capt. Turnley will be instructed to forward all transportation to Paducah that may be left after geting your Division aboard.

You being left senior here can take any steps deemed necessary to expedite embarcation of your command. It is desirable
that ~~they~~ you should arrive at Paducah by to-morrow morning.

> Respectfully
> your obt. svt.
> U. S. GRANT
> Brig. Gen.

ALS, McClernand Papers, IHi. On Feb. 2, 1862, Capt. William S. Hillyer wrote
to Capt. Parmenas T. Turnley. "Should more large Boats (not exceeding four,)
arrive here tomorrow send them immediately to Paducah." Copies, DLC-USG,
V, 1, 2, 85; DNA, RG 393, USG Letters Sent. Later the same day, Capt. John A.
Rawlins wrote to Turnley. "The troops that will arrive to-day will not be moved
to Paducah, as was first ordered, but will remain here; ~~except those accompanied
by Artillery~~; the Infantry to debark at Cairo, and the ~~other~~ Artillery subject to
orders." Copies, *ibid.*

To Brig. Gen. Eleazer A. Paine

> Head Quarters, Dist of Cairo
> Cairo, Febry 2nd 1862.

GEN. E. A. PAINE
COMMDG BIRD'S POINT, MO.
GENERAL:

As soon as practicable after the departure of Troops from
here, relieve the 10th Ills. Regt. from duty at Mound City, and
send them to Bird's Point. Two Companies will be detached from
the command at Cairo, to guard public property at Mound City.

Major Kuykendall will remain here as District Provost
Marshal, but will have no charge over the local duties. You can
appoint a suitable Officer for that position.[1]

~~Should~~ If no Troops arrive to ~~be~~ placed at Fort. Holt. before
my departure, it will be necessary for you to keep a Company

there to prevent the destruction of Public Property, until the place is can be garrisoned.

> Respectfully &c
> U S. GRANT.
> Brig. Genl. Commdg.

Copies, DLC-USG, V, 1, 2, 3, 85; DNA, RG 393, USG Letters Sent. On Feb. 2, 1862, 1st Lt. Clark B. Lagow wrote to Brig. Gen. Eleazer A. Paine. "I am directed by Gen. Grant, Commdg, to say to you, that you will send to Fort. Holt, Ky, and take possession of all the Teams and Horses at that Post, left by the Regiments that have gone on the present expedition, and have them brought to Cairo, to be taken care of until further orders." Copies, *ibid.* On Feb. 2, Capt. John A. Rawlins issued Special Orders No. 29. "Commanders at Fort Holt and Bird's Point will consolidate their Reports and forward to Brig Genl. E. A. Paine, Commanding Cairo, and these dependencies   All orders and instuctions necessary for the government of these Posts, will be given by Genl. Paine." Copies, DLC-USG, V, 15, 16, 82, 87, 89; DNA, RG 393, USG Special Orders.

1. On Jan. 31, Rawlins wrote to Maj. Andrew J. Kuykendall. "Your authority as Provost Marshal does not extend to prisoners confined by other Officers than yourself. You will therefore please to govern yourself accordingly." Copies, DLC-USG, V, 1, 2, 3, 85; DNA, RG 393, USG Letters Sent. On Feb. 1, Rawlins issued Special Orders No. 28. "Major A. J. Kuykendall Dist Provost Marshal is hereby relieved, temporarily, from the duties of Provost Marshal. The duties of the Office will be performed by Julius Carter 30th Ills. Vols." Copies, DLC-USG, V, 15, 16, 82, 87, 89; DNA, RG 393, USG Special Orders. See letter to Brig. Gen. George W. Cullum, Feb. 22, 1862.

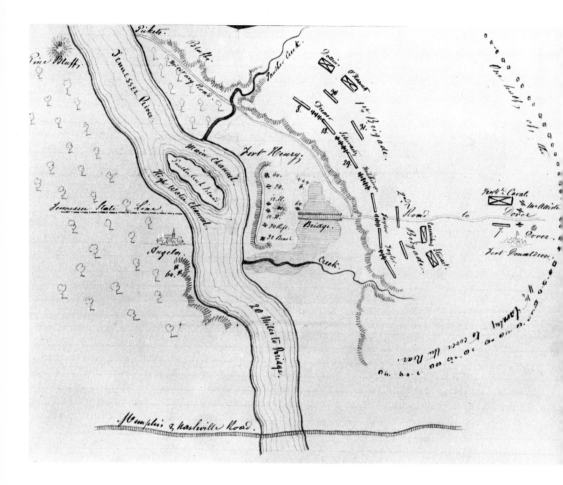

Fort Henry
Courtesy Illinois State Historical Library

To Maj. Gen. Henry W. Halleck

———

Paducah Feby 3. 1862

MAJ GEN HALLECK
SAINT LOUIS MO.

Will be off up the Tennesee at six (6) O'clock. Command twenty thre[e] (23) Regiments in all

U. S. GRANT

Telegram received, DNA, RG 94, Generals' Papers and Books, Telegrams Received by Gen. Halleck; copy, *ibid.*, RG 393, Dept. of the Mo., Telegrams Received. *O.R.*, I, vii, 581.

To Brig. Gen. John A. McClernand

———

Dist. of Cairo
Head Quarters, Camp in the Field
Paducah, Feb.y 3d 1862.

GEN J. A. MCCLERNAND
COMD.G 1ST DIV. ARMY IN FIELD
GEN.

On your arrival at Paducah you will proceed immediately up the Tennessee river debarking all your Cavalry excepting one company at the first Ferry above, on the side between the two rivers.[1]

The Cavalry will be instructed to march by the most practicable road to Pine bluffs,[2] seven miles below Fort Henry, should no further instructions reach them. The transports thus relieved will be returned immediately to Paducah to report to Brig. Gen. Smith.

With the balance of the transports you will proceed to Pine bluffs and debark your command and await the arrival of the

Division under Gen. Smith. In the absence of the remainder of the column this point is simply to be held, and for this purpose you will dispose your forces to the best advantage. Col. Cook, commanding one Brigade of Gen. Smith's ~~Command~~ Division, will be subject to your orders until the arrival of his forces and Division Commander.

The Cavalry going through by land will go without wagons, taking on their horses one days forage (grain) and rations.

The Cavalry being distributed over a number of transports, occupied by troops that do not debark at the same point, you will cause the space thus relieved to be filled up to the best advantage so as to entirely empty the greatest number of Steamers to be returned.

Capt. Phelps of the Gun boat Connestoga, who is familiar with the Tennessee, will indicate to you where the landings are both at the first ferry and at Pine bluff.

You will be convoyed by the old gun boats, the Iron clad ones having preceded you.

> Very respectfully
> your obt. Svt.
> U. S. GRANT
> Brig. Gen. Com

ALS, McClernand Papers, IHi. On Feb. 2, 1862, Maj. Gen. Henry W. Halleck had telegraphed to USG. "I think a column should move from Smithland between the rivers, if the road is practicable. Nearly all your available cavalry could take that route & be supplied, at least partly, by the boats on the river. Make your force as large as possible. I will send more regiments from here in a few days." ALS (telegram sent), CSmH; copies, DNA, RG 94, Generals' Papers and Books, Telegrams Sent in Cipher by Gen. Halleck; *ibid.*, RG 393, Dept. of the Mo., Telegrams Sent. *O.R.*, I, vii, 579.

1. The cav. disembarked at Patterson's Ferry on the Tennessee River approximately thirteen miles upriver from Paducah. *Ibid.*, p. 127.
2. Pine Bluff Landing was approximately seven miles downriver (north) from Fort Henry on the Ky. side of the Tennessee River. On Feb. 3, Flag Officer Andrew H. Foote wrote to Commander William D. Porter of the gunboat *Essex*. "You will proceed with the Gun Boat Essex & St. Louis, up the Tennessee as far as Pine Bluffs—a distance of about 65 miles and there wait my arrival in the Taylor for the purpose of protecting the landing of the troops on their arrival at that point." ADf, DNA, RG 45, Area 5. *O.R.* (Navy), I, xxii, 531.

To Maj. Gen. Henry W. Halleck

Head Quarters Disct of Cairo
Near Fort Henry, Tenn
February 4th 1862

GENL H. W. HALLECK
SAINT LOUIS

This morning the debarkation of one Division, under Genl McClernand took place, three miles below Fort Henry, nearly in view of the rebel batteries. Not having sufficient transportation for all the troops, the larger portion of the Steamers have to return to Paducah for the remainder of the command under Genl Smith. I went up on this Essex this morning with Capt Porter, two other iron clad boats accompanying, to ascertain the range of the rebel guns. From a point about one mile above the place afterwards decided on for place of debarkation several shells were thrown, some of them taking effect inside the rebel Fort. This drew the enemies fire, all of which fell far short, except from one rifled gun which threw a ball through the cabin of the Essex and several near it. I expect all the troops by 10 a. m. tomorrow. Enemy are represented as having reinforced rapidly during the last few days. Genl L Tilgham commands Fort Henry.

Respcty
Your Obt Servt
U S GRANT
Brig Genl Comdg

Telegram, copies, DLC-USG, V, 4, 5, 7, 8, 9; DNA, RG 393, USG Hd. Qrs. Correspondence. *O.R.*, I, vii, 581. The telegram was sent from Paducah on Feb. 5, 1862, and received at St. Louis the same day at 4 p.m. Telegram received, DNA, RG 94, Generals' Papers and Books, Telegrams Received by Gen. Halleck; copy, *ibid.*, RG 393, Dept. of the Mo., Telegrams Received. See letters to Brig. Gen. John A. McClernand, Feb. 3, 4, 1862, and to Julia Dent Grant, Feb. 4, 1862.

To Brig. Gen. John A. McClernand

Head Quarters, Dist. of Cairo,
On G. B. Essex
Feb.y 4th 1862.

GEN. J. A. MCCLERNAND
COMD.G 1ST DIV. IN THE FIELD
GEN.

Follow with the transports as rapidly as possible keeping below the advance gun boats and debark near where they may anchor.

Respectfully
your obt. svt.
U. S. GRANT
Brig. Gen. Com

ALS, McClernand Papers, IHi. See preceding letter. On Feb. 5, 1862, Brig. Gen. John A. McClernand wrote to USG. "I arrived on the advance transport at 9½ O'c'k transports with troops, commenced arriving at 12 O clock, until their arrival being without Infantry or Cavalry. Myself, Capts. Schwartz and Stewart and Lt Freeman, made a hasty reconnoisance. Pursuant to a determination arrived at as the result of reconnoisance, as fast as the troops were debarked I disposed them in 'line of battle' on a range of hills running parallel with the river opposite—the right consisting of 1st Brigade within three miles and one half of Fort Henry resting upon a point termined by Panther creek. The left being so disposed as in connexion with the left of the right to command the approaches by roads from Fort Henry. The left consisting of the 2nd Brigade under command of Col W H L Wallace. The trains of the whole division were disposed between the main line on the ridge and river about 400 yards distant from the same the whole being under cover of the Gun-boats. During our disembarkkation enemys pickets showed themselves oppisite and above on the other side of the river, were dispersed by the fire of the Gun boats. Capt. Osband 4th Cavalry (guards) being the first company to reconnoiter the roads to-wards Fort Henry under instruction to report the result of reconnoisance, from time to time, some sent back word 'have met enemy's pickets' ¾ of a mile ahead on Panther creek whom he drove in. In the meantime having given orders for the bivoacing of the men upon upon the line upon which they were firmed. I went forward accompanied by Col. J D Webster Chief &c and Lt. Col. McPherson, chief of Artillery Lt Freeman Engineer 1st Division; and reconnoitered Panther creek from mouth to the crossing of the road leading from our camp to Fort Henry, advancing beyond that point within a few rods of the fork of the Dover and Fort Henry roads, about 2¼ miles from the latter. This reconnoisance confirmed me in my precaution of the strength of the position I had taken and of the wide range commanded by the battery posted to the right. It is also suggested that the importance of taking advance positions with the support of Battery for the purpose of commanding the crossing of the creek above named, and accordingly I ordered forward two regiments, with 3 rifled pieces to occupy a commanding position about ½ [mi]le in advance of our line (near Panther creek)   Towards night my pickets of Infantry and cavalry reported non-appearance of the enemy or any of his pickets around his lines. Various reports reached me of recent re-inforcements of the garrison of Fort Henry indicating its strength variously from 6 to 20.000:—chiefly in the Fort the rest being across the river. The Steamer of the enemy was observed frequently during the day crossing and recrossing for the purpose of reconnoitering, and it may be for passing troops. The night was undisturbed except by the necessary labors of the embarkation, completing armaments &c''   Copy, McClernand Papers, IHi.

To Julia Dent Grant

On board Steamer, Uncle Sam
Tennessee river, Feb.y 4th/62

DEAR JULIA,

I am now just returning to Paducah after the troops from that place having landed the Cairo troops within three miles of Fort Henry in Tennessee. I went up this morning on one of the gun boats to reconnoiter the fort. A few shots were exchanged with what effect upon the enemy it is impossible to say. Some of our shells went into the fort while one of the enemies passed through the Cabin of of the boat I was on. Done no harm however. All the troops will be up by noon to-morrow, and Friday morning, if we are not attacked before, the fight will commence. The enemy are well fortified and have a strong force. I do not want to boast but I have a confidant feeling of success. You will soon hear if my presentiment is realized. I am sorry now that I did not let Fred.[1] come up and return on one of the boats that ~~are~~ will be going back.

My anxiety will be great to-night being at Paducah whilst my forces are almost within canon range of the enemy, and that too in inferior numbers.

Nothing further to write that can interest you. Dont know when you may look for me back. I will write you by every oppertunity.

Your ULYS.

P. S. Write to me and ask Capt. Du Barry[2] to send the letter. Is the Capt. living with us now? if not give him an invitation.

U. S. G.

ALS, DLC-USG.

1. Frederick Dent Grant was USG's oldest son. See letter to Frederick Dent, April 19, 1861, note 5.
2. Capt. Beekman Du Barry. See letter to Capt. Thomas J. Haines, Dec. 17, 1861. On Jan. 27, 1862, Capt. John A. Rawlins issued General Orders No. 4 assigning Du Barry as chief of the subsistence dept., District of Cairo. Copies, DLC-USG, V, 12, 13, 14, 95; DNA, RG 393, USG General Orders; (misdated Jan. 21) *ibid.*, RG 94, 9th Ill., Letterbook.

Field Orders No. 1

———

Head Quarters, Dist. of Cairo,
Camp in the field, near Fort Henry Ten
Feb.y 5th 1862.

FIELD ORDERS NO 1

The 1st Division, Gen. J. A. McClernand, Comd.g, will move at 11 O'Clock, a.m. to morrow under the guidance of Lieut. Col. McPherson[1] and take a position on the roads from Fort Henry to Fort Donaldson and Dover.

It will be the special duty of this command to prevent all reinforcements to Fort Henry, or escape from it. Also to be held in readiness to charge and take Fort Henry, by storm, promptly, on the receipt of orders.

Two Brigades of the 2d Division, Gen. C. F. Smith Commanding, will start, at the same hour, from the West bank of the river, and take and occupy the heights commanding Fort Henry.[2]

This point will be held by so much Artillery as can be made available, and such other troops as, in the opinion of the Gen. Comd.g, 2d Division, may be necessary for its protection.

The 3d Brigade, 2d Division,[3] will advance up the East bank of the Tennessee river, as fast as it can be securely done, and be in readiness to charge upon the Fort or to move to the support of the 1st Division, as may be necessary.

All of the forces on the West bank of the river, not required to hold the heights commanding Fort Henry, will return to their transports, cross to the East Bank and follow the 1st Brigade as rapidly as possible.

The West bank of the Tennesse river not having been reconnoitred, the Commanding officer entrusted with taking possession of the enemies works there, will proceed with great caution and such information as can be gathered, and such guides, as can be found in the time intervening before 11 o'clock to-morrow.

The troops will move with two days rations of bread and meat in their haversacks[4]

One company of the 2d Division, armed with rifles, will be ordered to report to Flag officer Foote as sharpshooters on board the Gunboats.

> By Order
> U. S. Grant
> Brig. Gen. Com

ADS, McClernand Papers, IHi; DS, DLC-Andrew H. Foote; DNA, RG 393, Dept. of the Mo., Letters Received. *O.R.*, I, vii, 125–26. Field Orders No. 1 are designated General Field Orders No. 1 in letterbook copies. DLC-USG, V, 12, 13, 14, 95; DNA, RG 393, USG General Orders. *O.R.*, I, vii, 585–86.

1. On Feb. 6, 1862, Brig. Gen. John A. McClernand wrote to USG. "Field Order No. 1, is just received, and will be as promptly and successfully carried into effect as possible. Of course, the words 'guidance of Lt. Col. McPherson' were not intended to interfere with my authority as commander." ADfS, McClernand Papers, IHi.

2. Fort Heiman was an unfinished earthen fortification on the bluffs opposite Fort Henry on the Ky. side of the Tennessee River.

3. Commanded by Col. John Cook, temporarily under command of McClernand. *O.R.*, I, vii, 219.

4. On Feb. 5, Capt. William S. Hillyer wrote to McClernand. "Have your entire command provided with two days cooked rations in their haversacks as

early to morrow morning as possible." ALS, McClernand Papers, IHi. On Feb. 5, Hillyer sent an identical message to Cook. Copies, DLC-USG, V, 1, 2, 3, 85; DNA, RG 393, USG Letters Sent. On the same day, McClernand wrote to USG. "Orders have been issued pursuant to your order directing the preparation of two days cooked rations. The 4th Ill Cavalry (Col Dickey) have arrived. My independent scouts coming in about dark bring important information. They report, that they made a near advance to Fort Henry—that they saw the Fort—a considerable encampment just above and out side of it the enemy widening his Abattis around the Fort and encampment—Several Steamers arriving at intervals of time, from above with reinforcements, but no formidable display on the opposite Shore. Is it not a question worthy of consideration, whether our greatest land forces should not be directed against the enemy on this side. Morever is not this a favorable night for the advance of the Gun-boats. Such an advance in the darkness and rain of the night take the enemy by surprize. They could almost certainly pass the Fort cut off all other re-inforcements and sink his transports." Copy, McClernand Papers, IHi.

To Brig. Gen. John A. McClernand

———

Head Quarters, Dist. of Cairo
Camp in the field Near Fort Henry
Feb.y 5th 1862.

GEN. J. A. MCCLERNAND
COMD.G 1ST DIVISION.
GEN.

It would be advisable to carry with you to-morrow all the Spades, Axes and other tools belonging to your command. For this purpose one or more wagons will be necessary.

Five or six Ambulances should also accompany you.

As success may depend to a great extent upon the celerity of our movements it is advisable to be encumbered as little as possible.

very respectfully
your obt. svt.
U. S. GRANT
Brig. Gen. Com

P. S. For excesses committed to-day by the Jessie Scouts Capt. Carpenter[1] and party will be arrested and confined to one of the transports of the fleet until further orders.

U. S. G.

ALS, McClernand Papers, IHi.

1. See letters to Col. Leonard F. Ross, Jan. 8, 1862, and to Brig. Gen. John A. McClernand, Feb. 8, 1862.

To Julia Dent Grant

———

Camp Near Fort Henry, Ten.
Feb.y 5th 1862

DEAR JULIA,

We returned to-day with most of the remainder of our troops. The sight of our camp fires on either side of the river is beautiful and no doubt inspires the enemy, who is in full view of them, with the idea that we have full 4,000 men.[1] To-morrow will come the tug of war. One side or the other must to-morrow night rest in quiet possession of Fort Henry. What the strength of Fort Henry is I do not know accurately, probably 10,000 men.[2]

To-day our reconnoitering parties had a little skirmishing resulting in one killed & two slightly wounded on our side and one killed and a number wounded on the side of the rebels, and the balance badly frightened and driven into their fortifications.[3]

I am well and in good spirits yet feeling confidance in the success of our enterprise. Probably by the time you receive this you will receive another announcing the result.

I received your letter last night just after I had written to you.

I have just written my order of battle. I hope it will be a report of the battle after it is fought.

Kiss the children for me. Kisses for yourself.

ULYS.

P. S. I was up til 5 o'clock this morning and awoke at 8 so I must try and get rest to-night. It is now 10½ however, and I cannot go to bed for some time yet.

U.

ALS, DLC-USG.

1. On Feb. 7, 1862, Maj. Gen. Henry W. Halleck wrote to Brig. Gen. Don Carlos Buell that USG had 15,000 troops. ALS (telegram sent), DNA, RG 107, Telegrams Collected (Unbound). *O.R.*, I, vii, 593. USG probably meant to write 40,000.
2. Brig. Gen. Lloyd Tilghman reported that he had 2,610 men at Fort Henry. *Ibid.*, p. 143.
3. The skirmish involved the cav. of Capt. James J. Dollins. *Ibid.*, p. 128.

To Brig. Gen. John A. McClernand

Head Quarters, Dist. of Cairo
Camp in the field Near Fort Henry Ten.
Feb.y 6th 1862

Gen. J. A. McClernand
Comd.g 1st Div.
Gen.

The Cavalry of the 2d Division not having yet come up it will be necessary to detach temporarily two companies of the 4th Cavalry for duty with it. Please designate two companies and order them over the river as speedily as possible.

If possible send over two or three ambulances for the use of 2d ~~Brig~~ Div.

Respectfully
your obt. svt.
U. S. Grant
Brig. Gen

ALS, McClernand Papers, IHi. See letter to Capt. John C. Kelton, Feb. 6, 1862.

To Brig. Gen. Charles F. Smith

———

Head Quarters, Dist. of Cairo,
On board Steamer "Brown" Feb 6th 1862

GEN. C. F. SMITH
COMMDG 2ND DIVISION
GENL:

A prisoner just in states that all the Troops from, the West bank of the river have been withdrawn to Fort Henry. It would be well to send Cavalry forward as rapidly as possible to ascertain, if such is the fact, and to save as much march as possible of such of your troops as may be required to cross to the east bank of the river. The tents of an Alabama Regt. are said to be left standing, but ~~no~~ are not occupied by troops.

U. S. GRANT
Brig Gen. Commdg.

Copies, DLC-USG, V, 1, 2, 3, 85; DNA, RG 393, USG Letters Sent. Brig. Gen. Lloyd Tilghman had transferred the troops at Fort Heiman to Fort Henry before 5:00 a.m. on Feb. 5, 1862. *O.R.*, I, vii, 138.

To Capt. John C. Kelton

———

Head Quarters, Dist. of Cairo
Fort Henry, Ten.
Feb. 6th 1862.

CAPT. J. C. KELTON
A. A. GEN. DEPT. OF THE MO.
ST. LOUIS MO.
CAPT.

Enclosed I send you my order for the attack upon Fort Henry.[1]

Owing to dispatches received from Maj. Gen. Halleck, and

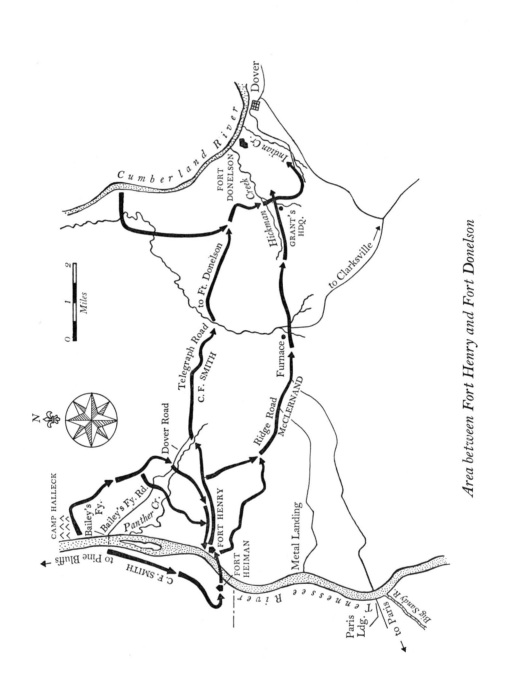

Area between Fort Henry and Fort Donelson

corroberating information here to the effect that the enemy were rapidly reinforcing, I thought it imperetively necessary that the fort should be carried to-day.[2] My forces were not up at 11 O'clock last night, when my order was written, therefore I did not deem it practicable to set an earlyier hour than 11 O'clock to-day to commence the investment. The Gunboats started up at the same hour to commence the attack and engaged the enemy at not over 600 yards.[3] In little over one hour all the batteries were silenced and the fort surrendered at discretion to Flag Officer Foote, giving us all their guns, camp & garrison equipage &c.—The prisoners taken are Gen. Tildghman & Staff,[4] Capt. Taylor[5] and company and the sick. The garrison I think must have commenced their retreat last night, or at an early hour this morning. Had I not felt it an imperitive necessity to attack Fort Henry to-day I should have made the investment complete and delayed until tomorrow so as to have secured the garrison. I do not now believe however the result would have been any more satisfactory.

The gunboats have proven themselvs well able to resist a severe canonading. All the iron clad boats received more or less shots, the Flag ship some twenty-eight, without any serious damage to any except the Essex. This vessel received one shot in her boilers that disabled her, killing and wounding some thirty two men, Capt. Porter among the wounded.[6]

I shall take and destroy Fort Donaldson on the 8th ~~returning~~ and return to Fort Henry with the forces employed unless it looks feasable to occupy that place with a small force that could retreat easily to the main body.[7] I shall regard it more in the light of an advance grand guard than as a perminant post.

For the character of the works at Fort Henry I will refer you to reports of the Engineers which will be required.[8]

Owing to the intolerable state of the roads no transportation will be taken to Fort Donaldson, and but little Artillery, and that with double teams.

Hoping that what has been done will meet with the approval of the Gen. Comd.g Dept. I remain

Your obt. svt.
U. S. GRANT
Brig. Gen

ALS, DNA, RG 94, War Records Office, Union Battle Reports. *O.R.*, I, vii, 124–25. The contents of the letter were telegraphed from Cairo, Feb. 8, 1862. Telegram received, DNA, RG 94, War Records Office, Union Battle Reports. On Feb. 6, USG telegraphed to Maj. Gen. Henry W. Halleck. "Fort Henry is ours   The Gun-boats silenced the batteries before the investment was completed. I think the Garrison must have commenced the retreat last night. Our cavalry followed finding two guns abandoned in the retreat. I shall take and destroy Fort Donaldso[n] on the eighth and return to Ft Henry." Telegram received, *ibid.*, Generals' Papers and Books, Telegrams Received by Gen. Halleck; copies, *ibid.*, RG 393, Dept. of the Mo., Telegrams Received; *ibid.*, USG Hd. Qrs. Correspondence; DLC-USG, V, 4, 5, 7, 8, 9. *O.R.*, I, vii, 124. On the same day, Brig. Gen. John A. McClernand reported to USG. "In compliance with your order of last night and to day, the 1st Division under my command was put in motion for advance upon Fort Henry. The heavy rains continuing through the night found a large portion of the force without tents and ill prepared for exposure, but they came up in the morning promptly and in good condition. The roads had become heavy and the streams swollen, rendering the march difficult   At eleven oclock the 1st Brigade Col. R. J. Oglesby commdg, was put in motion preceded by nine companies of Col. Dickeys Cavalry in advance, followed by five Regts of Infantry and Schwartz's and Drassers Batteryies and flanked on the right by three and on the left by one company of Cavalry. The 2nd Brigade Col W H L Wallace commdg followed comprising four Regiments of Infantry Taylors and McAllisters Batteries and one company of Dickeys cavalry as a rear guard. The forces were so disposed as to insure mutual support if attacked. The firing upon Fort Henry from the Gun Boats commenced at one oclock P M and continued until two, having the effect to hasten the march and increase the eagerness of the men to reach the Fort in time to cut off the retreat and secure the surrender of the enemy. About three oclock P M a report reaching me that the enemy were evacuating the Fort, I immediately sent orders to the advance cavalry guard to ascertain the fact and if true make vigorous pursuit. Col Oglesby however who was in the advance anticipated the order. The pursuit was made with great spirit and vigor by a portion of Colonels Dickeys command under Lt Col McCollough who followed for several miles and until nightfall. First overtaking the enemy's cavalry he engaged and dispersed it killing one man and losing one of his own. Then coming up with the rear of his Infantry, he also dispersed it taking 38 and causing the enemy to abandon his arms knapsacks blankets and everything calculated to impede his march. Although the letter of your order required the halting of my column near the fork of the Dover and Baileys Ferry road some two miles from the Fort, I did not deem it within its spirit, in view of the information I had received and accordingly pushing on the head of the column under the vigorous lead of Col Oglesby reached the Fort at half past three oclock P. M. having accomplished a march of seven miles over the worst possible roads cutting new roads a portion of the way through woods and bridging streams made too deep for fording by recent rain. Capt Stewart of my staff whom I had sent forward with the advance guard of Cavalry and a squad of his company, first coming up with the enemy, boldly charged ~~them~~ him hastening his flight. The 18th Regt being in the advance reached the Fort at half past three Oclock P. M. and were immediately followed by the remainder of the 1st Brigade. The second Brigade under the able and judicious lead of Col W. H. L Wallace although unavoidably detained by a battery of heavy siege guns and the aggravated condition of the roads followed close upon the first completing the arrival of my whole command, in the fort where it is all encamped for the night. On reaching the Fort I learned that the enemy in his flight had abandoned three pieces of Artillery beyond the outworks I instructed Col. Oglesby to detach two companies of Infantry with the necessary teams which were furnished by Capt S to bring them in. Col. Logan however volunteered his services with the required two companies and Capt Schwartz chief of Field staff the teams belonging to his Battery, making the necessary detachment which was placed in command of Col. Logan who hastened to the place where the guns had been abandoned   The The detachment pursuing the track of the enemy's flight for several miles found not only three guns but five others and the way strewn with the enemys wagons and other abandoned property. Col Logan brought in several prisoners but found it impossible in consequence of the approaching darkness and the state of the roads to haul in the cannon. I will cause them to [be] brought within the camp tomorrow morning. The fort was found to have been defended with seventeen heavy and effective guns, well mounted, and so commanding the river and land approaches as to render it formidable. With the eight field pieces found abandoned beyond the intrenchments, the whole number of the guns taken is twenty five. The fortifications are extensive, and give evidence of engineering skill, and great labor. Their defenses are far beyond expectations and the haste with which they were abandoned proves the efficiency of the cannonade and their apprehension of being cut off from retreat by my command, and being compelled to surrender the whole force. The troops of my command are now occupying the huts and tents abandoned by the enemy. A large amount of army stores were captured and will ~~proper~~ be accounted for by the proper Departments of the same for the benefit of the United States   The casualties of the day in my command are mostly confined to the loss and injury of animals and property in transportation by a circuitous route over roads in some parts ~~in~~ scarcely passable to this point. Only one man was killed a private in Col. Dickeys cavalry before referred to. The loss of the enemy except that caused by the fire of the Gunboats is confined as far as heard to two men one of whom was Shot upon the intrenchments. The other in the pursuit by Col Dickeys cavalry. The gallant and masterly manner in which the Gunboats under Flag officer Foote assailed and forced the enemy to surrender the Fort and abandon their entire works reflects the highest credit upon that officer, and his entire command, and proves the efficiency of that arm of the service. In compliment to this first naval engagement upon the western waters, I have taken the liberty of designating this camp as Fort 'Foote.' With reference to my own command, I am pleased to say that both officers and privates did their whole duty with the most commendable spirit and alacrity. It was the first of the land forces to enter the Fort, and having hoped to be able to come up in time to storm the Fort and capture the enemy, regret that his precipitate retreat prevented that wished for result." Df, McClernand Papers, IHi. See letter to Brig. Gen. John A. McClernand, Feb. 6, 1862. On Feb. 10, McClernand wrote to USG. "Herewith you will find my report of the part taken by my Division in the ~~movements~~ operations ending in the reduction of Fort Henry." ADfS, McClernand Papers, IHi. The lengthy detailed report was dated the same day. LS, DNA, RG 94, War Records Office, Union Battle Reports. *O.R.*, I, vii, 126–30. On Feb. 8, McClernand described his role in the capture of Fort Henry with no reference to USG's presence in a letter to President Abraham Lincoln. ALS, DLC-Robert T. Lincoln. McClernand's letter and letters of Flag Officer Andrew H. Foote and Col. William H. L. Wallace, describing the action at Fort Henry, are printed in *USGA Newsletter*, VII, 3 (April, 1970).

    1. See Field Orders No. 1, Feb. 5, 1862.

    2. On Feb. 5, Halleck telegraphed to the commanding officer at Paducah. "Ten thousand men have left Bowling Green to reinforce Fort Henry. Order forward all your available troops as rapidly as possible. I send down the 14th Iowa to-day; the 43d Ill. to-morrow, & the 2d Iowa in a few days." ALS (telegram sent), DNA, RG 107, Telegrams Collected (Unbound). *O.R.*, I, vii, 584–85. On the same day, Halleck telegraphed to the commanding officer at Cairo. "Send troops forward to Genl Grant as rapidly as possible. Fort Henry is being largely reinforced from Bowling Green. The 14th Iowa have left to-day; the 43d Ill will go to-morrow, & the 2d Iowa in a few days." ALS (telegram sent), DNA, RG 107, Telegrams Collected (Unbound). *O.R.*, I, lii, part 1, 206. Also on the same day, Halleck telegraphed to Asst. Secretary of War Thomas A. Scott. "I want all the Infantry regiments at Cairo you can possibly send me there, in order to reinforce the column now moving up the Tennessee river. Ten thousand men have been detached from Bowling Green by Rail Road to reinforce Fort Henry. Send me all the reinforcements you can, as I wish to cut the enemy's line before Beauregard arrives." ALS (telegram sent), Ritzman Collection, Aurora College, Aurora, Ill. *O.R.*, I, vii, 585.

    3. Foote's flotilla consisted of four gunboat ironclads—*Cincinnati, Essex, Carondelet,* and *St. Louis*—and three wooden gunboats—*Conestoga, Tyler,* and *Lexington. Ibid.*, p. 122; *O.R.* (Navy), I, xxii, 537–38.

    4. After ordering the evacuation of Fort Henry, Brig. Gen. Lloyd Tilghman remained with 11 officers, 66 enlisted men, and 16 wounded. Tilghman later explained he had remained in order to bolster the morale of the men manning the guns covering the retreat of the main body of his troops. In addition, he believed that by remaining he had demonstrated the value of land art. against gunboats. *O.R.*, I, vii, 141, 143. For C. S. A. reports on the fall of Fort Henry, see *ibid.*, pp. 130–52; *O.R.* (Navy), I, xxii, 552–69.

    5. Capt. Jesse Taylor of Lexington, Tenn., commanded Battery No. 11, Tenn. Art. Corps. Civil War Centennial Commission, *Tennesseans in the Civil War* (Nashville, Tenn., 1964–65), I, 118, 156.

    6. Gunboat *Essex* Commander William D. Porter was scalded when C. S. A. art. hit the boiler. *O.R.* (Navy), I, xxii, 538; *O.R.*, I, vii, 122. For the naval reports and related correspondence, see *ibid.*, pp. 122–24; *O.R.* (Navy), I, xxii, 534–51.

    7. A notation, "omit in copy for the press," covering the last four paragraphs of USG's original letter, was probably made at hd. qrs., Dept. of the Mo.

    8. A sketch of Fort Henry, prepared by Lt. Col. James B. McPherson, is in *O.R.* (Atlas), plate XI.

To Brig. Gen. John A. McClernand

———

Head Quarters, Dist. of Cairo
Fort Henry Ten.
Feb.y 6th 1862

GEN. J. A. McCLERNAND
COMD.G 1ST DIV.
GEN.

Place your men to occupy the grounds around Fort Henry to the best advantage for defence. An additional Brigade ~~haves~~ been ordered from the opposite side of the river.

To morrow a more extended reconnoisance will show the best grounds to be occupied.

I will send steamers to-night after the 13th Mo. and 17 Ill. to reinforce your command and will further reinforce you as rapidly as possible.

Respectfully
your obt. svt.
U. S. GRANT
Brig. Gen. Com

ALS, McClernand Papers, IHi. On Feb. 6, 1862, USG wrote to the commanding officer, 13th Mo., Smithland. "You will embark for Fort. Henry, Tenn. with as little delay as practicable. Bring with you all baggage and transportation. ~~You~~ Come prepared to remain." Copies, DLC-USG, V, 1, 2, 3, 85; DNA, RG 393, USG Letters Sent. On the same day, USG wrote to the commanding officer, Cape Girardeau, Mo. "Forward the 17th Ills. Regt. on the Steamer 'Illinois' to Fort. Henry. Tenn. with all dispatch. They will bring with them all baggage, transportation &c." Copies, *ibid.* On Feb. 7, USG telegraphed to the commanding officer, Cape Girardeau, Mo. "You will have 17th Ill's Vol's in readiness to move to this place at once—Steamer is now on the way for their transportation—Will be there to day—" Copy, *ibid.*, Post of Cape Girardeau, Telegrams. On Feb. 8, Col. William P. Kellogg telegraphed to USG. "Received Telegram this morning— 17th Regiment is ready—Off this afternoon" Copy, *ibid.*

To Brig. Gen. Eleazer A. Paine

Head Quarters, Dist of Cairo.
Fort. Henry, Febry 6th 1862

GEN. E. A. PAINE
COMMDG. CAIRO, ILLS.
GENL:

You will have to make the best disposition you can of the mutinous prisoners, sent from St Louis, until I return.[1] The prisoners of war, if you have no further instructions about them, will be placed in a ~~set~~ some of the ~~Company~~ quarters occupied by Gen. McClernand's Command, and will be closely guarded. They can have no better accommodations ~~better~~ than Soldiers are entitled to and must live upon Soldiers rations, cooked by themselves. Officers will receive the same rations, and will be allowed [*nothing extra*] unless paid for by themselves.

You can put ammunition in the casemate, in Fort. Cairo. If further facilities are ~~still~~ required, make inquiries of Mr. Sanford,[2] Ordnance Officer of the Navy as to the best means to adopt; and if ~~it~~ his suggestions conforms to your views, adopt them.

Respectfully,
Your Obt. Servant
U. S. GRANT
Brig. Gen. Commdg.

Copies, DLC-USG, V, 1, 2, 3, 85; DNA, RG 393, USG Letters Sent. *O.R.*, II, iii, 241.

1. On Feb. 2, 1862, Capt. Nathaniel H. McLean, asst. adjt. gen. to Maj. Gen. Henry W. Halleck, issued General Orders No. 28, Dept. of the Mo., ordering officers of several cos. of the 4th Mo. confined to Benton Barracks. Privates and non-commissioned officers were ordered to Cairo where they were to work on the fortifications. *Ibid.*, I, viii, 542. The cos. involved had formerly constituted the 3rd Reserve Corps, Mo. Vols., a German regt. formed Aug.-Oct., 1861, and were attached to the 4th Mo. on Jan. 18, 1862. [John B. Gray] *Annual Report of the Adjutant General of the State of Missouri, December 31, 1863* (Jefferson City, 1864), p. 220.
2. Act. Lt. Joseph P. Sanford.

To Julia Dent Grant

————

Fort Henry, Ten.
Feb.y 6th 1862.

DEAR JULIA,

Fort Henry is taken and I am not hurt. This is news enough for to-night. I have been writing until my fingers are tired and therefore you must excuse haste and a bad pen. I have written to you every day so far and you cant expect long letters.

Kiss the children for me.

ULYS.

ALS, DLC-USG.

To Maj. Gen. Henry W. Halleck

————

Fort Henry via
Paducah Feb. 7 1862

To GENL. H. W. HALLECK.

The amount of property left at Fort Henry is much larger than I expected. I send today all the prisoners to Paducah, for safe keeping. The number is larger than reported yesterday.[1]

U. S. GRANT.
Brig. Genl.

Telegram, copy, DNA, RG 393, Dept. of the Mo., Telegrams Received.

1. See letter to Capt. John C. Kelton, Feb. 6, 1862, note 4.

To Brig. Gen. John A. McClernand

Head Quarters, Dist. of Cairo
Fort Henry, Feb. 7th 1862

GEN. J. A. MCCLERNAND
COMD.G 1ST DIV.
GEN.

I would suggest the propriety of appointing an Acting Ordnance officer for the Advance Column and require him to collect and secure all ordnance and ordnance stores captured at and about Fort Henry.

I understand that a large amount of Ammunition has been picked up in the camps outside the forts which the ordnance officer, so appointed, should look after.

Respectfully
your obt. svt.
U. S. GRANT
Brig. Gen. Com.

ALS, McClernand Papers, IHi. On Feb. 7, 1862, Brig. Gen. John A. McClernand's hd. qrs. informed Capt. John A. Rawlins that 1st Lt. Erastus S. Jones, 27th Ill., who had been appointed ordnance officer before leaving Cairo, would continue to act in that capacity. Register of Letters, *ibid.*

To Brig. Gen. John A. McClernand

Head Quarters, Dist. of Cairo
Fort Henry, Ten.
Feb.y 7th 1862

GEN. J. A. MCCLERNAND.
COMD.G 1ST DIV. &c.
FORT HENRY, TEN.
GEN.

The horses of one of the artillery companies should accompany the party reconnoitering in the direction taken by the enemy for the purpose of bringing back the artillery abandoned by the enemy. It might also be advisable to send a few teams, without the wagons, to bring back abandoned wagons and plunder.

I would suggest that a heavy detail be made to bring up all property from the encampment left by our troops yesterday. Parties should be sent back on the road traveled yesterday to bring up all property left by the way.

> Respectfully
> your obt. svt.
> U. S. GRANT
> Brig. Gen.

ALS, McClernand Papers, IHi.

To Brig. Gen. John A. McClernand

> Head Quarters, Dist. of Cairo
> Fort Henry, Feb. 7th 1862

GEN. J. A. MCCLERNAND
COMD.G 1ST DIV.
GEN.

Notify all the Infantry and Cavalry on the East bank of the river to be prepared at any hour in the morning for a move, with two days rations in their haversacks

Owing to the impassable state of the roads it is entirely impracticable to move either baggage or Artillery and therefore if a movement is made it will be without encumbrance.

Gen. Smith will be instructed to move across the river with one Brigade of his command which, with having gunboats above us, will make this point secure.

A movement will depend upon the result of the reconnoisance made to-day and whether the baggage and Artillery on the road from the point of debarkation has all reached Camp, or is secured. I would like to be informed on these points as ~~rapidly~~ soon as possible

> Respectfully
> your obt. svt.
> U. S. GRANT
> Brig. Gen. Com

ALS, McClernand Papers, IHi. On Feb. 7, 1862, Maj. Mason Brayman wrote to USG. "Capt. Stewart, of the Cavalry, a member of my staff, in command of four companies of Cavalry, and accompanied by Col's Logan and Rearden returned about half an hour since from a reconnoisance extended along the Dover road to a point about one mile from Fort Donaldson. He reports that he met the enemys pickets about six miles and a half from this place and drove them forward. About a mile further on he came up with them again in stronger force—numbering probably one hundred mounted men, and drove them forward again. About a mile further on he came up with them again and drove them forward a third time. A half mile further on a body of Infantry was discovered who also dispersed and disappeared upon his advance. None of the enemy was seen after this during his march up to a point about two miles from Dover and about one mile from Fort Donaldson. Capturing a prisoner of war on the way, he learned from him that the enemy driven from Fort Henry, yesterday, had fallen back upon Fort Donaldson, and, by report, that that Fort was defended by more cannon than were taken here. Also; that a reënforcement of fifteen thousand men intended for this place had been diverted to Fort Donaldson and had probably reached there to-day. For the truth of this report, of course, Capt S. does not undertake to vouch, but only gives it for what it may be worth. He gives it as his opinion, however, that the enemy will make a stand there and that any movement made against the place ought to be accompanied by artillery, in the expediency of which I fully concur. I may add that Capt. Carpenter commanding independent scouts has come in from a reconnoisance in the same direction. He reports that he found the pickets of the enemy in such force some six and a half miles from here that he deemed it hazardous to go further. Capt. S. brought in twenty five head of beeves and five head of mules which had been abandoned by the enemy in their flight from this place. I have omitted to state that Capt. S. thinks from what he saw and heard that the enemy are turning their cannon so as to command a rear approach to the Fort, and therefore suggests that a fire should be opened upon the Fort from the river by a Gun boat about the time of the land attack. Capt. S. further states that the roads three miles from here are good from that point to Fort Donaldson. These particulars are given in response to your instructions upon this subject." Copy, *ibid.*

To Col. David Stuart

———

Head Quarters, Dist of Cairo.
Fort Henry, Febry 7th 1862.

COL. D. STEWART
COMMDG U. S. FORCES,
PADUCAH, KY.

Enclosed find a roll of Confederate prisoners taken at Fort. Henry, and sent forward for safe keeping, until ~~properly discharged.~~ finally disposed[1]

Security demands that the Officers should not be paroled in Paducah, but confined to a house, (you can select the property of any notoriously disloyal person, for the purpose) and not allowed to hold communication, by letter or otherwise, with citizens, except with such restrictions as you may deem prudent.

In accordance with orders from Head Quarters of the Department, Officers and Soldiers held as prisoners are allowed United States Soldiers allowance of rations, an[d] no more, and must cook, or provide cooks for themselves.[2]

Any articles of luxury wanted by the prisoners may be allowed them, where they have the means of purchasing them~~selves~~, subject to such restrictions only as the Commanding Officer of the Post may impose.

Respectfully,
Your Obt Servant
U. S. GRANT.
Brig. Genl Commdg.

Copies, DLC-USG, V, 1, 2, 3, 85; DNA, RG 393, USG Letters Sent. *O.R.*, II, iii, 245. On Feb. 7, 1862, Capt. John A. Rawlins issued Special Field Orders No. 2. "Capt. W. S. Hillyer, Aid-de-camp, will proceed to Paducah, Ky, on the Steamer 'Iatan,' with the prisoners of War taken at Fort Henry, and report with them to Col David Stuart, Commdg, who will take charge of and provide for the same.

The Commanding officer of 1st Division will cause to be detailed immediately one company to report on board the Steamer Iatan to take charge of prisoners of War to be sent to Paducah.

The detail will return by first steamer and will be provided with one days rations, reporting to the Comd.g officer at Paducah for more rations should they require them.

Capt H. S. Jones, Confederate prisoner being a Northern man will be kept in close confinement, seperate from the other prisoners, and will not be allowed to communicate with them." Copies, DLC-USG, V, 15, 16, 82, 89; DNA, RG 393, USG Special Orders. An extract containing the two middle paragraphs, in USG's hand and signed by him, is in the McClernand Papers, IHi.

1. On Feb. 19, Col. Robert C. Murphy, 8th Wis., wrote to Brig. Gen. George W. Cullum. "I have the honor to report that in obedience to Special Order No. 8, dated Cairo Feby 15th I proceeded with a guard of 100 men having in charge the prisoners of War taken at Fort Henry, and arrived by Rail at Alton on the 16th at 4 o'clock P. M. The conduct of the Prisoners, Officers as well as privates was most orderly and unexceptionable. I am happy to state that no indignity was offered them en route by any of our people. Enclosed is the receipt of the Comd'g Officer at Alton for all the Officers & their side arms, also for Six more privates than my lists called for. This the men state occured because when they first arrived at Paducah they were put in hospital & when turned over to the Provost Marshal their names were not added." ALS, DNA, RG 393, District of Cairo, Letters Received. On Feb. 17, Capt. Charles C. Smith, 13th Inf., gave Murphy a receipt for "one hundred and thirty privates, & fourteen officers prisoners of war,—two Derringer pistols two colts revolvers and four swords" DS, *ibid.*

2. General Orders No. 27, Dept. of the Mo., Dec. 16, 1861. *O.R.*, II, i, 153.

To Commander Henry Walke

———

Head Quarters of Cairo
Fort Henry Tenn.
Feby 7th 1862.

Capt Walke
Comd.g. G. B. Flotilla
Capt.

The party that went up the river last night for the purpose of destroying the R R Bridge¹ had to return without accomplishing their object in consequence of finding the bridge guarded.

I would request that you go up with your boat to day and take some twenty men, that I will furnish to do the job.

> Respectfully
> Your Obt. Sevt.
> U. S. GRANT
> Brigr Genl.

Copy, DNA, RG 45, Area 5. *O.R.* (Navy), I, xxii, 574–75. On Feb. 7, 1862, Maj. Gen. Henry W. Halleck telegraphed to USG or Flag Officer Andrew H. Foote. "Push the gun-boats up the river to cut the Rail Road bridges. Troops to sustain the gun-boats can follow in transports." ALS (telegram sent), DNA, RG 107, Telegrams Collected (Unbound). *O.R.*, I, vii, 591. Copies of the same telegram, misdated Feb. 10, are in DLC-USG, V, 4, 5, 7, 8; DNA, RG 393, USG Hd. Qrs. Correspondence. *O.R.*, I, vii, 601. On Feb. 7, Capt. William S. Hillyer wrote to Brig. Gen. John A. McClernand. "You will detail from your command two companies of sharpshooters to report to Col McPherson as soon as possible Let them take with them as many picks and axes as may be convenient—" ALS, McClernand Papers, IHi. On Feb. 8, Commander Henry Walke reported to Foote. "I have just returned from destroying the bridges of the Memphis and Bowling Green Railroad (up this river), where I was instructed to proceed by General Grant on the 7th instant. Colonel [J. D.] Webster, with other officers, and two companies of sharpshooters, accompanied me to do the job. We found the place deserted by rebel troops, who left their tents, wagons, etc., some of which we brought here." *O.R.* (Navy), I, xxii, 575. A special dispatch from Fort Henry, Feb. 8, 1862, in the *Chicago Tribune*, Feb. 10, 1862, reported that on Feb. 7, Col. Joseph D. Webster, Lt. Col. James B. McPherson, and John Riggin, Jr., vol. aide-de-camp to USG, had been to the Memphis and Clarksville Railroad bridge at Danville, Tenn. On Feb. 8, McClernand wrote to USG. "Capt Rockwood Comp E 4th Ill. Cavalry bringing up the rear of the detachment of Cavalry sent out yesterday to reconnoiter towards the Rail Road Bridge above on the Tennessee River has just come in (6½ oclock P. M.) and reports the capture of Five Prisoners of War taken near the bridge—the destruction of the telegraphe line along the bridge—the evacuation of the small Infantry camp on guard stationed at the Bridge—He also reports that the reconnoisancee was extended quite to the Bridge which was found impassable—At this point of this hasty report Lt Alshouse Co M. same Reg't comes to report the capture of another Prisoner—I have sent the six to the Officer in charge of the Prisoners on Board the 'New Uncle Sam'" Copies, McClernand Papers, IHi. See letter to Brig. Gen. George W. Cullum, Feb. 8, 1862.

1. The Memphis, Clarksville & Louisville Railroad bridge was located at Danville, Tenn., on the Tennessee River, approximately eleven miles upriver from Fort Henry.

To 1st Lt. William H. Heath

Head Quarters, Dist of Cairo.
Fort. Henry, Febry 7th 1862.

1ST LIEUT W H. HEATH, 18 ILL VOL.
A. A. C. S.
SIR:

Believing that your disobedience of orders this morning was more the result of ignorance of Military requirements, than an intention to treat with contempt orders from your superior Officers, you are released from arrest, and will resume your duties.

In future it is hoped you will require no more such admonitions, and certainly you cannot expect again the same leniency

U. S. GRANT.
Brig. Genl. Commdg.

Copies, DLC-USG, V, 1, 2, 3, 85; DNA, RG 393, USG Letters Sent. 1st Lt. William H. Heath, 18th Ill., who was mustered into the service on May 28, 1861, was act. asst. commissary of subsistence and an aide to Brig. Gen. John A. McClernand. The nature of Heath's violation is not known. Earlier on Feb. 7, 1862, Capt. John A. Rawlins had ordered Heath to issue two days' rations for forty prisoners of war taken at Fort Henry. Copies, *ibid*. In a letter probably received on Feb. 9, Heath wrote to McClernand. "By a verbal order of Capt Rawlins, I am under arrest, and ordered back to Cairo. The proceedings are unregular and not according to Military usage. There is not the slightest ground for my arrest, and if possible I would prefer not to return to Cairo, as the witnesses are all in the army and I cannot procure a trial for several months." Register of Letters, McClernand Papers, IHi.

To Maj. Gen. Henry W. Halleck

By TELEGRAPH FROM Paducah Feby 8 *1862*

To MAJ. GEN. HALLECK
GEN

Can Genl. Tilghman and other officers be placed on parole and confined to the limits of Paducah ? Answer Col Stuart, comdg. at Paducah.

I would suggest the privilege be given them.

U. S. GRANT
Brig. Genl

Telegram received, DNA, RG 94, Generals' Papers and Books, Telegrams Received by Gen. Halleck; copy, *ibid.*, RG 393, Dept. of the Mo., Telegrams Received. *O.R.*, II, iii, 247. On Feb. 8, 1862, Maj. Gen. Henry W. Halleck notified Col. David Stuart. "They can be released as proposed." *Ibid.* See letter to Capt. John C. Kelton, Feb. 10, 1862.

To Brig. Gen. George W. Cullum

Head Quarters, Dist. of Cairo
Fort Henry, Ten. Feb. 8th 1862.

GEN. G. W. CULLUM
CHIEF OF STAFF, DEPT. OF THE MO.
CAIRO, ILL.
GEN.

Yours of yesterdays date is received. The Cavalry which Gen. Halleck can spare from St. Louis might be used to advantage after a while, possibly as soon as they could be got here. At present we are perfectly locked in by high water and bad roads however and prevented from acting offensively as I should like to do. The banks are higher at the waters edge than further back leaving a wide margin of low land to bridge over before anything can be done inland. The bad state of the roads[1] will then prevent the transportation of baggage or Artillery.

I contemplated taking Fort Donaldson to-day, with Infantry & Cavalry alone, but all my troops will be kept busily engaged saving what we now have from the rapidly raising waters. Yesterday my Cavalry went to within a mile of Fort Donaldson. All the enemies pickets were driven in but no definite information received of the number of the enemy. The force from here however have all joined the force at Fort Donaldson and if any reinforcements were on the way for this place no doubt they have, or will, go there also.[2]

All ~~my~~ the Gunboats are gone from here. Capt. Phelps started with the three old boats the evening after the battle, or capture I should say, and will no doubt go to the head of navigation.[3] I sent after him a transport with some Infantry to disable the R. R. bridge, but geting off some hours later than the gunboats, and finding a rebel force at the bridge, they returned without accomplishing the object. I sent up yesterday the only remaining iron clad boat left here to do the work. She has not yet returned.—As this last sentence was finished the iron clad boat made her appearance. I will await her report and finish.~~ed~~

The R. R. bridge is disabled. Some Com.y stores and Qr. Mr's property was taken also.[4]

The steamer which will carry this will leave in a very short time so that I will not be able to send any additional report to Gen. Halleck. I would be obliged therefore if you would send this, or a copy, or such portion of it as you think might interest the Gen. Comd.g Dept.

> I am Gen. very respectfully
> your obt. svt.
> U. S. GRANT
> Brig. Gen

ALS, DNA, RG 393, Dept. of the Mo., Letters Received. *O.R.*, I, vii, 596–97. George W. Cullum of Pa., USMA 1833, ranked as capt., Corps of Engineers, at the outbreak of the Civil War. On April 9, 1861, he was appointed lt. col. and aide to Bvt. Lt. Gen. Winfield Scott. Promoted to brig. gen. on Nov. 1, he was announced as chief of staff and chief of engineers by General Orders No. 11, Dept. of the Mo., on Nov. 30. DNA, RG 94, Dept. of the Mo., General Orders. On Feb. 7, 1862, Cullum wrote to USG. "By direction of Maj. Genl Halleck I am here with his authority to give any Neccessary orders in his name to facilitate your very important operations—do you want any more Cavalry   if so Genl Halleck can send you a Regiment from Saint Louis   I have directed Genl Paine as soon as Transportation can be provided the 32d and 49 Ill. and 25 Indiana   the 57 Ill will be here on Wednesday en-route to join you. Several regiments are about Moving from Saint Louis to adde to your forces. Please ask Lt. Col. McPherson whether he wants intrenching tools or anything else ~~he~~ we can Supply"   Copies, DLC-USG, V, 4, 5, 7, 8, 9; DNA, RG 393, USG Hd. Qrs. Correspondence. *O.R.*, I, vii, 594. On Feb. 7, Maj. Gen. Henry W. Halleck had instructed Cullum, upon arrival in Cairo, to issue orders in the maj. gen.'s name. ALS (telegram sent), Ritzman Collection, Aurora College, Aurora, Ill. Misdated Feb. 6, *O.R.*, I, vii, 937.

    1. On Feb. 10, Halleck telegraphed to USG. "Report as soon as possible the condition of roads above Fort Henry. Can cavalry and artillery move over them? or can they get good camping ground near Fort Henry?" ALS (telegram sent), ICHi; copies, DNA, RG 94, Generals' Papers and Books, Telegrams Sent in Cipher by Gen. Halleck; *ibid.*, RG 393, Dept. of the Mo., Telegrams Sent.
    2. See letter to Brig. Gen. John A. McClernand, Feb. 7, 1862.
    3. For the reports of the Tennessee River expedition, see *O.R.* (Navy), I, xxii, 570–74; *O.R.*, I, vii, 153–57.
    4. See letter to Commander Henry Walke, Feb. 7, 1862.

To Brig. Gen. John A. McClernand

> Head Quarters District of Cairo
> Fort Henry, Feby 8th 1862

Gen. Jno. A. McClernand,
Com'd'g 1st Division,

    Will you do me the favor to send me the letter handed to you last night, by Col. Jno A. Logan. I desire to give such instructions to Col. Stewart, commanding Paducah, as will secure the arrest of the writer; and also to send the letter to Major Gen'l Halleck, St. Louis if agreable to you.

> Respectfully
> Your Obt Sev't
> U. S. Grant
> Brig. Gen. Com

LS, McClernand Papers, IHi. The circumstances surrounding the letter are not known. On Feb. 8, 1862, Brig. Gen. John A. McClernand wrote to USG. "In compliance with your written request of this date I have the honor herewith to enclose to you the letter desired—I have sent out scouts to reconnoiter the road above here, which I suppose to be the road leading from Paris to Dover." Copies, *ibid.*

To Brig. Gen. John A. McClernand

Head Quarters, Dist. of Cairo
Fort Henry, Feb.y 8th 1862.

GEN. J. A. MCCLERNAND
COMD.G 1ST DIV.
GEN.

I am so well satisfied of the irresponsible character of the reports brought by the Jessie Skouts, and their disposition to make exagerated and untrue statements that I have determined to send them back by the steamer Empress.

We have no men in our command calculated to bring so much discredit upon the service as these men. I therefore direct that they be sent aboard at once and sent to the rear with directions that they be not allowed to enter our lines again.

Respectfully
your obt. svt.
U. S. GRANT
Brig. Gen

ALS, McClernand Papers, IHi. See letter to Brig. Gen. John A. McClernand, Feb. 5, 1862. On Feb. 6, 1862, Capt. Charles C. Carpenter wrote to Brig. Gen. John A. McClernand. "I have to report the following property taking by the Jessie Scouts. . . . " LS, McClernand Papers, IHi. On the same day, Maj. Mason Brayman endorsed this letter to USG. AES, *ibid.* On Feb. 8, Brayman wrote to Capt. John A. Rawlins. "Genl. M'Clernand desires Genl. Grant to be informed, that his directions of this date, concerning the arrest, &c. of the 'Jessie Scouts' will be immediately complied with, on their return from a reconnoisance, upon which Genl. M'Clernand despatched them this morning, to find roads &c and the men sent on board the City of Memphis, to await Genl. Grants further order. Genl. M'Clernand instructs me to add, that he has also despatched Lt. Freeman,

Div. Engineer, up the river to examine points of landing, and roads leading from them, and Capt. Stewart, with another party, in the direction of Donaldson to find the direction and condition of approaches to that place." Copies, *ibid*. On the same day, McClernand issued Field Orders No. 60 for the arrest of Carpenter and the Jessie Scouts. Copy, *ibid*. On Feb. 10, Brayman wrote to Col. William H. L. Wallace. "In behalf of Genl. McClernand I advise you, that Capt. Carpenter, with his '*Jessie Scouts*,' were yesterday sent under arrest, by Genl. Grant down the river, not to return." LS, *ibid*. See letter to Maj. Gen. John A. McClernand, March 25, 1862.

To Brig. Gen. Charles F. Smith

——————

Head Quarters, Dist of Caio
Fort Henry, Tenn, Febry 8th 1862.

GEN. C. F. SMITH
COMMDG 2ND DIVISION
GENL:

If practicable to move one Brigade of your Command across the river tomorrow, you will do so, occupying the most suitable unappropriated grounds that you can find having an eye to defensive relations with Fort. Henry, ~~that you can find~~. The Engineer Officers with me being otherwise employed have not looked to the positions of the different camps.

I may move tomorrow on Fort. Donelson, but this will depend upon the result of a reconnoisance ordered this morning, and whether all the transportation, baggage, and particularly Artillery of the 1st Division ~~gets~~ is got up to-night.

Respectfully
Your Obt Servant
U. S. GRANT.
Brig. Gen. Commdg.

Copies, DLC-USG, V, 1, 2, 3, 85; DNA, RG 393, USG Letters Sent.

To Brig. Gen. John A. McClernand

————

Head Quarters, Dist. of Cairo,
Fort Henry, Feb. 9th/62

GEN. J. A. McCLERNAND
COMD.G 1ST DIV.
GEN.

You will please give directions for the removal of all the light Artillery ~~to~~ back of the low lands. It is highly important that the Artillery should be in a position where it can be promptly moved which is not the case whilst it is kept around the fort.

I have been over the ground for some ten miles and find the roads hard and good between the two rivers, after raising out of the bottom, and it may be quite an object to get our Artillery in a position where we can take advantage of this fact.

Respectfully
your obt. svt.
U. S. GRANT
Brig. Gen.

ALS, McClernand Papers, IHi. On Feb. 9, 1862, Capt. William S. Hillyer wrote to Brig. Gen. John A. McClernand. "You will send out four or five companies of cavalry to make reconnoisance towards Ft Donnelson this morning—" ALS, *ibid.* Later the same day, Hillyer wrote to McClernand. "I am instructed by Gen Grant to inquire whether the detachment of Cavalry ordered to make reconnoisance toward Donnelson have started yet? Gen Grant intends making reconnoisance in person and is ready to start but desires that party to precede him—" ALS, *ibid.* On Feb. 9, McClernand replied to USG. "In answer to your note this moment received, I have to say, that four companies of 2nd Cavalry, are now forming preparations to making the projected reconnoisance. If not inconvenient to yourself, please call by my Head Quarters on your way. Having ordered a reconnoisance yesterday, towards Fort Donelson which was very thoroughly made by Capt Stewart, I am almost assured, from his report, that the stories of the appearance of a company of the enemy's cavalry, some six miles from here, on yesterday, is totally unfounded. It is probable that some of our own cavalry, were mistaken for those of the enemy. Capt Stewart has furnished a drawing of the roads as a part of his report, and represents the practicability of marching in two colums over favorable roads against Fort Donelson. Maj Mudd at this point of connexion reports his four companies ready for the march." Copy, *ibid.* On the same day, Hillyer wrote to McClernand. "Gen Grant with Osbands Cavalry Company have already started on the reconnoisance—If Maj Mudds detachment have not already started, they had probably better push on—Your communication arrived after Gen Grant left—" ALS, *ibid.* Later the same day, McClernand replied to USG. "In reply to Capt Hillyers note just received, I have the honor to state, that Maj Mudd, 2nd Cavalry with four companies, left near an hour ago, for the purpose of reconnoitering near Fort Donelson. Capt Stewart of my Staff accompanied the detachment." Copy, *ibid.*

To Col. John Cook

Head Quarters, Dist of Cairo
Fort. Henry, Febry 9th 1862.

COL. J. COOK
COMMDG 3RD BRIGADE, 2ND DIVISION
COLONEL:

Some two or three hundred men of your Brigade, ~~embracing two or three hundred~~, have been out to-day, robbing and plundering most disgracefully. Some of them were of the 50th Ills. and some of the 7th,[1] and no doubt other Regiments were represented. I hope you will take active measures to ascertain what men have been out, and report their names to me. Officers will be sent immediately ~~off~~, and ~~be~~ recommended for dismissal without trial, and Non-Commissioned Officers will be reduced to the ranks, and otherwise punished.

Respectfully,
Your Obt. Servant.
U. S. GRANT.
Brig. Gen. Commdg.

Copies, DLC-USG, V, 1, 2, 3, 85; DNA, RG 393, USG Letters Sent. On Feb. 10, 1862, Capt. John A. Rawlins issued General Field Orders No. 7. "The pilfering and marauding disposition shown by some men of this command has determined the General Commanding to make an example of some one to fully show his disapprobation of such conduct. Brigade Commanders, therefore, will be held accountable for the conduct of their Brigades, Regimental Commanders for their Regiments, and Company Commanders for their Companies. If any one is found guilty of plundering, or other violation of orders, if the guilty parties are not punished promptly the Company officers will be at once arrested, or if they are not known the punishment will have to fall upon the Regimental or Brigade Commander. Every offence will be traced back to a responsible party   In an enemy's country, where so much more could be done by a manly and humane policy to advance the cause which we all have so deeply at heart, it is astonishing that men can be found so wanton, as to destroy, pillage and burn indiscriminately without enquiry. This has been done but to a very limited extent in this command, so far, but to[*o*] much for our credit has already occurred, to ~~pass without~~ be allowed to pass without admonition." DS, McClernand Papers, IHi; copy, DNA, RG 94, 9th Ill., Letterbook. Copies of the same orders, dated Feb. 9, and numbered General Field Orders No. *5*, are in DLC-USG, V, 12, 13, 14, 95; DNA, RG 393, USG General Orders. *O.R.*, I, vii, 599.

1. Lt. Col. Andrew J. Babcock then commanded the 7th Ill.; Col. Moses M. Bane commanded the 50th Ill.

To Salmon P. Chase

———

Fort Henry, Ten.
Feb.y 9th 1862.

Hon. S. P. Chase
Sec. of Treas. Washington, D. C.
Sir:

Should it be the intention of the Administration to open trade to the Southern states, as far as the Army goes, I would respectfully recommend Messrs N. Casey & Lelliott[1] as persons who it would be proper to extend such trading privileges to. They are both gentlemen who have been loyal to their government from the first, and would observe any restrictions placed upon them without the necessity of watching their actions.

I Am sir, very respectfully
your obt. svt.
U. S. Grant
Brig. Gen

ALS (facsimile), *The Flying Quill: Autographs at Goodspeed's* (May 15, 1968), p. 4. On March 5, 1861, President Abraham Lincoln had appointed Salmon P.

Chase secretary of the treasury. A life-long foe of slavery, Chase had belonged to various antislavery parties before the organization of the Republican Party. Chase, who had been a Republican presidential aspirant in 1856 and 1860, had been governor of Ohio and a U. S. Senator from that state. *DAB*, IV, 27–34; David Donald, ed., *Inside Lincoln's Cabinet: The Civil War Diaries of Salmon P. Chase* (New York, Toronto, London, 1954), pp. 1–45. Trade was prohibited with rebellious areas unless licensed by the secretary of the treasury. Act of July 13, 1861, *U. S. Statutes at Large*, XII, 255–58.

1. Probably John Lellyett; see USG endorsement concerning John Lellyett, Jan. 11, 1862.

To Mary Grant

Fort Henry, Ten.
Feb.y 9th 1862.

DEAR SISTER,

I take my pen in hand "away down in Dixie" to let you know that I am still alive and well. What the next few days may bring forth however I cant tell you. I intend to keep the ball moving as lively as possible and have only been detained here from the fact that the Tennessee is very high and has been raising ever since we have been here overflowing the back land making it necessary to bridge it before we could move.—Before receiving this you will hear, by telegraph, of Fort Donaldson being attacked.— Yesterday I went up the Ten. river twenty odd miles[1] and to-day crossed over to near the Cumberland river at Fort Donaldson.[2] —Our men had a little engagement with the enemie's pickets killing five of them, wounding a number and, expressively speaking, "gobbeling up" some twenty-four more.

If I had your last letter at hand I would answer it. But I have not and therefore write you a very hasty and random letter simply to let you know that I believe you still remember me and am carrying on a conversation whilst writing with my Staff and others.

Julia will be with you in a few days and possibly I may

accompany her.[3] This is bearly possible, depending upon having full possession of the line from Fort Henry to Fort Donaldson and being able to quit for a few days without retarding any contemplated movement. This would not leave me free more than one day however.

You have no conception of the amount of labor I have to perform. An army of men all helpless looking to the commanding officer for every supply. Your plain brother however has, as yet, had no reason to feel himself unequal to the task and fully believes that he will carry on a successful campaign against our rebel enemy. I do not speak boastfully but utter a presentiment. The scare and fright of the rebels up here is beyond conception. Twenty three miles above here some were drowned in their haste to retreat thinking us such Vandals that neither life nor property would be respected. G. J. Pillow commands at Fort Donaldson. I hope to give him a tug before you receive this.

U. S. G.

ALS, DLC-USG.

1. G. W. B. reported from Fort Henry, Feb. 8, 1862, that USG, his staff, and several newspaper correspondents, accompanied by a guard of sharpshooters, had visited the railroad bridge at Danville, Tenn. *Missouri Democrat*, Feb. 13, 1862.

2. A dispatch from Fort Henry, Feb. 9, reported that USG and his staff reconnoitered to within four miles of Fort Donelson. *Chicago Tribune*, Feb. 12, 1862. A dispatch from Fort Henry, Feb. 9, reported that Col. Joseph D. Webster and Lt. Col. James B. McPherson accompanied USG. *Missouri Republican*, Feb. 11, 1862.

3. Julia Dent Grant and the children arrived in Covington, Ky., on Feb. 22. *Cincinnati Commercial*, Feb. 24, 1862.

To Capt. John C. Kelton

Head Quarters, Dist. of Cairo
Fort Henry, Ten. Feb. 10th 1862.

Capt. J. C. Kelton,
A. A. Gen. Dept. of the Mo.
St. Louis Mo.
Capt.

After writing the dispatch to Gen. Halleck suggesting the propiety of paroling the prisoners of War (Commissioned officers) at Paducah Ky,[1] I received such reports of their conduct as to make me believe it was not prudent to leave them within our lines so near the enemy. Paducah being the home of Gen. Tilghman makes it particularly objectionable and I therefore gave orders, before the receipt of Maj. Gen. Hallecks reply, for the removal of all these prisoners to St. Louis or such other place as the Dept. Comdg. might direct.[2] I hope this will meet with approval.

Respectfully
your obt. svt.
U. S. Grant
Brig. Gen

ALS, DNA, RG 393, Dept. of the Mo., Letters Received. *O.R.*, II, iii, 252. On Feb. 13, 1862, Maj. Gen. Henry W. Halleck wrote to Brig. Gen. George W. Cullum. "The commissioned officers prisoners of war at Paducah will be permitted to go to Cincinnati on parole. If they decline to do this they will be sent under guard on one of the return steamers to Alton." *Ibid.*, p. 259. On Feb. 18, Halleck telegraphed to Brig. Gen. William T. Sherman, Cullum, and USG. "By order of the Secty of war, no parole will be given to Confederate officers prisoners of war. They will all be sent here under strong guards. All orders to the contrary revoked." ALS (telegram sent), DNA, RG 107, Telegrams Collected (Unbound); copies (to USG and Cullum), *ibid.*, RG 393, Dept. of the Mo., Telegrams Sent. *O.R.*, II, iii, 276. Copies (to USG, misdated Feb. 20, with notation "Telegram, forwd by Gen Sherman"), DLC-USG, V, 4, 5, 7, 8; DNA, RG 393, USG Hd. Qrs. Correspondence. *O.R.*, II, iii, 288.

1. See telegram to Maj. Gen. Henry W. Halleck, Feb. 8, 1862.
2. See letter to Col. David Stuart, Feb. 10, 1862.

To Flag Officer Andrew H. Foote

———

Head Quarters, Dist. of Cairo
Fort Henry, Ten, Feb.y 10th 1862.

FLAG OFFICER FOOTE
COMD.G FLOTILLA, CAIRO ILL.
FLAG OFFICER.

I have been waiting very patiently for the return of the gunboats under Commander Phelps[1] to go around on the Cumberland whilst I march my land forces across to make a similtanious attack upon Fort Donaldson. I feel that there should be no delay in this matter and yet I do not feel justifiable in going without some of your boats to co-opperate. Can you not send two boats from Cairo immediately up the Cumberland? To expedite matters any steamers at Cairo may be taken to tow them. Should you be deficient in men an Artillery company can be detached to serve on the gunboats temporarily.—Please let me know your determination in this matter and start as soon as you like. I will be ready to co-opperate at any moment.

I Am Flag officer, your obt. svt.
U. S. GRANT
Brig. Gen. Com

ALS, Fogg Collection, Maine Historical Society, Portland, Me. *O.R.*, I, vii, 600. On Feb. 10, 1862, Flag Officer Andrew H. Foote wrote to Lt. S. Ledyard Phelps or Commander Henry Walke that the gunboats should cooperate with the Army in the attack on Fort Donelson and then proceed up the Cumberland River in order to destroy the bridge at Clarksville. The letter was to be shown to USG or Brig. Gen. John A. McClernand. LS, DNA, RG 393, District of Cairo, Letters Received. *O.R.* (Navy), I, xxii, 583–84. On Feb. 11, Foote wrote to USG. "I have received your letter of yesterday's date, and in reply I will state that I shall be ready to start to morrow evening with two Boats. I am this morning very busy with Secretary Scott. It is possible that I may not get off before Wensday morning myself, but will try to send the Boats up to morrow evening. They will move slowly & I would like a steamer to accompany them. I want to see Capt Phelps & please send him to me when he comes to you from above. The Boats are so deep that they cannot be towed fast." ALS, DNA, RG 393, District of Cairo, Letters Received. On Feb. 10, Walke, at Paducah, wrote to Foote. "I received instructions from Genl Grant this evening to proceed with this vessel to Fort Donelson, on the Cumberland River, to co operate with our army in that vicinity. I expect to meet you before I reach there. The Alps will take me in tow. I will coal at this place. Genl Grant will send the Taylor Lexington and Conestoga after me. We heared that you were on your way to Fort Donelson, But I hear no tiding of you here to night. The Taylor had just returned from up the Tennessee River, as far as navigable. They with the Lexington and Conestoga destroyed or captured all the enemies boats, broke up their camps, and made a prise of their fine new gun Boat. I write this in anticipation of not seeing you before I leave hear, as I am, (or the Carondelet is) very slow, and Genl Grant desires that I should be ~~there~~, at Fort Donelson as soon as I can get there. But I hope you will overtake me, or send me your orders upon this occasion. as I am now acting upon your general instructions, repeated at Fort Henry. I expected to send this letter from here to night, but I am disappointed in this also." ALS, *ibid.*, RG 45, Area 5. *O.R.* (Navy), I, xxii, 583. On Feb. 11, Asst. Secretary of War Thomas A. Scott wrote to Foote. "Would it not be well for you to telegraph Genl. Halleck the order of Genl. Grant in regard to movement of the Gunboat 'Carondelet' & of the boats under Lt. Phelps—informing him that you will not be able to leave before tomorrow night or next morning under order of Genl. Grant and ask whether the boats now in Tennessee river—including the Carondelet—had not better remain there until you are ready & all forces in condition to make a successful move—He may be making arrangements with Genl. Buel that will render it necessary to have a few boats to sustain the column of his land forces within reasonabe distance of Fort Donelson" ALS, DNA, RG 45, Area 5. *O.R.* (Navy), I, xxii, 582–83.

1. The gunboats returned from the Tennessee River expedition late on Feb. 10. Dispatch from Fort Henry, Feb. 10, 1862, in *Missouri Democrat*, Feb. 12, 1862.

To Brig. Gen. John A. McClernand

Head Quarters Dist of Cairo
Ft Henry Feby 10. 1862

BRIG GEN JNO A. McCLERNAND
COM'G 1ST DIVISION U. S. FORCES

I am instructed by Brig Gen Grant Com'g to inform you that he desires to have a conference with you and your Brigade Commanders at his Head Quarters on board the Steamer "New Uncle Sam" at three o.clock this afternoon. You will please notify your Brigade Commanders and be prompt in attendance—

Very Respectfully
Your obt svt
WM S. HILLYER
Aid de Camp

ALS, McClernand Papers, IHi. Brig. Gen. Lewis Wallace later discussed a council
of war, at 2 P.M. on Feb. 10, 1862, attended by himself, Brig. Gen. John A.
McClernand, Brig. Gen. Charles F. Smith, and others whom he could not recall,
on board the *Tigress*. According to Wallace's account, USG said the purpose of
the meeting was to decide whether to march on Fort Donelson immediately, or
to await reinforcements. Those present agreed unanimously to move forward at
once. There was little discussion, but McClernand, to the apparent displeasure of
USG, read a paper outlining in detail his suggestions for the proposed movement.
Lew Wallace, *An Autobiography* (New York and London, 1906), I, 375–77. In
another account, Wallace wrote that the meeting took place on board the *New
Uncle Sam* during the morning of Feb. 11. Lew Wallace, "The Capture of Fort
Donelson," *Battles and Leaders of the Civil War*, eds., Robert Underwood Johnson
and Clarence Clough Buel (New York, 1887), I, 404–6. On Feb. 9, McClernand
wrote to USG. "According to reconnoisances made by the Cavalry under my
Command, and to information received from prisoners and private citizens, residing in this district, I propose the following manner of attack upon Fort Donelson,
viz:—Supposing that my Command consists of 3 Brigades, and that the Gunboats
will cooperate with us, I suggest the following order of march; *On the 'Ridge Road'*

1. 10 Companies of Cavalry
2. Advance Guard, 5 Co., 1st Brigade,
3. Pioneer Co. and wagon
4. 1st Brigade with Schwartz's and Dresser's Batts.
5. 1 Company of Cavalry
6. A. Battery of 20 Pdrs. Mos. Battalion
7. IId Brigade with Gaylor's and McAllister's Batts.
8. 1 Company of Cavalry as rear guard
9. 2 Companies of Cavalry as flankers on right and left of the column.

On the telegraph road.
1. 6 Companies of Cavalry
2. Advance Guard 4 Companies of Infty
3. Pioneer Co. and wagon
4. III Brigade including the two remaining Batt.s of Mo. Art.
5. 1 Company of Cavalry as rear guard
6. The balance of Cavalry as flankers.

Assuming that the Diagram annexed is correct, I suggest the following mode of
attack and disposition of the forces—supposing our forces to consist of 3 Brigades
including Batt Cavalry and as I have said before, our Gunboats to cooperate with
us—

1. That two Brigades, or the 1st Division advance upon the 'Ridge Road.'

2nd That the 3rd Brigade advance upon the telegraph road

3rd that the 1st Division halting form a line of battle near and parallel with
the road leading from A. to B—resting its right at the point on the upper creek
where it ceases to be fordible.

4th That the 3rd Brigade extend the line of the 1st Division so as to rest its
left upon the lower creek where it ceases to be fordible, or near it.

5   That if the space between A & B will only receive the 1st Division that
the 3rd Brigade be formed as a reserve in column of Companies or Divisions to
move in any direction in support of the attacking line

6th   That a reserve in all circumstances be placed so as to support the attacking line, and probably at the point indicated by the letter D.

7th   That the largest rifle pieces be planted near the spot indicated by letter C, which is supposed to be a commanding ridge"   Copies, McClernand Papers, IHi.

On Feb. 10, Capt. John A. Rawlins issued General Field Orders No. 10. "The 17th, 43d, and 49th Regiments of Illinois Volunteers, Commanded by the Senior Colonel, will form the Third Brigade, First Division of the Army in the Field. The 14th Iowa, 25th and 52nd Indiana Volunteers, Birge's Sharp Shooters, and one Battillion of Curtis's Horse will form the Fourth Brigade, Second Division." DS, *ibid.;* Brayman Papers, ICHi. Copies of the same orders, numbered General Field Orders No. 8, are in DLC-USG, V, 12, 13, 14, *95;* DNA, RG 393, USG General Orders. *O.R.,* I, vii, 601. On the same day, McClernand wrote to USG. "I think it would ~~contribute~~ tend much to secure efficiency to the administration of the affairs of this Post, if the unbrigaded troops here were brigaded. With a view to that object I would suggest that, the 17 Ill. Col. Ross; the 52nd ~~Ill~~ Ia. Col Smith; the 43d Ill. Col. Raith and the 49th Ill. Col. Morrison with one Company of Maj Cavender's Artillery be organized into one brigade. Also; that the 14th Iowa Col. Shaw; the 25th Ia. Col. Veatch and the ~~25 Ky~~ 16. Mo. Col. Birge ~~be organized~~ with another ~~batter~~ Company of Col. Cavender's Artillry be organized into another brigade." ADfS, McClernand Papers, IHi. On Feb. 10, Rawlins wrote to the commanding officer, 25th Ind. "Will report to Brig Gen. Jno. A McClernand for location and orders." DS, *ibid.;* copies, DLC-USG, V, 1, 2, 85; DNA, RG 393, USG Letters Sent.

On Feb. 11, Rawlins issued General Field Orders No. 11. "The following changes and additions are made to present Brigade organizations: The 23d Ill. Vols. will be added to 3d Brigade, 1st Division. The 52nd Indiana will be transferred to 3d Brigade 2nd Division, and, 7th Iowa from the 3d Brigade 2d Division, to 4th Brigade, 2nd Division. The 2d Iowa Regiment will be added to this Brigade, immediately upon arrival"   DS, Brayman Papers, ICHi. Copies of the same orders, numbered General Field Orders No. 9, are in DLC-USG, V, 12, 13, 14, 95; DNA, RG 393, USG General Orders. *O.R.,* I, vii, 605.

To Col. David Stuart

Head Quarters, Dist of Cairo
Fort Henry, Febry 10th 1862.

COL. D. STEWART.
COMMDG U. S. FORCES,
PADUCAH, KY.

COL:

My dispatch ~~was~~ suggesti~~ng~~ed the propriety of paroling the Officers taken prisoners at this place, confining them to the limits of the town. It seems that Gen. Halleck has consented to the arrangement. Since sending that dispatch, however, I have changed my views in consequence of the reported conduct of the captured officers. You will see by an order sent before this, that I have directed that all the prisoners be sent to St Louis for disposal. I will write to Genl—Halleck, ~~explaining~~ giving my reasons.

> Respectfully,
> Your Obt. Servant.
> U. S. Grant.
> Brig. Genl. Commdg.

Copies, DLC-USG, V, 1, 2, 3, 85; DNA, RG 393, USG Letters Sent. *O.R.*, II, iii, 252–53. See letters to Maj. Gen. Henry W. Halleck, Feb. 8, 1862, and to Capt. John C. Kelton, Feb. 10, 1862.

To Col. David Stuart

> Head Quarters, Dist. of Cairo.
> Fort. Henry, Febry 10th 1862.

Col. David Stuart Commdg U. S. Forces.
Paducah, Ky.
Col:

Enclosed you will find a roll of Prisoners of War, ordered to St Louis, escort to report to Major Gen. Halleck, Commdg Department. The prisoners sent to your charge a few days since will also be sent.

A description roll, such as that accompanying will be sent with the prisoners.

> Respectfully,
> Your Obt. Servant.
> U. S. Grant.
> Brig. Genl. Commdg.

Copies, DLC-USG, V, 1, 2, 3, 85; DNA, RG 393, USG Letters Sent. *O.R.*, II, iii, 252. On Feb. 10, 1862, Capt. John A. Rawlins issued Special Field Orders No. 8. "The prisoners of War now held here will be sent to-day on board Steamer 'Chancellor,' for transmittal to St. Louis, or such other point as the Maj. Gen. Comd.g the Department may designate. An escort of one commissioned officer and ten private will accompany them. The party going from here will turn the prisoners over to the commanding officer at Paducah, together with such packages and instructions as he may be furnished with, and return to Fort Henry by the first steamer coming up." This copy, in USG's hand, is signed by Rawlins. AD, McClernand Papers, IHi. Copies of the same orders, numbered Special Orders No. 5, are in DLC-USG, V, 15, 16, 82, 89; DNA, RG 393, USG Special Orders. See preceding letter.

To Col. David Stuart

Head Quarters, Dist of Cairo.
Fort Henry, Febry 10th 1862.

COL. D. STEWART
COMMDG U. S. FORCES,
PADUCAH, KY

The Steamer "Iatan" has now on board some Six hundred barrels of Powder, which has been transported up and down the river several trips, for want of Storage at Cairo. I wish you would make some disposition of it in Paducah, to save carrying it longer. For the purpose, a suitable store house near the river might be rented down near the water, and a guard kept to prevent fire, either accidental or by design.

Respectfully
Your Obt. Servant
U. S. GRANT
Brig. Gen. Commdg

Copies, DLC-USG, V, 1, 2, 3, 85; DNA, RG 393, USG Letters Sent.

To Julia Dent Grant

———

Fort Henry, Ten.
Feb.y 10th 1862.

DEAR JULIA,

Fred arrived this evening all well. I will let him remain here for a few days but will not take him into danger. On the 12th I shall go to Fort Donelson where quite an engagement may be expected. This of course will prevent my return at the time I told you.—I do not expect to be back much more for the present an active campaign being probably the order of the day.—Our gunboats have just returned from an expedition up the Tennessee to Florance Alabama. The Union sentiment up there is much stronger than we have found it through Missouri. Twenty-five men enlisted in our gunboat service up there and many more could have been got if there had been time to devote in that way.

I write you so often that there is not much to write about but it serves the purpose to let you know that I am alive and where I am.—Kiss the children for me and continue to write often.

Your ULYS.

ALS, DLC-USG. For the reports of the Tennessee River expedition of Feb. 6–10, 1862, see *O.R.* (Navy), I, xxii, 570–74; *O.R.*, I, vii, 153–56.

To Elihu B. Washburne

———

DATED Fort Henry Via Cairo [*Feb.*] 10 *1861*2

TO HON E B WASHBURN

For Gods sake get the Senate to reconsider Gen Smiths Confirmation. There is no doubt of his loyalty & efficiency   We Cant spare him now.

U. S. GRANT.
Brig Genl

Telegram received, DLC-Elihu B. Washburne. On Feb. 10, 1862, Brig. Gen. John A. McClernand telegraphed to Elihu B. Washburne. "Having entire confidence in Gen Grants representation I take great pleasure in concurring in his recommendation." Telegram received, *ibid.* On Feb. 10, Lt. Col. Augustus L. Chetlain wrote to Washburne. "Why was not Gen C F Smith not confirmed by the Senate?—He is one of the best officers in the army." ALS, *ibid.* On Feb. 12, Maj. Gen. Henry W. Halleck telegraphed to Senator Milton S. Latham of Calif. "Dont permit C. F. Smith's nomination to be rejected. He is the best officer in my command, and there is not the slightest ground for suspecting his loyalty." ALS (telegram sent), Victor Jacobs, Dayton, Ohio.

Brig. Gen. Charles F. Smith's Aug. 31, 1861, recess appointment, referred to the Senate Committee on Military Affairs on Dec. 24, was not confirmed until Feb. 14, 1862. *Senate Executive Journal*, XII, 57, 66, 118–19. The delay probably resulted from political pressure brought by supporters of two of Smith's detractors, Brig. Gen. Eleazer A. Paine and Brig. Gen. Lewis Wallace. After Paine disobeyed orders during the battle of Belmont, Smith requested a court of inquiry. See General Orders No. 22, Dec. 23, 1861, note 2; *O.R.*, I, iii, 300, 303–4; Smith to asst. adjt. gen., Dept. of the Mo., Nov. 25, 1861, copy, DNA, RG 94, Letters Received; Halleck to Brig. Gen. Lorenzo Thomas, Nov. 27, 1861, LS, *ibid.;* Halleck to Thomas, Jan. 15, 1862, ALS, *ibid.* Smith believed that Paine was conspiring to have him removed from command. Bruce Catton, *Grant Moves South* (Boston and Toronto, 1960), p. 60. On Jan. 14, James J. Ferree, former chaplain of the 9th Ill., wrote to Senator Lyman Trumbull. "In connection with Gen Grant he maneuvered the removal of Gen Paine from Paducah to Birds Point, & since that he has bent all his energies and used all the influence which his position gives him to alienate from Gen P his (Paines) old Regiment (the 9th infantry), & to create a feeling in his (Smiths) favor among the the officers under his command, and doubtless this is to be used to keep him in command of the Post and to secure his confirmation by the Senate. This and *this alone* is the source of any feeling in his favor   His course is unhesitatingly condemned by every loyal man, and he he is held in the same contempt among the secessionists that Pillow is among us. All the truly loyal men of that region are devoted to Gen Paine.   he is looked upon by them as *peculiarly* their friend & they regard his removal as a calamity only equalled by that of retaining Gen Smith in command of the Post." ALS, DLC-Lyman Trumbull.

Correspondents for the *Chicago Tribune* and others accused Smith of sympathy for the C. S. A. He refused to allow the forcible removal of a Confederate flag and the raising of a U. S. flag at the home of Robert Owen Woolfolk of Paducah, by Ind. troops in Wallace's brigade. This led to fisticuffs between Wallace's asst. adjt. gen., Capt. Frederick Knefler, and Smith's asst. adjt. gen., Capt. Thomas J. Newsham. The same sources accused Smith of permitting trade with the South while hampering the trade and travel of loyal citizens. His dilatory tactics were alleged also to have led to the murder of a Unionist at Columbus. In addition, Smith was condemned for following a policy on fugitive slaves required by General Orders No. 3, Dept. of the Mo., Nov. 20, 1861. *Chicago Tribune*, Nov. 27, Dec. 1, 6, 1861; *Cincinnati Gazette*, Dec. 7, 12, 1861; *O.R.*, II, i, 778; Catton, *Grant Moves South*, pp. 87–89; *Lew Wallace: An Autobiography* (New York and London, 1906), I, 350–51. Enclosing an article from the *Chicago Tribune*, on Dec. 6, 1861, Joseph Medill wrote to Secretary of War Simon Cameron. "This man Smith is doubtlessly a secession sympathizer—if not worse." ALS, DLC-Simon Cameron.

On Dec. 10, Secretary of the Treasury Salmon P. Chase wrote in his diary.
"I directed the attention of the President to complaints made against Gen. Smith
at Paducah, and was glad to learn that Gen. McClellan had already directed him
to be superseded." David Donald, ed., *Inside Lincoln's Cabinet: The Civil War
Diaries of Salmon P. Chase* (New York, London, Toronto, 1954), p. 50. On the
same day, Brig. Gen. Lorenzo Thomas wrote to Halleck. "The General-in-Chief
has learned from several sources that Brig. Genl. C. F. Smith, Comdg. at Paducah,
has not, at this time, the confidence of the forces under his command or of the loyal
citizens of Kentucky. He desires that you withdraw this officer and devolve the
command on Brigadier General Grant, the next in command." Copy, DNA,
RG 94, Letters Sent. On Dec. 17, however, Thomas telegraphed to Halleck.
"The order concerning General Smith may be suspended as you desire." Copy,
ibid. Aware of the allegations against him, on Jan. 10, 1862, Smith wrote to
Thomas. "I have long known that a base conspiracy was on foot in this place orrigi-
nating with and formented by some of my subordinates and others, Citizens of the
County, who were the dirty tools of the Chief conspirators to oust me from the
Comand, with a view of placing Brig. Genl. Paine in it. Truth was no obstacle
with this party. Anything that would strike me down that would ruin me was
sufficient. An underbred, vulgar, and impudent fellow by the name of *Ferree*
miscalled the Revd. late the chaplain of the 9th Ills. Regt. from which he has been
driven with marked contempt, was the first dirty instrument he being employed,
to write me down in the Chicago Tribune. A person by the name of *Lucien
Anderson* of Mayfield was another dirty tool. He is I am told the author of certain
articles of the worst type in a Cincinaty paper (The Comercial) I believe I have
never seen them. This Mr. Anderson who makes now quite a parade of his loyalty
(with the view of being a Candidate for Congress from this District—in April
last immidiatly after the proclamation of the President, consequent on the fall of
Fort Sumpter made violent and determined harangues at public Meetings in this
City against the Governement of the U.S. and proposed armed resistance to the
passage of Federal troops through the State of Ky, denouncing the Proclamation
& its Author all of the abolition type, to be resisted by every Kentuckian. Deputa-
tions have been send from here by the Chief Conspirators to the Comander of
the Dept of St. Louis to urge my removal, he also I have been told sent a similair
deputation to Washington for a like purpose, all of which time this said Conspirators was adressing letters to polititians in Illinois and in Washington urging my
removal, and his great merits and his exceeding fitness for the Comand. I all this
time I have been quietly pursuing the even tenor of my way—doing my duty to
the best of my ability, never noticing the attackts upon me in the belief that my
past history and reputation would shield me from base aspersions, at least they
would guarantee to me a fair hearing before I was stricken down. In this it seems
I have been mistacken. It has come to my knowledge that an order for my removal
from here was issued from the Headquarters of the Army. That this implied
censure upon me was not carried into effect I am, I understand indebted to the
manliness and just appreciation of a distinguished officer of the Govt. I request
to be informed what allegiations have been made against me for I am intirely
ignorant   Comon justice gives me the right to demand this. The miscreants who
have orriginated the Cry against me, continue to have insinuations inserted in
the papers about my loyalty. Presuming this to be one of the allegiations against
me I take this occasion to meet that issue at once; and to brand any one be he who
he may, who dares to say that I am not as loyal to my Country as the most loyal,

to be an unmitigated liar and scoundrel. I am not conscious of having done ought here or elsewhere at any time—on any occassion that could by the remotest chance induce any fair minded Person to suspect my loyality. The charge if made to the Governement against me is an infamous falsehood & Calumny. I renew my request to be furnished with the allegiations against me, with copies of all correspondence. It is due to my age, past service and reputation, to justice to charity, this should be done." Copy, The Filson Club, Louisville, Ky. On Dec. 26, 1861, Smith had written a letter to Brig. Gen. George W. Cullum in which he discussed other charges against him. Copy, *ibid.*

On January 13, 1862, President Abraham Lincoln referred to Cameron a petition bearing the names of Henry S. Lane of Ind., Garrett Davis of Ky., and others, asking for Smith's removal. DNA, RG 107, Register of Letters Received. It is possible that Wallace may have had something to do with the petition. Lane was a fellow townsman of Wallace and his wife's brother-in-law. On Jan. 8, Wallace wrote to Ind. Governor Oliver P. Morton. "Nothing new. 'All quiet in Paducah.' *Gen. Smith is not removed.*" ALS, Wallace Papers, InHi. More evidence that Wallace was part of the effort is contained in a Feb. 19 letter to his wife. "I am now in command of these forts, (Henry and Heiman) with fourteen regiments. In other words, I am acting Major Genl commanding a division. All which is not so satisfactory as the happy riddance of Gen. Smith, which is at last accomplished. He is at Donelson, I here. He left me behind on the marching of the troops, thro' jealousy." ALS, *ibid.* See also General Field Orders No. 12, Feb. 11, 1862.

On Jan. 15, Halleck explained to Thomas that Smith had not been removed because his command, far from being disgruntled, was "reported in the best discipline and order of any one in the Department." He wrote further that partisans of another officer, probably Paine, had attempted for several months to remove him, and that USG agreed that Smith should remain. "This was done for the purpose of having him removed to give place for another aspirant, who, by all accounts, is totally unfit for any command." ALS, DNA, RG 94, Letters Received. *O.R.*, I, vii, 929. On Jan. 21, Halleck again wrote to Thomas. This time he buttressed his case for Smith's efficiency by forwarding an extract from a report on Smith's command by Capt. John P. Hawkins, inspecting commissary officer. "The condition of the Dept. at Paducah is superior to that of any place I have visited—I ascribe this to the watchfulness of Genl. C. F. Smith Commdg, ably seconded by the Commissary of Subsistence, Capt Cox" Copy, DNA, RG 94, Letters Received.

General Field Orders No. 12

Head Quarters, Dist. of Cairo
Fort Henry, Ten. Feb.y 11th 1862.

GEN. FIELD ORDERS NO 12

The troops designated in Gen. Field Orders No 9,[1] will move to-morrow as rapidly as possible in the following order:

One Brigade of the 1st Division will move by the Telegraph

road directly upon Fort Donaldson, halting for further orders, at a distance of two miles from the fort. The other Brigades of the 1st Division will move by the Dover, or ridge, road, and halt at the same distance from the fort, and through out troops so as to form a continuous line between the two wings.

The two Brigades of the 2d Division, now at Fort Henry, will follow as rapidly as practicable by the Dover road and will be followed by the troops from Fort Heiman, as fast as they can be ferried across the river.

One Brigade of the 2d Division should be thrown into Dover to cut off all retreat by the river, if found practicable to do so.

The force of the enemy being so variously reported it is impossible to give exact details of attack but the necessary orders will be given on the field.

> By Order of Brig. Gen. U. S. Grant, Com
> JNO. A. RAWLINS
> Asst. Adjut General.

AD (in USG's hand), McClernand Papers, IHi. Copies of the same orders, numbered General Field Orders No. 11, are in DLC-USG, V, 12, 13, 14, 95; DNA, RG 393, USG General Orders. *O.R.*, I, vii, 605. See letter to Brig. Gen. John A. McClernand, Feb. 11, 1862. On Feb. 11, 1862, Capt. John A. Rawlins wrote to Capt. Algernon S. Baxter. "You will furnish one four horse or mule team and driver, early tomorrow morning, to transport the baggage of the Hd. Qrs. on the Fort. Donelson expedition." Copies, DLC-USG, V, 1, 2, 3, 85; DNA, RG 393, USG Letters Sent.

1. On Feb. 10, Rawlins issued General Field Orders No. 9. "The troops from Forts Henry and Heiman will hold themselves in readiness to move on Wednesday morning, the 12th inst, at as early an hour as practicable. Neither tents nor baggage will be taken, except such as the troops can carry. Brigade and Regimental Commanders will see that all their men are supplied with forty rounds of ammunition in their Cartridge boxes, and two days rations in their Haversacks. Three days additional rations may be put in wagons to follow the expedition, but will not impede the march of the main column. Two Regiments of Infantry will remain at Fort Henry, to be designated from the First Division and one Brigade at Fort Heiman Ky. to be designated by General Smith Com'd'g" DS, McClernand Papers, IHi; Brayman Papers, ICHi. Copies of the same orders, numbered General Field Orders No. 7, are in DLC-USG, V, 12, 13, 14, 95; DNA, RG 393, USG General Orders. *O.R.*, I, vii, 601. On Feb. 11, Brig. Gen. Lewis Wallace wrote to his wife. "The whole force, except my brigade, marched this morning to attack Ft. Donelson. Through old Smith, I am left behind in command of this Fort and Ft. Henry. Nice arrangement! I have been sick from rage since yesterday. Still I cannot repress my anxiety about the expedition. It is wonderful how little

we know in advance of the condition of the enemy. The force at the Fort is represented as between 12 & 20.000. It will turn out, I think, that it will not exceed eight thousand. . . . My patience with old Smith is now 'played out.' I have been too modest and patient. He has abused both. I will change policy—in fact, have done so." ALS, Wallace Papers, InHi. On the same day, Capt. William S. Hillyer wrote to Wallace. "I received your note on my return from an expedition up the river—I was surprized to hear that you were to be left behind—and so was *Gen Grant*—He designed in arranging the troops to give you a Division, but said he could not do so and throw your old Brigade into it, and he supposed you would not desire to be seperated from your old Brigade, for which he knew you had a great affection—~~Gen Smith~~ He left to Gen McClernand and Gen Smith to designate the forces to be left behind—He told me to day that he would give you a Division as soon as the new troops arrive and that he would see that you should have a good position in the next fight. Let me beg of you as your friend that you keep quiet for a day or two—and you will have a position that will suit you *in every particular—having no intermediate commander*. Be assured that you have my warmest condolence, and had I thought it possible that a General would be left behind and 7 colonels ordered forward I should have made a more active effort to change it. P. S. 'All things work together for those &c'—This thing will operate to your advantage—Gen Grant has given positive assurance to me that you shall have a Division in a few days—Donnelson will be only the first *skirmish*. You will be in at *the tug of war—*" ALS, *ibid.*

To Maj. Gen. Henry W. Halleck

BY TELEGRAPH FROM Ft Henry via Cairo
[*Feb.*] 11th *1862*

To MAJ GEN HALLECK

Every effort will be put forth to have Clarksville[1] within a few days   there are no Negros in this part of the Count[ry] to work on Fortifications

U. S. GRANT
Brig Genl

Telegram received, DNA, RG 94, Generals' Papers and Books, Telegrams Received by Gen. Halleck; copy, *ibid.*, RG 393, Dept. of the Mo., Telegrams Received. *O.R.*, I, vii, 604. On Feb. 8, 1862, Maj. Gen. Henry W. Halleck wrote to USG. "If possible, destroy the bridge at Clarksville; it is of vital importance & should be attempted at all hazards. Shovels & picks will be sent you to strengthen Fort Henry. The guns should be transferred & arranged so as to resist an attack by land. The redan on south bank should be arranged for the same object. Some of the guns from Fort Holt will be sent up. Reinforcements will reach you daily. Hold on to Fort Henry at all hazards. Impress ~~all~~ slaves of secessionists in vicinity to work on fortifications. It is of vital importance to strengthen your position as rapidly as possible. Where slaves are so impressed they should be kept under guard & not allowed to communicate with the enemy; nor must they be allowed to escape. Where supplies are taken from union men they should be paid either in money or proper vouchers; where taken from secessionists, they must be receipted for and duly taken up on the proper returns. You must cut the enemy's telegraph lines wherever you can. Keep me informed of all you do, as often as you can write & telegraph." ALS, DNA, RG 94, Generals' Papers and Books, Henry W. Halleck, Letters Sent (Press). *O.R.*, I, vii, 595–96. On the same day, Halleck telegraphed to USG substantially the same instructions. ALS (telegram sent), DNA, RG 107, Telegrams Collected (Unbound). Copies of the same telegram, misdated Feb. 10, are in DLC-USG, V, 4, 5, 7, 8, 9; DNA, RG 393, USG Hd. Qrs. Correspondence. *O.R.*, I, vii, 600.

    1. Clarksville, Tenn., on the Cumberland River, about thirty-eight miles upriver from Fort Donelson.

To Brig. Gen. John A. McClernand

Head Quarters, Dist. of Cairo
Fort Henry, Ten. Feb.y 11th 1862.

GEN. J. A. MCCLERNAND
COMD.G 1ST DIV.
GEN.

    The 2d Cavalry and three batteries of rifled guns belong to the 2 Division[.] These three batteries are all the Artillery Gen. Smith can take with him and the two companies of 2d Cavalry, and two of regulars, was all that he had of that arm of service until ~~until~~ a battalion addition was attached this morning.

    Col. Cook with his Brigade will follow immediately in rear of the 1st Division, on the ridge road, so that practically the guns spoken of will be along with your command.

    It only becomes necessary that Brigades should be composed of all arms of service when they act independently. As parts of a Division it is well to have one Brigade exclusively Infantry.

Respectfully
your obt. svt.
U. S. GRANT
Brig. Gen. Com

ALS, ICHi. On Feb. 11, 1862, Brig. Gen. John A. McClernand wrote to USG. "The 3rd Brigade of the 1st Division is without ~~both~~ either Cavalry and Artillery. I have ordered one battery of 20 pdrs. of Maj Cavender's Battallion to join the brigade, also two companies of 2nd Cavalry, here; and the two companies of Regular Cavalry now with the 2nd Cavalry, subject to your approval. Please advise me at the earliest moment, as my dispositions will be affected by your decision. It is desirable that an additional battery of heavy pieces from the same Battallion should be attached to what will be my advance brigade on the 'Ridge Road.' Leaving the 32nd and 43rd Regiments of the 3rd Brigade of the 1st Division behind according to your order, I will move the 2nd Brigade on the 'Telegraph Road' instead of the 3rd Brigade—sending the latter in the rear of the 1st Brigade on the 'Ridge Road.' I hope these dispositions will meet with your approbation. . . . P. S. Field order No. 12., issued by you, is just received and will be attended. You will discover, however, that this communication proposes a slight modification." LS, DNA, RG 393, District of Cairo, Letters Received. See General Field Orders No. 12, Feb. 11, 1862.

To Maj. Gen. Henry W. Halleck

By TELEGRAPH FROM Ft Henry
[*Feb.*] 12th via Cairo 13th *1862*

To GEN HALLECK

We start this morning for Fort Donaldson in heavy force.[1]

Four Regts from Buell's command and two from St Louis arrived last night, and were sent around by water.[2]

I hope to send you a despatch from Fort Donaldson tomorrow.[3]

U. S. GRANT
Brig Genl.

Telegram received, DNA, RG 94, Generals' Papers and Books, Telegrams Received by Gen. Halleck; copy (misdated Feb. 14, 1862), *ibid.*, RG 393, Dept. of the Mo., Telegrams Received. *O.R.*, I, vii, 612.

    1. See General Field Orders No. 12, Feb. 11, 1862.
    2. On Feb. 8, Maj. Gen. Henry W. Halleck telegraphed to Brig. Gen. George W. Cullum that the brigade being sent to Smithland by Brig. Gen. Don Carlos Buell should be sent "up the Tennessee to Grant." ALS (telegram sent), DNA, RG 107, Telegrams Collected (Unbound); copy, *ibid.*, RG 94, Generals' Papers and Books, Telegrams Sent in Cipher by Gen. Halleck. *O.R.*, I, vii, 596. On Feb. 11, Capt. John A. Rawlins wrote to Col. Charles Cruft, 31st Ind. "You

will proceed with your Brigade, consisting of the 31st Indiana, 25th Kentucky, 44th Indiana, and 17th Kentucky. Volunteers to Fort Doneldson, by way of the Cumberland, on the Steamers you are now embarked on. You will not pass the Gun Boats, already directed to precede you. It is expected that the Troops from Fort Henry will arrive near Fort Doneldson to-morrow evening, ready to commence the engagement on the following morning. The force going by water should effect a landing as near the Fort as practicable, and be in readiness to co-operate with the forces from here." LS, DNA, RG 393, Dept. of the Mo., Telegrams Received. On the same day, Rawlins wrote substantially the same thing to Col. Silas D. Baldwin, 57th Ill. Copies, DLC-USG, V, 1, 2, 3, 85; DNA, RG 393, USG Letters Sent. Also on the same day, Rawlins wrote substantially the same thing to Col. John M. Thayer, 1st Neb., but added "Each Regiment, will be under ~~their~~ its immediate Commander, the Senior officer however, taking direction of the whole, until Brigaded by orders from these Head Quarters. . . . P. S. Col. John M. Thayer will assume command of all the forces preceding, and directed in the above order to proceed to Fort Donelson, by way of the Cumberland, on river transports, until further orders." Copies, *ibid.*

3. On Feb. 13, Halleck telegraphed to Buell that USG would attack Fort Donelson on Feb. 13 or Feb. 14. He added: "Why not come down and take the immediate command of the cumberland column yourself? If so, I will transfer Sherman & Grant to the Tenn. column." ALS (telegram sent), *ibid.*, RG 107, Telegrams Collected (Unbound). *O.R.*, I, vii, 609. On Feb. 11, Halleck had telegraphed to Buell. "Cant you come with all your available forces and command the column up the cumberland. I shall go to the Tennessee this week." ALS (telegram sent), DNA, RG 107, Telegrams Collected (Unbound). *O.R.*, I, vii, 605. On Feb. 12, Halleck telegraphed to Buell. "If you conclude to lead the column on the cumberland, come at once with your spare forces." ALS (telegram sent), DNA, RG 107, Telegrams Collected (Unbound). *O.R.*, I, vii, 607.

On Feb. 7, Maj. Gen. George B. McClellan had suggested by telegram to Halleck that either he or Buell should take command of the Cumberland expedition. *Ibid.*, p. 591. On Feb. 8, Halleck wrote to McClellan. "I have considered, with due deliberation, that part of your telegram of yesterday in relation to Genl. Buell's coming to the Cumberland river & taking command of the expedition against Nashville. Genl. Sherman ranks Genl. Buell, & he is entitled to a command in that direction—I propose, with due deference to your better judgement, the following plan as calculated to produce unity of action, & to avoid any difficulties about rank & command: create a *Geographical Division*, to be called '*Western Division*,' or any other suitable name, & to be composed of three Depts., viz: 'Dept. of the 'Missouri,' including the present Dept of Kansas, & the states of Minnesota, Iowa, Missouri, & Arkansas; 'Dept. of the Mississippi,' including the remainder of the present Dept. of the Missouri, & West Tennessee; 'Dept. of the Ohio,' to be the same as at present with the addition of East Tennessee—If we penetrate into Alabama or Mississippi, they can be assigned according to circumstances—Genl. Buel would then retain his present command with a small addition; Genl Hunter could take the new 'Dept. of the Missouri,' which, I have no doubt, would be more agreeable to him than his present position, and Genl. Hitchcock if you can get him appointed, could take the new 'Dept. of the Mississippi—' I have no desire for any larger command than I have now; but it seems to me that this would produce greater concert of action, give more satisfaction to Genl. Hunter, & economize your labor, as all your orders for the West, would then go through a single channel—Moreover, where troops of different Depts. act together, as they must on the Cumberland & Tennessee, & on the frontiers of Kansas, Missouri, & Arkansas, they would be under one general head. This would avoid any clashing of interests, or difference of plans & policy. I make these suggestions for your consideration. If Genl. Hitchcock cannot be appointed, Genl. Sherman could take the Dept. of the Mississippi—His health is greatly improved." LS, DNA, RG 94, Letters Received. *O.R.*, I, vii, *595*. On the same day, Halleck telegraphed to Secretary of War Edwin M. Stanton. "Brig Genls Sherman, Pope, Grant, Curtis, Hurlbut, Sigel, Prentiss & McClernand, are all in this Dept, are of same date and each unwilling to serve under the other. If Brig Genl E. A. Hitchcock could be made Major Genl of vols & assigned to this Dept., it would satisfy all & reconcile all differences. If it can be done there should be no delay, as an experienced officer of high rank is wanted immediately on the Tennessee line." ALS (telegram sent), Ritzman Collection, Aurora College, Aurora, Ill. *O.R.*, I, vii, *594*. As early as Jan. 24, Halleck had urged that Ethan Allen Hitchcock be appointed a maj. gen. Hitchcock diary, Feb. 20, 1862, Hitchcock Papers, Gilcrease Institute, Tulsa, Okla. On Feb. 2, Hitchcock wrote. "Genl. Halleck told me this morning that he had received a letter from Gen. McClellan and that I would 'certainly' be appointed a Major General—of volunteers, I suppose of course, as there are no vacancies in the regular army. This news does not please me." *Ibid.* According to W. A. Croffut, ed., *Fifty Years in Camp and Field: Diary of Major-General Ethan Allen Hitchcock, U. S. A.* (New York and London, 1909), p. 434, on Feb. 5, Bvt. Lt. Gen. Winfield Scott informed Hitchcock that he would be appointed a maj. gen. and replace USG in command of operations on the Tennessee and Cumberland rivers. No entry for this date is in the Hitchcock diary, Gilcrease Institute; Scott was then retired. On Feb. 10, Hitchcock was confirmed. *Senate Executive Journal*, XII, 115. On Feb. 12, Brig. Gen. William T. Sherman wrote to his wife from Benton Barracks, Mo. "Gen Hitchcock first declined peremptorily his appointmt but the pressure on him was so great that he has accepted but will remain in St Louis and Halleck will go to Paducah. I saw him last night and he said we would all go down very soon. how soon I cannot tell." ALS, Sherman Family Papers, InNd. See General Orders No. 1, Feb. 17, 1862. On Feb. 17, Halleck asked McClellan to telegraph Hitchcock of his appointment and assignment to the Dept. of the Mo. *O.R.*, I, vii, *628*. On Feb. 20, Hitchcock declined the appointment on grounds of ill health. Hitchcock diary, Gilcrease Institute. Eventually he accepted the appointment, but served in the War Dept. in Washington.

To Brig. Gen. Lewis Wallace

Head Quarters, Dist of Cairo.
Fort. Henry, Febry 12th 1862.

GEN. L. WALLACE.
COMMDG FORTS HEIMAN AND HENRY
GENL.

You will cause the first troops arriving here to debark on the Ky. side of the river, until three Regts of Infantry and at least one Company of Artillery are there. Directions should then be left for all other troops arriving to debark at Fort. Henry.

You will hold your Brigade in readiness to follow the advance, and to assume command of a Division, which will be composed of new arrivals, six Regiments of which have already been sent around by the Cumberland, where orders may reach you.

Should no Artillery arrive one Company of what you now have will be left.

Respectfully,
Your Obt. Servant
U. S. GRANT.
Brig. Gen. Commdg.

Copies, DLC-USG, V, 1, 2, 3, 85; DNA, RG 393, USG Letters Sent. On Feb. 11, 1862, Capt. John A. Rawlins issued Special Field Orders No. 6. "Brig. Gen. L. Wallace having been designated to remain behind, during the expedition ~~upon~~ against Fort Donelson, will assume command of all the Forces at Fort. Heiman and Fort Henry. He will encamp all Troops arriving ~~will be placed in camp~~ to the best advantage for self-defense, ~~under the immediate instructions of the Commdg Officer of Forts Henry & Heiman~~" Copies, DLC-USG, V, 15, 16, 82, 89; DNA, RG 393, USG Special Orders. *O.R.*, I, vii, 606. On Feb. 12, Rawlins issued Special Field Orders No. 7. "The two companies of regular Cavalry "C" and "I" of the 2nd Brigade, 2nd Division, will immediately return to Fort Henry, and report to Gen L. Wallace for ~~instructions~~ orders" Copies, DLC-USG, V, 15, 16, 82, 89; DNA, RG 393, USG Special Orders.

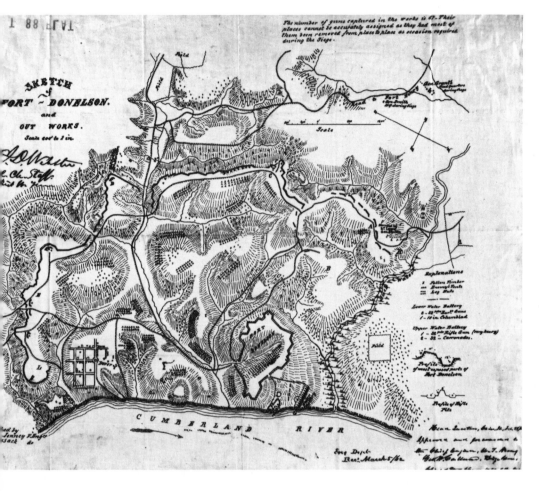

Fort Donelson
Courtesy National Archives

To Maj. Gen. Henry W. Halleck

———

Near Fort Donaldson Feb. 13/62

GEN. HALLECK.

Send all troops to arrive to Fort Henry. They can be transferred here if required, and there is now, appearance that that point is in danger. One gun-boat should be there.

U. S. GRANT.
Brig. Gen.

Telegram, copy, DNA, RG 393, Dept. of the Mo., Telegrams Received. *O.R.*,
I, vii, 609.

To Maj. Gen. Henry W. Halleck

———

Near Ft. Donaldson via Cairo,
14th [*13*] Feb. 1862.

MAJ. GEN. HALLECK.

Floyd[1] arrived at Donaldson, today with four thousand men. Genls. Johnson,[2] Buckner, Floyd and Pillow are said to be there. I have but one gun-boat today.[3] We have had considerable skirmishing, losing some ten or twelve killed, and about one hundred and twenty wounded. Rebel loss probably much heavier. I am hourly looking for more gun-boats and reinforcements.[4]

U. S. GRANT.
Brig. Gen.

Telegram, copy, DNA, RG 393, Dept. of the Mo., Telegrams Received. *O.R.*,
I, vii, 613. This telegram was probably dated Feb. 13, 1862, for the gunboats arrived during the night of Feb. 13. See letter to Maj. Gen. Henry W. Halleck, Feb. 14, 1862.
   1. John B. Floyd, a Va. Democrat, had been governor of his state, and under President James Buchanan had been secretary of war, a position from which he resigned on Dec. 29, 1860. After Va. seceded, Floyd raised a brigade, entered the Va. military service, and, on Aug. 28, 1861, he was confirmed as a C. S. A. brig. gen. On Feb. 12, 1862, Gen. Albert Sidney Johnston ordered Floyd to Fort

Donelson where he arrived before daylight on Feb. 13. *DAB*, VI, 482–83; *O.R.*, I, vii, 267; *ibid.*, I, lii, part 2, 271.

2. Bushrod R. Johnson of Ohio, USMA 1840, resigned from the army in 1847 and in 1848 joined the staff of the Western Military Institute of Ky., which was later absorbed by the University of Nashville. In May, 1861, Johnson received a commission as a maj. in the Tenn. militia, and later, as col., commanding engineers in the Tenn. Provisional Army, he participated in the site selection and construction of Fort Henry and Fort Donelson. Appointed a C. S. A. brig. gen. on Jan. 24, 1862, and assigned to command of Fort Donelson on Feb. 7, he was superseded by Brig. Gen. Gideon J. Pillow on Feb. 9. Charles M. Cummings, "Forgotten Man at Fort Donelson: Bushrod Rust Johnson," *Tennessee Historical Quarterly*, XXVII, 4 (Winter, 1968), 380–81.

3. The *Carondelet*.

4. On Feb. 13, Brig. Gen. John A. McClernand wrote to USG. "A prisoner taken last night reports that some of our Gun boats were seen near here yesterday Col. Oglesby's Brigade is considerably extended towards Dover He thinks a large force of the enemy is between him and the river and so reports to me and also that they have been intrenching themselves there and at work all night His position is necessarily somewhat embarrassed by the thick brush and the timber I will order forward at daylight the balance of my Division to join his left for the purpose of supporting him, which will vacate the hights on the left of Indian Cr. near the redoubt. These hights ought to be immediately occupied A Battery of 20 pounders might be so disposed to the right or left as to obstruct the retreat of the enemy Without asking for any information not proper to be communicated, I would be pleased to be advised of any plan of operations and attack which you may have digested and decided upon" Copy, Brayman Papers, ICHi.

To Brig. Gen. John A. McClernand

Feb.y 13th 1862

GEN. MCCLERNAND
COMD.G 1ST DIV.

A dispatch just rec'd from below informs me that four gunboats and ten steamers[1] have left for the Cumberland river. Men on the left have charged up to the Abattis but found it impossible to get through.[2]—No word yet from the gun boats here.[3]

Respectfully &c.
U. S. GRANT
Brig. Gen.

ALS, McClernand Papers, IHi.

1. See letter to Maj. Gen. Henry W. Halleck, Feb. 14, 1862.

2. On the morning of Feb. 13, 1862, Brig. Gen. Charles F. Smith ordered the left wing of the 4th Brigade, 2nd Division, under Col. Jacob G. Lauman, to advance toward the enemy. After reaching the abatis, Lauman's troops were forced to fall back under heavy fire. *O.R.*, I, lii, part 1, 7–9.

3. Apparently only one gunboat—the *Carondelet*—was in the vicinity of Fort Donelson at the time. See following letter.

To Commander Henry Walke

————

Head Quarters, Camp in the field
Near Fort Donelson, Feb 13th 1862

Capt. Walke

Comdg Carondelet Flotilla

I arrived here yesterday and succeeded in getting positions almost entirely investing the enemies works. Most of our batteries are now established and the remainder soon will be. If you will advance with your gun boats. at 10 Oclock A.M, we will be ready to take any advantage of every diversion in our favor.

> Respectfully
> your Obt Sevt.
> U S Grant
> Brig Genl.

Copy, DNA, RG 45, Correspondence of Henry Walke. *O.R.* (Navy), I, xxii, 594. On Feb. 15, 1862, Commander Henry Walke, "near Fort Donelson," wrote to Flag Officer Andrew H. Foote. "I arrived here (towed by the *Alps*) on the 12th instant, about 11:20 a.m., and seeing or hearing nothing of our army, I threw a few shell into Fort Donelson to announce my arrival to General Grant, as he had previously desired. I then dropped down the river a few miles and anchored for the night, waiting General Grant's arrival. On the morning of the 13th instant, I weighed anchor and came again to this place, when I received a dispatch from General Grant notifying me of his arrival the day before, and succeeded in getting position almost entirely investing the enemy's works. 'Most of our batteries' (he writes) 'are [now] established, and the remainder soon will be. If you will advance with your gunboats at 10 o'clock a.m., we will be ready to take advantage of every diversion in our favor.' I immediately complied with these instructions by throwing some 139 15-second and 10-second shell into the fort, receiving on return the enemy's fire from all their batteries, most of their shot passing over us, and but two striking us, one of which was 128 pounds solid [shot]. It passed through our port casemate forward, glancing over our barricade at the boilers, and again over the steam drum, it struck and, bursting our steam heater, fell into the engine room without striking any person, although the splinters wounded slightly some half dozen of the crew. I then dropped down to this anchorage, but, the sound of distant firing being heard, we again attacked the fort, throwing in some 45 shell and receiving but little damage. I returned to this place to await for further orders, when I received a second dispatch from General Grant that you were expected on the following morning." *Ibid.*, pp. 587–88. See following letter.

To Commander Henry Walke

————

Head Quarters near Fort Donelson
Feb 13th 1862

Capt Walke
Capt
    A dispatch just received states that four more gunboats are on their way from Cairo. Will probably arrive to morrow morning.
Respectfully &c
U S Grant.
Brig Genl.

P. S. We are dowing well on the land side   how are you.

Copy, DNA, RG 45, Correspondence of Henry Walke.

To Julia Dent Grant

————

Near Fort Donaldson Ten
Feb. 13th 1862

Dear Julia.
    I am still well and out side the fort. We have a large force to condend against but I expect to accomplish their subjugation. Do not look for it for three days yet however. To-day our loss

has probably been 120 wounded and 12 or 15 killed. The enemies works are large embracing probably 1000 acres. Kiss the children for me.

ULYS.

ALS, DLC-USG.

To Absalom H. Markland

———

Head Quarters, &c.
[*Feb. 13, 1862*]

MARKLAND,
SPECIAL MAIL AGT.

Send the Mail steamer as soon as possible after receiving this.

All is well here but we have a powerful force. Johnson, Buckner Floyd and Pillow are all said to be here.

U. S. GRANT.

(ALS facsimile?), Herman Dieck, *The Most Complete and Authentic History of the Life and Public Services of General U. S. Grant, "The Napoleon of America"* (Boston, 1885), facing p. 152. *O.R.*, I, vii, 609. The handwriting of the facsimile is not exactly that of USG, but bears a strong resemblance, suggesting that the original document may have been traced or copied in order to prepare a facsimile. Below the facsimile is printed a statement of USG, dated May 3, 1867. "This was written from the front of Fort Donelson the 13th or 14th of February, 1862. After the words 'powerful force' the words 'in front of us' should have followed." Absalom H. Markland, born in Clark County, Ky., had been a classmate of USG at Maysville Seminary, Maysville, Ky., and had lived in Maysville and Paducah. In 1849, he went to Washington, D. C., where he became an employee of the Office of Indian Affairs for a time. About the time USG assumed command at Cairo, in the fall of 1861, Markland was sent there as a special agent of the Post Office Dept. with instructions to investigate and remove postmasters, and others connected with the postal service, who were disloyal to the U. S. In early Feb., 1862, while en route to the attack on Fort Henry, aboard the *New Uncle Sam*, USG and Markland discussed the possibility of organizing mail service for troops in the field. *New York Times*, Feb. 16, 1885; *Report of the Proceedings of the Society of the Army of the Tennessee, at the Twenty-First Meeting, held at Toledo, Ohio, September 5th and 6th, 1888* (Cincinnati, 1893), pp. 179–80; Arthur Hecht, "Union Military Mail Service," *The Filson Club History Quarterly*, 37, 3 (July, 1963), 238. On Feb. 6, Capt. John A. Rawlins issued Special Field Orders No. 1.

"A. H. Markland, Esq, Special U. S. Mail Agent, will take charge of all mail matter from and to ~~the camp~~ the troops composing the present expedition, and make such arrangements as he may be authorized by the Department to make, to forward the same ~~as addressed~~. All Government Boats are commanded to ~~take~~ carry all mail matter ~~directed by Agt. Markland, or persons duly authorized by him,~~ and ~~to carry~~ such persons as may have charge of the same, free, to any point where such boats may be plying." Copies, DLC-USG, V, 15, 16, 82, 89; DNA, RG 393, USG Special Orders. *O.R.*, I, vii, 586. On Feb. 11, Rawlins issued General Field Orders No. 10. "Here after there will be a daily line of steamers between this place and Cairo, running as follows, to wit: Leaving at 10 o'clock A. M. each terminous; and touching at all intermidate military posts, taking on the mails. Two good boats will be put on the line for this purpose, and the regular Cairo and Paducah steamers will be discontinued." Copies, DLC-USG, V, 12, 13, 14, 95; DNA, RG 393, USG General Orders. Instructions to Markland from the Post Office Dept. are in *O.R.*, I, x, part 2, 3–4.

General Field Orders No. 14

Head Quarters, Army in the Field
Camp Near Donaldson, Feb. 14th/62

GEN. ~~ORDER~~ FIELD ORDERS NO 14

The 46th, 57th & 58th regiments Ill. Vol. Infantry, and ~~one Squadron of~~ 2d Battalion of Curtis horse[1] will constitute the 2d Brigade 3d Division Army in the Field. The Senior Col. will command.[2]

The 3d Brigade will be composed of the 1st Nebraska, 58th 76th and 78th Ohio and one Battalion of Curtis horse, Commanded by Senior Col.[3]

The 1st Brigade will remain as organized under Gen. Buell[4] and is composed of the 17th and 25th Kentucky and 31st and 44th Ia[5] regiments, Col. Cruft commanding.[6]

Brig. Gen. L. Wallace will command the 3d Division of the Army in the Field.[7]

By Order
U. S. GRANT
Brig. Gen. Com

ADS, Wallace Papers, InHi. Copies of the same orders, numbered General Field Orders No. 12, are in DLC-USG, V, 12, 13, 14, 95; DNA, RG 393, USG General Orders.

1. On Dec. 18, 1861, by Special Orders No. 74, Dept. of the Mo., Brig. Gen. Samuel R. Curtis was ordered to organize the Curtis Horse at Benton Barracks, Mo., later the 5th Iowa Cav., composed of existing cos. from Iowa, Minn., Mo., and Neb. On Feb. 11, 1862, the regt. arrived at Fort Henry. See letter to Col. William W. Lowe, March 11, 1862.

2. Brig. Gen. Lewis Wallace, commander of the 3rd Division, attached the 2nd Brigade to the 3rd Brigade. *O.R.*, I, vii, 236.

3. Col. John M. Thayer, 1st Neb., commanded the 3rd Brigade, although, on Feb. 14, Capt. John A. Rawlins issued Special Field Orders No. 8, transferring the 1st Neb. to the 2nd Brigade. Copies, DLC-USG, V, 15, 16, 82, 89; DNA, RG 393, USG Special Orders.

4. Brig. Gen. Don Carlos Buell. See telegram to Maj. Gen. Henry W. Halleck, Feb. 12, 1862, note 2.

5. USG's abbreviation for Indiana.

6. Charles Cruft of Terre Haute, Ind., graduated from Wabash College in 1842, and practiced law before becoming president of the Terre Haute and Alton Railroad in 1855. On Sept. 20, 1861, he was appointed col., 31st Ind.

7. On Feb. 13, 1862, Wallace wrote to his wife. "It is 12 o'clock at night. I have just recd orders to march two Regiments to Ft. Donelson. The regts selected are the 8th Mo. and the 11th Ind. A desperate fight has been going on there till late to night, with no result. Buckner, Johnson, Pillow and ~~Polk~~ Floyd are present. If we win, this rebellion goes under at once, and there shall be no such word as fail." ALS, Wallace Papers, InHi.

To Maj. Gen. Henry W. Halleck

———

Near Fort Donelson Ten.
Feb.y 14th 1862.

GEN. H. W. HALLECK
COMD.G DEPT. OF THE MO.
ST. LOUIS, MO.
GEN.

Five Gun boats & twelve transports arrived this morning[1] and will materially strenthen us. The enemy have been receiving heavy reinforcements every night since the investment commenced. They are now all driven inside their outer works which however cover an extensive area. It was impossible, in consequence of the high water and deep sloughs to throw a force in above Dover to cut off these reinforcements. Any force sent for such a purpose would be entirely away from support from the main body.[2]

Last night was very severe upon the troops. At dusk it commenced raining and in a short time turned cold and changed to snow and sleet. This morning the thermometer indicated 20° below freezing.

Respectfully
your obt. svt.
U. S. GRANT
Brig. Gen.

ALS, DNA, RG 393, Dept. of the Mo., Letters Received. *O.R.*, I, vii, 613. On Feb. 14, 1862, USG telegraphed the substance of this letter to Maj. Gen. Henry W. Halleck. "Our troops now invest the works of Fort Donaldson. The enemy have been driven into their works at every point. A heavy abattis all around prevents carrying the works by storm at present. I feel every confidence of success, and the best feeling prevails among the men." Copy, DNA, RG 393, Dept. of the Mo., Telegrams Received. *O.R.*, I, vii, 613.

1. On Feb. 13, three iron clad gunboats—the *Louisville, St. Louis,* and *Pittsburg*—and two wooden gunboats—the *Conestoga* and *Tyler*—arrived at a point two miles downriver from Fort Donelson at midnight and tied up near the *Carondelet.* The transports arrived a little later. Letter of "Try Again," Cairo, Feb. 16, 1862, in *Missouri Democrat,* Feb. 18, 1862.

2. See telegram to Maj. Gen. Henry W. Halleck, Feb. 13, 1862, note 4.

To Maj. Gen. Henry W. Halleck

Head Quarters, Dist. of Cairo.
Near Fort Donelson, Feb. 14th 1862.

GEN. H. W. HALLECK
COMD.G DEPT. OF THE MO.
ST. LOUIS MO.
GEN.

Your letter of the 4th of Feb.y enquiring by what authority Capt. Baxter, Asst. Qr. Mr. was absent is just received.

I ordered Capt. Baxter to Washington to get funds for the use of this District. His mission was successful he geting $150,000 which by the way was most of it taken, by Capt. Turnley's orders, immediately upon his return, and applied differently from what was intended.

Every effort has been made to get funds for this Military District through the Chief Quartermaster in St. Louis, without success, and although departing from strict Military rule I deemed the urgency of the case justified the step taken. I should however have reported the fact at once and would have done so but did not think of it.

> Respectfully
> your obt. svt.
> U. S. GRANT
> Brig. Gen.

ALS, DNA, RG 393, Dept. of the Mo., Letters Received. On Feb. 4, 1862, Maj. Gen. Henry W. Halleck had written to USG. "[It] is reported to me that Capt A. S. Baxter has left his duties as Qrmaster in your district & gone to Washington. By whose authority has he done this? If Capt. Baxter is absent without leave, arrest him on his return. Also report the facts of the case." ALS, *ibid.*, RG 94, Generals' Papers and Books, Henry W. Halleck, Letters Sent (Press). On Feb. 4, Brig. Gen. Montgomery C. Meigs telegraphed to Maj. Robert Allen. "Telegram of Feb. 3d relative to draft in favor of Capt. Baxter Q Mr. at Cairo, referred to Secrety of the Treasury I have urged prompt action in the matter" LS (telegram sent), *ibid.*, RG 107, Telegrams Collected (Unbound). On Feb. 5, Meigs telegraphed to Halleck. "A requisition for $150.000 for services in the Quarter-Master's Department at Cairo, was made under orders of the Secretary of War in favor of Captain Baxter upon his urgent representations to the President and Secretary of the absolute necessity of sending funds to Cairo. As Capt. Turnley has now been assigned to the charge of that post, I advise you to send orders to Capt Baxter to turn over these funds to Capt. Turnley as soon as they are received." LS (telegram sent), *ibid.* See letter to Elihu B. Washburne, Jan. 23, 1862. On Feb. 19, Capt. Nathaniel H. McLean wrote to USG. "I am instructed by the Major General Commanding to say that, your sending Capt Baxter Asst Qr Master to Washington was irregular, unauthorized, and is disapproved; and such things must not be done in future without his authority." ALS, DNA, RG 393, Dept. of the Mo., Letters Sent (Press).

To Brig. Gen. George W. Cullum

Head Quarters, Army in the field
Near Fort Donelson Feb. 14th 1862

GEN. G. W. CULLUM,
COMD.G CAIRO.
GEN.

Special Order No 6 is just received directing Capt. Baxter to be sent back to Cairo to close his Acts, &c. I have to state that Capt. Baxter come up here by order of Capt. Turnley, for a specific purpose, and was to have returned the next day. Being without a Quartermaster I ordered him to remain for the present.[1] I shall now have to retain him until some one is taken to fill his place.

Matters here look favorable in one sense. We have the works of the enemy well invested and they do not seem inclined to come out. They are very strong however being well fortified and having not less than 30,000 troops.[2] All statements places their numbers much higher.[3]

I will direct my dispatches to you in future to be forwarded to the Comd.r of the Dept.

Respectfully
your obt. svt.
U. S. GRANT

P. S. I should have a Com.y of Subsistence here. Capt. W. W. Leland whos leave of absence expired near two weeks ago has not returned.[4]

U. S. G.

ALS, DNA, RG 393, Dept. of the Miss., Letters Received. On Feb. 15, 1862, Brig. Gen. George W. Cullum wrote to USG. "Genl Halleck telegraphs Me that you are assigned to the New Military Dist of West Tenn and Genl W. T. Sherman to relieve you of the charge of this—Another Quartermaster will be sent you in a few days to relieve Capt Baxter. Capt Leland—W. W. asst. Com of Sub was ordered by me on the 13th inst. to report to you for duty in the field without a Moments delay. Go on as you have Commenced in your Glorious work   I expect to learn to Morrow that Ft. Donnelson is ours, and the Centre of the enemy's line is broken, and their right and left Isolated and in retreat leaving no hostile foot on the Soil of Kentucky. You are in the great Strategic line   The telegraphic line is Completed and in working order to Smithland and is being rapidly pushed on to your Head Quarters—Tell Lieut Col McPherson that his Engineers should strengthen the land defences at Fort Henry, and remove his heavy Guns there. I have Sent two 32 pds. from Fort Holt"   Copies, DLC-USG, V, 4, 5, 7, 8, 9; DNA, RG 393, USG Hd. Qrs. Correspondence. *O.R.*, I, vii, 619. On Feb. 14, Maj. Gen. Henry W. Halleck informed Cullum by telegraph of the changes in command organization. ALS (telegram sent), Oglesby Papers, IHi. *O.R.*, I, vii, 614. See General Orders No. 1, Feb. 17, 1862.

1. On Feb. 10, Capt. John A. Rawlins issued General Field Orders No. 6. "Capt. A. S. Baxter, A. Q. M. is hereby appointed Chief Quartermaster, with the Army in the Field. He will accompany Head Quarters, and have special charge of all captured property in addition to such other duties as necessarially pertain to his office." DS, DNA, RG 94, Staff Papers, A. S. Baxter; copies, *ibid.*, RG 393, USG General Orders; DLC-USG, V, 12, 13, 14, 95. On Feb. 19, Cullum wrote to USG. "You will order Captain A. S. Baxter Asst. Quarter Master to report to Capt Turnley at this post with the least possible delay. He is required to close his accounts here, and he cannot act through his clerks here but will in all cases receive his instructions through Capt Turnley the District Quarter Master." ALS, DNA, RG 94, Staff Papers, A. S. Baxter. On Feb. 21, USG wrote to Cullum. "No officer of the Quartermaster's Department has yet reached here to temporarily relieve Capt. Baxter whilst he goes to Cairo to turn over his property there. I nevertheless send him and hope he will be allowed to return as soon as he can possibly turn over his property there." ALS, *ibid.*

2. There is no certainty concerning the number of Confederates at Fort Donelson. In his *Memoirs*, I, 315, USG estimated that there were 21,000 men in the fort on Feb. 15. Adam Badeau, *Military History of Ulysses S. Grant, from April, 1861, to April, 1865* (New York, 1868–81), I, 51*n*–52*n*, gave the number as 21,123. Although Brig. Gen. Gideon J. Pillow claimed that there were never more than 13,000 men in Fort Donelson, Gen. Albert Sidney Johnston estimated that there were 17,000 men in the fort on Feb. 13. *O.R.*, I, vii, 283, 922. An extension of figures for regts. for which numbers are given in C. S. A. reports to others for which figures are lacking tends to support Johnston's estimate. A list of Union and Confederate regts. at Fort Donelson may be found in Robert Underwood Johnson and Clarence Clough Buel, eds., *Battles and Leaders of the Civil War* (New York, 1887), I, 429. After analysis, Thomas L. Livermore, *Numbers & Losses in the Civil War in America: 1861–65* (Bloomington, Ind., 1957), pp. 78–79, accepted USG's estimate of 21,000.

3. On Feb. 15, Halleck telegraphed to Brig. Gen. Don Carlos Buell. "The forces from Bowling Green are concentrating at Clarksville. The garrison of Fort Donaldson is estimated at thirty thousand. Unless I can have more assistance the attack may fail. The place is completely invested, and four sorties have been repulsed. If possible send me more aid. ~~The~~ No more troops can be sent from Cairo without danger from Columbus. The gun boats are all at Fort Donaldson, but we find great difficulty in getting up the Mortar-boats against the currant." ALS (telegram sent), DNA, RG 107, Telegrams Collected (Unbound). *O.R.*, I, vii, 621.

4. On Jan. 20, Rawlins issued Special Orders No. 19, granting Capt. William W. Leland leave of absence for seven days with permission to apply for an additional five days' leave. Copies, DLC-USG, V, 15, 16, 82, 87, 89; DNA, RG 393, USG Special Orders. On Feb. 15, Rawlins issued Special Field Orders No. 9. "1st Lieut W. Pinckard, Regimental Qr Master 9th Ills. Vols is hereby appointed Acting Com. of Sub. ~~for the~~ Army in the field. He will immediately report on board Steamer 'T. H. McGill,' and receipt for such supplies as may be in possession of Capt Cox, C. S. ~~He will be guided in his duties for the present by Special Field Orders No.~~" Copies, *ibid*.

To Julia Dent Grant

Near Fort Donelson, Ten.
Feb.y 14th 1862

DEAR JULIA,

The taking of Fort Donelson bids fair to be a long ~~job~~. The rebels are strongly fortified and are in very heavy force. When this is to end is hard to surmise but I feel confidant of ultimate success.

I see no prospect of going back so I think you had better pack up and go to Covington.[1] You will hear from me, through the papers, one day earl~~y~~ier than where you now are. Draw all the money I have in bank. Ask Captain Du Bar[r]y to take charge of my horse and give all my clothing in charge of one of the clerks ready packed so that I can send for them. Dont send them up here until I send for them.

Turn over the keys of the house to Mrs. Hillyer.[2] ~~and~~ She can turn them over if she should leave either to Mr. Safford[3] or any officer who may take possession.

Take the bedding with you. I shall not want it. The Matress you might leave in charge of the clerk.

Tell Capt. Du Barry that my horse is perfectly gentle and requires spurs.

I have had two or three letters from you since Fred. was sent back. I suppose he reached you all safe.

Give my love to all enquiring friends. Kiss the children for me and accept the same for yourself. I intend no blame shall attach to me whether successful or not. But with the public it would make great difference on not.

Good night

ULYS.

ALS, DLC-USG.

1. See letter to Mary Grant, Feb. 9, 1862.
2. Wife of Capt. William S. Hillyer.
3. Alfred B. Safford, born in Vt., had been a lawyer and merchant in Joliet, Ill., and St. Louis, Mo., before becoming cashier of a Shawneetown, Ill., bank in 1854. In 1858, the bank was moved to Cairo where it became the Cairo City Bank with Safford remaining cashier. USG's Cairo hd. qrs. office was located in the bank. William Henry Perrin, ed., *History of Alexander, Union and Pulaski Counties, Illinois* (Chicago, 1883), 56A–56E; testimony of James C. Smith before the Commission on War Claims at St. Louis (Davis-Holt-Campbell Commission), DNA, RG 217. See letter to Alfred B. Safford, Feb. 21, 1862.

To Brig. Gen. George W. Cullum

———

Head Quarters, Army in the Field
Camp Near Fort Donelson, Feb.y 15th 1862.

GEN. G. W. CULLUM
CHIEF OF STAFF, DEPT. OF THE MO.
CAIRO ILL.
GEN.

I hope you will direct Capt. Turnley to forward the transportation belonging to the troops here as rapidly as possible. It is now almost impossible to get supplies from the landing to where our troops are.

We will soon want ammunition for our 10 & 20 pound Parrot guns; already require it for the 24 pound howitzers. ~~and~~

I have directed my ordnance officer to keep a constant watch upon the supply of ammunition and to take steps in time to avoid a deficiency.[1]

Appearances now indicate that we will have a protracted siege here. The ground is very broken and the fallen timber extending far out from the breast works I fear the result of attempting to carry the place by storm with raw troops. I feel great confidance however of ultimately reducing the place. As yet I have had no batteries thrown up hoping with the aid of the Gunboats to obviate the necessity.[2] The present high water has prevented my extending the right to the river.[3] Col. Webster is now making a reconnoisance with the view of sending a force above the town of Dover to occupy the river bank.

Please inform Gen. Halleck the substance of this.

> Respectfully
> your obt. svt.
> U. S. GRANT
> Brig. Gen.

ALS, DNA, RG 393, Dept. of the Mo., Letters Received. Copies of this letter, dated Feb. 14, 1862, are in DLC-USG, V, 4, 5, 7, 8, 9; DNA, RG 393, USG Hd. Qrs. Correspondence. *O.R.*, I, vii, 613–14. On Feb. 16, Brig. Gen. George W. Cullum wrote to USG. "Glad to have Your encouraging letter of Yesterday which I will forward to Genl Halleck. Dont be rash for having the place Completely invested   You can afford to have a little patience   I have ordered all the transportation I can lay my hands upon. The ammunition you want is not here, and Scarce any ordinance Stores of any kind. I have sent an urgent Telegram to Genl Halleck. You must not Keep the Steamers I send up to You or Ill be deprived of all Means of Supplying you with troops ammunition Forage Wood &c   every boat I have taken and am wooding everything but there are No Steamers now disposable" Copies, DLC-USG, V, 4, 5, 7, 8, 9; DNA, RG 393, USG Hd. Qrs. Correspondence. Dated Feb. 15 in *O.R.*, I, vii, 619.

1. On Feb. 12, Cullum wrote to USG. "Like yourself I am most to[o] busy to write a word. I am now sending every thing up the Cumberland by Gen. Halleck's direction.—Flag Officer Foote left at 9 last night with three armored gun boats and must now be on the way to Fort Donelson, which with their aid I hope to hear you have taken in a few days, and the back-bone of secession broken. I am sending re-inforcements up very fast.—Let me know your wants. I will write Lt. Col. McPherson in a short time." ALS, DNA, RG 393, District of West Tenn., Letters Received. *O.R.*, I, vii, 608.

2. See following letter.

3. On Feb. 15, Capt. William S. Hillyer wrote to Brig. Gen. John A. McClernand. "You will if practicable push on a portion of your column to the river, otherwise remain in *statu quo* till further orders—maintaining your present position You will direct that each regimental quartermaster proceed to our transports on the river and draw rations for the regiment receipting for them in gross. Provision

returns can be made out hereafter—Those regiments which have waggons with them will send their waggons for the rations—Waggons ~~can be procured at the river and~~ will be furnished at the river for those who have not got them—Have each brigade commander designate some regimental quartermaster to procure rations for the artillery attached to the Brigade—Have five days rations provided if there is sufficient transportation and *not less than three days*—"   ALS, Brayman Papers, ICHi; LS (signed 1st Lt. Clark B. Lagow), DNA, RG 393, Dept. of the Mo., Letters Received; copies (signed Capt. John A. Rawlins), *ibid.*, USG Letters Sent; DLC-USG, V, 1, 2, 3, 85.

To Commanding Officer, Gunboat Flotilla

Head Quarters, Army in the Field,
Camp near Ft. Donelson, Febry 15th 1862.

COMMDG OFFICER G. B. FLOTILLA

If all the Gun Boats that can, will immediately make their appearance to the enemy, it may secure us a Victory.[1] Otherwise all may be defeated. A terrible conflict ensued in my absence, which has demoralized a portion of my command. ~~and~~ I think the enemy is much more so.[2] If the Gun Boats do not show themselves it will reassure the enemy and still further demoralize our troops. I must order a charge to save appearances. I do not expect the Gun Boats to go into action, but to make their appearance, and throw ~~a few~~ shells at long range.

Respectfully &c
U. S. GRANT
Brig Gen. Commdg.

Copy, DLC-USG, V, 85. Copies of the same letter, recorded as addressed to Flag Officer Andrew H. Foote, are *ibid.*, V, 1, 2, 3, 9; DNA, RG 393, USG Letters Sent. *O.R.*, I, vii, 618. On Feb. 16, 1862, Commander Benjamin M. Dove wrote to Foote. "At 2:30 p.m. yesterday, shortly after your departure, I received the enclosed dispatch (No. 1) from General Grant. It seemed of so much importance for us to keep up a show of force that I decided not to accompany the *Pittsburg* down the river. I immediately went on board the *Carondelet* and *St. Louis* to see their condition and consult with their commanders. The *Carondelet* could not well be moved, but I ordered up the *St. Louis* and followed up with this vessel. The *St. Louis* threw a few shells, and toward dark both vessels returned to their former anchorage." *O.R.* (Navy), I, xxii, 588.

1. On Feb. 15, Foote telegraphed to Maj. Gen. Henry W. Halleck. "I made an attack on Fort Donaldson yesterday at three o'clock P. M. with four iron clad gun-boats and two wooden ones, and after one hour and a quarter severe fighting, —the latter part within less than four hundred yard[s] of the Fort,—the wheel of this boat and the tiller-ropes of the Louisville were shot away, rendering the two boats unmanageable. They then drifted down the river. The two remaining boats were also greatly deranged between wind and water, this vessel alone having received fifty-nine shots, and the others about half that number each. There were fifty-four killed and wounded in this attack, which we have reason to suppose would in fifteen minutes more,—could the action have been continued,—have resulted in the capture of the Fort bearing upon us, as the enemy was running from his batteries, when the two gun-boats helplessly drifted down the river from dis-abled steering apparatus, as the relieving tackles could not steer the vessels in the strong current, when the fleeing enemy returned to the river battery guns, from which they had been driven, and again hotly opened fire upon us. The enemy must have brought over twenty guns to bear upon our boats from the upper battery, and the main fort on the hill, while we could only return the fire with twelve bow guns from the four boats. One rifle gun aboard the Carondelet burst during the action. The officers and men, in the hotly contested, but unequal fight behaved with the greatest gallantry and determination; all deploring the accident rendering two of our gun-boats suddenly helpless in the narrow and swift current. On consultation with Gen Grant, and my own officers, as my services here, until we can repair damages by bringing up a complete force from Cairo to attack the fort, are much less required than they are at Cairo, I shall proceed to that place with two of the disabled gun-boats, leaving the two others here to protect the transports, and with all despatch prepare the mortar boats and Benton, with other boats, to make an effectual attack upon Fort Donaldson. I sent the Tyler to the Tennessee river to render impassible the bridge, so as to prevent the rebels at Columbus reinforcing their army at Fort Donaldson." Telegram received, DNA, RG 94, Generals' Papers and Books, Telegrams Received by Gen. Halleck; copies, *ibid.*, RG 45, Area 5. On the same day, Foote conveyed substantially the same information in letters to Halleck and to Secretary of the Navy Gideon Welles. *O.R.*, I, vii, 166–67; *O.R.* (Navy), I, xxii, 585–86. See following letter.

Also on Feb. 15, Brig. Gen. William T. Sherman, Paducah, wrote to USG. "I am just arrived here by order of Gen Halleck prepared to hasten all reinforcements & supplies. Gen Halleck has just enquired if reinforcements sent to Fort Henry could reach you across the intervening land and have answered they can— He says two Batteries of artillery and a Regiment of Infantry leave St Louis to day. I am ordered to send up the Regt from Smithland, and shall send it up tomorrow.—I have seen Commodore Foote who told me of the Repulse of his Gunboats, and that he is compelled to go to Cairo for repairs. I am advised by telegraph that Bowling Green is evacuated—Either its Garrison will reinforce Ft Donelson & Clarksville, or will go to Nashville in case Buell is moving on Nashville via Glasgow & Gallatin. Scouts have been out today as far as Blandville, & Mayfield, but nothing is reported. The safety of Paducah is all important— there are three Regiments here, and I may send one to you if necessary. I should like to hear from you, and will do everything in my power to hurry forward to you reinforcements and supplies, and if I could be of service myself would gladly come, without making any question of Rank with you or General Smith whose commissions are of the same date   The Gun boat Taylor is here on her way up the

Tennessee to more effectually destroy the R R bridge. If you think Smithland should be occupied send orders at once to Col. Sweeny who will be on the Aleck Scott coming up the Cumberland." ALS, DNA, RG 393, District of West Tenn., Letters Received. On the same day, Sherman again wrote to USG. "Enclosed is a telegraph just received from Genl McLellan. Any message can be sent from Smithland or here [*Paducah*]. Commodore Foote telegraphs substantially that he had attacked the Fort with four of his Gunboats, that he got within four hundred yards when his steering aparatus and Rudder were shot away, and he and his companion boats were compelled to drift out of range of fire, that he had returned to Cairo for repairs, but would soon return to Donelson He spoke confidantly of your ability to hold your own. The wounded men & officers who came down in the Minnehaha, report that yesterday you had several severe fights and that you drove the enemy within his intrenchments. I feel anxious about you as I know the great facilities they have of concentration by means of the River & R Road, but have faith in you—Command me in any way." ALS, *ibid.* A copy, with the notation "The original & dispatch sent—by Post—copied in case of failure," and dated Feb. 16, is *ibid.* On Feb. 15, at 10:00 p.m., Maj. Gen. George B. McClellan telegraphed to USG. "Telegraph in full the state of affairs with you" ALS (telegram sent), *ibid.*, RG 107, Telegrams Collected (Bound). *O.R.*, I, lii, part 1, 212. Copies dated Feb. 16 are in DLC-USG, V, 4, 5, 7, 8, 9, 81; DNA, RG 393, USG Hd. Qrs. Correspondence; *ibid.*, District of West Tenn., Letters Received. The letterbook copy in DLC-USG, V, 81, was entered with the notation: "Note: This dispatch was received at Fort Donelson March 3d being forwarded from Paducah by Gen. Sherman, with instructions from Genl Halleck dated 1st March."

2. On Feb. 14 (received 4:00 a.m., Feb. 15), Foote wrote to USG. "Will you do me the favor to come on board at your earliest convenience, as I am disabled from walking by a contusion and cannot possibly get to see you about the disposition of these vessels, all of which are more or less disabled." Copies, DLC-USG, V, 1, 2, 3, 9; DNA, RG 393, USG Letters Sent. On the morning of Feb. 15, while USG was conferring with Foote on board the flagship *St. Louis*, the Confederates attempted to cut their way out of Fort Donelson. Brig. Gen. Simon B. Buckner had attacked on the Union right and driven back Brig. Gen. John A. McClernand's troops when their supply of ammunition was exhausted. C. S. A. forces had fallen back after their initial success. At this point, USG returned from his conference with Foote. Upon learning of the situation, USG ordered McClernand's men supplied with ammunition. Then he ordered Brig. Gen. Charles F. Smith to attack on the left. Smith was successful in driving the enemy into the fort, while McClernand was able to retake the position lost earlier in the day. *Memoirs*, I, 304–8; Bruce Catton, *Grant Moves South* (Boston, Toronto, 1960), 164–69; Kenneth P. Williams, *Lincoln Finds a General: A Military Study of the Civil War* (New York, 1949–1959), III, 244–47. See letter to Brig. Gen. George W. Cullum, Feb. 16, 1862, notes.

To Commanding Officer, Fort Henry

Head Quarters, Dist of Cairo,
Camp, near Fort. Donelson, Feb 15th 1862.

Commdg Officer
Fort Henry, Tenn.

Sir:

Send a Company of Cavalry[1] on one of the transports up the Tenn. river to destroy Rail Road Bridges—the position of which will be indicated by Capt. Gwin,[2] Commander of Gun Boat "Taylor" Charge the Officer of Commanding the Company sent, that the District of Country into which they are going is strongly Union, and they should be on their good behavior, and disprove the lying reports made against our forces by the Secessionists.

I hope to hear a good report from this expedition, not only of the favorable impression made, but work done.

Respectfully,
Your Obt. Servant.
U. S. Grant.
Brig. Genl. Commdg.

Copies, DLC-USG, V, 1, 2, 3, 85; DNA, RG 393, USG Letters Sent. *O.R.*, I, vii, 618–19. The copies cited above and the *O.R.* mistakenly address the letter to Brig. Gen. Lewis Wallace, who was then commanding the 3rd Division before Fort Donelson. The letter was probably received by Col. William L. Sanderson, 23rd Ind.

1. On Feb. 15, 1862, Lt. Col. Matthewson T. Patrick, with one hundred men of the Curtis Horse, destroyed the Memphis and Ohio Railroad bridge across the Tennessee River at Danville, Tenn. Wm. H. Thrift and Guy E. Logan [Iowa AGO], *Roster and Record of Iowa Soldiers in the War of the Rebellion, together with Historical Sketches of Volunteer Organizations, 1861–1866* (Des Moines, 1908–11), IV, 847. See letter to Brig. Gen. Lewis Wallace, Feb. 19, 1862.

2. Lt. William Gwin of Columbus, Ind., assumed command of the *Tyler* on Jan. 16.

To Brig. Gen. Simon B. Buckner

Hd Qrs, Army in the Field
Camp near Donelson, Feb.y 16th 1862

GEN. S. B. BUCKNER,
CONFED. ARMY,
SIR;

   Yours of this date proposing Armistice, and appointment of commissioners, to settle terms of capitulation is just received. No terms except an unconditional and immediate surrender can be accepted.

   I propose to move immediately upon your works.

I am sir; very respectfully
your obt. servt.
U. S. GRANT
Brig. Gen.

ALS, Smithsonian Institution, Washington, D. C.; ADfS, Dreer Collection, PHi. *O.R.*, I, vii, 161; *O.R.* (Navy), I, xxii, 596–97. On Feb. 16, 1862, Brig. Gen. Simon B. Buckner wrote to his asst. adjt. gen., Maj. George B. Cosby. "Maj. Cosby will take or send by an Officer to the enemy the accompanying communication to Genl Grant, and request information of the point where further communications will reach him. Also inform him that my Head Quarters will be for the present in Dover. Have the White flag hoisted on Fort Donelson, not on the Batteries." Copies, DLC-USG, V, 4, 5, 7, 8, 9; DNA, RG 393, USG Hd. Qrs. Correspondence. *O.R.*, I, vii, 160–61; *O.R.* (Navy), I, xxii, 596. On Feb. 16, Buckner wrote to USG. "In consideration of all the circumstances governing the present situation of affairs at this station I propose to the Commanding officer of the Federal forces the appointment of commissioners to agree upon terms of capitulation of the forces and post under my command, and in that view suggest an armistice until 12 o'clock to-day." ALS, Dreer Collection, PHi. *O.R.*, I, vii, 160; *O.R.* (Navy), I, xxii, 596. On the same day, Buckner again wrote to USG. "The ~~condition~~ distribution of the forces under my command, incident to an unexpected change of commanders, and the overwhelming force under your command, compel me, notwithstanding the brilliant success of the Confederate armies yesterday, to accept the ungenerous and unchivalrous terms which you propose." ALS, Dreer Collection, PHi. *O.R.*, I, vii, 161; *O.R.* (Navy), I, xxii, 597. See letter to Brig. Gen. George W. Cullum, Feb. 16, 1862.

   Upon receipt of Buckner's letter requesting surrender terms, USG drafted a reply. After showing it to Brig. Gen. Charles F. Smith, USG copied the letter and sent the copy to Buckner. USG then gave the draft to Capt. John A. Rawlins. Later, in Buckner's hd. qrs., Rawlins found on the floor the letter sent to Buckner and retained it also. On Nov. 28, 1868, he gave the letter sent to his wife's relative, Dr. James K. Wallace of Litchfield, Conn. On July 27, 1885, Charles L. Webster (publisher of USG's *Memoirs*) purchased the letter from Wallace and used it in facsimile for the *Memoirs*. Rawlins retained the original draft until his death in 1869. Shortly thereafter, Ferdinand J. Dreer of Philadelphia, Pa., a prominent autograph collector, obtained the draft, and the letters sent by Buckner to USG, from the executors (USG and Bvt. Maj. Gen. John E. Smith) of Rawlins' estate. The three letters pertaining to the surrender were copied in USG's register of letters received, the only letters copied there, presumably because the original letters were given away by USG at the time. DLC-USG, V, 10; DNA, RG 393, USG Register of Letters Received. Signed statement by Charles L. Webster, n. d., Smithsonian Institution; Robert Underwood Johnson and Clarence Clough Buel, eds., *Battles and Leaders of the Civil War* (New York, 1887), I, 427; *The Century Magazine*, XXX, 5 (September, 1885), 766; *New York Herald*, April 26, 1896; James Grant Wilson, "Grant's Historic Utterances," *The Outlook*, 55, 14 (April 3, 1897), 883–84; Smith to Dreer, Aug. 5, 1885, ALS, Dreer Collection, PHi; William R. Rowley to Smith, Nov. 13, 1885, ALS, *ibid.*; Smith to Dreer, Nov. 15, 1885, ALS, *ibid.*; Wilson to Dreer, April 26, 1896, ALS, *ibid.* Facsimiles of the "unconditional surrender" letter now in the Smithsonian Institution were published in: *Memoirs*, I, opposite p. 312; Robert Underwood Johnson and Clarence Clough Buel, eds., *Battles and Leaders of the Civil War* (New York, 1887), I, 427. Facsimiles of the "unconditional surrender" letter now in the Dreer Collection, PHi, were published in: *Richardson*, pp. 228–29; James Grant Wilson, *General Grant* (New York, 1897), opposite p. 114. USG wrote out his "unconditional surrender" letter for friends several times in the years after the surrender of Fort Donelson. ALS, Gratz Collection, PHi; ALS (dated Feb. 16, 1863), Utica Public Library, Utica, N. Y.; LS, USMA; LS, IaHA.

General Field Orders No. 16

Head Quarters, Army in the Field
Fort Donelson, Feb. 16th 1862

GEN. FIELD ORDERS NO 16

The 2 Division will occupy the right of the work including Fort Donelson and will be located to the best advantage for defence and comfort. Gen. C. F. Smith, Comdg Division will designate the place for each Brigade.

The 1st Division will occupy grounds at the South end of the works and will be located by Brig. Gen. J. A. McClernand, Com.

All public property will be collected and turned over to Capt. A. S. Baxter A. Q. M.[1]

Pillaging and appropriating public property to private purposes is positively prohibited. ~~and~~ officers are particularly enjoined to see to the enforcement of this order.[2]

By order

U. S. GRANT

Brig. Gen. Com

ADS, McClernand Papers, IHi. Copies of the same orders, numbered General Field Orders No. 13, are in DLC-USG, V, 12, 13, 14, 95; DNA, RG 393, Dept. of the Miss., Letters Received; *ibid.*, USG General Orders. *O.R.*, I, vii, 625–26.

1. On Feb. 16, 1862, Capt. John A. Rawlins issued special field orders. "Gens. McClernand and Smith will detail from their respective commands four full companies each, to report at 7½ o.clock, to-morrow morning for fatigue duty in the Quartermaster, Commissary and Ordnance Departments" DS, McClernand Papers, IHi. The same orders are numbered Special Field Orders No. 21, DS, DNA, RG 393, Dept. of the Miss., Letters Received. Copies of the same orders, numbered Special Field Orders No. 10, are in DLC-USG, V, 15, 16, 82, 89; DNA, RG 393, USG Special Orders.

2. On Feb. 16, Rawlins wrote to Brig. Gen. Charles F. Smith. "You will cause to be detailed from your command, 25 men, to report to Capt. A. S. Baxter, A. Q. M. for the purpose of preventing the shipment, of property captured at Fort Donelson; and to search for and put off, any such property, that may be now shipped." LS, *ibid.*, Dept. of the Miss., Letters Received. On the same day, Rawlins wrote to the commanding officer, Forts Heiman and Henry. "You will allow no horses, or arms, or captured property of any kind to be shipped by boat from Fort Henry, without the written permission of the Quartermaster or General Commanding Division." LS, Wallace Papers, InHi.

General Field Orders No. 17

———

Head Quarters, Army in the Field
Fort Donelson, Feb.y 16th 1862

GEN. FIELD ORDERS No 17

During the detention of prisoner[s] of war at this place, and to facilitate in collecting them and supplying their wants passes signed by Brig. Gen. Buckner, Confederate Army, will be respected by all inside guards.

By Order

U. S. GRANT

Brig. Gen.

ADS, McClernand Papers, IHi. Copies of the same orders, numbered General Field Orders No. 14, are in DLC-USG, V, 12, 13, 14, 95; DNA, RG 393, USG General Orders. *O.R.*, II, iii, 268. On Feb. 16, 1862, Capt. John A. Rawlins issued Special Field Orders No. 10. "All Prisoners taken at the surrender of Fort Donelson will be collected as rapidly as practicable, near the village of Dover, under their respective Company and Regimental Commanders, or in such manner as may be deemed best by Brig. Genl. S. B. Buckner, and will receive two days rations, preparatory to embarking for Cairo. Prisoners are to be allowed their Clothing, Blankets, and such private property as may be carried about their person, and Commissioned Officers will be allowed their side arms." Copies, DLC-USG, V, 15, 16, 82, 89; DNA, RG 393, USG Special Orders. *O.R.*, I, vii, 626; *ibid.*, II, iii, 267. Other portions of the same orders are numbered Special Field Orders No. 20 and Special Field Orders No. 21, DS, DNA, RG 393, Dept. of the Miss., Letters Received. On Feb. 16, C. S. A. Col. James E. Bailey, 49th Tenn., wrote to Brig. Gen. Simon B. Buckner. "I understood from Major Casseday that by the terms of capitulation the officers were to be permitted to retain their side arms, but the U. S. officer in charge of my officers & men has demanded that they should be deliverd to him, agreeing however that the arms should remain in my custody until tomorrow morning. My officers & men have been brought from their camp at the Fort to this place to night; much of their clothing and baggage has been left behind, & the side arms of officers are all at the Fort. The men will tonight be placed on a transport & their property may be lost. Will you have this corrected" ALS, *ibid.*, District of West Tenn., Letters Received. *O.R.*, II, iii, 799. Buckner sent this letter to USG. "Forwarded to Brig. Gen. Grant for his orders and correction. Major Bain? was the officer who seized the arms." AES, DNA, RG 393, District of West Tenn., Letters Received. On the same day, Buckner wrote to USG. "It is with much regret that I am forced to call your attention again to the cruel situation in which my men are placed by the ignorance of some of your executive officers, on guard. Thousands of these men have been standing nearly all day in the mud, without food, and without fire. Whenever my officers attempt to collect their men they are arrested at almost every corner of the street by some of your guards. The arrangement suggested by me this evening to employ four or five of your officers to assist in this collection is ~~inoperative~~ ineffectual. Fifty messengers could not accomplish it. If you wish to give effectual relief to my men your police orders will necessarily have to undergo material modifications. On my way from your Hd. Qrs. this evening, I met opposite my quarters, Capt. Dodge of one of your cavalry regiments having in charge two of my ~~regiments~~ colonels, who by the orders of some officer for some unknown purpose, were to be marched ~~to~~ through the mud to your Hd. Qrs, although one of the officers was paroled specially by Gen. Smith. There seems to be no concert of action between the different departments of your army in reference to these prisoners. As a means of remedying this and the other existing evils I suggest ~~that~~

either that your *interior* guards be permitted to respect my pass; or that you appoint a Provost Marshal or other officer who shall hold his office in my Hd. Qrs, vested with authority to issue passes for ~~the~~ all necessary purposes ~~of~~ connected with the administrative duties of the prisoners. . . . P.S. I will thank you to decide also the question ~~of~~ in reference to private horses, whether or not transportation will be allowed for them. If not their private property necessarily falls into the hands of your army." ALS, *ibid.*, District of Cairo, Letters Received. *O.R.*, II, iii, 267–68.

To Maj. Gen. Henry W. Halleck

Fort Donelson, Feb.y 16th 1862

GEN. H. W. HALLECK
COMD.G DEPT. OF THE MO.
GEN.

If you will permit Col. McPherson to accompany me in any future movement to be made against the rebels I will esteem it as a personal favor to myself and feel that the service can also be benefited.

You know the Col. better than I do therefore an expression of opinion of his merits is unnecessary from me.

The Col. is well qualified to supply a deficiency which would otherwise be felt for want of Engineers.

> Respectfully
> your obt. svt.
> U. S. GRANT
> Brig. Gen.

ALS, DNA, RG 393, Dept. of the Mo., Letters Received. On Feb. 21, 1862, Lt. Col. James B. McPherson wrote to USG. "Here I am in St Louis but under the Dr's care who says I must not go out for some time yet. My throat is very much better, at least I can breathe more freely, but the swelling is far from having gone down—I hope however to be able to join you next week. To give you an idea of the joy and excitement which pervaded this community on the receipt of the news would be impossible. Genl. Halleck is exceedingly gratified and says you could not have done better—Immediately on the receipt of the news he telegraphed to the President to nominate you for a *Major General*. You will not be troubled any more by *Kountz* His character is found out and I think he will be dismissed   I am in hopes that the Qr. Masters & Commissary depts. will be arranged to suit you—Genl. Halleck says Genl. Hunter behaved nobly, but Buel acted like a dog in the manger—The former transferred nearly all his troops to Missouri and placed them at Hallecks disposal—while the latter would not coperate at all—Genl. Halleck telegraphed to him his position, and told him the rebels were reinforcing Donelson from Bowling Green and asked him to advance, and he replied he could not on account of the mud—the Genl. then telegraphed to him to make a demonstration & he replied that he *never made* demonstrations, now I suppose he will claim all the credit of having forced the rebels to evacuate Bowling Green—For the life of me in times like this I cannot see why men are not willing to act for the good of the cause and not self—My hand is not very steady as I have been taking medicine & I don't know whether you can make this out—Give my regards to all the members of your staff & hoping soon to be with you again I am"   ALS, USG 3.

To Brig. Gen. George W. Cullum

Head Quarters, Army in the Field
Fort Donelson, Feb. 16th 1862

GEN. G. W. CULLUM
CHIEF OF STAFF, DEPT. OF THE MO.
GEN.

I am pleased to announce to you the unconditional surrender this morning of Fort Donelson, with twelve to fifteen thousand prisoners,[1] at least forty pieces of Artillery and a large amount of stores, horses, mules and other public property. I left Fort Henry on the 12th inst. with a force of about 15000 men, divided into two Divisions under the commands of Gens. McClernand and Smith. Six regiments were sent around by water the day before, convoyed by a gun boat, or rather started one day later than one of the gunboats, and with instructions not to pass it.

The troops made the march in good order, the head of the colum arriving within two miles of the Fort, at 12 o'clock M. At this point the enemies pickets were met and driven in.

The fortifications of the enemy were from this point gradually approached and surrounded with occational skirmishing on the line. The following day owing to the nonarrival of the Gunboats and reinforcements sent by water no attack was made but the investment was extended on the flanks of the enemy and drawn closer to his works, with skirmishing all day. The evening of the 13th the Gunboats and reinforcements arrived. On the 14th a gallant attack was made by Flag Officer Foote, upon the enemies works, with his fleet. The engagement lasted probably one hour and a half and bid fair to result favorably to the cause of the Union when two unlucky shots disabled two of the Armoured boats so that they were carrid back by the tide. The remaining two were very much disabled also having received a number of heavy shots about the pilot houses and other parts of the vessels.

After these mishaps I concluded to make the investment of Fort Donelson as perfect as possible and partially fortify and await repairs to the gunboats. This plan was frustrated however by the enemy making a most vigorous attack upon our right wing, commanded by Gen. J. A. McClernands ~~command~~ with a portion of the force under Gen. L. Wallace. The enemy were repelled after a closely contested battle of several hours in which our loss was heavy. The officers, and particularly field officers, suffered out of proportion. I have not the means yet of determining our loss even aproximately but it cannot fall far short of 1200 killed wounded and missing.[2] Of the latter I understand through Gen. Buckner about 250 were taken prisoners.—I shall retain enough of the enemy to exchange for them as they were immediately shipped off and not left for recapture.[3]—About the close of this action the ammunition in cartridge boxes gave out, which with the loss of many of the Field officers produced great confusion in the ranks. ~~And~~ Seeing that the enemy did not take advantage of it convinced me that equal confusion, and possibly great demoralization, existed with him. Taking advantage of this fact I ordered a charge upon the left,—Enemies right,—with the Division under Gen. C. F. Smith which was most brilliantly executed and gave to our arms full assurance of victory. The battle lasted until dark giving us possession of part of the entrenchments.—An attack was ordered from the other flank, after the charge by Gen. Smith was commenced, by the Divisions under Gens. McClernand & Wallace, which, notwithstanding the hours of exposure to a heavy fire in the fore part of the day, was gallantly made and the enemy further repulsed.

At the points thus gained, night having come on, all the troops encamped for the night feeling that a complete victory would crown their labors at an early hour in the morning.

This morning at a very early hour a note was received from Gen. S. B. Buckner, under a flag of truce, proposing an armistice &c. A copy of the correspondence which ensued is herewith accompanying.[4]

I cannot mention individuals who specially distinguished themselvs but leave that to Division and Brigade Commanders, whos reports will be forwarded as soon as received.

To Division Commanders however, Gens McClernand, Smith and Wallace I must do the justice to say that each of them were with their commands in the midst of danger and were always ready to execute all orders no matter what the exposure to themselvs.

At the hour the attack was made on Gen. McClernand's command I was absent, having received a note from Flag Officer Foote requesting me to go and see him he being unable to call ~~upon~~ me in consequence of a wound received the day before[5]

My personal staff, Col. J. T. Webster, Chief of Staff Col. J. Riggin Jr Vol. Aid. Capt. J. A. Rawlins, A. A. Gen. Capts C. B Lagow & W. S. Hillyer Aids, and Lt. Col. J. B. McPherson Chief Engineer all are deserving of personal mention for their gallantry and services.

For full details see reports of Engineers, Medical Director[6] and Commanders of Brigades & Divisions to follow.

> I am Gen. very respectfully
> your obt. svt.
> U. S. GRANT
> Brig. Gen

ALS, DNA, RG 94, War Records Office, Union Battle Reports. *O.R.*, I, vii, 159–60; *O.R.* (Navy), I, xxii, 595–96. On Feb. 16, 1862, USG telegraphed to Maj. Gen. Henry W. Halleck. "We have taken Ft. Donaldson, and from twelve to fifteen thousand prisoners including Gens. Buckner and Bushrod Johnson, also about twenty thousand stand of arms, forty eight pieces of artillery, seventeen heavy guns, from two to four thousand horses, and large quantities of commissary stores." Copy, DNA, RG 393, Dept. of the Mo., Telegrams Received. *O.R.*, I, vii, 625. On Feb. 23, USG forwarded the report, with a map of Fort Donelson, drawn by Col. Joseph D. Webster, to Brig. Gen. George W. Cullum. "Approved and respectfully forwarded to Head Quarters, Dept. of the Mo." AES, DNA, RG 393, Dept. of the Mo., Letters Received. Manuscript copies of the following reports on the capture of Fort Donelson: Brig. Gen. Lewis Wallace to Capt. John A. Rawlins, Feb. 25, 1862; Lt. Col. James B. McPherson to USG, Feb. 25, 1862; Brig. Gen. John A. McClernand to USG, Feb. 28, 1862, are *ibid.*, RG 94, War Records Office, Union Battle Reports. Reports of the various division, brigade, and regt. commanders are in *O.R.*, I, vii, 161–253; *ibid.*, I, lii, part 1, 7–13. USG took exception to portions of McClernand's report of Feb. 28. See letter to Capt. Nathaniel H. McLean, April 21, 1862. C. S. A. reports are in *O.R.*, I, vii, 254–416.

1. Uncertainty remains concerning the number of men captured at Fort Donelson. On Feb. 16, Brig. Gen. Simon B. Buckner told USG that the number surrendered was between 12,000 and 15,000. *Memoirs*, I, 313. On Aug. 11, Buckner wrote to C. S. A. Adjt. and Inspector Gen. Samuel Cooper that his army was composed of fewer than 9,000 men when surrendered. *O.R.*, I, vii, 335. Buckner's q. m., Maj. Samuel K. Hays, estimated that 9,929 men were surrendered. *Cincinnati Commercial*, Feb. 26, 1862. USG noted that rations for 14,623 prisoners had been issued at Cairo as they passed through on their way to prison camps. *Memoirs*, I, 314; Adam Badeau, *Military History of Ulysses S. Grant* (New York, 1868–81), I, 51, 51*n*–52*n*. On Feb. 19, Cullum wrote to Halleck that nearly 11,000 prisoners had been sent up the Mississippi River on steamers and an additional 500 were scheduled to leave for Camp Douglas, Chicago, the following morning. *O.R.*, I, vii, 944; *ibid.*, II, iii, 282. But, on the same day, Cullum telegraphed to Halleck that 9,000 prisoners had been forwarded to St. Louis; 1,000 had been sent to Chicago; 500 were to follow. *Ibid.* On the same day, Rawlins wrote to Buckner that USG wanted 6,000 prisoners to leave for Cairo that evening while the remainder were to stay in their camps until morning. *Ibid.*, p. 283. Apparently, then, from 16,500 to 17,500 prisoners passed through Cairo. In addition, USG exchanged some 250 C. S. A. prisoners for an equal number of Union prisoners. For an estimate of the size of the C. S. A. army in Fort Donelson, see letter to Brig. Gen. George W. Cullum, Feb. 14, 1862, note 2. On the numbers escaping, see letter to Julia Dent Grant, Feb. 16, 1862.

2. Union losses at Fort Donelson: killed, 500; wounded, 2,108; captured or missing, 224; total, 2,832. *O.R.*, I, vii, 169. USG estimated the men in his army at 27,000. *Memoirs*, I, 315.

3. See letter to Brig. Gen. Simon B. Buckner, Feb. 17, 1862.

4. See letter to Brig. Gen. Simon B. Buckner, Feb. 16, 1862.

5. See letter to Commanding Officer, Gunboat Flotilla, Feb. 15, 1862.

6. No report from the Medical Director, Surgeon Henry S. Hewit, has been found. Accounts of the activities of various medical officers at Fort Donelson may be found in *The Medical and Surgical History of the War of the Rebellion* (Washington, 1870–88), I, part 1, appendix, 24–36.

To Brig. Gen. George W. Cullum

———

Head Quarters, Army in the Field
Fort Donelson, Feb.y 16th 1862

GEN. G. W. CULLUM
CHIEF OF STAFF, DEPT. OF THE MO.
GEN.

Will you be pleased to direct Capt. Turnley to have the regular steamer for the Cumberland leave Cairo at 10 O'Clock A.M. daily.[1] One boat, ~~for this pla~~ regular, will be sufficient for the two rivers and I would prefer it should come here. The mail for Fort Henry can be sent on irregular boats when they happen to be running and when not I will send it across the country. Daily communication must be kept up between the two places.[2]

If our gunboats were ready[3] I would move upon Clarkesville on Teusday[4] but not I suppose it will be impossible.

Respectfully &c.
U. S. GRANT

ALS, DNA, RG 393, Dept. of the Miss., Letters Received.

1. See letter to Absalom H. Markland, Feb. 13, 1862.
2. See letter to Brig. Gen. Lewis Wallace, Feb. 16, 1862.
3. The gunboats had been badly damaged in the attack on Fort Donelson. See letter to Commanding Officer, Gunboat Flotilla, Feb. 15, 1862, note 1.
4. Feb. 18, 1862.

To Brig. Gen. Lewis Wallace

————

Head Quarters, Army in the Field
Fort Donelson Feb. 16th 1862.

GEN. L. WALLACE
COMD.G U. S. FORCES
FORTS HENRY & HEIMAN.
GEN.

Send the Steamer City of Memphis to this place without delay. She is much required as a hospital boat for the wounded. All the sick on board, not fit to join their regiments, may be left on board and sent to Hospital in Paducah. Surgeon Hewitt,[1] Medical Director,[2] will send the surgeon written directions in this matter.

I Am Gen. Very respectfully
your obt. svt.
U. S. GRANT
Brig. Gen.

ALS, Wallace Papers, InHi. On Feb. 16, 1862, Capt. John A. Rawlins issued Special Field Orders No. 20. "In order to secure the glorious victory acquired by our arms, and to perpetuate it, the General Commanding deems it highly important that the utmost vigilence should be observed to guard all points captured. It is ordered, therefore, that Gen. L. Wallace return to Fort Henry, Tenn. with two Brigades of his command, and Williard's & Bullis' Batteries. Curtis Horse is attached to the command of Genl. Wallace." DS, DNA, RG 393, Dept. of the Miss., Letters Received. Copies of the same orders, numbered Special Field Orders No. 10, are in DLC-USG, V, 15, 16, 82, 89; DNA, RG 393, USG Special Orders. *O.R.*, I, vii, 626. On Feb. 16, Rawlins wrote to Brig. Gen. Lewis Wallace. "I am directed by Gen. Grant to say to you that your orders are to proceed to Fort Henry (with only two Brigades of your command; and that the 8th Missouri and 11th Indiana are not of your Division. They will remain at this place." LS, Wallace Papers, InHi. On the same day, Capt. William S. Hillyer wrote to Wallace. "Yours received—You are *not going to be left behind*—I know Gen Grants views. He intends to give you a chance to be shot in every important move—We cannot advance for some days—We must fortify as we move—You will not be left at Ft Henry *unless it be to defend against a threatened attack*—I *speak advisedly*—God bless you. You did save the day on the right—" ALS, *ibid.* On Feb. 17, Wallace wrote to Rawlins. "Say to the Genl that I beg his pardon for having brought the 11th Indiana & 8th Mo back with me. I asked them of Genl Smith in presence of Genl Grant, as I thought, and no objection being made I ordered them along.

Upon receipt of the order to come here with two Brigades of my Division, I instantly issued the proper orders to Col Cruft, comdg 1st Brigade and to Col Thayer comdg 3rd Brigade. This morning Col Cruft started with his command, and they are now straggling in. Col Thayer has made no demonstration of compliance; probably because he could not have his regiments assembled for the march. Under the circumstance I would be very much obliged to the Genl if he would leave me my two old regiments. If he cannot I would be gratified if you would order Col Thayer to proceed here at once with the regiments of the 3rd Brigade. As the 8th & 11th on the way and their tents & equipage on the other side of the river, I will have them secure their effects and return to Ft Donaldson. In his disposition of them, I hope the Genl will consider the 'exceeding great love' I bear them. . . . P. S. I should have stated that I did not receive the Genls prohibiting order until I reached the Ft *a few minutes ago*" Copy, *ibid.*

1. Henry S. Hewit of Conn. was an asst. surgeon from 1849 to 1851, when he resigned and entered private practice. In 1861, he was commissioned brigade surgeon of vols. and assigned to the staff of Brig. Gen. Charles F. Smith at Paducah.

2. On Feb. 6, 1862, Rawlins issued General Field Orders No. 2. "Surgeon H. S. Hewitt, Senior Surgeon of the Fort Henry expedition, will act as Medical Director to the command. He will, if necessary, organize hospitals and make such details of the Medical Corps as, in his judgement, may be most conducive to the public interest." AD (in USG's hand), McClernand Papers, IHi.

To *Julia Dent Grant*

———

Head Quarters, Fort Donelson Ten.
Feb.y 16th 1862

DEAR WIFE

I am most happy to write you from this very strongly fortified place, now in my possession, after the greatest victory of the season. Some 12 or 15 thousand prisoners have fallen into our possession to say nothing of 5 to 7 thousand that escaped in the darkness of the night last night.[1]

This is the largest capture I believe ever made on the continent.

You warn me against Capt. Kountz.[2] He can do me no harm. He is known as a venimous man whose hand is raised against every man and is without friends or influance.[3]—My impression is that I shall have one hard battle more to fight and will find easy sailing after that. No telling though. This was one of the most desperate affairs fought during this war. Our men were out three terrible cold nights and fighting through the day, without tents. Capt. Hillyer will explain all to you. Kiss the children for me. I will ~~write~~ direct my next letter to Covington.

ULYS.

ALS, DLC-USG.

    1. Brig. Gen. John B. Floyd reported that on the morning of Feb. 16, 1862, before the surrender of Fort Donelson, he had escaped, with about 1,300 men, on two steamers; others of his brigade also had been ferried across the Cumberland River and joined him at Murfreesborough, Tenn. *O.R.*, I, vii, 275. Brig. Gen. Nathan B. Forrest stated that he escaped with the cav. under his command, except for Lt. Col. George Gantt's Ky. cav. battalion and two cos. of Ky. cav. which refused to leave. Forrest escaped with approximately 1,500 men. *Ibid.*, pp. 295, 386–87; John Allan Wyeth, *Life of General Nathan Bedford Forrest* (New York and London, 1899), p. 71. Additionally, an unknown number of individuals escaped during the night by wading through the sloughs on the Union right near Dover, Tenn. *O.R.*, I, vii, 364. Brig. Gen. Gideon J. Pillow also escaped. *Ibid.*, p. 288. The total number of men who escaped during the night was probably about 3,000.
    2. Capt. William J. Kountz. See letter to Capt. William J. Kountz, Dec. 21, 1861, and endorsement to Kountz, Jan. 29, 1862.
    3. Ten lines crossed out and illegible.

General Orders No. 1

———

Head Quarters Dist of West Tenn
Fort Donelson Feby 17th 1862

GENERAL ORDERS No 1

    By virtue of directions from Head Quarters Department of the Mo., dated Feby 15th 1862 the undersigned has been assigned to the Command of the new Military District of West Tennessee. Limits not defined.

By Order
U. S. GRANT
Brig Genl Commanding

DS, McClernand Papers, IHi. *O.R.*, I, vii, 629. See letter to Brig. Gen. George
W. Cullum, Feb. 14, 1862. On Feb. 14, 1862, Capt. Nathaniel H. McLean issued
General Orders No. 37, Dept. of the Mo. "Brig. Gen. U. S. Grant is assigned to
the command of the District of West Tennessee and Brig. Gen. W. T. Sherman
to the command of the District of Cairo." *O.R.*, I, viii, 555. On Feb. 17, Brig.
Gen. William T. Sherman, Paducah, wrote to USG. "Yours of yesterday is just
received. Gen Halleck has made another District, West Tennessee of which you
are the Commander. I have that of Cairo.—Cairo, Paducah and Smithland have
all been much reduced to reinforce you, and Gen Halleck telegraphs me that I
must detain 'all reinforcements to resist Beauregard' He may have information
from Columbus which I have not—Our scouts go 15 miles out & report nothing.
I am pushing the work at the Fort, and have three Regiments. I understand from
Gen Cullum that 12000 men are coming down the Ohio from Buells Column for
you. Do you want them up the Tennessee or Cumberland. You express a preference for Henry, but I suppose that relates to the Illinois & Missouri troops coming
up stream. As the Cumberland is the Dept Line it may work a temporary difficulty
but of course Buell & Halleck can arrange that. Your wounded are landed here
and comfortably provided for. We now have over 1300 in hospital and must send
those which arrive hereafter to Cairo. Your eminent success ensures your fortune,
and I suppose your next step will be Clarksville—Several large mortar Boats have
passed up—two of them in tow of the W H Brown have just passed—" ALS,
DNA, RG 393, District of West Tenn., Letters Received. On the same day,
Sherman wrote to his wife. "On Sunday last a week I received a despatch from
Gen Halleck to prepare to come to the Tennessee or Cumberland—I sent a copy
to you at once. On Thursday I received a despatch to come at once to Paducah
and assume command—I started same day telegraphing you at Lancaster." ALS,
Sherman Papers, InNd.

General Orders No. 2

Head Quarters District of West Tenn
Fort Donelson Feby 17th 1862

GENERAL ORDERS No 2

The General Commanding takes great pleasure in congratulating the Troops of this Command for the triumph over rebellion
gained by their valor on the 13th, 14th and 15th inst

For four successive nights, without shelter, during the most
inclement weather known in this latitude, they faced an enemy
in large force, in a position chosen by himself. Though strongly
fortified by nature, all the additional safeguards suggested by
science were added. Without a murmur this was borne, prepared

at all times to receive the attack and with continuous skirmishing by day, resulted ultimately in forcing the enemy to surrender without conditions.

The victory achieved is not only great in the effect it will have in breaking down rebellion, but has secured the greatest number of prisoners of war ever taken in any battle on this continent.

Fort Donelson will hereafter be marked in Capitals on the maps of our United country, and the men who fought the battle will live in the memory of a grateful people.

By Order

U. S. Grant

Brig Genl Com'dg

DS, Stephenson County Historical Society, Freeport, Ill. *O.R.*, I, vii, 629.

To Brig. Gen. Simon B. Buckner

Head Quarters, Dist of West. Tenn.

Fort. Donelson, Febry 17th 1862.

Gen. S. B. Buckner, C. S. A.

At the request of Major Glandville,[1] I am about sending a Flag of Truce, up the river as far as Clarkesville, for the purpose of carrying the bodies of two Officers of your Army. If you have still a desire to effect a release of a portion of the prisoners held here, an opportunity presents itself, of doing so.

I will release just the same number of your men, that you do of Federal troops, rank for rank. Any arrangement that you may suggest as to the place of making the exchange, will be agreeable to me.

I am, Sir, Very Respectfully,

Your Obt. Servant.

U. S. Grant.

Brig. Gen. Commdg.

Copies, DLC-USG, V, 1, 2, 3, 85; DNA, RG 393, USG Letters Sent. *O.R.*, II, iii, 272–73. On Feb. 17, 1862, Brig. Gen. Simon B. Buckner wrote to USG. "In reply to your communication of this date, I suggest that the prisoners taken by the Confederate army at this place be exchanged for an equal number of prisoners of the 2nd Ky. Regiment now here, and that the place of exchange be at some point on the Cumberland River,—say Clarksville. Permit me also to ask if as your flag is about to start, if I can be permitted to send a brief dispatch to Gen. Johnston; and also if officers can send private letters (open) to their friends in the Confederate States. If your answer should be affirmative please inform me of the time of departure of your flag." ALS, DNA, RG 393, District of West Tenn., Letters Received. *O.R.*, II, iii, 273.

1. Surgeon T. J. Vanderville, 51st Tenn.

To Brig. Gen. George W. Cullum

Head Quarters, Dist. of West Ten.
Fort Donelson, Feb.y 17th 1862

GEN. G. W. CULLUM
CHIEF OF STAFF, DEPT. OF THE MO.
GEN.

I am now forwarding prisoners of war to your care and I shall be truly glad to get clear of them.[1] It is a much less job to take than to keep them.

In the midst of confusion there has been a greatdeel of plundering notwithstanding all the precautions taken to prevent it. I ordered guards over all captured property before marching the troops into the works of the enemy but it seemed to do no good. All steamers leaving are searched to recover such as can be found and guards placed to prevent such property from being carried aboard.[2] I would suggest that precautions be taken also to prevent landing any captured property except to be taken charge of by a proper officer.

Several regiments of my command, Gen. McClernands Division, were repulsed for a time on the morning of the 15th and lost their blankets fell into the hands of the enemy. I am trying to have these collected and returned.[3] All those lost I believe are grey with the letters U S in the center. All such, found upon the prisoners, I would recommend should be taken from them and returned here.

I am not in want of Commissary stores nor any supplies as yet except Ammunition already written for. I would like however if you would urge the Quartermaster to hurry up the teams left by different regiments from Cairo & Paducah. I permitted no regiment to bring over four teams on account of limited transportation and many of the new regiments from other points have come without any.[4]

The teams captured here will I think supply all our remaining wants if those already assigned to regiments are sent.

I am Gen. Very respectfully
your obt. svt.
U. S. GRANT
Brig. Gen.

ALS, DNA, RG 393, Dept. of the Mo., Letters Received. *O.R.*, II, iii, 271.

1. On Feb. 17, 1862, John Riggin, Jr., wrote to Col. Thomas W. Sweeny, 52nd Ill. "You will take charge of the prisoners to be transported to Cairo, from whence the guard will return here, furnishing the necessary number to guard each Steamer not now provided for. You will provide two days rations for the prisoners, and four days rations for the guards. The arms of the Commissioned Officers will be kept seperate, and returned to them at Cairo, unless otherwise ordered, i. e: Pistols and swords; All other arms will be turned over to the Qr. Master at Cairo." Copies, DLC-USG, V, 1, 2, 3, 85; DNA, RG 393, USG Letters Sent. *O.R.*, II, iii, 272.

2. See General Field Orders No. 16, Feb. 16, 1862. On Feb. 16, Capt. John A. Rawlins wrote to Col. Charles Whittlesey, 20th Ohio. "You will instruct the officers of the Guard, detailed for the several boats, transporting Prisoners to Cairo, to watch the boats on their downward trip, and seize all guns, horses, and other captured property, which the claimant has not the authority of Capt. A. S. Baxter, A. Q. M. or of the Commanding General, to transport." LS, DNA, RG 393, Dept. of the Mo., Letters Received.

3. On Feb. 17, Rawlins issued Special Orders No. 1. "Officers of the several Brigades, composing this command will detail a sufficient number of men from the respective Regiments composing their Brigades, to proceed on board the Transports, on which prisoners are being embarked, and recover from them all blankets previously belonging to the Government, and all having more than two blankets, the excess will be taken from them" Copies, DLC-USG, V, 15, 16, 82, 87, 89; DNA, RG 393, USG Special Orders.

4. Brig. Gen. George W. Cullum noted on the letter "Attended to by me."

To Brig. Gen. George W. Cullum

————

Head Quarters, Dist. of W. Ten.
Fort Donelson, Feb. 17th 1862

Gen. G. W. Cullum
Chief of Staff &c.
Gen.

I am geting off the prisoners captured as rapidly as possible. Think the last will be off to-morrow. I fear they will prove an Elephant. I would suggest the policy of paroling all prisoners hereafter and taking a receipt for them from the commanding officer so that exchanges may all be made on paper.

Seeing the trouble I have had myself I began to pity you the moment the first cargo started.

Send me 5000 blankets and 1000 overcoats as soon as possible. Many were lost on the battle field and the men are now without.

We want blanks of all kinds and particularly Muster rolls for the approaching muster.

Respectfully &c.
U. S. Grant

P. S. If everything looks favorable I will take and garrison Clarkesville in a few days. At present I am not ready.
U. S. G.

ALS, DNA, RG 393, Dept. of the Mo., Letters Received. *O.R.*, II, iii, 271–72. On Feb. 20, 1862, Brig. Gen. George W. Cullum wrote to USG. "I have received with the highest gratification your reports and letters from Fort Donelson, so galliantly captured under your brilliant leadership. I, in common with the whole country, warmly congratulate you upon this remarkable achievement which has broken the enemy's centre, dispersed the rebels, and given a death blow to secession   The prisoners by thousands have arrived here, and will be sent off by to morrow to their respective destinations   I have directed the 5.000 blankets and 1.000 overcoats to be sent to you. Very few blanks are in this office, Gen McClernand having taken them all. If none are to be found to supply your wants, here, I will order them sent from Headquarters. Supplies of nearly all kinds have been forwarded to you. The teams you wish, have been sent. The sick and wounded are well provided for at Paducah, Mound City and here. If we have too many to look after, we will send them to Cincinnatti and St. Louis   Doctors, nurses, and all kinds of assistance and sympathy have been freely and generously offered.

Your letter of the 19th gives glorious news, and an earnest of continued success. We have newspaper reporters who state that 2.000 Tennesseeans have come in to you and laid down their [*arms.*] Again congratulating you, assuring you of my continued esteem, I am" LS, DNA, RG 393, Dept. of the Mo., Telegrams Received. *O.R.*, I, vii, 643–44.

To Brig. Gen. Stephen A. Hurlbut

Head Quarters, West Ten.
Fort Donelson, Feb. 17th 1862

GEN. S. ЈA HURLBUT
GEN.

Will you please order twenty men under one commissioned and two noncommissioned officers to report immediately to Surgeon Brinton on board the Steamer Univers for the purpose of carrying sick and wounded on board.

I call upon you because it would take to great a time to send out to Camp for a regular detail and the men are now laying on the bank waiting.

Respectfully
your obt. svt.
U. S. GRANT
Brig. Gen.

ALS, Stephenson County Historical Society, Freeport, Ill. On Feb. 16, 1862, Brig. Gen. Simon B. Buckner wrote to USG. "The medical director of my command, Surgn. Griffin, desires to confer with the Med. Director of your army, ~~The~~ in reference to the disposal of sick prisoners. The Office of Surgn. Griffin is at the 'Union Inn' at this place, where any communication from your officer will reach him" ALS, DNA, RG 393, District of West Tenn., Letters Received. *O.R.*, II, iii, 268. On Feb. 17, USG endorsed this letter. "Refered to Surgeon Hewitt, Medical Director." AES, DNA, RG 393, District of West Tenn., Letters Received. See letter to Brig. Gen. Lewis Wallace, Feb. 16, 1862.

To Brig. Gen. John A. McClernand

Head Quarters, Dist. of West Ten.
Fort Donelson, Feb.y 17th 1862

Gen. J. A. McClernand
Comd.g 1st Div.
Gen.

It appears that during the night a large number of captured animals have been run off and many prisoners escaped. As the larger portion of the Cavalry force of this command is in your Division I wish you would form patrolls to prevent further escape and also send a party into the country to recapture such as may be found.

Direct your patrolls to take all horses and other captured property found in possession of our troops and turn the same over to Capt. Baxter A. Q. M. In case of officers having such property they must be arrested and the names reported to these Head Quarters.

Respectfully
your obt. svt.
U. S. Grant
Brig. Gen.

ALS, McClernand Papers, IHi. *O.R.*, II, iii, 272. See letter to Brig. Gen. John A. McClernand, Feb. 18, 1862.

General Orders No. 4

Head Quarters, Dist of West Tenn
Fort Donelson, Feby 18, 1862

General Orders No 4

Hereafter, until otherwise ordered, Guard Duty will be performed by the 1st and 2d Divisions and Col. McArthur's Brigade which for the present will be attached for orders to the 2nd Division.[1]

The 1st Division will guard all roads and passes into the entrenchments from the river above Dover, to the road leading West to Fort Henry.

The 2nd Division, with the Brigade attached, will guard from the Fort Henry road to the river below the Fort, and furnish the Guard for the Fort.

The 4th Division, now organizing will furnish all other Guards, such as for Commissary and Quarter Masters Stores, at Steam Boat Landing, Hospitals, &c.

Brig Gen. S. A. Hurlburt will have especial charge of the interior police regulations of the camps inside of the grounds occupied by the other Divisions.

By order,

U. S. GRANT

Brig. Gen. Com

DS, McClernand Papers, IHi. *O.R.*, I, vii, 633–34.

1. Col. John McArthur, commanding the 1st Brigade, 2nd Division, had been assigned to the 1st Division during the attack on Fort Donelson. One copy of General Orders No. 4 includes a note: "Cruft's instead of McArthur's." DLC-USG, V, 95.

General Orders No. 5

Head Quarters, Dist. of W. Ten.

Fort Donelson, Feb. 18th 1862.

GEN. ORDERS No 5

All horses, mules and other captured property will be immediately turned over to the Dist. Quartermaster, Capt. A. S. Baxter, or to Regimental Quartermasters, reporting the property received by them to the District Quartermaster.

Brigade and regimental commanders are expected to give
their personal attention to this matter and see that this order is
faithfully executed.

Ordnance, and ordnance stores will be turned over to Capt.
Brinck, ordnance officer.

All commanders are expected to see that all property within
the range of their regimental or Brigade grounds ~~are~~ is collected
and guarded until taken away by the proper officers.

All firing in and around camp is positively prohibited.

By Order
U. S. Grant
Brig. Gen.

ADS, McClernand Papers, IHi; DS, Brigham Young University, Provo, Utah;
copies, DLC-USG, V, 12, 95; DNA, RG 393, Dept. of the Mo., Letters Received;
ibid., USG General Orders. A different version of General Orders No. 5 appears
in two USG order books. "1. Division, Brigade and Regimental Commanders are
especially directed to see that all property captured at this place is immediately
turned over to the proper officers. 2. All Ordnance and Ordnance Stores will be
turned over to Capt. Brinck, Ordnance Officers; and all horses, mules and other
property will be turned over to Capt. A. S. Baxter Chief Quartermaster   3. All
Commanding Officers are required to give their personal attention to gathering
up and guarding all property within their camp lines until the same can be diliv-
ered to the officers designated to receive it   4. All firing in and around Camp is
positively prohibited"   Copies, DLC-USG, V, 13, 14.

On Feb. 19, 1862, Brig. Gen. John A. McClernand wrote to USG. "Capt.
Baxter informs me that there is much confusion in his department growing out of
surrounding circumstances. I write to suggest that if the captured animals within
and near the lines of my division were committed to the care of Capt. J. B. Russell,
who is acting for Captain Dunlap here, the labor falling on Captain Baxter would
be lessened and the animals preserved. Captain Russell displayed geart energy in
collecting and safe keeping, property captured at Fort Henry, preparatory to its
transfer to Capt. Baxter. This task is not invited, but suggested with a view to
the promotion of the public interest. There is now a large number of animals near
my Head Quarters under guard." Copies, McClernand Papers, IHi. On the same
day, McClernand wrote to USG. "Maj Bacon's hors[e] has become disabled in
consequence of hard service during the operations around this Fort. The horse
which Major Granbury delivered to him upon our entrance into the Fort and which
he intended to turn over to Capt. Baxter, has been taken by the latter, together
with the Majors saddle &c. Will it be agreeable to you that the Major should take
the horse either as a substitute for his or at his appraised value. The Major is
willing to pay for him. I will assign the Major to the command of the 18th Regt
—being one of my best officers." Copies, *ibid.*

To Brig. Gen. George W. Cullum

Head Quarters, Dist. of W. Ten.
Fort Donelson, Feby 18th 1862

GEN. G. W. CULLUM
CHIEF OF STAFF &c.
GEN.

If the bearer P. K. Stankiewitz should propose to give his parole I wish you would have him released. He has not asked me for this but I know him as an old and faithful soldier and have no doubt but his heart has always been with the Union cause. Living South at the time our present difficulties broke out and having been a soldier for many years in this country and in Europe I have no doubt he was virtually forced into his present position.

Respectfully
your obt. svt.
U. S. GRANT
Brig. Gen

ALS, DNA, RG 109, Union Provost Marshals' File of Papers Relating to Individual Civilians.
    Peter K. Stankiewicz, born in Cracow, Poland, around 1810 (there are discrepancies concerning his age), first enlisted in the U.S. Army in 1835, was promoted to sgt. in 1840, and was discharged at Camp Matamoros, Mexico, June 18, 1846. Stankiewicz was sgt. of Co. I, 4th Inf., in Sept., 1843, when USG joined this co. as bvt. 2nd lt. Captured at Fort Donelson as capt., 1st Tenn. Light Art., Stankiewicz was imprisoned at Camp Chase and Johnson's Island, Ohio, until exchanged in Nov., 1862. His petition for discharge from the C.S. Army was disapproved, and he was again captured and exchanged in 1863. Records of his military career are *ibid.*, RG 94 and RG 109.

To Brig. Gen. Stephen A. Hurlbut

———

Head Quarters, Dist of West. Tenn.
Fort. Donelson, Febry 18th 1862.

GEN. S. A. HURLBUT.
GENL:

You will encamp one Regiment of the troops, just arrived, or ~~both~~ 2 if you choose, near the village, with instructions to throw out guards and patrols, to prevent Officers and Soldiers, from entering any house without authority, and to prevent plundering generally. I would suggest that patrols, and strong ones at that, be sent out at once.

Respectfully,
Your Obt. Servant.
U. S. GRANT.
Brig. Gen. Commdg.

Copies, DLC-USG, V, 2, 3, 85; DNA, RG 393, USG Letters Sent. On Feb. 18, 1862, Capt. John A. Rawlins issued General Orders No. 3. "All commissioned officers, non-commissioned officers and soldiers are prohibited from entering the town of Dover, or any houses therein situated, without permission, in writing, of their Regimental Commanders. All captured property belongs to the Government, and no officers, non-commissioned officers or soldiers will be permitted to have or retain possession of captured property of any kind. Any officer violating the above order, will be at once arrested. Any non-commissioned officers or soldiers will be arrested and confined in the Guard House. And all captured property taken from them and turned over to the District Quarter Master. Col. Leggett is hereby appointed to see to the strict enforcement of the above, useing his whole command for that purpose if necessary." Copies, DLC-USG, V, 12, 13, 14, 95; DNA, RG 393, USG General Orders. *O.R.*, I, vii, 633. Copies of the same orders, numbered Special Orders No. 3, are in DLC-USG, V, 87; DNA, RG 94, 9th Ill., Letterbook.

To Brig. Gen. John A. McClernand

—————

Head Quarters, Dist. of West Tennessee
Fort Donelson, Feb. 18th 1862

GEN. J. A. McCLERNAND
COMD.G 1ST DIV.
GEN.

Your note in regard to details is just received. Details are necessarily very heavy just at this time consequent upon the large amount of property to be collected, the distance much of it has to be brought, state of the roads &c. They are equalized however between the two Divisions here and some made from the odd regiments belonging to neither Div.

I would suggest the plan of making details by regiments and commencing with those not in the engagement. A few days hard work is not going to hurt fresh men and particularly where it is a matter of so much importance.

Respectfully
your obt. svt.
U. S. GRANT
Brig. Gen

ALS, McClernand Papers, IHi. On Feb. 17, 1862, Brig. Gen. John A. McClernand wrote to USG. "The details for fatigue, Extra duty and Guard duty for Quarter Master, Commissary and Ordnance Department, have been so heavy today on my Division as to be oppressive and almost cruelly to the men. The calls upon my Div, today from your head quarters have amounted to about 600 men in addition to the Cavalry detailed for patrols. The men under my command have been out several days and nights, under arms most of the time in the face of the enemy and without shelter in two snow storms. Last night many were without shelter and no blankets during the rain. I would further state that it appears as if the same detail had been ordered a second time. It would very much facilitate the duty of the officers in charge of details for the Quarter Masters Department if he had some place at which they could report for duty. I am inclined to think that there is some want of method and deliberation in the Quarter Masters department." Copy, *ibid.*

To Brig. Gen. John A. McClernand

Head Quarters, Dist. of W. Ten.
Fort Donelson, Feb. 18th 1862

GEN. J. A. MCCLERNAND
COMD.G 1ST DIV.
GEN.

Send me a Company of Cavalry as soon as possible and I will send up the river and investigate the matter of which you make mention in your note.

I have ordered four companies of Infantry from the other ~~Brig~~ Division.

Respectfully
your obt. svt.
U. S. GRANT
Brig. Gen.

ALS, McClernand Papers, IHi. On Feb. 18, 1862, Brig. Gen. John A. McClernand wrote to USG. "I am informed that there are 500 negroes lately sent from the Iron Foundry, some eight or ten miles above to work on the entrenchments here who are now on their way to Clarksville. The Foundry alluded to is located about half a mile from the opposite shore of the Cumberland. A considerable quantity of property belonging to the enemy is reported to be in the same vicinity. If you should decide to make an effort to rescue the negroes and property belonging it~~o the enemy in~~ would be advisable to send a steamer bearing detachments both of Infantry and Cavalry. It is said but few white men are in charge of the negroes. The negroes, if forfeited under the law might be made to relieve our men from a portion of the heavy amount of fatigue duty required of them" Copy, *ibid*. See letter to Capt. John C. Kelton, Feb. 22, 1862.

To Edwin M. Stanton

Fort Donelson, Tennessee,
February 18th 1862

Hon. E. M. Stanton,
Secretary of War,
Washington, D. C.

We would respectfully recommend the promotion of Capt. W. W. Leland, Commissary of Subsistance on General U. S. Grant's Staff, to the rank of Major, as a benefit to the public service[1]

Your Very Respectful and Ob't Serv'ts.
Richd Yates Gov.[2]
O. M. Hatch Sec. State.[3]
Jesse K. Dubois, Auditor.
U. S. Grant Brig Gen

LS, IHi. Edwin M. Stanton, Pa. Democrat, was confirmed as secretary of war on Jan. 15, 1862. He had served as attorney general under President James Buchanan, Dec. 20, 1860–March 4, 1861.

1. On March 7, 1862, President Abraham Lincoln endorsed this letter. "Respectfully submitted to the War Department with the remark that I think the appointment would be a good one." AES, *ibid.* On April 16, Asst. Secretary of War Peter H. Watson wrote to Warren Leland. "The Secretary of War directs me to acknowledge the receipt of your letter of the 13th instant, and to state that, the meritorious services of your brother shall not be overlooked or go unrewarded after being officially made known by his Commanding officer to this Department." Copy, DNA, RG 107, Letters Sent. Capt. William W. Leland was not appointed maj. See letters to Capt. William W. Leland, Dec. 17, 1861, and to Brig. Gen. Lorenzo Thomas, July 25, 1862.

2. On Feb. 17, Ill. Governor Richard Yates telegraphed to Chicago that Ill. Auditor Jesse K. Dubois, Ill. Secretary of State Ozias M. Hatch (brother of USG's former q. m., Capt. Reuben B. Hatch), and Ill. Q. M. John Wood (former Ill. governor) were on their way to Fort Donelson. Yates concluded: "Send surgeons, friends and clothing for the wounded." *Illinois State Register*, Feb. 18, 1862. On Feb. 18, several surgeons were sent to Fort Donelson. *Illinois State Journal*, Feb. 19, 1862; [Allen C. Fuller], *Annual Report of the Adjutant General of the State of Illinois* (Springfield, 1863), pp. 50–51.

3. On Feb. 23, John Riggin, Jr., wrote to Capt. Wilbur F. Brinck. "Will

furnish Hon. O. M. Hatch with one dozen assorted captured arms, to be selected by Mr. Hatch, to be deposited in the Secretary of State's Office, Springfield, Illinois, as trophies taken at this place, from the rebel enemy." Copies, DLC-USG, V, 1, 2, 85; DNA, RG 393, USG Letters Sent.

To Brig. Gen. George W. Cullum

Head Quarters, Dist. of W. Ten.
Fort Donelson, Feb.y 19th 1862

GEN. GEO. W. CULLUM
CHIEF OF STAFF, DEPT. OF THE MO.
GEN.

Clarkesville is evacuated[1] and I shall take possession on Friday next[2] with one Division under Gen. Smith.[3] If it is the desire of the Gen. Comd.g Dept. I can have Nashville on Saturday week.[4] To do this I will have to retain transportation as it arrives. Please inform me early of the desire of the Gen. Comd.g on this point at as early a day as possible.

As soon as I got possession of Fort Donelson I commenced sending the sick and wounded to Paducah as seems to have been the desire of Gen. Halleck. No distinction has been made between Federal and confederate sick and wounded.[5] Generally the prisoners have been treated with great kindness and I believe they appreciate it.—Great numbers of of Union people have come into see us and express great hope for the future. They say secessionests are in great trepidation some leaving the country, others expressing anxiety to be assured that they will not be molested if they will come in and take the oath.[6]

The amount of supplies captured here is very large, sufficient probably for twenty days for all my army. Some articles will be deficient such as coffee. Of rice I dont know that we will want any more during the war.

I think I will send you the tail of the elephant to-night, or in the morning at furthest.[7]

Respectfully
your obt. svt.
U. S. GRANT
Brig. Gen.

ALS, DNA, RG 393, Dept. of the Mo., Letters Received. *O.R.*, I, vii, 637–38; *ibid.*, II, iii, 283.

1. On Feb. 20, 1862, Flag Officer Andrew H. Foote wrote a report evidently intended for Maj. Gen. Henry W. Halleck. "Yesterday on the 19th. instant I came up the river on an armed reconnoisance with the Conestoga and Cairo, having Col. Webster of the Engineer Corps and chief of Genl Grant's staff on board. On nearing Fort Defiance near Clarksville we found a white flag displayed and on landing found the fort deserted. Lieut. Com'd'g Phelps and Col. Webster took possession of the fort—the former hoisting the American flag. There were three guns mounted on this fort, three in the fort near the city and two in a fort a short distance up the Red river. On reaching Clarksville I sent for the authorities of the city and soon after the Hon. Cave Johnson, the Mayor and Judge Wisdom came aboard stating that the rebel soldiers had left the city and with the portion of the defeated army which had escaped from Fort Donelson, had fled to Nashville, after having wantonly burned the splendid rail-road bridge near the city—against the remonstrance of the citizens. I further ascertained that two-thirds of the citizens had fled from the place, panic stricken. In short the city was in a state of the wildest commotion from rumors that we would not respect the citizens either in their persons or their property. I assured those gentlemen that we came not to destroy anything but tents, military stores and army equipments. With this assurance they earnestly importuned me to issue a proclamation embodying my views and intentions to the citizens, that the confidence and quiet of the community might be restored. I was constrained contrary to my pre-determination of never writing such a document to issue the proclamation of which the enclosed is a copy. I leave this morning with the Conestoga to bring up one or two iron-clad Gun-Boats with this vessel and six mortar boats and then proceed with all possible dispatch up the Cumberland river, to Nashville and in conjunction with the army make an attack on Nashville. The rebels have great terror of the GunBoats as will be seen in their papers. One of them a short distance above Fort Donelson had previously fired an iron rolling mill belonging to the Hon. John Bell." LS, DNA, RG 393, Dept. of the Mo., Letters Received. *O.R.*, I, vii, 422–23; *O.R.* (Navy), I, xxii, 617–18. The text of the proclamation appears *ibid.*, p. 618.

2. Feb. 21.

3. See letter to Brig. Gen. Charles F. Smith, Feb. 19, 1862.

4. March 1.

5. On Feb. 18, Brig. Gen. William T. Sherman wrote to USG. "I have this moment received this Despatch from Genl Halleck. 'You will send Five hundred of the sick and wounded to Cincinati our men and the enemy to be treated precisely the same. Fit up boats and send them up. Remainder to be sent to Mound

City and to St. Louis. Inform Genl Grant all sick & wounded must be withdrawn from Fort Henry and Fort Donelson.—H W HALLECK, Maj Genl Comd' Nothing new here." ALS, DNA, RG 393, District of West Tenn., Letters Received. On the same day, Sherman again wrote to USG. "I am this moment in receipt of these Dispatches from Gen Halleck. 'Send five hundred sick & wounded to Cincinati consigned to Sanitary Committee the sick & wounded of our own troops and of the enemy to be treated precisely alike The boats which take them to Cincinati to be fitted up as comfortably as possible for our own men & the Rebels' 'All troops from Ky will be sent up the Cumberland, all others will be stopped at Paducah to await further orders. Watch Beauregard's movements from Columbus & report by Telegraph your force at Paducah (3200) also report all you stop there. We must now prepare for a still more important movemt.' Our scouts have been to Blandville and Lovelaceville, but I cannot observe that any change has taken place at Columbus. I learn that Camp Beauregard is abandoned and all men drawn inside of the Lines at Columbus, also that they have forbidden to citizens access to or egress their Lines. I understand heavy reinforcements are expected down from Kentucky but am not advised what troops if any are coming up." ALS, *ibid.*, Dept. of Kan., Letters Received. The first telegram quoted in the letter immediately preceding, dated Feb. 17, was addressed to USG, Sherman, and Brig. Gen. George W. Cullum. ALS (telegram sent), *ibid.*, Dept. of the Mo., Letters Received. *O.R.*, II, iii, 270.

On Feb. 19, Halleck telegraphed to Sherman. "Give Gov Morton the Indianna wounded. Use your discretion in this matter. No paroles will be given to Rebel officers. Divide them. Send a part here & a part to Cincinatti under strong guards. Telegraph above to Cullum & Grant." ALS (telegram sent), DNA, RG 107, Telegrams Collected (Unbound). *O.R.*, II, iii, 281.

6. There was no loyalty oath prescribed by army regulations for civilians, and military commanders used a variety of them. Harold M. Hyman, *To Try Men's Souls: Loyalty Tests in American History* (Berkeley and Los Angeles, 1959), p. 168.

7. On Feb. 19, Capt. John A. Rawlins wrote to Brig. Gen. Simon B. Buckner. "I am instructed by Brig. Gen. U. S. Grant, Comdg to say to you that there is transportation now in readiness for 6000 men, which number he desires may embark this evening. The remainder will be allowed to remain in their camps until morning." Copies, DLC-USG, V, 1, 2, 3, 85; DNA, RG 393, USG Letters Sent. *O.R.*, II, iii, 283. On the same day, Rawlins wrote to Col. Jacob G. Lauman. "Will detail Capt. Walker and Company, 25th Ind. Vols. to accompany Prisoners of War, as guards to Cairo, on board Steamer 'Continental.' " Copies, DLC-USG, V, 1, 2, 85; DNA, RG 393, USG Letters Sent.

To Brig. Gen. George W. Cullum

———

Head Quarters, Dist. W. Ten.
Fort Donelson, Feb. 19th 1862
I made it a point to discharge all citizens found in the fort at the time of surrender and had the case of Mr. Lurton been reported he also would have been released. I would recommend that he be now released if among the prisoners at Cairo.

U. S. GRANT
Brig. Gen.

AES, DLC-Horace H. Lurton. Written on a letter of Feb. 19, 1862, from Brig. Gen. Simon B. Buckner to Brig. Gen. George W. Cullum. "You will please release Horace H Lurton who was sent as a prisoner from this place as I learn from his father that he is not in the army being under age he was discharged at Bowling Green and whilst on a visit to his parents in Clarksville came to the Fort without their knowledge as a spectator, and being dressed in uniform was taken prisoner—By releasing him you will oblige" LS, *ibid*. Horace H. Lurton of Clarksville, Tenn., left the University of Chicago and enlisted in the 5th Tenn., from which he was released as a sgt. maj. for physical disability at the age of seventeen in early 1862. A few weeks later he joined the 2nd Ky. and was captured with the regt. at Fort Donelson. In April, 1862, he escaped from Camp Chase, Columbus, Ohio.

To Brig. Gen. William T. Sherman

———

Head Quarters, Dist. of West. Tenn.
Fort. Donelson, Febry 19th 1862.
GEN. W. T. SHERMAN
COMMDG DIST OF CAIRO,
PADUCAH, KY.
GENL:
Send all reenforcements up the Cumberland. I shall occupy Clarkesville, on Friday, and Nashville Saturday week, if it meets the approval of Gen. Halleck. I have written him to that effect.[1]

I feel under many obligations to you for the kind tone of your letter, and hope that should an opportunity occur you will win for yourself the promotion, which you are kind enough to say belongs to me.[2] I care nothing for promotion so long as our arms are successful, and no political appointments are made.

Respectfully,
Your Obt. Servant.
U. S. Grant.
Brig. Gen. Commdg.

Copies, DLC-USG, V, 1, 2, 3, 85; DNA, RG 393, USG Letters Sent. *O.R.*, I, vii, 638.

1. See letter to Brig. Gen. George W. Cullum, Feb. 19, 1862.
2. On Feb. 21, 1862, Brig. Gen. William T. Sherman wrote to USG. "Congratulating General Grant on his promotion" DLC-USG, V, 10; DNA, RG 393, USG Register of Letters Received.

To Brig. Gen. Charles F. Smith

Head Quarters, Dist. of W. Ten.
Fort Donelson, Feb. 19th 1862

Gen. C. F. Smith
Comd.g 2d Division &c.
Gen.

Hold your command in readiness to take possession of Clarkesville and garrison it.

I would suggest the propriety of appointing some Lieut. to Act. as Division Com.y and one to Act. as Div. Qr. Mr. Ten days rations should be taken to issue after arrival besides what the troops may have when they leave here.

There are no Confederate troops at Clarkesville at present but it may be a matter of importance to us to move there as rapidly as possible.

You can commence the movement as soon as practicable ~~and~~ after transportation can be provided.

> Respectfully
> your obt. svt.
> U. S. GRANT
> Brig. Gen.

ALS, James S. Schoff, New York, N. Y. *O.R.*, I, vii, 638.

To Brig. Gen. Lewis Wallace

———

> Head Quarters, Dist of West. Tenn.
> Fort. Donelson, Febry 19th 1862.

GEN. L. WALLACE
COMMDG AT, FORTS HENRY & HEIMAN.
GENL:

I understand that much more destruction has been done the R. R. Bridge, across the Tenn. river than was authorized by my order.

I wish you would direct the Officers who had charge of the job, to make a written report of what was done, and forward it to me.

Where long forage can be got ~~through~~ in the country, you may send after it provided you think men can be got who will not disgrace our cause by acts of vandalism, such as are too frequent.

Our men going into houses and taking any thing they want; killing Stock, poultry, &c. is calculated to do our cause great injury.

Where it is necessary to take property for the use of the Government, the amount taken should be fairly estimated and a

Certificate given for the amount, and purpose for which it ~~was~~ is taken.

> Respectfully
> Your Obt. Servant.
> U. S. GRANT.
> Brig. Genl. Commdg.

Copies, DLC-USG, V, 1, 2, 3, 85; DNA, RG 393, USG Letters Sent. See letter to Commanding Officer, Fort Henry, Feb. 15, 1862. On Feb. 24, 1862, Capt. John A. Rawlins wrote to Brig. Gen. Lewis Wallace. "Your communication of date 23rd inst, is just received. In answer thereto, I am instructed by Brig. Gen. Grant, Commanding to say that he had given directions to the Commdg. Officer of Fort. Henry, on the 15th inst. through Capt. Gwin, of the Gun Boat 'Taylor,' to send a sufficient force of Infantry and Cavalry up the river to effect the purpose mentioned in your communication, and had hoped the same had succeeded. But from present appearances the road will soon fall into our hands, and it is not deemed advisable therefore to destroy it now." Copies, DLC-USG, V, 1, 2, 3, 86; DNA, RG 393, USG Letters Sent.

To Brig. Gen. George W. Cullum

> Head Quarters, Dist. of W. Ten.
> Fort Donelson, Feb. 20th 1862

Respectfully forwarded to Gen. Cullum at Cairo. As I understand the Ordnance alluded to was sent to fill up the original Brigade of Gen. McClernand to a standard promised by the President over his own signature.[1]

> U. S. GRANT
> Brig. Gen.

AES, DNA, RG 393, District of West Tenn., Letters Received. Written on a letter of Feb. 19, 1862, from Brig. Gen. John A. McClernand to USG. "I understand that an order has been made by General Cullom, in the name of General Halleck, the scope of which will require the Ordnance, provided by the President for my original brigade, to be transferred to Lt. Col. Duff, Ordnance officer, at Cairo. You will recollect that the Ordnance thus provided consists of twelve 6 pdrs. and two 12 pds (James' rifled pieces), with ammunition etc. It was the purpose to make two batteries of these pieces—6 of which are now here, in the hands of Capt Dresser, another remaining to be brought up: while the remaining seven were to be assigned to Capt. McAllister whose company was assigned, by your order, to my original brigade. After the delay, personal efforts and expense incident to the obtaining of these pieces, it would be hard and, I think, unjust, to take them from me. I am persuaded you will agree with me in this; nor shall it be done except by General Halleck, and then only against my solemn & earnest protest. The accompanying copy of this communication you will please forward with any communication you may be pleased to make upon the subject." LS, *ibid.* On Feb. 22, Brig. Gen. George W. Cullum endorsed the letter. "Upon my arrival here I found ordnance property scattered in different hands, among them Quartermaster Dunlap's—the father-in-law of Gen. McClernand. To bring the Ordnance Dept. out of the chaos in which I found it, I appointed a Chief of Ordnance and directed all ordnance and ordnance stores to be turned over to him, which order was necessary for the good of the service and will not be changed except by the direction of the Major General Commanding the Dept. of the Missouri"   AES, *ibid.*

1. See endorsement to Brig. Gen. John A. McClernand, Oct. 30, 1861.

To Brig. Gen. Stephen A. Hurlbut

————

Head Quarters, Dist. of W. Ten.
Fort Donelson, Feb. 20th 1862.

GEN. S. A. HURLBUT U. S. A.
GEN.

I shall be absent from this command to-day. Am going to Clarkesville and will return in the evening.[1]

I understand from Gen. Sherman that 12000 troops are on their way here. Should they arrive in my absence you will assign them grounds.

Respectfully
your obt. svt.
U. S. GRANT
Brig. Gen.

ALS, Stephenson County Historical Society, Freeport, Ill. See letter to Brig. Gen. George W. Cullum, Feb. 21, 1862.

1. On Feb. 20, 1862, Col. William H. L. Wallace wrote to his wife. "It is 11 o'clk at night—I have just returned from a trip up the river to Clarksville— Genls. Grant & McClernand with several of their staff went up & I took up two

companies of my brigade (Co. D of the 11th & a company from the 20th) with the band of the 11th—It was a pleasant trip and a great relief from the constant & heavy cares incident to our dearly bought victory—Clarksville is a beautiful village or town of 5 or 6000 inhabitants on the North side of the Cumberland 40 miles above this & within 60 miles of Nashville—We marched through the streets but met no welcome except from the negros—Most of the white inhabitants have left—One house, where there were pleasant looking ladies at the door had the British flag hung out—On the way up we met one of our gun boats with Flag officer Foote on board—I went aboard his boat with the Genls—The commodore met us on crutches—He was slightly wounded at the bombardment of Ft. Donelson—He enquired about you & I gave him your congratulations on his success at Ft. Henry—" ALS, Wallace-Dickey Papers, IHi.

General Orders No. 6

Hd. Quarters District of West Tenn.
Fort Donelson, Feby 21st 1862.

GENERAL ORDERS No. 7.

The troops in this Military District are hereby Brigaded and assigned to Divisions in the following order to-wit:

First Division—Brig. Gen. J. A. McClernand Com'd'g

1st Brigade:

8th, 29th, 30th and 31st Illinois Infantry, Dresser's Battery, and Dollins, O'Harnett's and Carmichaels Cavalry.

2nd Brigade:

11th, 18th 20th and 45th Illinois Infantry, the 1st Battallion of 4th Illinois Cavalry, and Taylor's Battery.

3d Brigade:

17th, 43rd, 49th and 52d Illinois Infantry, and McAllister's and Schwartz's Batteries.

Second Division—Brig. Gen. C. F. Smith, Com'd'g

1st Brigade:

2nd, 7th, 12th and 14th Iowa Infantry and 2d Battallion 4th Illinois Cavalry.

2nd Brigade:

9th and 12th Illinois and 13th and 16th Missouri Infantry, Willard's Battery and detachment—Reg. Cav.[1]

3d Brigade:

7th, 50th, 57th, and 58th, Illinois Infantry, and 2 companies 2d Illinois Cavalry.—The Battallion of Artillery commanded by Major Cavander will be attached to the Second Division, at large.

Third Division—Brig. Gen. L. Wallace, Com'd'g.[2]

1st Brigade:

8th Missouri, 11th, 24th and 25th Indiana Infantry and Bullis's Battery

2nd Brigade:

1st Nebraska, and 58th, 68th and 78th Ohio Infantry, and 4 companies Curtis's Horse.

3d Brigade:

20th, 56th and 78th Ohio and 23d Indiana Infantry and the remainder of Curtis's Horse.

Fourth Division—Brig Gen. S. A. Hurlburt Com'dg

1st Brigade:

15th, 28th, 32d, and 41st Illinois Infantry and Barron's Battery of Light Artillery

2nd Brigade:

25th Indiana, 14th, 46th, 48th Illinois Infantry, and Mann's Battery of Light Artillery[3]

3d Brigade:

31st and 44th Indiana, and 17th and 25th Kentucky Infantry and 3d Battallion of 4th Illinois Cavalry.

The Senior Colonels of Brigades will command them in all instances.

Brigade Commanders will select from their Regimental Quartermasters of their commands one to act as Brigade Commissary

By order of Brig Gen U. S. Grant, Com'd'g
JNO. A. RAWLINS
A. A. Gen'l

DS, McClernand Papers, IHi. The copy received by Brig. Gen. John A. McClernand was mistakenly numbered General Orders No. 7, but the other copies are numbered General Orders No. 6. DLC-USG, V, 12, 13, 14, 95; DNA, RG 393,

USG General Orders; McClernand Papers, IHi. *O.R.*, I, vii, 649-50. On Feb. 22, 1862, McClernand wrote to USG. "General Orders No 7, brigading the troops under your command, is just received. Upon examination I find the 27th Regm.t (Col. Buford) is omitted. I ~~have~~ ordered him, several days ago, to join me, and would be pleased to have him attached to some one of my brigades. The great loss in battle, sustained by my original brigade, would seem to sanction such a measure. I also find that the 41st Ills. is assigned both to the 3rd Brigade of my Division and to the 1st Brigade of the 4th Division. Was it your intention to assign the 48th instead of the 41st to my Division? If satisfactory to you, either that or the 32nd (composed in large part of my neighbors) would be acceptable to me. Capt. Warren Stewart's Company of Cavalry who ~~has been~~ was assigned to my original brigade, is not mentioned in your Order. I suppose he is regarded as belonging to the 1st ~~Brigade, together with Delano's, O'Harnett's and Carmichael's~~. Division. The Captain is a member of my Staff, which his Company has for sometime past accompanied." DfS, McClernand Papers, IHi. On Feb. 22, Capt. John A. Rawlins wrote to McClernand. "I am instructed by Brig Genl Grant to say to you that the 41st Ill. Vols. is not assigned to your Division. It was the 43d Ill. that was assigned to you. The mistake was made by the clerk in copying." LS, *ibid.* On Feb. 26, McClernand wrote to USG. "Painful and severe sickness confining me to my bed for some days past has left me to conjecture, what is going on. As a consequence of the reduction of this place, Nashville has fallen into the hands of Genl. Buell's column. I suppose he is now pursuing the fugitive enemy. What are we to do? If we are to march against Columbus or Memphis or both, I trust it will be consistent with Department instructions and your own views, early, to send forward my division. Besides, a personal and somewhat thorough reconnoissance of the country about Columbus, I have, from the breaking out of the rebellion, attentively and carefully studied the immediate valley of the Mississippi as a principal field of military operations. These considerations may reasonably be supposed to afford some assurance of the efficiency of my command if employed in that field, or if danger and duty call in another direction I trust you send me with my command, there. I am sparing no pains to organize and consolidate my division conformably to your General Order No. 7." Copies, *ibid.* On March 2, Rawlins issued General Orders No. 20. "The following changes in General Orders, No. 6, Brigading and assigning to Divisions, the troops of this command, are hereby made. The 48th Ill. Vols. is transferred from the 2d Brigade, 4th Division, to the 2d Brigade, 1st Division   The 18th Ill. Vols. from the 2d Brigade, 1st Division, to the 1st Brigade, 1st Division. And the 52d Ill. Vols. from the 3d Brigade, 1st Division, to the 2d Brigade, 4th Division." DS, *ibid. O.R.*, I, vii, 678.

1. On Feb. 18, Brig. Gen. Charles F. Smith wrote to Rawlins. "Cos. C & I of the 2d. and 4th. regular cavalry respectively and Co. A, Chicago Light Art.y (Willard's battery), belonged to my Div.n at Paducah and at Fort Henry, in ~~Wall~~ Genl. *Wallace's* brigade; I request to know if I am to consider them still as attached to my command. These Cavalry Cos. are still here; I do not know if the battery is or not. A squadron of the 2d. Ills. Cav.y and a squadron of the 4th. Ills. Cav.y were assigned to the 1st & 2d. brigades of the Div.n respectively, but did not join; at least a small squadron of one of these regt.s did join at Ft. Heiman and was subsequently ordered away. I have no cavalry with my command at present." ALS, DNA, RG 393, District of West Tenn., Letters Received.

2. On Feb. 24, Rawlins wrote to Brig. Gen. Lewis Wallace. "I am instructed by Brig. Gen. Grant, to say to you that the Steamer 'Tigress' has been ordered to proceed from this place to Fort. Henry, (touching at no intermediate points) for the purpose of transporting the baggage, and camp equipage, including that of Officers, as well as men of the different Regiments now here, and formerly at Fort. Henry. She will arrive there ~~by~~ tomorrow morning. You will have all tents, camp equipage, baggage, &c. both at Fort Henry and Fort. Heiman, in readiness for shipping, that there may be no detention." Copies, DLC-USG, V, 1, 2, 3, 86; DNA, RG 393, USG Letters Sent. On Feb. 26, Rawlins wrote to Wallace. "Your orders addressed to the several Regiments, assigned as your Division, have just been received at these Head Quarters for distribution. I am directed by the General Commdg. to say to you that they are all countermanded for the present. The Regiments will remain as now located, until further orders." Copies, *ibid*.

3. Capt. Charles Mann commanded Mann's Independent Battery Light Art., organized in St. Louis on Nov. 4, 1861, later Co. C, 1st Mo. Light Art. On Feb. 20, 1862, McClernand wrote to USG. "Capt. Mann commanding two sections of Mo. Independent Artillery finding himself in the vicinity of my Head Quarters called on me to assign a place for his encampment. I accordingly did so—attaching his battery to the 3rd Brigade, Col Ross, for the time. This disposition will the better enable me to guard the passway near the river above town [*Dover*]. I trust, in all this, I have but anticipated your wish" Copies, McClernand Papers, IHi.

General Orders No. 7

Head Quarters, Dist. of West Ten.
Fort Donelson, Feb. 21st 1862

GEN. ORDERS No 7

Division and Brigade Commanders will take immediate steps to prevent soldiers of their respective commands from passing beyond the limits of the Field works of Fort Donelson.

All depridations committed upon citizens must be summarily punished.

Patrolls will be sent out daily by Division Commanders and all soldiers found out side the works without a pass approved by a Division Commander will be brought into camp and punished by regimental Commanders.

By order of
Brig. Gen. U. S. Grant
JNO A RAWLINS
A. A. Genl.

AD (in USG's hand), McClernand Papers, IHi. *O.R.*, I, vii, 650.

To Brig. Gen. George W. Cullum

Head Quarters, Dist. of W. Ten.
Fort Donelson, Feb. 21st 1862

GEN. G. W. CULLUM
CHIEF OF STAFF, DEPT. OF THE MO.
GEN.

I am now in possession of Clarkesville but will move no force there except Gen. Smith's Div. until I hear from Gen. Halleck. There is a conciderable amount of Army stores at Clarkesville, particularly flour and bacon, which it will be necessary to move if the Army is to fall back this way.

I would suggest however that points above Forts Henry and Donelson would be more advantageous for us to occupy than where we now are. I would say about the R. R. crossing on the two rivers.

It is my impression that by following up our success Nashville would be an easy conquest but I only through this out as a suggestion based simply upon information from people who have no sympathy with us.[1] White flags are flying from here to Clarkesville and rumor says the same thing extends to Nashville. At Nashville I understand one party put the white flag on the State House but it was torn down by another party.

I wrote you some days ago to have forwarded blankets and overcoats to issue to troops who lost theirs on the field of battle.[2] The men are suffering for them.

Shoes and other clothing is begining to be wanted to some extent.

I am ready for any move the Gen. Commanding may order.

I am Gen. very respectfully
your obt. svt.
U. S. GRANT
Brig. Gen.

ALS, DNA, RG 393, Dept. of the Mo., Letters Received. *O.R.*, I, vii, 423–24.
A postscript was added by Col. Joseph D. Webster. "By desire of Gen. Grant I

add a word. I went up to Clarksville with Flag Officer Foote on Wednesday at his request. While there an intelligent man told us that Gen. Johnson had left Nashville for Columbia. Another gentleman in town told me that Nashville had made offers to capitulate to some Federal Army which was near them. He said he has seen a man from N. who told him this. The first informant above referred to who is certainly our friend, begged us to push on to Nashville as fast as possible.—We took possession of two forts at Clarksville. In one were two 12 pdr guns on field carriges and a 42 on barbette carrige. In the other two 24 pdrs on siege carriages and one 42 on barbette carriage—none spiked. There was some powder at the lower fort which we threw into the river." ALS, DNA, RG 393, Dept. of the Mo., Letters Received.

1. On Feb. 21, 1862, Flag Officer Andrew H. Foote telegraphed to Brig. Gen. George W. Cullum. "Genl Grant and my self consider this a good time to move on Nashville, six Mortar boats and two iron clad steamers can ~~preceed~~ precede the troops and shell the forts, we were about moving for this purpose, when Genl Grant to my astonishment received a telegram from Genl Halleck 'not to let the Gunboats go higher than Clarksville,' no telegram sent to me— The Cumberland is in a good stage of water, and Genl Grant and I believe that we can take Nashville—Please ask Genl. Halleck if we shall do it—We will talk per telegraph. Capt Phelps representing me in the office, as I am still on crutches" Copy, *ibid.*, RG 45, Letters from Officers Commanding Squadrons, Miss. Squadron. *O.R.*, I, vii, 648; *O.R.* (Navy), I, xxii, 622–23. On Feb. 21, Maj. Gen. Henry W. Halleck telegraphed to Asst. Secretary of War Thomas A. Scott. "Advices just received from Clarksville represent that Genl A. S. Johnston has fallen back on Columbia & that there is very little preparation for a stand at Nashville. Genl Grant and Commodore Foote say the road is now open & are impatient. Cant you come down to the Cumberland & divide the responsibility with me. If so, I will immediately prepare to go ahead. I am tired of waiting for action in Washington. They will not understand the case; it is as plain as day light to me." ALS (telegram sent), Ritzman Collection, Aurora College, Aurora, Ill. *O.R.*, I, vii, 648. On the same day, Halleck telegraphed to Cullum. "Let me know result of reconnaissance as early as possible. Every thing must remain in *statu quo* till to-morrow. I am waiting messages from Kentucky & Washington. If possible notify Grant, Phelps & Com Foote to make no further moves till they receive orders." ALS (telegram sent), DNA, RG 107, Telegrams Collected (Unbound). *O.R.*, I, vii, 648.

2. On Feb. 26, Capt. Nathaniel H. McLean endorsed this letter. "Respectfully referred to Major R. Allen, about blankets and overcoats—" AES, DNA, RG 393, Dept. of the Mo., Letters Received. At the bottom of the letter is the notation "2000 Blankets   2000 Inf Overcoats"   See letter to Brig. Gen. George W. Cullum, Feb. 17, 1862.

To Capt. John C. Kelton

Head Quarters, Dist. of W. Ten.
Fort Donelson, Feb. 21st 1862.

CAPT. J. C. KELTON
A. A. GEN. DEPT. OF THE MO.
ST. LOUIS MO.
CAPT.

I understand, unofficially, that several fragments of regiments from Illinois have been ordered to St. Louis and are now subject to be assigned wherever they may be needed. If such is the case I would respectfully request that one thousand of them be sent here to fill up regiments that suffered severely in the late engagement, and were weak before.

Respectfully
your obt. svt.
U. S. GRANT
Brig. Gen.

ALS, DNA, RG 393, Dept. of the Mo., Letters Received.

To Brig. Gen. William T. Sherman

Head Quarters, Dist. W. Ten.
Fort Donelson, Feb.y 21st 1862.

GEN. W. T. SHERMAN
COMD.G DIST. OF CAIRO,
PADUCAH, ILL.
GEN.

I am sending off the sick and wounded as rapidly as possible and commenced doing so immediately after the battle. Owing however to the continuous wet and cold weather we are much retarded in the operation.

I want to see as few citizens here as possible They embarass us very much. Ladies are still worse than men and particularly if they are the wives of officers. I would esteem it a special favor if you would allow no officers wifeves to come up except where the officers ~~may be~~ are wounded.

I am at a loss to know what the next move is going to be. Yesterday I was in Clarkesville and expected by to-morrow week to be in Nashville. Gen. Halleck's telegram indicates a different move.

We want no more Surgeons here.

> I am Gen. very respectfully
> your obt. svt.
> U. S. GRANT
> Brig Gen

ALS, DLC-William T. Sherman. On Feb. 19, 1862, Brig. Gen. William T. Sherman wrote to USG. "I despatched a small boat up the Cumberland this afternoon with dispatches for you. These consisted of Telegraphic Despatches sent to Smithland, but no opportunity offered, and I therefore sent the Boat up. Governor Morton of Indiana has just arrived in a small boat the Cousin, with a party of citizens & physicians, and will proceed forthwith to Donelson.—Lest any mistake has occurred I will here repeat—General Halleck orders you to send down all wounded & disabled men—and not to advance beyond Clarksville, and even then to confine your operations to the destruction of the Railroad there—All the Prisoners including those of the McGill have passed down—The wounded are divided between Cairo and Paducah, but many are being furloughed and in the end we shall be compelled to allow friends to take them away—The Thos E Tutt came down disabled in tow of the Alps, and being full of the baggage of a Brigade including tents & knapsacks, and there being no opportunity to send them to Mound City, I on consultation with officers concluded the wounded would be more comfortable on board than to be twice transferred. As soon as they return they will be taken care of. I write in haste." ALS, DNA, RG 393, District of West Tenn., Letters Received.

On Feb. 18, Maj. Gen. Henry W. Halleck telegraphed to USG. "Dont let gun boats ~~or mortars~~ go higher up than Clarksville. Even there they must limit their operations to the destruction of the bridge & rail-road, and return immediately to Cairo, leaving one at Fort Donaldson. Mortar boats to be sent back to Cairo as soon as possible." ALS (telegram sent), *ibid.*, RG 107, Telegrams Collected (Unbound); copies, *ibid.*, RG 45, Area 5; *ibid.*, RG 94, Generals' Papers and Books, Telegrams Sent in Cipher by Gen. Halleck; *ibid.*, RG 393, USG Hd. Qrs. Correspondence; *ibid.*, Dept. of the Mo., Telegrams Sent; DLC-USG, V, 4, 5, 7, 8, 9. *O.R.*, I, vii, 633; *O.R.* (Navy), I, xxii, 616. Halleck sent this telegram to Sherman with instructions to forward it to USG "with all possible despatch." On the same day, Halleck telegraphed to the operator at Smithland. "When will line reach Fort Henry or some point where I can communicate with Genl Grant?" ALS (telegram sent), DNA, RG 107, Telegrams Collected (Unbound). On Feb. 19, Sherman wrote to USG. "The intense anxiety of the People to learn the names and condition of the dead and wounded of your army is such that many have come here, with the wish that they be allowed to proceed to Fort Henry or Donelson. As a general Rule I have thought you would be embarrassed by their presence and have withheld passes, because the number of boats going down with prisoners and wounded is so great that we have none here, or none at Cairo. I have ordered a boat which arrived with grain to get ready to go up, this afternoon.—Three boats arrived at Smithland yesterday with troops from General Buells command, but were recalled to the mouth of Green River by Gen Buells order. The Garrison there is very small, and I have sent to Shawneetown for a Cavalry Regiment a part of which will be placed there and remainder here. General Halleck is looking to your communications and orders me to stop all troops arriving here, and place them at Cairo or Paducah. Scouts are out all the time in the direction of Columbus but the enemy there keeps close. We have now several men employed to ascertain if any part of Beauregards forces have been withdrawn and sent either in your direction or Cairo. General Halleck has telegraphed you the dispatch having been forwarded, to send down all your sick wounded and disabled. Some of your wounded are here, and no efforts have been or will be spared to make them as comfortable as possible. Those by the Chancellor have been sent to Mound City, and all as they arrive will be sent either to the General Hospital at Mound City or to Cincinati. The whole country is alive to the necessity of caring for the wounded. Do you wish surgeons, nurses—the wives of officers, Laundresses or any thing. I should know your wishes as I am compelled to exercise a supervision over the Boats. If allowed to carry up all who apply, you would have no room left for transporting of the wounded and prisoners. Please communicate your wishes on this point as the ladies of several officers are here." ALS, *ibid.*, RG 393, District of West Tenn., Letters Received.

To Brig. Gen. Charles F. Smith

Head Quarters, Dist. of W. Ten.
Fort Donelson, Feb. 21st 1862

GEN. C. F. SMITH
COMD.G 2D DIV. &c
GEN.

You will proceed to Clarkesville Ten. with so much of your command as transportation is now ready for[1] and occupy grounds about the forts on the North bank of the river.

I have no special directions to give that wont naturally suggest themselvs to you, such as keeping the men from going into private houses and annoying the citizens generally.

There is said to be a large quantity of Army stores at Clarkesville[2] which, by calling upon the Mayor of the City,[3] will be given up to our use.

> very respectfully
> your obt. svt.
> U. S. GRANT
> Brig. Gen.

ALS, James S. Schoff, New York, N. Y. *O.R.*, I, vii, 649.

1. On Feb. 21, 1862, Capt. John A. Rawlins wrote to George W. Graham. "You will order the Steamers W. H. B' and 'Alps,' or some other suitable boats, in readiness to, at once tow the Mortar Boats to Clarkesville." Copies, DLC-USG, V, 1, 2, 85; DNA, RG 393, USG Letters Sent. On Feb. 21, Flag Officer Andrew H. Foote, Paducah, wrote to any naval officer commanding, or USG, Brig. Gen. Charles F. Smith, Brig. Gen. John A. McClernand, or any army commanding officer. "You will immediately *order down to Cairo* with the utmost haste and in ~~tow~~ *tow* of *steamers*, all the Mortar Boats, and one of the Gun Boats, either Capt. Dove or ~~M~~Capt. Byrant. They must leave immediately as they are wanted in Cairo by or before Sunday. I prefer the Cairo to come down if she can leave as soon as the Louville can leave. The Gun Boat & Mortar Boats must leave immediately as they are wanted this moment in Cairo to be instantly prepared for service. hasten, hasten, 'bear a hand' & follow me" ALS, *ibid.*, RG 45, Area 5. On Feb. 22, Foote wrote to USG. "I have been telegraphing with Genl. Cullum, who says that Genl. Halleck is waiting instructions from the War Dept. and Kentucky, and directs that every[*thing*] remains in 'Statu quo' or as they now are. Therefore please hold on to the Gun & Mortar Boats till you hear further from me. If they are at Clarksville now, all the better, as in that case, if we move up to Nashville, they are that far on their way, whereas if we are ordered not to proceed to Nashville they can, in tow of steamers, easily be sent down to Cairo,—retaining for your use only the Gun Boat 'Cairo.' With hearty congratulations for your well earned Major Generalship. Please have a barge of coal at Clarksville." Copy, *ibid.*, Correspondence of Joshua Bishop. *O.R.* (Navy), I, xxii, 624.
2. See letter to Brig. Gen. George W. Cullum, Feb. 21, 1862.
3. C. George Smith. Letter of Ursula S. Beach, Clarksville, June 16, 1970, USGA.

To Alfred B. Safford

Fort Donelson Ten.
Feb.y 21st 1862

MR. A. B. SAFFORD
CAIRO ILL.
DEAR SIR:

I wrote to Mrs. Grant last week to go to Covington and among other things directed her to draw out of bank any money I might have remaining there. Since that a letter from her states that she has no directions from me what to do from which I infer that my letter was lost. Will you be kind enough to send her a draft on New York or Cincinnati, directed to the care of J. R. Grant, Covington, Ky. for what ever may still be due me.

Capt. Brinck will send the draft if you will give it to him.

Your obt. svt.
U. S. GRANT

ALS, OClWHi. See letter to Julia Dent Grant, Feb. 14, 1862.

To Elihu B. Washburne

Fort Donelson Ten.
Feb.y 21st 1862

HON. E. B. WASHBURN
WASHINGTON D. C.
DEAR SIR;

Since receiving your letter at Fort Henry events have transpired so rapidly that I have scarsely had time to write a private letter. That portion of your letter which required immediate attention was replied to as soon as your letter was read.[1] I mean that I telegraphed Col. C. C. Washburn,[2] Milwukee Wis. asking him to accept a place on my Staff. As he has not yet arrived I fear my dispatch was not received. Will you be kind enough to say to him that such a dispatch was sent and that I will be most happy to publish the order the moment he arrives assigning him the position you ask.[3]

On the 13th 14th & 15th our volunteers fought a battle that would figure well with many of thos fought in Europe where large standing armies are maintained. I feel very greatful to you for having placed me in the position to have had the honor of commanding such an army and at such a time. I only trust that I have not nor will not disappoint you.—The effect upon the community here is very marked since the battle. Defeat, disastrous defeat, is admitted.—Yesterday I went to Clarkesville with a small escort two of our gun boats having preceded me. Our forces now occupy that place and will take possession of a large amount of Commissary stores, ammunition and some artillery. The road to Nashville is now clear but whether my destination will be there or further West cant yet be told. I want to move early and no doubt will.

I want to call your attention to Gen. C. F. Smith. It is a pity that our service should loose so fine a soldier from a first command. If Maj. Generals are to be made a better selection could not be made than to ~~take~~ appoint C. F. Smith.[4]

Truly yours
U. S. GRANT

ALS, IHi.

 1. Not found.
 2. Col. Cadwallader C. Washburn, younger brother of Congressman Elihu B. Washburne, was born in Me., and settled at Mineral Point, Wis., in 1842. There he began a successful career as lawyer, banker, and Republican U. S. Representative (1855–1861). On Feb. 6, 1862, he was appointed col., 6th Wis. Cav.
 3. See General Orders No. 19, March 2, 1862.
 4. On March 21, the Senate confirmed Brig. Gen. Charles F. Smith as a maj. gen. *Senate Executive Journal*, XII, 179. See letter to Elihu B. Washburne, Feb. 22, 1862, note.

General Orders No. 7

Head Quarters Dist of West Tenn.
Fort Donelson, Feby 22d 1862

General Orders No. 7.

Col. M. D. Leggett,[1] 78th Ohio Vols is appointed Acting Provost Marshall, until a suitable person for the position can be designated, and will be obeyed and respected accordingly.

In all cases where it may be deemed necessary to refer to higher authority, Brig Gen. S. A. Hurlburt second in authority will be appealed to.

Tenneessee, by her rebellion, having ignored all laws of the United State[s] no courts will be allowed to act under State authority, but all cases coming within the reach of the Military Arm, will be adjudicate[d] by the authorities the Government has established within the State.

Martial law is therefore declared to extend over West Tennessee. Wheraever a sufficient number of citizens of the State return to their allegiance to maintain law and order, over this Territory, the military restriction here indicated will be removed.

By order of Brig Gen U. S. Grant Com'd'g
Jno. A. Rawlins
A A Gen'l

DS, McClernand Papers, IHi; copy, *ibid.* Copies of the same orders, numbered General Orders No. 8, are in DLC-USG, V, 12, 13, 14, 95; DNA, RG 393, USG General Orders. *O.R.*, I, vii, 654–55.

The capture of Fort Henry and Fort Donelson, and the occupation of Clarksville, by USG's forces marked the first time that any portion of a seceded state had come under U. S. control in the Dept. of the Mo. Under martial law, military authority is substituted for civil authority; the commander, who becomes the source of law, can suspend, continue, or modify existing law and government. J. G. Randall, *Constitutional Problems Under Lincoln* (Rev. ed., Urbana, Ill., 1951), pp. 142, 170–74. Precedents for the government of conquered territory had been brought together by Maj. Gen. Henry W. Halleck, a leading authority on international law. He held that once hostile territory was seized, the President had the authority to establish temporary government and to provide laws to govern the territory. *International Law; or, Rules Regulating the Intercourse of States in Peace and War* (San Francisco, 1861), pp. 783–85.

On March 3, 1862, President Abraham Lincoln appointed Tenn. Senator Andrew Johnson a brig. gen., and the Senate confirmed the appointment the next day. *Senate Executive Journal*, XII, 147–48. On March 3, Secretary of War Edwin M. Stanton wrote to Johnson. "You are hereby appointed Military Governor of the State of Tennessee, with authority to exercise and perform, *within the limits of that state*, all and singular, the powers, duties and functions pertaining to the office of Military Governor (including the *power* to *establish all necessary offices and tribunals*, and *suspend* the *writ of Habeas Corpus*) during the pleasure of the President, or until the loyal inhabitants of that state shall organize a civil government in conformity with the Constitution of the United States" Copy, DLC-Andrew Johnson. War Dept. General Orders No. 100, April 24, 1863, prepared by Francis Lieber, codified the rules for governing occupied territory. *O.R.*, III, iii, 148–64. See also Frank Freidel, "General Orders 100 and Military Government," *Mississippi Valley Historical Review*, XXXII, 4 (March, 1946), 541–56.

1. Mortimer D. Leggett of Zanesville, Ohio, educated at Kirtland Teachers School and Western Reserve College before being admitted to the bar in 1844, taught law for a brief period at Ohio Law College, Poland, and later became superintendent of schools at Zanesville, where he continued to practice law. He served briefly on the staff of Maj. Gen. George B. McClellan before returning to Ohio to recruit the 78th Ohio. On Jan. 21, 1862, Leggett was appointed col. of the 78th Ohio, which arrived at Fort Donelson on Feb. 13.

To Brig. Gen. George W. Cullum

Headquarters District of West Tennessee,
Fort Donelson, February 22, 1862.

GENERAL G. W. CULLUM,
CHIEF OF STAFF, DEPARTMENT OF THE MISSOURI,
CAIRO, ILL.

GENERAL: Inclosed I send you a petition of surgeons now held as prisoners at this place. There are still here some 200 sick and wounded prisoners and probably 120 wounded at Clarksville. These latter were not taken prisoners at the fort but fell into our hands by taking possession of Clarksville. I would suggest the propriety of liberating such of the prisoners as are not likely to be fit for duty soon and a sufficient number of surgeons to take care of them. I would respectfully request that Major Kuykendall, of the Thirty-first Illinois Volunteers, now at Cairo,

be ordered to join his regiment, now without a field officer.[1]
There is now but little doubt but that the enemy have fallen back
from Nashville to a point about forty miles south on the Chatta-
nooga Railroad. What is the news from General Buell?

Very respectfully, your obedient servant,
U. S. GRANT,
Brigadier-General.

O.R., II, iii, 299. On Feb. 19, 1862, Surgeon John Patterson, 18th Tenn., and
seventeen others, addressed a petition to USG. "The memorial of the undersigned
surgeons and assistant surgeons of the respective regiments that have surrendered
at this point respectfully suggests that a number of the prisoners who were seriously wounded in the late actions at this place—arms and legs shot off, disabling
shots through chest, shoulder and abdomen—will be totally unable for any military duty during life or a long period of years. If permitted to return to their
respective homes [they] could be well cared for by their friends and relieve the
United States Government of the trouble and expense with them. That for ourselves we would ask to be released, pledging our honor as gentlemen that in the
event of surgeons and assistant surgeons of the U. S. Army being taken prisoners
by the Confederate forces and held as such to cause ourselves to be exchanged for
them, or report ourselves as prisoners of war at the nearest garrison of the U. S.
Army." Ibid., p. 300.

1. On Feb. 15, at Fort Donelson, Col. John A. Logan, 31st Ill., was wounded
and Lt. Col. John H. White was killed. See letter to Elihu B. Washburne, Feb. 22,
1862; O.R., I, vii, 177. Maj. Andrew J. Kuykendall was provost marshal at Cairo.
See letter to Brig. Gen. Eleazer A. Paine, Feb. 2, 1862.

To Capt. John C. Kelton

Head Quarters, Dist. of West Ten.
Fort Donelson, Feb.y 22d 1862.

CAPT. J. C. KELTON
A. A. GEN. DEPT. OF THE MO.
ST. LOUIS, MO.
CAPT.

Enclosed I send you ~~copy~~ of report of Capt. E. P. Barrett[1] of
50th Ill. Vols. sent up the Cumberland[2] to return property

improperly taken by Capt. Moses Cline[3] of the 13th Mo. Vols. Capt. Cline has been ordered to report himself at Hd Qrs. in arrest.

On the 19th I ordered a detail of one Comp.y of Cavalry and three companies of Infantry to proceed up the river to apprehend several hundred negroes said to be on their way to Nashville to work in the fortifications there and who had been employed in like manner at this place.[4] Also to get a large quantity of bacon which was said to be on the river above here and belonging to the Confederate Army.—Capt. Cline was the senior officer of the expedition and had written instructions, which he can show, what to do. I gave him very full verbal instructions what he was not allowed to do. He was not to molest private property nor allow his men to insult citizens.

Pillaging and burning was expressly to be avoided. When the Capt. returned his report showed the capture of two citizens taken from their homes, twenty-five or thirty negroes, mostly old men, women and children taken from their Cabins and such stores as had been provided for their maintainance. A considerable amount of property also was burned.

I immediately ordered the return of such of the property as had not been disposed of by Capt. Cline and he to report himself in arrest at Head Quarters.

> Very respectfully
> your obt. svt.
> U. S. GRANT
> Brig. Gen.

ALS, DNA, RG 393, Dept. of the Mo., Letters Received. *O.R.*, II, iii, 300. On Feb. 22, 1862, 1st Lt. Edward P. Barrett wrote to USG. "In compliance with your order, I, with my command returned to Bell-wood Furnace the property therefrom taken, by Capt Cline, with the following exceptions, viz   About Five Thousand pounds of Bacon, (fifteen hundred pounds of which was put upon the Iatan, some three hundred pounds given to some travelers, & the rest used & disposed of in such ways as I could not get it)   Also one Beef given by Capt Cline to the Iatan valued at $30.00 Thirty Dollars. Also a lot of Carpenters and Black Smith Tools, part burned and a part taken on board the Iatan as near a[s] I can learn, valued at $500 00 Five hundred Dollars. Also a lot of Farming Tools viz   Plows Cultivators &Co, valued at $1000 00 One Thousand Dollars, which were burned.

Also one Bbl Lard put upon the Iatan, and two bbls Engine Lard missing. Also one Bbl molasses used by Capt Clines. command together with some 50 lbs Sugar. Also one Negro man, Bill Casey, a low, dark brown negro about 5 ft 6 in high & 30 years old or upwards. The following property was burned The Furnace building & moulding room, Coal Shed & Coal house full of Coal, Casting house & negro house I resptly submit this to your consideration" ALS, DNA, RG 393, Dept. of the Mo., Letters Received. On Feb. 22, W. W. Yarrell, J. D. Green, and N. G. Morris, Bellwood Furnace, Tenn., wrote to USG. "We in behalf of the owners and citizens of this place, return you our sincere thanks, for the kind, gentlemanly and efficient manner in which Capt. Barrett executed your orders in regard to us, also to his entire command." Copy, *ibid.*

 1. Edward P. Barrett of Avon, Ill., was appointed 1st lt., 50th Ill., on Dec. 12, 1861. On Feb. 9, 1862, Capt. John A. Rawlins issued Special Field Orders No. 4. "1st Lieut. Edward P. Barrett, Co. "D" 50th Ills. Vols. is hereby appointed Captain of Company "A" 50th Ills. Vols. the Commission to be made out by the subject to the approval of the Governor of the State of Ills. if it meets with his approval. This appointment from to-day." Copies, DLC-USG, V, 15, 16, 82, 89; DNA, RG 393, USG Special Orders. On April 1, Col. Moses F. Bane, 50th Ill. wrote to Ill. Governor Richard Yates. "Respectfully asked, that you commission Geo R. Tippett 1st Lieut of Co 'G' 50th Regt Ill Vols in place of 1st Lieut Ed P Barrett, who is acting Captain of Company 'A' 50th Ill Regt, by field order of Maj Gen Grant issued Feby 8th at Fort Henry Tenn to fill the place of Capt Picket Co A whose resignation was accepted by Major Gen Halleck to take effect Feby 5th 1862. Please date the commission of Geo R Tippett, the 8th Feby 1862, as he has been acting in that capacity from that date by order of Gen Grant" ALS, Records of 50th Ill., I-ar. On July 13, Capt. Nathaniel H. McLean issued Special Orders No. 154, Dept. of the Miss., accepting Barrett's resignation. DS, *ibid.*

 2. Probably in the vicinity of Bellwood Creek which flows into the Cumberland River from the north, approximately five miles upriver from Fort Donelson.

 3. Moses Klein of Ohio was appointed capt., 13th Mo., on Sept. 6, 1861.

 4. See letter to Brig. Gen. John A. McClernand, Feb. 18, 1862. On March 24, Capt. William R. Rowley wrote to Elihu B. Washburne. "By the By I notice that some of our northern papers of the Chicago Tribune Kidney are circulating the report that Gen'l Grant returned some 25 or 50 slaves that had been employed on fortifications to their owners. Now as I happen to know all about that matter I deem it due to the Gen'l that I explain it. On the day after we entered Fort Donelson a report was brought to the Gen that during the fight the rebels had sent a number of slaves (who had been employed on Fortifications) across the river under a guard with instructions to work their way towards Clarksville. deeming it his duty to intercept them if possible he ordered a company of Cavalry to embark on a Steam boat and proceed up the River until they should get ahead of them, and then to disembark and proceed into the country & intercept & bring them back. but on *no account to interfere with citizens* or their private property. The Cavalry proceeded up the river—disembarked & went back into the Country but *failed* to find the party they were sent after—and in returning to the boat commenced pillaging on their *own* hook taking from one of the settlements about 25 negroes all of whom were *Old* men & women and *small* children taking in addition a Quantity of bacon & provisions and some mules &c *all* private property consumating the outrage by burning some of the Cabins &c. When the boat arrived

at Donelson and the Gen. learned the facts of the case he ordered the boat to return direct with the same Company with negroes mules & provisions to ~~return~~ the place where they wer taken and the officer commanding the company was sent under arrest to St Louis to report to Gen Halleck, which is the sum and substance of the great sensation story" ALS, DLC-Elihu B. Washburne.

To Brig. Gen. John A. McClernand

Head Quarters, Dist. of W. Ten.
Fort Donelson, Feb.y 22d 1862

Gen J. A. McClernand
Comd.g 1st Div.
Gen.

Hereafter expeditions will not be sent to the country for the purpose of Arresting citizens and taking their property without first having authority from these Head Quarters. It leads to constant mistakes and embarassment to have our men runing through the country interpreting confiscation acts[1] and only strengthens the enthusiasm against us whilst it has a demoralizing influance upon our own troops.

> Very respectfully
> your obt. svt.
> U. S. Grant
> Brig. Gen.

ALS, McClernand Papers, IHi. On Feb. 22, 1862, Brig. Gen. John A. McClernand wrote to USG. "Your communication condemning expeditions for the seizure of citizens and private property is recd. I am not aware that any such expeditions have been ordered; certainly they have not by me; on the contrary I condemn them. Denying any complicity in any such order, you will pardon me for repelling the implication that I am guilty. Such expeditions as have been ordered by me, since the battle were for the purpose of reconnoisance up the river and to capture fugitive rebels and enemy's property; in all of which I trust I have your approbation as well as my order" Copies, *ibid.*

1. The Confiscation Act of Aug. 6, 1861, *U. S. Statutes at Large*, XII, 319, provided for the confiscation of property used to aid the rebellion. Even then, however, the property first had to be condemned by a federal court. J. G. Randall, *Constitutional Problems under Lincoln* (Rev. ed., Urbana, Ill., 1951), p. 276. Gen-

eral Orders No. 8 and 13, Dept. of the Mo., Nov. 26, Dec. 4, 1861, contained instructions concerning the seizure of private property. *O.R.*, I, viii, 381, 406. See preceding letter.

To *Julia Dent Grant*

———

Fort Donelson Ten.
Feb.y 22d 1862

DEAR JULIA,

You no doubt received a letter from me immediately on your arrival in Covington. I will write to you frequently but short. How long I shall be here is uncertain but not many days I am confidant.

I see from the papers, and also from a dispatch sent me by Mr. Washburn, that the Administration have thought well enough of my administration of affairs to make me a Maj. General. Is father afraid yet that I will not be able to sustain myself? He expressed apprehensions on that point when I was made a Brigadier.

There is but little doubt but that Fort Donelson was the hardest fought battle on the Continent. I was extremely lucky to be the Commanding officer. From the accounts received here it must have created a perfect furor through the North.

I am in most perfect health and ready for anything even to chasing Floyd & Pillow. There is but little hope however of ever overhawling them. They are as dead as if they were in their graves for any harm they can do.

To go over the works here it looks as if the enemy had nothing to do but stand in their places to hold them. I have no doubt but you have read of Fort Donelson until you have grown tired of the name so I shall write you no more on the subject. Hope to make a new subject soon. Give my love to all at home. Kiss the children for me and write me all the news.

Tell Mary to write to me also.

ULYS.

ALS, DLC-USG. On the evening of Feb. 16, 1862, Secretary of War Edwin M. Stanton brought the nomination of USG as maj. gen., dated Feb. 17, to President Abraham Lincoln, who remarked as he signed the nomination: "If the Southerners think that man for man they are better than our Illinois men, or Western men generally, they will discover themselves in a grievous mistake." Helen Nicolay, *Lincoln's Secretary: A Biography of John G. Nicolay* (New York, London, Toronto, 1949), pp. 132–33; *Senate Executive Journal*, XII, 120–21. On Feb. 19, the Senate confirmed USG's promotion to maj. gen. to date from Feb. 16. On Feb. 19, Congressman Elihu B. Washburne telegraphed to USG. "You are appointed Major General." Copy, DNA, RG 393, Dept. of the Mo., Telegrams Received. On Feb. 17, Maj. Gen. Henry W. Halleck had telegraphed to Maj. Gen. George B. McClellan. "Make Buell, Grant, and Pope major-generals of volunteers, and give me command in the West. I ask this in return for Forts Henry and Donelson." *O.R.*, I, vii, 628. On the same day, Asst. Secretary of War Thomas A. Scott wrote to Stanton. "I have had a long and confidential interview with General Halleck this morning, and have gone over all the practical troubles in the way of united action in the armies of the West. After a full discussion I am now satisfied that his views and aims are thoroughly patriotic and proper. He wants the following organisation to make our armies effective in the shortest possible time, and with it, the additional forces as stated below—Major General Hunter to remain in command of his present Department. Major General Hitchcock to assume the command of the Department of Missouri (now Department of the West.) Brigadier General Buell to be promoted to the rank of a Major General, and to have the command of his present Department, with all the forces belonging thereto—those now on the Cumberland river to be restored to him. The whole of these commands to be thrown into One Department or Division—to be called 'The Department of the West', 'The Division of the West' or 'The Armies of the West', as may be thought best; and under such consolidation to be under the immediate direction of Major General Halleck as the senior officer in command —he, in that event, taking the field in person and assuming command of the Center Column, or of the army as it may be organised for movement on the Cumberland and Tennessee rivers; he, Maj. Genl. Halleck, with his organisation of the West, to be of course under the command and direction of the General Commanding the Army and of the military heads of the Government. This will provide a working organisation that must be effective and will make the armies of the West an entire success. General Halleck desires (and in this General Buell coincides) that 50.000 well disciplined troops, consisting of infantry and artillery from the army of the Potomac be sent West immediately, and with them about two (2) regiments of well equipped Cavalry—the forces to come West to such points on the Cumberland and Tennessee rivers as may be designated—brigaded, with active and efficient officers ready for active service—With these additions to the armies of the West, Major General Buell can concentrate his forces in Kentucky for movement upon Nashville and other points in Tennessee, restoring it to the Union, while Maj. Genl Halleck can restore to Missouri a portion of the forces now on the Cumberland and Tennessee rivers—which forces are much needed here. He can also detach a column to cut off communication on the Mississippi river below Columbus, about New Madrid where the rebels have a small fort of 9 guns & 1200 men, to prevent supplies and forces from reaching or leaving Columbus by river: This would be done while Columbus was threatened—but not attacked—by a column on the river, with gunboats, mortar fleet and transports, from above: while this is being done the main portion of the Center Column (being the Potomac forces) could move up the Tennessee river & by rapid movements from points on the Tennessee River cut off all railroad communications between Nashville, Memphis, New Orleans, and other points that now connect with the rebel force at Columbus and by which communications they are now able to supply and reinforce all their armies in the west: having their several western armies thus divided they can be crushed out in detail. A portion of this force (the Center Column) to penetrate far enough up the Tennessee river to sever all railroad communication between the extreme South and the rebel armies in Virginia and other states on the Atlantic seaboard—in short, effectively dividing the Southern Confederacy. With this organisation as set forth there can be no such thing as fail. Can it be done and done promptly? . . . P. S. General Halleck has seen this report and approves the programme as stated. He desires that Genl. Grant be promoted to the rank of Major General for meritorious services and that he shall be assigned to duty with him in movements of Center Column—he believes his promotion would have a good effect upon all Brigadiers in service—stimulating them to unusual efforts for distinction." ALS, DLC-Edwin M. Stanton. See telegram to Maj. Gen. Henry W. Halleck, Feb. 12, 1862, note 3. On Feb. 19, Capt. Nathaniel H. McLean issued General Orders No. 43, Dept. of the Mo. "The major-general commanding the department congratulates Flag-Officer Foote, Brigadier-General Grant, and the brave officers and men under their commands, on the recent brilliant victories on the Tennessee and Cumberland. But the war is not yet ended. Prepare for new conflicts and new victories. Troops are concentrating from every direction. We shall soon have an army which will be irresistible. The Union flag must be restored everywhere, and the inthralled Union men in the South must be set free. The soldiers and sailors of the Great West are ready and willing to do this. The times and places have been determined on. Victory and glory await the brave." *O.R.*, I, vii, 638–39.

To Orvil L. Grant

————————

[*Feb. 22, 1862*]
As the papers have been full of the capture of Fort Donelson for the last few days, it is not necessary for me to say much on that point. There is no doubt but it was the hardest fought battle on this continent, and reflects great credit on our volunteer corps. Fort Donelson is a very strong point naturally and an immense deal of labor has been added to strengthen it. Strangers who have looked upon the works express great astonishment that our troops ever took the place. The enemy had evidently prepared

for a long siege. Their supplies of munitions of war and provisions were very large.

Galena Daily Advertiser, March 3, 1862.

To Elihu B. Washburne

Fort Donelson, Feb.y 22d 1862.

Hon. E. B. Washburn M. C.
Washington, D. C.
Sir:

Allow me to call your attention to a fact that has just been made known to me to day for the first time. It is this. In bestowing appointments not a single Brigadier General has been made from Illinois south of about the Central part of the state. Now this portion of the state has contributed not only her proportion of troops but a more gallant set of men cannot be found to day batteling for the preservation of the Union. Among the Cols. commanding these regiments, or any others, a braver or more gallant man is not to be found than Col. John A. Logan. To him perhaps more than to any other one man is to be attributed the unanimity with which south Illinois has gone into this war.[1] His capacity for filling any position you are aware of.

You perhaps remember my telling you that I never would recommend the appointment of any man, for any position, on personal grounds but solely on grounds that the service would be benefited, in my judgement, by the appointment recommended.

Col. Logan I consider eminantly qualified and equally deserving of promotion his gallantry having stood the test of Belmont and Fort Donelson, at the latter of which he was severely wounded.[2]

Should Col. Logan be promoted I want him left with the

Division of the Army I may have the honor of commanding, nor
do I believe such a disposition would be disagreeable to him.

                                    I am very respectfully
                                    your obt. svt.
                                    U. S. GRANT

ALS, DNA, RG 94, Letters Received. On March 1, 1862, Elihu B. Washburne
wrote to President Abraham Lincoln. "In compliance with your request I send
you a list of the Brigadier Generals who I understand were acting Major-Generals
at Fort Donelson, and also a list of those Colonels who were acting as Brigadier
Generals. I also enclose you a letter I have received from Major General Grant,
asking that Jack Logan be appointed a Brigadier which I hope will be done. I hope
also that all the acting Brigadiers will be made Brigadiers. If any of these men
were particularly my friends, I should prefer they would remain as Colonels rather
than have them only breveted as Brigadiers. I do not believe they would want the
shadow without having the substance. If these promotions are to be made at all,
I beg leave to suggest that they be made at once, on the ground that which is given
quickly and graciously, is twice given. The prompt recognition of the service of
Grant was hailed with acclamation by the country." LS, *ibid*. Washburne enclosed
a "List of acting Major Generals and acting Brigadier Generals at the capture of
Fort Donelson.

> The following Brigadier Generals were acting as Major Generals
>   Ulysses S. Grant senior & in command,
>   John A. McClernand,
>   Lewis Wallace,
>   Charles Ferguson Smith, Col.1 3d Infantry
> The following Colonels were acting as Brigadier-Generals:
>   John Cook, 7th Ills. Vols,
>   Richard J. Oglesby, 8th Ills. Vols,
>   William H. L. Wallace, 11th Ills. Vols,
>   John McArthur, 12th Ills. Vols,
>   Isham N. Haynie, 48th Ills. Vols,
>   Jacob G. Lauman, 2d Iowa Vols."

Copy, *ibid*. On March 2, Washburne wrote to John G. Nicolay, Lincoln's private
secretary. "At the request of the President I made out and sent him last night, a
list of the acting Major Generals and acting Brigadier Generals at the capture of
Donelson   Among the acting Brigadiers I classed Haynie, but I find I was wrong,
and that he really was *not* an acting Brigadier. It is important that his name should
be stricken from the list, and will you be good enough to get the list and strike
the name off. I think I put down on the same list that Lauman belonged to the *2d*
Iowa. If so, that was a mistake. He is colonel of the *7th* Iowa. Please Mr. Nicolay
attend to these two matters. . . . P. S. I send this because I leave town this P. M."
ALS, *ibid*. On March 3, Lincoln directed Secretary of War Edwin M. Stanton to
have Brig. Gen. Don Carlos Buell, Brig. Gen. John A. McClernand, Brig. Gen.
Charles F. Smith, and Brig. Gen. Lewis Wallace appointed maj. gens. of vols.
"Also, let John Cook, Richard J. Oglesby, William H. L. Wallace[,] John
McArthur, Jacob G. Lauman and John A. Logan, (all of whom fought at Fort

Donnelson, with commissions of Colonels, but all except the last, commanded brigades) be appointed Brigadier generals of volunteers." Lincoln, *Works*, V, 142. On March 21, the Senate confirmed the above appointments. *Senate Executive Journal*, XII, 179.

1. See letters to Julia Dent Grant, June 27, 1861, note 2, and to Capt. Reuben B. Hatch, Nov. 1, 1861, note 1; *Memoirs*, I, 244–46.
2. Logan was wounded three times in the fighting on Feb. 15: in the shoulder, the side, and the thigh. James P. Jones, "*Black Jack:*" *John A. Logan and Southern Illinois in the Civil War Era* (Tallahassee, 1967), pp. 126, 129.

To Brig. Gen. George W. Cullum

Head Quarters, Dist. of West Ten.
Fort Donelson, Feb.y 23d 1862.

GEN. G. W. CULLUM,
CHIEF OF STAFF DEPT. OF THE MO.
CAIRO ILL.
GEN.

Reports have just reached me from Clarkesville that a powerful change is taking place in the minds of the people through this state. The Capt. of a steamer just down says that some two hundred people wanted to come down to see me to give assurances of ~~of~~ obedience to such rules as may be laid down by the Military authorities and to ask protection.—I will go up to Clarkesville to-morrow[1] and return in the evening. Of course I shall not tie the hands of myself or any future commander by any promise or proclaimation.

I am Gen. very respectfully
your obt. svt.
U. S. GRANT
Brig. Gen.

ALS, DNA, RG 393, Dept. of the Mo., Letters Received.

1. On Feb. 23, 1862, Capt. John A. Rawlins wrote to Brig. Gen. Stephen A. Hurlbut. "I am instructed by Brig. Gen. U. S. Grant, to say to you, that he will

be absent from here, until tomorrow evening. During his Absence you will assume command of this Post." Copies, DLC-USG, V, 1, 2, 3, 85; DNA, RG 393, USG Letters Sent.

General Orders No. 10

———

Head Quarters Dist. of West Tenn.
Fort Donelson, Feby. 24th 1862

GENL. ORDERS NO. 10

1st Lieut W. R. Rowley, 45th Ills. Vols. is herby appointed Aid-de-Camp to rank as such from this date. He will be obeyed and respected according.

U. S. GRANT
Brig. Gen.

DS, ICHi. Copies of the same orders, numbered General Orders No. 11, are in DLC-USG, V, 12, 13, 14, 95; DNA, RG 393, USG General Orders.

William R. Rowley, born in Gouverneur, N.Y., was a prominent Galena, Ill., Republican, and clerk of the Jo Daviess County Circuit Court. On Nov. 20, 1861, Rowley was appointed 1st lt., 45th Ill. On Jan. 30, 1862, Rowley wrote to Congressman Elihu B. Washburne. "Presuming that you would be glad to hear from us occasionally I take the liberty of boreing you with another letter (the second within two weeks.) We are still as when I last wrote at Cairo 'The City of Mud' and judging from outward appearances are likely to remain here for some time to come unless there is a great improvement in the weather, as it is now snowing and blowing like the very mischief and the roads *must* be impassable for some time to come. More troops are constantly arriving from St Louis & other points and are immediately sent up to Paducah and Smithland. I have had an excellent opportunity of learning as to the truth or falsetity of the reports which have without a doubt reached you concerning Gen'l Grant and I have no hesitation in saying that any one who asserts that he is becomeing dissipated is either mis-informed or else he lies. he is the same cool, energetic and unassumeing man that you supposed him to be. I think you will have no cause to be ashamed of the Brigadier you have manufactured. I wrote you, ~~last~~ week before last upon a matter of personal interest to me, and presume Col Smith has written you on the same subject but I presume you have been so busy you have had no time to attend to it Since then I have had a conversation with the Gen'l upon the subject and he assures me that if permission can be obtained from the War department for him to add an additional aid to his Staff that he would be (as he expressed it, more than glad to have me there. And he says he thinks he ought considering the extent of his command to be permitted to have more. as he is now necessarily compelled to leave much to be attended to by volunteer aids. I would like the position much better than the one I now occupy for a number of reasons   One of which is that I know I could be much more useful to the country and to my own Regiment than I can in the position I now occupy.   the Gen'l informed me that he should make an effort to obtain permission to make the addition but I am satisfied that you can bring it about easier than any one else: I do not like to trouble you in the matter but hope to be able to reciprocate at some time—I do not like to have Rawlins and Maltby steal all the thunder out of our county. Col Smith started this morning for Chicago to try and get some volunteers for our Regiment out of the Fusileers who we understand are disbanded   Maj Smith and Maltby are with us   The Maj is a Tip Top officer—a soldier every inch.   of Maltby *more anon*   I am afraid 'we are slightly bit' but hope all will end well. A Barrel head makes a poor desk which will explain a multitude of blots." ALS, DLC-Elihu B. Washburne.

On Feb. 26, Rowley was appointed capt. and aide-de-camp to USG. On March 14, Rowley wrote to Washburne. "I to day recd your communication of the 26th informing me of my appointment and confirmation as Capt & Aid De Camp to Gen'l Grant. I also recd from the Secretary of War notice of the same (to which bye the bye he omitted to affix his signature)   I will forward my acceptance and also the necessary oath as soon as I can find a man in this God forsaken country, who is authorized to administer oaths. I need not not say to you how much gratification the appointment gives me nor the amount of obligation I feel myself under to you for the interest you have manifested in my welfare & advancement. I will endeavour that you shall have no cause to regret it. We are now lying at Fort Henry oweing I think to the petty jealousies of some interested parties but from the appearances we are emerging from under the cloud and I think to morrow or next day will see us on the road again   I would write you more particularly but am pressed for time" ALS, *ibid.*

To Brig. Gen. George W. Cullum

Head Quarters Disct of West Tenn.
Fort Donelson, Feby 24th 1862

GENL G. W. CULLUM
CHIEF OF STAFF, DEPT OF THE MO.
CAIRO, ILL
GEN

Enclosed I send you a dispatch from Genl Buell, sent through to Clarksville yesterday.[1] As requested, the Gun-boats have gone up to Nashville   The Mortar Boats, I am sending back to Cairo, because it would be with great difficulty that they could be got to Nashville and could be of no service there. Yesterday a Steamer, was down from Nashville, with quite a delegation of the citizens.

Their ostensible object, was to bring Surgeons to attend their wounded at Clarksville; real object, probably, to have some assurance that their property would be protected. Johnson with his army has fallen back to Mumfreesboro,[2] first destroying all bridges, Commissary stores, and such Artillery as could not be carried along.[3] The troops wanted to destroy the City, but were restrained by the citizens, and a speech from Pillow.

I have just returned from Clarksville[4] where I arrived last evening, some hours after the departure of the Nashville Delegation and Gun boat Cairo. Genl Nelson[5] reported to day with his Division. I fowarded them immediately to Nashville with verbal instructions to have the men under wholesome restraint, and written instructions, a copy of which is herewith ~~accompanying~~ forwarded.[6]

I have only sent four small regiments to Clarksville and do not propose sending more, until I know the pleasure of Genl Halleck on the subject.[7] A large Garrison is not required.

Genl C. F. Smith is in command at Clarksville.[8]

> Very Respcty
> Your Obt Servt
> U. S. GRANT
> Brig Genl Comdg

Copies, DLC-USG, V, 4, 5, 7, 8, 9; DNA, RG 393, USG Hd. Qrs. Correspondence. *O.R.*, I, vii, 662.

1. On Feb. 22, 1862, Brig. Gen. Don Carlos Buell wrote to the commanding officer, Clarksville. "I am marching on Nashville. My advance will probable be within 9 miles of that place to-night. Your gunboats should move forward instantly. I believe they will meet no serious opposition." *Ibid.*, p. 653.

2. Murfreesborough, Tenn., about thirty-five miles southeast of Nashville.

3. On Feb. 23, Commander Benjamin M. Dove wrote to USG. "I have to report that I had reached as far down as the destroyed rolling mill when I turned back, by a verbal order from some one on board the Transport McClellan. I was detained a few hours behind the Mortar boats, which I despatched early this morning, by attending to a delegation of Surgeons and citizens from Nashville, who came down to attend to the sick and wounded confederate forces. They represented that Nashville is in very bad condition. The confederates had all evacuated it having previously burned two fine bridges and cut the wires of the suspension bridge. They wish our forces to push on up there and restore confidence to the people very few of whom have left town. I hardly think under these circumstances

that the Mortar boats will be required. I send the Tug down with this, and a few letters, some of them from Genl Smith   The Tug will require a little coal, and it is very necessary that a barge of coal should be towed up to clarksville. The Cairo has very little. I have enough to get up to Nashville, but after I arrive I will find none there, as I was informed by the delegation of surgeons and citizens. The confederates retreated in great disorder towards Murfreesboro." ALS, DNA, RG 393, District of West Tenn., Letters Received. On the same day, Brig. Gen. Charles F. Smith wrote to Capt. John A. Rawlins. "From the bearer an intelligent Mulatoo man who resides in Louisville, by the name of Cox, who has been detained by the rebels for many months I gain the following: That on the day we marched into Ft. Donelson (Sunday the 16th.) the rebel force some 15 to 20000 commenced to move from Nashville to Murfreesboro, 40 miles S. E. of ~~Nashv~~ N. on the Nashville & Chatannoogo rail way—burning the bridge over the river at Nashville. They were moving from Sunday unto Thursday, under Genl. Sidney Johnston. They intend to make a stand at Murfreesboro. In destroying a wire bridge at Nashville they put on it all the artillery they could not carry off & burnt the carriages—This Cox came in this morning on board a steamer with a flag of truce. Govr. Isham Harris went off with Johnston carrying off all the public records. Beauregard was sick with diptheria at Nashville a short time since and it is said has left for Columbus." ALS, *ibid.* Again on Feb. 23, Smith wrote to Rawlins. "Since writing my information by *Cox* (the mulato) ten mounted men from Bowling Green (72 miles) brought in the enclosed note from Genl. Buell. His advance 2,000 left by rail for Nashville at 10 o'c yesterday morning. I shall send a gun boat up." ALS, *ibid.* For C. S. A. reports on the evacuation of Nashville, and the move to Murfreesborough, see *O.R.*, I, vii, 426–33.

4. See letters to Brig. Gen. George W. Cullum, Feb. 23, 1862, and to Julia Dent Grant, Feb. 24, 1862.

5. William Nelson of Maysville, Ky., appointed a midshipman, Jan. 28, 1840, and a lt., April 18, 1855, was stationed at the Washington Navy Yard in spring, 1861. In May, President Abraham Lincoln sent Nelson to Ky. to distribute 5,000 guns to the loyal men of the state; in Aug., Nelson established and commanded Camp Dick Robinson in Garrard County, Ky. On Sept. 16, he was appointed a brig. gen. Arthur A. Griese, "A Louisville Tragedy—1862," *The Filson Club History Quarterly*, 26, 2 (April, 1952), 133–54; John G. Nicolay and John Hay, *Abraham Lincoln: A History* (New York, 1890), IV, 235–37, 240.

6. See following letter.

7. On Feb. 24, 1862, Rawlins wrote to Brig. Gen. Stephen A. Hurlbut. "I am instructed by Brig. Gen. U. S. Grant, Commanding, to say to you that all the troops belonging to Genl. C. F. Smith's and Gen. L. Wallace's Divisions, now at this place, will be under your command, while they remain here, and, will report to you." Copies, DLC-USG, V, 1, 2, 3, 86; DNA, RG 393, USG Letters Sent. On the same day, Rawlins wrote to the commanding officer, Birge's Sharpshooters. "The order for your command to move to Clarkesville is countermanded. That part, if any, which has embarked, will immediately debark, and your command will go into quarters at this place." Copies, *ibid.* On Feb. 23, Maj. Gen. Henry W. Halleck telegraphed to Brig. Gen. William T. Sherman and Flag Officer Andrew H. Foote. "All available gun boats to be sent to clarksville prepared for a movement up the cumberland. I think Mortar-boats will be of little use on this expedition. If Com. Foote agrees with me, let them be sent down for defense of Cairo. I am waiting for telegraphic line to be opened to Fort ~~Me~~ Henry to communicate

with Genl Grant. In the mean time tell him that I wish to have about twenty thousand men concentrated at clarksville, including Smith's & Nelson's Divisions. Proper garrisons should be detailed for Forts Henry & Donelson. All other forces should be encamped opposite Danville bridge, to await further orders. Cavalry & field artillery to be ready to move between the two rivers. One gun boat to be stationed ~~between~~ near Danville Bridge. All others not required for defence of Cairo to be at Clarksville ready for service. Abundant ammunition to be taken along. See to this. There is a great & decisive contest awaiting us. Be ready for it. Answer, and give all you know of present state of affairs. Encouraging news continually coming in from the South west." ALS (telegram sent), *ibid.*, RG 107, Telegrams Collected (Unbound); copy, *ibid.*, RG 393, USG Hd. Qrs. Correspondence. *O.R.*, I, vii, 655; *O.R.* (Navy), I, xxii, 625. Copies (dated Feb. 25), DLC-USG, V, 4, 5, 7, 8, 9, 81; (undated) DNA, RG 393, District of West Tenn., Letters Received. On Feb. 25, Halleck telegraphed to Brig. Gen. George W. Cullum, Foote, and Sherman. "The possession of Nashville by Genl Buell renders it necessary to countermand the instructions sent to Foote & Sherman yesterday morning (dated 23d). Grant will send no more forces to Clarksville   Genl Smith's division will come to Fort Henry or a point higher up on the Tenn. River. Transports will also be collected at Paducah and above. All Mortar boats to be immediately brought back to Cairo. Two gun-boats to be left in the Cumberland at Clarksville to precede Nelsons Division up the river to Nashville. Having [done] this they will return to Cairo. Two gunboats in Tenn. River with Genl Grant. The latter will immediately have small garrisons detailed for Forts Donelson & Henry, and all other forces made ready for the field." ALS (telegram sent), *ibid.*, RG 107, Telegrams Collected (Unbound); copies, *ibid.*, RG 45, Area 5; *ibid.*, RG 393, USG Letters Received; DLC-USG, V, 9. *O.R.*, I, vii, 667–68; *O.R.* (Navy), I, xxii, 637–38. Copies (dated Feb. 24), DLC-USG, V, 4, 5, 7, 8; DNA, RG 393, USG Hd. Qrs. Correspondence. Capt. John H. Hammond, Sherman's asst. adjt. gen., added: "The preceding are telegrams sent to Genl Grant to day. These Duplicates are forwarded to insure their earliest reception possible—Beauregard *is said to be* sick at Jackson Tenn—Polk in command at Columbus. All negroes captured sent in to the town   Bridges burnt between here & the Miss R. & close to Columbus   trees cut down—R R Track torn up from May field towards to Tenn line—streams high & Roads bad very! Gen'l Sherman being at Cairo I send the above direct—Please excuse letter in my own name"   ALS, *ibid.*, District of West Tenn., Letters Received.

8. See letter to Brig. Gen. Charles F. Smith, Feb. 21, 1862.

To Brig. Gen. William Nelson

Head Quarters, Dist of West. Tenn.
Fort Donelson, Febry 24th 1862.

BRIG. GEN. NELSON
COMMDG. DIV, ~~DEPT~~. ARMY OF THE OHIO.
GEN:

You will proceed with the Division under your command to Nashville, Tenn, keeping in rear of the Gun Boat "Carondelet," with all your transports. From Nashville you will put yourself in immediate communication with Gen. Buell, and if you find that his command is not within two days march of you, your command will not debark, but fall back (down the river some miles) on the transports, and remain to form a junction, with Gen. Buell, when he does arrive.[1]

I am, General, Very Respectfully
Your Obt. Servant
U. S. GRANT,
Brig. Gen. Commdg.

Copies, DLC-USG, V, 1, 2, 3, 86; DNA, RG 393, USG Letters Sent. *O.R.*, I, vii, 662–63; *O.R.* (Navy), I, xxii, 631. See preceding letter. On Feb. 22, 1862, Capt. John H. Hammond issued Special Orders No. 32. "Brig. Genl. Nelson having reported in person his Division from the Dept. of the Ohio, will in pursuance of orders from Genl. Halleck, Comdg. Dept. of the Mo. proceed in his present transports to Clarksville Tenn. and there report to Major Genl. Grant, Comdg. the Army in the field—" Copy, DLC-USG, V, 83. On Feb. 24, Brig. Gen. William Nelson wrote to USG. "I have the honor to enclose the consolidated morning Report of 4th Division, Army of the Department of the Ohio for Feb 22d 1862. Since this report was made the remaining three companies of the 34th Ind & the remaining three companies of 46th Ind have left the Division for Cairo. Four Regiments of this Division have been detached for duty at Cairo. The aggregate of Infantry present with the Division is now 5947. I have the honor to enclose a report of the ammunition, etc. with the Division. This report does not include the ammunition train.—which went to Cairo on boat with troops and has not yet been allowed to return. the circumstances are fully set forth in an accompanying letter. I have the honor also to enclose lists of the officers under my command." Copy, DNA, RG 393, 4th Division, Dept. of the Ohio, Letters Sent. *O.R.*, I, vii, 661–62. On Feb. 23, Nelson had written to USG. "The ammunition of this Division sorted according to the calibre of arms with which the several Regiments are armed went down to Cairo in the steamers that carried the Indiana Regiments ordered to that point. The Commanding officer on board each of the steamers and the master of each of them were particularly charged to return promptly with the ammunition. They have been detained at Cairo. It is unnecessary for me to point out the embarrassment this occasions. Permit me nevertheless to express my indignation at the conduct of the commanding officer at Cairo in the premises. I will endeavor to find the enemy with the bayonets of my division if my boxes are empty." Copy, DNA, RG 393, 4th Division, Dept. of the Ohio, Letters Sent.

1. On the night of Feb. 24, Brig. Gen. Don Carlos Buell arrived at Edgefield, Tenn., across the Cumberland River from Nashville. Nelson disembarked at Nashville later the same night. *O.R.*, I, vii, 425, 668–69. See letter to Brig. Gen. George W. Cullum, Feb. 25, 1862.

To Surgeon Henry S. Hewit

Head Quarters, Dist. of W. Ten.
Fort Donelson, Feb.y 24th 1862

SURGEON H. S. HEWITT
MEDICAL DIRECTOR, DIST OF WEST TEN.
FORT DONELSON TEN.
SIR;

You will proceed with as little delay as practicable to Paducah, Mound City & Cairo and visit the Hospitals ~~and~~ for the purpose of collecting such facts as are necessary for the completion of your report of the battles of Forts Henry & Donelson.

Having performed this duty you may report to Maj. Gen. Halleck for further orders or return here at your own option.

The *prompt* and *efficient* manner in which the duties of your Corps have been performed, under your direction, induces me to request however that your services may be retained with the Army in the field.

very respectfully
your obt. svt.
U. S. GRANT
Brig. Gen. Com

ALS, ViU. See letter to Brig. Gen. Lewis Wallace, Feb. 16, 1862, notes 1, 2.

To Julia Dent Grant

Fort Donelson, Feb. 24th 1862.

DEAR JULIA,

I have just returned from Clarkesville. Yesterday some citizens of Nasville come down there ostensibly to bring surgeons to attend their wounded at that place but in reality no doubt to get assurances that they would not be molested. Johnson with his army of rebels have fallen back about forty miles south from Nashville[1] leaving the river clear to our troops   To-day a Division of Gen. Buells Army reported to me for orders. As they were on Steamers I ordered them immediately up to Nashville.[2] "Secesh" is now about on its last legs in Tennessee. I want to push on as rapidly as possible to save hard fighting. These terrible battles are very good things to read about for persons who loose no friends but I am decidedly in favor of having as little of it as possible. The way to avoid it is to push forward as vigorously as possible.

Gen. Halleck is clearly the same way of thinking and with his clear head I think the Congressional Committee for investigating the Conduct of the War will have nothing to enquire about in the West.[3]

I am writing you in great haste a boat being about leaving here. I will write you often to make up for the very short letters I send.

Give my love to all at home and write frequently. Tell me all about the children. I want to see rascal Jess already. Tell Mary she must write to me often. Kiss the children for me and the same for yours[elf]

ULYS.

ALS, ICarbS.

    1. Murfreesborough, Tenn.
    2. See letter to Brig. Gen. William Nelson, Feb. 24, 1862.
    3. On Dec. 10, 1861, the U.S. House of Representatives approved a resolution passed the previous day by the Senate: "That a joint committee of three

members of the Senate and four members of the House of Representatives be appointed to inquire into the conduct of the present war; that they have power to send for persons and papers, and to sit during the sessions of either house of Congress." *House Journal*, 37–2, p. 56; *Senate Journal*, 37–2, p. 32. On Jan. 10, 1862, the controversial committee began taking testimony on the conduct of the war in the Western Dept. under Maj. Gen. John C. Frémont. For accounts of the committee, see William Whatley Pierson, Jr., "The Committee on the Conduct of the Civil War," *The American Historical Review*, XXIII, 3 (April, 1918), 550–76; T. Harry Williams, *Lincoln and the Radicals* ([Madison,] 1941), *passim;* Hans L. Trefousse, "The Joint Committee on the Conduct of the War: A Reassessment," *Civil War History*, X, 1 (March, 1964), 5–19. The major report covering the early phases of the war is *HRC*, 37–3–108.

General Orders No. 12

Head Quarters Dist. of West Tenn.
Fort Donelson Feby. 25th 1862

GENL. ORDERS No. 12

Soldiers are positively forbid going beyond the line of Sentinals out side the entrenchments.

The Genl. Comdg. is again obliged to call the attention of Division, Brigade and Regimental commanders to orders restraining their men from committing depredations upon private property.

Such restrictions must be placed upon the actions of the men of this command as to prevent complaints in future of them killing stock or depridating in any manner.

By order of Brig. Genl. U. S. Grant
JNO A RAWLINS
A. A. Genl.

P. S. The above order must be inforced at once.

DS, McClernand Papers, IHi. *O.R.*, I, vii, 667. See General Orders No. 7, Feb. 21, 1862. On Feb. 25, 1862, Capt. John A. Rawlins wrote to Maj. William W. Sanford, 48th Ill. "A list of Articles from one of your men, with permission to send them to Cairo, Ills, has just come to my notice. You have no authority to grant permission to send away property from this place, and in future will not attempt to do so." Copies, DLC-USG, V, 2, 86; DNA, RG 393, USG Letters Sent. On

Feb. 28, Capt. William S. Hillyer wrote to Lt. Col. William Swarthout, 50th Ill., commanding at Clarksville, Tenn. "Enclosed find the pass which was taken with the man who had the arms. You will have Capt Estabrook, arrested as already ordered, and removed from the Office of Provost Marshal. If Capt. Estabrook denies the genuineness of the enclosed paper you will ascertain who has committed the forgery, and have such party arrested. Mr. W. C. Noell further stated that the captured arms were presented to him by Dr. Metcalf, Surgeon of the 3rd Brigade who told him that they were arms captured at Fort Donelson. You will investigate the truth of this statement and report to these Head Quarters, for further action." Copies, DLC-USG, V, 1, 2, 3, 86; DNA, RG 393, USG Letters Sent. An LS, signed by Rawlins, is *ibid.*, Dept. of the Mo., Letters Received. On Feb. 28, USG wrote to hd. qrs., Dept. of the Mo. "In reference to dismantling the Forts. Has great difficulty in preventing captured property from being stolen &c." *Ibid.*, Register of Letters Received.

To Brig. Gen. George W. Cullum

Head Quarters Disct of West Tenn
Fort Donelson Feby 25th 1862

Genl G W. Cullum
Chief of Staff, Dept of the Mo
Cairo, Ill
Genl

I wrote you that Genl Nelsons Div had been sent to Nashville.[1] Since that I have learned that the head of Genl Buells column arrived there on Monday evening.[2] The rebels have fallen back to Chatanooga, instead of Mumfreesboro, as stated in a former letter.[3] I shall go to Nashville immediately after the arrival of the next Mail, should there be no orders to prevent it.[4]

Two soldiers of the 8th Mo Vols who were disguised and sent to Memphis, have just returned.[5] They went by the way of Nashville and Decatur.[6] Saw Beauregard at Decatur, sick. He has since gone to Columbus.[7] They were in Fort Donelson before the attack commenced, and say the force was estimated at Forty thousand. (40.000).

Since the battle, the people thro' the country are much disposed to return to their allegiance   Orders have been given for the evacuation of Columbus.[8] This I learn not only from the men themselves, but from Memphis papers, which they bring with them. I send two of these papers to Genl Halleck

I am growing anxious to know, what the next move is going to be[9]

The Southern papers advise the Columbus forces to fall back on Island No 10,[10] and to Fort Pillow.[11] The force at Memphis is said to be about 12.000.

I am General Very Respcty
Your Obt Servt
U. S. GRANT
Brig Genl Comdg

Copies, DLC-USG, V, 4, 5, 7, 8, 9; DNA, RG 393, USG Hd. Qrs. Correspondence. *O.R.*, I, vii, 666.

1. See letter to Brig. Gen. George W. Cullum, Feb. 24, 1862.
2. Feb. 24, 1862. See letter to Brig. Gen. William Nelson, Feb. 24, 1862, note 1.
3. See letter to Brig. Gen. George W. Cullum, Feb. 24, 1862, note 2. Gen. Albert Sidney Johnston's forces remained at Murfreesborough until Feb. 28. *O.R.*, I, vii, 911.
4. See letter to Brig. Gen. George W. Cullum, Feb. 28, 1862.
5. See following letter.
6. Decatur in northern Ala., on the Tennessee River about 110 miles south of Nashville at the junction of the Memphis and Charleston Railroad and the Nashville and Decatur Railroad.
7. Gen. P. G. T. Beauregard was in Jackson, Tenn., at this time, suffering from a throat inflammation. *O.R.*, I, vii, 890, 895–96, 899–901, 905–10. He did not go to Columbus, but instructed Maj. Gen. Leonidas Polk to come to Jackson for consultation. Alfred Roman, *The Military Operations of General Beauregard in the War between the States* (New York, 1883), I, 233.
8. On Feb. 18, Beauregard suggested to C. S. A. Adjt. and Inspector Gen. Samuel Cooper that Columbus should be evacuated. *O.R.*, I, vii, 890. On Feb. 19, Secretary of War Judah P. Benjamin telegraphed to Beauregard that Columbus should be evacuated. *Ibid.*, p. 892. On Feb. 20, Benjamin informed Polk that President Jefferson Davis had decided on the evacuation of Columbus. *Ibid.*, p. 893. On Feb. 21, Beauregard sent a confidential circular to the governors of Tenn., Ala., Miss., and La., informing them of the decision to abandon the Ky. fort. *Ibid.*, p. 899. On March 2, Polk telegraphed to Benjamin that Columbus had been evacuated. *Ibid.*, p. 437.
9. See letter to Brig. Gen. George W. Cullum, Feb. 24, 1862, note 7. On Feb. 24, Maj. Gen. Henry W. Halleck telegraphed to Brig. Gen. George W. Cullum. "The reason that Cairo has no blanks is that no requisitions have not been made. There is a screw loose in that command; it had better be fixed pretty

soon or the commander will hear from me. Nashville has been abandoned   Genl Buell marches in this afternoon without opposition. This enables me to withdraw my column from the Cumberland. I was holding the Cumberland forces to await Buell's movement   All O. K. and now for a decisive movement. Tell Flag officer Foote not to move till I give him further orders. The sending of steamers to Genl Buell was all wrong. It disconcerts my plans. You should not have done it, without my orders. If you can stop them by telegraph, do so, & order them to rendezvous at Paducah. You are too fast at Cairo. Consult me before you order any other movements. I have held every thing in check till I could have positive information about the abandonment of Nashville   It is now certain." ALS (telegram sent), DNA, RG 107, Telegrams Collected (Unbound). *O.R.*, I, vii, 661. On Feb. 26, Halleck telegraphed to Cullum. "Send to Paducah transports sufficient to move Grant's army up either the Cumberland or Tennessee. Accounts of Johnston's movements are very conflicting, & we must be ready for any contingency. As soon as we know positively where he is a movement will be made." ALS (telegram sent), DNA, RG 107, Telegrams Collected (Unbound).

10. Island No. 10 in the Mississippi River about forty miles below Cairo.

11. Fort Pillow, Tenn., about seventy miles southwest of the Ky., Tenn., Mo. border, on the Mississippi River. On Feb. 21, Beauregard wrote to Cooper that in consultation with Johnston, it had been decided that "Island No. 10 and Fort Pillow would be fortified for defense to the last extremity." *O.R.*, I, vii, 895–96.

To Brig. Gen. William T. Sherman

Head Quarters, Dist. of W. Ten.
Fort Donelson, Feb.y 25th 1862

Gen. W. T. Sherman,
Comdg Dist. of Cairo
Paducah, Ky.
Gen.

Your letter of the 23d asking what disposition I will have made of large reinforcements now on their way is just received. I do not know what work Gen. Halleck intends me to do next therefore cannot say where it is best to have them. Probably they had better remain at Paducah until further orders are received from Head Quarters of the Department.

Our troops are now occupying Nashville. The rebels have fallen back to Catanooga, only three miles from Georgia state line. Two soldiers from the 8th Mo. regiment who were sent as spies have just returned from Memphis. They describe the feeling of the people as much inclined to return to their allegiance.

Orders have been given for the evacuation of Columbus. This I get not only from the men themselve but from a Memphis paper of the 19th which they bring with them   There is a detachment of troops belonging to my command at Henderson Ky.[1] which there can be no further use of detaining there. If you have an opportunity of having them transported I would like them to join their regiments.

> I am Gen. very respectfully
> your obt. svt.
> U. S. GRANT
> Brig. Gen.

ALS, DLC-William T. Sherman. *O.R.*, I, vii, 667. See preceding letter. On Feb. 25, 1862, Brig. Gen. William T. Sherman wrote to USG. "Enclosed is a copy of dispatch from General Halleck, to Commodore Foote and myself, of so much importance that I send this large boat up without delay. In a few days there will be a large fleet of boats at Paducah ready to be sent up to you and to carry up reinforcements if they are deemed necessary for the accomplishment of the end in view. I hope that by today the Telegraph will be finished to Fort Henry, and you be placed in communication with all parts of the country. As near as we can ascertain Columbus is still occupied in force. The Guns on the River front are still mounted and in position. Genl Polk was in command yesterday. The day before Genl Cullum went down to make an armed Reconnoissance and when within two miles was met by a flag of truce, born by an officer Blake, who proposed to permit the families of Buckner Hanson and others to join them.—To answer this Gen Cullum proposed to send back a flag yesterday which was done, and the families are now in Cairo, but Gen Halleck will not concent to the families joining their husbands, and they are still at Cairo. Buckner & his Staff have reached Indianapolis. That you may understand the sources whence you are to draw your supplies of troops I will mention that, at Smithland is the small detachmt left by you and a Battalion of the 6th Illinois Cavalry. At Paducah 3 armed Regiments and 9 unarmed Ohio Regiments. At Cairo three Regts & three detached Companies

at Birds Point	10 Regiments
" Capt Girardeau	3 Regiments
" Fort Holt	5 "

at Commerce a large force is assembling under General Pope, to operate on New Madrid.—I have no Report from there but suppose he has about 10000 men. There are more men than arms, but these are promised us from the States & arsenal at St Louis. The sick & wounded are being furloughed and discharged. Still our hospitals are very full, and will be relieved by sending them to St Louis and Cincinati. There is great sympathy everywhere and the wounded will be well cared for. I hope you will command my services any time you please   I will brigade the Regiments at Paducah at once, and trust to getting arms very soon. I have no doubt of the move contemplated, but think Columbus will be evacuated very soon—The Memphis papers announced that its evacuation had already been determined on." ALS, DNA, RG 393, District of West Tenn., Letters Received. See preceding letter, and letter to Brig. Gen. George W. Cullum, Feb. 24, 1862, note 7. For the correspondence relating to Maj. Gen. Halleck's refusal to allow wives to visit C. S. A. officers who were prisoners of war, see Maj. Gen. Leonidas Polk to Commanding Officer, Cairo, Feb. 22, 1862, copy, DNA, RG 45, Area 5; Polk to Flag Officer Andrew H. Foote and Brig. Gen. George W. Cullum, Feb. 23, 1862, LS, *ibid.;* Halleck to Cullum, Feb. 25, 1862, ALS (telegram sent), *ibid.*, RG 107, Telegrams Collected (Unbound). *O.R.*, II, iii, 312–15, 321; *O.R.* (Navy), I, xxii, 627–31.

1. Henderson, Ky., on the Ohio River, about ten miles downriver from Evansville, Ind.

General Orders No. 14

———

Head Quarters, Dist of West. Tenn.
Fort. Donelson Feby 26th 1862.

GENERAL ORDERS No 14

General Orders. No. 3. of the series of 1861, from Head Quarters, Department of the Missouri, are still in force and must be observed.[1]

The number of citizens who are applying for permission to pass through the camps, to look for their fugitive slaves, proves the necessity of the order, and its faithful observance. Such permits cannot be granted, therefore the great necessity of keeping out fugitives.

Such slaves as were within the lines at the time of the capture of Fort Donelson, and such as have been used by the enemy, in building the fortifications, or in any way hostile to the Government, will not be released or permitted to return to their Masters, but will be employed in the Quarter Masters Department, for the benefit of Government[2]

All officers and companies now keeping slaves so captured, will immediately report them to the District Quartermaster.

Regimental Commanders will be held accountable for all violation of this order, within their respective commands

> By order of Brig. Gen. U. S. Grant, Com'd'g
> JNO A RAWLINS
> A. A. Genl.

P. S. You will promulgate the above order to your command, at
once.

DS, McClernand Papers, IHi; DLC-Elihu B. Washburne. *O.R.*, I, vii, 668. On
March 5, 1862, Col. Cadwallader C. Washburn wrote to his brother, Congressman Elihu B. Washburne. "I have read that part of your letter to Gen. Grant
where you speak of fugitive slaves, and the printed slip containing the remark of
Mr. Wickliffe, on that subject. I am advised by Genl. Grant that there is no truth
whatever in the allegation that he had returned fugitives to their masters—On the
contrary he expressly forbid persons from coming within his lines in pursuit of
fugitives. His action is shown by the order made by him at the time, a copy of
which I enclose. No action was taken inconsistent with that. A number of colord
men were found in the fort or within the lines who represented themselves to be
free men, and desired to return to their homes, and were permitted to do so."
ALS, DLC-Elihu B. Washburne. On Feb. 25, Union Whig Charles A. Wickliffe
of Bardstown, Ky., remarked in the House of Representatives: "I see by the evidence which has been furnished, that General Grant captured at Fort Donelson,
I think it was, twelve negro slaves among the prisoners there taken. They were
returned by him to their loyal owners in Kentucky, from whom they had been
forced by the rebel power." *CG*, 37–2, p. 956.

1. Issued on Nov. 20, 1861. *O.R.*, I, viii, 370. See letter to Col. John Cook,
Dec. 25, 1861. On Feb. 22, 1862, Capt. Nathaniel H. McLean issued General
Orders No. 46, Dept. of the Mo. "Orders heretofore issued in this department in
regard to pillaging, marauding, the destruction of private property, and the stealing and concealment of slaves must be strictly enforced. It does not belong to the
military to decide upon the relation of master and slave. Such questions must be
settled by the civil courts. No fugitive slave will, therefore, be admitted within
our lines or camps, except when specially ordered by the general commanding. . . .
These orders will be read at the head of every regiment, and all officers are commanded to strictly enforce them." *O.R.*, I, viii, 564.

2. A *New York Tribune* correspondent, present at a meeting between USG
and Brig. Gen. Simon B. Buckner after the fall of Fort Donelson, reported on
Feb. 17: "In their business, the negro question came up, and Gen. Grant decided
that no negroes found within the lines should be suffered to depart for the reason
that 200 had long worked on the fortifications; officers could take their servants
along, but they could not be liberated. 'We want laborers, let the negroes work
for us.' I saw a master receive this decision—he retired silent and sullen." *New
York Tribune*, Feb. 22, 1862.

To Julia Dent Grant

———

Fort Donelson, Feby. 26th, 1862.

DEAR JULIA:

I am just starting to Nashville and will drop you a line before starting. Gen. Buell is there, or at least a portion of his command is, and I want to have an interview with the comdg. officer and learn what I can of the movements of the enemy. I shall be back here to-morrow evening and remain until some movement takes place.[1] Since my promotion some change may take place in my command, but I do not know. I want however to remain in the field and be actively employed. But I shall never ask a favor or change. Whatever is ordered I will do independantly and as well as I know how. If a command inferior to my rank is given me it shall make no difference in my zeal. In spite of enemies, I have so far progressed satisfactorily to myself and the country and in reviewing the past can see but few changes that could have bettered the result. Perhaps I have done a little too much of the office duties and thereby lost time that might have been better employed in inspecting and reviewing troops.

I want to hear from you. I have not had a word since you left Cairo. My clothing &c. came up all right except the saddle cover.[2] Do you know anything about it? Those covers cost $30 00 and I shall be compelled to buy another if that one is lost. I have written to Gen. Cullum to look it up. I am anxious to get a letter from Father to see his criticisms. I see his paper the Gazette gets off whole numbers without mentioning my name That paper and the Cincinnati Commercial for some reason inexplicable to me have always apparently been my enemies   It never disturbed me however[3]

Give my love to all at home. I write to you so often that you must be satisfied with short letters.

ULYS.

Copies, ICHi; Algernon Sartoris, "Unpublished Letters by Grant after First Victory," *New York Times*, April 6, 1913.

1. See letters to Brig. Gen. William Nelson, Feb. 24, 1862, to Brig. Gen. Don Carlos Buell, Feb. 27, 1862, and to Brig. Gen. George W. Cullum, Feb. 28, 1862.

2. Gen. officers had saddle covers of dark blue cloth trimmed with two rows of gold lace, with a gold-embroidered spread eagle, and stars according to rank. AGO General Orders No. 6, March 13, 1861.

3. Murat Halstead edited the *Cincinnati Commercial* and Richard Smith edited the *Cincinnati Gazette*, both Republican papers. The *Gazette* had published most of USG's letter to his father after the battle of Belmont. See letter to Jesse Root Grant, Nov. 8, 1861. A *Commercial* correspondent reported: "When I was introduced to General Grant, as corresponding for the Commercial, don't you think the General was so ungenerous as to say: 'the Commercial never did say a good thing about me, I believe.' Now will you oblige me by saying, without advice, that General Grant stands high with officers and men in these quarters. . . . I find him every inch a gentleman, and in the management of this expedition, which has so far, been the great event of the war, he has displayed Generalship that some of his superior officers might covet." Letter of E. J., Feb. 18, 1862, in *Cincinnati Commercial*, Feb. 22, 1862.

To Brig. Gen. Don Carlos Buell

Nashville, Feb. 27th 1862

GENL. D. C. BUELL
COM'D'G DEPT OF THE OHIO.
GENERAL.

I have been in the City since an early hour this Morning, anxious and expecting to see you. When I first arrived I understood that you were to be over today, but it is now growing too late for me to remain longer.[1]

If I could see the necessity of more troops here, I would be most happy to supply them. My own impression is, however, that the enemy are not far north of the Tennessee line. I was anxious to know what information you might have on the subject. Gen. Smith will be here this evening, with probably, 2000 men as requested by you.[2] and should still more be required, address me, at Clarksville. Tonight I shall return to Fort Donelson, but will take up my Head Quarters at Clarksville the next day.[3] Should you deem the command under Genl. Smith unnecessary to

your security I request that they be ordered back.[4] I am in daily
expectation of orders that will require all my available force.

> I am, General, very respectfully
> Your Obt. Servt.
> U. S. GRANT
> Maj. Gen. Com'd'g

Copies, DLC-USG, V, 1, 2, 3, 88; DNA, RG 393, USG Letters Sent. *O.R.*, I,
vii, 670–71.

1. Upon arriving at the river for the return to Fort Donelson, USG met
Brig. Gen. Don Carlos Buell. *Memoirs*, I, 321.
2. See letter to Capt. John C. Kelton, Feb. 28, 1862.
3. Feb. 28, 1862. USG's hd. qrs. remained at Fort Donelson until March 5,
when he moved to Fort Henry by direction of Maj. Gen. Henry W. Halleck. See
letters to Maj. Gen. Henry W. Halleck and to Brig. Gen. Charles F. Smith,
March 5, 1862.
4. On March 1, Buell reported to Halleck that Brig. Gen. Charles F. Smith
had been ordered back to Clarksville. *O.R.*, I, vii, 675.

To Brig. Gen. George W. Cullum

Fort Donelson, Feb.y 28th 1862

GEN. G. W. CULLUM
CHIEF OF STAFF, DEPT. OF THE MO.
CAIRO ILL.
GEN.

It is due to myself, having heard of strictures that you have
made upon the manner of moving the troops in my command
from Cairo, that you should hear the explaination.

When I was ordered to Fort Henry I took all the transportation (river) that was at Cairo. Even with leaving all the regimental teams but four to a regiment, and having the Cavalry
march through, it took two trips to move my forces.[1]

The Tennessee river being very much swolen it was a matter
of the very greatest difficulty to discharge the steamers, and
being no store houses such articles as would be injured by rain

was obliged to remain on board steamers. There was no houses
for Hospitals and as you are aware the weather has been the most
inclement of the Winter. Hence the necessity of using boats for
Hospitals.—My Hd Qrs. have been kept on a steamer[2] because
the steamer used as such has necessarily been kept as a store boat
and has probably had an average of 70.000 rations on board all
the time. All boats used for Hospital purposes have been sent
below as soon as filled.

I do not make these explainations because I feel it so much
necessary for my own vindication but because I do not want you
to think that when the expenses of Government are so excessive
as at this time I would add to them, even by thoughtlessness,
~~even~~ one dollar.

As soon as I was ready to receive freight I ~~orde~~ requested
that the transportation left behind should be sent forwarded. I
believe it has not yet come.

Some captured arms were sent to Cairo because we have no
use for them here. There are still more and I designed sending
them also. At this place and Clarkesville there is probably over
fifty pieces of Light Artillery. This I think should be sent down
but will now await Gen. Halleck's orders on the subject.

I am Gen. very respectfully
your obt. svt.
U. S. GRANT
Brig. Gen

ALS, DNA, RG 393, Dept. of the Mo., Letters Received. In a matter related to
the discharge of steamboats, USG sent an undated endorsement, presumably written about this time, to hd. qrs., Dept. of the Mo. "It seems to me Captain Turnley
is more disposed to thwart my movements than to further them, at all events I
know he cannot give me any advice. The rivers are full many places out of banks,
and I need the steamers as floating storehouses and barracks, until the waters
subside." *Reminiscences of Parmenas Taylor Turnley* (Chicago, [1892]), p. 369.
This was written on a letter of Capt. Parmenas T. Turnley. "To the masters of
steamers who have left the port of Cairo: This will be handed to you by Clerk
Ed. E. Whitehouse, and you are directed to return to this port with your boat
without delay. All boats that fail to report at this depot within six days after
reading this order will not receive any daily pay after the six days, unless the
master can show written authority from the general commanding to remain
longer." *Ibid*. The letter was returned to Turnley by Maj. Robert Allen. Turnley

endorsed the letter and forwarded copies to the q. m. gen. and the secretary of war. "In reply to General Grant's most incomprehensible endorsement, I have simply to say, first, that seventeen steamers had gone up river to his command, and none had returned to this depot. I had no river transport for service elsewhere, and that is why I sent notice to masters to return with their boats. General Grant says in the last part of his endorsement all he need have said at all, and had he done so, and returned it to me by my clerk, it would have been my duty and my pleasure to have fully acquiesced in his action. But General Grant went out of his official line to indulge in language as to my *motives* or *desires*, and is as unjust and as far from the truth as his method of expressing the same is *infamous* and *unworthy of a sober man*, which charity inclines me to think Grant *was not* when he wrote the endorsement. However, I shall say no more; 'soft words turneth away wrath.' " *Ibid.*, pp. 370–71. Since Turnley does not discuss the status of the document he used for his text, and no manuscript copy has been found (though Turnley stated that he sent two copies to Washington), the authenticity of this exchange remains open to question.

1. See telegram to Maj. Gen. Henry W. Halleck, Feb. 4, 1862.
2. The *W. H. Brown.*

To Brig. Gen. George W. Cullum

Head Quarters, Dist. of W. Ten.
Fort Donelson, Feb.y 28th 1862

GEN. G. W. CULLUM,
CHIEF OF STAFF, DEPT. OF THE MO.
CAIRO ILL.
GEN.

I have just returned from Nashville.[1] Gen. Buell has arrived with a portion of his command.[2] Nelsons Division, as you have before been informed, I forwarded immediately to Nashville.[3] — Gen. Buell was in possession ~~was in possession~~ of information which he believes reliable to the effect that Johnson was at Murphreesboro' with his entire force and might conclude to attack him whilst his force is still weak. Acting upon this Gen. Buell ordered Gen. Smith from Clarkesville with all his available force up the river.[4] To-day a number of boats went up loaded with troops belonging to Buell's command so that Nashville may now, if it was not before, be concidered safe. I had no apprehension from the start.

I will hold my force in readiness for a move on very short notice. At present there are no transports here, and I suppose you are aware that I have no wagon train.

There are a great many sick and wounded Confederates in Nashville.

> I am Gen. very respectfully
> your obt. svt.
> U. S. Grant
> Brig. Gen.

ALS, DNA, RG 393, Dept. of the Mo., Letters Received. On March 2, 1862, Brig. Gen. George W. Cullum telegraphed to USG via Brig. Gen. William T. Sherman. "Gen. Halleck, Feb. 25th telegraphs me Grant will send no more forces to Clarksville. Gen. Smith's Division will come to Fort Henry or a point higher up the Tennessee River Transports will also be collected at Paducah Two gunboats in Tennessee River with Gen. Grant Grant will immediately have small garrisons detailed for Forts Donelson and Henry, and all other forces made ready for the field. From your letter of 28th I learn you were at Fort Donelson and Gen. Smith at Nashville, from which I infer you could not have received order. Halleck's telegram of last night says, Who sent Smith's Division to Nashville.— I ordered it across to the Tennessee where they are wanted immediately. Order them back.—Send all spare transports up Tennessee to Gen. Grant. Evidently the general supposes you on the Tennessee.—I am sending all the transports I can find for you reporting to Sherman for orders to go up Cumberland for you, or if you march across to Fort Henry, then to send them up Tennessee." ALS (telegram sent), *ibid.*, District of West Tenn., Letters Received; telegram received, DLC-William T. Sherman; copies, *ibid.*; DNA, RG 393, USG Hd. Qrs. Correspondence; DLC-USG, V, 4, 5, 7, 8, 9, 81. *O.R.*, I, vii, 677. On March 2, Sherman wrote to USG. "I have just received the Dispatch which I send forward by two Special messengers. The Gun boat Louisville passed down today and the Captain told me that Gen Smiths Division had gone to Nashville, but that you were at Dover. Still by the time this reaches Fort Henry I take it you will be there—In case you are not, these messengers will come to you wherever you are. My force here is 12 Regiments, 5 of which are partially without arms. Arms are en route from St Louis. I will telegraph Gen Halleck to know if you send if I may not send some up to you.—At present they are designed to operate against Columbus which is still occupied in force. Beauregard is not at Columbus, but at Jackson Tennessee. Polk is in Columbus. The Enemy is fortifying Island No 10, and we cannot yet tell what they design at Columbus to fight there, or abandon it. Pope is organizing an army at Commerce, Mo, and there are about 10000 men in and around Cairo. I have received no orders about provisions, but suppose General Halleck has attended to this. I will send by one of the transports all the ammunition I have, which was left ashore here, and deposited at the request of Captain Brink Ordnance officer.—The assemblage there of so large a fleet of empty boats will attract attention so that I suppose you will have to move pretty promptly." ALS, DNA, RG 393, Dept. of the Mo., Telegrams Received. On March 3, USG prepared a receipt for Sherman. "Despatches from Gen Halleck, date March 2/62 received last night. Duplicate received this morning" DS, DLC-William T. Sherman.

1. On Feb. 28, Col. William H. L. Wallace wrote to his wife. "I have just returned from Nashville—I went up on the Steamer 'W H. B.' with Genls. Grant & McClernand & staffs, Col. Lauman 7th Iowa, Capt. Taylor of Chicago & others —The weather was beautiful & the trip a very pleasant one—We found Nashville a most beautiful city, with a magnificent capitol building, & better than all, the old flag waving over it—The city had been occupied two days before by a part of Genl. Buels army—the last of the 'sesech' army moving out as our troops came in sight—There were unfinished fortifications below the city—the guns were left standing—Our victory here is a very great one—Bowling Green, Clarksville & Nashville all strong places, have all been evacuated as the result of our success here—and it now seems probablye, that Columbus will fall from the effects of the same blow—'Te Deum laudamus'—'Let the people praise Him'—At Nashville I found some 85 of our wounded soldiers who had been taken prisoners & carried away by the enemy—Among them were about 40 belonging to the 11th— . . . In company with Genl. McClernand I called on Mrs Polk, the widow of President Polk—She is 'sesech' but a very lady like person—I plucked a daffodil from her garden & enclose it to you in this letter—" ALS, Wallace-Dickey Papers, IHi. Although a *New York Times* correspondent reported that USG had visited Mrs. James K. Polk on Feb. 27, there is no other evidence that he did so. Other correspondents failed to mention it at the time, and USG does not allude to it, either in his *Memoirs*, or in extant letters. Letter of Galway [Franc B. Wilkie], Feb. 27, 1862, in *New York Times*, March 5, 1862; *Memoirs*, I, 321.

2. Feb. 24. See letter to Brig. Gen. William Nelson, Feb. 24, 1862, note 1.
3. See letter to Brig. Gen. George W. Cullum, Feb. 24, 1862.
4. See following letter, note 3.

To Capt. John C. Kelton

Head Quarters, Dist. of W. Ten.
Fort Donelson, Feb.y 28th 1862

CAPT. J. C. KELTON
A. A. GEN. DEPT. OF THE MO.
ST. LOUIS, MO.
CAPT.

There are many men of this command who will have to be discharged on Surgeons Certificates of Disability. As it will take a conciderable length of time to refer these to St. Louis can I not act on them at once? As commander of an "army in the field" I would have the right. As Comd.r of a Dist. I have not. Whether to concider this as an army in the field is respectfully refered to the Maj. Gen. Comd.g Dept.[1]

I have informed Gen. Cullum that Gen. Buell ordered Gen. Smith from Clarkesville to join him at Nashville.[2] I enclose herewith Gen. Buells order on the subject.[3]

I just returned from Nashville this morning.[4] My impression is, from all that I can learn, that the enemy have fallen back to Decatur or Chatanooga.[5]

> very respectfully
> your obt. svt.
> U. S. GRANT
> Brig. Gen. Com

ALS, DNA, RG 393, Dept. of the Mo., Letters Received.

1. U. S. Army regulations allowed the commander of an army in the field to discharge soldiers on certificate of disability. *Revised Regulations for the Army of the United States* (Philadelphia, 1861), p. 30. On March 4, 1862, Capt. Nathaniel H. McLean wrote to USG. "The Commanding General directs me to inform you, that you are hereby authorized to discharge soldiers upon certificates of disability." LS, DNA, RG 393, Dept. of the Mo., Letters Sent (Press). Volume 92, DLC-USG, contains a record of the 1,460 medical discharges from USG's army, March 15–May 29, 1862.

2. See preceding letter.

3. On Feb. 25, Brig. Gen. Don Carlos Buell wrote to Brig. Gen. Charles F. Smith. "The landing of a portion of our troops, contrary to my intention, on the South side of the river, has compelled me to hold this side at every hazard. If the enemy should assume the offensive, and I am assured by reliable persons, that in view of my position such is his intention, my force present is altogether inadequate, consisting of only 15,000 men. I have to request you therefore to come forward with all the available force under your command. So important do I consider the occasion, that I think it necessary to give this communication, all the force of orders, and I send four boats, the Diana, Woodford, John Rain, and Autocrat, to bring you up. In five or six days my force will probably be sufficient to relieve you." Copy, DNA, RG 393, Dept. of the Mo., Letters Received. *O.R.*, I, vii, 944–45.

4. See preceding letter.

5. On Feb. 25, Gen. Albert Sidney Johnston, Murfreesborough, wrote to Secretary of War Judah P. Benjamin. "I will move this corps of the army, of which I have assumed the immediate command, towards the left bank of the

Tennessee, crossing the river near Decatur, in order to enable me to co-operate or unite with General Beauregard for the defense of Memphis and the Mississippi." *O.R.*, I, vii, 427.

To Capt. James Dunlap

Head Quarters, Dist. of W. Ten.
Fort Donelson, Feb.y 28th 1862
Capt. Dunlap[1] will commence unloading the Steamer City of Memphis[2] at once and when the freight is all out discharge her. Capt. Turnley cannot say how long it will take to discharge a boat at this place with all the inconveniences attending and his limitations will receive no attention. If the boat can be unloaded in half the time specified all the better.

U. S. GRANT
Brig. Gen.

AES, McClernand Papers, IHi. Written on a letter of Feb. 26, 1862, from Capt. Parmenas T. Turnley to master, steamer *City of Memphis.* "You will proceed, at once up the River—leave about half your Grain at Paducah the other half at Smithland, take balance of freight & Troops up Cumberland and deliver as per instructions from Capt J. Dunlap a. q. m. after discharging your freight & Troops (which must be done within 12 hours of landing) you will then load with such freight as the commanding officer, or Quarter Master then & there may direct, and return to this post, with all dispatch *In this fail not.*" ALS, *ibid.* On Feb. 28, Brig. Gen. John A. McClernand endorsed the letter to USG. "Respect fully refered to Maj Genl Grant, with the statement of Mr Stewart—Capt Dunlap's Clerk who says it is impossible to unload the boat within the time herein mentioned—" ES, *ibid.*

1. Capt. James Dunlap served as brigade q. m. for McClernand. See letter to Brig. Gen. John A. McClernand, Nov. 16, 1861, note 1.
2. On Feb. 28, George W. Graham wrote to Capt. John A. Rawlins. "The following boats I employed at Cairo on the present expedition, and have been employed day and night in the service, vis—Sr 'New Uncle Sam' 'Fanny Bullett' 'Chancellor' 'Alps' 'Aleck Scott' 'Lake Erie' 'Illinois' Keystone 'Emerald' The above boats have been in Govt. service from two to six months prior to this expedition—excepting about three weeks—no charter price was asked for, or agreed upon when we started, simply the fact, that the rate paid should be satisfactory to the Govt. was the only understanding—boats are fully manned and always ready for any port day or night—The City of Memphis is the only steamer that I know

of, chartered at a rate where the Crew is stipulated   in order to run her day and night, she should be manned with thirty additional men. I cannot get along pleasantly with her officers, and as her time for the second month is out on the sixth of March, Respectfully suggest the propriety of dismissing her from your command —" ALS, DNA, RG 393, District of West Tenn., Letters Received.

To Maj. Gen. Henry W. Halleck

Head Quarters, Dist. of W. Ten.
Fort Donelson, March 1st 1862.

Respectfully refered to Hd Qrs. Dept. of the Mo. I would state that every effort has been made to get fresh beef in this country, without avail. The contractor for furnishing fresh beef in the field reports that he has the beef but cannot get the transportation up the river. I have to request that facilities be allowed to obviate these difficulties and also that potatoes be sent here for issue.

U. S. GRANT
Brig. Gen. Com

AES, DNA, RG 393, Dept. of the Mo., Letters Received. Written on a letter of March 1, 1862, from Brig. Gen. John A. McClernand to USG. "I beg leave to call your attention to the increasing ill health of our troops, and I must ascribe the cause to the want of *fresh beef* and *potatoes*. I am informed that camp diarehoea and debility are becoming almost universal, and are only to be attributed to a continued diet of *salt meats without vegetables*. Confident that in calling your attention to this serious evil, every effort in your power will be used to remedy it." LS, *ibid*. Attached to this letter is a letter of March 3 from Capt. Beekman Du Barry, Cairo, to Brig. Gen. George W. Cullum. "I have the honor to return herewith the letter of Brig Genl McClernand endorsed by Brig: Genl Grant, in relation to the supply of Fresh Beef and Potatoes at Fort Donelson, and by you referred to me. In reply I have to state that the contractor (Mr Pearce) for supplying Fresh Beef in the field was notified to supply Genl Grants force a few days after the contract was signed (contract dated Feb.y 8th)   I have no doubt that he has difficulty in obtaining transportation and would recommend that any facilities possible not involving expense to the U. S. be provided him. Five thousand bushels of potatoes were at my request forwarded from St Louis. these as I learn were taken to Fort Donelson thence back to St Louis, a part of them having been landed at Cairo on the return trip of the steamer, and part of these latter (about 40000 pounds) were again shipped from Cairo for Fort Donelson. Had the five thousand bushels been landed at Fort Donelson there would have been an ample supply for the time being." ALS, *ibid*. On March 1, 1st Lt. Clark B. Lagow wrote to Capt. Algernon S. Baxter. "You will furnish six horses to Butchers (for the purpose of bringing in Beef cattle) tomorrow." Copies, DLC-USG, V, 2, 86; DNA, RG 393, USG Letters Sent.

To Brig. Gen. George W. Cullum

Head Quarters, Dist. of W. Ten.
Fort Donelson, March 1st 1862

Gen. G. W. Cullum
Chief of Staff, Dept. of the Mo
Cairo Ill.
Gen.

Some ten days ago I wrote to have the regimental teams left behind forwarded. I do not know that any of them have as yet come. As I have no quartermaster I cannot keep myself as thoroughly posted on such matters as I would like to be however.

I hope you will order all teams belonging here forwarded at once. If harness was sent for thirty or forty teams I could rig out that number from captured mules and wagons. The rebels destroyed all their harness nearly; what was not destroyed has already been put to use in fitting out additional teams.

A number of the regiments sent here during the siege of Donelson were entirely without wagons.

I hope at least one Quartermaster will be assigned me without delay. The good of the service most assuredly demands it.

I am Gen. very respectfully
your obt. svt.
U. S. Grant
Brig. Gen. Com.

ALS, DNA, RG 393, Dept. of the Mo., Letters Received. Brig. Gen. George W. Cullum endorsed this letter to Capt. Parmenas T. Turnley. "Have you any work harness. Is the transportation for Grant's regiments sent from here forwarded.— When will Capt. Dunlap report to Grant." AE, *ibid*. On March 5, 1862, Turnley replied to Cullum. "About ten days after Genl: Grant left Cairo, I found a large number of teams about Cairo, Birds point & Ft. Holt—reported as belonging to the service of Regiments that had gone with Genl: Grant. I had *all* of them assembled and *shipped* on steamers for the *Cumberland & the Tenn: Rivers.—They left here,* some seven days before the date of this letter, and must have got in the neighborhood of Forts Donelson & Henry, but, perhaps without Genl: Grants knowledge   In all I sent up about *176* teams complete"   AES, *ibid.* On March 2, Capt. John A. Rawlins issued General Orders No. 18. "Division Commanders will make out, and furnish to these Head Quarters immediately a full and complete list of the number of teams of their commands, including Regimental and Detachment, as well as general trains; and captured, as well as purchased teams." DS, *ibid.*; (2), McClernand Papers, IHi.

On March 5, Cullum wrote to USG. "The Yates Sharp Shooters have been sent to Brig Genl Pope now before New Madrid and until they return no disposition can be made of that force. The guards of Prisoners of War have received instruction direct from Genl Halleck except in a few Cases. Genl Thomas states that several Companies of them have passed Paducah on their return to their regiments—All the transportation of the regimts You Took from here was Sent to you some time since three Steamer loads. Capt Baxter was ordered to return to You and Capt Dunlap has also been ordered to report to You. If the Quartermaster here can find any such harness I will send it you"   Copies, DLC-USG, V, 4, 5, 7, 8, 9; DNA, RG 393, USG Hd. Qrs. Correspondence. *O.R.,* I, lii, part 1, 219. On Feb. 23, Maj. Frederick W. Matteson, Yates Sharpshooters (later 64th Ill.), Cairo, wrote to Brig. Gen. John A. McClernand. "I am requested by the officers of the 'Yates Sharp Shooters' to write to you on a subject of considerable importance to us. The officers without a single dissenting voice, have expressed their desire to join your column in the field. The condition of the Battalion is as follows:—Six companies commanded by Lieut Col. David. E. Williams— 550 men, armed with good long range rifles, with sabre bayonets, well equipped, well drilled, and prepared to act as 'Sharp Shooters,' Skirmishers and Light Infantry. As far as *physique* and *morale* are concerned they yield to no other corps in the service." Copy, McClernand Papers, IHi. On Feb. 28, McClernand wrote to USG. "Following is the copy of a letter which explains itself. If you can accommodate the 'Yates Sharp Shooters' and me by having them assigned to my Command (Ross' Brigade) I would be much pleased and obliged." Copy, *ibid.*

To Capt. John C. Kelton

———

Head Quarters, Dist. of W. Ten.
Fort Donelson, March 1st 1862.

CAPT. J. C. KELTON
A. A. GEN. DEPT. OF THE MO.
ST. LOUIS, MO.
CAPT.

I have informed the Gen. Comd.g Dept. generally through the Chief of Staff, every day since leaving Cairo of my wants, what information was obtained of the movements of the enemy &c. I will now recapitulate partly my wants.

When I left Cairo for the want of transportation it took two trips of the boats at hand to move the troops, leaving the Cavalry to march and leaving behind all the regimental trains but four wagons to each regiment. A number of the regiments sent to reinforce me come without wagons.—Since geting into Fort Donelson I have written to have the wagons left forwarded. None of them have as yet come, I think none. As I have no Quartermaster to look out for these matters I may be mistaken partly.

My command are now suffering from Camp Dysentery the result, according to report of surgeons, of being compelled to live on salt meat.

I have had this country scoured for miles for beef cattle but without being able to obtain them. The contractors for supplying fresh beef say they have the cattle but are unable to procure transportation.

If I am compelled to move suddenly it will be with a very week force compared with what the Maj. Gen. Comd.g probably expects. The loss in battle and the number who have sickened since reduces my force conciderably. I will probably have to leave a garrison at Clarkesville, Fort Henry and at this place. Gen. Buell ordered Gen. Smith with the force at Clarkesville, five regiments of Infantry and some Artillery; to join his Column at Nashville.¹ Two regiments that were sent as a guard to the prisoners have not been returned to me.

I most respectfully lay these matters before the Gen. Comd.g Department not to make suggestions but that my true condition may be known.

There are now two or three cases of small pox among the men. Every effort has been made to prevent the spread of the disease.

Very respectfully
your obt. svt.
U. S. GRANT
Brig. Gen.

ALS, DNA, RG 393, Dept. of the Mo., Letters Received. *O.R.*, I, vii, 674–75.

1. On March 1, 1862, Brig. Gen. Don Carlos Buell wrote to Maj. Gen. Henry W. Halleck. "I am now in sufficient force to feel secure, and this morning sent General Smith back to Clarksville." *Ibid.*, p. 675.

To Julia Dent Grant

Fort Donelson, Ten.
F̶e̶b̶.̶y̶ March 1st 1862

DEAR JULIA.

Enclosed I send you seven hundred dollars which with as much as you can spare from money you already have you may lend to the store taking a note payable to yourself. In sending this I am anticipating my March pay but I will be able to send you one hundred every month for your support and when all is paid up I can send you four hundred per month for you to apply the savings for your own benefit. I want you to accumulate all you can against any accident that may arise. I hope this War will not continue long and when it does end I want to have a few hundred dollars at least independent of every body. My pay now is over $6000 per year and I can live off of one thousand even as a Maj. Gen. Keeping my horses is necessarily somewhat expensive but in other particulars I spend but very little.—Should I not be where you can join me this Summer I want you to visit your friends and mine.—Send the children to school and tell them to be good and not annoy anybody. Dear children tell them their pa thinks of them every day notwithstanding he has so much els to think of. I have done a good job at Forts Henry and Donelson but I am being so much crippled in my resources that I very much fear that I shall not be able to advance so rapidly as I would like. When I left Cairo steam transportation was so scarce that it took two trips to bring up my force leaving behind nearly all my wagons and leaving the cavalry to march. Since that I have been unable to get up these teams. Besides this Gen. Buell ordered to his column some of my troops that were at Clarkesville; the loss in battle and from fatigue and exposure takes of a number of thousands; I sent off two regiments to guard prisoners who have not been returned, and if I leave, garrisons will have to be left here, at Clarkesville and Fort Henry. This will weaken me so much that great results cannot be expected. I shall write to Gen. Halleck to-day however stating all these facts. I have written to those at Cairo who should have rectified this matter but without much response. Remember this is a private letter and is not to be made public. You had better keep it however. I do hope that I will be placed in a seperate Department so as to be more independent, not that I have any fault to find with Gen. Halleck on the contrary I regard him as one of the greatest men of the age and there are not two men in the United States who I would prefer serving under to McClellan & Halleck. They would be my own chois for the positions they fill if left to me to make. Kiss the children for me. The same for yourself.

Ulys.

ALS, DLC-USG.

General Orders No. 19

———

Head Quarters, Dist of West. Tenn
Fort Donelson March. 2d 1862.

GENERAL ORDERS, No. 19

By virtue of authority from Head Quarters of the Army, Washington, D. C. Col. C. C. Washburn, of the 2d Wisconsin Cavalry, is appointed, Aid-de-Camp, to the undersigned.

He will be obeyed and respected accordingly.

By order.

U. S. GRANT
Maj. Gen. Com'd'g

DS, McClernand Papers, IHi. See letter to Elihu B. Washburne, Feb. 21, 1862. On March 3, 1862, Col. Cadwallader C. Washburn wrote to his older brother, Congressman Elihu B. Washburne. "I arrived here last night, and found Genl Grant very cordial. Have not had time to go out & examine the Fort, & battle ground. It looks to me to be a very strong position, and the wonder is that we ever captured it. Genl. Grant is quite ill this morning, but preperations are on foot for moving on to the Tennessee River. The weather here is the worst you ever saw. Raining constantly, & cold & disagreeable. The prospect for another big battle immediately is not brilliant. Buel is at Nashville with a large force. There are reports that the rebels are making a stand at Murfresboro, but Genl. Grant thinks that it is not so to any great extent. The only show for a great battle is now at Columbus. If they do not evacuate that point, there will no doubt be music there by the entire band before long. As I came here I stopd and saw Gen. Halleck at St Louis & got an order to remove my Regt to St. Louis where it will be armed and mounted. Consequently I shall remain here but a few days. I wish it was here now, as it might have been, and ought to have been. The public cannot overestimate the importance of the victory here. It is in my judgment of more practical importance than all other battles that have been won by our army. The capture of this point was the capture virtually of Nashville, and settles the rebellion throughout the valley of the Mississippi. The vast preparations at Cairo no doubt carry with them a great moral force, but I much doubt whether they will be used to any great extent. The plan in regard to Columbus, I think is to surround them, & cut off their communications & compel them to come out & fight. If they do not the 40 mortars will then pepper them. I dont believe they will ever stand that. The Galena Regt. is here, but I have seen nobody connected with it. It behaved well in the battle. I may go up to Nashville for a day, in case we do not get away from here immediately—I will send you a plan of the battle as soon as I can get one made. I have noticed that ~~some~~ a correspondent for the N. Y. World says that it was bad Generalship that Floyds retreat was not cut off. An examination of the ground will satisfy any man of sense that it was impossible, a~~t~~s the river was wholly unapproachable, above the enemys lines, and had it been otherwise with nothing but light field Artillery, it would not have been possible to have prevented them from running away—"   ALS, DLC-Elihu B. Washburne.

To Brig. Gen. John A. McClernand

Head Quarters, Dist. of W. Ten.
Fort Donelson, March 2d 1862

GEN. J. A. MCCLERNAND
COMD.G 1ST DIV.
GEN.

Will you please send by the bearer a map you borrowed from me before the Kentucky reconnoisance of the state of Tennessee.

If you have not got it please send me any such map as you may have. I require one immediately

Very respectfully
your obt. svt.
U. S. GRANT
Maj. Gen.

ALS, McClernand Papers, IHi.

To Brig. Gen. William T. Sherman

Head Quarters, Dist of W. Ten
Fort Donelson, March 2d 1862

GEN. W. T. SHERMAN
COMD.G DIST. OF CAIRO
PADUCAH ILL.
GEN.

Dispatches from Gen. Halleck, per express from Paducah just received.

I will commence moving as soon as boats arrive. Gen. Smith

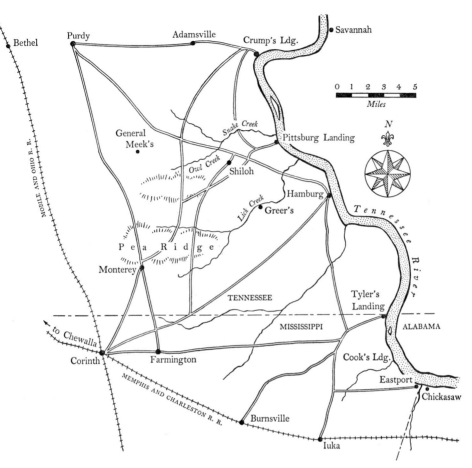

Area around Shiloh

is at Clarkesville and I dont much like to move him at present and yet, as suggested, would like to take him along.

If steamers have not left when this reaches you they had probably better go up the Tennessee, or at least most of them had.

The rivers are still very high making it difficult to embark or debark. It has now been raining for twenty-four hours and bad roads and deep branches will have to be encountered.

> I am Gen. very respectfully
> your obt. svt.
> U. S. GRANT
> Maj. Gen.

ALS, DLC-William T. Sherman. On March 2, 1862, Brig. Gen. William T. Sherman had written to USG. "I send by two special messengers on separate steamboats telegraphic instructions from Maj Genl Halleck; and with the messengers, I order the Qr Master to send you up ten Steam Boats, capable of transporting about 8 or 10000 men   These Steam Boats are seized as they pass, and I will send all that arrive today—The Telegraph No 3 is up the Tennessee & will be held for you, as also any boats that arrive to day, to be at Fort Henry during the night so that you will have transportation for ten thousand men"   LS, DNA, RG 393, Dept. of the Mo., Telegrams Received.
    On March 1, Maj. Gen. Henry W. Halleck telegraphed to USG. "A̶l̶l̶ Transports will be sent you as soon as possible to move your column up the Tennessee River. The main object of this ex[pedi]tion will be to destroy [the] R R Bridge over Bear Creek near Eastport, Miss, and also the connexions at Corinth, Jackson & Humbolt. It is thought best that these objects be attempted in the order named. Strong detachments of cavalry & light artillery supported by infantry may, d̶e̶s̶t̶r̶ by rapid movements, reach these points from the river without very serious opposition. Avoid any general engagement with strong masses. It will be better to retreat than to risk a general battle. This should be strongly imp[ressed] upon the officers w̶h̶o̶ ̶c̶o̶m̶m̶a̶n̶d̶ sent with expeditions from the river. Genl. C. F. [Smith] or some very discreet officer should be selected for such commands. Having accomplished these objects, or such of them as may [be] practic[able], you will [return to Danville] & move on Paris. Perhaps the troops sent to Jac[kson &] Humbolt can r̶e̶t̶u̶r̶n̶ ̶t̶o̶ reach Paris by land as w̶e̶l̶ easily as to return to the f̶i̶v̶e̶ transports. This must depend upon the character of the roads and the position of the [enemy.] All telegraph lines which can be reached must be cut. The Gun boats s̶h̶o̶u̶l̶d̶ will accompany the transports for their protection. Any loyal Tennesseeans who desire it may be enlisted & supplied with arms. Competent officers should be left to command the garrisons of Forts Henry & Donelson in your absence. I have indicated in general terms the object of this." ALS (telegram sent), *ibid.*, RG 107, Telegrams Collected (Unbound); telegram received, DLC-William T. Sherman. *O.R.*, I, vii, 674. On the same day, Halleck telegraphed to Sherman. "Send all transports to Gen Grant up the Tennessee.   orders have been sent to him to move up that River. You can retain Ohio Regts for the present." Telegram received, DLC-William T. Sherman.

To Brig. Gen. Charles F. Smith

——

Head Quarters, Dist. of W. Ten.
Fort Donelson, March 2d 1862

GEN. C. F. SMITH
COMD.G U. S. FORCES
CLARKESVILLE TEN.
GEN.

Herewith I send you copy of instructions just received from Head Quarters of the Dept.[1]

Instead of carrying out the instructions according to the plan laid down I think it will be preferable to divide it and let the expedition on Paris[2] start from Fort Heiman.

I will leave here on the transports provided and execute the commands on the upper Tennessee taking with me two Brigades of each the 1st & 4th Divisions and the Brigadiers commanding them.[3]

The Paris expedition will be left to you and the force to do it can be organized out of Gen. Wallace's Division and such portion of the remaining Brigades of the other two Divs. as you may deem necessary.

Leave the force you now have at Clarkesville and assume command of the forces at Forts Donelson, Henry & Heiman on my departure and prepare the expedition. It should not leave Heiman earlyer than three or four days after my departure.

I am Gen. very respectfully
your obt. svt.
U. S. GRANT
Maj. Gen.

ALS, James S. Schoff, New York, N. Y. On March 5, 1862, Brig. Gen. Charles F. Smith, Fort Donelson, wrote to Capt. John A. Rawlins. "Say to the General if you please that I am in the receipt of his dispatch of the 2d inst., enclosing a copy of Genl. Halleck's telegram of the 1st. inst., on the relating to proposed movements on the Tennessee, and that I arrived here last night pursuant to said the instructions in his dispatch. I shall leave here for Fort Henry as soon as possible —say tomorrow. I beg to be favored with an interpretation of the telegram, &c.,

as to what I am expected to do on arriving at Paris. Am I simply to destroy the rail-way bridge at that point? and then retire upon Fort Heiman? or am I to remain there awaiting a junction with ~~your forces Gen~~the General or ~~your~~ his further orders? I am sorry to appear so very stupid but I am a little puzzled in this matter. I send this by two of my mounted orderlies, who will bring back any message the General may be pleased to send me. What garrison shall I leave here?" ALS, DNA, RG 393, District of West Tenn., Letters Received. On the same day, Smith wrote another letter to Rawlins, "Acknowledging receipt of orders to proceed to Fort Henry." DLC-USG, V, 10; DNA, RG 393, USG Register of Letters Received.

    1. See preceding letter.
    2. Paris, Tenn., on the Memphis, Clarksville and Louisville Railroad, about twenty-five miles southwest of Fort Henry.
    3. On March 2, Rawlins issued Special Orders No. 14. "Two Brigades of each of the 1st and 4th Divisions, will proceed without delay to the Tennessee River, by what is known as the 'Ridge or Furnace road, and go into camp at the nearest accessible point for embarking on Steamers. Three days rations will be taken and forty rounds of ammunition, besides what is contained in Cartridge boxes. All weak and disabled soldiers are to be left behind. Camp and garrison equippage will be taken, but soldiers are to be limited as per General Orders No 17. No officer or soldier not entitled to forage, will be permitted to ride on horseback or to have a horse with them. Attention of Division, Brigade and Regimental Commanders is particularly called to the execution of this order." DS, McClernand Papers, IHi; DNA, RG 393, Dept. of the Mo., Letters Received. *O.R.*, I, vii, 678–79.

To Capt. John C. Kelton

Head Quarters, Dist of West Tenn.
Fort Donelson March 3d 1862.

Capt. J. C. Kelton
A. A. Gen. Depart. of the Mo.
St. Louis, Mo.
Capt.

I have ordered Capt. Z. S. Main of the 52d Ia. Regt. to St. Louis under arrest, for gross violation of orders, and conduct highly prejudicial to good order and Military Discipline.

I have done every thing possible to prevent public plunder, both by publishing orders, and trying to enforce them. In spite

of all, the Capt. has been caught in attempting to pass, per
Steamer, the articles of which you have herewith an enclosed list.

> I am, Capt. Very Respectfully
> Your. Obt. Servt.
> U. S. GRANT
> Maj. Gen. Com'd'g

Copies, DLC-USG, V, 4, 5, 7, 8, 9, 88; DNA, RG 393, USG Hd. Qrs. Corre-
spondence. On March 3, 1862, Capt. William S. Hillyer wrote to Capt. Zalmon S.
Main, 52nd Ind. "You will proceed immediately to St Louis, Mo. and report
yourself to Major Gen. Halleck, Commdg. Dept of the Mo, as under arrest.
Charges will be forwarded to Capt. J. C. Kelton Asst. Adjt. Genl." Copies, DLC-
USG, V, 1, 2, 3, 86; DNA, RG 393, USG Letters Sent. On March 9, Capt.
John C. Kelton issued Special Orders No. 210. "Capt. Zamlin S. Main 52nd Regt.
Inda. Vols. is herby discharged from the service of the United States to take effect
this day" Copy, DLC-USG, V, 83.

To Flag Officer Andrew H. Foote

Fort Donelson, March 3d/62

FLAG OFFICER FOOTE U. S. N.
COMD.G WESTERN FLOTILLA
CAIRO ILL.
SIR:

I start to-morrow for Fort Henry thence up the river on a
new mission and I regret to say feeling much as you must have
before the attack on Fort Donelson. I am bearly able to be out of
my bed. I have had a severe cold ever since leaving Cairo and it
has now settled on my chest which, with a severe head ache,
nearly destroys my energy.

When you and I conversed last Capt. Phelps was the subject
and I then expressed a willingness to add all I could in my humble
way to his advancement. Feeling that the Capt. is deserving in
an eminant degree I am anxious to do all in my power for him
and you have only to suggest to whom I am to write and it will

be done at once.[1]—Thank the Capt. for me for the very handsome manner in which he notices my advancement.

I send herewith a letter from a young sister of mine from which you will see how you are appreciated, deservedly, by the people of Covington as well as the remainder of this broad country.

I am Flag Officer your obt. svt.

U. S. GRANT

ALS, War Library and Museum, Military Order of the Loyal Legion, Philadelphia, Pa. On March 8, 1862, Flag Officer Andrew H. Foote wrote to USG. "In your letter to me enclosing your sisters touching & beautiful note showing a highly cultivated and delicate mind armed with strong religious faith, you mention Phelps' congratulatory letter but make no allusion to mine. I also wrote you as earnest if not as good an effusion of congratulation at being promoted as it were on that sanguinary field where you have placed your name so high in the pages of your country's history, but it seems you did not receive this, therefore take this as a substitue, and give my love, the love of an old man to your accomplished sister who I know will take it from the friend of her distinguished brother. I send a copy of my telegram and shall be most happy to enlarge upon it giving the details if you wish, as we were anxious to proceed against Fort Henry before I ever heard of its being the intention to do so from any higher quarter. Excuse my chirography & composition as I am in a hurry & believe me as ever"   ALS, DNA, RG 45, Area 5. *O.R.* (Navy), I, xxii, 661–62.

1. It was not until Dec. 1, 1862, that President Abraham Lincoln nominated S. Ledyard Phelps as lt. commander to rank from the previous July 16.

To Brig. Gen. William T. Sherman

Head Quarters, Dist of West Tenn
Fort Donelson March 3d 1862

GENERAL W. T. SHERMAN
COM'D'G DIST OF CAIRO,
PADUCAH, KY.
GENERAL:

I send by the "City of Memphis" three iron 24 pounders, belonging to McAllisters Battery. These guns are somewhat out of order, besides being heavy and cumbersome for the field. May

I ask you the favor to exchange them for the brass 24s at Paducah ?
I ask this at the suggestion of Gen. Totten who is now here. If
you will make the exchange please send them up the Tennessee
as soon as practicable.

> I am, General,
> Very Respectfully
> Your Obt Servt.
> U. S. GRANT
> Maj. Genl.

Copies, DLC-USG, V, 1, 2, 88; DNA, RG 393, USG Letters Sent. On March 3,
1862, Capt. John A. Rawlins wrote to Brig. Gen. John A. McClernand. "You will
hold your Artillery ready for inspection immediately, by Gen. Totten who is now
here for that purpose." LS, McClernand Papers, IHi. On the same day, McClernand wrote to USG. "Capt McAllisters Battery consisting of 3, 24 pds Howitzers
is disabled, the trail of one of the carriages, and a wheel of another have been shot
away by the enemy in the battle of Fort Donelson—At the suggestion of Genl
Totten I would recommend that Capt McAllisters Battery be immediately sent on
board of a steamer to Paducah, there to be exchanged so far as necessary to give
it efficiency for similar Guns and carriages at that place   The Battery is also in
need of Artillery harniss, Ammunition &c which might be supplied at the same
place. After the battery has been thus refitted I hope you will cause it to be sent
forward to me wherever I may be without delay   If requested Genl Sherman
commanding at Paducah would doubtless afford every facility in power to effect
the object in view." Copy, *ibid.* Also on the same day, Rawlins wrote to Capt.
Edward McAllister. "You will proceed on board the Steamer, 'City of Memphis,'
at once with your Battery as now existing, to Paducah, Ky, and there exchange it,
for four new twenty four pounder Guns, and Artillery equipments complete, and
rejoin your Brigade at Fort. Henry, or wherever it may be, as soon as practicable.
The Commdg. General at Paducah, will afford you every facility." Copies, DLC-
USG, V, 1, 2, 86; DNA, RG 393, USG Letters Sent. See following letter.

To Brig. Gen. William T. Sherman

———

Head Quarters, Dist of West. Tenn
Fort. Donelson, March 3d 1862

GEN. W. T. SHERMAN
COM'D'G DIST OF CAIRO,
PADUCAH, ILL.
GENERAL.

I send you, by steamer, "City of Memphis," McAlisters Battery of 24 pound Howitzers, which is in want of some repairs. I hope you will afford the necessary facilities for making the required repairs and forward the Battery to me as soon as practicable.

I am, Gen. Very Respectfully
Your Obt Servt.
U. S. GRANT
Maj. Gen. Com'd'g

Copies, DLC-USG, V, 1, 2, 3, 88; DNA, RG 393, USG Letters Sent. See preceding letter.

To Brig. Gen. William T. Sherman

———

Head Quarters, Dist. of West Tenn.
Fort. Donelson March 3d 1862

GEN. W. T. SHERMAN
COM'D'G DIST. OF CAIRO,
PADUCAH KY.
GEN.

I would respectfully request that you send me two companies of the 2d. Ill. Cavalry of which I now have two companies, and with them Lieut. Col. Hogg.[1] I am deficient in Cavalry, and if consistent with the interest of service would like to have Col.

Hogg to command the detachment of the 2d. I have, with what is here asked. Send them to Fort Henry if they can be dispensed with.

I am, General,
Very Respectfully
Your Obt. Servt.
U. S. GRANT
Maj. Gen. Com'd'g.

Copies, DLC-USG, V, 1, 2, 3, 88; DNA, RG 393, USG Letters Sent.

1. Lt. Col. Harvey Hogg of Bloomington, 2nd Ill. Cav. On March 2, 1862, Hogg led a portion of the 2nd Ill. Cav. from Paducah to Columbus. Through Shiloh only Cos. A and B served with USG. *Ill. AG Report*, VII, 526.

To Maj. Gen. Henry W. Halleck

Head Quarters, Dist. of W. Ten.
Fort Donelson, March 5th/62

MAJ. GEN. H. W. HALLECK
COMD.G DEPT. OF THE MO.
ST. LOUIS, MO.
GEN.

Your dispatch of yesterday[1] is just received. Troops will be sent under Com.d of Maj. Gen. Smith as directed.

I had prepared a different plan intending Gen. Smith to command the forces which would go to Paris & Humboldt[2] whilst I would command the expedition upon Eastport, Corinth & Jackson[3] in person. Information received this morning however would have changed my plan even if your orders had not done it. Forces going to East Port must go prepared to meet a force of 20,000 men. This will take all my available troops after garrisoning Clarkesville Forts Donelson & Henry.

By your instructions I do not know whether I am to abandon

Clarkesville entirely or not. There are some captured stores there and heavy ordnance that must be disposed of before the place can be abandoned.

I am not aware of ever having disobeyed any order from Head Quarters, certainly never intended such a thing. I have reported almost daily the condition of my command and reported evry position occupied. I have not however been able to get returns from all the troops from which to consolidate a return for Dept. Hd Qrs. All have come in except from Gen. Smiths command at Clarkesville, five small regiments of Infantry, and two companies of Artillery. The Gen. has probably been unable to get his in in consequence of being ordered to Nashville by Gen. Buell.

Gen. Smith has been relieved by Gen. Buell and was ordered immediately to the Tennessee by me.

As soon as I was notified that Gen. Smith had been ordered to Nashvill I reported the fact and sent a copy of Buell's order.[4]

My reports have nearly all been made to Gen. Cullum, Chief of Staff, and it may be that many of them were not thought of sufficient importance to forward more than a telegraphic synopsis of.

The Tennessee is now so high that there are but few points on the river where troops can be embarked. Fort Henry is under water. ~~the guns~~ The water is about six feet deep inside the fort. The continuous rains have made it almost impossible to get from Fort Donelson to the Tennes[see.] It is now very difficult to move across the country.

I will leave at Fort Donelson four regiments of Inf.y all of them very small having suffered severely at Donelson and from sickness since.

I will leave two regiments at Clarkesville until further directions are received.

I have 46 Infantry regiments, 3 Cavalry regiments 8 independent companies & ten batteries of Light Artillery. The average available strength of regiments, fit for the field, is about 500 men

In conclusion I will say that you may rely on my carrying

out your instructions, in every particular, to the very best of my ability.

> I am Gen. Very respectfully
> your obt. svt.
> U. S. GRANT
> Maj. Gen.

ALS, DNA, RG 393, Dept. of the Mo., Letters Received. *O.R.*, I, x, part 2, 4–5. On March 9, 1862, Maj. Gen. Henry W. Halleck wrote to USG. "Your letter of the 5th inst, just recd, contains the first & only information of your actual forces. If you have reported them before, I have not seen them. Genl McClellan has repeatedly ordered me to report to him daily the numbers & positions of your forces. This I could not do; and the fault certainly was not mine, for I telegraphed to you time & again for the information, but could get no answer. This certainly indicated a great want of order & system in your command, the blame of which was partially thrown on me, and perhaps justly, as it is the duty of every commander to *compel* those under him to obey orders & enforce discipline. Dont let such neglect occur again, for it is equally discreditable to you & to me. I really felt ashamed to telegraph back to Washington time & again that I was unable to give the strength of your command. But to business. I think the guns & stores at Clarksville should be brought down to Paducah. We require no garrison there. Fragmentary regiments, equivalent to one regt, will be sufficient to garrison Fort Donelson. The same for Fort Henry. All other troops should be sent up the ~~cumb~~ Tennessee as rapidly as possible. As soon as these things are arranged, you will hold yourself in readiness to take the command. There will probably be some desperate fighting in that vicinity, and we must be prepared. See that stores, ammunition, entrenching tools, &c, are forwarded. Messengers should be sent at least twice a day to the telegraph line to keep me informed of every thing. I am required to report to Washington, at least once a day, the condition of affairs. Your district was the only one heretofore from which I could not obtain the required information. I shall organize an[d] send you reinforcements as rapidly as possible, and when I get them under way I shall join you myself." ALS, DNA, RG 94, Generals' Papers and Books, Letters Sent by Gen. Halleck (Press). *O.R.*, I, x, part 2, 22. On March 9, Halleck telegraphed to Maj. Gen. George B. McClellan. "From Genl Grant's letter of the 5th inst just received, I learn that his force consists of forty six regiments of infantry, three regiments of cavalry, and ten batteries of light artillery. This is the first & only information on this subject I have received from him. The regiments, he says, will not average more than five hundred men each. You will percieve from this that without Buell's aid, I am too weak for operatio[ns] on the Tennessee." ALS (telegram sent), Ritzman Collection, Aurora College, Aurora, Ill.; copy, DNA, RG 94, Letters Received. *O.R.*, I, x, part 2, 22.

1. On March 4, Halleck telegraphed to USG, via Paducah. "You will place Major Genl C. F. Smith in command of expedition, & remain yourself at Fort Henry. Why do you not obey my orders to report strength & positions of your command?" ALS (telegram sent), DNA, RG 107, Telegrams Collected (Un-

bound); telegram received, DLC-William T. Sherman; copies, *ibid.;* DNA, RG 94, Generals' Papers and Books, Telegrams Sent in Cipher by Gen. Halleck; *ibid.*, RG 393, Dept. of the Mo., Telegrams Sent; *ibid.*, USG Hd. Qrs. Correspondence; DLC-USG, V, 4, 5, 7, 8, 9, 81. *O.R.*, I, x, part 2, 3. On March 3, Halleck had telegraphed to McClellan. "I have had no communication with General Grant for more than a week. He left his command without my authority and went to Nashville. His army seems to be as much demoralized by the victory of Fort Donelson as was that of the Potomac by the defeat of Bull Run. It is hard to censure a successful general immediately after a victory, but I think he richly deserves it. I can get no returns, no reports, no information of any kind from him. Satisfied with his victory, he sits down and enjoys it without any regard to the future. I am worn-out and tired with this neglect and inefficiency. C. F. Smith is almost the only officer equal to the emergency." *Ibid.*, I, vii, 679–80. On the same day, McClellan telegraphed to Halleck. "Your dispatch of last evening received. The future success of our cause demands that proceedings such as Grant's should at once be checked. Generals must observe discipline as well as private soldiers. Do not hesitate to arrest him at once if the good of service requires it, & place C F Smith in command. You are at liberty to regard this as a positive order if it will smooth your way. I appreciate the difficulties you have to encounter & will be glad to relieve you from trouble as far as possible" ALS (telegram sent), DNA, RG 107, Telegrams Collected (Bound). *O.R.*, I, vii, 680. McClellan's retained copy is endorsed "Approved" by Secretary of War Edwin M. Stanton. On March 4, Halleck wrote to McClellan. "A rumor has just reached me that since the taking of Fort Donelson General Grant has resumed his former bad habits. If so, it will account for his neglect of my often-repeated orders. I do not deem it advisable to arrest him at present, but have placed General Smith in command of the expedition up the Tennessee. I think Smith will restore order and discipline." *Ibid.*, p. 682.

Although Halleck complained that USG had failed to report his strength and position, there are no specific requests for this information either in USG's hd. qrs. records or those of the Dept. of the Mo. On Feb. 16, McClellan had telegraphed to Halleck. "Give me in detail Grant's force & positions—the last report from him—all that you heard reliably in regard to enemy. What left at Fort Henry." ALS (telegram sent), DNA, RG 107, Telegrams Collected (Bound). On the preceding day, McClellan had requested the information directly from USG, but the telegram was not received until March 3. See letter to Commanding Officer, Gunboat Flotilla, Feb. 15, 1862. *Memoirs*, I, 325. On Feb. 21, McClellan complained that Halleck had not reported "either often or fully enough," though this telegram did not refer specifically to USG's command. *O.R.*, I, vii, 646. In his reply of the same date, Halleck explained that he had encountered difficulties with the telegraph. *Ibid.*, p. 647.

On Feb. 21, Halleck telegraphed to Brig. Gen. William T. Sherman. "Give me strength of forces at Smithland & Paducah; also obtain & send me strength of Gen. Grant's forces as soon as possible." Copy, DNA, RG 393, Dept. of the Mo., Telegrams Sent. On Feb. 23, Halleck noted that the telegraph line to Fort Henry was still not complete. *O.R.*, I, vii, 655. On Feb. 24, Halleck telegraphed to McClellan. "Lines down. Can get nothing south of the Ohio. To day line down to Cairo." ALS (telegram sent), Victor Jacobs, Dayton, Ohio. USG later explained that some of his difficulties with Halleck were caused by the telegraph operator at Fort Henry. See letter to Maj. Gen. Henry W. Halleck, March 21,

1862. *Memoirs*, I, 325. This is somewhat doubtful in view of the delay in completing the telegraph line to Fort Henry. USG's communication with hd. qrs. was principally by boat, and even regular letters went astray. On Feb. 25, USG informed Brig. Gen. George W. Cullum that he intended to go to Nashville "should there be no orders to prevent it." On Feb. 28, USG reported his return from Nashville to Cullum, who wrote to Halleck on March 2. "Grant writes from Fort Donelson on 28th just returned from Nashville. Supposed him and army yet at Donelson." *O.R.*, I, vii, 676.

McClellan and Halleck discussed superseding USG after the fall of Fort Henry. See telegram to Maj. Gen. Henry W. Halleck, Feb. 12, 1862, note 3. On Feb. 19, Halleck wrote to McClellan. "Brig. Gen. Charles F. Smith, by his coolness and bravery at Fort Donelson when the battle was against us, turned the tide and carried the enemy's outworks. Make him a major-general. You can't get a better one. Honor him for this victory and the whole country will applaud." *O.R.*, I, vii, 637. On March 3, Charles F. Smith was nominated for promotion to maj. gen., and Halleck gave him that rank in his telegram to USG the following day. *Senate Executive Journal*, XII, 144. USG later concluded that Halleck believed Smith to be "a much fitter officer for the command of all the forces in the military district than I was," and added: "I was rather inclined to this opinion myself at that time." *Memoirs*, I, 328. See John M. Schofield, *Forty-Six Years in the Army* (New York, 1897), p. 361.

2. Humboldt, Tenn., about forty-seven miles southwest of Paris, Tenn., the junction point for the Mobile and Ohio and the Memphis, Clarksville and Louisville railroads.

3. Eastport, Miss., on the south side of the Tennessee River just across the Ala. state line; Corinth, Miss., five miles south of the Tenn. state line and about fifteen miles west of the Tennessee River, the junction point for the Mobile and Ohio and the Memphis and Charleston railroads; Jackson, Tenn., about fifteen miles south of Humboldt, the junction point of the Mobile and Ohio and the Mississippi Central railroads.

4. See letter to Capt. John C. Kelton, Feb. 28, 1862.

To Maj. Gen. Charles F. Smith

Head Quarters, Dist of West. Tenn.
Fort Henry, March 5th 1862.

MAJOR GEN. C. F. SMITH
COMMDG U. S. FORCES,
CLARKESVILLE, TENN.
GENL:

By directions just received from Head Qrs. of the Dept, you are to take command of the expedition which I designed Commanding in person. You will repair to Fort. Henry with as little delay as practicable.

> I am, Gen. Very Respectfully,
> Your Obt. Servant.
> U. S. GRANT.
> Major General.

Copies, DLC-USG, V, 1, 2, 3, 86; DNA, RG 393, Dept. of the Mo., Letters Received; *ibid.*, USG Hd. Qrs. Correspondence. *O.R.*, I, x, part 2, 5–6. See preceding letter.

To Maj. Gen. Charles F. Smith

> Head Quarters, Dist of West. Tenn.
> Fort. Henry, March 5th 1862.

MAJOR GEN. C. F. SMITH
FORT. DONELSON, TENN.
GENL:

By direction of ~~the~~ Major Genl. Halleck, you will take command of the entire expedition, and carry out the instructions of the Dept. Commander, whilst I am directed to remain at Fort. Henry. I am now having arrangements made for embarking troops as rapidly as possible, but with the present stage of water, it must take several days to embark them.

I have sent orders to day for three Regts, from Clarkesville, and all the troops at Donelson except Oglesby's Brigade.[1] I will be here when you arrive and give you all the information I am in possession of.

> I am, Genl, Very Respectfully &c
> U. S. GRANT
> Major Genl

Copies, DLC-USG, V, 1, 2, 3, 86; DNA, RG 393, USG Letters Sent. *O.R.*, I, x, part 2, 6.

1. On March 5, 1862, Capt. John A. Rawlins wrote to Col. Richard J. Oglesby. "You will immediately order forward all the forces of every arm, not

belonging to your immediate Brigade, to the Tennessee River above Fort Henry, and to the same point started for by Genl. McClernand's forces. You will direct them to move out on the 'Ridge Road' (the *same* as a portion of our forces marched to Ft. Donelson) to the Iron Furnace, between here and Fort Donelson, and from thence follow on the same track over which Genl. McClernand moved. They will move with the Camp and Garrison Equippage, Officers Baggage, and transportation, as limited in Gen'l Orders No. 17 (a copy of which is herewith enclosed), and three days rations. They will move immediately and with all possible dispatch. . . . P. S. So as to materially lighten the loads on their teams, you will direct that a portion of their Baggage be loaded on the Steamer 'New Uncle Sam' which you will order around to this place, as soon as the baggage is received on Board." LS, DNA, RG 393, Dept. of the Mo., Letters Received. *O.R.*, I, x, part 2, 5. On the same day, Rawlins wrote to George W. Graham. "You will send Steamers to Clarksville sufficient for transportation of three Regiments of Infantry, and Major Cavender's Battallion of Artillery to a point six miles above Fort Henry on the Tennessee. If you should be short of transportation debark the Cavalry and Artillery Horses at Ft. Donelson, from whence they will march by land. Send Steamers immediately and without delays, also, accompanying dispatches" LS, DNA, RG 393, Dept. of the Mo., Letters Received.

On March 5, Brig. Gen. John A. McClernand, Metal Landing, Tenn., wrote to USG. "My Division is nearly all arrived and a portion of it embarked preparatory to a forward movement. Additional boats suited to the transportation of wagons and Cavalry are indispensible to the complete embarkation of all my Command. A want of Haversacks and the nature of the service before us make it necessary that the wagons attached to my command should not be left behind, but should go with it. May I ask that you will immediately order up a number of such boats as are adapted to the purpose named ? . . . P. S. The enclosed communication forwarded by Col Oglesby is just recd. Will you please forward an answer to him by a Special Courier ?" Copy, McClernand Papers, IHi.

To Maj. Gen. Charles F. Smith

Head Quarters, Dist. of W. Ten.
Fort Henry, March 5th 1862

MAJ. GEN. C. F. SMITH
FORT HENRY TEN.
GEN.

By directions from Head Quarters, Dept. of the Mo. you have been assigned to the command of the Expedition up the Tennessee river. For instructions see enclosed letter from Maj. Gen. Halleck.

Information that seems to be reliable places the rebel forces at Eastport, and Corinth at 20,000 men with rolling stock between the two places sufficient to throw all the troops to either place in a short time.

If this should prove true I can hardly say what course should be pursued to carry out the instructions. A general engagement is to be avoided while the bridges are to be destroyed, if possible. The idea probably is there must be no defeat and rather than to risk one it would be better to retreat.

I will remain at Fort Henry and throw forward all the troops that can be provided with transportation. The Com.y of Subsistence is directed to take along 300.000 rations and all the forage here is to go. It will probably be necessary to procure forage on the road.

Allow me to congratulate you on your richly deserved promotion and to assure you that no one can feel more pleased at it than myself.

> I am Gen. very respectfully
> your obt. svt.
> U. S. GRANT
> Maj. Gen.

ALS, James S. Schoff, New York, N. Y. *O.R.*, I, x, part 2, 6. On March 7, 1862, Capt. John A. Rawlins issued Special Orders No. 19. "In pursuance of directions, from Head Quarters, Dept. of the Mo, Maj. Gen. C. F. Smith is assigned to the command of the expedition now about moving up the Tenn. river." DS, DNA, RG 393, Dept. of the Miss., Letters Received; Stephenson County Historical Society, Freeport, Ill. *O.R.*, I, x, part 2, 17. On March 6, Brig. Gen. John A. McClernand, Metal Landing, Tenn., wrote to USG. "Having crossed from Fort Donelson to this place, yesterday, in pursuance of your order, I have the honor to report the fact. You had returned to Fort Henry before my arrival—leaving word that you had been ordered to place Genl C. F. Smith in command of the expedition of which my Division forms a part. If Genl Smith has been promoted to the rank of Maj Genl I can cordially congratulate him and am ready cheerfully, to obey orders. On the other hand, if he has not been promoted, I rank him as a brigadier and cannot recognize his superiority without self-degradation, which no human power can constrain me to do. In all this, doubtless, I shall have the sympathy and approval of Genl Smith as a soldier and man of honor." Copy, McClernand Papers, IHi.

To Brig. Gen. William T. Sherman

———

Head Quarters, Dist. of W. Ten.
Fort Henry, March 5th 1862

GEN. W. T. SHERMAN
COMD.G DIST. OF CAIRO
PADUCAH KY.
GEN.

I have just learned that a large force of rebels have collected at East Port, or at the bridge near there, and also at Corinth. Force estimated at 20,000. Engaged fortifying at both places.

U. S. GRANT
Maj. Gen.

Please send by telegraph to Gen. Halleck
U. S. G.

ALS, DLC-William T. Sherman. On March 6, 1862, Maj. Gen. Henry W. Halleck telegraphed to Brig. Gen. William T. Sherman and USG. "Genl Sherman may join Genl Smith's column. [Smith must] advance with great caution, if the enemy is in force at Corinth or Eastport, our landing must be below. [I agree with Genl] Grant that water [batter]ies at Fort Donelson [should be dismantled], and captured [field artillery sent to Paducah or Cairo.]" ALS (telegram sent), DNA, RG 107, Telegrams Collected (Unbound); Telegram received, DLC-William T. Sherman. *O.R.*, I, x, part 2, 12.

To Brig. Gen. Lewis Wallace

———

Head Quarters, Dist of West. Tenn.
Fort. Henry March 5th 1862.

BRIG. GEN. L. WALLACE,
COMMDG. U. S. FORCES,
FORT. HENRY, TENN.

You will please embark, on board Transports, at once, all the troops, including one Battery of Light Artillery, at this place, excepting those designated for garrison duty.

Instead of one hundred and fifty thousand (150.000) as per ᵇ directions this morning, you will place on board Steamers to proceed up river three hundred thousand (300.000) rations.

Land transportation will be limited as per Genl. Order. No 17.[1]

> By order of Major Gen. U. S. Grant.
> JNO RAWLINS
> Asst. Adjt. Genl.

Copies, DLC-USG, V, 1, 2, 3, 86; DNA, RG 393, USG Letters Sent. *O.R.*, I, x, part 2, 6–7.

1. On March 1, 1862, Capt. John A. Rawlins issued General Orders No. 17. "All Regiments having extra arms will turn them over to the Ordnance Officer. Those having extra clothing will turn them over to such Regiments as are without, and all extra baggage will be placed in boxes, marked and turned over to Quartermaster for shipment to Cairo. No room will be allowed in wagons for any extra Baggage of Soldiers. Officers will be limited to One hundred pounds each, in wagons including Mess-Chest. One wagon, only, will be allowed to each company, for transportation of camp and Garrison equippage, and Officers Bagage. Three additional wagons will be allowed to each Regiment, for Head Quarters, Medical Department and Quarter Master. It is important that this should be attended to immediately. Should an order be received to move, private property will be first thrown out in order that the transportation designated may be sufficient." DS, DNA, RG 393, Dept. of the Miss., Letters Received; (3), McClernand Papers, IHi.

To Julia Dent Grant

Fort Henry, March 5th 1862

DEAR JULIA,

Father is just going back and I will take this occation to write you a few lines. I want you to send me a statement of how much money you had when you got home. My recollection is that you had enough over $400 to pay all expenses and leave about that amount clear. You can lend father all you have keeping about $100 for yourself to last until I can send you more. Take a note payable to yourself bearing interest. I feel myself worse used by my own family than by strangers and although I do not think father, of his own accord, would do me injustice yet I believe he is influanced, and always may be, to my prejudice.

Kiss the children for me. I am in a very poor humor for writing. I was ordered to command a very important expedition up the Tennessee river and now an order comes directing one of my juniors to take the command whilst I am left behind here with a small garrison.

It may be all right but I dont now see it.

ULYS.

ALS, DLC-USG.

To Maj. Gen. Henry W. Halleck

———

By TELEGRAPH FROM Fort Henry Mch 6 *1862*

TO MAJ. GEN HALLECK

All the transports here will be loaded and off today if the gunboat arrives to convoy them. One gunboat has gone to Savannah. The transports here will not take all the troops now in rediness to move. Your instructions contemplated my commanding expedition in person.[1] Despatch yesterday changed it.[2]

U. S. GRANT
Maj. Genl

Telegram received, DNA, RG 94, Generals' Papers and Books, Telegrams Received by Gen. Halleck; copy, *ibid.*, RG 393, Dept. of the Mo., Telegrams Received. *O.R.*, I, x, part 2, 9–10.

1. On March 5, 1862, Maj. Gen. Henry W. Halleck telegraphed to USG. "It is exceedingly important that there should be no delay in destroying the [bridge] at Corinth or Bear creek. Dont delay the matter a moment. If successful, the expedition will not return to Paris but [will encam]p at Savanna, [unless threatened] by superior numbers. P[repare] every thing to reinforce him there. Dismount the water bat[teries] at Henry & Donelson, & remove a[ll] stores except for a small garrison at Donelson. Travellers can pass to Nashville, but no one will be permitted to land at the forts, except in extreme cases. None must be allowed to go up the Tennessee. See to this. What we do there must not be communicated to the public." ALS (telegram sent), DNA, RG 107, Telegrams Collected (Unbound); copies, *ibid.*, RG 94, Generals' Papers and Books, Telegrams

Sent in Cipher by Gen. Halleck; *ibid.*, RG 393, USG Hd. Qrs. Correspondence; *ibid.*, Dept. of the Mo., Telegrams Sent; DLC-USG, V, 4, 5, 7, 8, 9, 88. *O.R.*, I, x, part 2, 7.
    2. See letter to Maj. Gen. Henry W. Halleck, March 5, 1862, note 1.

To Maj. Gen. Henry W. Halleck

Fort Henry Mch. 6th/62

MAJ GENL. HALLECK.

Union City is said to be strongly garrisoned by rebels. I will keep a lookout to prevent surprise from that direction, while the garrison is weak here.

U. S. GRANT.
Maj. Genl.

Telegram, copy, DNA, RG 393, Dept. of the Mo., Telegrams Received. *O.R.*, I, x, part 2, 11.

To Brig. Gen. George W. Cullum

BY TELEGRAPH FROM Ft Henry via Paducah 6½
[*March 6*] *1862*

TO GEN G W CULLUM

It is highly important that I should have another Gun Boat The Rebels are fortifying near Savannah[1] where the only Gun Boat I have now is

U S GRANT.

Telegram received, DNA, RG 107, Telegrams Collected (Unbound). On March 6, 1862, Flag Officer Andrew H. Foote, Cairo, wrote to Secretary of the Navy Gideon Welles. "I have the honor to forward a report just received from Lieut Comdg Gwin of the 'Taylor' communicating important information, which with a telegram just received from Genl. Grant Comdg at Fort Henry stating that the rebels were fortifying Savannah on the Tenessee river, and calling for an additional Gunboat has been communicated to Genl. Halleck. I shall probably send an additional Gunboat—making three boats on that river—The Asst. Secretary of War is now in my office and is informed of the state of things, and we shall be able to meet the demands, I trust, by having a force at hand sufficient to prevent any fortifications being erected on the Tenessee as far up as the stage of water will permit the Gunboats to ascend the river." LS, *ibid.*, RG 45, Letters Received, Mississippi Squadron. *O.R.* (Navy), I, xxii, 647. Foote enclosed a letter of March 5 from Lt. William Gwin. LS, DNA, RG 107, Letters Received. *O.R.* (Navy), I, xxii, 647–48.

1. Savannah, Tenn., on the east bank of the Tennessee River, about 130 miles upriver from Fort Henry.

To Brig. Gen. Stephen A. Hurlbut

Head Quarters, Dist. of W. Ten.
Fort Henry, March 6th 1862

GEN. S. A. HURLBUT
COMD.G 4TH DIV.
GEN.

Embark your forces on the transports now awaiting you as rapidly as possible. The number of transports furnishe[d] being inadequate to the number of troops to be shipped you will place as many on each boat as can be taken having a due regard to the health and comfort of the men. Any transports that may remain after geting your force aboard will be sent back to Fort Henry to take on the troops there.

There will be a supply of provisions and forage with the fleet to issue on the route, but all troops should start out with at least five days rations issued three days of which would be better cooked.

There is also a supply of ammunition on one of the transports for future issue should it be required.

I am, Gen. very respectfully
your obt. svt.
U. S. GRANT
Maj. Gen. Com

ALS, DNA, RG 393, 16th Army Corps, Miscellaneous Papers. Copies, misdated March 7, 1862, in DLC-USG, V, 1, 2, 3, 86; DNA, RG 393, USG Letters Sent. *O.R.*, I, x, part 2, 16.

To Col. Richard J. Oglesby

Head Quarters, Dist of West. Tenn.
Fort. Henry, March 6th 1862.

COL. R. OGLESBY
COMMDG. U. S. FORCES,
FORT. DONELSON, TENN.
COL:

Surgeon Brinton will make arrangements for the sick at your post. All who are not likely to be able for duty within a week or two, I want sent to Cairo. You will maintain discipline at your Post, and protect it from all assaults of the enemy. Captured property is to be kept for the benefit of the Government.

All the Field Artillery is to be sent to St Louis, and all other property that cannot be used advantageously in the Field will be sent to Cairo. I directed 25,000 rations to be left at your Post. This will be sufficient, as I intend to order most of the Troops to Ft. Henry.

I am, Col. Very Respectfully,
Your Obt. Servant.
U. S. GRANT.
Major General. Commdg

P. S. Genl. Orders. will be sent you as soon as they can be copied.

Copies, DLC-USG, V, 1, 2, 3, 86; DNA, RG 393, USG Letters Sent; *ibid.*, Dept. of the Mo., Letters Received.

To Maj. Gen. Henry W. Halleck

Fort Henry, March 7th 1862

MAJ. GEN. H. W. HALLECK,

Your dispatch of yesterday just received.[1] I did all I could to get you returns of the strength of my command. Evry move I made was reported daily to your Chief of Staff, who must have failed to keep you properly posted. I have done my very best to obey orders, and to carry out the interests of the service. If my course is not satisfactory remove me at once. I do not wish to impede in any way the success of our arms. I have averaged writing more than once a day, since leaving Cairo, to keep you informed of my position; and it is no fault of mine, if you have not received my letters. My going to Nashville was strictly intended for the good of the service, and not to gratify any desire of my own.

Believeing sincerely that I must have enemies between you and myself who are trying to impair my usefulness, I respectfully ask to be relieved from further duty in the Dept.

U. S. GRANT
Maj. Gen.

Telegram, copies, DLC-USG, V, 4, 5, 7, 8, 9, 88; DNA, RG 393, USG Hd. Qrs. Correspondence; DLC-Elihu B. Washburne. *O.R.*, I, x, part 2, 15. Misdated March 8, 1862, telegram received, DNA, RG 94, Generals' Papers and Books, Telegrams Received by Gen. Halleck; copy, *ibid.*, RG 393, Dept. of the Mo., Telegrams Received. See telegram to Maj. Gen. Henry W. Halleck, March 9, 1862.

1. On March 6, Maj. Gen. Henry W. Halleck telegraphed to USG. "Genl McClellan directs that you report to me dayly the numbers and positions of the forces under your command. Your neglect of repeated orders to report the strength of your command has created great dissatisfaction, & seriously interfered with military plans. Your going to Nashville without authority & when your presence with your troops was of the utmost importance, was a matter of very serious complaint at Washington, so much so that I was advised to arrest you on your return." ALS (telegram sent), DNA, RG 107, Telegrams Collected (Unbound); copies, *ibid.*, RG 94, Generals' Papers and Books, Telegrams Sent in Cipher by Gen. Halleck; *ibid.*, RG 393, USG Hd. Qrs. Correspondence; *ibid.*, Dept. of the Mo., Telegrams Sent; DLC-USG, V, 4, 5, 7, 8, 9, 88. *O.R.*, I, x, part 2, 15. (Misdated Feb. 6) DLC-Elihu B. Washburne.

To Maj. Gen. Charles F. Smith

_____

Head Quarters, Dist of West. Tenn.
Fort. Henry, March 7th 1862.

MAJOR GEN. C. F. SMITH
COMMDG TENN. RIVER EXPEDITION.
GENL:

All the transports now have more or less troops aboard, but many of them evidently have a less number than can be healthfully carried. I would advise the appointment of a suitable Officer, as master of transportation, and have the capacity of all the Boats inspected, and where they are capable of taking more troops, require them to return, and take them on. The Steamer I am now on will be sent tomorrow.

I am, Gen. Very Respectfully,
Your Obt Servant
U. S. GRANT
Major Gen. Commdg.

Copies, DLC-USG, V, 1, 2, 3, 86; DNA, RG 393, USG Letters Sent; *ibid.*, Dept. of the Mo., Letters Received. On March 7, 1862, Maj. Gen. Henry W. Halleck telegraphed to USG. "Intrenching tools should be sent to Genl Smith to enable him to secure his position wherever he may land." ALS (telegram sent), *ibid.*, District of West Tenn., Letters Received; copies, *ibid.*, RG 94, Generals' Papers and Books, Telegrams Sent in Cipher by Gen. Halleck; *ibid.*, RG 393, Dept. of the Mo., Telegrams Sent.

To Brig. Gen. William T. Sherman

_____

BY TELEGRAPH FROM Fort Henry [*March*] 7th *1862*

TO W. T. SHERMAN
BRIG GEN

All the transports are loaded, but not having all the troops aboard, I have dirrected the appointment of a master of transportation to inspect the steamers and put aboard any additional number they may hold.   additional forces can be got aboard at an early hour tomorrow.

U. S. GRANT

Telegram received, DLC-William T. Sherman; copies, DLC-USG, V, 2, 86; DNA, RG 393, USG Letters Sent. On March 7, 1862, Brig. Gen. William T. Sherman telegraphed to USG. "I sent up four regiments last night   have boats enough for 3 more & will send up in all eleven Regts & one battery   do you want anything special"   Copy, *ibid.*, Dept. of the Mo., Telegrams Received.

To Col. Richard J. Oglesby

Head Quarters, Dist of West. Tenn.
Fort. Henry, March 7th 1862.

COL R. OGLESBY
COMMDG. U. S. FORCES,
FORT. DONELSON, TENN.
COLONEL:

Dismount all the Guns in the Fortification, and ship them to Cairo, if practicable. If not practicable to ship, at least dismount the Guns. Send to Cairo, as rapidly as possible, all public and captured property not required for the service. Citizens may be permitted to pass up and down the river, but should be excluded as far as practicable, from the Post. I will order over here, in a few days, all but one Regt. of your command.

Respectfully &c.
U. S. GRANT
Major Gen. Commdg.

Copies, DLC-USG, V, 1, 2, 3, 86; DNA, RG 393, USG Letters Sent; *ibid.*, Dept. of the Mo., Letters Received. *O.R.*, I, x, part 2, 16–17. On March 7, 1862, Capt. John A. Rawlins wrote to Col. Richard J. Oglesby. "Your communication of the 7th, also, a telegraphic dispatch received. I am instructed by Major Gen. U. S. Grant, Commdg, to say to you that he has made application to the Department to have Paymaster Cooke sent to this District, immediately to pay off the troops of this command. Leaves of Absence and furloughs in proper cases, will be approved by you as per existing orders, but will require his further approval. The sick will not be fuloughed except in very extreme cases, but will be sent to the Hospitals. The two companies of Cavalry, will remain in your command until further orders." Copies, DLC-USG, V, 1, 2, 3, 86; DNA, RG 393, USG Letters Sent.

To Maj. Gen. Henry W. Halleck

By Telegraph from Ft Henry Mch 9 *1862*

To Maj. Genl Halleck

Your dispatch of yesterday is just received.[1] I will do all in my power to advance the expedition now started.

You had a better chance of knowing my strength whilst surrounding Ft Donelson than I had. Troops were reporting daily by your order & immediately assigned to brigades. There was no orders received from you until the 28th Feby, to make out returns, and I made every effort to get them in as early as possible. I have always been ready to move anywhere regardless of consequences to myself, but with a disposition to take the best care of the troops under my command.

I can renew my application to be relieved from further duty. Returns have been sent.

U. S. Grant
Major Genl.

Telegram received, DNA, RG 94, Generals' Papers and Books, Telegrams Received by Gen. Halleck; copies, *ibid.*, RG 393, USG Hd. Qrs. Correspondence; *ibid.*, Dept. of the Mo., Telegrams Received; DLC-USG, V, 4, 5, 7, 8, 9, 88; ICHi. *O.R.*, I, x, part 2, 21. On March 6, 1862, Maj. Gen. Henry W. Halleck telegraphed to USG. "Please inform me immediately the number of Infantry, artillery & cavalry up the Tennessee, as near as you can." ALS (telegram sent), Victor Jacobs, Dayton, Ohio; copy (misdated March 7), DNA, RG 393, Dept. of the Mo., Telegrams Sent. On March 9, USG telegraphed to Halleck. "Infantry present and for duty thirty-five thousand one hundred and forty seven. Cavalry three thousand one hundred and sixty-nine—artillery twelve batteries—aggregate number of pieces fifty-four—men twelve hundred and thirty-one—Location —embarked on expedition twenty-five thousand two hundred and six. At landing above Ft Henry awaiting transportation five thousand seven hundred and forty. At Clarksville eleven hundred seventy three—Ft Donelson twenty-three hundred and twenty-eight, twelve hundred and sixteen of whom are under marching orders for the Tennessee as soon as transportation can be had at Ft Henry. Seven hundred cavalry embarked on expedition—nineteen hundred at Ft Henry—one Regiment poorly armed at Fort Donelson. Two companies of artillery embarked on expedition—all except one battery of two pieces, at Fort Donelson. This includes Genl. Sherman's division of seven thousand eight hundred and twenty-nine infantry and one battery. A full return of the forces and location in this district was mailed to you from Paducah the 6th inst." Telegram received, *ibid.*, RG 94, Generals' Papers and Books, Telegrams Received by Gen. Halleck; copies, *ibid.*, RG 393, USG Hd. Qrs. Correspondence; *ibid.*, Dept. of the Mo., Telegrams Received; DLC-USG, V, 4, 5, 7, 8, 9, 88. *O.R.*, I, x, part 2, 21. On March 7, Capt. John A. Rawlins wrote to Brig. Gen. William T. Sherman. "Herewith I send you the Consolidated Returns of the Dist of West. Tenn, which, you will do me the kindness to forward to Major Gen. Halleck, Commdg, Department. Thinking that possibly you might desire to be informed as to the location and effective strength of said troops, I leave the letter open for your perusal." Copies, DLC-USG, V, 1, 2, 3, 86; DNA, RG 393, USG Letters Sent.

1. On March 8, Halleck telegraphed to USG. "You are mistaken; there is [*no*] enemy between me & you. There is no letter of yours stating the number & position of your command since the capture of Fort Donelson. Genl McClellan has asked for it repeatedly, in reference to ulterior movements, but I could not give him the information. He is out of all patience waiting for it. Answer by telegraph, in general terms." ALS (telegram sent), Mr. and Mrs. Philip D. Sang, River Forest, Ill.; copies, DLC-USG, V, 4, 5, 7, 8, 9, 88; DNA, RG 94, Generals' Papers and Books, Telegrams Sent in Cipher by Gen. Halleck; *ibid.*, RG 393, USG Hd. Qrs. Correspondence; *ibid.*, Dept. of the Mo., Telegrams Sent. *O.R.*, I, x, part 2, 21. On March 8, Halleck telegraphed to Maj. Gen. George B. McClellan. "Strange to say I have not yet received any returns whatever from Grant showing the number & position of his forces. I ordered on the 1st of March, one week ago, a movement up the Tennessee to destroy bridges, &c. I can get no official information of how many have gone or where they now are" Copy, DNA, RG 107, Telegrams Collected (Unbound). *O.R.*, I, x, part 2, 20.

To Maj. Gen. Charles F. Smith

———

Head Quarters, Dist of West. Tenn.
Fort. Henry, March 9th 1862.

GEN. C. F. SMITH
COMMDG. EXPEDITION ON UPPER TENN.
GENERAL:

You will oblige me by discharging the Steamer "Uncle Sam" as soon as possible, and ordering her to return and report to me at Fort. Henry. With the balance of the transports, I have no directions to give, knowing that you being on the spot, can tell much better what should be done with them, than any person at a distance possibly could do.

> I am, Gen. Very Respectfully,
> Your Obt. Servant.
> U. S. Grant.
> Major. Genl. Commdg.

Copies, DLC-USG, V, 1, 2, 3, 86; DNA, RG 393, USG Letters Sent; *ibid.*, Dept. of the Mo., Letters Received.

To Maj. Gen. Charles F. Smith

———

> Head Quarters, Dist of West. Tenn.
> Fort. Henry, March 9th 1862.

Gen. C. F. Smith
Commdg Expedition up the Tenn.
General—

I just learned through my Qr. Master, that there are yet quite a number of teams, complete, at Henry, that can be given you should you require them. Any thing you may require, send back transports for, and if within my power, you shall have it.

> I am, Genl. Very Respectfully,
> Your Obt. Servant.
> U. S. Grant.
> Major Genl.

Copies, DLC-USG, V, 1, 2, 3, 86; DNA, RG 393, USG Letters Sent; *ibid.*, Dept. of the Mo., Letters Received.

To Brig. Gen. John A. McClernand

Head Quarters, Dist. of W. Ten.
Fort Henry, March 9th 1862

GEN. J. A. MCCLERNAND
COMD.G 1ST DIV.
GEN.

Col. Oglesby will follow you just as soon as it is possible to provide transportation for him. At present I see no opportunity but for him to await the return of some of the transports now going up.

I am Gen. very respectfully
your obt. svt.
U. S. GRANT
Maj. Gen. Com

ALS, McClernand Papers, IHi. On March 10, 1862, Capt. John A. Rawlins wrote to Col. Richard J. Oglesby. "Your communication is just received. You will not delay your movements, but proceed to the Tennessee river, as designated in Special Orders, No 22. with all possible dispatch. When uniforms arrive they will be forwarded." Copies, DLC-USG, V, 1, 2, 3, 86; DNA, RG 393, USG Letters Sent. On the same day, Rawlins issued Special Orders No. 22. "Col. R. J. Oglesby, commanding U. S. Forces at Fort Donelson, will immediately proceed with 8th Ill. Vols. and one other Infantry Regiment, to be designated by him from the forces at that place, together with Capt Dressers Battery, and Two Companies of 2d Ill. Cavalry to Metal Landing on the Tennessee river, a point four miles above Fort Henry, with their camp and garrison equippage. Land transportation will be limited as per. General Orders, No. 17." DS, *ibid.*, Dept. of the Mo., Letters Received.

To Brig. Gen. John A. McClernand

Head Quarters, Dist. of W. Ten.
Fort Henry March 9th 1862

I did not mean to give any directions about the order of moving. Gen. Smith being in command of the expedition I will give no order further than for the preperation.

U. S. GRANT
Maj. Gen

AES, McClernand Papers, IHi. Written on a letter of March 9, 1862, from Brig. Gen. John A. McClernand to USG. "Did you mean in our late interview that I would follow with my Division the Gunboat when she passes, or that I am to await a specific order to [move]" LS, *ibid.* On the same day, McClernand wrote to USG. "Genl. McClernand informs Genl. Grant that Lt Freeman of my staff awaits on you, for any order you may choose to send In a conversation with you this evening, leads me to doubt whether I am to wait further orders or move" Register of Letters, *ibid.*

Also on the same day, a letter to USG was prepared at hd. qrs., 1st Div., Pine Landing, Tenn. "We have heard with deep regret of your having been deposed from your authority as Commander in the field of the forces in this district. Whether, in fact, this be true, we do not pretend to say; much less to make it occasion for censure or reflection upon any. On the contrary, we disclaim not only the feeling but the purpose to do so. Our object is far different—it is simply and singly to perform an act which justice to ourselves as well as to you, equally, requires. Not to perform it would prove ourselves wanting in the sympathy and generosity which become fellow soldiers, who have fought and suffered together. This is our explanation and apology for this hasty note. Reverting to the past, we cannot forbear the expression of our thanks for the uniform urbanity and kindness you have extended to us. Nor in the sterner realities of war are we wanting in reason for awarding you our gratitude and respect. As our Commander at Belmont and Forts Henry and Donelson, besides in numerous mere skirmishes, you were successful. Under your lead the flag of the Union has been carried from the interior further towards the seaboard than by any other hands. You have slain more of the enemy, taken more prisoners and trophies, lost more men in battle and regained more territory to the Union than any other leader. If we have born a part in achieving these results we are proud of it, and are, therefore, naturally concerned in what may darken or disparage them. We place this spontaneous tribute at your disposal for such use as you may think proper to make of it." LS, DNA, RG 94, Generals' Papers and Books, Ulysses S. Grant. This letter was signed by McClernand, Col. William H. L. Wallace, Col. Leonard F. Ross, and eight officers of McClernand's staff.

To Maj. Gen. Henry W. Halleck

BY TELEGRAPH FROM Ft Henry Mch 10 *1862*

To MAJ. GENL HALLECK

Tomorrow is the day when all persons of proper age are to be enrolled in this State in the rebel army. Troops are now in Paris to enforce the order of Governor Harris.[1] I am concentrating the small force at my command on the west bank of the river to defeat their object as far as lays in my power.

U. S. GRANT
Major Genl

Telegram received, DNA, RG 94, Generals' Papers and Books, Telegrams Received by Gen. Halleck; copies, *ibid.*, RG 393, USG Hd. Qrs. Correspondence; *ibid.*, Dept. of the Mo., Telegrams Received; DLC-USG, V, 4, 5, 7, 8, 9, 88. *O.R.*, I, x, part 2, 25.

1. Isham G. Harris, sympathetic to the C. S. A., continued to consider himself governor of Tenn. despite the fall of Nashville. U. S. authorities recognized Andrew Johnson, appointed military governor of Tenn.

To Maj. Gen. Henry W. Halleck

BY TELEGRAPH FROM Ft Henry [*March 10*] 186[*2*]

To MAJ GEN HALLECK

Third Iowa ~~Regt~~ Infantry Just arrived effective strength 676, ordered to join Gen Smith   advance of expedition started last evening

U S GRANT
Maj Genl

Telegram received, DNA, RG 94, Generals' Papers and Books, Telegrams Received by Gen. Halleck; copies, *ibid.*, RG 393, USG Hd. Qrs. Correspondence; *ibid.*, Dept. of the Mo., Telegrams Received; DLC-USG, V, 4, 5, 7, 8, 9, 88. *O.R.*, I, x, part 2, 25.

To Brig. Gen. George W. Cullum

By Telegraph from Ft Henry [*March 10*] 186[*2*]

To Genl Cullum

No steamers will be detained here   as fast as they return from above I will send them to report to you

U. S. Grant
Maj Genl

Telegram received, DNA, RG 107, Telegrams Collected (Unbound); copies, *ibid.*, RG 393, USG Hd. Qrs. Correspondence; DLC-USG, V, 4, 5, 7, 8, 9, 88. *O.R.*, I, x, part 2, 26. On March 10, 1862, Brig. Gen. George W. Cullum had telegraphed to USG. "Send back Steamers as soon as they can be spared—No Transports here and very few in St. Louis." Copies, DLC-USG, V, 4, 5, 7, 8, 9, 88; DNA, RG 393, USG Hd. Qrs. Correspondence. *O.R.*, I, x, part 2, 26.

To Maj. Gen. Charles F. Smith

Head Quarters, Dist of West. Tenn.
Fort. Henry, March 10th 1862.

Gen. C. F. Smith
Commdg Expedition on upper Tenn.
General:

Herewith, ~~accompanying~~, find Invoice of Clothing, &c. sent for use of expedition. Please direct your Quarter Master to receipt for the same, and have it issued to the best advantage, to satisfy the wants of your command.

I am, Gen, Very Respectfully,
Your Obt. Servant
U. S. Grant.
Major Gen. Commdg.

Copies, DLC-USG, V, 1, 2, 3, 86; DNA, RG 393, USG Letters Sent.

To Maj. Gen. Henry W. Halleck

By Telegraph from Ft Henry Mch 11 *1862*

To Maj. Genl. Halleck

I just learn there is a disposition to carry on a guerilla war-fare in Kentucky, north of this point. It has assumed small proportions as yet, but may become more formidable. I would advise sending a few companies of cavalry to Eddyville, with instructions to go to interior of Hopkinsville

U. S. Grant
Brig Genl

Telegram received, DNA, RG 94, Generals' Papers and Books, Telegrams Received by Gen. Halleck; copies, *ibid.*, RG 393, USG Hd. Qrs. Correspondence; *ibid.*, Dept. of the Mo., Telegrams Received; DLC-USG, V, 4, 5, 7, 8, 88. *O.R.*, I, x, part 2, 29. On March 11, 1862, Maj. Gen. Henry W. Halleck telegraphed to USG. "General Buel has been notified of the Guerrilla organizations in Kentucky and also that I purposed to withdraw the garrison from Clarkesville. As the coun-try north of the Cumberland belongs to his Dept, we cannot interfere without his request." ALS (telegram sent), DLC-Henry W. Halleck; copies, DLC-USG, V, 4, 5, 7, 8, 88; DNA, RG 94, Generals' Papers and Books, Telegrams Sent in Cipher by Gen. Halleck; *ibid.*, RG 393, USG Hd. Qrs. Correspondence; *ibid.*, Dept. of the Mo., Telegrams Sent. *O.R.*, I, x, part 2, 30. Halleck's telegram of March 11 to Brig. Gen. Don Carlos Buell is *ibid.*

To Maj. Gen. Henry W. Halleck

By Telegraph from Ft Henry Mch 11 *1862*

To Maj. Gen Halleck

Your dispatch of yesterday is just received. The transports sent here have not been able to take all the troops, coal being much wanted.[1] I shall run down to Paducah tonight. There is but one Steamer retained here and she is being used in transporting troops to the west bank of the river. The people of Tennessee are much in want of protection today against the Governor's conscription orders. I wish we were in condition to afford them the protection they require.

U. S. Grant
Maj. Genl. Comdg

Telegram received, DNA, RG 94, Generals' Papers and Books, Telegrams Received by Gen. Halleck; copies, *ibid.*, RG 393, USG Hd. Qrs. Correspondence; *ibid.*, Dept. of the Mo., Telegrams Received; DLC-USG, V, 4, 5, 7, 8, 9, 88. *O.R.*, I, x, part 2, 29. On March 10, 1862, Maj. Gen. Henry W. Halleck telegraphed to USG. "The hard fought Battle and signal victory by Gen. Curtis in the South West, relieves the reserves intended for his support.—They will be sent to you immediately—Transports with cavalry and artillery can each take an Infantry Regiment, from Fort Henry, up the Tennessee. Arrange for them as they arrive & be ready yourself to take the general command." Copies, DLC-USG, V, 4, 5, 7, 8, 9, 88; DNA, RG 94, Generals' Papers and Books, Telegrams Sent in Cipher by Gen. Halleck; *ibid.*, RG 393, USG Hd. Qrs. Correspondence; *ibid.*, Dept. of the Mo., Telegrams Sent. *O.R.*, I, x, part 2, 27. See following letter.

1. On March 10, Col. Silas Noble, Paducah, telegraphed to USG. "Please send Steamer 'Rocket' or 'City of Memphis' here immediately to tow coal. Keystone disabled and gone to Cairo." Telegram, copy, DLC-USG, V, 88. On March 11, USG telegraphed to Noble. "If possible forward coal, at once, by any Steamers passing. The expedition will be wanting it, and I have no Steamer to send down." Copies, *ibid.*, V, 1, 2, 3, 86; DNA, RG 393, USG Letters Sent. On the same day, USG telegraphed to Brig. Gen. George W. Cullum. "You will please send Steamer W. H. B & alps with two barges each of Coal up Tennessee River to report to maj Genl C. F. Smith there being No boat here to send down and they must have it at once" Telegram received, *ibid.*, RG 107, Telegrams Collected (Unbound); copies, *ibid.*, RG 393, USG Hd. Qrs. Correspondence; *ibid.*, USG Letters Sent; DLC-USG, V, 1, 2, 3, 4, 5, 7, 8, 9, 88. *O.R.*, I, lii, part 1, 222. On the same day, Cullum telegraphed to USG. "Steamer 'W. H. B' disabled (boilers bursted) 'Alps' in hands of navy, wanted to tow mortar boats to attack Island 10. Cant send the ten steamers. Have not a single one. Every thing up Tennessee. Quartermaster says plenty of coal at Paducah. 'White Cloud' and 'John Warner' left St. Louis last night for Tennessee not arrived—will send coal by them if you cant obtain it at Paducah. Cant you get steamers from Cumberland." Copies, DLC-USG, V, 4, 5, 7, 8; DNA, RG 393, USG Hd. Qrs. Correspondence. *O.R.*, I, lii, part 1, 222. On the same day, USG again telegraphed to Cullum. "Nine Regiments ready to embark no river transportation send ten (10) Steamers immediately" Telegram received, DNA, RG 107, Telegrams Collected (Unbound); copies, *ibid.*, RG 393, USG Hd. Qrs. Correspondence; *ibid.*, USG Letters Sent; DLC-USG, V, 1, 2, 3, 4, 5, 7, 8, 9, 88. *O.R.*, I, lii, part 1, 222. Also on the same day, USG wrote to Col. Jacob G. Lauman, Metal Landing. "All transports sent from here, you will load to the best advantage, and have them follow, to report to Major Gen. C. F. Smith, as rapidly as possible." Copies, DLC-USG, V, 2, 88; DNA, RG 393, USG Letters Sent. Also on the same day, USG wrote to the commanding officer, Fort Donelson, Col. Philip B. Fouke.

"Press into service all boats coming down, ~~into service~~ and send them up the Tennessee, with guard of ten men to ~~a~~ each boat to enforce the order." Copies, DLC-USG, V, 1, 2, 3, 86; DNA, RG 393, USG Letters Sent.

To Maj. Gen. Charles F. Smith

———

                     Head Quarters, Dist of West. Tenn.
                     Fort. Henry, March 11th 1862.
GEN. C. F. SMITH
COMMDG. EXPEDITION TO UPPER. TENN.
GENERAL:

Send back Steamers as rapidly as possible, to enable me to forward balance of troops. Gen. Halleck telegraphs me this morning that since the signal success of Gen. Curtis in the South West,[1] the troops held as a reserve for him, will be sent to me; and when they arrive I may take the General direction. I think it exceedingly doubtful whether I shall accept; certainly not until the object of the expedition is accomplished.

                     I am, Gen, Very Respectfully,
                     Your Obt. Servant.
                     U. S. GRANT.
                     Major Gen. Commdg.

Copies, DLC-USG, V, 1, 2, 3, 86; DNA, RG 393, USG Letters Sent; *ibid.*, Dept. of the Mo., Letters Received. *O.R.*, I, x, part 2, 29. On March 14, 1862, Maj. Gen. Charles F. Smith, Savannah, wrote to USG. "I wrote you yesterday to say how glad I was to find from your letter of the 11th. inst., that you were to resume your old command from which you were so unceremoniously and (as I think) improperly stricken down. I greatly fear your coming here will be a matter of necessity in consequence of my lameness. I cannot mount a horse. In jumping into a yawl two days ago I mis-calculated the distance and the seat scraped my leg and shin in a rude manner—hurting the bone. I hope for the best but it is with great difficulty that I limp thro' the cabin from one chair to another. Capt. *Lyman*, asst. qr. mr. brought up this morning a story of a reverse to our arms at Paris ~~by~~ in ~~wh~~ which Capt. *Bullis* was shot. I hope the story is unfounded or greatly exagerated. Can you give me any news of *Buel's* movements? I heard yesterday he was about 40 miles from Decatur. I shall send you down to day 6 or 8 steamers—and two more tomorrow. Please do not forget we need coal very much and in ~~small or~~ great quantities. The river is falling *fast*—two feet of a night." ALS, DNA, RG 393, District of West Tenn., Letters Received.

On March 17, Smith wrote to an unidentified person. "The public are all astray about Gen. Grant. His habits (drink) are unexceptionable. His absence during the engagement to see Flag-Officer Foote was explained to the satisfaction of Gen. Halleck, and his going to Nashville was perfectly proper if he thought fit to go. The reason why both McClellan and Halleck were down upon him was they had no information from him for two weeks, although he always wrote once and sometimes twice or thrice a day and sent daily reports of the strength of his force. Why these reports were not received is not known, but the moment Halleck had Grant's explanation he was restored to command. Grant is a very modest person. From old awe of me—he was one of my pupils from 1838 to 1842 (I think) —he dislikes to give me an order and says I ought to be in his place. Fancy his surprise when he received no communication from the General for two weeks after the fall of Donelson, and that a telegram of bitterest rebuke! He showed it to me in utter amazement, wondering at the cause, as well he might." *Chicago Tribune*, Aug. 10, 1885.

1. On March 6–8, C. S. A. Maj. Gen. Earl Van Dorn, Army of the West, with about 14,000 troops, attacked Brig. Gen. Samuel R. Curtis, Army of the Southwest, with about 11,250 troops, in the battle of Pea Ridge or Elkhorn Tavern, Ark. Although U. S. losses were heavier, Curtis drove Van Dorn's army from the field in such disorder that the battle was a clear U. S. victory.

To Maj. Gen. Charles F. Smith

———

Head Quarters, Dist of West. Tenn.
Fort. Henry, March 11th 1862.

Gen. C. F. Smith
Commdg Ex up the Tenn.
Genl:

The Steamer "Dunbar" (I think I am not mistaken in the name) is still above us. She may possibly have run in some creek, to get below our transports and destroy them. That would be my plan, but I do not believe they have adopted it. It would be well however, to keep a look out, taking your sense of what should be done, and what you would do under the same circumstances.

I am, Gen, Very Respectfully
Your Obt. Servant.
U. S. Grant.
Major. Gen. Commdg

Copies, DLC-USG, V, 1, 2, 3, 86; DNA, RG 393, USG Letters Sent.

To Col. Philip B. Fouke

———

Head. Quarters, Dist of West. Tenn
Fort Henry, Mar 11th 1862

Col. P. Fouke,
    Receive the Twenty-Five (25) Head Beef Cattle, and load Steamer with Baggage and captured property, with as little delay as possible

U. S. Grant
Maj. Gen. Comdg

Telegram, copies, DLC-USG, V, 1, 2, 3, 88; DNA, RG 393, USG Letters Sent. Philip B. Fouke, a lawyer of Belleville, Ill., was then serving his second term as a Democratic U. S. Representative. On Aug. 28, 1861, he entered the army as col., 30th Ill. He was wounded at Belmont, and resigned on April 22, 1862. On March 11, Fouke, Fort Donelson, telegraphed to Capt. John A. Rawlins. "Col. Oglesby has turned the command of this Post over to me—Beef Contractor has delivered twenty five (25) Beef-Cattle here to day—I will ~~not~~ receive them all. If I am to remain here long enough to Eat so many—(two (2) Regiments)— there is now enough Baggage & captured Property here to load Boat, and I will not detain her unless under the Generals Orders"   Copy, DLC-USG, V, 88.

To Col. William W. Lowe

———

Head Quarters, Dist of West. Tenn.
Fort. Henry, March 11th 1862.

Col. W. W. Lowe
Commdg Curtis' Horse.
Colonel:
    The reports of E. Y. Shelly[1] and Lieut. M. M. Wheeler,[2] are just received. From their fulness they are most satisfactory, and you may say to those gentleman, that when subordinates, take such pains to ~~state a full~~ ascertain the condition of affairs, their course will always meet with a most hearty approval from their Commander, no matter who he may be.

You will move towards Paris, Tenn, with your forces, as soon as possible, and protect the citizens as far as possible from conscription.³ I will not probably be here to say just when you should return, so that in this matter, you will have to use your own discretion. In your absence it may be necessary to get forage from citizens. In all such cases receipts will be given, for the amount taken, and the forage accounted for, as if obtained in the regular way.

> I am, Sir, Very Respectfully,
> Your Obt Servant.
> U. S. Grant.
> Major Gen. Commdg.

Copies, DLC-USG, V, 1, 2, 3, 86; DNA, RG 393, USG Letters Sent. *O.R.*, I, x, part 2, 30. William W. Lowe of Iowa, USMA 1853, served with the 2nd Cav. in Tex. through most of the years before the Civil War, rising to the rank of capt. In late 1861, he organized the Curtis Horse, later the 5th Iowa Cav., including cos. from Iowa, Minn., Mo., and Neb., and was appointed col. on Jan. 1, 1862.

1. On March 10, 1st Lt. Erwin Y. Shelley of St. Paul, Minn., Curtis Horse, commanding telegraph guard, wrote to Lowe. "In accordance with instructions, I proceeded on the 4th Inst., with a detachment of seventy men, consisting of parts of companies, K & L. of your Regiment, along the route of the telegraph line, between this Post and Smithland, with view of protecting and keeping in repair said line. I now respectfully report that I have established posts along the entire route at intervals of from three to six miles. At each post there are sta- tion[ed] four or six men, who divide evry morning, part of them patroling half way to the next post towards Smithland, and the other patrol half way to the next post, in the direction of Fort Henry, thus meeting each other half way between the different posts. They start out in the morning, and return in the evening, so that the whole line is thoroughly inspected twice a day. I adopted this plan for the reason that I thought it the safest for the men, and in case there should be any interruption to the line it would be discovered with more certainty. In a number of instances, we found the insulators off, and the brackets broken from the trees; limbs of trees in many cases had to be cut in order to free the wires. I feel bound to report that this line is most miserably constructed. In a number of instances there is no difficulty at all for a man to reach the wire from the ground, and pull it down. There are as a general thing only two nails to hold the brackets, and numbers of them are thus insecurely attached to dead trees, that are liable to fall to the ground at any moment. It is my opinion that the line would require but little guarding by troops, if it were properly put up, and if the trees were trimmed where a strong wind is liable to carry the limbs upon the wire. The men now guarding the line, all have definite instructions, in regard to a careful scrutiny of the line, in making repairs when found necessary, and in removing obstructions   I further report, that when I reached within twenty-

five miles of Smithland, I found the line guarded for that distance by Cavalry from said town, but they were withdrawn immediately after I had passed, although they led me to believe that is was their intention to take care of that end of the line. Thus the entire line is now guarded by my detachment. P. S.—My men draw upon the inhabitants, along the line for the necessary provisions and forage, with the understanding that they will be renumerated when the Guards are withdrawn." Copy, DLC-USG, V, 88.

2. On March 8, 1st Lt. Mortimer M. Wheeler of Dubuque, Iowa, Curtis Horse, wrote to Lowe. "Persuant to your order of the 7th I reported to Colonel Kruft, 31st Ind. Vols. & was directed by him to proceed with the men under my command, to Linton Ferry, on the Cumberland & arrest all deserters from the 17th & 25th Kentucky regiments. I accordingly proceeded to Linton Ferry, which was reached yesterday about 4. P. M., where I found waiting for the Ferry boat, six of the deserters of the 25th Kentucky, whom I arrested. Subsequently four of the 17th Kentucky were arrested, and still later two of the 25th Kentucky. I then quartered the men on the premises of Mr. Champion, near the Ferry, and returned today with the prisoners, whom I delivered to Col. McReynolds, 52d Indiana. From Mr. Champion and other loyal citizens, I ascertained that a Captain Wm Harris, of the rebel cavalry—one Alex Utley & Thos. Handy are now on the other side of the river, between Linton and Hopkinsville, about 25 miles from Linton, committing depredations on the property of loyal citizens. Utley was prominent in disarming the Home Guards near Hopkinsville. I was furnished with a list of forty-two deserters, and have ascertained that they reside along the road running from Linton to Hopkinsville, commencing about eight miles from the former place. The men arrested had with them about 80 lbs of musket balls, put up in canteens, which I was obliged to leave in possession of Mr. Champion. They also had two revolvers, and two single barrell pistols which I delivered up to Col. McReynolds, but no other arms." Copy, *ibid*.

3. On March 11, Capt. John A. Rawlins wrote to Lowe. "Your communication in reference to command of the Expedition towards Paris, just received. The General commanding instructs me to say that the Two Battallions of your Regiment on West Bank of the river, are expected to go. Instructions have been given. The expedition will, of course, be under command of the 'Senior Officer' accompaning it. You need not necessarially go yourself." Copies, *ibid.*, V, 1, 2, 79; DNA, RG 393, USG Letters Sent. See telegram to Maj. Gen. Henry W. Halleck, March 13, 1862.

To Commanding Officer, Fort Heiman

————

Head Quarters, Dist of West. Tenn.
Fort. Henry, March 11th 1862.

COMMDG OFFICER
FORT HEIMAN, KY.
SIR:

With the troops now at your disposal give the citizens of Tenn. who are disposed to be loyal, the best protection, you can. It is impossible for us to send a force to Paris, to-day, but you can go in that direction, and encamp for the night. You need not return tomorrow unless the approach of an enemy, in superior force, make such a course necessary.

U. S. GRANT.
Major Gen. Commdg.

Copies, DLC-USG, V, 1, 2, 3, 86; DNA, RG 393, USG Letters Sent. The commanding officer at Fort Heiman may have been Capt. John T. Croft, Curtis Horse, who led the expedition from Fort Heiman to Paris, Tenn. *O.R.*, I, x, part 1, 18.

To Julia Dent Grant

————

Fort Henry Mach 11th/62

MY DEAR JULIA,

I am just going down to Paducah looking after the interest of the expedition now gone up the Tennessee. Soon more troops will join us then I will go in command of the whole. What you are to look out for I cannot tell you but you may rely upon it that your husband will never disgrace you nor leave a defeated field. We all volunteered to be killed, if needs be, and whilst any of us are living there should be no feeling other than we are so far successful. This is my feeling and believe it is well inculcated among the troops.

My dear Julia I have but little idea from what point I shall next write you. If I knew I would hardly tell but I hope another mark will be made against rebelion.

There is a greatdeel that might be said, in a Military way, but that cannot be properly discussed. If I was ahead of the telegraph however I might say that I believe that I have the whole Tennessee river, to Florance Alabama, safe from any immediate attack. The enemy have pr[eserv]ed one Gunboat, the Dunbar, and may have run her up some creek, during the present high water, to bring out and destroy our transports. That would be my policy yet I do not think it has been adopted. Of course the steamer would be lost but she is lost anyhow and individuals should never take that into account.—We have such an inside track of the enemy that by following up our success we can go anywhere. To counteract us Tennessee at least is trying to bring out all her men. She is doing so so much against the feeling of the men themselvs that within my limited sphere I am giving all the protection possible to prevent forced enlistments. I have written you a military letter when only my love and kisses to the children, and to yourself, was intended. Tell Mary that her last letter was received and she must continue to write. Some day I will find a chance of answering

ULYS.

ALS, DLC-USG.

To Commanding Officer, Clarksville, Tenn.

Head Quarters, Dist of West. Tenn.
Fort. Henry, March 12th 1862.

COMMDG OFFICER
CLARKESVILLE TENN.

You will immediately proceed to dismantle the works at Clarkesville and come to Fort. Donelson, and cross over to the

Tennessee River as soon as possible. You will there find orders
for you further actions.

> I am, Very Respectfully,
> Your Obt. Servant
> U. S. GRANT
> Major Gen. Commdg.

P. S. You will avail yourself of the first Steamer comeing down
the Cumberland to transport your command.

> U. S. G.

Copies, DLC-USG, V, 1, 2, 3, 86; DNA, RG 393, USG Letters Sent. Probably
intended for Col. Crafts J. Wright, 13th Mo. See letters to Col. Philip B. Fouke
and to Col. Crafts J. Wright, March 15, 1862.

To Maj. Gen. Henry W. Halleck

————

BY TELEGRAPH FROM Ft Henry [*March 13*] *1862*

TO MAJ GEN HALLECK

Just arrived and ordered to proceed up the Tennessee and
there report to Maj Gen Smith commanding expedition thir-
teenth Iowa effective force eight hundred forty eight 848 fifth
Ohio battery effective strength one hundred forty nine with four
six pounders rifled & two six pounder smooth guns and Minn
battery Capt Munch[1] four six pounder rifled guns & two twelve
pounder howitzers effective strength one hundred forty—I have
also learned unofficially that the 20th Ohio sent from Fort
Donelson as an escort to prisoners proceeded up the tennes[see.]
they did not report to me—I suppose their orders were to report
to General Smith

> U. S GRANT

Telegram received, DNA, RG 94, Generals' Papers and Books, Telegrams
Received by Gen. Halleck; copies, *ibid.*, RG 393, USG Hd. Qrs. Correspondence;
ibid., Dept. of the Mo., Telegrams Received; DLC-USG, V, 4, 5, 7, 8, 9, 88.
O.R., I, x, part 2, 33.

1. Capt. Emil Munch commanded an independent battery of Minn. light art. On March 13, 1862, Capt. William S. Hillyer wrote to Munch. "You will proceed to the landing on the east bank above here, and report to Col. Lauman, who will assign such additional force, as the boat, you are on can transport." Copies, DLC-USG, V, 2, 86; DNA, RG 393, USG Letters Sent.

To Maj. Gen. Henry W. Halleck

By Telegraph from Ft Henry [*March 13*] *1862*

To Gen Halleck

Learning that rebel troops[1] had assembled at Paris for the purpose of enforcing conscription orders of Gov Harris I sent night before last a portion of Curtis horse fifty second Ind & Bullis[2] battery—The enemy were driven from their works situated about one & one half miles beyond the town with a loss of probably one hundred 100 killed & wounded our loss was Capt Bullis & four men killed & five men wounded—we have taken eight prisoners—I am now engaged in sending more troops to the west bank of the river The enemy are in force at Humbolt & might reinforce their ~~paris~~ Paris troops in one day

U. S. Grant
Maj Genl

Telegram received, DNA, RG 94, Generals' Papers and Books, Telegrams Received by Gen. Halleck; copies, *ibid.*, War Records Office, Union Battle Reports; *ibid.*, RG 393, USG Hd. Qrs. Correspondence; DLC-USG, V, 4, 5, 7, 8, 9, 88. *O.R.*, I, x, part 1, 16–17. On March 13, 1862, Capt. John A. Rawlins wrote to the commanding officer, Fort Heiman. "You will please make out and send to these Head Quarters, a report of the expedition towards Paris yesterday. The Genl. Commdg. desires telegraphing its results, to Head Quarters, Dept of the Mo." Copies, DLC-USG, V, 1, 2, 3, 86; DNA, RG 393, USG Letters Sent. On March 13, Capt. John T. Croft, Curtis Horse, wrote to USG. "In accordance with Your Instructions I left Ft Heiman During the night of the 11th, proceeded with Bullice Batty of St Louis and the 1st Batt of Curtis Horse To Henry County Tenn to afford protection to union men friends and Citizens of that county who wished protection from being drafted on the 12th at Paris Tenn Large Numbers fell in and travelled in our rear for such protection our advance Guard came up the outer Pickets about 6 miles from the Town we secured them killing 2 and taking ther arms I then detail 20 Men and Lt Williams to advance causiouly and Secure the inpickets   this he did successfuly surprising them taking Eight prisoners with their horses and equipments   among them was Capt Coats of Stocks Mounted Infantry   ascertaining about the enemies force I made a charge upon the Town about 5 oclock P M   I order one Secion of Bullice Batty the Cavalry in advance for a charge on the Town which we did successfuly driving the enemy before we passed down Main Street with white flags hanging in every window driving the enemy into their entrenchments about a Mile and a half West of the Timber on a high hill   then we planted our Batty and soon shelled them from that portion of their grounds   thinking it vacated I order a charge up the hill with two companies of Cavalry Co A and B under Capt Lower and Lt Summers   about two thirds the way up the hill we discovered the Ambuscade   about 300 opened a terrible fire on us but it passed over our heads   Co A and B much to their credit retured a successfull fire with revolvers and carbine of three vollies Retiring with a loss of 5 killed and 3 wounded I had the Batteries open a fire on them causing a sad havoc among them   Capt Bullice was mortally wounded in this fire   the action lasted a little more than an hour   their firing now ceased. we fell back upon the Town cut off the Telegraph Communication took possesion of the Court house and a large Hotel for our sick and wounded   during the night I thought best to fall back here   we expected to find Genl Grant with a force of infantry" ALS, *ibid.*, RG 94, War Records Office, Union Battle Reports. *O.R.*, I, x, part 1, 18. On March 13, Rawlins issued Special Orders No. 23. "Sergt Trouppe & 3 men will proceed to Cairo Ill. and there report to the commanding officer of the post with eight prisoners taken at Paris on the 11th inst. A roll showing names and regiments to to which they belonged will be made out on the way down and delivered with the prisoners to the commanding officer at Cairo." AD (in USG's hand), DNA, RG 393, Dept. of the Mo., Letters Received. For an account of the encounter at Paris, see John S. Ezell, ed., "Excerpts from the Civil War Diary of Lieutenant Charles Alley, Company "C," Fifth Iowa Cavalry," *Iowa Journal of History*, 49, 3 (July, 1951), 255.

On March 13, Maj. Gen. Henry W. Halleck telegraphed to USG. "Dont bring on any general engagement at Paris. If enemy appear in force our troops must fall back. It is not the proper point of attack. When you go up the river to assume the general command direct the officer at Fort Henry to report all troops that pass. Inform me as early as possible where Genl Smith has landed. Some of the Ponton boats at Paducah should be towed up the Tennessee for depot of commissary stores." ALS (telegram sent), DNA, RG 107, Telegrams Collected (Unbound); copies, *ibid.*, RG 94, Generals' Papers and Books, Telegrams Sent in Cipher by Gen. Halleck; *ibid.*, RG 393, USG Hd. Qrs. Correspondence; *ibid.*, Dept. of the Mo., Telegrams Sent; DLC-USG, V, 4, 5, 7, 8, 9, 88. *O.R.*, I, x, part 2, 32–33.

On March 14, Rawlins wrote to Col. William W. Lowe. "You will send an ambulance with two or three men to proceed under a flag of truce, towards Paris, to recover the wounded men mentioned in your communication. If they are claimed as prisoners you can agree to send back an equivalent number of their men, who are our prisoners." Copies, DLC-USG, V, 1, 2, 3, 86; DNA, RG 393, USG Letters Sent. On the same day, Rawlins issued Special Orders No. 24. "Col. W. W. Lowe Com'd'g Curtis Horse and Forces at Ft. Heimen Ky, will call in all troops he has in the direction of Paris to Ft. Heimen, keeping out only sufficient Pickets, and Guard to prevent surprise" Copies, DLC-USG, V, 15, 16, 82, 87, 89; DNA, RG 393, USG Special Orders. On March 15, Lowe sent USG a report

of the expedition to Paris. DLC-USG, V, 10; DNA, RG 393, USG Register of
Letters Received.

1. According to C. S. A. Maj. Gen. Leonidas Polk, the force at Paris consisted of a battalion of mounted rifles commanded by Maj. Henry C. King and
two cos. of cav. *O.R.*, I, x, part 1, 19.
2. Capt. Robert E. Bulliss had commanded a battery of Mo. light art. previously commanded by Capt. James T. Buel.

To Maj. Gen. Henry W. Halleck

———

Head Quarters, Dist. of W. Ten.
Fort Henry March 13th 1862.

MAJ. GEN. H. W. HALLECK
COMD.G DEPT. OF THE MO.
ST. LOUIS MO.

Yours of the 6th inst. enclosing an anonimous letter to Hon.
David Davis[1] speaking of frauds committed against government
is just received. I refer you to my orders to suppress marauding
as the only reply necessary.

There is such a disposition to find fault with me that I again
ask to be relieved from further duty until I can be placed right
in the estimation of those higher in authority.

I am Gen. very respectfully
Your obt. svt.
U. S. GRANT
Maj. Gen.

ALS, DNA, RG 393, Dept. of the Miss., Letters Received. On the same day,
USG telegraphed the same message. Telegram received, *ibid.*, RG 94, Generals'
Papers and Books, Telegrams Received by Gen. Halleck; copy, *ibid.*, RG 393,
Dept. of the Mo., Telegrams Received. Copies (misdated March 11, 1862),
DLC-USG, V, 4, 5, 7, 8, 9, 88; DNA, RG 393, USG Hd. Qrs. Correspondence.
O.R., I, x, part 2, 30. On March 6, Maj. Gen. Henry W. Halleck wrote to USG.
"I enclose herewith a copy of a letter addressed to Judge Davis, Prest of the
Westn. Investigating commission. Judge Davis says, the writer is a man of
integrity and perfectly reliable. The want of order & discipline, and the numerous
irregularities in your command since the capture of Fort Donelson, are matters

of general notoriety, and have attracted the serious attention of the authorities at Washington. Unless these things are immediately corrected, I am directed to relieve you from the command." ALS, DNA, RG 94, Generals' Papers and Books, Letters Sent by Gen. Halleck (Press). *O.R.*, I, x, part 2, 13. The enclosure was an unsigned letter of March 2, addressed to David Davis from Cairo. "As you are engaged in the business of investigating Army Contracts, and frauds practised on the Government, it may not be out of place, for me to state a few facts, as they have been told to me, and that by parties most interested. At the taking of Fort Henry there was a large amount of Sugar, Coffee, and rice, captured, besides a lot of Horses, wagons, and other property. Now I would like to know who is to take charge of the property captured from the enemy? In the case above mentioned, the property went into the hands of the Qr. Master of one of the Illinois Regiments and he turned it over to the suttlers (the sugar, coffee & rice) and the Suttlers repacked the goods in Bbls. with different marks, so as to deceive the Steam Boat men, and shipped them to Cairo, and from there to Bloomington, Ills. I asked one of the suttlers, what the sugar, coffee and rice cost them, and he said the coffee cost about 8 cts per. lb., the sugar 4¢ pr. lb. and the rice about 2 cts. pr. lb. and when I asked him how they came to get them so cheap, he said that they (the Sutlers) were to run it off, and divide the profits with the Qr. Master. One of the Sutlers bought a Jack-ass, but who from, I am not informed, for seven dollars. They say if he can get him home, he will be worth five or six hundred Dollars   The Suttlers were here, when they heard of the surrender of Fort Donelson, and they were in a great hurry to get up there, for fear the property would all be gone, before they got there. If you can have the patience to read a little further I will try to explain how it is all done. Col. Jno. Cook of Springfield, has a command of a Brigade, and when there is any property captured, he puts his own Regiment in the lead, and therefore the property goes into the hands of his Qr Master, and the Government is none the better of it. They say if Cook can get a Brigadiers commission (and they think he will) they can make six or eight thousand dollars by just such operations, as the sugar, coffee & rice operation. When they come to ship this sugar, coffee and rice to Cairo, Col Cook gives them a free pass for them and their goods to Cairo, and Cook takes the pass to a Mr. G. W. Graham, and gets him to endorse it, though I dont think Graham knew what they were doing, and further they tell me that Cook has no part of the profits, but is very clever and accommodating to his friends, one of which is a personal friend of Cook's and lives at Springfield, Ill. These same Suttlers, are selling whiskey, at the most extravagant prices ever heard of.—$1.50 pr bottle, which is about nine dollars pr. Gallon. There has been lots of property carried off by individuals, such as dirks, pistols, and guns of evry description rifles, double barreled shot guns, Sharps Rifles &c. If all the property captured from the enemy could be taken care of, and sold for what it would bring, it would put several thousand Dollars into the Treasury where it is so much needed. There are a great many other little things I would like to mention, but I fear your patience will be exhausted, before you get through reading so long a letter and of so little interest. Hoping things will all come right in the end." Copies, DLC-USG, V, 4, 5, 7, 8, 9, 88; DNA, RG 393, USG Hd. Qrs. Correspondence. *O.R.*, I, x, part 2, 14.

On March 13, Halleck telegraphed to USG. "You cannot be relieved from your command. There is no good reason for it. I am certain that all which the authorities at Washington ask, is, that you enforce discipline & punish the disorderly. The power is in your hands; use it, & you will be sustained by all above you. Instead of relieving you, I wish you, as soon as your new army is in the field, to assume the immediate command & lead it on to new victories" ALS (telegram sent), DNA, RG 393, Dept. of the Mo., Telegrams Received; copies, *ibid.*, USG Hd. Qrs. Correspondence; *ibid.*, RG 94, Generals' Papers and Books, Telegrams Sent in Cipher by Gen. Halleck; DLC-USG, V, 4, 5, 7, 8, 9, 88. *O.R.*, I, x, part 2, 32.

1. David Davis of Bloomington, Ill., had served for fourteen years as judge of the Eighth Circuit Court of Ill., in which Abraham Lincoln practiced law. A close friend and adviser to Lincoln, Davis was appointed on Oct. 25, 1861, to the Commission on War Claims at St. Louis along with former Secretary of War Joseph Holt and Hugh Campbell of St. Louis. The committee report is *HED*, 37–2–94. Willard L. King, *Lincoln's Manager David Davis* (Cambridge, Mass., 1960), pp. 186–87.

To Col. Philip B. Fouke

Head Quarters, Dist of West. Tenn.
Fort. Henry, March 13th 1862.

COL. P. B. FOUKE
FORT. DONELSON, TENN.

Direct the Quartermaster to sell the Gunny-bags. The heavy Artillery should be dismounted and turned with the vent down, to prevent spiking.

Respectfully &c.
U. S. GRANT.
Major. Gen. Commdg.

Copies, DLC-USG, V, 1, 2, 3, 86; DNA, RG 393, USG Letters Sent. On March 12, 1862, Col. Philip B. Fouke, Fort Donelson, had telegraphed to USG. "I send you Steamers Poe Lancaster No 4 & Autocrat today. What shall I do with the heavy guns. Thirty five hundred (3500) gunny bags been under the water two weeks The water has receded from them They are very muddy—Quarter Master is offered one hundred & fifty (150) dollars for them Shall he sell or ship. The Sacks are in bad condition." Telegram received, *ibid.*, Dept. of the Mo., Telegrams Received. On the same day, Fouke again telegraphed to USG. "Out of rations I will draw on Paducah Advise me how many to draw for." Telegram received, *ibid.*

To Col. Jacob G. Lauman

Head Quarters, Dist of West. Tenn.
Fort. Henry March 13th 1862.

Col. J. G. Lauman,
Commdg U. S. Forces
Metal Landing, Tenn.
Col:

Order a large detail of men to make a Coral or pen to hold a thousand mules, arrived and to arrive. Your detail should be at work at an early hour in the morning, as some of the mules have already arrived, and being so crowded, have neither been fed or watered for several days.

I am, Col. Very Respectfully, &c
U. S. Grant.
Major Genl. Commdg.

Copies, DLC-USG, V, 1, 2, 3, 86; DNA, RG 393, USG Letters Sent.

To Edwin M. Stanton

Fort Henry, March 14th 1862

Hon. E. P. Stanton
Sec. of War
Washington D. C.
Sir:

I have been waiting for reports of subcommanders at the battle of Fort Donelson to make some recommendations of officers for advancement for meritorious services. These reports are not yet in and as the troops under my command are actively engaged may not be for some time. I therefore take this occation to make some recommendations of officers who, in my opinion, should not be neglected. I would particularly mention the names of Cols. J. D. Webster, Morgan L. Smith, W. H. L. Wallace and John Logan.

The two former are old soldiers and men of decided merit. The two latter are from civil pursuits but I have no hesitation in fully endorsing them as in every way qualified for the position of Brigadier General, and think they have fully earned the position on the field of battle.

There are others who also may be equally meritorious but I do not happen to no so well their services.

> I am sir, very respectfully
> your obt. svt.
> U. S. GRANT
> Maj. Gen.

ALS, DNA, RG 107, Letters Received. *O.R.*, I, x, part 2, 35. Cols. John A. Logan and William H. L. Wallace had been nominated as brig. gens. on March 3, 1862, and were confirmed on March 21. Col. Morgan L. Smith was promoted to brig. gen. on July 16, and Col. Joseph D. Webster on Nov. 29, 1862. On Feb. 25, Capt. William S. Hillyer wrote to U. S. Representative William M. Dunn of Ind. urging the promotion of Webster to brig. gen. Hillyer stated that: "His name has already been submitted by Gen. Grant with a recommendation for his promotion to a Brigadier Generalship—" ALS, DNA, RG 94, Letters Received. See letter to Henry Wilson, July 1, 1862.

To Maj. Gen. Henry W. Halleck

BY TELEGRAPH FROM Fort Henry [*March*] 14th *1862*

To MAJ GENL HALLECK

The garrison at Clarksville has been entirely broken up and Fort dismantled. Two small regiments numbering less than seven hundred effective men in the aggregate are left at Donelson. Forts Henry and Heiman are garrisoned by 52d Indiana & Curtis Horse.

> U. S. GRANT.
> Maj Genl

Telegram received, DNA, RG 94, Generals' Papers and Books, Telegrams
Received by Gen. Halleck; copies, *ibid.*, RG 393, USG Hd. Qrs. Correspondence;
ibid., Dept. of the Mo., Telegrams Received; DLC-USG, V, 4, 5, 7, 8, 9, 88.
O.R., I, x, part 2, 36. See telegram to Maj. Gen. Henry W. Halleck, March 15,
1862.

To Maj. Gen. Henry W. Halleck

By Telegraph from Fort Henry [*March*] 14th *1862*

To Maj. Gen Halleck

The Steamer J. H. Dickey passed down as I was going to the
landing above. Orders were given the Capt to remain at Ft
Henry until a mail could be made up and put aboard. On my
return I found her gone, thus disobeying my order, and depriv-
ing me of sending you a mail.

U. S. Grant
Maj. Genl.

Telegram received, DNA, RG 94, Generals' Papers and Books, Telegrams
Received by Gen. Halleck; copies, *ibid.*, RG 393, USG Hd. Qrs. Correspondence;
ibid., Dept. of the Mo., Telegrams Received; DLC-USG, V, 4, 5, 7, 8, 88.

To Maj. Gen. Henry W. Halleck

Head Quarters, Dist. of W. Ten
Fort Henry March 14th 1862

Maj. Gen. H. W. Halleck
Comd.g Dept. of the Mo.
Gen.

After your telegraph enclosing copy of an anonymous letter
upon which severe sensure was based[1] I felt as though it would
be impossible for me to serve longer without a court of enquiry.
Your telegraph of yesterday[2] however places such a different
phase upon my position that I will again resume command and

give every effort to the success of our cause. Under the worst circumstances I would do the same.

I have just received the first word from Gen. Smith since he left.[3] The troops were debarked at Savana, why I dont know. There are eight regiments here awaiting transportation yet. I had expected the return of transports from above to take them before this.

The supply of Com.y Stores sent forward is abundant but of forage rather short. Under my directions Capt. Baxter, Qr. Mr. is using every effort to keep up the supply.

> I am Gen. very respectfully
> your obt. svt.
> U. S. Grant
> Maj. Gen.

P. S. Since writing the above yours of the 9th inst.[4] is received. I certainly received but one telegraphic despatch up to the 28th of Feb.y to furnish report of my strength. I had done my best however previous to that to get in field returns in order that consolidated returns might be made out to send you.

Now I am not in communication with Gen. Smith's command to report fully as I should like to do but all that I learn, directly or indirectly you shall be made acquainted with.[5]

I feel a doubt about when I should proceed up the river. Gen. Smith landing at Savana indicates that fortifications have been encountered above that point and the enemy in force.

> U. S. G.

ALS, DNA, RG 393, Dept. of the Miss., Letters Received. *O.R.*, I, x, part 2, 36.

    1. See letter to Maj. Gen. Henry W. Halleck, March 13, 1862.
    2. *Ibid.*
    3. On March 14, 1862, Maj. Gen. Henry W. Halleck telegraphed to USG. "Have our troops landed? If so when & where. As soon as any transports can be spared they should be sent to Cairo." ALS (telegram sent), DLC-Henry W. Halleck; copies, DNA, RG 94, Generals' Papers and Books, Telegrams Sent in Cipher by Gen. Halleck; *ibid.*, RG 393, Dept. of the Mo., Telegrams Sent. On the same day, USG telegraphed to Halleck. "The first word received from Gen. Smith to-day. He has debarked at Savannah. Sent me no report, but his landing there would indicate fortifications and enemy in force above." Telegram received,

ibid., RG 94, Generals' Papers and Books, Telegrams Received by Gen. Halleck; copies, *ibid.*, RG 393, USG Hd. Qrs. Correspondence; *ibid.*, Dept. of the Mo., Telegrams Received; DLC-USG, V, 4, 5, 7, 8, 88. *O.R.*, I, x, part 2, 35.

4. See letter to Maj. Gen. Henry W. Halleck, March 5, 1862.

5. On March 14, USG telegraphed to Halleck. "Report and field return from Gen Smith just received and battery of a dozen pieces or more found at Eastport. —The Genl thinks Corinth will have to be left alone for the present, but will learn more, and report probably by next Steamer. An expedition is organizing from Pittsburg in the direction of Corinth but east of it." Telegram received, DNA, RG 94, Generals' Papers and Books, Telegrams Received by Gen. Halleck; copies, *ibid.*, RG 393, USG Hd. Qrs. Correspondence; *ibid.*, Dept. of the Mo., Telegrams Received; DLC-USG, V, 4, 5, 7, 8, 9, 88. *O.R.*, I, x, part 2, 35. On March 13, Maj. Gen. Charles F. Smith wrote to Capt. John A. Rawlins. "Please say to the Genl. that I arrived here at noon tewo days since with the view of returning steamers   I have ordered Genl. *McClernand's* division to disembark and opp occupy this place. I sent yesterday Genl. *Wallace's* division to *Crump's* Landing about 3½ miles above on the West bank to make a dash with a battalion of cavalry (4 troops) south of Purdy to cut the communication. It is about 17 miles. The cavarly cavalry with will be supported by Infantry, Arty. & a gun boat. I expect to hear of them from this force tonight. I went up yesterday afternoon on the gun boat Tyler to look at Pittsburgh on the West bank from whence the road leads directly to Corinth—say 19 miles off. It is a good place to hold & from whence to operate. On the same day before the two gun boats went up and engaged the enemy's batteries at Eastport, some dozen guns or more—2 of them rifled 24 or 32 pounders—to draw their fire & convey the impression that that was the true point of attack. I am unable to speak of the strength of the enemy at Corinth, but shall know more tonight. I am organizing an expedition from Pittsburgh in the direction of Corinth but East of it. In view of the restrictive nature of my orders I think that I shall have to cut the rails as I have above indicated & let Corinth alone. I send herewith a field return of this command." ALS, DNA, RG 393, District of West Tenn., Letters Received.

On March 14, USG telegraphed to Halleck. "Arrived last night and proceeded up the Tennessee, Eleventh Iowa Volunteers—Col A. M. Hare Comdg. Effective strength twenty-five commanding officers, seven hundred seventy-five men—aggregate eight hundred." Telegram received, *ibid.*, RG 94, Generals' Papers and Books, Telegrams Received by Gen. Halleck; copies, *ibid.*, RG 393, USG Hd. Qrs. Correspondence; *ibid.*, Dept. of the Mo., Telegrams Received; DLC-USG, V, 4, 5, 7, 8, 9, 88. On the same day, USG again telegraphed to Halleck. "Just arrived and proceeded up the Tennessee, Sixth Iowa Vols, Col McDowell Comdg. Effective strength six hundred men." Telegram received, DNA, RG 94, Generals' Papers and Books, Telegrams Received by Gen. Halleck; copies, *ibid.*, RG 393, USG Hd. Qrs. Correspondence; *ibid.*, Dept. of the Mo., Telegrams Received; DLC-USG, V, 4, 5, 7, 8, 9, 88.

To Brig. Gen. Don Carlos Buell

Head Quarters, Dist of West. Tenn.
Fort. Henry, March 14th 1862.

GEN. D. C. BUELL,
NASHVILLE, TENN.
GENERAL:

I am authorized by Flag Officer Foote, to request that you send up the Tennessee River the Gun Boat Carondelet. Her services are much needed on this river.

Respectfully &c
U. S. GRANT.
Major Gen. Commdg.

Telegram, copies, DLC-USG, V, 1, 2, 3, 86; DNA, RG 393, USG Letters Sent. On March 15, 1862, USG telegraphed to Maj. Gen. Henry W. Halleck. "Yesterday I telegraphed Genl Buell . . . Would it not be well to have an Iron Clad bo[at] on this River. The river i[s] now very high & rising" Telegram received (misdated March 16), *ibid.*, RG 94, Generals' Papers and Books, Telegrams Received by Gen. Halleck; copy (misdated March 16), *ibid.*, RG 393, Dept. of the Mo., Telegrams Received; copies (dated March 15), *ibid.*, USG Hd. Qrs. Correspondence; DLC-USG, V, 4, 5, 7, 8, 9, 88. Misdated March 16 in *O.R.*, I, x, part 2, 41.

On March 13, Capt. William S. Hillyer wrote to Maj. Gen. Charles F. Smith. "If you think you can safely dispense with the Gun Boat Conestoga, let her run regularly between your transports and Fort. Henry, in order to keep the river banks free from Batteries, and to protect our boats conveying reenforcements." Copies, DLC-USG, V, 1, 2, 3, 86; DNA, RG 393, USG Letters Sent.

To Col. Philip B. Fouke

———

Head Quarters, Dist of West. Tenn.
Fort. Henry, March 14th 1862.

Col. P. B. Fouke,
Fort. Donelson, Tenn.
Colonel:

Report to me what you have done in the way of dismantling
the Fort, and in shipping captured property below. You need not
send any Steamers, ~~around~~ here.

Respectfully &c
U. S. Grant.
Major Gen. Commdg

Copies, DLC-USG, V, 1, 2, 3, 86; DNA, RG 393, USG Letters Sent. On March
14, 1862, Col. Philip B. Fouke telegraphed to USG. "The Guns will all be dismantled tomorrow   I have shipped all public property as fast as collected to
Paducah—I have ~~found~~ at least two (2) days work to get the balance off—I have
found five (5) six (6) Pounders which I will ship tomorrow—Can send up everything by Monday—Will the force here be ordered away soon?" Telegram
received, *ibid.*, Dept. of the Mo., Telegrams Received.

To Col. Richard J. Oglesby

———

Head Quarters, Dist of West. Tenn.
Fort. Henry, March 14th 1862.

Col. Oglesby
Commdg 1st Brig. 1st Div.

You will immediately embark your command on board the
Steamer, "Henry Choteau," ordered to report to you at Metal
Landing.[1] See that as many are put on board, as she can carry,
having regard for health, and when embarked, proceed up the

Tenn. until you overtake the expedition, Commanded by Major
Gen. C. F. Smith to whom you will report.

By order of Major Gen. U. S. Grant

JNO A RAWLINS

Asst. Adjt. Genl.

Copies, DLC-USG, V, 1, 2, 3, 86; DNA, RG 393, USG Letters Sent. *O.R.*, I, x,
part 2, 36. On March 15, 1862, Capt. John A. Rawlins wrote to Col. Richard J.
Oglesby. "You will immediately embark your command on board Steamer 'Belle
Memphis,' ordered to report to you at Metal Landing. See that as many are put
on board as she can carry, having regard for health, and when embarked proceed
up the Tennessee until you overtake the expedition commanded by Major Gen.
C. F. Smith, to whom you will report. You will also see that no negroes are permitted to be carried off by any of your command. If there are any with you, who
were captured at Fort. Donelson. The Orders are that they be turned over to the
Quartermaster's Department. If not so captured leave them on the shore. This
order must be strictly complied with." Copies, DLC-USG, V, 1, 2, 3, 86; DNA,
RG 393, USG Letters Sent. *O.R.*, I, x, part 2, 40.

On March 20, Col. Joseph D. Webster wrote to the commanding officer,
Paducah, Ky. "A few days since a Mr. Ryan (of the firm of Yates & Ryan) Sutler
of the 31st Regt. Ind. Vols., was detected in selling liquor to Soldiers, and was
very properly set on shore with his goods at Clifton, Tenn. It is reported that he
subsequently left that place taking away a Negro, belonging to a Mr. Hughes,
and a skiff. It is thought proper that the goods, which more subsequently sent to
Paducah, Ky. by Capt Shink of the Steamer Lexington, who did not know the
circumstances, should be detained until further information from these Head
Quarters, or until Mr. G. B. Hughes of Clifton, Tenn, signifies his assent to these
being restored to Mr. Ryan. His goods are marked (wrong of course) as belonging to the Qr. Master's Dept. and were sent to Paducah yesterday afternoon on
the Steamer 'Boston,' with directions, that they be delivered to the Master of
transportation at your Post. The selling of the liquor to the Soldiers was done
under circumstances of aggravated deception and falsehood, and was fully punished by Col. Oglesby, who set Ryan a shore." Copies, DLC-USG, V, 1, 2, 3, 86;
DNA, RG 393, USG Letters Sent. According to a diary kept jointly by 1st Lt.
William D. Harland and Sgt. Thomas C. Watkins, 18th Ill., the sutler of the
31st Ind. brought on board a steamboat headed up the Tennessee River boxes
containing liquor but mislabeled to indicate legitimate sutler's wares. During
the night of March 17–18, some of the troops discovered the liquor. "About ½
of the men got drunk and it was a free fight all around." One drunken soldier fell
overboard and drowned. Typescript, IHi.

1. Metal Landing, Tenn., on the east bank of the Tennessee River, about
one mile upriver from Fort Henry.

General Orders No. 21

———

Head Quarters Dist of West Tenn.
Fort Henry March 15th 1862.

GENL ORDERS NO 21

The necessity for order, and regularity about Head Quarters, espeacially in keeping the records, makes it necessary to assign particular duties to each member of the Staff.

The following are the duties which will be assigned to each. Capt J. A. Rawlins A. A. Genl. assisted by Capt W. R. Rowley Aid-de-Camp will have special charge of the books of records, consolidating returns, and forwarding all documents to their proper destination.

Capt W. S. Hillyer, Aid-de-Camp, will see that returns are furnished by all Division and other commanders whose duties it may be to furnish said returns direct to these Head Quarters.

Capt Clark B Lagow A. D. C. and Col Jno Riggins Jr. will act upon applications for passes, both of persons and property, and also have a care to the amount of supplies on hand, both of Commissary stores and articles of daily consumpsion in the Qr M. Dept, such as coal forage &c.

Col. J. D. Webster chief of staff & Engnr will be the adviser of the Genl Comdg—and will give his attention to any portion of duties that may not receive proper attention.

Capt J. P. Hawkins inspecting Commy—for the Dept of the Mo, having been ordered to report to these Head Quarters for duty is hereby assigned in the same capacity for this District.[1]

He will also have a General superintendence over the Quarter Master Dept; for the entire Military Dist, and as such will be obeyed and respected by all Commanders.—

Asst and Regimental Qr—Masters Commissaries and acting Commissaries of Subt.

By order of Maj Genl U. S. Grant
JNO A RAWLINS
A. A. Genl.

Copies, DLC-USG, V, 12, 95; DNA, RG 393, USG General Orders. *O.R.*, I, x, part 2, 41. A condensed version of the same orders is in DLC-USG, V, 13, 14.

1. Capt. John P. Hawkins of Ind., USMA 1852, had served as commissary under USG earlier, then had been assigned to duty as inspecting commissary, Dept. of the Mo. See letter to Brig. Gen. Lorenzo Thomas, Oct. 20, 1861. Special Orders No. 211, Dept. of the Mo., March 7, 1862, assigned him the same duty in the District of West Tenn.

To Maj. Gen. Henry W. Halleck

Fort. Henry, March. 15th 1862

MAJ. GEN. H. W. HALLECK
ST. LOUIS, MO.
GENERAL.

I think the troops will be away from here so as to enable me to start tomorrow. morning. Col. Lowe, Curtis Horse, will be in command here; Col. P. B. Fouke at Donelson.

U. S GRANT
Maj. Gen. Com'dg

Telegram, copies, DLC-USG, V, 4, 5, 7, 8, 9, 88; DNA, RG 393, USG Hd. Qrs. Correspondence; *ibid.*, Dept. of the Mo., Telegrams Received.

To Maj. Gen. Henry W. Halleck

BY TELEGRAPH FROM Ft Henry [*March 15*] 1862

TO GEN HALLECK

Before leaving Donelson I directed all artillery except heavy guns shippe[d] to St Louis—I understan[d] however it was stopped a[t] Paducah   here there is but one 1 howitzer it spiked before the fort fell—at Clarksville there were tw[o] twenty four 24 pounder gun[s] & four 4 of heavy calibre—I ordered the garrison from there to ship everything & come up the Tennessee themselves   three times I have communicated but learn this evening my instructions were not receiv[ed.] I will try again immediat[ely.]

U. S. GRANT.

Telegram received (misdated March 16, 1862), DNA, RG 94, Generals' Papers and Books, Telegrams Received by Gen. Halleck; copies (dated March 15), *ibid.*, RG 393, USG Hd. Qrs. Correspondence; *ibid.*, Dept. of the Mo., Telegrams Received; DLC-USG, V, 4, 5, 7, 8, 9, 88. *O.R.*, I, x, part 2, 39–40. On March 15, Maj. Gen. Henry W. Halleck telegraphed to USG. "Field Howitzers are wanted to complete a couple of batteries here. Have you any captured pieces suitable for that purpose? If so how many & where are they?" ALS (telegram sent), DLC-Henry W. Halleck; copies, DNA, RG 94, Generals' Papers and Books, Telegrams Sent in Cipher by Gen. Halleck; *ibid.*, RG 393, Dept. of the Mo., Telegrams Sent.

To Maj. Gen. Henry W. Halleck

BY TELEGRAPH FROM Ft Henry [*March*] 15 1862.

To MAJ GEN HALLECK

In my telegrap[h] yesterday I state that Clarksvi[lle] was abandoned by our force[s.] I ordered the abandonment four days ago but have not y[et] heard from the troops there   Mules & Harness are arrivin[g] fast from Cincinnatti but as yet no waggons. It is no[w] raining & has been continually for forty eight hours   Weather cold & roads Impassable[1]

Gen. Wallace has destroyed a long piece of trestle work between East Port and Corinth.[2] Rebel force at Corinth, East-Port, and points East represented at from 50 to 60 thousand.

U S GRANT
Maj Genl

Telegram received, DNA, RG 94, Generals' Papers and Books, Telegrams Received by Gen. Halleck; copies, *ibid.*, RG 393, USG Hd. Qrs. Correspondence; *ibid.*, Dept. of the Mo., Telegrams Received; DLC-USG, V, 4, 5, 7, 8, 88. *O.R.*, I, x, part 2, 40. See telegram to Maj. Gen. Henry W. Halleck, March 14, 1862.

1. The remainder of the telegram does not appear on the copies received in St. Louis.

2. See letter to Capt. Nathaniel H. McLean, March 15, 1862.

To Maj. Gen. Henry W. Halleck

BY TELEGRAPH FROM Ft Henry [*March 15*] 1862

TO GEN HALLECK—

An expedition under Gen Wallace have cut o[ne] half a mile of trussel work north of Purdy.[1] Cheatham[2] with a force estimated at about 13.000 probably will not exceed twelve thousand 12.000, i[s] to the left of Wallace. th[e] probable estimated strength of the enemy from the point referred to Eastp[ort] & near there east is estim[ated] at from fifty to sixty thousand. I am much exercised to know if it will be prudent to leave the garrison intended for this place mostly at the Heiman—the latte[r] point commands the river effectually even with light artillery & is accessible by good roa[ds] from the interior. a sma[ll] garrison would be perfect[ly] secure at Henry & might not be at the other

U. S. GRANT

Telegram received, DNA, RG 94, Generals' Papers and Books, Telegrams Received by Gen. Halleck; copies, *ibid.*, RG 393, USG Hd. Qrs. Correspondence; *ibid.*, Dept. of the Mo., Telegrams Received; DLC-USG, V, 4, 5, 7, 8, 9, 88. *O.R.*, I, x, part 2, 40. On March 16, 1862, Maj. Gen. Henry W. Halleck telegraphed to USG. "As the enemy is evidently in strong force, my instructions, not to advance so as to bring on an engagement, must be strictly obeyed. Genl Smith must hold his position without exposing himself by detachments, till we can strongly reinforce him. Genl Buell is moving in his direction, and I hope in a few days to send ten or fifteen thousand more from Missouri. We must strike no blow till we are strong enough to admit no doubt of the result. If you deem Fort Heiman best for defense occupy it instead of Fort Henry. You must [decide upon all details] from your better local information. What captured field pieces have you?" ALS (telegram sent), DNA, RG 107, Telegrams Collected (Unbound); copies, *ibid.*, RG 94, Generals' Papers and Books, Telegrams Sent in Cipher by Gen. Halleck; *ibid.*, RG 393, USG Hd. Qrs. Correspondence; *ibid.*, Dept. of the Mo., Telegrams Sent; *ibid.*, Telegrams Received; DLC-USG, V, 4, 5, 7, 8, 9, 88; Oglesby Papers, IHi. *O.R.*, I, x, part 2, 41.

1. Purdy, Tenn., about fifteen miles west of Savannah, Tenn.
2. Benjamin F. Cheatham of Tenn. rose to col. of Tenn. Vols. in the Mexican War and to maj. gen. of Tenn. militia later. A C. S. A. brig. gen. since July 9, 1861, he was appointed C. S. A. maj. gen. as of March 10, 1862, and on March 12 was assigned to command the 2nd Division under Maj. Gen. Leonidas Polk at Humboldt, Tenn.

To Capt. Nathaniel H. McLean

Head Quarters, Dist. of W. Ten.
Fort Henry March 15th 1862.

CAPT. N. H. MCLEAN
A. A. GEN. DEPT. OF THE MO.
ST. LOUIS MO.
CAPT.

A steamer has just returned from above but I have nothing official but learn from Maj. McDowel[1] that Gen. Sherman with his Division has left Savanna for some point higher up the river.

The union sentiment seems to be strong in the south part of the state. Already sixty men had organized themselvs into a company to serve the United States and a number had enlisted in the ranks of our reduced regiments.

I will have consolidated returns ready to mail to-morrow morning and will then leave for the scene of action, or where the troops are.

Our supply of rations and ammunition is good. The amount of coal & forage consumed is so great that these articles should be sent in great quantities.

The unusual stage of water for the last few weeks has washed away all the wood prepaired for steamboat purposes so that coal must be relied on entirely.

I am Capt. very respectfully
your obt. svt.
U. S. GRANT
Maj. Gen.

ALS, DNA, RG 393, Dept. of the Miss., Letters Received. *O.R.*, I, x, part 2, 39. Nathaniel H. McLean of Ohio, USMA 1848, served continuously in the U. S. Army after graduation, ranking as 1st lt. on the eve of the Civil War. On Aug. 3, 1861, he was appointed capt. and asst. adjt. gen., and on Jan. 31, 1862, began to serve on the staff of Maj. Gen. Henry W. Halleck.

1. Probably Maj. Malcolm McDowell of Ohio, appointed additional paymaster of vols. on June 1, 1861. In a letter to his wife, March 12, 1862, Brig. Gen. William T. Sherman mentioned McDowell's presence at Savannah. ALS, InNd.

To Capt. Nathaniel H. McLean

Head Quarters, Dist. of West. Tenn.
Fort Henry, Mar. 15th 1862

CAPT. N. H. MCLEAN,
A. A. G., DEPT. OF THE MO.
ST. LOUIS, MO.
CAPT.

Enclosed please find reports of Brig. Gen. L. Wallace, of expedition fitted out under his charge, also, letter of Gen. Smith accompanying same.

I am, Capt.
Very Respectfully
Your Obt. Servt.
U. S. GRANT
Maj. Gen.

Copies, DLC-USG, V, 4, 5, 7, 8, 9, 88; DNA, RG 393, USG Hd. Qrs. Correspondence. On March 14, 1862, Maj. Gen. Charles F. Smith wrote to Capt. John A. Rawlins. "From the enclosed reports of Brig. Gen. Wallace, numbered one, and two, of yesterday's date it will be perceived, that the expedition to injure the Rail way communication, north of Purdy, has been successful. (Please see enclosed my orders on the subject) Another expedition, on the same principle, will leave under Brig. Gen. Sherman in an hour or so, to operate between Corinth and Eastport, at a point about 12 miles from the river, in the neighborhood of Burnville. I have not been able to get any thing like the desired information, as to the strength of the enemy, but it seems to be quoted at 50 to 60.000, from Jackson through Corinth, Eastport and farther east. Their principal force is at Corinth: that which has induced me not to attempt to cut the communication at that place, as that would inevitably lead to a collision in numbers that I am ordered to avoid, and hence my efforts North of Purdy and east of Corinth. In order to furnish the Steamers called for by Gen. *Grants* recent instructions, I have caused Brig. Genl. McClernand's division to debark and occupy Savannah, and the surrounding country. From a scouting party, east of the town, two days since, it was ascertained that the only force of the enemy in that quarter is a body of 5 to 600 cavalry, about 15 miles, S. E. We need coal very much. Two barges filled with it arrived this morning, but the two Gun Boats here, consume nearly or quite ⅔ of the quantity brought: say 8.000 out of 12.000 Bu.   Our sick list is increasing. As the Hospital Steamer (City of Memphis) is nearly full, I have ordered her below to get rid of her freight and then to return." Copy, DLC-USG, V, 88. *O.R.*, I, x, part 1, 8–9. Smith enclosed two letters, both dated March 13, from Brig. Gen. Lewis Wallace to Capt. William McMichael. Copies, DLC-USG, V, 88. *O.R.*, I, x, part 1, 9–10. On March 15, Wallace wrote to his wife. "I returned from the expedition (mentioned in my last letter) yesterday. The object was to cut the Railroad leading from Jackson, Tennessee, to Corinth, Mississippi I was successful. It proved, contrary to my belief, a hazardous affair, as may be judged when I tell you that I lay with my command, barely five thousand strong, two nights and a day, within three miles of Gen. Cheatem with fifteen thousand men. Of course, nothing saved me from attack but an exaggerrated idea of my force; which exaggerration I kept up by such little tricks as changing my lines in the day and multiplying fires by night The tapping of the Railroad was done by a battalion (four companies) of Ohio Cavalry, who rode twenty miles off the river with strong detachments of the enemy quartered at several places around them." ALS, Wallace Papers, InHi.

Wallace later forwarded to USG a report of Maj. Charles S. Hayes, 5th Ohio Cav., March 18, of a subsequent expedition toward Purdy. "Pursuant to Special Order No 26 from Headquarters I proceeded with my command at 12 m o clock to Adamsville, on arriving at which place I learned that the rebels had abandoned their camp four and a half miles from the town, upon the receipt of which information I deemed it expedient to proceed futher into the country in the direction of Purdey and make a reconnoissance of the enemy W I first met the enemy, most probably a foraging party, three miles this side of Purdey, which I pursued inside their pickets, also driving in the pickets to almost with range of the enemys infantry drawn up in line just outside of Purdey. One of the rebel pickets I captured and hold subject to orders, and at the same place Lieutenant Murray of Co II commanding my advance guard had his horse shot from under him As the result of my reconnoissance I report that the country is clear of the enemy to Purdey, that at Purdey there is stationed two regiments of rebel infantry from 800. to 1.000 strong each, well armed, and also one or two companies of cavalry" LS, DNA, RG 393, District of West Tenn., Letters Received.

To Capt. Nathaniel H. McLean

Head Quarters, Dist of West. Tenn.
Fort Henry, Mar. 15th 1862

CAPT. N. H MCLANE.
ASST. ADJ'T. GENL.
SIR.

I herewith transmit to you, General and Special Orders. of this District. Also letters of direction to Division and Brigade Commanders. accompanying Expedition up the Tennessee.

I am Sir Very Respectfull
Your Obt. Servt.
U. S. GRANT
Maj. Gen.

LS, DNA, RG 393, Dept. of the Miss., Letters Received. The documents enclosed are printed elsewhere in this vol.

To Col. Philip B. Fouke

————

Head Quarters, Dist of West. Tenn.
Fort. Henry, March 15th 1862.

COL. P. B. FOUKE
FORT. DONELSON, TENN.

Send a Steamer up to Clarkesville, and direct Col. Wright[1] by my order to load on all public property, captured and otherwise, and send the boat to Paducah to be discharged. As soon as public property can be removed, all troops at Clarkesville, are to come up the Tenn. river, and report to me. Owing to the impassable state of the roads, they will come round by Steamers.

It is important that this dispatch should go through at once unless the troops have left Clarkesville.

U. S. GRANT
Major. Gen. Commdg.

Copies, DLC-USG, V, 1, 2, 86; DNA, RG 393, USG Letters Sent. See following letter.

1. See letter to Col. Crafts J. Wright, March 15, 1862.

To Col. Philip B. Fouke

————

Fort Henry March 15th/62

COL P B FOUKE FORT DONELSON TENN

Ship all the Ammunition & Artillery to Paducah. Did you receive & forward my instructions to Col Wright, Clarksville.

U S GRANT
Maj Genl.

Copies, DLC-USG, V, 1, 2, 3, 88; DNA, RG 393, USG Letters Sent. On March 15, 1862, Col. Philip B. Fouke, Fort Donelson, telegraphed to USG. "The magazines in the Fort are full of solid shot ~~shell~~ shell and Powder enough to load a Boat   the quantity is immense   what shall I do with it—where send it—where shall I ship the six (6) Pounders"   Telegram received, *ibid.*, Dept. of the Mo., Telegrams Received. On March 15, Fouke again telegraphed to USG. "I received your instructions for Col Wright—I Telegraphed Him and also sent a written order   authorized Him to press into his service first Boat down the River and to report his command to you as soon as He shipped all captured property—I will ship everything here as soon as possible"   Telegram received, *ibid.* See letter to Col. Crafts J. Wright, March 15, 1862.

To Col. William W. Lowe

Head Quarters Dist of West Tenn
Fort Henry March 15th 1862.

COL W. W. LOWE
COMMANDING FTS HENRY & HEIMAN.
COL.

During my absence, and untill further orders you will have command as above. You will continue the guard on the line of telegraph, as now performed.

It will be necessary to have at least two companies as a garrison to Fort Henry, who will be held by you strictly responsible for the proper care of all public property. The magazine and captured amunition have been grossly neglected by the troops put there to guard them.

All boats passing up the river are to be hailed by the Steamer "Cricket," a boat from which your commissary supplies will be issued, and her cargo, number of troops, name of commander, and regiment and corps ascertained and reported by telegraph to Head Quarters of the Dept St. Louis Mo without delay.

Prevent all marauding and destroying of private property. The citizens are not to be molested by our troops. Makes severe examples of company commanders, whose companies are guilty of such conduct. If necessary ship them to Head Quarters, St Louis, with charges and a request that they be mustered out of service. You will make or cause to be made, requisitions upon the Quartermaster and Commissary at Paducah for such supplies as may be required for your Command, being careful to have at least fifteen days of rations, and at least eight days forage, on hand at all times.

Hurry up steamers destined for above, and report all apparent delinquency of Steamboat Capts. or other agts.

Your particular attention is called to Gen, Orders No. 3. from Head Quarters of the Dept of series of 1861 and to accompanying orders from these Head Quarters.

Should you, at any time, receive such information as in your judgement would make it unsafe to occupy your present position with your limited command, you move to Fort Henry.

All information obtained report to me, sending a copy direct to Dept, Head Quarters.

> Very Respectfully
> Your Obt Servt.
> U. S GRANT Maj. Gen Comdg.

LS, DNA, RG 393, Dept. of the Miss., Letters Received.

To Col. Crafts J. Wright

Fort Henry March 15th/62

CO'L C J WRIGHT CLARKESVILLE TENN

I have sent orders three times to break up the Garrison at Clarkesville. Ship to Paducah all ordinance and captured property of no use in the field   Balance bring with you by water and report to me on the Tennessee

> U S GRANT
> Maj Gen'l Com

Copies, DLC-USG, V, 1, 2, 3, 88; DNA, RG 393, USG Letters Sent. Crafts J. Wright of Ohio, USMA 1828, resigned from the U. S. Army almost immediately after graduation. An Ohio lawyer, and editor of the *Cincinnati Gazette* (1847–1853), he was appointed col., 13th Mo., on Aug. 13, 1861. The 13th Mo., composed largely of Ohioans, was renamed the 22nd Ohio on July 7, 1862. On March 15, Wright telegraphed to USG. "There are one thousand (1000) effective men here and a large population without one Union or not hostile man—There is a large amount of what was at the surrender Public stores to select which we have no orders nor have we any for our Government—If we [m]ove away the property will pass into the hands of the Enemies unless others take our place—The Rail Road between the Rivers can easily be opened & even now passed over by Hand Cars—" Telegram received, *ibid.*, Dept. of the Mo., Telegrams Received. On March 16, Wright again telegraphed to USG. "I have received no orders except this Telegram   Considerable Stores here and will take several days to ship   have 40 sick and wounded of the Enemy and 121 sick of our own   What shall be done with the Enemy—Clarksville people burnt down our Wharf Boat last night and set fire to one Fort   Will the 50th Illinois and other detachments move with me." Telegram received, *ibid.* On the same day, USG wrote to Wright. "Do as ordered—ship public property. The 50th Ills. and other forces will move with you. Make all possible dispatch." Copies, DLC-USG, V, 1, 2, 3, 86; DNA, RG 393, USG Letters Sent.

To Alfred F. Goodman

On board Steamer Tigress
Upper Tennessee river
March 15th 1862

ALFRED F. GOODMAN, ESQ.
SEC. TO FOREST CITY UNION CLUB
CLEVLAND OHIO.
MY DEAR SIR:

Your favor of the 4th of March enclosing resolutions highly complimentary to myself, passed by your association on the 1st inst. was received whilst I was at Fort Henry, Ten. busily engaged in getting off a large expedition for the upper Ten. which I sincerely hope you will hear a good account from before many days.

I acknowledge the compliment with feelings that they are more than I deserve   As a soldier however I shall endeavour never to disappoint you.

With sincer thanks to the Assosiation, of which you are an honorable member, for their expression of confidance I remain,

> very respectfully, your obt. svt.
> U. S. GRANT
> Maj. Gen.

ALS, OClWHi.

To Julia Dent Grant

―――――

Fort Henry March 15th 1862

DEAR JULIA

I have an opportunity of sending a letter to Cairo and avail myself of it. I can write you but a short letter however having to get other mail matter ready to go by the same boat.—I am much better than when father was here but not by any means well yet. A few days will restore me entirely. I now have orders to proceed up the river in command of the whole force on the Ten. What you may look for is hard to say, possibly a big fight. I have already been in so many that it begins to feel like home to me.

Kiss the children for me and give my love to all at home.

> ULYS.

ALS, DLC-USG. On March 15, 1862, USG also wrote to Jesse R. Grant. "I have been ordered to go up the Tennessee river and take command of the forces there, and shall start immediately." *Galena Daily Advertiser*, March 22, 1862.

To Julia Dent Grant

―――――

Fort Henry March 15/62

DEAR JULIA,

A boat is just going down to Cairo a little unexpectedly to me and gives but a moment to write. I can say however that I am well something that I could not say for the last three weeks. I will send by this boat a present made to me by some of the officers of my command for safe keeping. You will see that is very beautiful. I start to-morrow up the river to resume command of the army in the field.

You will probably hear from me again soon, either that I or some one els is whipped. It does not look much now as if you would be able to join me soon. I have no time to write more.

ULYS.

Kiss all the children for me and give my love to all at home.

ALS, DLC-USG. The present mentioned is probably the ornamental sword given to USG by George W. Graham, 1st Lt. Clark B. Lagow, Col. C. Carroll Marsh, and Col. John Cook on March 10, 1862, in a ceremony on board the *Tigress*. In a speech of presentation, Marsh said that fortunately the sword had been delayed, "fortunately, I say, because at this moment when the jealousy caused by your brilliant success has raised up hidden enemies who are endeavoring to strike you in the dark, it affords us an opportunity to express our renewed confidence in your ability as a commander." After receiving the sword, USG said he was unable to reply, and a speech of acknowledgment was delivered by Capt. William S. Hillyer. Dispatch from Fort Henry, March 10, 1862, in *Chicago Tribune*, March 11, 1862; dispatch from Fort Henry, March 10, 1862, in *Cincinnati Gazette*, March 11, 1862. The sword, now in the Smithsonian Institution, is shown in Lawrence A. Frost, *U. S. Grant Album* (Seattle, 1966), p. [147]. See *Personal Memoirs of John H. Brinton* (New York, 1914), p. 149.

To Maj. Gen. Henry W. Halleck

BY TELEGRAPH FROM Ft Henry [*March 16*] 1862

TO MAJ GEN HALLECK

I have made out a full return of the forces of this district & location which will be forwarded by first steamer—would send by telegraph but fear it might be taken off the wires for benefit of the enemy as I have reason to believe such has been done— the eighty first 81st Ohio effective strength five hundred fifty 550 arrived last ~~night~~ evening & proceed up the river   all the troops are embarking   those at Clarksville are ordered to avail themselves of first steamer passing for transportation   I shall leave for Savannah immediately

U. S. GRANT

Telegram received, DNA, RG 94, Generals' Papers and Books, Telegrams Received by Gen. Halleck; copy, *ibid.*, Dept. of the Mo., Telegrams Received.

To Col. Philip B. Fouke

Head Quarters, Dist of West. Tenn.
Fort. Henry March 16th 1862

COL. P. FOUKE,

Ship Powder—don't destroy it. Obey orders No 3. Dept of the Mo, in reference to negroes. None will be allowed within your lines or camps, except when specially ordered by the Genl. Commdg.

U. S. GRANT.
Major. Genl. Commdg.

Copies, DLC-USG, V, 1, 2, 86; DNA, RG 393, USG Letters Sent. On March 16, 1862, Col. Philip B. Fouke, Fort Donelson, telegraphed to USG. "I have about two (2) tons of Powder in sacks   Boats are here to take it   shall I destroy it— Contrabands whose masters are in the Confederate Army are continually applying for passes   What shall I do with them"   Telegram received, *ibid.*, Dept. of the Mo., Telegrams Received.

To Capt. Nathaniel H. McLean

———

Head Quarters, Dist. of W. Ten.
Savanna Ten. March 17th 1862

Capt. N. H. McLean,
A. A. Gen. Dept. of the Mississippi
St. Louis Mo.
Capt.

I have the honor of reporting my arrival, but a few minuets since, at this place. Just as I arrived a report was received from Gen. Sherman which ~~is~~I herewith enclose.[1] A man employed by Gen. Smith as scout also come in reporting the enemy very strong from Chickasaw[2] to Corinth. Their number was estimated at 150.000, about one third of them being at Corinth.   Gen. Johnson, with his force, is said to be with them. The number is of course very much exagerated and Johnson being there was very much against my expectation.

This country is so overflown that but few roads can be traveled and all are most impassable for artillery. A few dry days however would remedy this and it is certainly time to look for a change of weather.

I shall order all the forces here, except McClernand's Division, to Pittsburg and send back steamers as rapidly as possible.

It is with great difficulty that Quartermasters at Paducah & Cairo can be impressed with the magnitude of our wants in coal & forage. We are now short in both these articles. Corn can be procured here for a few days but not for a long period.

I would respectfully suggest to the Gen. commanding the importance of having funds in the hands of the Quartermaster to pay these people for such supplies as we get from them.

All the troops ~~here~~ of my command except those left to garrison Forts Henr[y] and Donelson, ~~and~~ two regiments at Clarkesville yet to arrive, and McClernands Division will be at Pittsburg. The accompanying report of Gen. Sherman, with the above statement shows the present distribution of my forces.

The 52d Ill. Col. Sweeney[3] commanding, has just arrived.

> I am Capt. very respectfully
> your obt. svt.
> U. S. GRANT
> Maj. Gen.

ALS, DNA, RG 393, Dept. of the Miss., Letters Received. *O.R.*, I, x, part 2, 42–43.

1. On March 16, 1862, Maj. Gen. Charles F. Smith wrote to Capt. John A. Rawlins. "I enclose for the information of the Maj. Genl. Commanding the Dist. the report of Brig. Genl. Sherman in reference to an expedition, the contemplated object of which was the destruction of the line of Railroad between Corinth and Eastport, but which was not accomplished for reasons which Genl. Sherman has fully explained in his report. — Brig Genl. Sherman's Division is now at Pittsburg, a point upon the river nine miles above Savannah; and in view of the importance of the position I have directed him to remain there for the present making such fortifications as may be neccessary for temporary defence, and making frequent and extended recconaisances, and also to keep well informed of the strength and movements of the Enemy—Genl. Sherman is supported by the Division commanded by Brig. Genl Hurlbut. I send also the report of a successful expedition commanded by Brig. Genl. Wallace. . . . P. S. Since writing the above I have information from Genl. Sherman that he intends carrying out the original intention by making a demonstration upon Corinth and moving to the left with his cavalry" LS, DNA, RG 393, District of West Tenn., Letters Received. Enclosed was a letter of March 16 from Brig. Gen. William T. Sherman, Pittsburg Landing, to Capt. William McMichael. Copies, *ibid.*; DLC-USG, V, 88. Dated March 17 in DNA, RG 94, War Records Office, Union Battle Reports. *O.R.*, I, x, part 1, 24–25. On March 17, Sherman wrote to Rawlins. "I have just returned from an extensive reconnaissanc[e] towards Corinth & Purdy and am strongly impressed with the importance of the position both for its land advantages and its strategic position The ground itself admits of easy defense by a small command and yet affords admirable camping ground for a hundred thousand men I will as soon as possible make or cause to be made a Topographal sketch of the position The only drawback is that at this stage of water the space for landing is contracted too much se for the immense fleet now there discharging I will push the landing & unloading but suggest you send at once here (Capt Dodd if possible) the best Quarter master, you can, that he may control & organize this whole matter. I have good commissarys & will keep as few provisions afloat as possible." Copies, DNA, RG 94, Generals' Papers and Books, William T. Sherman, Letters Sent; *ibid.*, War Records Office, Union Battle Reports. *O.R.*, I, x, part 1, 27. On the same day, Sherman again wrote to Rawlins. "The object indicated by Gen Smith for me to accomplish is, to cut the Charleston & Memphis Road, without a General or serious engagement—This

is impossible from here, because the ground is well watched and a dash cannot be made. I have tried it twice the first time defeated by Rains, storm & High Water, the Second, by coming in contact with a cavalry force of the enemy which was defeated routed, and dispersed in utter confusion, evidences of which met us at every foot of the Road beyond the scene of conflict to the extent of our Reconnoissance. Horses loose, or mired in the bottoms, saddles, sabres, shot guns, scattered through the woods and along the several roads and bye-paths, by which they retreated towards Purdy. The mode of accomplishing the important object first indicated is this. To advance with considerable display on the Corinth Road, by a large force, as far as Pea Ridge—then dispatch by a good steamer under convoy of the Gunboat to Tylers Landing about 200 cavalry, and a Regt of Infantry, to reach that point at 6 P M and to take its immediate departure for the Railroad 19 miles off, at a place called Burnville. We attempted this but were defeated by the Rain. The small streams have now run out, and I think the plan practicable. The enemy knows, that we have abandoned Tylers Landing & have concentrated here—Crumps Landing is a good point also, as there is a considerable force at Purdy—I was well out there today and think there is some mistake about the Road being broken to the North of Purdy, for a very inteligent man says he saw the Train leave Purdy for Jackson yesterday. This Road can easily be reached now from here. The difficulty is with the other Road, which is watched because of its great importance. To advance on Corinth in force, we should make use of several Roads, our troops drag out too long on a single country Road— From Tylers Landing, Pittsburg, and Crumps as well as Hamburg troops could move concentrically on Corinth, or could cross the Road at any other point. I am trying my best to find out the strength of the enemy at these points but thus far am unsuccessful—" ALS, DNA, RG 94, War Records Office, Union Battle Reports. *O.R.,* I, x, part 1, 26–27. On March 17 and 18, Sherman wrote to his wife. "I started in command of eleven (11) Regiments, landed at Tylers Landing 18 miles above this and in the midst of a perfect flood attempted to cross over the intervening space of 17 miles to break the Memphis & Charleston Road. The Rains fell in torrents and streams began to rise, and the Cavalry which led had to turn back for the swollen water. It was very unfortunate. So I had to retain the Boats. The Tennessee River rose 15 ~~miles~~ feet in one day and the Landing was under water. I was compelled to drop down again to this place where there is a high Bluff Landing. Troops are passing in to my command, and again I attempted to make for the Road sending a Cavalry force ahead—Mr Bowman took part in this movement—The force had only gone 5 miles when in the dark they had a fight with some secession Cavalry, which retired in disorder. My Infantry force was on the point of starting but as I depended on the Cavalry to travel the 20 miles before daylight which was impossible, I determined to convert my attempt on the Road into a Reconnaissance. This was done, and I have been out two days and have obtained pretty accurate notions of the Road on which we are to move. Genl Grant & Smith are at Savanna 19 miles below, and I command here, but as the Force has swollen to 25000 men, and more are coming I take it for granted that some one else will come to command. I hear Halleck is coming, may be Grant, and on the whole we are furthest advanced into Secessia." ALS, Sherman Papers, InNd.

On March 17, USG wrote to hd. qrs., Dept. of the Miss., "Inclosing reports of Maj's Hayes & Rickers & one from Genl Sherman." DNA, RG 393, Dept. of the Miss., Register of Letters Received. Two reports of Maj. Charles S. Hayes,

5th Ohio Cav., both dated March 14, to Capt. Fred Knefler, asst. adjt. gen. for Brig. Gen. Lewis Wallace, are in *O.R.*, I, x, part 1, 10–11. They describe the destruction of a bridge of the Mobile and Ohio Railroad across Beach Creek and a reconnaissance toward Purdy, Tenn. The report of Sherman, March 15, addressed to McMichael, described a reconnaissance southward from Pittsburg Landing which was unsuccessful due to high water, bad weather, and impassable roads. Copy, DNA, RG 94, War Records Office, Union Battle Reports. *O.R.*, I, x, part 1, 22–24. On March 15, Maj. Elbridge G. Ricker, 5th Ohio Cav., reported to Sherman that his assignment to cut the Memphis and Charleston Railroad between Corinth and Iuka, Miss., had been unsuccessful for the same reasons. *Ibid.*, pp. 28–29.

    2. Chickasaw, Ala., on the south bank of the Tennessee River at the Miss. state line.

    3. Thomas W. Sweeny, born in Ireland in 1820, served as a 2nd lt., 2nd N. Y., in the Mexican War, then joined the U. S. Army at the same rank despite the fact that he had lost an arm. At the start of the Civil War he commanded the U. S. Arsenal, St. Louis, and served as second-in-command in the capture of Camp Jackson. On May 20, 1861, he was appointed brig. gen., Mo. Vols., but resigned that position, and was appointed col., 52nd Ill., on Jan. 21, 1862.

To Brig. Gen. William T. Sherman

Head Quarters, Dist of West. Tenn.
Savanna, March 17th 1862.

GEN. W. T. SHERMAN,
COMMDG U. S. FORCES,
PITTSBURG, TENN.
GENL:

I have just arrived and although sick for the last two weeks, begin to feel better at the thought of again being along with the troops.

I have ordered all troops here to report to you immediately, except McClernand's Division. Among those to report you will find a number of Regiments not of my command formerly, and consequently not yet Brigaded.

Organize them into Brigades, and attach them to Divisions as you deem best.

Enclosed is a list of all such regiments[1] some of which must be with you already.

> I am, Genl, Very Respectfully,
> Your Obt. Servant.
> U. S. GRANT.
> Major Genl. Commdg.

Copies, DLC-USG, V, 1, 2, 3, 86; DNA, RG 393, USG Letters Sent. *O.R.*, I, x, part 2, 43.

1. Not found. On March 19, 1862, Capt. John H. Hammond issued Special Orders No. 7 brigading previously unattached troops at Pittsburg Landing. *Ibid.*, I, lii, part 1, 226–27.

To Brig. Gen. William T. Sherman

> Head Quarters, Dist of West. Tenn.
> Savanna, March 17th 1862.

GEN. SHERMAN
COMMDG U. S. FORCES
PITTSBURG, TENN.
GENL.

The 7th Ills Vols. is just arrived from Clarkesville, Tenn. and I am told ~~with~~ has twenty odd slaves ~~aboard~~ with ~~them~~ it. The same complaint has been made before of this regiment and several times, I have been compelled to give them special ~~order~~ directions, to carry out General Orders No 3. from Head Quarters of the Dept, series of 1861, and my own orders in support of that order.

Make inquiries ~~if~~ whether the charge is true and if so, arrest the Commdg Officer, and any others who may be implicated in the transaction. Should these slaves be found improperly in camps, or on board Boats, carry out Gen. Halleck's Order in your own way.

The slaves should not be allowed to remain with the 7th. If

they are ~~men, or so many of them as may~~ be able bodied men possibly, had better be turned over to the Qr. Master, and employed as teamsters until higher Authority can decide their status.

> I am, Gen. Very Respectfully,
> Your Obt. Servant.
> U. S. GRANT
> Major. Gen. Commdg.

Copies, DLC-USG, V, 1, 2, 3, 86; DNA, RG 393, USG Letters Sent. On March 22, 1862, Brig. Gen. William T. Sherman wrote to Capt. John A. Rawlins. "I have the honor to acknowledg the receipt of General Orders No 23 and 24 which hasve been published to my Division and shall be duly enforced. I am investigating the matter of the negroes brougt away from Clarksville and am statisfied that the Captain of the Fairchild exaggerated the facts very much. The number is now reduced to two, and they are in the hands of the Regimental Quarter Master. I remit a Report of the Major Commanding Reg't (7th Illinois) to comply with General Grants orders" Copy, *ibid.*, RG 94, Generals' Papers and Books, William T. Sherman, Letters Sent. On March 29, Sherman wrote to Rawlins. "I was ordered by Gen Grant to make inquiry ~~of~~ into the charge that the 7th Ills Ift Maj Rowell commanding had brought from Clarksville a number of run-a-way slaves. The charge originated with the Captain of the steamer 'Fairchild' Fawcett, who said about twenty slaves had come passengers on board his boat from Clarksville under the sanction of the officers of the 7th Illinois. I ordered that he should be more specific in his charge, and gave him every facility for a personal inspection of the Regiment, that he might designate the slaves. His number gradually fell away from twenty to four, and at last one. Major Rowell asserts positively that all the negroes in his camp are free negroes, that were in the employment of the officers before the Regiment came from Illinois and all being strange to me, I am unable to question the truth of their assertion. I enclose herewith the written Report of Major Rowell with the receipt of the Regimental Quarter Master for the one negro slave admitted to have been received on board the Fairchild. I am satisfied that Capt Fawcett made his charge against this Regiment loosely and recklessly. When I faced him with Major Rowell he fell down in his number of slaves from twenty to four, and I cannot discover that more than one slave was brought away. That one slave is in the possession of the Regimental Qr Master employed for account of the U. S. The 7th Illinois does not belong to my Division and any further investigation should I suppose pass through the Commander of the Division to which the 7th Illinois belongs" ALS, *ibid.*, RG 393, District of West Tenn., Letters Received.

To Col. Marcellus M. Crocker

———

Head Quarters, Dist of West. Tenn.
Savanna, March 17th 1862.

COL. CROCKER
COMMDG 13TH IOWA. VOLS.
COL:

It is reported to me that you have on board the Steamer with your Regiment, two negroes, the property of a citizen of this place. You will not permit the Steamer to leave the landing, until the negroes are put ashore, and if possible the parties who induced them aboard found and reported to these Head Quarters.

There is but little doubt of the fact of the negroes being on your Steamer, and you will be held responsible for the compliance of this order.

It may be possible, and even is probable, that some of the Officers of the boat are the guilty parties and for the credit of the service I hope it may prove so.

I am, Col, Very Respectfully,
Your Obt Servant.
U. S. GRANT
Major Gen. Commdg.

Copies, DLC-USG, V, 1, 2, 3, 86; DNA, RG 393, USG Letters Sent. On March 14, 1862, Capt. John A. Rawlins wrote to Col. William W. Lowe. "The Commanding General has just been informed that Capt. Kidd, of Co. M of your Regiment has two negro women and a boy, fugitives, whom he has brought from Fort. Henry in violation of orders of the Dept of the Mo. and he directs me to request, that you have the matter investigated, at once; and if it should be true, the fugitives be sent back to Fort. Henry, and put out side our lines, and the Captain to report himself in person to the General Commanding. You will send A full report of the facts ~~you will send~~ to these Head Quarters." Copies, *ibid.*

To Commanding Officer, Pittsburg Landing

Head Quarters, Dist of West. Tenn.
Savanna, March 17th 1862

COMMDG OFFICER
PITTSBURGH TENN.
SIR:

You will immediately cause the debarkation of all troops now at or to arrive at Pittsburgh,[1] and discharge all boats except such as have on board Army stores.

Very Respectfully,
Your Obt Servant.
U. S. GRANT.
Major Gen. Commdg.

Copies, DLC-USG, V, 1, 2, 3, 86; DNA, RG 393, USG Letters Sent.

1. Pittsburg Landing, Tenn., on the west bank of the Tennessee River, about eight miles upriver from Savannah.

General Orders No. 23

Head Quarters, Dist of West Tenn.
Savanna March 18th 1862.

GEN ORDER NO 23

Troops now being in this field, all encampments will conform as near as practicable to Army Regulations.

Where soldiers are required to live in Tents, the same will be required of all Regimental officers.

Brigade Commanders will not be allowed to occupy Houses at the expense of the United States, on any account, nor at all unless they should occupy ground contigous to their Brigades.

A better state of discipline than has been maintained heretofore with much of this command, is demanded, and will be enforced.

By order of
Maj Gen U. S. Grant
Jno. A. Rawlins
A. A. Genl—

The Division commanders will see that the above order is publish to their respective commands, and that the same is strictly enforced.

DS, McClernand Papers, IHi; copies, DLC-USG, V, 12, 13, 14, 95; DNA, RG 94, 9th Ill., Letterbook. *O.R.*, I, x, part 2, 46–47.

To Maj. Gen. Henry W. Halleck

Head Quarters, Dist. of W. Ten.
Savanna March 18th 1862

Maj. Gen. H. W. Halleck,
Comd.g Dept. of the Mississippi
St. Louis, Mo.
Gen.

Your Dispatch of the 16th[1] is just received and replied to by telegraph from Fort Henry. I arrived here last evening and found that Gens. Sherman's & Hurlbut's Divisions were at Pittsburgh partially debarked. Gen. Wallace at Crump's Landing,[2] six miles below, same side of the river. Gen. McClernands Division at this place encamped and Gen. Smith's with unattached regiments on board transports also here.

I immediately ordered all troops except McClernands command to Pittsburgh and to debark there at once and discharge the steamers to report at Paducah for further orders.

All your instructions will be carried out to the best of my ability. There is no doubt a large force is being concentrate[d] at Corinth and on the line of the R. R.

Troops of Cavalry are all over the state impressing men into the service most of whom would rather serve with us. Refugees are coming in here and to other points on the river for protection. Some enlist and others ask for transportation to a safe retreat North.

I have not been here long enough to form much idea of the actual strength of the rebels but feel satisfied that they do not number 40.000 armed effective men at this time.

I shall go to-morrow to Crumps Landing and Pittsburg and if I think any change of position for any of the troops needed will make the change. Having full faith however in the judgement of Gen. Smith who located the present points of debarcation I do not expect any change will be made. There are no intermediate points where a steamer can land at the present stage of water.

This is an elevated piece of ground, probably forty feet above the present water level. The opposite side is covered with water to the depth of six or eight feet on the bank and much more further back, extending far beyond where Field Artillery would reach.

I will send with this a copy of my instructions to Col. Lowe on leaving Fort Henry.[3]

Over Fifty[4] pieces of Light Artillery were captured at Forts Henry & Donelson all of which was ordered shipped to St. Louis, afterwards I understand stopped at Paducah. There has been so much absolute theft however, ~~after property~~ in spite of all my exertions to prevent it, that I cannot say that all reached its destination. Many steamers are commanded in whole or in part by secessionests that there is no certainty of honest shipments being made. I ~~have~~ instructed however that Invoices be sent and receipts required from Steamers to give all the security possible.

I have found that there was much truth in the report that captured stores were carried off from Fort Henry improperly. I will make you a report, probably to-morrow.

> I am Gen. very respectfully
> your obt. svt.
> U. S. GRANT
> Maj. Gen. Com

ALS, DNA, RG 393, Dept. of the Miss., Letters Received. *O.R.*, I, x, part 2,
45–46. On March 18, 1862, USG telegraphed to Maj. Gen. Henry W. Halleck.
"Despatch of 16th just received. Your instructions are being fully carried out.
On my arrival here, last night, I found Sherman and Hulburt at Pittsburg, Wallace
at a landing six miles lower down—same side of river. Gen Smith and McClernand
here—McClernand in camp; balance on transports. I ordered to Pittsburg, Smith's
division, and all unattached regiments   Also ordered the immediate debarkation
of all troops, and return of Steamers to Paducah to report. Several have gone down
today. Some sixty field pieces—six and twelve pounders—have been shipped."
Telegram received, DNA, RG 94, Generals' Papers and Books, Telegrams
Received by Gen. Halleck; *ibid.*, RG 393, USG Hd. Qrs. Correspondence; *ibid.*,
Dept. of the Mo., Telegrams Received; DLC-USG, V, 4, 5, 7, 8, 9, 88.

    1. See telegram to Maj. Gen. Henry W. Halleck, March 15, 1862.
    2. Crump's Landing, Tenn., on the west bank of the Tennessee River,
approximately midway between Savannah and Pittsburg Landing.
    3. See letter to Col. William W. Lowe, March 15, 1862.
    4. "Fifty" written over "sixty."

To Brig. Gen. William T. Sherman

Head Quarters, Dist of West. Tenn.
Savanna, March 18th 1862.

GEN. W. T. SHERMAN
COMMDG U. S. FORCES
PITTSBURG TENN.
GENL:

    In Brigading the new ~~arrival of~~ troops I would advise attach-
ing the 8th Iowa to the 1st Brigade, 2nd Divn, and one Regt. to
each of the 2nd and 3rd Brigades, same Division, Major Gen.
Smith to command. This is advised because the 1st Brigade is
very weak in numbers and one Regt. ~~and one Regt.~~ from each of
the other two was left behind to garrison Posts.

I am, Genl, Very Respectfully
Your Obt. Servant.
U. S. GRANT.
Major Gen. Commdg.

Copies, DLC-USG, V, 1, 2, 3, 86; DNA, RG 393, USG Letters Sent.

To Julia Dent Grant

———

Savanna Tennessee
March 18th 1862

MY DEAR JULIA,

You will see by the above that I am far up South in the State of Ten. When you will hear of another great and important strike I cant tell you but it will be a big lick so far as numbers engaged is concerned. I have no misgivings myself as to the result and you must not feel the slightest alarm.—It is now 3 O'Clock in the morning but as a boat will be going down to-morrow and having just arrived I will have to much to do to write private letters in the morning. We got here about 4 O'Clock in the afternoon and I had necessarily many orders to write.

There is a strong manifestation of Union feeling in this section. Already some 500 have come in voluntarily and enlisted to prevent being drafted on the other side. Many more have come in to get the protection of our army for the same purpose.—With one more great success I do not see how the rebellion is to be sustained. War matters however must be an uninteresting subject to you so I will close on that.—I have been poorly for several weeks but I began to feel better the very moment of arriving where there is so much to do and where it is so important that I should be able to do it.

I will try and have you hear from me often but it will not be possible to communicate as often as heretofore. I'm getting further from home. You are spending a pleasant time in Covington are you not? I should love very much to be there a day or two with you and the children. Does Jess talk of his pa? Kiss all the children for me and give my love to all at home.

Good night dear Julia.

ULYS.

ALS, DLC-USG.

General Orders No. 24

Head Quarters Dist of West Tenn
Savanna March 19th 1862.

GENERAL ORDERS NO 24

Hereafter issues of subsistence stores to the Troops of a Division will be made by the Division Commissary on Consolidated returns presented by each Regimental. Commissary.   Issues to Brigade commissaries are forbidden except in cases of extreme necessity.

Whenever the duties of this Regimental Quarter Master are arduous it is recommended that Regimental commanders detail a suitable commissiond officer to act as commissary.

The troops often suffer by reason of the Regt Quarter-Master being over-worked, obliging him to give up almost entirely the Commissary business to the Commissary Sergeant; who not being a commissioned officer cannot properly perform the duties.

The Division commissaries will see that the Regimental commissaries are attentive to their duties, and that their Department is conducted in a manner to insure the greatest possible comfort and health of the troops: they will particularly see that proper supplies are kept on hand for Hospital use.

Supplies needed in Hospital are frequently not supplied to Regimental Hospital on account of the incapacity or indifference of some of the Regtl commissaries; in such cases it is requested that surgeons make a report of the ~~same~~ case.

While making arraingements for, or during an action commissaries and Quarter-Masters will on no account leave their appropriate duties to engage in the fight, but will remain with their supplies and wagons trains and enforce the presence of those belonging to and detached for these departments. It is highly necessary that all Commanders enforce the observance of this as the labour of these staff Depts. commences when the battle has been fought. All property of the enemy captured in Battle must be properly secured and guarded, for this purpose as soon as the action is over. Brigades Commanders will detail a strong detail under charge of commissioned officers, who will report to the Quarter Master of the Brigade, under whose direction the property will be collected and stored near Division Head Quarters or at some other suitable place that may be designated while it is being collected. Brigade guards will be detailed to prevent pillage, and all commanders will use their utmost endeavor to restrain those under them from the improper appropriation of Captured property:

For one person to take possession for himself, what has been gained by the United Bravery and exertion of all is nothing less than pilfering.

Whenever orders are issued from these Head Quarters Division commanders will make out, and transmit a copy to each of their Brigade commanders, who will publish it to his company at the next parade, or roll call:

Each commander will furnish his staff officers with a copy of all orders that may in any manner interest their Department.

> By Order of Maj Genl U. S. Grant
> Jno A Rawlins
> A. A. Genl.

P. S. all general orders of Division to Brigade & Regimental commanders must be forwarded to these Head Quarters.

Copies, DLC-USG, V, 12, 13, 14, 95; DNA, RG 94, 9th Ill., Letterbook; *ibid.*, 48th Ill., Letterbook; *ibid.*, RG 393, USG General Orders. *O.R.*, I, x, part 2, 49–50.

To Maj. Gen. Henry W. Halleck

By Telegraph from Savannah [*March*] 19, 1. P. M.
                                                via Cairo 20th *1862*

To Maj. Genl. Halleck

Gen Smith received orders to have a gun-boat ply between R. R. bridge and here constantly. He did not deem it prudent however, the gun-boat Dunbar being up Duck Creek and possibly another gun-boat afloat further up. One of the two gun-boats in this river is now below.

Immediate preparations will be made to execute your perfectly feasible order. I will go in person, leaving Genl McClernand in command here.

U. S. GRANT

Maj. Gen. Comdg

Telegram received, DNA, RG 94, Generals' Papers and Books, Telegrams Received by Gen. Halleck; copies, *ibid.*, RG 393, USG Hd. Qrs. Correspondence; *ibid.*, Dept. of the Mo., Telegrams Received; DLC-USG, V, 4, 5, 7, 8, 9, 88. *O.R.*, I, x, part 2, 49. On March 18, 1862, Maj. Gen. Henry W. Halleck telegraphed to USG or the commanding officer, Fort Henry. "Transports in ascending the Tennessee River should in all cases be convoyed by a gun boat. It is reported that enemy has moved from Corinth to cut off our transports below Savanna. If so, Genl Smith should immediately destroy R. R. connexion at Corinth." ALS (telegram sent), DLC-Henry W. Halleck; copies, DLC-USG, V, 4, 5, 7, 8, 9, 88; DNA, RG 94, Generals' Papers and Books, Telegrams Sent in Cipher by Gen. Halleck; *ibid.*, RG 393, USG Hd. Qrs. Correspondence; *ibid.*, Dept. of the Mo., Telegrams Sent. *O.R.*, I, x, part 2, 46. On March 20, Halleck telegraphed to USG. "Your telegram of yesterday just received   I do not fully understand. By all means keep your forces together until you connect with Genl Buell who is now at Columbia & will move on Waynesboro with three divisions. Dont let the enemy draw you into an engagement now. Wait till you are properly reinforced & you receive orders." ALS (telegram sent), DNA, RG 107, Telegrams Collected (Unbound); copies, *ibid.*, RG 94, Generals' Papers and Books, Telegrams Sent in Cipher by Gen. Halleck; *ibid.*, RG 393, USG Hd. Qrs. Correspondence; *ibid.*, Dept. of the Mo., Telegrams Sent; DLC-USG, V, 4, 5, 7, 8, 9, 88. *O.R.*, I, x, part 2, 50–51.

To Capt. Nathaniel H. McLean

Head Quarters, Dist. of W. Tenn

Savanna, March 19th 1862.

CAPT. N. H. MCLEAN

A. A. GEN. DEPT. OF THE MISSISSIPPI,

ST. LOUIS MO.

CAPT.

I have just returned from Pittsburg and Crumps Landing. I find these two positions are the only ones where a landing can be effected on the West bank of the river, as far as I saw, and learn that there is no other point from there to East port, Miss. This of course only applies to the present stage of water.

From information to Gen. Sherman received whilst I was there the enemy cannot be over 20.000 strong at Corinth but haves troops scattered at all stations and important points. Some heavy artillery arrived at Corinth on Monday[1] but the informant saw no signs of fortifications.

Buell seems to be the party most expected by the rebels. They estimate his strength all the way from 20 to 150 thousand.[2]

> I am Capt. very respectfully
> your obt. svt.
> U. S. GRANT
> Maj. Gen.

ALS, DNA, RG 393, Dept. of the Miss., Letters Received. *O.R.*, I, x, part 2, 48–49.

1. March 17, 1862.
2. On March 23, Maj. Gen. Don Carlos Buell informed Maj. Gen. Henry W. Halleck that he expected to lead about 35,000 men to Savannah. *O.R.*, I, x, part 2, 60.

To Brig. Gen. Don Carlos Buell

Head Quarters, Dist of West. Tenn
Savanna, March 19th 1862.

GENL. D. C. BUELL,
COMMDG. ARMY IN THE FIELD.

Feeling a little anxious to learn your whereabouts, and as much as possible of your present movements I send two scouts, Breckenridge and Carson,[1] to you. Any information you will send by them I will be glad to ~~learn~~ receive. I am massing troops at Pittsburg, Tenn. There is every reason to suppose that the Rebels have a large force at Corinth, Miss. and many at other points on the road towards Decatur.

> I am, Gen. Very Respectfully,
> Your Obt Servant.
> U. S. GRANT.
> Major. Gen.

Copies, DLC-USG, V, 1, 2, 3, 86; DNA, RG 393, USG Letters Sent. *O.R.*, I, x, part 2, 47. On March 23, 1862, Brig. Gen. Don Carlos Buell replied to USG. "I received your letter of the 19th this morning. I some days ago directed my advance to open communication with you. My advance is at Columbia. Our progress has been retarded by high water and the absence of bridges, almost every one on the road, however small, having been destroyed by the enemy. I shall be at Columbia myself by the time the bridge there is ready for crossing, probably three or four days yet. The information I get indicates that Johnston is withdrawing the principal part of his force from Decatur and concentrating at Tuscumbia. I find there is still a gunboat here. If needed she can be sent to you, though if you had not immediate use for her it might be well to let her remain until you have. I do not deem it safe to give detailed information in this way in regard to my force, dispositions, &c. I shall soon be able to communicate more fully on that point. Please inform me whether the bridge at Florence has been destroyed." *Ibid.*, p. 58. A register of "Documentary Evidence for Defense," in Buell Papers, TxHR, lists a letter from Buell to USG of March 22 and none for March 23.

1. A newspaper article, written after the death of Irving W. Carson at Shiloh, stated that he was born in Scotland, worked for the Illinois Central Railroad in Chicago in its machine shops and as an engineer, then studied law. He enlisted in Barker's Dragoons, an organization which served from April 19 to Aug. 18, 1861, when the men refused to enlist for three years. Carson then served as a scout for Brig. Gen. Benjamin M. Prentiss, later for USG. According to a letter of Carson, dated March 26, 1862, he traveled for four days and passed through three C. S. A. camps to reach Buell. *Chicago Tribune*, May 4, 1862. See telegram to Maj. Gen. Henry W. Halleck, March 26, 1862.

To Brig. Gen. Lewis Wallace

———

Head Quarters, Dist of West. Tenn.
Savannah, March 19th 1862.

BRIG. GEN. L. WALLACE,
COMMDG 3RD DIVISION
GENL:

Debark all the troops of your Division and dismiss all Steamers, except such as have stores aboard, and those detailed by my order to remain. All Steamers leaving will be required to report at ~~Savanna~~ to Head Quarters at Savanna as they pass.

Very Respectfully,
Your Obt Servant.
U. S. GRANT,
Major Gen. Commdg.

Copies, DLC-USG, V, 1, 2, 3, 86; DNA, RG 393, USG Letters Sent.

To Brig. Gen. Lewis Wallace

———

Head Quarters, Dist of West. Tenn.
Savanna, March 19th 1862.

BRIG. GEN. L. WALLACE
COMMDG 3RD DIVISION
GENL:

Enclosed is a copy of an order taken to day from Steamer Telegraph. By what authority do you send sick of your Division to Evansville, or out of the District at all?

By what authority do you direct Steamers from the course they were ordered to take by higher authority?

I am, Gen. Very Respectfully,
Your Obt. Servant.
U. S. GRANT.
Maj. Gen. Commdg.

Copies, DLC-USG, V, 1, 2, 3, 86; DNA, RG 393, USG Letters Sent. See letter to Brig. Gen. Lewis Wallace, March 21, 1862.

To Capt. Nathaniel H. McLean

Head Quarters, Dist. of W. Ten.
Savanna, March 20th 1862.

Capt. N. H. McLean
A. A. Gen. Dept. of the Mississippi,
St. Louis Mo.
Capt.

Last night at 11 O'Clock dispatch of Maj. Gen. Halleck stating that the enemy would probably attempt to cut off the river navigation[1] was received and immediately replied to to go from Fort Henry by telegraph.

Some time ago I directed Gen. Smith to let one of the gunboats ply between Fort Henry and this place to keep the river open[2] but the Gen. did not think it prudent to spare one at that time. One boat went down yesterday and returned to-day and will go back again this evening.

Owing to the high stage of water there are but few points on the river where light artillery could be taken to annoy our transports.

I will go with the expedition to Corinth in person should no orders received hereafter prevent it. Owing to the limited space where a landing can be effected it will take some days yet to ~~get off.~~ debark the troops now there. I was in hopes of starting on the 22d but now think the 23d or 24th will be as early as I can get off.

There is no enemy on this side of the river much before reaching Florence.—I sent yesterday two scouts to find Gen. Buell.[3] They will probably be back to-morrow.

A deserter from the rebel army just in says that Bethel[4] is deserted and the troops from there gone to Corinth. Some troops at Jackson & Humboldt and in fact small parties all along the

Railroad. He represents the panic as very great among the troops, but few of them wanting to fight.

I will take no risk at Corinth under the instructions I now have. If a battle on anything like equal terms seems to be inevitable I shall find it out in time to make a movement upon some other point of the railroad, or atleast seem to fill the object of the expedition without a battle and thus save the demoralizing effect of a retreat upon the troops.

I am very much in hopes of receiving further instructions by Mail.

> I Am Capt. very respectfully
> your obt. svt.
> U. S. GRANT
> Maj. Gen

ALS, DNA, RG 393, Dept. of the Miss., Letters Received. *O.R.*, I, x, part 2, 51.

1. See telegram to Maj. Gen. Henry W. Halleck, March 19, 1862.
2. See letter to Maj. Gen. Charles F. Smith, March 11, 1862.
3. See letter to Brig. Gen. Don Carlos Buell, March 19, 1862.
4. Bethel, Tenn., about twenty miles northwest of Pittsburg Landing on the Mobile and Ohio Railroad.

To [*Maj. Gen. Charles F. Smith*]

[*March 20, 1862*]

GEN.

Th[e] above is copy of a telegraphic dispatch [ju]st received. As an attack does not appear [to threa]ten us I do not see that this need i[nterfere wi]th Gen. Shermans contemplated move.— Lo[oking] at the map I do not see but that Buell will have to come to this point to cross the river

Instruct Gen. Sherman to fortify himself partially and to make no stand against a superior force shou[l]d he be attacked.

> Very respectfully
> U. S. GRANT
> Maj. Gen

AES, Oglesby Papers, IHi. Written on a copy of a telegram of March 20, 1862, from Maj. Gen. Henry W. Halleck to USG. See telegram to Maj. Gen. Henry W. Halleck, March 19, 1862.

To Maj. Gen. Charles F. Smith

Head Quarters, Dist of West. Tenn.
Savanna, March 20th 1862.

MAJOR GEN. C. F. SMITH
COMMDG. U. S. FORCES,
PITTSBURG, TENN.
GENL:

Hold all the command at Pittsburg subject to marching orders at any time. Troops will march with three days rations in Haversack, and seven in wagons. Each wagon will take five days forage of grain for the teams that draw it, and a forage train will accompany with the same number of days allowance for all other animals. Baggage will be cut down to make the transportation on hand carry the supplies indicated.

Very Respectfully
Your Obt. Servant
U. S. GRANT
Major Genl.

Copies, DLC–USG, V, 1, 2, 3, 86; DNA, RG 393, USG Letters Sent. *O.R.*, I, x, part 2, 52. On March 20, 1862, USG again wrote to Maj. Gen. Charles F. Smith. "You will assign the 16th Wisconsin, Col. B. Allen for duty" Copies, DLC–USG, V, 2, 86; DNA, RG 393, USG Letters Sent.

To Brig. Gen. John A. McClernand

——————

Head Quarters, Dist of West. Tenn.
Savanna, March 20th 1862.

GEN. J. A. MCCLERNAND.
COMMDG 1ST DIVISION
GENL:

Make immediate preperations for shipping two Brigades of your Command to Pittsburg, Tenn. The other Brigade will follow as soon as sufficient new ~~arrivals of~~ troops for a proper garrison arrive here will admit of their leaving, probably quite as soon as they could be landed, was every thing ready now.

I am, Gen, Very Respectfully,
Your Obt. Servant.
U. S. GRANT.
Maj Gen. Commdg.

Copies, DLC-USG, V, 1, 2, 3, 86; DNA, RG 393, USG Letters Sent. *O.R.*, I, x, part 2, 52. On March 21, 1862, Brig. Gen. John A. McClernand wrote to USG. "Col. Ross has nearly completed the embarkation of his entire command and will hasten forward to the point of debarkation. As fast as the remainder of my division shall have been embarked, according to your instruction by Lt. Freeman, it will be ~~hastened~~ sent forward." ADfS, McClernand Papers, IHi. On the same day, McClernand again wrote to USG. "I shall be delayed beyond 9 o'clock A. M. in embarking my troops, in consequence of the want of necessary transports. There being only two now here (8. o'clock) and one of them a small boat: upon the arrival of others of which I am to be advised by Commodore Graham, I will immediately commence embarking. In the mean time in view of the weather, I will avoid striking tents—" Copy, *ibid*. Also on March 21, Capt. John A. Rawlins wrote to McClernand. "Maj Genl U. S. Grants directs me to informed you that but one steamer can convienently unload or debark troops at the Pittsburgh Landing, and that as soon as a boat is loaded here, you will order her to proceed to place of Destination so as to facilitate your move ment" LS, *ibid*.

On March 20, Capt. William R. Rowley wrote to Brig. Gen. Lewis Wallace. "You will hold the Troops under your command in readiness to march at a moments notice. (not probably, however before day after tomorrow). They will provide themselves with three days rations in Haversacks, and seven in wagons. All tents and personal baggage, except what the men can carry, will be left behind. No portion of rations drawn for this purpose, are to be consumed before marching. In the mean time let the work of debarkation go on as rapidly as possible." Copies, DLC-USG, V, 1, 2, 3, 86; DNA, RG 393, USG Letters Sent. *O.R.*, I, x, part 2, 52–53.

To Maj. Gen. Henry W. Halleck

Head Quarters Dist of W Ten
Savanna March 21st 1862

MAJ GEN H W HALLECK
DEPT OF THE MISSISSIPPI
ST LOUIS MO
GEN

I have just returned from Pittsburg. The roads back are next to impassible for artillery or baggage wagons. I have certain information that thirteen trains of cars arrived at Corinth on the 19th with twenty cars to each train, all loaded with troops. This would indicate that Corinth cannot be taken without a general engagement, which from your instructions is to be avoided. This taken in connection with the impassible state of the roads, has determined me not to move for the present without further orders

The temper of the rebel troops is such that there is but little doubt but that Corinth will fall much more easily than Donelson did, when we do move. All accounts agree in saying that the great mass of the Rank and file are heartily tired. One thing I learn however is against us. Most of the impressed troops from this state are being sent to the Sea coast and older soldiers brought from there.

I do not think as yet any steps are being taken to interfere with the navigation of the river. Bands of Cavalry are prowling all over West Ten, Collecting men who have been drafted into the service and such supplies as they can get. Some nine or ten men made their escape from the Cars at Bethel and came in here yesterday. From them I learn there are about 400 men at Union City; Two Regiments of infantry and probably some Cavalry at Humbolt; a force not estimated at Jackson, and small forces at various points on the road. Paris & Bethel are deserted. They think the force at Union City is anxious to be captured. I have just learned to day that your dispatches to me, after the taking of Fort Donelson, reached Fort Henry, some of them at least, but were never sent to me. What has become of the operator then at Henry, I dont know. At present a soldier detailed from the ranks, is filling the station[1]   I have received no Mail matter from below for several days though boats are arriving constantly. My returns for the 20th will be ready to mail to morrow

> I am Gen very respectfully
> Your Obt Servt
> U S GRANT
> Maj Gen

Copies, DLC-USG, V, 4, 5, 7, 8, 9, 88; DNA, RG 393, USG Hd. Qrs. Correspondence. *O.R.*, I, x, part 2, 55–56. On March 21, 1862, USG telegraphed the substance of the first paragraph to Maj. Gen. Henry W. Halleck. "It will be impossible to move now with any celerity, taking artillery. Corinth cannot be taken without meeting a large force—say thirty thousand. A general engagement would be inevitable, therefore I will wait a few days for further information. I have just returned from Pittsburg." Telegram received, DNA, RG 94, Generals' Papers and Books, Telegrams Received by Gen. Halleck; copies, *ibid.*, RG 393, USG Hd. Qrs. Correspondence; *ibid.*, Dept. of the Mo., Telegrams Received; DLC-USG, V, 4, 5, 7, 8, 9, 88. *O.R.*, I, x, part 2, 55.

1. On March 11, Capt. John A. Rawlins wrote to the post q. m., Fort Henry. "You will furnish Horace Stokes, of the 17th Ills. Vols. (now acting telegrapher at this place) with such clothing as necessary for his use. You will take his receipt for the same and notify the Commander of his Regiment." Copies, DLC-USG, V, 2, 86; DNA, RG 393, USG Letters Sent.

To Brig. Gen. Lewis Wallace

> Head Quarters, Dist of West. Tenn.
> Savanna, March 21st 1862.

BRIG. GEN. L. WALLACE,
COMMDG 3RD DIVISION
GENL:

Your attention is called to the fact that my note of the 19th inst asking for information, as to your authority for sending the sick of your command out of this Dist. has received, no answer. Yesterday more sick of your command were ordered to Cincinnatti by Col. Stedman,[1] with your apparent knowledge, a Surgeon having been sent to attend them. An explanation is required.

I am, Genl. Very Respectfully,
Your Obt. Servant.
U. S. GRANT.
Major Genl.

Copies, DLC-USG, V, 1, 2, 3, 86; DNA, RG 393, USG Letters Sent. See letter to Brig. Gen. Lewis Wallace, March 19, 1862. On March 21, 1862, Brig. Gen. Lewis Wallace, Crump's Landing, wrote to Capt. John A. Rawlins. "This morning I received a note from Gen. Grant, dated Mar. 19th 1862, enclosing a copy of an order of mine, directed to Capt. Godman, of the Steamer 'Telegraph,' and instructing him to 'Fire up, and proceed with his boat to Evansville, Ind., as fast as possible, stopping at no intermediate point;' and to 'land the sick there, and return to Paducah for orders.' In his note the Gen. asks me—'By what authority do you send sick of your division to Evansville or out of the District at all? By what authority do you direct steamers from the course they were ordered to take by higher authority?' I beg you will submit to the General the following explanation. I. Special Order No. 27 directs the troops of the 3rd Division not yet debarked and at Pittsburg to return to the lower landing and report to Genl. Wallace, and concludes by saying Genl. Wallace 'will cause their debarkation and *discharge of the steamers with as little delay as possible.'* The General will understand, at a glance, how easily the language of that order might be construed as authority for my discharge of the Steamer Telegraph. A mistake growing out of it I am satisfied he will pardon. II. In addition to that order I will ~~add~~ say, in justification, that the sending the Steamer to Evansville was, in my opinion, a military necessity. It had on board about two hundred and sixty sick men from my command, many of them in a dying condition. On Monday last, I think, in charge of my Staff officer, Dr. Fry, I sent the boat to Savannah to land the sick there for lodgement in the Hospital. They were sent back to me the same day. On Tuesday I again sent ~~them~~ Telegraph ~~for~~ to Savannah for the same purpose. Again the crowd of suffering men were sent back to me, one of them having died while the boat was at the town. Upon the return of the Steamer I boarded her, and have no hesitation in saying that I never saw such a scene of disease and misery. *Believing* that, under Order No. 27, I could discharge the Telegraph; that, from the fact of twice sending her sick back to me, there were no Hospital accomodations at Savannah; and *knowing* that I had none here, not even medicines, not even lumber to make coffins for the dead; that, in one instance, the planking of a berth in a steamboat state-room was taken and used for burial purpose; I supposed the intention of the medical authorities was to leave me to my own judgment to do the best I could. Under the circumstances, I never for a moment doubted that the General, when he came to be informed of the facts, would, as he has done, justify my proceeding. It may be further said, that the dying condition of so many soldiers on board the Steamer, would not allow time for a correspondence with Head Quarters on the subject. It is but an honest expression of opinion on my part when I say, I thought the General's character for tender solicitude for his sick soldiers would not only sustain me in my action in the premises, but even gain me his hearty commendation. I knew his humanity could be depended on; and it makes me inexpressably glad to know I was not mistaken. In conclusion, Captain, pardon me for observing, in the way of assurance, that you need not fear or expect that I will at any time march my Division without orders. . . . P. S. Herewith I append report of Dr. Fry. I should have added to the above that I sent the sick to *Evansville* because, as I had been informed, the hospitals at Paducah, Mound city, and Cairo, were already crowded. A letter, addressed by me to the Mayor of Evansville, accompanied the boat, earnestly asking him and his citizens to receive and take care of the unfortunate sufferers." ALS, DNA, RG 393, District of West Tenn., Letters Received. Wallace enclosed a letter of March 21 of Surgeon Thomas W. Fry explaining that sick troops had been sent to Evansville because of a shortage of doctors and hospital facilities at Crump's Landing. ALS, *ibid.* On March 21, Wallace wrote to his wife. "The sick are legionary—it is truly awful to read the morning reports. Very likely I shall have trouble for presuming to send to Evansville a boatload of diseased and dying men, who had been twice sent back on my hands, when I had no places to shelter them, but few Doctors to tend them, and not enough plank to make coffins for them when dead. In fact, for one poor soldier in the Eleventh Regiment the lumber in a steamboat berth was taken for coffin-material. The General commanding (Grant,) this morning demands by what authority I presumed to send the poor fellows out of the District. It will all come right however He will hardly make issue with me in that business." Copy, Wallace Papers, InHi.

1. Samuel H. Steedman, appointed col., 68th Ohio, on Nov. 29, 1861, was mustered out on July 5, 1862.

To Col. Philip B. Fouke

———

Savannah March 21st 1862

COL. P. B. FOUKE
FT. DONELSON TENN.

Has the force from Clarksville yet moved? Are there still boats up the Cumberland to bring them?

Make your requisitions for forage and rations on Paducah. Send reports direct to St. Louis, but send copies here

U. S. GRANT
Maj Genl. Com'd'g

Copies, DLC-USG, V, 1, 2, 3, 88; DNA, RG 393, USG Letters Sent. On March 23, 1862, Col. Philip B. Fouke telegraphed to USG. "Captured property nearly all shipped from Clarksville—I have two (2) large Boats up there to take the Troops—I have been there and given my personal attention They ought to leave there today plenty of Boats up the Cumberland how many Days rations would you advise for this Post" Telegram received, *ibid.*, Dept. of the Mo., Telegrams Received. On the same day, Col. Crafts J. Wright, Clarksville, tele-graphed to USG. "Detained by new discoveries of uncured Bacon valued at one hundred thousand (100000) Dollars to be shipped at once to Cincinnati to be cured and also other stores are found daily   shall have all now on hand shipped by Monday Evening and be ready—should like to have permission to march the strong men over the country to the Tenn River via Charlotte or via Rail Road track and ship the Baggage & feeble and send my Boat around to meet us—believe we would disperse enimies and find Property" Telegram received, *ibid.*

On March 25, USG wrote to Fouke. "Draw twenty days rations always, and never allow yourself to get below ten days on hand." Copies, DLC-USG, V, 1, 2, 3, 86; DNA, RG 393, USG Letters Sent. On the same day, Capt. John A. Rawlins wrote to Fouke. "No return of the forces of your command having been received at these Head Quarters, since the Genls. departure from Fort. Henry, I am instructed by him to say to you that you will immediately make out and send to these Head Quarters a return of the forces under your command, giving the name and strength of each regiment, detachment or Corps; and that the same be forwarded daily hereafter." Copies, *ibid.*

To Maj. Gen. Henry W. Halleck

By Telegraph from Savanna [*March*] 22 1862

To Maj Genl Halleck

The acting medical director reports that medical supplies of every description are ou[t.]   a sufficient quantity for ten thou-sand sick shou[ld] be sent—alternate day[s] of rain and sun-shine pleasant & very cold weather is telling unfav[orably] upon the health of this command—Requisitions have been made but not responded to—Can two hospital boa[ts] be sent here

U. S. Grant
Maj Genl

Telegram received, DNA, RG 94, Generals' Papers and Books, Telegrams Received by Gen. Halleck; copies, *ibid.*, RG 393, USG Hd. Qrs. Correspondence; *ibid.*, Dept. of the Mo., Telegrams Received; DLC-USG, V, 4, 5, 7, 8, 88. *O.R.*, I, x, part 2, 57. On March 24, 1862, Maj. Gen. Henry W. Halleck wrote to USG. "Your telegram of 22d in relation to medical stores was referred to Medical Director who replies that your 'acting Medical Director' is not a commissioned officer & that such requisitions could not be filled. If you have appointed a citizen to such a position you will immediately discharge him, and have your requisitions hereafter made by a proper officer. The Medical officer at Cairo is now forwarding the proper supplies up the Tenn. I call your attention to gross irregularities in your district in regard to the disposition of the sick & wounded. A telegram from New Albany to day says that 200 sick & wounded of Genl Wallace's division had just been landed in that place & that there were no hospital arrangements there. By whose order were these sent to New Albany? I ordered them to be sent to Cincinnati, where preparations were made to receive them. Again, large numbers of sick & wounded, which were ordered to be sent to Cincinnati, were sent to St Louis, where the hospitals are full to overflowing & no room for the sick & wounded from Curtis army. It is impossible for me to have proper provisions made for the sick and wounded where no regard is paid to my orders, and where each one assumes to act upon his own authority. Again colonels of regiments in your command have been giving furloughs on surgeons certificates for 60 & 90 days, and in many cases to men who are not sick at all! Of 180 who arrived here a few days ago, a medical board decided that more than three quarters were fit for duty & should be returned to their regiments. There seems to be collusion between the officers & men to give sick leaves to well & healthy men who wish to visit their homes. This should be immediately stopped, & furloughs should be given only by yourself & after a proper examination by a trustworthy Medical officer. If this abuse of the furlough system [is] not promptly checked, half of the army will be on furlough." ALS, DNA, RG 94, Generals' Papers and Books, Letters Sent by Gen. Halleck (Press). *O.R.*, I, x, part 2, 63.

On March 22, Capt. John A. Rawlins issued Special Orders No. 32. "Surgeon J. H. Brinton will proceed to St Louis Mo without delay and procure through the Medical Director & Purveyor of the Department the necessary Medical stores and supplies for the growing wants of this District." Copies, DLC-USG, V, 15, 16, 82, 87, 89; DNA, RG 393, USG Special Orders. See *Personal Memoirs of John H. Brinton* (New York, 1914), pp. 153–55.

To Capt. Nathaniel H. McLean

Head Quarters Dist of West Tenn
Savanna March 22d 1862.

CAPT N. H MCLEAN
ASST ADJT GENL
ST LOUIS MO.

Enclosed find requisitions for Printed Blanks, upon the adjt Genl of the Army, for the use of this District, which please foward.

The Muster and pay rolls, certificate of disability, and to enable discharge soldiers to draw pay. Division returns and descriptuve rolls are greatly needed, if they can be supplied from St Louis, I would like that they ~~would~~ be sent immediately.

I am Sir
Very Respectfully
Your obt Servt
U. S. GRANT
Maj. Gen.

LS, DNA, RG 393, Dept. of the Miss., Letters Received.

To Julia Dent Grant

———

Savanna, March 22d 1862

DEAR JULIA,

Have you found out yet where Savanna is? Well I am away down in Dixie myself and Staff living with a very nice family who, for a wonder, have been Union through all the troubles.[1] It is not so much of a wonder here however as it would be in many other parts of the state. This county is largely Union and quite a number of citizens are coming in and enlisting in our army.

The weather continues wet and cold up here. The river is over all the farms in the Tennessee valley and roads are so bad that Artillery can not be moved until we have a few days of dry weather.—The amount of sickness is so great among the troops that I am anxious to move for the health of the men.

Soon I think the public may look for important news. If we are successfull all along the line, I mean McClellan in the East, Buell & myself in the middle and Pope, Steel[2] & Curtis in the West *secesh* will be about dead. We will be successful. Curtis may have a hard time of it but I think he will come out right.

I have had the longest siege of being unwell that I ever had in my life. I ~~have~~ now ~~got a~~ have a fine appetite and think there is but little els to do but to get strong.—It is about midnight and Dr. Brinton, who will take this letter to Cairo, is probably seting up waiting.[3]

Has Jess made up with his aunt Mary? How is Buck and all the children? I have not heard from you for about ten days and when you do write you say but little about the children. Are they going to school? Did you get a letter from me with a key in it? and the box by express that it fits?[4]

I will send you a couple of hundred dollars at the end of this month. We ought now to save $800 per month after supporting both of us. Give my love to all at home and kiss the children for me. I shall always regret that I did not take Fred. with me to Fort Donelson. Kisses for yourself dear Julia.

Good night

ULYS.

ALS, DLC-USG.

1. USG lived with William H. Cherry, a prosperous merchant and farmer of Savannah, Tenn., and a strong Unionist. Bruce Catton, *Grant Moves South* (Boston and Toronto, 1960), p. 222; "Gen. Grant at Shiloh," *Confederate Veteran*, I, 2 (Feb., 1893), 44–45; "Mrs. Annie Irwin Cherry," *ibid.*, IX, 1 (Jan., 1901), 33; William H. Cherry to Andrew Johnson, Feb. 23, 1861, March 27, April 23, May 2, 1862. ALS, DLC-Andrew Johnson. On April 3, 1862, Capt. John A. Rawlins issued Special Orders No. 44. "The District Quartermaster will vacate the Blacksmith Shop belonging to Mr. Wm. H Cherry, removing all Government property, and occupy the shop owned by Mr. J. J. Williams, now in possession of Post Quartermaster permitting Post Quarter Master, if there is sufficient room, to occupy and use so much of said last mentioned shop as will be necessary for his Department." Copies, DLC-USG, V, 89; DNA, RG 393, USG Special Orders. On April 6, Capt. William S. Hillyer issued orders. "The residence of Mrs. Nancy Irwin in Savanna, will not be taken for Hospital or any other purpose and the family will not be in any manner disturbed. The same order will be observed with reference to the Residence of Mr. W. H. Cherry." Copies, DLC-USG, V, 2, 86; DNA, RG 393, USG Letters Sent. See letter to Capt. Nathaniel H. McLean, March 30, 1862.

2. Frederick Steele of N. Y., USMA 1843, had served in the U. S. Army continuously, ranking as capt. when the Civil War began. On Jan. 29, 1862, he was appointed brig. gen. and on March 1 assigned to command troops in southeastern Mo. *O.R.*, I, viii, 578. Steele had been USG's classmate at USMA, a guest at his wedding, and his host at Benicia, Calif., in 1852. *PUSG*, I, 257.

3. See telegram to Maj. Gen. Henry W. Halleck, March 22, 1862.

4. See letter to Julia Dent Grant, March 15, 1862.

To Elihu B. Washburne

Savanna, Tennessee
March 22d 1862.

Hon. E. B. Washburn
Washington D. C.
Dear Sir:

I have received two or three letters from you which I have not answered, because, at the time they were received I was unwell, and busy, and because at the time they were received either your brother[1] or Rowley were about writing. I am now getting nearly well ~~again~~ and ready for any immergency that ~~that~~ may arise. A severe contest may be looked for in this quarter before many weeks, but of the result feel no alarm.

There are some things which I wish to say to you in my own vindication, not that I care one straw for what is said, individually, but because you have taken so much interest in my wellfare that I think you entitled to all facts connected with my acts.

I see by the papers that I am charged with giving up a certain number of slaves captured at Fort Donelson!

My published order on the occation shows that citizens were not permitted to pass through our camps to look for their slaves.[2] There were some six or seven negroes at Donelson who represented that they had been brought from Ky. to work for officers, and had been kept a number of months without receiving pay. They expressed great anxiety to get back to their families and protested that they were free men. These I let go and none others.—I have studiously tried to prevent the running off of negroes from all outside places as I have tried to prevent all other marauding and plundering.

So long as I hold a commission in the Army I have no views of my own to carry out. Whatever may be the orders of my superiors, and law, I will execute. No man can be efficient as a commander who sets his own notions above law and those whom he is sworn to obey. When Congress enacts anything to[o] odious for me to execute I will resign.

I see the credit of attacking the enemy by the way of the Tennessee and Cumberland is variously attributed! It is little to talk about it being the great wisdom of any Gen. that first brought forth this plan of attack.

Our gunboats were running up the Ten. and Cumberland rivers all fall and winter watching the progress of the rebels on these works. Gen. Halleck no doubt thought of this route long ago and I am shure I did.[3] As to how the battles should be fought both McClellan and Halleck are too much of soldiers to suppose that they can plan how that should be done at a distance. This would presuppose that the enemy would make just the moves laid down for them. It would be a game of Chess the right hand against the left determining before hand that the right should win.

The job being an important one neither of the above Generals would have entrusted it to an officer that who they had not confidance in. So far I was highly complimented by both.

After geting into Donelson Gen. Halleck did not hear from me for near two weeks. It was about the same time before I heard from him. I was writing every day and sometimes as often as three times a day. Reported every move and change, the condition of my troops &c. Not getting these Gen. Halleck very justly become dissatisfied and was, as I have since learned, sending me d[a]ily repremands. Not receiving them they lost their sting. When one did reach me not seeing the justice of it I retorted and asked to be relieved. Three telegrams passed in this way each time ending by my requesting to be relieved. All is now understood however and I feel assured that Gen. Halleck is fully satisfied. In fact he wrote me a letter saying that I could not be relieved and otherwise quite complimentary. I will not tire you with a longer letter but assure you again that you shall not be disappointed in me if it is in my power to prevent it.

> I am sir, very respectfully
> your obt. svt.
> U. S. GRANT

ALS, IHi.

1. Col. Cadwallader C. Washburn.
2. See General Orders No. 14, Feb. 26, 1862.
3. Much discussion of who deserves the credit for originating the Tennessee River campaign is summarized in Bruce Catton, *Grant Moves South* (Boston and Toronto, 1960), pp. 123–26; Kenneth P. Williams, *Lincoln Finds a General* (New York, 1949–1959), III, 448–56. Both authors believe that the idea of attacking on the Tennessee River had been discussed by many people for several months before the campaign began and that USG's statement is appropriate.

To Maj. Gen. Henry W. Halleck

By Telegraph from Savannah [*March 23*] *1862*

To Maj Gen Halleck

Your dispatch of twentieth Just recv'd   troops from here except one regt all sent to Pittsburg   no movement making except to advance Gen Shermans division to prevent rebels from fortifying Pea Ridge.[1]   weathe[r] here cold with some snow

U. S. Grant
Maj Genl

Telegram received (misdated March 25, 1862), DNA, RG 94, Generals' Papers and Books, Telegrams Received by Gen. Halleck; copies, *ibid.*, RG 393, Dept. of the Mo., Telegrams Received; (misdated March 22), *ibid.*, USG Hd. Qrs. Correspondence; DLC-USG, V, 4, 5, 7. *O.R.*, I, x, part 2, 57. Copies (dated March 23), DLC-USG, V, 9, 88. See telegram to Maj. Gen. Henry W. Halleck, March 19, 1862.

1. Pea Ridge, or Monterey, Tenn., about ten miles southwest of Pittsburg Landing.

To Maj. Gen. Charles F. Smith

———

Head Quarters, Dist of West. Tenn.
Savannah, March 23rd 1862.

Major Gen. C. F. Smith
Commdg. U. S. Forces,
Pittsburg, Tenn.
Genl:

Carry out your idea of occupying and partially fortifying Pea Ridge. I do not hear one word from St Louis. I am clearly of the opinion that the enemy are gathering strength at Corinth quite as rapidly as we are here, and the sooner we attack, the easier will be the task of taking the place. If Ruggles[1] is in command it would assuredly be a good time to attack. I have made no change yet in the command, so soon as sufficient troops arrive to form another Brigade, I will do so and assign Artillery and Cavalry to Divisions and leave them subject to the control of Division Commanders.

I am, Gen, Very Respectfully,
Your Obt Servant.
U. S. Grant.
Major Genl. Commdg.

Copies, DLC-USG, V, 1, 2, 3, 86; DNA, RG 393, USG Letters Sent. *O.R.*, I, x, part 2, 62. On March 23, 1862, Maj. Gen. Charles F. Smith wrote to Capt. John A. Rawlins. "Please say to the General that I have directed Brigr. Genl. *Sherman*, whose brigade is in the advance, to make a reconnaissance in strong force about Pea Ridge. He will move at daylight tomorrow. By ~~report~~ rumor the enemy proposes to fortify this ridge: I will prevent this if possible. I think it might be advisable for us to hold and fortify (slightly) for the present this ridge. The proper point is ~~prop~~ probably 12 to 13 miles off. I perceive by a quotation from a Memphis paper in the St. Louis Republican of the 17th that *Bragg* is at Memphis and Brigr. Genl. *Dan.l Ruggles* is in command at Corinth. The latter is a weak vessel." ALS, DNA, RG 393, District of West Tenn., Letters Received.

1. Daniel Ruggles of Mass., USMA 1833, served in the U. S. Army until his resignation as bvt. lt. col. on May 7, 1861, although his last two years were on sick leave of absence. His decision to join the C. S. A. may have been based on long residence in Tex. and the fact that his wife was from Va. On Aug. 9, he was

confirmed as C. S. A. brig. gen. and was soon sent to New Orleans. On Feb. 20, 1862, Ruggles assumed command of forces based at Corinth guarding the Memphis and Charleston Railroad.

To Julia Dent Grant

Savanna, March 23d/62

DEAR JULIA,

Two letters from you are just received. One of them a business letter and the other not. You do not say a word about the $700 00 I sent you since you left Cairo. I see plainly from your letter that it will be impossible for you to stay in Covington. Such unmittigated meanness as is shown by the girls makes me ashamed of them. You may go to Columbus and board or to Galena and keep house. It will be impossible for you to join me. It will be but a short time before I shall be in the tented field, *without a tent*, and after the enemy.

What the papers say about relieving me is all a falshood. For some reason to me entirely inexplicable Gen. Halleck did not hear from me for about two weeks after the fall of Donelson, nor did I hear from him for about the same time. I was writing daily and sometimes two or three times a day and the Gen. doing the same. At last a repremand come for not reporting as I had been frequently ordered.

I replied sharply that that was the first order I had but to relieve me. Gen. Halleck declined though he said my course had caused him to be repremanded from Washington. As I had been reporting daily I stated so and again asked to be relieved, and so again for the third time. All was understood however afterwards and though I say it myself I believe that I am the very last man in the Dept. Gen. Halleck would want to see taken out of it. Through some misrepresentations of ~~from~~ jealous and disappointed persons, not belonging with my Army, false rumors were set afloat about what was done with captured property. I done all in my power to prevent any of it being carried off. I had sentinels placed to prevent it being carried aboard of boats, and send persons aboard of boats leaving to search and bring off all captured property they could find. This maddened the rascals engaged in the business and as much escaped my vigilence they have no doubt given currency to reports prejudicial to me. I am so consious of having done all things right myself that I borrow no trouble from the lies published. I say I dont care for what the papers say but I do. It annoys me very much when I see such barefaced falshoods published and then it distresses you.

I want to whip these rebels once more in a big fight and see what will then be said. I suppose such a result would make me a host of enemies.

I wrote to you last night and Capt. Lagow wrote the night before. Some day a big lot of letters will be turning up as I write from two to four letters a week.

If you go to Columbus to spend the summer put the children to school at once. I am sorry you cannot stay in Covington pleasantly for it is such a good place for the children. But it is too mortifying to me to hear of my sisters complaining about the amount paid for the board of their brothers children. If I should name the subject of board for one of them I could not raise my head again. How much better it would appear if they should never say a word on the subject. It would cost nothing either for them to hold their tongues.

You had better leave at once for some place. Tell them I direct it and the reason why.

Kiss the children for me and accept the same for yourself. It looks now as if the first place you could join me would be far down in Dixie.

ULYS.

ALS, DLC-USG.

To Maj. Gen. Henry W. Halleck

———

Savanna, March 24th 1862

MAJ. GEN. H. W. HALLECK
COMD.G DEPT. OF THE MISS.
ST. LOUIS MO.
GEN.

Your letter enclosing correspondence between yourself and Adj. Gen. Thomas is just received.[1] In regard to the plundering at Fort Donelson it is very much overestimated by disappointed persons who failed in getting off the trophies they had gathered. My orders of the time show ~~great~~ that I ~~doneid~~ did all in my power to prevent marauding. To execute these orders I kept a company on duty searching boats about leaving and to bring off all captured property found.

My great difficulty was with the rush of citizens, particularly the sanitary committee, who infested Donelson after its fall. They thought it an exceedingly hard case that patriotic gentleman like themselvs, who had gone to tender their services to the sick and wounded could not carry off what they pleased. Most of the wounded had reached hospitals before these gentlemen left Cairo. One of these men, a Dr. Fowler of Springfield,[2] swore vengeance against me for this very act, of preventing trophies being carried off. How many more ~~doneid~~ did the same thing I cant tell.

My going to Nashville I did not regard particularly as going beyond my District. After the fall of Donelson from information I had I knew that the way was clear to Clarkesville & Nashville. Accordingly I wrote to you, directed to your Chief of Staff, as was all my correspondence from the time of leaving Fort Henry until I learned you were not hearing from me, that by Friday following the fall of Donelson I should occupy Clarkesville, and by Saturday week following should be in Nashville if not prevented by orders from Hd Qrs. of the Dept. During all this time not one word was received from you and I accordingly occupied

Clarkesville on the day indicated and two days after the time I was to occupy Nashville Gen. Nelson reported to me with a Division of Buell's Army. They being already on transports and knowing that Buells Column should have arrived opposite Nashville the day before, and having no use for these troops myself I ordered them immediately to Nashville.

It is perfectly plain to me that designing enemies are the cause of all the publications that appear and are the means of getting extracts sent to you. It is also a little remarkable that the Adj. Gen. should learn of my presence in Nashville before it was known in St. Louis where I reported that I was going before starting.

I do not feel that I have neglected a single duty. My reports to you have averaged at least one a day since leaving Cairo and there has been scarsely a single day that I have not either written or telegraphed to Hd Qrs.

I most fully appreciate your justness Gen. in the part you have taken and you may rely upon me to the utmost of my capacity for carrying out all your orders.

> I Am Gen. very respectfully
> your obt. svt.
> U. S. GRANT
> Maj. Gen. Com

ALS, DNA, RG 393, Dept. of the Miss., Letters Received. *O.R.,* I, x, part 2, 62–63.

1. On March 17, 1862, Maj. Gen. Henry W. Halleck wrote to USG. "I enclose you a letter and a slip from a newspaper, as a sample of what I am almost daily receiving in relation to the general plunder of public property which, it is alleged, took place at Fort Donelson. Representations of these robberies by our soldiers & the general neglect of the officers, were made to Washington, & I have been called on time & again to have the officers & men arrested & punished. Of course I could act only through you, and as you had full power to order courts, I deemed it *your* duty to bring these plunderers to justice. Officers of companies, regiments brigades & divisions should be held strictly accountable for the conduct of their men, and where they fail to prevent such misconduct, they should be arrested & tried for neglect of duty. In justice to myself as well as to you, I enclose herewith copies of a letter received from the Adjt Genl in relation to this matter, and of my answer. I have been directed that hereafter where any plunder of this kind occurs to arrest every officer in command of the troops engaged in it." ALS,

DNA, RG 94, Generals' Papers and Books, Letters Sent by Gen. Halleck (Press). *O.R.*, I, x, part 2, 42. On March 10, Brig. Gen. Lorenzo Thomas wrote to Halleck. "It has been reported that soon after the battle at Fort Donelson, Brigadier General Grant left his command without leave. By direction of the President, the Secretary of War desires you to ascertain and report—Whether General Grant left his command at any time without proper authority, and if so, for how long? Whether he has made to you proper reports and returns of his force? Whether he has committed any acts which were unauthorized, or not in accordance with military subordination, or propriety? and if so, what?" LS, DNA, RG 94, Generals' Papers and Books, Ulysses S. Grant. *O.R.*, I, vii, 683. On March 15, Halleck replied to Thomas. "In accordance with your instructions of the 10th inst. I report that Genl Grant and several officers of high rank in his command, immediately after the battle of Fort Donelson, went to Nashville without my authority or knowledge. I am satisfied, however, from investigation that Genl Grant did this from good intentions and from a desire to subserve the public interests. Not being advised of Genl Buell's movements, and learning that Genl B. had ordered Smith's Division of his (Grants) command to Nashville, he deemed it his duty to go there in person. During the absence of Genl Grant and a part of his General officers, numerous irregularities are said to have occurred at Fort Donelson. These were in violation of the orders issued by Genl Grant before his departure, and probably, under the circumstances, were unavoidable. Genl Grant has made the proper explanations and has been directed to resume his command in the field. As he acted from a praise-worthy, although mistaken zeal, for the public service, in going to Nashville & leaving his command, I respectfully recommend that no further notice be taken of it. There never has been any want of military subordination on the part of Genl Grant, and his failure to make returns of his forces has been explained as resulting partly from the failure of col.s of regiments to report to him on their arrival, and partly from an interruption of telegraphic communication. All these irregularities have now been remedied." ALS, DLC-Edwin M. Stanton. *O.R.*, I, vii, 683–84.

2. Probably Dr. Edwin S. Fowler, born in Belleville, Pa., in 1828, who graduated from medical school in 1851, and in 1855 began to practice medicine in Springfield, Ill. *The Biographical Encyclopaedia of Illinois of the Nineteenth Century* (Philadelphia, 1875), p. 333.

To Maj. Melancthon Smith

———

Head Quarters, Dist. of W. Ten.
Savanna, March 24th 1862

MAJ. M. SMITH
COMD.G EXPEDITION,
MAJ.

You will proceed with the force under your command to Nichol's landing two miles back of which it is understood that a large quantity of Govt. (Southeren Confederacy) bacon is stored. You will get it and return.

Nichol's Landing is ten miles below Clifton.[1] Mr. H. Gibbs of Clifton will accompany you to that place and furnish a guide there who will show you where the bacon is.

You will avoid all delay but remain until your expedition has completed the object for which it is sent.

Private property is on no account to be molested nor citizens annoyed. The troops under your command should be impressed with the idea that the neighborhood where they are going is almost entirely Union. It was a citizen of the country, or rather a deligation of citizens, who gave the information of the bacon being where it is, and of of its ownership.

No large bodies of troops are supposed to be near where you are going but small bodies of Cavalry are known to be there. You will therefore keep your men from stragling and at all times keep a guard at the boat to prevent accident there.

You are particularly cautioned against engaging an enemy of your own, or superior, force. You are not going to fight the enemy but for a different object, where nothing could be gained by a small victory which would cost us a single man. Should the enemy appear therefore in sufficient force to make a stand against your weak numbers you will return and a larger number of men will be sent.

very respectfully
your obt. svt.
U. S. GRANT
Maj. Gen Com

ALS, St. Mary's of the Barrens Library, St. Mary's Seminary, Perryville, Mo. *O.R.*, I, x, part 2, 63–64. Melancthon Smith, born at Rochester, N. Y., in 1828, settled at Rockford, Ill., in 1854 as a merchant. He soon turned to law and was postmaster at Rockford at the time he raised a co. for the 45th Ill. He was appointed maj., 45th Ill., on Oct. 31, 1861. On March 24, 1862, Capt. John A. Rawlins wrote to Smith. "You will have for the Infantry and Cavalry of your command four days rations, except the bacon." Copies, DLC-USG, V, 2, 86; DNA, RG 393, USG Letters Sent. On the same day, Rawlins wrote to Capt. William W. Leland. "You will furnish Major Smith with four days rations, with the exception of Bacon, for two companies of Infantry, and one Company of Cavalry without any delay or excuse." Copies, DLC-USG, V, 1, 2, 86; DNA, RG 393, USG Letters Sent. Also on the same day, Rawlins wrote to George W. Graham. "Will please have a large sized steamer in readiness to embark two companies, and place on board the same, at once, as many teams as the Regt. from which the two companies detailed, and as the Qr. Master at this place can spare, and await orders." Copies, DLC-USG, V, 2, 86; DNA, RG 393, USG Letters Sent. On the same day, Rawlins wrote twice to Brig. Gen. John A. McClernand. "You will detail Two Companies of 45th Ills Inft to proceed on board steamer to be designated by Commodore Graham, to Clifton Tenn ~~river~~ under such instruction as will be furnish from these Head Quarters. ~~and~~ when they return they will debark at Pittsburgh" "Will place the Teams and teamters of the 45th Regiment Ills Vols. on board Steamer to be designated by Commodore Graham for embarkation of the Two Companies, which the Genl Commanding requested you to detail from said Regt to proceed to Clifton Tenn." LS, McClernand Papers, IHi; copies, DLC-USG, V, 1, 2, 3, 86; DNA, RG 393, USG Letters Sent.

1. Clifton, Tenn., on the Tennessee River about thirty-two miles downriver from Savannah.

To Julia Dent Grant

Savanna March 24th 1862

DEAR JULIA

I have received four letters from you since yesterday running from the 4th of March to the 16th. As I am writing every day you cannot expect me to write much. All I write for, now, is to tell you to take the children and make a visit to Louisville if you wish. If I was to put of[*f*] writing long I should forget it. Lend your money to the store and take the note in your own name. I want you to save all you can in case any accident should overtake me, and for us, when I get back should nothing happen.

You need not give yourself the least trouble about what the papers say. All is the work of env~~y~~ious persons and the ultra Abolition press. You may rest assured, though I say it myself, Gen. Halleck would rather loose almost any other officer in his Department, that is have them sent elswhere for duty, than your husband.

I will send you some more money soon.

Mr. & Miss Safford[1] are here, or rather at Pittsburg nine

miles above here.—How many days I shall be here yet I cant tell. Not long I hope.

Kiss the children for me. Love to all at home. Kisses for yourself dear Julia.

ULYS.

ALS, DLC-USG.

1. See letter to Alfred B. Safford, Feb. 21, 1862. Mary Jane Safford of Cairo, sister of Alfred B. Safford, was active in voluntary military hospital relief service. LeRoy H. Fischer, "Cairo's Civil War Angel, Mary Jane Safford," *Journal of the Illinois State Historical Society*, LIV, 3 (Autumn, 1961), 229–45.

To James W. Singleton

Head Quarters, Dist of West Tenn
Savanna March 24th 1862

Hon Jas W Singleton
Chairman of Committee on Mily Affairs
Constitutional Convention
Springfield Ill
Sir

Your Circular of the 23d of Jany is just received   In reply I would state that so far as my observation has extended Illinois volunteers have entered the United States well clothed and equipped   When it was impossible to procure clothing from the Government, after wearing out their first suit clothing could generally be obtained from State Authority

I am Sir Very respectfully
Your Obt Servt
U S Grant
Maj Gen

Copy, ICHi. James W. Singleton of Quincy, born in Va., was a Democratic politician, then strongly opposing the war effort. *DAB*, XVII, 191. On Jan. 23, 1862, Singleton addressed a circular letter to commanders of Ill. regts. "I am instructed by the committee on militray affairs to inclose you a copy of the subjoined resolution, adopted by the Constitutional Convention now in session in this city, and to request your immediate answer, in order that the committee may report to the Convention at an early day. In responding to this communication I am instructed to request you to make such suggestions as your observation and experience may dictate with reference to the present and future comfort of your command." "*Resolved*, That the committee on military affairs be instructed to inquire whether the soldiers sent into the field from this state have been and continue to be provided for in all respects as the troops sent into the field from other states have been provided for, and if the committee find that the Illinois troops have not been thus provided for that they be instructed to inquire further, whether the neglect is justly chargeable to any person or persons holding office under this state, and to report the facts to this Convention." *Journal of the Constitutional Convention of the State of Illinois, Convened at Springfield, January 7, 1862* (Springfield, 1862), p. 834. On March 13, Singleton reported that the Ill. troops had been properly equipped. *Ibid.*, p. 833.

To Maj. Gen. Henry W. Halleck

────────

Head Quarters Dist. of West. Tenn.
Savannah March 25th 1862

Maj. Gen'l H. W. Halleck
St. Louis Mo.

Oxen can be got here, though we may be obliged to go far ~~in~~ into the Country for the number that will be required. There are surplus mules enough here to partly supply a siege battery. 6th Wisconsin, 53rd Ia and Mich. Battery arrived.

U. S. Grant
Maj. Gen'l Com'd'g

Telegram, copies, DLC-USG, V, 4, 5, 7, 8, 9, 88; DNA, RG 393, USG Hd. Qrs. Correspondence; *ibid.*, Dept. of the Mo., Telegrams Received. *O.R.*, I, x, part 2, 66. On March 22, 1862, Maj. Gen. Henry W. Halleck telegraphed to USG. "Several Regiments of Infantry and Batteries will leave to day and to morrow for the Tenn. I have several Artillery Companies without Horses or Batteries. I propose to fit out one or more heavy Siege Batteries to be drawn by oxen. Can you supply oxen for this purpose if I send the batteries." Copies, DLC-USG, V, 4, 5, 7, 8, 9, 88; DNA, RG 94, Generals' Papers and Books, Telegrams Sent in Cipher by Gen. Halleck; *ibid.*, RG 393, USG Hd. Qrs. Correspondence; *ibid.*, Dept. of the Mo., Telegrams Sent. *O.R.*, I, x, part 2, 57.

To Maj. Gen. Henry W. Halleck

Savannah, March 25, 1862.

MAJ. GEN. H. W. HALLECK,
COMMANDING DEPARTMENT OF THE MISSISSIPPI,
SAINT LOUIS, MO.:

GENERAL: Inclosed I send you a sketch of the country about Pittsburg, which will explain the location of Smith's, Sherman's, Hurlbut's, and McClernand's divisions. General Wallace is six miles below, with a good road out, enabling them to form a junction with the main column, when a move is made, six or seven miles before reaching Corinth.

I am, general, very respectfully, your obedient servant,

U. S. GRANT,
Major-General.

O.R., I, lii, part 1, 230. Two maps accompanying this letter are reproduced in *O.R.* (Atlas), LXXVIII, 3, 6.

To Maj. Gen. John A. McClernand

Head Quarters, Dist of West. Tenn.
Savanna, March 25th 1862.

GEN. J. A. MCCLERNAND
COMMDG. 1ST DIVISION
GENL:

I have just had arrested and confined here one of the Jessie Scouts who was going to Cairo in possession of a very fine horse, with your pass. I would call your attention to the fact that I have already been severely reprimanded from Washington for the acts of Officers and men under me, for taking or permitting to be taken, captured property. I hold the horse and man awaiting your report as to the manner in which the horse was obtained.

> I am, Very Respectfully,
> Your Obt. Servant.
> U. S. GRANT.
> Major Gen. Commdg.

Copies, DLC-USG, V, 1, 2, 3, 86; DNA, RG 393, USG Letters Sent. On March 25, 1862, John Riggin, Jr., wrote to Maj. Gen. John A. McClernand. "You will send by first Steamer, Carpenter, the 'Jessie Scout' to these Head Quarters in charge of a proper guard." Copies, DLC-USG, V, 1, 2, 86; DNA, RG 393, USG Letters Sent. On the same day, McClernand wrote to USG. "I sympathize with you in the mortification and regret you have experienced, in ~re~ respect to the gross disregard of the rights of person, by individual officers and men, in our army. I have denounced, in more than one order, the penalty of death, as the punishment for pillage and plunder of private property. While my Division was at Savannah, Capt Carpenter of the 'Jessie Scouts,' came and reported to me for duty, as, from Maj. Genl. Halleck. Your note informs me that Scott, one of these Scouts was found in possession of a horse, on board of a steamer. I cannot say, not knowing, where he got the horse; nor ~can~ am I able to give any information about his ownership. My Aids, one and all, deny giving any authority to take ~any horse~ any horse to Cairo. Of course, no one of them, would claim or control a horse not his. They have had nothing to do with the horse. One of the Scouts, probably, Scott, stating that he was unable for service, asked me for a pass to Cairo. A pass was written for him by my Clerk, and signed by me. No horse was included in it. My Clerk informs now, for the first time, that Scott afterwards returned with the pass, and asked to have it amended so as to include a horse, and that he accordingly so amended it. I have not the least recollection of authorizing the alternation; although, in the absence of suspicion, I might, originally, given such a pass, if it had been asked for. I repeat however, that I have no recollection, whatever, of having authorized the alteration. It is proper to add, however, that I do not think my clerk acted from any bad motive, in the matter, although he acted without my my authority. Another horse—a black one—was brought to Savannah, by one of the Scouts, which is now in my Camp. Whether he was rightfully obtained I do not know; but I advise you of the fact, that you may make such order for his disposal as you may think proper. If you think these Scouts ought not to be with the army, I trust you will send them away." ALS, *ibid.*, District of West Tenn., Letters Received. See letter to Capt. Nathaniel H. McLean, March 29, 1862.

To Maj. Gen. Charles F. Smith

Head Quarters, Dist. of W. Ten.
Savanna, March 25th 1862

MAJ. GEN. C. F. SMITH
COMD.G U. S. FORCES
PITTSBURG TEN.
GEN.

I send the 21st Mo. Regt. to report to you.[1] All the regiments that arrive, unattached, place in one Brigade and attach to your Division. I cannot yet make an assignment of Cavalry and Artillery to Divisions because I do not know what is to arrive. I am officially informed of one more Mo. regt. on the way, and three batteries. Also understand, unofficially, that a Regt. of Cavalry is on the way.

Buells three Divisions destined for this place left Columbia[2] eight days ago. They are detained however building a bridge which they expected to take five days in the construction.

Send the cotton you have, with orders to report here, and I will give instructions for its disposal.

I am Gen. very respectfully
your obt. svt.
U. S. GRANT
Maj. Gen.

ALS, James S. Schoff, New York, N. Y.

1. See letter to Maj. Gen. Henry W. Halleck, March 28, 1862.
2. Columbia, Tenn., on the Central Alabama Railroad, about forty miles south of Nashville, and about seventy-five miles northeast of Savannah.

To Maj. Gen. Henry W. Halleck

By Telegraph from Savannah via Paducah
[*March*] 26 1862

To Maj Gen Halleck

I understand through refugees from Perryville[1] 50 miles
below that the rebels intend to establish a battery at that point
—one regiment of infantry & four Companies cavalry could prevent it & afford great relief to that section

U. S. Grant
Maj Genl

Telegram received, DNA, RG 94, Generals' Papers and Books, Telegrams
Received by Gen. Halleck; copies, *ibid.*, RG 393, USG Hd. Qrs. Correspondence;
ibid., Dept. of the Mo., Telegrams Received; DLC-USG, V, 4, 5, 7, 8, 9, 88.

1. Perryville, Tenn., about fifty-four miles by river below Savannah.

To Maj. Gen. Henry W. Halleck

By Telegraph from Savannah [*March*] 26 1862

To Maj Gen Halleck

My scouts are Just in with a letter from Genl Buell[1]   the
3 divisions coming this way are yet on east side of duck river
detained bridge building   Rebel cavalry are scattered through
from here to Nashville gathering supplies—Through some citizens I learn that a large quantity of pork for the southern army
is in store forty miles below here. I have a boat & detail now
getting it[2]   no news from Corinth

U. S. Grant
Maj Genl

Telegram received, DNA, RG 94, Generals' Papers and Books, Telegrams
Received by Gen. Halleck; copies, *ibid.*, RG 393, USG Hd. Qrs. Correspondence;
ibid., Dept. of the Mo., Telegrams Received; DLC-USG, V, 4, 5, 7, 8, 9, 88.
O.R., I, x, part 2, 67.

1. See letter to Brig. Gen. Don Carlos Buell, March 19, 1862.

2. See letters to Maj. Melancthon Smith, March 24, 1862, and to Capt. William W. Leland, March 26, 1862.

To Maj. Gen. Charles F. Smith

Head Quarters, Dist of West. Tenn.
Savanna, March 26th 1862.

MAJOR GEN. C. F. SMITH,
COMMDG. U. S. FORCES,
PITTSBURG, TENN.
GENL:

I have released Messrs. Farnsworth, Wilson & Peterson. Mr. Peterson left a mule at Pittsburg, which will be returned. Also the three mules and Horse taken from Gen. Meeks, without authority,[1] will be returned to the released prisoners, to be taken back, where they were taken from.

You may place such restrictions as you may deem proper and prudent, on the return of these men to their homes. Probably it would be prudent to keep these men about the landing, and have them and their Animals returned here to make their way home, by the way of Eastport, or the best they can from this side.

I am sorry there is such a propensity on the part of our Officers to arrest citizens whenever they get out. It is embarrassing to have prisoners against whom there are no charges, brought in, and from the fact that they must be released it is virtually admitting spiees within our lines.

I am, Gen, Very Respectfully,
Your Obt Servant.
U. S. GRANT.
Major Gen. Commdg.

Copies, DLC-USG, V, 1, 2, 3, 86; DNA, RG 393, USG Letters Sent. See following letter.

1. On March 24, 1862, C. S. A. Brig. Gen. Bushrod R. Johnson, Bethel, Tenn., wrote to Maj. R. N. Snowden. "Squire Meeks, living about 10 miles from Purdy, on the Purdy and Pittsburg road, was taken prisoner on Saturday by the enemy. They also carried off 24 bales of his cotton, 3 mules, 1 horse, 12 barrels of corn, and 1,000 bundles of fodder." *O.R.*, I, x, part 2, 359.

To Brig. Gen. William T. Sherman

Head Quarters, Dist of West. Tenn.
Savanna, March 26th 1862.

GEN. W. T. SHERMAN
PITTSBURG, TENN.
GEN:

Gen. Meeks reports to me that the party sent to bring in Cotton, in addition to executing what they were there for, carried off three mules and a horse; also set fire to one of his houses. Some of the men put out the fire before much injury was done, however. Our men must learn not to exceed their orders. The horse and mules must be returned, and the Officers in charge of the party arrested and tried, or reprimanded, if guilty, according to the degree of guilt.

I am, Gen, Very Respectfully
Your Obt Servant
U. S. GRANT.

Copies, DLC-USG, V, 1, 2, 3, 86; DNA, RG 393, USG Letters Sent. On March 28, 1862, Brig. Gen. William T. Sherman wrote to Capt. John A. Rawlins. "I have the honor herewith Reports from Col John A. McDowell and Col Taylor concerning the taking of the cotton & arrest of Meeks and his three neighbors. I am satisfied that no harsh treatment has been experienced by any of them. The three men with their mules & Saddles have been sent to their homes. Meeks is still at your head qrs, and his animals are safly held subject to his order. The enemy's cavalry is engaged in burning the small parcels of cotton held by the farmers, and taking their horses wagons &c. and it is a question for you whether we should not anticipate them. Capt W. H. Harland is under arrest—He exceeded his orders in bringing in as prisoners any other than meeks, but as no harm befel them, I recommend he be released with an admonition that such arrests are wrong" Copy, *ibid.*, RG 94, Generals' Papers and Books, William T. Sherman, Letters Sent. On the same day, Rawlins issued Special Orders No. 38 for Capt. William H. Harland, 6th Iowa. "Capt. W. H Horland, 6th Iowa. vol. Inf is hereby released from arrest. Capt. Horland should bear in mind for the future that instructions are given to junior officers to be obeyed. In this particular instance it does not appear that any particular harm has been done, but the greatest evil might result from disobedience no greater than that of which Capt Horland has been guilty" Copies, DLC-USG, V, 15, 16, 82, 87, 89; DNA, RG 393, USG Special Orders.

To Col. Crafts J. Wright

———

Head Quarters, Dist of West. Tenn.
Savanna, March 26th 1862.

COL. C. J. WRIGHT. 13TH MO
CLARKESVILLE, TENN.

Tear down the walls of the Forts. Injure them as much as possible.

U. S. GRANT.
Major. Gen.

Copies, DLC-USG, V, 1, 2, 3, 86; DNA, RG 393, USG Letters Sent. On March 19, 1862, Col. Crafts J. Wright, Clarksville, telegraphed to USG. "Shall I leave the Walls of the Fort—The Ordnance is out   have filled two (2) Boats   shall fill two More before shipping Regiment" Telegram received, *ibid.*, Dept. of the Mo., Telegrams Received.

To Capt. William W. Leland

———

Head Quarters, Dist of West. Tenn.
Savannah, March 26th 1862.

CAPT. W. W. LELAND,
DIST. COMMISSARY.

You will cause the captured meat brought by the Steamer "John Rain" to be distributed between the different Divisions Commissaries with instructions to issue it before any now in their hands is issued.

U. S. GRANT.
Major. Genl.

Copies, DLC-USG, V, 1, 2, 86; DNA, RG 393, USG Letters Sent. See letter to Maj. Melancthon Smith, March 24, 1862.

To Capt. Nathaniel H. McLean

Head Quarters Dist of West Tenn
Savanna March 27th 1862

Capt N H McLean
A A Gen Dept of the Mississippi
St Louis Mo
Capt

The Steamer "John Raine" sent with two companies of Infantry and forty Cavalry to Nichols landing after the balance of Confederate Pork left there has returned bringing in with them from one hundred to one hundred and twenty thousand pounds that was found   The pork is in good order and has been distributed between the different Division Commissaries with directions to issue it on the first returns sent in

The telegraph wire ordered here has arrived and has been put up to day through town and some ways into the country. I have ordered up three companies of Curtis' Horse, from Fort Henry to guard the line as it is being laid.[1] I have no news yet of any portion of Gen Buells command being this side of Columbia. I visited the different divisions at Pittsburg to day. The health of the Troops is materially improveing under the influence of a genial sun which has blessed us for a few days past   News having arrived of the promotion of Gen. McClernand to the rank of Maj Gen. without the date of promotion of either him or Gen Smith being known makes it necessary for me to move my Hd Qrs from this place to Pittsburg.[2] I will not go up however until something further is heard from Buells command and until furtherll directions are given for their transfer from this place.

I would respectfully request that Capt Waterhouse's Battery be sent from Cairo to this place.[3] I make the request at the suggestion of Col Webster who says the battery requires drilling which they cannot have at Cairo where they now are. And here would be a good place for it

I am Sir very Respty
Your Obt Servt
U. S. GRANT
Maj. Gen.

P S. The 8th Independant Battery Ohio Vols (Capt Lewis Margroff)[4] has just arrived and will proceed to Pittsburg in the morning

U. S. G.

LS, DNA, RG 393, Dept. of the Miss., Letters Received. *O.R.*, I, x, part 2, 70.

1. On March 26, 1862, USG wrote to Col. William W. Lowe. "Send three companies of your Cavalry under an efficient Field Officer, with the least possible delay to this place. I send a Steamer herewith to transport them." Copies, DLC-USG, V, 1, 2, 3, 86; DNA, RG 393, USG Letters Sent.

2. On March 26, Maj. Gen. John A. McClernand wrote to Maj. Gen. Charles F. Smith. "Your communication of this date is recd., requiring me to detail certain privates from my command, as nurses. While entertaining the highest respect for you, both, as an officer and a man; yet as I understand my relations to Maj. Genl. Grant, I can only receive orders from him. If I am in error, I will be happy to correct it, upon the receipt of official information to that effect. Accepting your communication as a suggestion of the importance of the detail, I will make it upon my own authority." LS, *ibid.*, District of West Tenn., Letters Received. On the same day, Smith endorsed the letter to USG. "Respectfully referred to the Hd. Qrs. of the District. I do not understand the views of Genl. McClernand. If I am his senior he is, as a part of the force at this post under my command; if he is mine I am bound to obey his orders. I shall not notice this communication of Genl. McClernand, awaiting Genl. *Grant's* decision. I presume he did not know I am the senior." AES, *ibid.* On March 26, Capt. John A. Rawlins issued Special Orders No. 36. "Major Gen'l C. F. Smith the senior officer at Pittsburgh is herby appointed to command that post during the continuance of Head Quarters of the Dist. at this place or until properly relieved He will be obeyed and respected accordingly" Copies, DLC-USG, V, 15, 16, 82, 87, 89; DNA, RG 393, USG Special Orders; McClernand Papers, IHi. *O.R.*, I, x, part 2, 67. On March 27, McClernand wrote to USG. "To day, at 11 oClock, a. m. I had the honor to receive your Special order No 36, which is as follows: . . . This order is evidently founded upon the idea that Genl Smith is my senior and hence ranks me. Lately, I was Genl Smiths senior, as a Brigadier. I wish to be advised how he became *my* senior. I am, unofficially, advised that he has been promoted to a Major Generalship; and I am so advised with regard to myself. If his promotion gives him seniority, very well. If it does not, I cannot recognize him as my superior in rank or command; and no earthly power can make me do so. I say this with all respect for General Smith, whom I regard as a gallant, experienced, and skillful commander,

and whom under proper circumstances, if left to me, I would probably choose, as such. Having made this order, the fair presumption is that you are warranted in it; Yet, as the facts upon which it is founded, are not accessible to me, or the public, and are inconsistent with the antecedent relations between Genl Smith and myself, I ask for the facts—the legitimate, determinate facts, upon which it is founded. Regarding your order, however, as only intended to cover the time intervening between its date and the early disposition of the point I have presented —I will consider, and execute, such orders as may come from Genl Smith, as included within your own, and coming from yourself; he being the official medium through whom you think proper to convey them to me. By this means, your wishes will be carried into effect in a manner, entirely respectful to General Smith, bringing no detriment to the service, and reserving for adjustment, the considerations I have urged. I have respectfully to request, that you will afford me, as early as possible, the information I desire. In making this request, I am only obeying a dictate of self-respect, which, I am confident, you will fully appreciate" LS, DNA, RG 94, Generals' Papers and Books, John A. McClernand. On March 29, USG endorsed this letter. "Respectfully refered to Hd Qrs. of the Dept. I shall move my Hd Qrs. to Pittsburg on Monday which will obviate present difficulty on the subject of rank, but I would like to know if Maj. Gen. McClernand and Maj. Gen. Smith are commissioned on the same day to guide me in future." AES, *ibid.* On the same day, McClernand again wrote to USG. "I avail myself of Capt. Stewart's, temporary, return to Savannah, to offer a suggestion or two, prompted by observation and reflection. Our proximity to the enemy makes it, at least, proper that the various camps here should be formed upon some general and connected plan. Such a precaution might be necessary to avoid confusion and self destruction in case of a possible night attack. Your presence, here, too, as Commander-in-Chief of the Army, would tend to avoid differences between Subordinate Commanders, and to secure uniformity and efficiency in their several administrations. Some of the rebel cavalry were seen about five miles from my camp yesterday and the day before. If you should think proper to direct me to send out the entire cavalry force here, or such portion of it as may be necessary, I will do it tomorrow, and with the prospect of dispersing the rebel cavalry. Lt. Col. McCullough is anxious to take part in the expedition." Copies, McClernand Papers, IHi.

On March 31, Maj. Gen. Henry W. Halleck wrote to USG. "The question of rank between Genls Smith & McClernan has been referred to the Secty of War & will probably be answered to-morrow. I know nothing about it, except that Genl McClellan directed me to place Genl Smith in command of the expedition until you were ordered to join it. I hope to get most the troops fitted out & forwarded so as to reach you about the time Buell's main force gets within supporting distance. Give me more information about enemy's numbers and positions. Your scouts & spies ought by this time to have given you something approximating to the facts of the case. A pontoon train will probably be shipped to-morrow or the day after. A number of regiments have been sent without the usual means of transportation. It is suppose[d] that you may be able to supply them there from those sent from Cincinnati. If not they will serve to guard the depot till transportation can be sent from here. We have completely exhausted present supply" ALS, DNA, RG 94, Generals' Papers and Books, Letters Sent by Gen. Halleck (Press). *O.R.*, I, x, part 2, 82.

On April 5, Halleck telegraphed to USG. "The rank of Maj Genls is Grant

Buell Pope McClernand C F Smith Wallace. Genl Buells force will concentrate
at Waynesboro; you will act in concert, but he will exercise his separate command, unless the enemy should attack you. In that case you are authorized to take
the general command. I hope to join you early next week" Copies, DLC-USG,
V, 4, 5, 7, 8, 9, 88; DNA, RG 94, Generals' Papers and Books, Telegrams Sent
in Cipher by Gen. Halleck; *ibid.*, RG 393, USG Hd. Qrs. Correspondence; *ibid.*,
Dept. of the Mo., Telegrams Sent. *O.R.*, I, x, part 2, 94.

    3. The battery organized by Capt. Allen C. Waterhouse, later Battery E,
1st Ill. Light Art., was mustered into service on Dec. 19, 1861, and sent to Cairo
on Feb. 13, 1862. On March 22, Halleck wrote to Brig. Gen. William K. Strong.
"As soon as horses are received, Waterhouse's battery will be sent to Genl
Grant." Copy, DNA, RG 94, Generals' Papers and Books, Telegrams Sent in
Cipher by Gen. Halleck. The battery left Cairo on March 27 and arrived at
Pittsburg Landing on March 30.

    4. The 8th Ohio Independent Battery, commanded by Capt. Louis Markgraf,
was organized at Camp Dennison, Ohio, on March 10. On March 22, by Special
Orders No. 31, Dept. of the Miss., it was ordered from Benton Barracks, Mo.,
to join USG at Savannah. *O.R.*, I, lii, part 1, 228.

To Brig. Gen. Stephen A. Hurlbut

Head Quarters, Dist of West. Tenn.
Savanna, March 27th 1862.

    Referred to Brig. Gen. Hurlbut who will enquire by what
authority Col. Reed grants passes on Steamers, and by what
authority the Surgeon of his Regt. orders patients out of this
Dist. If the explanation is not very satisfactory, Col. Reed should
be arrested, and tried by Court. Martial.

U. S. GRANT.
Major. Gen.

Copy, DLC-USG, V, 86. Written on a certificate of March 26, 1862, prepared
by Asst. Surgeon John W. Renick, 44th Ind., acting for Surgeon W. W. Martin.
"This is to certify that Capt. W. S. Brigham, Co. "H" and Act Major 44th Regt.
Ind. Vols. is at present unfit for duty, owing to Chronic Dysentery and is ordered
to General Hospital, Evansville Ind. for treatment." Copy, *ibid.* On the same day,
the certificate was endorsed by Col. Hugh B. Reed, 44th Ind. "Capt. of Steamer
Will pass Major Brigham, 44th Regt. Ind. Vols. to Evansville or to such place
as he may desire." Copy, *ibid.* On March 28, Reed sent to USG a "Statement in
reference to a pass given to Major Bingham." *Ibid.*, V, 10; DNA, RG 393, USG
Register of Letters Received. Reed resigned on Nov. 26; Maj. William B. Bingham resigned on Sept. 7.

General Orders No. 28

Head Quarters, Dist. of West Ten.
Savanna, March 28th 1862

GEN. ORDERS No 28

The attention of Division, Brigade and Regimental commanders is again called to the fact that no leaves of absence or furloughs can be granted, or passes given, either for persons or property without approval at these Hd Quarters.

The Gen. Commanding has learned with astonishment that the habit of giving furloughs and passes has been previlent among regimental commanders, and in some instances Captains of Companies have been guilty of the same assumption of authority.

Where leaves or furloughs are asked the application must come through all intermediate commanders, to Hd Quarters of the District, and in no instance will the applicant come in person to press his claim.

By Order of Maj. Gen. U. S. Grant, Com.
JNO A RAWLINS
A. A. Genl

To Gen. John A. McClernand
through Maj Gen C. F Smith.

AD (in USG's hand), McClernand Papers, IHi. See endorsement to Brig. Gen. Stephen A. Hurlbut, March 27, 1862. On March 29, 1862, Capt. John A. Rawlins issued General Orders No. 29. "Regimental and detachment commanders will make out, and forward to these Head Quarters without delay, the names of all absent officers of their respective commands, by what authority they are absent, and how long they have been so absent. All enlisted men absent without competent authority will be ordered to join their companies without delay, and such as have absented themselves without authority charges will be preferred against for desertion, and brought to trial immediately on their return." DS, McClernand Papers, IHi.

To Maj. Gen. Henry W. Halleck

———

Head Quarters, Dist. of West Ten
Savanna, March 28th 1862

MAJ. GEN. H. W. HALLECK
COMD.G DEPT. OF THE MISS.
ST. LOUIS MO.
GEN.

Your letter of the 24th inst. is just rec'd. Surgeon Hewit is my Acting Medical Director, and is the senior surgeon within this District according to the Army register.

I never ordered any sick to New Albany nor have I received orders to send any to Cincinnati.

In the absence of orders on the subject sick and wounded men have been sent down the river to be disposed of. They could be sent from Paducah to any other point.

I ordered no sick to St. Louis, the Medical Director may have done so however.

In regard to Col.s. or others than myself giving furloughs all my orders on that subject are most stringent. Steamboats also are forbidden to ~~for~~ carry soldiers or citizens without a pass approved by my order.

This Army is mostly new to me and it is impossible that I should correct all irregularities, or know of them, at once, especially as I receive such feeble support from many of the officers.

A few days ago a soldier who was about leaving on a furlough given by his Col. was stopped here and sent back and orders given for the arrest of the Col.

I find great difficulty in getting my orders disseminated though all in my power has been done to insure it.

The sick here have been entirely out of some important medicines for a week although requisitions, properly made and properly signed, by a *Commissioned Act. Medical Director* were forwarded in time to prevent it.

> I am Gen. very respectfully
> your obt. svt.
> U. S. GRANT
> Maj. Gen Com

ALS, DNA, RG 393, Dept. of the Miss., Letters Received. *O.R.*, I, x, part 2, 73. See telegram to Maj. Gen. Henry W. Halleck, March 22, 1862.

To Maj. Gen. Henry W. Halleck

Head Quarters, Dist. of West Ten.
Savanna, March 28th 1862

MAJ. GEN. H. W. HALLECK
COMD.G DEPT. OF THE MISSISSIPPI
ST. LOUIS MO.
GEN.

Since the receipt of your letter this morning[1] I have caused boats leaving here to be visited and all persons leaving on them to be required to show their passes. This course led to the discovery that a number of persons were going North without my authority, on leaves and passes given in one instance by a Brig. Gen. in one by a Captain and all the others by Regimental Commanders.

As this course of proceedure is in violation of my orders I have ordered the arrest of all these parties and will prefer charges against them.

I acknowledge the justness of your rebuke in this respect, although I thought all proper measures had been taken to prevent such abuse, and will see that no such violations occur in future.

As I shall prefer the charges myself in these cases it will be necessary to forward the charges to you to order the Court.[2]

I forward herewith the names of officers proposed to compose the Court,[3] should you deem fit to order one. I would respectfully recommend however that these officers be released with a reprimand which will probably do more good than to try them by Court-Martial.

News received here from a Union man who has been a prisoner at Corinth showes that the rebels have been evacuating Island No 10 for the last eight days and concentrating at Corinth.[4] I give this for what it is worth.

One of the Gunboats make daily trips as far down the river as Perryville, the point on the river where there is the most probability of a battery being established to annoy our transports.

The conduct of the 21st Mo. on their way up here has been reported to me as infamous. A constant fire was kept up all the way on the trip and in some instances the citizens on shore were fired at. I caused charges to be prefered against the Col. and the Court is now in session trying him.[5]

> I am Gen. very respectfully
> your obt. svt.
> U. S. GRANT
> Maj. Gen.

ALS, DNA, RG 393, Dept. of the Miss., Letters Received. *O.R.*, I, x, part 2, 73–74.

1. See preceding letter.
2. See letters to Capt. Nathaniel H. McLean, March 29, 30, 1862. On April 1, 1862, Col. Joseph C. McKibbin wrote to USG. "I am ordered to call your attention to Gen Orders. 'No 111' dated 'Head Quarters of the Army, Adjt Genls Office Washington, December 30th. 1861.'.—embodying, an act relative to Courts Martial. Division & Brigade Commanders are empowered to dispose of all cases, provided for by the Article of War, except those extending to loss of life, or the dismission of a Commissioned officer. Such cases after trial will be sent to these Head Quarters for review, excepting such where the Division or Brigade commander, is the accusee.—Charges refered by you to this Dept. are respectfully returned.—" LS, DNA, RG 393, District of West Tenn., Letters Received.
3. On March 28, USG sent to Capt. Nathaniel H. McLean a list of proposed members for a court-martial, with Maj. Gen. Lewis Wallace designated president. LS, *ibid.*, Dept. of the Miss., Letters Received.
4. On March 28, Col. William W. Lowe, Fort Henry, wrote to Capt. John A. Rawlins. "I have the Honor to report the arrival at this Post of a Gentleman who left Memphis on the morning of the 26th: inst:. He brings some information with reference to the position and movements of the Rebel Troops, that may be of service to the General Commanding.—He says that there were not more than

Eight regular regiments in the Vicinity of Island No. 10, and that the people of Memphis had no hope of being able to hold the place any length of time; in fact that they looked for the City itself to be taken in the course of a week or ten days. From all the information he could gather he comes to the conclusion that they are bending all their energies to the concentration of a large force at Corinth, where they expect to make a desperate stand. They are even bringing to that point some forces from Virginia. Beauregard is in command. Since my last communication the Scouting parties of my Regiment have captured fifteen additional prisoners, among them one Lieutenant. Citizens continue to arrive here daily from the interior, to avoid impressment. As it is likely to prove very unhealthy, now that the water is falling rapidly, inside the Post of Fort Henry, I should like permission to move the companies now there to the Fort Heiman side, sending over daily a sufficient Guard. Several Citizens here wish to ship Tobacco and other articles down the River—from whom can the license be obtained? Will you be kind enough to furnish me with a copy of Dep't: General Order No 3. Series 61, with accompanying orders based thereon from District Head Qrs:" LS, *ibid.*, District of West Tenn., Letters Received. *O.R.*, I, x, part 2, 74. Lowe enclosed a report of March 28 of 1st Lt. Mortimer Neely, Curtis Horse, concerning his capture of ten men at Agnew's Ferry, Tenn. *Ibid.*, I, x, part 1, 46. Ten prisoners are listed on a receipt for their delivery at St. Louis, April 4, McClernand Papers, IHi. See letter to Brig. Gen. William K. Strong, March 30, 1862. On March 29, Rawlins wrote to Lowe. "Major Gen. U. S. Grant, Commdg. directs me to acknowledge the receipt of your communication of the 28th inst and in reply to say. that You will cause to be made out lists of prisoners of War captured by you as required in General Orders No 50. of the Dept. of the Mo. (Current Series), and send them prisoners together with such lists on board first Steamer to Cairo, Ills. Send none but those who were actually in the Confederate Service. You will make such disposition of the forces under your command as you may deem best. The regulation adopted by the Secretary of the Treasury not having been received, the Genl. Commdg. cannot give you a definite answer as to the procuring of License to ship the Tobacco referred to, but supposes it would be proper to ship to Paducah, Ky, where the license, if any, is required, may be obtained. Enclosed find General Orders No 3. & 46., Dept of the Mo. and those upon subject herein referred to. Also General Orders No 14. of this Dist." Copies, DLC-USG, V, 1, 2, 3, 86; DNA, RG 393, USG Letters Sent.

5. On March 25, John Riggin, Jr., wrote to Col. David Moore, 21st Mo. "It has been reported here that while your Regiment was being transported on Steamer, 'J. C. Swan' between Fort. Henry and this point several of the men of your Regt. fired a into a house on, or near the bank of the river in which were unoffending people. You will cause an immediate investigation to be made and if such firing did take place, you will arrest the guilty parties for punishment, and you will also arrest any Officer having a Knowledge of the act, and countenancing the same, by not preventing and arresting the guilty parties. You will make a report of the facts, and proceedings to these Head Quarters." Copies, DLC-USG, V, 1, 2, 3, 86; DNA, RG 393, USG Letters Sent. On March 26, Maj. Gen. Charles F. Smith wrote to USG: "Returning charges against Col. Moore and the order for trial of the same." DLC-USG, V, 10; DNA, RG 393, USG Register of Letters Received.

On April 2, USG issued General Orders No. 32. "Befor a General Court Martial which assembled at Savannah Tenn., March 28th 1862 and of which Brig.

Gen'l W. H. L. Wallace is President was arraigned and tried Col. David Moore 21st Mo. Vols. on the following Charge and Specification

Charge

Conduct unbecoming an Officer and a Gentleman

Specification

In this, that Col. David Moore of the 21st Mo Vols permitted the most abusive course of conduct on the part of his command towards citizens, and Steamboat Employees from paducah Ky. to Pittsburg Tenn. in allowing firing on peaceful citizens on the bank of the River, in abusind Stewards and Servents on the Boat, and interfering with officers in the discharge of their duty, trying to prevent this reckless course of conduct. This on the Tennessee River between the 23rd and 26th days of March 1862. To which the Prisoner pleaded as follows

Of the Specification—Not Guilty

Of the Charge   Not Guilty

The Court finds the Prisoner as follows

Of the Specification—'Guilty of allowing firing on peaceable Citizens on the bank of the river: Of the other parts of the Specification, 'Not Guilty—[']

Of the Charge—'Not Guilty,' but Guilty of conduct prejudicial to good order and Military Disipline

Sentence

To be repremanded in Gen'l Orders by the Commanding General of the Dist. of West Tenn. The proceedings, finding and sentence in the foregoing case are approved.

The Gen'l Comd'g Regrets that it becomes his duty to reprimand an officer of high rank for conduct in his command disgraceful to the Service and Calculated to produce enemies where it was reasonable to expect to make friends. Col. Moore is herby released from arrest and will resume Command of his regiment. It is hoped that the conduct of this Regiment in future will wipe out the stain attached to them for their bad behavior on the trip from Paducah to Pittsburg. Col. Moore is released from arrest and returned to duty.

The Gen'l Court Martial of which Brig. Gen'l W. H. L. Wallace is President is desolved"   Copies, DLC-USG, V, 12, 13, 14, 95; DNA, RG 393, USG General Orders.

To Maj. Gen. John A. McClernand

Head Quarters, Dist of West. Tenn.
Savannah, March 28th 1862.

MAJOR GEN. J. A. McCLERNAND
COMMDG. 1ST DIVISION
GENL:

Complaints have been made that your command on leaving here carried off with them to Pittsburg a number of Negroes, belongin to Citizens of this place and vicinity.

This is in violation of orders from Head Quarters of the Dept, and of my orders. You will please enforce the standing orders, and if the parties who have violated them, can be discovered, arrest and prefer charges against them.

I am, Gen, Very Respectfully,

Your Obt. Servant.

U. S. GRANT.

Major Gen. Commdg.

Copies, DLC-USG, V, 1, 2, 3, 86; DNA, RG 393, USG Letters Sent. What appears to be the reply of Maj. Gen. John A. McClernand to USG is dated the preceding day, March 27, 1862. "Your communication of this date conveys the first and only intelligence I have received upon the subject to which it relates. If the fact alleged, be true, it deserves condemnation and its authors the punishment due for the violation of an express order. I will cause immediate inquiry to be made: whether the negroes alleged to have been 'carried off' are in my camp, and if found will turn them out of it. In the absence, however, of a responsible author for the complaint made and proof identifying the negroes, you will perceive it may be difficult, perhaps, impracticable to deal with them. If it be your wish that they should be returned to their claimants, it may be suggested: whether it is not necessary that you should give a letter of authority to the claimants to come, identify, and take them away. In my view of the late article of war enacted by Congress, I could not do it, particularly, if the negroes are fugitives coming into camp of their own motion." Copies, McClernand Papers, IHi. On March 29, McClernand again wrote to USG. "The subject of properly disposing of negroes found within our lines, has been productive of repeated orders, and frequent correspondence. I have endeavoured to enforce fully, your orders, and my own on this subject in conformity with law, and am not conscious of failing in my duty in that respect. The acts of Congress confiscating property (including slaves) and forbidding officers to employ the U. S. forces, in returning them to their claimants—the question whether they be slaves—and if ~~if~~ so, the slaves of rebels —how the facts shall be ascertained by proofs—under what law a proceeding is to be had, when the whole matter is within a single state:—all these present difficulties, which accumulate, as we proceed, and for the solution of which, an army in the field affords no competent tribunal. It would seem, that a civil commission, accompanying the army, clothed by the President, with sufficient powers, would afford a remedy, and relieve commanding officers from a duty not contemplated in the articles of war, and which they cannot now undertake, except under great constraints. I wish to say with respect to my command, that whenever the presence in my camp, of any person of the description mentioned, ~~in my camp~~ is known to me, from your Head Quarters or otherwise, I will place him in custody and report the fact to you, prepared to deliver him to your order, for such investigation and disposal as you may deem proper. I hope this will meet your views. It will enable me to rid my command of a class of men unwelcome and unprofitable to me, and place the whole matter within the reach of such uniform and safe rule, as you may adopt." Copies, *ibid.*

To Maj. Gen. Charles F. Smith

Head Quarters, Dist of West. Tenn.
Savanna, March 28th 1862.

MAJOR GEN. C. F. SMITH
COMMDG. U. S. FORCES,
PITTSBURG, TENN.
GENL:

Every boat that leaves Pittsburg, brings away Soldiers with leaves and passes given by the Col. of their Regiments, and in some instances by Capts of Companies, only.

My attention has just been called to this by Gen. Halleck, in severe terms. My orders have been that boats should carry no one, citizens or Soldiers, who is not provided with a pass at least countersigned at these Head Quarters. A boat just down has men aboard from seven or eight different Regts. passed and furloughed without proper authority, leading to the arrest of one Brig. Gen. four Colonels and two Captains. Please require some proper person to visit every boat leaving Pittsburgh and examine all passes and when improperly given, arrest the parties giving them, and cause charges to be preferred.

I am, Gen, Very Respectfully,
Your Obt. Servant.
U. S. GRANT.
Major. Gen. Commdg.

Copies, DLC-USG, V, 1, 2, 3, 86; DNA, RG 393, USG Letters Sent. See letter to Maj. Gen. Henry W. Halleck, March 28, 1862.

To Capt. Nathaniel H. McLean

Head Quarters Dist of West Tenn
Savanna, March 29th 1862

CAPT N. H. MCLEAN
A. A. GEN DEPT OF THE MISSISSIPPI
ST LOUIS MO
CAPT

I send back to St Louis, for such disposition as the Gen Comdg Dept, may deem fit, the two scouts Carpenter and Scott. They profess to be here by Gen Halleck's order, but I have seen nothing to warrant belief in their statement.

They are an intolerable nuisance with the army. Stealing and plundering seems to be the object of their mission. The particular act which I am able to fix upon them is stealing two horses and appropriating them to their own use. One of them, a very fine horse, they attempted to sell here, and afterwards to ship off. I have had the horse restored to his owner; ~~this one, and~~ The other one is in the hands of the Quartermaster.

Very Respectfully
U. S. GRANT
Maj Genl Comdg—

Copies, DLC-USG, V, 4, 5, 7, 8, 88; DNA, RG 393, USG Hd. Qrs. Correspondence. See letter to Maj. Gen. John A. McClernand, March 25, 1862. On March 29, 1862, Capt. John A. Rawlins issued Special Orders No. 39. "Capt W. S. Hillyer A. D. C. will proceed to St Louis Mo. with as little delay as practiable and take with him Carpenter & Scott of the 'Jessie Scouts' as prisoners. At St Louis they will [be] turned over to the provost marshal and report made to Maj Gen Halleck Comdg Dept" Copies, DLC-USG, V, 15, 16, 82, 87, 89; DNA, RG 393, USG Special Orders.

On April 10, Rawlins issued Special Orders No. 50. "The Scout known as Carpenter of the 'Jessie Scouts' being in Camp against positive orders from these Head Quarters will be immediately sent here a prisoner." Copies, *ibid.* In a letter undated in a letterbook, entered as April 1 in a register of letters, but probably of April 10 or 11, Maj. Gen. John A. McClernand wrote to USG. "Among a number of orders received this morning, I find one for the arrest of 'the Scout known as Carpenter. He has just returned with three of his company, John Crone, Dock Green and Carter—from scouting in the vicinity of the enemys lines; and reports that the enemys camp has been advance[d] a half mile nearer our lines since yesterday evening—and that too of our them were killed by the enemys cavalry about a half a mile from our pickets. He further reports that he slipped through the enemys picket line, and approached close to the enemys tents.—the substance of which particulars he reported about an hour ago to Genl. Buell, whose troops and Genl. Shermans in that vicinity are in line of battle. Lt. S R Tresilian of Co. "I" 49th Ills. Infantry brings Carpenter to deliver him according to your order. These particulars are reported for what they may be worth, in pursuance of my order. I send Carpenter in charge of Lt Trasilian for delivery subject to your order." Copy, McClernand Papers, IHi. On April 11, Rawlins wrote to Capt. Breckinridge. "You will take such force as you may require from Capt. Osband's Company of Cavalry and scour the camp and arrest one Carpenter 'Jessie Scout' bringing him at all hazards to these Head Quarters. You will notify Regimental Commanders of your orders that they may facilitate your search." Copies, DLC-USG, V, 1, 2, 86; DNA, RG 393, USG Letters Sent.

To Capt. Nathaniel H. McLean

Head Quarters Dist of West Tenn
Savanna March 29th 1862

CAPT N H McLEAN
A A GEN. DEPT OF THE MISSISSIPPI
ST LOUIS MO
CAPT
    I would respectfully recommend that 2nd Lieut Charles Speak of the 23d Indiana Infantry be dismissed the service for deserting his regiment after having been refused a leave of absence
    He is now absent without leave
Very Respectfully
Your Obt Servt
U S GRANT
Maj Gen—

Copies, DLC-USG, V, 4, 5, 7, 8, 88; DNA, RG 393, USG Hd. Qrs. Correspondence. 2nd Lt. Charles W. Speake, 23rd Ind., was discharged from the service on April 1, 1862.

To Capt. Nathaniel H. McLean

Head Quarters Dist of West Tenn
Savanna March 29th 1862

CAPT N H MCLEAN
A A GEN DEPT OF THE MISSISSIPPI
ST LOUIS MO
CAPT

Enclosed herewith I send you a number of passes and furloughs given to men of this command which will explain in part the cause of so many being absent from their Regiments

After the battle of Fort Donelson a great many men and officers were sent to Paducah & Cairo to be disposed of because it was impossible to give them proper attention there

Very respectfully
Your Obt Servt
U S GRANT
Maj Gen

Copies, DLC-USG, V, 4, 5, 7, 8, 88; DNA, RG 393, USG Hd. Qrs. Correspondence.

To Col. Crafts J. Wright

Head Quarters, Dist of West. Tenn.
Savanna, March 29th 1862.

COL. C. J. WRIGHT
CLARKESVILLE TENN.

Come immediately with your command by Steamer. Do not march across the country.

U. S. GRANT
Major Gen. Commdg.

Copies, DLC-USG, V, 1, 2, 3, 86; DNA, RG 393, USG Letters Sent. On March 27, 1862, Col. Crafts J. Wright had telegraphed to USG. "We shall ship fully I

think one hundred thousand (100,000) pounds of uncured bacon which to prevent
being spoiled should go at once to Cincinnati   We have no special orders—We
embark tomorrow and break up the Post"   Telegram received, *ibid.*, Dept. of
the Mo., Telegrams Received.

To Julia Dent Grant

Savanna, March 29th 1862

DEAR JULIA,

I am again fully well. I have had the Diaoreah for sever[*al*]
weeks and an inclination to Chills & Fever. We are all in *statu
qua*. Dont know when we will move. Troops are constantly
arriving so that I will soon have a very large army. A big fight
may be looked for someplace before a great while which it appears
to me will be the last in the West. This is all the time supposing
that we will be successful which I never doubt for a single
moment.

I heard of your arrival at Louisville several days ago through
some Steamboat Capt. and before your letter was received stating
that you would start the next day.

All my Staff are now well though most of them have suffered
same as myself. Rawlins & myself both being very unwell at the
same time made our labors hard upon us. All that were with me
at Cairo are with me here, substuting Dr. Brinton for Dr. Simons,
and in addition Capt. Hawkins & Capt. Rowley. Rowley has also
been very unwell. Capt. Hillyer will probably return home and
go to Washington. His position on my Staff is not recognized
and he will have to quit or get it recognized.[1]

Capt. Brinck is in the same category.[2] All the slanders you
have seen against me originated away from where I was. The
only foundation was from the fact that I was ordered to remain
at Fort Henry and send the expedition under command of Maj.
Gen. Smith. This was ordered because Gen. Halleck received no
report from me for near two weeks after the fall of Fort Donelson.
The same occured with me   I received nothing from him. The

consequence was I apparently totally disregarded his orders. The fact was he was ordering me every day to report the condition of my command, I was not receiving the orders but knowing my duties was reporting daily, and when anything occured to make it necessary, two or three times a day. When I was ordered to remain behind it was the cause of much astonishment among the troops of my command and also disappointment. When I was again ordered to join them they showed, I believe, heartfelt joy. Knowing that for some reason I was relieved of the most important part of my command the papers began to surmize the cause, and the Abolition press, the New York Tribune particularly, was willing to hear to no solution not unfavorable to me. Such men as Kountz busyed themselvs very much. I never allowed a word of contridiction to go out from my Head Quarters, thinking this the best course. I know, though I do not like to speak of myself, that Gen. Halleck would regard this army badly off if I was relieved. Not but what there are Generals with it abundantly able to command but because it would leave inexperienced officers senior in rank. You need not fear but what I will come out triumphantly. I am pulling no wires, as political Generals do, to advance myself. I have no future ambition. My object is to carry on my part of this war successfully and I am perfectly willing that others may make all the glory they can out of it.

Give my love to all at home. Kiss the children for me.

Ulys.

ALS, ICarbS.

1. On March 1, 1862, USG wrote to Secretary of War Edwin M. Stanton. "Requests the promotion of several officers of his Staff." DNA, RG 107, Register of Letters Received. On March 1, Capt. John A. Rawlins wrote to Elihu B. Washburne. "After thanking you for your continued friendship to our favorite Genl Grant & previous kindness to me, without further prefacing my remarks I will call your attention to the enclosed letter of the Generals a duplicate of which he has sent to the Secretary of War. My doing so, is at the General's suggestion and for the purpose of asking your urgent influence in securing the appointment of Captains Lagow and Hillyer as Aides Decamp with the rank of Colonel under the act of Congress, approved August 5th 1861. these gentlemen have been within him throughout his campaigns, the former was a Lieut. in the Regiment of which he was Col. and the latter was an intimate & tried friend of his in Saint Louis,

they were each in the Battle of Belmont & there, by personal coolness and courage proved themselves to be worthy, and well trusted, they were with him at the Battles of Forts Henry & Donelson, the general earnestly desires their appointment to the position and with the rank before designated if it can possibly be done. Should the President be not disposed to grant more than two Aides with the rank of Col. it is Lagow & Hillyer whom the General desires should have the appointment. Our mutual Friend Wm R. Rowley, Lieut. of the 'Lead mine Regt.' has been appointed Aide under the Act of Congress approved July 22nd, 1861, entitling a major genl. to three—Aides, the genl asks to have him appointed asst. adjt. genl. with the rank of Capt. he also asks that your humble servant be promoted to the rank of major in the asst adjt. genl's Dept. on his Staff under the last mentioned 'Act,' authorising a Major general to have one asst. adjt. genl. with the rank of Major. From your friendship toward me so marked and manifest since the commencement of the present terrible conflict of loyalty against treason, I feel assured whatever you may deem necessary ~~for~~ to my interest without injury to the public good you will cause to be done; also you will not forget the advancement of our Friend Rowley. The general would like to have Col. Riggin recognised, as asked for in his letter but not to in any manner ~~to~~ interfere with the promotion of Lagow & Hillyer   I See by the papers that Col Washburne, your brother has applied for and obtained permission to serve on Genl Grants staff. I hope this is true. He had been telegraphed to come previous to the capture of Ft. Donelson, the Genl. is in daily expectation of his arrival, I trust it will be before we move. The forces here are now under marching orders and I hope 'ere the lapse of many days, the country will again, be rejoicing in the victory of our arms, and additional evidence furnished you of having selected & stood by through evil as well as good report the right man in Illinois to lead the advance, and victorious column of the army of the mighty West, to reassert the supremacy of our laws & institutions over every inch of American soil; I tell you Friend Washburne I have ever felt hopeful, I have no doubt now of the final result. All honor to the President who dared to maintain and the People resolved to uphold the Constitution & laws of Washing. & his compeers. P. S. Please telegraph result" ALS, DLC-Elihu B. Washburne. On March 18, Asst. Secretary of War Peter H. Watson wrote to USG. "The Secretary of War directs me to acknowledge your communication of the 1st instant and in reply to say that on refering it to the adjutant General, that officer reports as follows; 'Of the five requests made by Major General. Grant One only can be *lawfully* granted—that for the appointment of his present assistant adjutant General to the rank of Major, from that of Captain, with which he was appointed at a time when General Grant was but a Brigadier General.' " Copy, *ibid*.

On March 29, Capt. William R. Rowley wrote to Washburne. "My attention has just been called to a letter sent by the Secretary of War to Gen Grant. of which the enclosed is a copy. At the time the Gen sent the request it was my impression from reading the army Regulations that the request could not be acceded to except in reference to the appointment of Capt Rawlins as Major which was really more desired by the Gen (in my opinion) than any other portion of it. Rawlins is justly entitled to the promotion for if any one ever earned it he has. he works night and day and probably performs as much or more hard labor than any other Staff officer in the service of the United States. I hope you will interest yourself sufficiently in the matter to see that the appointment is made. I was fortunate in getting the appointment of Capt in the manner I did. I have sent in my acceptance but have recd no notice as to whether the oath I sent accompanying it was deemed sufficient or not as it was sworn to before a Provost Marshall no. Justices or other Civil Officers living in this God forsaken Country. Will you make for me the enquiry as to whether it was deemed sufficient or not. We are now stopping at Savanna   the main part of the army are at Pittsburg, where we shall go on Monday. The Rebels are posted in force at Corinth about 20 miles from Pittsburg   from the best information I can get at I think their force is probably from 50.000 to 70.000 men   Beauriguard is said to be in command   We are awaiting the arrival of Buells forces when we shall undoubtedly 'Move on their works'   I presume we shall have a lively time   listen for Music.   the Gen'l & Rawlins send compliments to you   Col John E. is here all right and sends his compliments"   ALS, *ibid.*

2. See letter to Maj. Gen. Henry W. Halleck, April 27, 1862.

To Maj. Gen. Henry W. Halleck

Head Quarters, Dist. of West Ten.
Savanna, March 30th 1862

MAJ. GEN. H. W. HALLECK
COMD.G DEPT. OF THE MISSISSIPPI
ST. LOUIS, MO.
GEN.

Frequent complaints come to me of officious detention of Steamers and Mails at Paducah by the Master of transportation at that place.

The last complaint is by H. P. Treat, Mail Agt. and Deputy P. M. at Paducah.

I am Gen. very respectfully
your obt. svt.
U. S. GRANT
Maj. Gen.

ALS, DNA, RG 393, Dept. of the Miss., Letters Received.

To Capt. Nathaniel H. McLean

———

Head Quarters, Dist. of West Ten.
Savanna, March 30th 1862

CAPT. N. H. MCLEAN,
A. A. GEN. DEPT. OF THE MISSISSIPPI,
ST. LOUIS, MO.
CAPT.

Yesterday I sent you, through mistake, a number of passes granted by unauthorized persons upon which I have based charges against the persons granting them. I now send the papers intended to be sent and would respectfully request that the others be returned, especially if a Court is ordered for the trial of those officers granting them.

I am Capt. very respectfully
your obt. svt.
U. S. GRANT
Maj. Gen.

ALS, DNA, RG 393, Dept. of the Miss., Letters Received. Enclosed were five irregular passes. On the docket is a note of April 2, 1862, indicating that USG's letter to Capt. Nathaniel H. McLean of March 29 and its enclosures had been returned.

To Capt. Nathaniel H. McLean

———

Head Quarters, Dist. of West Ten.
Savanna, March 30th 1862

CAPT. N. H. MCLEAN
A. A. GEN. DEPT. OF THE MISSISSIPPI
ST. LOUIS, MO.
CAPT.

Some half dozen deserters from Corinth come in to Pittsburg to-day. One represents the number of troops there at seventy-five regiments and the others say the whole number is usually represented at 80.000 men.[1] They describe the discontent as being very great among the troops and rations short. Many men will desert if an opportunity occurs.

The rebels are burning Cotton and Gins without regard to the proclivities of owners on the Union question. I permitted some forty bails to be shipped to Louisville to-day, on account of owners, seventeen of which is the property of a secessionest. There is no evidence however of hims having given aid and comfort to the enemy and he now pledges himself not to do so. The majority belongs to a Mr. Cherry,[2] a promimant citizen, and one who had taken a promimant stand for the Union from the start.

The secessionests have already burned some sixty bales for him and will likely burn much more, as the greater part of it is some eight miles West of the river and below here. Under the instructions I have I could not give all the protection to this species of property that seems needful.

The health of this command is materially improving under a genial Sun and influance of good water.

I would respectfully ask for instructions as to privileges to be allowed citizens in shipping their produce North. If I have done wrong in this matter the necessary correction can be made as this will, or should, reach St. Louis before the Cotton arrives at Louisville. The Cotton was shipped on the steamer John Raine.

> very respectfully
> your obt. svt.
> U. S. GRANT
> Maj. Gen. Com

ALS, DNA, RG 393, Dept. of the Miss., Letters Received. *O.R.*, I, x, part 2, 80. On April 2, 1862, Maj. Gen. Henry W. Halleck telegraphed to USG. "I send you a Pontoon Bridge to day. Genl Buell has sent another around by Nashville Some of the Regiments sent to you are not well drilled   They should be Brigaded and drilled every day. There is no restriction on shipping goods from disloyal states. Give all possible encouragement to shippers of Cotton and Tobacco." Copies, DLC-USG, V, 4, 5, 7, 8, 9, 88; DNA, RG 94, Generals' Papers and Books, Telegrams Sent in Cipher by Gen. Halleck; *ibid.*, RG 393, USG Hd. Qrs. Correspondence; *ibid.*, Dept. of the Mo., Telegrams Sent.

1. C. S. A. forces then at Corinth were probably close in number to the 40,335 who attacked USG one week later at Shiloh. *O.R.*, I, x, part 1, 396.

2. See letter to Julia Dent Grant, March 22, 1862, note 1. On April 17, William H. Cherry wrote to USG. "I have Just learned that the Cotton shipped by me from this landing has been detained at Paducah by the Collector or Marshall I do not know which and that he refused to permit the Boat to carry it to Louisville as shipped—Will you please give me such Authority as will secure me the right to Control it. I speak of the first Lot shipped including the Meek Cotton which can be placed to my Credit and subject to your order— . . . P S. Perhaps it would be better to order the proper Porters at Paducah to Ship the Cotton to its destination—" ALS, DNA, RG 56, Letters from Executive Officers, War Dept. No. 3, Miscellaneous Officers. Somebody writing for USG added an undated and unsigned endorsement. "The cotton referred to in the within communication was shipped by my authority and the circumstances stated in a letter from myself to Maj Gen Halleck." AE, *ibid.* On April 23, Halleck wrote to Secretary of the Treasury Salmon P. Chase. "It is officially reported to me that cotton shipped on the Tennessee River, by order of Genl Grant, to Ports on the Ohio, has been siesed at Paducah by the Collector or Marshall. This, it seems to me, is very bad policy. The object of shipping this cotton was to prevent its destruction by the enemy. The rebel authorities have directed that all cotton likely to fall into our hands be destroyed, and large quantities have already been burned. Unless we encourage the planters in the vicinity of our armies to bring their cotton within our lines for shipment, it will all be destroyed. And if when shipped under military permits it is to be siesed by custom house officers, no cotton will be brought within our lines, & every pound will be destroyed by the planters themselves, as we advance. By allowing the planters to ship it to our ports, we not only get the cotton for our manufactories, but get the planters on our side, for no one who makes a shipment can venture to return to the enemy for fear of punishment. I do not regard such shipments *from* enemy's territory as *trade*, because the proceeds are always subject to our direction." ALS, *ibid.*

To Brig. Gen. William K. Strong

Head Quarters, Dist. of West Ten.
Savanna, March 30th 1862

BRIG. GEN. STRONG
COMD.G CAIRO, ILL.
GEN.

I send in charge of the bearer four rebel Cavalrymen and a notorious old secessionest who has been engaged guiding rebel Cavalry to the premises of Union men for the purpose of impressing them and their property into the service of the rebel army.

I send them no further than Cairo because I do not know to what point Gen. Halleck might wish to have them sent.

> I am Gen. very respectfully
> your obt. svt.
> U. S. GRANT
> Maj. Gen.

ALS, IHi. William K. Strong, born in Duanesburg, N. Y., in 1805, was a retired New York City wool merchant living at Geneva, N. Y., on the eve of the Civil War. His position as both an active Democrat and an active supporter of the war led to his appointment as brig. gen. on Sept. 28, 1861. While assigned to Benton Barracks his eagerness to learn military procedures won him the favorable opinion of Brig. Gen. William T. Sherman. *Personal Memoirs of Gen. W. T. Sherman* (3rd ed., New York, 1890), I, 247. On March 6, 1862, by Special Orders No. 207, Dept. of the Mo., Strong was assigned command at Cairo. *O.R.*, I, liii, 514. On March 8, Maj. Gen. Henry W. Halleck telegraphed to Brig. Gen. George W. Cullum. "Genl Strong has been assigned to the Command of Cairo. Genl Paine will not be permitted to command any depôt. He is continually violating my orders & throwing everything into confusion. When Genl Strong is installed, you can return to St Louis. No more reinforcements to be sent to Genl Pope unless he asks for them." ALS (telegram sent), Victor Jacobs, Dayton, Ohio. On March 21, by Special Orders No. 28, Dept. of the Miss., Strong was assigned command of the District of Cairo. *O.R.*, I, lii, part 1, 227. On April 1, 1st Lt. A. H. Holt, aide-de-camp to Strong, issued Special Orders No. 125. "Lt. Mortimer Neely Curtis Horse having reported to these Hd Qurs with 10 prisoners from Gen Grants command is hereby ordered to proceed with them and 18 others from this Post to St Louis Mo and report for orders to Major General Halleck commanding Department of the Mississippi"   ADS, IHi. See letter to Maj. Gen. Henry W. Halleck, March 28, 1862, note 4.

General Orders No. 30

> Head Quarters, Dist. of West Ten.
> Savanna, March 31st 1862

GEN. ORDERS No 30

Head Quarters of the District of West Tennessee is hereby changed to Pittsburg. An office will be continued at Savanna

where all official communications may be left by troops having
easyier access with that point than Pittsburg.

By Command of Maj. Gen. Grant
JNO. A. RAWLINS
A. A. Gen

AD (in USG's hand), McClernand Papers, IHi. *O.R.*, I, x, part 2, 84.

To Capt. Nathaniel H. McLean

Head Quarters, Dist. of West Ten.
Savanna, March 31st 1862

CAPT. N. H. McLEAN
A A. GEN. DEPT. OF THE MISSISSIPPI,
ST. LOUIS MO.
CAPT.

Two soldiers from the head of Gen. McCooks[1] Column come
in this evening bearing Gen. Hallecks dispatch of the 24th inst.[2]
but no other message. Some of the command crossed Duck river
on the 29th and established Guards eight miles out that night.—
This is the sum and substance of information collected from the
messengers sent.

The telegraph will probably be through from here to Columbia this week. This is what the Superintendent says.

The armored gunboat from Nashville arrived here this evening. I have ordered her, with the two others, up the Tennessee
to-morrow to take and destroy the batteries established near
Chickasaw. Gen. Sherman accompanies with one regiment of
Infantry, two companies of Cavalry and one section of Artillery.

Gen. Sherman's instructions are not to engage any force that
would likely make a stand against him but if the batteries are

unsupported by other than Artillery troops to take or destroy
~~their batteries~~. them.[3]

> very respectfully
> your obt. svt.
> U. S. GRANT
> Maj. Gen. Com

ALS, DNA, RG 393, Dept. of the Miss., Letters Received. *O.R.*, I, x, part 2, 82.

    1. Alexander M. McCook of Ohio, USMA 1852, served continuously in the
U. S. Army after graduation, and was asst. instructor of inf. tactics at USMA,
1858–1861. On April 16, 1861, he was appointed col., 1st Ohio, and on Feb. 3,
1862, was confirmed as brig. gen. to rank from Sept. 3, 1861. He then commanded
the 2nd Division, Army of the Ohio.
    2. On March 24, 1862, Maj. Gen. Henry W. Halleck telegraphed to Maj.
Gen. Don Carlos Buell. "It is reported that Jackson & Humbolt have been evacuated & that the enemy has concentrated his forces at Corinth with the intention
to give battle. A battle should be avoided for the present & until we can concentrate a larger army against him. But, if possible without a very serious engagement, the R. R. at Jackson & Humbolt should be cut. Please send copy of this
to Genl Grant, as he can be reached sooner from Columbia than from Fort Henry."
ALS (telegram sent), DNA, RG 107, Telegrams Collected (Unbound); copies,
DLC-USG, V, 4, 5, 7, 8, 9, 88; DNA, RG 393, USG Hd. Qrs. Correspondence.
    3. On March 31, 6 P. M., Brig. Gen. William T. Sherman wrote to USG.
"Your orders of this date are received   I will be at the Landing in an hour, with
a Regt of Infantry and 1 Squadron 2 Cos of Cavaly ready to embark on board the
Gladiator and Tecumsah at once. We should move at night & I will use all
celerity" Copy, *ibid.*, RG 94, Generals' Papers and Books, William T. Sherman,
Letters Sent. On April 2, Sherman wrote to Capt. John A. Rawlins. "In obedience
to General Grants instructions of March 31, received at 6 P M. I detached one
section of Capt Munch's Minnesota Battery of two (2) Twelve pounder Howitzers, a detachment of the 5th Ohio Cavalry of one hundred and fifty (150) men
under Major Ricker, and two Battalions of Infantry from the 57, and 77 Ohio
under command of their respective Colonels Hildebrand, and Mungen. These
were marched to the River and embarked on the Transports Empress and Tecum-
seh, the Gladiator not having arrived. The Gunboat (iron clad) Cairo, did not
reach Pittsburg Landing until after Midnight, and at 6 a m. her Commander
Captain Bryant, notified me he should proceed up the River at once, followed by
the Gun boats Tyler and Lexington. I followed with the Transports Keeping
about three hundred yards in rear of the Gunboats. About 1 P M, the Cairo
commenced shelling the Battery near to and above the mouth of Indian Creek
but elicited no reply. She proceeded up the River steadily and cautiously followed
close by the Tyler and Lexington, all throwing shells at the points where on former
visits of the Gun boats the enemy's batteries were found, and in this order proceeded to and above Chickasaw where it was demonstrated that the enemy had
abandoned all his batteries and removed the Guns. I then ordered the Battalion
of Infantry under Colonel Hildebrand to disembark at the town of Eastport, and
with the other Battalion proceeded up to Chickasaw and landed. The Battery at

this point had evidently been abandoned some time; and consisted of the remains of an old Indian mound partly washed away by the River, which had been fashioned into a two Gun Battery with a small covered magazine. The ground to its Rear had evidently been overflowed during the late Freshet, and this had probably led to its abandonment, and the removal of the Guns to Eastport, where the Batteries were on high elevated ground, accessible at all times from the country in their rear. Upon personal inspection I attach little importance to Chickasaw as a Military position   The People who had fled during the approach of the Gun boats returned to the village as soon as the firing ceased, and said that the troops which had garrisoned the place were one Tennessee Regt. of Infantry, and a company of Artillery from Pensacola. After remaining some hours at Chickasaw, & conferring with Capts Bryant and Gwin, we all dropped down to Eastport Landing one mile below. This Landing at the present stage of water is the best I have seen on the Tennessee River.   during the late Freshet the shore & land back for three hundred yards were from 12 to 15 feet under water, but now the whole is hard, firm and dry. The Levee is clear of trees & stumps, and a hundred boats could discharge troops there without delay or confusion. The road leading back to Iuca is the best of any that reaches the Charleston and Memphis Railroad, being only from 8 to 10 miles distant. Col Hildebrand had sent out scouts for about two miles and discovered the enemy's pickets, and although I could find no one who had been recently at the Railroad yet the pickets of the enemy are relieved daily at Eastport from Iuca, and it is universally believed there is a considerable force of Infantry & Cavalry there and at the Bear Creek Bridge. My orders being to dislodge the enemy from the Batteries recently erected near Eastport and these being already abandoned, I have returned to Pittsburg, and report the River all clear of Batteries between us and Chickasaw. Not a hostile shot was fired at any of the Boats during the trip." ALS, *ibid.*, RG 393, District of West Tenn., Letters Received. *O.R.*, I, x, part 1, 83–84. For the report of Lt. William Gwin, gunboat *Tyler*, see *O.R.*, I, viii, 121–22.

To Capt. Nathaniel H. McLean

Head Quarters Dist of West Tenn
Savanna March 31st 1862

CAPT N H MCLEAN
A. A. GEN DEPT OF THE MISSISSIPPI
ST LOUIS MO
CAPT

Herewith I forward to Hd Qrs of the Dept. charges made against Col C. J. Wright 13th Mo Vol. Inf'y

These charges have just been handed me. I will have an immediate investigation and should the result warrant it, will prefer charges against Col Wright

Under the recently added "Article of War."[1] ~~added~~, I would respectfully ask if it would be prohibited to send these negroes back to Clarkesville, to turn them out of our Camp, ~~If~~ if these charges should prove true. My own opinion is they should be sent back.

> Very respectfully
> Your Obt Servt
> U S GRANT
> Maj Gen

Copies, DLC-USG, V, 4, 5, 7, 8, 88; DNA, RG 393, USG Hd. Qrs. Correspondence. On March 30, 1862, Col. Philip B. Fouke, Fort Donelson, wrote to USG. "Inclosed you will find a note to you from Honl. J. M. Quarles, a member of the 36th Congress & one of my personal friends & highly esteemed by Mgr. Genl. McClernand & Brigr Genl. Logan—Every reliance can be placed on his statement of facts—In good truth Genl. I have investigated this case carfully, at Clarksville & find that *all* said by Mr. Quarles is *true*. I found a very bad state of feeling at Clarkville—The citizens attributed it all to the administration of Col Wright —(I hope Genl. this is not, unmilitary—I wish merely to state facts)   They have lost a large number of slaves—& in consequence of the exasperated state of feeling in & about Clarksville, I am assured that not less than 200 men had gone off in a fit of desperation & joined the Confederate army, who never would have gone, if protection to their property could have been afforded. The two negroes refered to by Mr. Quarles are the property of Mrs. Thomas & her children & I am satisfied that the return of those two negroes would do more good, & go further to cultivate a union sentiment in & about Clarksville than any other act—a liberal policy, such as you inaugerated here, & instructed me to pursue will be of infinitely more value than a victory with arms—all is quiet here, all satisfied, commerce & buisniss begining to move & I have no doubt but in a short time, a large majority will wish to vote for the 'old union' again—I send you two other memorandums, which are very hard cases indeed—I feel deeply the importance of the step I have ventured to lay before you & *know* the benefits that will result from it. I have two Companies of my Regt. stationed at Clarkville by order of Maj. Genl. Halleck. Upon the subject of negroes, I gave them your instructions to me—The citizens are satisfied with them & seem to desire a friendly intercourse with them   With a hope, Genl that I have said nothing out of place I subscribe myself your Sincere friend & admirer"   ALS, *ibid.*, District of West Tenn., Letters Received. Fouke enclosed a letter of March 27 to USG from former U. S. Representative James M. Quarles, Clarksville, who later served in the C. S. army. "Mrs R W Thomas. had Two Negro-boys—carried off by Col. Wright when his command left this place. by. Name James &. Stephen—James. is about. 22. years of age. and very Black and weighs. about. 150 pounds. Stephen is Liter complected. and inclind to be fat—and is about. 18 years of age.—These negroes. are all the property She has. and they were given to her. and her—Children (eight in number) by her. brother in Law—and they are her sole support—Her husband. is a cripple—and totally unable to perform physical Labour—but the Editor of a paper at this place and a man of great popularity—and I know the fact to be True, that neither of them were ever employed on any government work of any sort. My information is that they were taken by Col Wright as body servants Mrs Thomas is my. mother in Law and I Know every fact that I state—all I ask is that Genl. Grant will send them back to Col Fouke and if these facts are not. clearly and conclusively—proven then I do not ask their release It is a great Injustice. and should at once be rectified—and I trust it will be done—for they have never been. used in any way so as to. forfeit them to the United States Government—They are stemmers of Tobacco. and have always been employed at it—and I appeal to the Gen Commanding to see that the Col here does not violate justice right fair dealing—and the general orders of the Commander—I. refer the Gen to Col Fouke Col Logan and Major Genl. McClernand to know who I am and whether my Statements are to be relied on" ALS, *ibid*.

1. Article 102, approved March 13, prohibited soldiers from returning fugitive slaves. *O.R.*, II, i, 810.

To Brig. Gen. Alexander M. McCook

Head Quarters, Dist of West. Tenn.
Savanna, March 31st 1862.

GEN. McCOOK
COMMDG. ADVANCE FORCES,
ARMY OF THE OHIO
GENL:

The two Cavalry men sent by you have arrived. I have been looking for your column anxiously for several days so as to report it to Head Quarters of the Dept., ~~and~~ thinking some move may depend on your arrival.

I am, Gen, Very Respectfully
Your Obt. Servant.
U. S. GRANT.
Major Gen.

Copies, DLC-USG, V, 1, 2, 3, 86; DNA, RG 393, USG Letters Sent. *O.R.*, I, x, part 2, 83. See letter to Capt. Nathaniel H. McLean, March 31, 1862, note 1.

Calendar

1862, JAN. 8. Capt. William S. Hillyer to Brig. Gen. Eleazer A. Paine. "I am instructed by Gen. Grant, to say to you that Mr. R. F. Fitzgerald, who was arrested, and relieved by you, will not be permitted to return. You will have his team taken care of, and used for Government purposes till further orders."—Copies, DLC-USG, V, 1, 2, 3, 85; DNA, RG 393, USG Letters Sent. On Feb. 12, Richard F. Fitzgerald, Cairo, wrote to I. Edward Wilkens, British consul at Chicago, asserting that he was a British subject who had lived sixty miles below Cairo on the Mississippi River, and that he had been imprisoned since bringing a load of family furniture to Cairo in Jan.— Copy, *ibid.*, RG 109, Union Provost Marshals' File of Papers Relating to Individual Civilians. Other documents in the same place do not reveal what happened to Fitzgerald.

1862, JAN. 8. Col. Nicholas Perczel, 10th Iowa, to USG, reporting "an engagement with the rebels."—DLC-USG, V, 10; DNA, RG 393, USG Register of Letters Received. USG may have received a copy of Perczel's report to Brig. Gen. Eleazer A. Paine, Jan. 8, concerning the ambush of his command the previous night near Charleston, Mo., in which five of his men were killed, two mortally wounded, and fifteen severely wounded.—*O.R.*, I, viii, 47–48.

1862, JAN. 9. L. A. Louis, Ill. Central Railroad agent, Ashley, Ill., to USG. "Four recruits here for forty Eighth Ills Regt send transportation by telegraph"—Telegram received, DNA, RG 393, Dept. of the Mo., Telegrams Received.

1862, JAN. 11. Col. John J. S. Wilson, Springfield, Ill., to USG. "Have you any orders that you wish me to Execute Any time soon operator will send to me in cypher if you desire it"—Telegram received, DNA, RG 393, Dept. of the Mo., Telegrams Received.

1862, JAN. 12. To hd. qrs., Dept. of the Mo. "Approved and respectfully forwarded to Hd Qrs. Dept. of the Mo"—ES, DNA, RG 393, Dept. of the Mo., Letters Received. Written on a letter of Jan. 8 from Col. Leonard F. Ross to Maj. Gen. Henry W. Halleck. "In accordance with Genl Order No 1. Jany 1st 1862. I herewith transmit for your approval and appointment as a 'Board or commission, under said order

The following officers, and will state that an imperative necessity requires their immediate appointment.

Major. Jonas Rawalt	7th Ill Cavalry
Captain Thomas A Boyd	17th Ill. Vol Reg
Captain C. M Carter	11th Mo '' ''
Captain J. Elliott ~~Artillery Co~~	11th Mo.'' ''
Lieut William Pearce	11th Mo Vol Reg

The above names are submitted, with the belief that they will do full and ample justice to parties concerned.''—ALS, *ibid.*

1862, Jan. 12.   Capt. John A. Rawlins to Capt. Charles D. Townsend, 4th Ill. Cav., Big Muddy Bridge, Ill. "Information having been received at these Head Quarters, that Mr. Kellogg, a representative in the legislature of the State of Ills. at its last session from Washington County is buying and shipping Powder from Chicgo to some point for the use of the Rebels (it is said to be put up in boxes and marked Dry Goods.) Brig. Genl. Grant, Commdg, directs me to say you will go, or send a competent Officer, with the requisite number of men, along the line of said Rail Road both ways, as far as you may deem practicable, and by proper search and investigation discover if possible the truth or falsity of the above charge, and if found to be true, you will have Mr. Kellogg arrested, and sent to the Provost Marshal of the District at this place. You will be governed in this case as far as may be compatible, with instructions priviously furnished you, in regard to the breaking up of illicit and contraband trade, seizing all contraband articles and arresting all persons implicated by proof with the same." —Copies, DLC-USG, V, 1, 2, 3, 85; DNA, RG 393, USG Letters Sent. Representative Orson Kellogg of Perry County served in the Ill. General Assembly 1860–1862. His loyalty was questioned in a letter of "Clay," Bridgeport, Ill., Nov. 11, 1861, in *Missouri Democrat,* Nov. 16, 1861.

1862, Jan. 12.   Capt. John A. Rawlins to Valentine B. Horton, Jr. "I am instructed by the Genl. Commdg to say, he gave verbal orders to Capt. W. J. Kountz, A. Q. M. to retain the Steamer 'Key Stone' in the Government service, and is surprised at his order discharging the same. She will be retained in the service, until otherwise ordered by the Genl. Commdg."—Copies, DLC-USG, V, 1, 2, 3, 85; DNA, RG 393, USG Letters Sent. On Jan. 11, Capt. William J. Kountz wrote to

Horton. "Your Steambots, the 'Keystone' and 'Lake Erie' are hereby discharged from further service as Government Transports"—LS, *ibid.*, District of Cairo, Letters Received.

1862, JAN. 13.   Maj. Gen. George B. McClellan to USG. "Have you provided ammunition for the Enfield & other new rifles?"—ALS (telegram sent), DNA, RG 107, Telegrams Collected (Bound). The telegram is undated; the date is provided in copies, DLC-USG, V, 4, 5, 7, 8; DNA, RG 393, USG Hd. Qrs. Correspondence.

1862, JAN. 13.   Capt. Richard McAllister to USG. "I require the services of an authorized inspector for the purpose of inspecting between five and six hundred barrels of Flour on Williamson & Haynes Wharf-boat; and as there is none here I would respectfully request you to appoint one. My instructions from Capt. Haines, Chief Com. Subs. at St. Louis, are to receive none but such as will pass 'as the highest grade of extra superfine,' and the inspector should be instructed accordingly."—LS, DNA, RG 393, District of Cairo, Letters Received.

1862, JAN. 14.   USG Special Orders No. 16. "The Negro sent to General Hospital at Mound City, from the Fleet at this point, will be transfered to a private Hospital or, private Quarters, agreable to paragraph 1217, U. S. A. Regulations, and attended by the Medical Officers of the Hospital."—Copies, DLC-USG, V, 15, 16, 82, 87, 89; DNA, RG 393, USG Special Orders. "The expenses of a soldier placed temporarily in a private hospital, on the advice of the senior surgeon of the post or detachment, sanctioned by the commanding officer, will be paid by the Subsistence Department, not to exceed seventy-five cents a day."—*Revised Regulations for the Army of the United States, 1861* (Philadelphia, 1861), p. 246.

1862, JAN. 14.   Col. Leonard F. Ross to USG. "I desire to call your attention to the enclosed letter from Captain Norton, which will explain itself. Captain Taggart, Commissary of Subsistence at this Post, refuses as I understand him upon the ground that P—1218, as well as the entire section relating to the commutation of rations, relate to the recruiting service. He will pay the commuted price at cost of ration, no more. Evidently this am't (About 11¢ a day) would leave the clerk but ill fed while on detached duty—I submit the question for your determination—Please advise as soon as practicable."—Copy, DNA, RG 393, Post of Cape Girardeau, Letters Sent.

1862, JAN. 16.   To Secretary of State William H. Seward. "The persons named are very dangerous men & ought to be permanently secured. No safe custody for them here."—Copy, DNA, RG 107, Telegrams Received (Press). Written on a telegram of Jan. 16 from David L. Phillips, U. S. marshal for the southern district of Ill., to Seward. "Genl Grant commanding district of Cairo has delivered into my hands as marshall, Col. Ogden & Jas M Perkins of Kentucky W. H. Childs of Alabama & Patrick Brady of Mo as traitors they must be held   Where shall I put them   One guard in former case other an officer on furlough   No charge for him"—Copy, *ibid.* See *O.R.*, II, ii, 1357–60.

1862. JAN. 17.   Maj. Gen. Henry W. Halleck to USG. "One S. L. Casey has telegraphed me from Evansville, asking that troops be sent from Shawneetown, into Union & Crittenden counties, Ky. to protect the Union men from a body of marauders. I do not know the man; but have referred him to you for such action as you may deem proper."— LS (telegram sent), DNA, RG 393, Dept. of the Mo., Telegrams Received. The telegram probably refers to Samuel L. Casey of Casey-ville, Ky., a member of the Ky. House of Representatives, about this time elected to the U. S. House of Representatives to fill a vacancy.

1862, JAN. 19.   Capt. John A. Rawlins to Maj. Andrew J. Kuykendall. "Hereafter when you find persons violating, or ~~having~~ who have vio-lated General Orders No 22. issued by the Post Commander, prohib-iting the sale, barter or Exchange of intoxicating liquors to any and all persons, whatsoever, quartered, resident, or being within the incor-porated limits of the City of Cairo, you will enter the premises, and take possession of, and destroy all liquors, therein found."—Copies, DLC-USG, V, 1, 2, 3, 85; DNA, RG 393, USG Letters Sent.

1862, JAN. 20.   To Brig. Gen. Montgomery C. Meigs requesting that $100,000 be deposited to his credit at New York.—DNA, RG 92, Register of Letters Received.

1862, JAN. 21.   Col. Leonard F. Ross to USG. "Our ferry boat was snagged this morning & sunk in 18 inches Water. We must have a small boat here. The Iatan is now here. Shall I use her?"—Telegram received (punctuation added), DNA, RG 393, Dept. of the Mo., Telegrams Received; copy, *ibid.*, Post of Cape Girardeau, Telegrams. On Jan. 23, Ross telegraphed to USG. "We have raised the 'Luella,' but in damaged condition. Shall we send her to Cairo for repairs?—What shall we have to take her place?—"—Copy, *ibid.* On Jan. 24, Ross wrote to USG. "I will be compelled to send 'Luella' to Cairo for repairs. We greatly need a boat in her place: What course shall I pursue to procure one in her place until repaired?"—Copy, *ibid.*, Letters Sent. On Jan. 28, Capt. John A. Rawlins wrote to the asst. q. m., Cairo. "Will furnish transportation by the Steamer Ferry Boat 'Luella' as soon as she is off the ways at Mound City, where she is being repaired, for John C. Vanduzen and one man, and Telegraph Cable, from this place to Cape Girardeau, Mo."—Copies, DLC-USG, V, 2, 85; DNA, RG 393, USG Letters Sent.

1862, JAN. 21. Col. Leonard F. Ross to USG. "Many of the Mo S. Militia Capt Murdock Commanding, now stationed here—are without horses or arms. We are constantly taking horses and arms from enemy. Would it not be as well to have the same appraised and sold to these men who are properly mustered into Service. In this way these men can be rendered efficent. There are also in possession of Q M. Shields at this post, saddles, & holsters—turned over by Maj Abby 'Fremont Rangers' Could they not be disposed of in same Way. I sent report, by Express I will forward Inventory of Captured property—as soon as completed. We have Twenty Six Horses"—ALS, DNA, RG 393, District of Cairo, Letters Received.

1862, JAN. 22. Brig. Gen. John A. McClernand to USG, "in reference to a Squad of men now at Cave-in-rock—men returned this morning."—Register of Letters, McClernand Papers, IHi.

1862, JAN. 22. Col. James D. Morgan, 10th Ill., Mound City, Ill., to USG. "I have Just received information that I think entitled to credit That a rebel force of two thousand are at Pin hook in Poverty hollow a point five miles South of Blandville"—Telegram received, DNA, RG 393, Dept. of the Mo., Telegrams Received.

1862, JAN. 22. Capt. Richard McAllister to USG. "I enclose for your approval bill of Coffee furnished 45th Regt. Ill. Vols. I am ordered by the late commander of the post to pay the bill but before doing so I prefer having your approval. The price pr. gallon (36½ cts) is high but the claimants aver that they were ordered to make it in haste without previous preperation and that the price but barely compensates for their labor. I am much in favor of furnishing the troops arriving here in the present inclement season with cooked rations and shall be most happy to second any order you may make on that subject."—ALS, DNA, RG 393, District of Cairo, Letters Received.

1862, Jan. 22. Capt. Charles D. Townsend, 4th Ill. Cav., Carbondale, Ill., to USG. "Send me pass from Big Muddy to Cairo for a non commissioned officer under arrest & two men for guard   Telegraph here as soon as convenient."—Telegram received, DNA, RG 393, Dept. of the Mo., Telegrams Received.

1862, Jan. 23. Brig. Gen. John A. McClernand to USG. "The acceptance of Genl. McClernand of the resignation of Lieut Geo W Green was accompanied with a letter of explanation—that Lt. Green resigned Aug 9 1861, and a successer elected and commissioned, and has been in service and paid,—when Lt Green left the service and has been engaged in other business—by some mistake Lt Greens resignation was sent to Springfield instead of St Louis—should not his resignation been accepted Aug 9, instead of 'this day' "—Register of Letters, McClernand Papers, IHi.

1862, Jan. 25. Col. John J. S. Wilson, Springfield, Ill., to USG. "The Paducah and Cape Girardeau lines together with the Cable now at Cairo belong to the Government; the Telegraph Company having henceforward nothing whatever to do with them. Please afford Mr. Van Duzer the necessary facilities for the repair of the lines and the laying of the Cable."—Telegram received, DNA, RG 393, Dept. of the Mo., Telegrams Received.

1862, Jan. 26. To Brig. Gen. John A. McClernand. "Wishes to know if Genl McClernand has any special charge against G Thompson who was taken a prisoner on Coffee's farm. He is quite a youth and general good character his mother a widow, was at Coffees going to school   Judge Marshall wishes him released."—Register of Letters, McClernand Papers, IHi.

1862, JAN. 27.   Col. Leonard F. Ross to USG. "Refugees are daily arriving from Bloomfield and not a few are enlisting in the U. S. Army —A band of desperadoes below Bloomfield, about eighteen miles are represented as having hoisted the 'Black flag' and engaged in murdering and driving out Union men—We are very much in want of *Armed Cavalry* to disperse these bands—Our Cavalry have nothing but sabres and the *enemy know it*. At first we did effective Service by Capturing them without arms—but as they are now aware of our unarmed condition it would be unsafe to attack them—Yesterday twenty five rebels were reported as being at Jackson—I could order no pursuit because of *this lack*—Must loyal citizens continue to be murdered and driven from their homes and we be able to offer no protection?—I have made representations so frequently in regard to this matter that I am reluctant in calling your attention to it again—With Five or Six Companies of well armed Cavalry I know that I can maintain peace and quiet within a radius of fifty or sixty miles of this post—Had they been furnished when the call was first made, I am satisfied that many valuable lives could have been saved—I know that hundreds of men now fleeing for their lives, leaving their property behind them might now be enjoying the peace and quiet of home. The expidition to Benton & Commerc[e] returned. The substance of Report I have already telegraphed. I can add nothing, until a written report is rec'd from the officer in command—"—Copy, DNA, RG 393, Post of Cape Girardeau, Letters Sent.

1862, JAN. 28.   Brig. Gen. John A. McClernand to USG. "Genl. McClernand informs Genl. Grant, that the Steamer W H Brown needs repairs and that the Steamer Champion could take her place."—Register of Letters, McClernand Papers, IHi.

1862, JAN. 29.   USG endorsement: "explains . . . seizure of flatboats on the Mississippi used for smuggling."—American Art Association Anderson Galleries Sale No. 4292, Jan. 20–21, 1937. On Jan. 28, Thomas H. Clark, Mound City, wrote to Brig. Gen. John A. McClernand. "The petition of Thos H. Clark Respectfully sheweth That petitioner was the lawful, and Sole Owner of a Covered Flat Boat 80 feet long 16 feet wide fitted up for Store purposes and value for Same $250 00   That Said Boat was removed from her moorings and taken charge of by U. S. authorities in common with other Boats for the

better Security against traitors, which petitioner thinks was very prudent. That on the 20th day of the present Month of Jan. 1862 at 11.
O clock P. M. Said Boat broke her moorings at the port of Cairo, from
pressure, of heavy drift, from the present flood, and despite the exertions of Mr. Engineer Nye of the Steamer Alps, & petitioner, She got
away.   feeling it our imperative duty to Save this, or any other property, in charge of our Government. That the Capt. of the *Rob Roy* used
every exertion to overhaul Said Boat but in vain, on account of the
darkness of the Night at ½ past 11 O clock, P. M. That Said Boat
passed the lower Blockade, little after 8 Bells, as reported by the
Officers of the Deck, to petitioner and by petitioner to you. How on
Same day whilst embarking your Command to Cairo, &c. you kindly
referring petitioner to the Office. 'That' you were then engrossed'
That your petitioner is a poor man, and feeling that the dignity of his
Country, does not desire Sacrifice of this Kind, from her faithful Citizens, of which Class he is Known truly to be. He is respectfully before
your Honor Claiming Compensation for Said boat. That your petitioner feeling the Justice of the Act prays that your Honor, will Order
the Division Q. M. at Cairo to pay to petitioner, an equvalent equal
in value to his Boat, ~~to him~~. Out of any rebel property or money, that
may be on hand from Kentucky, as they directly led to this loss by
their Rebellion."—AD, DNA, RG 109, Union Provost Marshals' File
of Papers Relating to Individual Civilians. One-third of the docket
sheet is torn away, presumably the portion on which USG's endorsement was written. On Jan. 29, McClernand endorsed this letter to
USG. "Respectfully refer.d to Genl U. S. Grant, Comg Dis of Cairo,
as a just and politic application."—ES, *ibid*. On Jan. 31, Capt. John C.
Kelton endorsed this letter. "At this time the Commanding General
cannot act upon such claims."—ES, *ibid*. On Feb. 8, Clark wrote to
USG. "A few days before you left Cairo for Fort Henry, your servant
made application for indemnification for a flat Boat belonging to him.
It was presented to you with Gen McClernands remarks thereon which
you kindly endorsed for adjustment, and sent the same to Gen Halleck
for instructions.   you told me to call for an answer in six days from
that time but when I called you were gone—I have filed the claim
before the Commission now in Session at Cairo—They instruct me to
write to you with a request that you will please send me the application
with its endorsements—that I may place it before them as testimony
that an order issued from your Office to put all those boats on the Ohio

River under Serveilance (in this neighborhood) by Sending me this class of testimony you will confer a great favor on your very faithful Servant."—ALS, *ibid.*

1862, JAN. 29. Capt. John A. Rawlins to Brig. Gen. John A. McClernand. "The enclosed Special Order No 21 issued from these Head Quaters has not yet been complied with. Will you please see to its enforcement at once"—LS, McClernand Papers, IHi. In a letter misdated Jan. 27, but probably written on Jan. 29, Maj. Mason Brayman wrote to USG. "In reply to yours of to-day enclosing copy of your order No 21 respecting vacation of a building occupied by the Quarter Master of the 27th Regt., I am instructed by Genl McClernand to advise you that the order was sent to Col. Buford on its receipt but that on representations made by him, its operation was suspended, by an order of which a copy is enclosed. Genl. McClernand awaits your further direction"—Copy, *ibid.* On Jan. 30, Rawlins wrote to McClernand. "I am instructed by Brig. General Grant to inform you that he has just received information that the Building mentioned in Special Orders. No. 21. issued from these Head Quarters, a copy of which was sent you yesterday, is not yet vacated. You are again requested to have it vacated ~~at once~~, or the reason why it is not done made known to these Head Quarters, that the order may be suspended by the same authority that originated it."—LS, *ibid.*

1862, JAN. 29. Brig. Gen. John A. McClernand to USG. "Herewith you will find a special requisition from Capt Schwartz, accompanied by what appears to me to be a very satisfactory letter of explanation. To meet the contingency of an order for a forward movement, I ~~I~~ am striving to complete the equipment and armament of my command. Hence, ~~I trouble you with~~ the apology for troubling you with this notice of the fact, and the reference of the requisition ~~named~~ mentioned for your confermatory approval."—DfS, McClernand Papers, IHi.

1862, JAN. 29. Brig. Gen. Eleazer A. Paine to Capt. John A. Rawlins. "By order of Brig. Genl. McClernand, issued to me on Saturday the 25th Inst, I sent a cavalry force of about 275. men under command of Major Hall of the 7th Ill cavalry Regt. to Charleston Mo. and also by Rail Road detatchments of the 8th 11th and 20th Regts. Ill Infantry under the command of Col Wallace, of the 11th to the same place. The next morning with a detachment from the 10th Iowa Infantry Regt. I proceeded by Rail Road to the same place. Also Capt. Nolemans, and Burrels companies, under command of Major Jenkins, of the 1st Ill Cavalry Regt; making the entire force about 1400 men. On my arrival at Charleston I received what we believed to be reliable information, that rebels were encamped in the neighborhood of Bertrand, a small village on the Rail Road, six miles from Charleston. Leaving the 10th Iowa at Charleston in command of Lieut Col Small, I proceeded to Bertrand; but was unable to find the location of the rebels. Monday morning the 27nth I sent Major Hall with 250 of his command by way of the north cut Bridge: to Andersons Mill, a locality much infested by rebels and proceeded with Col Wallace and Major Jenkins commands leaving the 8th Ill under command of Major Post at Bertrand. By following the Rail Road the men marching on the track, and the horses being rode through the swamp to said Mill. I there found reliable authority that none of the organized military rebels, had been concerned in firing into the Steamer D. A. January near Prices Landing. But the fact is some ten or twelve citizen rebels living near to Prices Landing were guilty of the act. I have all of the facts and as soon as I can cause three or four arrests, I will make a more extended report. From Andersons Mill the Infantry returned by Bertrand and the Cavalry by the north cut road to Charleston.   at this time all of the troops have returned, to this post, except the command of Lieut Col Small which is still at Charleston. The Topographical information obtained by the march, is of much value. The ridges of land on which troops can be marched extend from Cape Girardeau towards New Madrid. The spaces intervening large too, are swamps and lakes impassable at this season of the year. It is much easier for troops to reach Sykeston, 25 miles from here on the Rail Road by way of Cape Girardeau, than direct from this point"—LS, DNA, RG 393, District of Cairo, Letters Received.

1862, JAN. 30.   Brig. Gen. John A. McClernand to USG. "Although having a clear opinion, thereon, I desire to be assured by your advise upon the following statement of law and fact. War Department General Order No 15. May 4th 1861—provides:—'The adjutant and Regimental Quartermaster will be selected from the Company Officers of the regiment, by the Colonel, and may be re-assigned to Companies at his pleasure.' War Department decision—September 25th. 1861:—

'The adjutants and Quartermasters are extra Lieutenants, by law.' War Department General Order No 44 July 13th 1861.:—'Commanding Officers of regiments are reminded that the appointment, resignation and removal of regimental adjutants are to be reported immediately to this office.' Revised Regulations, paragraph 466:—Same point. The facts are:—A Colonel appoints his adjutant and Quartermaster from persons, outside—not Lieutenants. The Governor commissions them:—'having been appointed' 'do Commission' 'as Lieutenants in the 00th Regiment.' Enquiry:—Has the Colonel the right to remove them at pleasure? If so, do they remain Lieutenants.? If so, may he assign them to duty in Companies? In the case under consideration there are vacancies ready. Or is the rank and pay only given as an appendage to the office of adjutant, ceasing when the removal takes place?''—Copy, McClernand Papers, IHi.

1862, Jan. 30. Maj. Mason Brayman to USG. "Genl. M'Clernand desires the enclose provision return sent to you; for the reason that he has no knowledge of the 'contract' referred to, and no means of comparison, to ascertain the accuracy of the return. He suggests that the requisitions of this kind be approved at Dist. Head Quarters, or that he be furnished with copies of the contracts."—ADfS, McClernand Papers, IHi.

1862, Jan. 30. Maj. Mason Brayman to USG. "Capt. F. Evans recently mustered out of service at Big Muddy Bridge informs Genl. McClernand that some of his unsettled accounts were in the hands of Capt R. B. Hatch at the time of his arrest, and that Capt. Hatch informs him he has not access to them. Capt. Evans desiring adjustment &c, respectfully enquires, through Genl. McClernand, if the officer now in charge can dispose of the matter."—DfS, McClernand Papers, IHi. See endorsement to Brig. Gen. John A. McClernand, Oct. 30, 1861.

1862, Jan. [30]. Col. Thomas H. Cavanaugh, Shawneetown, to USG. "Will you please grant Maj. Grierson leave of absence to go to Jacksonville, Ills., his family being sick. Also, I would state, he has never been absent from his duties prior to this time."—ALS, McClernand Papers, IHi. On Jan. 31, by Special Orders No. 27, Capt. John A. Rawlins granted leave to Maj. Benjamin H. Grierson.—DS, *ibid.*

1862, Jan. 31.   USG endorsement, "Approved" on an application for leave of absence for Private Charles Pasley, 27th Ill., wounded at Belmont.—AES, McClernand Papers, IHi.

1862, Jan. 31.   Col. John Cook, Fort Holt, to USG. "I am informed that the 28th Reg't. are removing lumber from their present quarters on board City of Memphis, which evidently causes their delay in embarking. Orders having been issued to embark at seven A M., Have issued notice to the Captain, a copy of which he will show you on his arrival. I will hold the boat for your instruct[ion]s. Many of the quarters [a]re covered with clap boards. Can they not as well take those off also?"—Telegram received (punctuation added), DNA, RG 393, Dept. of the Mo., Telegrams Received. On Feb. 1, Cook telegraphed to USG. "Should the water Continue rising the Quarters of the 28th cannot be occupied after a few days   If from your knowledge of the river an Early fall may be expected the quarters of the 28th would make a Regt very comfortable—"—Telegram received, *ibid.* On Feb. 1, Brig. Gen. Charles F. Smith telegraphed to USG. "Am I to put the 28th Regt in camp here   Answer"—Telegram received, *ibid.*

1862, Jan. 31.   Robert Forsyth, Chicago, to USG. "Contractors to Govt. at Cairo do not take their freight, but consign to Quarter Master, thus compelling us to take vouchers from Govt. They must pay cash. The vouchers would subject us to a deduction of 33 per cent. I know your intention is to have Contracts filled at Cairo & not do us the injustice of giving Contractors benefit of road as enjoyed by Govt. Will you please see to this?"—Telegram received (punctuation added), DNA, RG 393, Dept. of the Mo., Telegrams Received. On Feb. 7, Capt. John A. Rawlins wrote to Forsyth. "I am directed by Brig. Gen. Grant to say to you that it is not inteded that Contractors to deliver supplies at Cairo, for the Army, shall have any benefit, or be parties to the arrangements for carrying Freight between the Government, and the Illinois Central Rail Road. ~~If they have not the money to pay the full price of Freight they should~~"—Copies, DLC-USG, V, 2, 85; DNA, RG 393, USG Letters Sent.

1862, Jan. 31.   Ill. AG Allen C. Fuller to USG. "The thirty second (32d) Regt Col Logan Eight hundred & seventy four (874) strong

leave today for Cairo & will report to you   will send the forty ninth
Col Morrison Saturday or Sunday"—Telegram received, DNA, RG
393, Dept. of the Mo., Telegrams Received.

1862, [JAN.]   USG endorsement. "The object of having a Medical
Director is that he shall be supreme in his own Department. The
decision of Surgeon Brinton is sustained."—*Personal Memoirs of John
H. Brinton* (New York, 1914), p. 104. Surgeon John H. Brinton
recalled from memory this endorsement on a letter of Brig. Gen. John
A. McClernand withdrawing able-bodied men from hospital details.
Brinton believed this would paralyze hospital services, and had already
endorsed the order with a challenge to its validity.—*Ibid.,* pp. 103–4.

1862, FEB. 1.   USG General Orders No. 6. "Troops leaving the
various posts of this command will take with them, when ordered into
the Field none but well men. Each Regiment will leave either their
surgeons or assistant Surgeon, in charge of the sick. When there is
but one, he will accompany the Regiment, reporting first to the Medical
Director, who will provide attendance for the Sick, or transfer them
to the General Hospital."—Copies, DLC-USG, V, 12, 13, 14, 95;
DNA, RG 393, USG General Orders.

1862, FEB. 1.   To Brig. Gen. John A. McClernand. "Respectfully
refered to Gen. McClernand Comd.g"—AES, McClernand Papers,
IHi. Written on a letter of Jan. 23, from James Holmes, General Hospital, Mound City, to Maj. Gen. Henry W. Halleck. "As a soldier in
the service of the U. S. I feel it my duty to report to you a case that
happens to come under my notice and one that is a violation of army
order No 3. issued by you (I may be mistaken as to the number of the
order.) During the late Reconnisance by Gen. Grant into KY two
Captains of the 10th Ill Vol. was guilty of abducting slaves from that
state. The owner of a certain slave came into the camp on the hunt of
his property   The slave was secreted, and the owner was arrested but
upon his producing evidence that he was a good union man was liberated   When the army left their encampment on their home ward
march the Negro was wrapped in a tent cloth and put on a wagon   The
names of the guilty parties are Capt.s Cowens and Smith   It is currently reported that two slaves were stolen by this Regiment and

brought over into this state   For reference in regard to this matter
I give you the following names

> Capt Lusk   10th Reg Ill Vol
> Lieut Man   ”   ”   ”   ”
> Capt Wood   ”   ”   ”   ”

(Drs Thorp & Goddard of Mound City Gen Hospital and others heard
some of the officers of the Reg acknowledge to the above charge   Hoping that these Negro thieves will be dealt with in a proper manner I
subscribe myself”—ALS, *ibid.* On Jan. 30, Capt. Nathaniel H. McLean
endorsed the letter. "Respectfully referred to Brig. Genl. Grant for
report."—ES, *ibid.*

1862, FEB. 1.   Brig. Gen. Charles F. Smith to Capt. John A. Rawlins.
"Soon after the general hospital at this place was put on a good footing
some half-a-dozen Sisters of Charity residing in St. Mary's academy
here tendered their services as nurses in the same, with the sanction of
their Bishop, and were accepted. Their duties have been admirably
performed, and one, quite young, has fallen a victim to disease contracted from exposure and labor in the discharge of duty. With the
exception of a ration they receive no compensation; refusing it by
direction of the Bishop. Not long after their instalation as nurses the
building in which they formerly resided—their home—the St. Mary's
Acad.y, was forcibly entered by some of the Volunteer troops and
stores and other articles carried off. I had an investigation made and
the property was, in great degree, restored. I directed Brigr. Genl.
Paine to have a guard stationed at the house to protect the property,
but this, it would seem, was soon discontinued; why I have yet to
learn. Soon after this the house was again forcibly entered by Volunteers and '*gutted.*' Altho' it was known to have been done by Vols. of
the 40th. or 41st. Ills. regts., one or both, the investigation I ordered
Genl. *Paine* to make in the matter ~~soon~~ resulted in nothing. The
accompanying list of articles taken was prepared by 'Sister *Martha,*'
the head of the establishment, at my request, in the hope that its payment may be ordered. As they refuse compensation for their personal
services I endeavored to induce them to allow themselves to be mustered for payment to the extent of the loss claimed, but they steadily
refuse to do this. The services of these women have been invaluable,
and I most earnestly hope that they will not be allowed to be the sufferers of the outrage perpetrated upon them: that the Commander of

the Dept. will order prompt payment for the loss incurred."—ALS, DNA, RG 393, District of Cairo, Letters Received.

1862, FEB. 1. Col. John Cook to USG. "Can the Sick in my Hospital be sent to Hospital in Cairo or M[*ound*] City? All will be in readiness if the Hospital Can be provided for. My Asst. Surgeon is on hand. By permission from head quarters, surgeon present for duty."—Telegram received (punctuation added), DNA, RG 393, Dept. of the Mo., Telegrams Received.

1862, FEB. 2. Brig. Gen. John A. McClernand to USG. "I understand that Genl. M. C. Meigs Qr. Mr. U. S. has ordered large quantities of India rubber goods—consisting of blankets &c. for the use of U. S. troops. The Army on the Potomac is amply supplied with such goods. They are a great protection against rain and snow—conducing much to the comfort and healthfulness of the men. Cannot some of these goods be procured for distribution among the troops of this District? I hope so. I would respectfully urge it."—Copies, McClernand Papers, IHi.

1862, FEB. 2. Surgeon Edward C. Franklin, Mound City Hospital, to USG. "Three hundred & twenty five comfortably, four hundred on an emergency."—Telegram received, DNA, RG 393, Dept. of the Mo., Telegrams Received. Apparently in relation to hospital facilities available. See letter to Capt. John C. Kelton, Dec. 24, 1861.

1862, FEB. 4. Capt. John A. Rawlins to Col. John J. S. Wilson. "You will make arrangements to have the Telegraph Office, at Cairo, kept open night and day during the next three days. Have an operator at his post at all hours."—Copies, DLC-USG, V, 1, 2, 3, 85; DNA, RG 393, USG Letters Sent.

1862, FEB. 5. Col. William P. Kellogg, 7th Ill. Cav., Cape Girardeau, to USG. "Our Cavalry are scouting the country some thirty or forty miles west of this point. Some thirty persons, several of them deserter[s] from Jeff Thompsons army—came in this morning and took the oath. Persons are constantly arriving from the counties west of this place and voluntarily delivering themselves up. A detachment of our Cavalry are now in the Vicinity of Bloomfield—with a View of intercepting a drove of cattle said to be in that Vicinity on their way

to New-Madrid. Via plank road Pt Pleasant—I will advise you as soon
as I ascertain the result"—Copy, DNA, RG 393, Post of Cape Girar-
deau, Letters Sent. On Jan. 28, by Special Orders No. 24, District of
Cairo, one battalion of the 7th Ill. Cav. was sent from Bird's Point to
Cape Girardeau.—Copies, DLC-USG, V, 15, 16, 82, 87, 89; DNA,
RG 393, USG Special Orders. See *Calendar*, Feb. 8, 1862.

1862, FEB. 6.   Flag Officer Andrew H. Foote to [Commander William D. Porter]. "General Grant has referred a letter to me addressed
by ~~Mr~~. Capt. Graham to him asking that the *Alps* may tow your vessel
the Essex immediately to Cairo, at your request. ~~This~~ This request
should have been made to me as the Flag Officer, ~~and I would readily
have granted it~~. I give you permission to go to Cairo in tow of the
Alps, ~~whenever you deem it necessary to do so~~   ~~Unless you deem~~ If
you deem it necessary, but as I intend going down to night, I wish
you to remain till this vessel reaches you as we are so badly cut up
I do not like to go down alone."—ADfS, DNA, RG 45, Area 5. *O.R.*
(Navy), I, xxii, 545–46.

1862, FEB. 7.   Capt. William S. Hillyer to Brig. Gen. John A.
McClernand. "I am instructed by Gen Grant to say to you that during
the present expedition and in order to avoid confusion Capt G. W.
Graham will have the charge of all steamboats and all orders to the
steamboats will pass through him. This suggestion is made on account
of an order having been given by Quartermaster Dunlap which con-
flicted with an order previously given by me—This was done inno-
cently and no blame is attached to any one—"—ALS, McClernand
Papers, IHi.

1862, FEB. 8.   USG Special Field Orders No. 5. "Hereafter details
called for from these Head Quarters, will be considered as being asked
from the First Division exclusively, and not from the Second Division,
unless expressly designated. Details from the Second Division will be
made through Gen. Smith Com'd.g   This is intended to apply during
the continuance of Head Quarters at this Fort; after leaving, as the
senior officer, you will necessarily command all the troops"—DS,
McClernand Papers, IHi. Copies of the same orders, designated Special
Field Orders No. 3, are in DLC-USG, V, 15, 16, 82, 89; DNA, RG
393, USG General Orders. On Feb. 8, Brig. Gen. John A. McClernand
wrote to USG. "Special Order No. 5. restricting details called for by

You to the 1st Division is received, and will be observed. The language however leaves me to infer that details called for by the Commissary, Quarter Master, and Ordnance Officer of the Forces here will continue to be made by me as equally as practicable, from all of them. Otherwise, in as much as all of these calls are made upon me, the whole weight of the fatigue duty of the Post, except in so far as your calls might mitigate it, would fall upon the 1st Division. If this inference is erroneous please advice me. Againe if erroneus: would it not be adviceable to equalize their calls as far as practicable upon both Divisions. Unwilling, however, to make an inference the basis of action in this regard, I have taken the liberty to enclose herewith the answer to two calls for details, which you will cause to be communicated, or not, according to your pleasure"—Copies, McClernand Papers, IHi.

1862, FEB. 8. Col. William P. Kellogg, Cape Girardeau, to USG. "I went out an expedition mainly composed of Cavalry, as I had the honor to report to you on the 4th inst. They went to Bloomfield and surrounded the town, about, daylight on the morning of the 5th instant, and Captured severel Notorious Rebels. A detachment then proceeded to Millen's Mill and Distillery, the place of rendezvous of a company forming under one Boot: and encountered a rebel force of about 80 men, routing and pursuing them. ~~Killing~~, Killing 7, wounding severel, and taking twenty prisoners. Also destroying the *mill* and Distillery heretofore much used by the Rebels. We had two men missing, both their Horses being Killed. One of the missing has since been heard from, and is supposed to have escaped. The expedition brought in about forty prisoners. They also, found the remains of five union men, shot by the Rebels some time since. Persons, many of them deserters, from Thompsons Army, are continually coming in, and taking the Oath. There is an Opportunity for a good field of operations for Cavalry in the Country west, especially beyond Bloomfield; where we are credibly informed, Cattle, Hogs and large amount produce, are continually transmitted over the Plank Road, thirty miles beyond Bloomfield, Point Pleasan[t] New Madrid &c. I intend if it shall meet your approbation to intercept and prevent, as far as possible, the Carrying off, Cattle, and produce, over this Road, and break up bands of Marauding parties, particularly organizing and constantly organizing, in aid of the Rebellion"—Copy, DNA, RG 393, Post of Cape Girardeau, Letters Sent.

1862, FEB. 9.   USG General Field Orders No. 3. "All Regimental Officers will immediately take up quarters with their Commands, and not lodge and board on steamers as the General Commanding regrets to see has been done. No officer will be allowed to go aboard any steamer except where his duty carries him. Commanders of Regiments will see that this order is properly executed."—DS, McClernand Papers, IHi. *O.R.*, I, vii, 598.

1862, FEB. 9.   Brig. Gen. John A. McClernand to USG. "In addition to the suggestions which I made to you this afternoon on the subject, I advise you that I have learned that some 75 Beeves which have been fattening for the rebel army, are now on a point of land on the river bank above, now surrounded by high water. The distance is about four miles. Sergeant *Duke* of Co. E. 12th Iowa, Regt. says a black man who had been feeding them, informed him. A prisoner, who had been in the rebel commissary Department here, confirmed the statement. A steamer and party of men could bring them in."—Copies, McClernand Papers, IHi. On Feb. 10, Capt. William S. Hillyer wrote to McClernand. "I am instructed by Gen Grant to say to you that if you will send him the guide you spoke of he will send a boat for those beef cattle—"—ALS, *ibid.*

1862, FEB. 10.   Capt. John A. Rawlins to Brig. Gen. John A. McClernand. "You will cause to be detailed from your Command, at once, one hundred armed men, to proceed on Board the Str. 'Gladiator' to the mouth of Big Sandy. Reporting to Col. Jno Riggin for duty"—LS, McClernand Papers, IHi. On Feb. 10, Maj. Mason Brayman wrote to Rawlins. "The detail for 100 men for 'Gladiator' came to me this afternoon from Genl. M'Clernand who had it. The detail was made, and I hope the men will soon report."—ALS, *ibid.* A correspondent stated that large quantities of tobacco, flour, corn, wheat, salt, tents, clothing, and leather had been seized by John Riggin, Jr., at the mouth of the Big Sandy River at Paris Landing, eight miles upriver from Fort Henry.—Letter of "W. K. P.," Fort Henry, Feb. 13, 1862, in *Missouri Democrat*, Feb. 17, 1862.

1862, FEB. 10.   Brig. Gen. Montgomery C. Meigs to USG. "I have received your letter of the 5th instant, enclosing an account for Horses &c. lost in the battle of Belmont. The Act of March 3 1849, which provides for the payment of Horses and other Property lost or destroyed in the Military service of the United States, also provides that the claim shall be adjusted by the third auditor, to whom, therefore, you should transmit your accounts, which are herewith returned."—LS, DNA, RG 393, District of Cairo, Letters Received. On Jan. 5, USG had written to the q. m. gen.'s office concerning his claim for two horses killed at Belmont.—*Ibid.*, RG 92, Register of Letters Received. See letter to Jesse Root Grant, Nov. 8, 1861.

1862, FEB. 13.   Maj. Gen. Henry W. Halleck to USG. "Announce to your troops the splendid victory gained by our land & naval forces at Roanoke Island North Carolina."—Telegram, copies, DNA, RG 94, Generals' Papers and Books, Telegrams Sent in Cipher by Gen. Halleck; *ibid.*, RG 393, Dept. of the Mo., Telegrams Sent.

1862, FEB. 13.   Maj. Gen. Henry W. Halleck to USG. "Look out for Birge's sharp shooters; they have been committing numerous robberies. I have the Col locked up in the Military prison."—Telegram, copies, DNA, RG 94, Generals' Papers and Books, Telegrams Sent in Cipher by Gen. Halleck; *ibid.*, RG 393, Dept. of the Mo., Telegrams Sent.

1862, FEB. 14.   Maj. Gen. Henry W. Halleck to USG. "The flag of the Union floa[ts] over the Court house in Springfiel[d.] The enemy retreated after a short engagement leaving a large ammount of stores & equipage, which was captured by Genl Curtiss. Our cavalry are in close pursuit."—LS (telegram sent), DNA, RG 107, Telegrams Collected (Unbound); copies, *ibid.*, RG 94, Generals' Papers and Books, Telegrams Sent in Cipher by Gen. Halleck; *ibid.*, RG 393, Dept. of the Mo., Telegrams Sent.

1862, FEB. 15.   Capt. John A. Rawlins to Capt. William W. Leland. "You will furnish to Brig. Gen. U. S. Grant. for the use of himself and Staff, six hams, one hundred and fifty pounds of Hard Bread; fifty pounds of Coffee; thirty pounds of Coffee, and ten pounds Candles, and charge the same to him."—Copies, DLC-USG, V, 2, 85; DNA, RG 393, USG Letters Sent.

1862, FEB. 15.   Capt. John A. Rawlins to Capt. William W. Updegraff, 20th Ohio. "You will at once cause all Soldiers of the Army that you may find on any of the Government transports, except the Sick who have been sent on board, and those who are there on duty, to rejoin their Regiments wherever they may be, and see that neither Officers or Soldiers go on board any of the Boats, unless on Special business."—Copies, DLC-USG, V, 1, 2, 3, 85; DNA, RG 393, USG Letters Sent.

1862, FEB. 18.   Brig. Gen. Simon B. Buckner to USG. "I learn that a report is current amongst your troops, inducing the highest excitement amongst them, and occasioning threats of vengeance on their part towards my soldiers. It is reported that a number of Federal prisoners who had been wounded had been found dead in the jail, and their bodies tied hand and foot. There is not, as I find after an investigation of the subject by a member of my staff in connection with Capt. ~~Osborn~~ Ormsby and Capt. Baxter of your staff, any foundation for this absurd rumor. In justice to the Confederate army I request that you will at once institute a rigid investigation of the matter with a view both of doing justice to the honor of the Confederate army, and of preventing the perpetration on my soldiers, of any acts of cruelty from yours. I will thank you, after the investigation to furnish me with the result of your inquiries and publish the facts to your army. I enclose a statement of Gen. Johnson's."—ALS, DNA, RG 393, District of West Tenn., Letters Received. On Feb. 17, Brig. Gen. Bushrod R. Johnson wrote to Buckner. "On the day of Capitulation, the 16th inst. I gave the keys of the prison to Capt Osburn and requested him to examine it and see if there were any prisoners confined therein. He return the keys to me and reported that there was no one confined in the prison. I am not aware that there ever was but one prisoner confined in the county prison. Indeed I am not sure that even one was therein confined ~~therein~~ About the 14th inst. when there was no guard on duty in the town, it was contemplated to place one man in the prison for a time. I do not know that he was so confined. If he was it is evident that he had been released on the 16th when Capt Osburn made the examination"—ALS, *ibid.* Buckner wrote on the bottom of this letter. "The prisoner alluded to above as probably have been placed in the jail, was actually taken to my quarters and is now there."—AES, *ibid.*

On Feb. 19, Maj. Alexander Casseday wrote to Buckner. "According to your request I reduce to writing what I know of my own knowledge as to the charge that some Federal soldiers had been tied, stripped of their clothing & cast into the jail at Dover to die. On Yesterday as I was passing the jail in Dover I noticed unusual excitement among the Federal soldiers gathered there. Capt. Baxter A. Q. M. U. S. A. told me several Federal soldiers had been tied & left in the jail to die. I assured him that it could not be true & insisted on his going with me to investigate the matter. ~~We found~~ Capt. Osborne of 'the Body Guard' & three other Federal officers—unknown to me—accompanied us. We found that four dead men were lying upon the floor of one of the vaults. Three of them were evidently Federal soldiers & the other I am satisfied from his uniform was a Confederate soldier. Neither of them was tied; they all had their clothing on & I think their Blankets were under them. With the exception of the one appearing to be a confederate they were carefully laid out ready for ~~inter~~ burial, cotton being placed on the mouths of two of them to conceal and absorb the froth—They had ~~been~~ evidently received medical attention, the bandages carefully placed on the wounds of some of them were visible without removing their clothing. Every indication showed that they had been placed there, after careful attention, laid out for decent burial. Whether the door of the vault had ~~even~~ been locked I do not know. It ought to have been, enough ~~of blood~~ horrible sights had been seen upon the battle field, without exposing the bloody wounds of ghastly corpes, to every curious eye that might wander into a public jail in a crowded street. All of the Federal officers with me expressed themselves satisfied that the charge of inhumanity against the Confederates in this instance was unfounded. The corpses I am satisfied were placed there by some of the U. S. Army"—ALS, *ibid.* On the same day, Buckner endorsed this letter to USG. "This communication is forwarded to Gen. Grant, with the view of correcting the erroneous impression left upon his mind in reference to the care bestowed upon the wounded soldiers found in the cell of the jail."—AES, *ibid.*

1862, Feb. 19.   Maj. Charles T. Larned, chief paymaster, District of Ky. and Tenn., to USG. "The troops under your command being now in my district which embraces Kentucky and Tennessee, I am desirous to obtain information concerning their condition as to pay. If unpaid to Dec. 31st 1861, I wish to make arrangements for immediate payment to include that date, if so paid I would like to have data upon which to base an estimate for payment to include Feb. 28th. The desired information embraces a list of Regts in your division, date to which last paid, the number and if practicable the period of service including Dec. 31st of unpaid regiments, if payment has not been made to Dec. 31st and rolls therefor. are prepared, they should be forwarded at once to this office; if not prepared I will send the necessary blanks and if desired, paym'rs. to assist in their preperation   Another muster is near at hand, and I would like to dispose of the payment due before a second shall fall upon me. I have written to St. Louis for the desired data but, as yet, have not received a reply; if you will direct a statement to be furnished this office without delay, your kind attention thereto will greatly oblidge."—ALS, McClernand Papers, IHi.

1862, FEB. 19.   Capt. Adolph Schwartz, acting chief of staff and aide for Brig. Gen. John A. McClernand, to USG. "I propose to name the battle fought from Feb. 13 to Feb. 16., '*The Battle of the Cumberland*', and wish to know, if this designation meets your approval, or if you have already given an other name to this great historical event."—ADfS, McClernand Papers, IHi.

1862, FEB. 22.   Capt. John A. Rawlins to Brig. Gen. Charles F. Smith. "Your communication just received. I am instructed by Brig Gen. Grant to say to you, that his note, was written under the supposition, that you might have possibly go[t] off last evening."—Copies, DLC-USG, V, 1, 2, 3, 85; DNA, RG 393, USG Letters Sent.

1862, FEB. 22.   Brig. Gen. John A. McClernand to USG. "Maj Bowman 4th Ills Cavalry brings before you Col George Stocker for orders respecting the manner in which he shall be disposed of. Col. Stocker was arrested about fifteen miles from here and is now detained as a prisoner. Maj Bowman will impart all information within his possession relative to the Case."—Copies, McClernand Papers, IHi.

1862, FEB. 24.   USG General Orders No. 8. "In accordance with the Requirements of Army Regulations, the Troops of this command will be mustered for pay on Friday, the 28th inst commencing at 10 O'Clock, A. M. Each Regimental or Detachment Commander, will act as Inspecting Officer for his immediate command, under the supervision of Division or Brigade Commanders."—DS (Capt. John A. Rawlins), McClernand Papers, IHi. Copies of the same orders, numbered General Orders No. 10, are in DLC-USG, V, 12, 13, 14, 95; DNA, RG 393, USG General Orders.

1862, Feb. 24. Capt. John A. Rawlins to George W. Graham. "I am directed by Brig. Gen. Grant, Commdg, to notify you to provide no transportation for troops or Citizens, without orders from these Head Quarters."—Copies, DLC-USG, V, 2, 85; DNA, RG 393, USG Letters Sent.

1862, Feb. 25. Capt. John A. Rawlins to Brig. Gen. John A. McClernand. "I am instructed by Brig. Genl. U. S. Grant to mention to you that a soldier has just presented to these Head Quarters a furlough granted by you through your Asst. Adjt. Genl. without being sent to him for his approval; and in connection therewith to call your attention to enclosed Genl. Orders No. 9, and further to say, that all furloughs or leaves of absence after receiving your Personal endorsement (not that of your Asst. Adjt. Genl. by order) of approval or disapproval will be forwarded to Dist. Head Quarters, addressed to the Asst. Adjt. Genl. (see par. 451 Revised Army Regulations); and not delivered to the applicant to present in person, and when they have been acted upon they will be returned to you or forwarded to Dept. Head Quarters as the particular case may require."—LS, McClernand Papers, IHi. On Feb. 24, Rawlins had issued General Orders No. 9. "Furloughs to enlisted men, and leaves of absence to Commissioned officers are positively prohibited unless approved by the Genl. Comdg. Dist."—DS, *ibid.*

1862, Feb. 25. Capt. William S. Hillyer to Capt. Adolph Schwartz. "I am instructed by Gen Grant that having ascertained since he saw you that Capt Taylor is gathering together the artillery in pursuance of orders, the special order given to you this morning in reference to the same is rescinded."—ALS, McClernand Papers, IHi. On Feb. 25, Capt. John A. Rawlins had issued Special Orders No. 9. "All Artillery captured will be collected, and brought in to near the village of Dover, where a Park of Artillery and ammunition will be established under the superintendence of Capt. A. Schwartz Chief of Staff 1st Division. The grounds for establishing the Park will be selected by Capt. Schwartz Such teams as may be required for collecting the Artillery will be furnished by the different batteries when called for by Capt. Schwartz."—DS, *ibid.* On the same day, Brig. Gen. George W. Cullum telegraphed to USG. "Secretary of war orders inventory to be made of all captured arms & those not serviceable, to be sent to Pittsburgh arsenal"—Copies, DLC-USG, V, 4, 5, 7, 8, 9, 81; DNA, RG 393, USG Hd. Qrs. Correspondence.

1862, FEB. 27. Asst. U. S. Treasurer John J. Cisco to USG. "YOUR FAVOR OF THE 21 February IS RECEIVED WITH ITS INCLOSURE OF A. S. Baxter's DRAFT NO. 25 FOR Two thousand, four hundred DOLLARS, WHICH AMOUNT HAS BEEN PLACED TO THE CREDIT OF YOUR DISBURSING ACCOUNT ON THE BOOKS OF THIS OFFICE. Check & Book sent."—DS, DNA, RG 393, District of West Tenn., Letters Received.

1862, FEB. 28. Brig. Gen. John A. McClernand to USG. "I am informed that 20,000 ~~Bbls~~lbs of bulk Pork ~~is~~ are concealed in a cave about six miles southwest from this place, of which it is supposed that a man in the neighborhood can speak more definitely. Shall I investigate the matter?"—LS, McClernand Papers, IHi. On Feb. 28, Capt. William S. Hillyer endorsed the letter to McClernand. "Investigate the matter"—AES, *ibid.*

1862, FEB. 28. Capt. Wilbur F. Brinck to Capt. John A. Rawlins. "In pursuance of the order of Major Gen U. S. Grant, I proceeded to Cairo Illinois for the purpose of turning over the Ordnance Stores formerly in my charge at Cairo. I would very respectfully inform you that I found Lieut Col Duff had been placed in charge of the Department   The Steamer John Gault on which I had my office and store room, I found had been permited to ground, and partially copacise, the stores falling into the River, others thrown on the Levee in the mud, and scattered in several places without guard, and exposed to the inclement wether   Finding this state of things I could not turn over the property, as it could not be gotton togather to take Invoices, even of such as was not lost, as no transportation could be secured to move the stores to a proper place for examination   I consider it would be very unjust to hold me responsiable for the loss and damage to the stores, after they had been placed in charge of another and by him permitted to be lost, damaged, and scattered   I would therefor very respectfully request that I may be releived from all responsibility in the premises"—ALS, DNA, RG 393, District of West Tenn., Letters Received.

1862, MARCH 1. USG General Orders No. 15. "All Officers of this command now under arrest in this District are hereby released, and will resume their swords and return to duty with their companies or regiments."—DS (Capt. John A. Rawlins), McClernand Papers, IHi.

1862, MARCH 1. USG General Orders No. 16. "Capt. Smith D. Atkins 11th Ills. Vols., being physically disabled from performing the duties of Company commander, is herby detailed as acting Asst. Adjt. Genl. on the Staff of Brig. Genl. S. A. Hurlburt. He will perform the duties appertaining to said office, and will be obeyed and respected accordingly."—DS (Capt. John A. Rawlins), McClernand Papers, IHi. The same orders appear in DLC-USG, V, 12, 95.

In two other letterbooks, however, General Orders No. 16, March 1, is an entirely different document. "The attention of all officers of this command is directed to paragraphs 449, 450 and 451, Army Regulations in regard to official correspondence. The mode there prescribed must be adhered to in future   The careless and unsoldierly manner in which Guard Duty is generally performed calls for the serious displeasure of the General Commanding. Officers in immediate command of troops are alone responsible for for this, and they are again urgently requested to give their personal attention to the subject and see that the neglect of this important duty that now prevails is promptly corrected."—Copies, *ibid.*, V, 13, 14.

1862, MARCH 1. Brig. Gen. John A. McClernand to USG. "Capt. D. H. Fetter, charged with the examination of the Dover and Paris road to the mouth of sandy reports that the road is good to the back water of the Tennessee river, which renders the immediate landing inaccessible. He says, however, that the Ridge or Tennessee road leads to the Metal landing, twelve miles distant which is accessible but adds that this road this side of the Tennessee is considerably cut by waggons, but fine beyond. Falling as the Tennessee is, he thinks the former road will be practicable in two, three or four days. By it the distance would be about the same as by the other road."—Copy, McClernand Papers, IHi.

1862, MARCH 1. Brig. Gen. John A. McClernand to USG. "Henry Rice, a man of strict integrity and large fortune, whose appointment as Brigade Sutler, at Cairo you approved, and whom you recommended for Post Sutler for that place, wishes your written permission to vend goods in the City of Nashville. I hope it may be within your power

and consistent with your views to give him authority to do so."—
Copy, McClernand Papers, IHi. See *Calendar*, [Oct. 29], 1861.

1862, March 3.   Brig. Gen. John A. McClernand to USG. "Having
been informed by you this morning that the 'B.' and 'Tigress' would
take around to the proper point on the Tennessee river, such baggage
and Forage belonging to my division as could not be conveniently
transported overland, I directed Capt. Dunlap to ~~transport~~ transfer
the same on board of one or both of the boats named for that purpose.
Capt Baxter, I am informed, objects to it—desiring that the forage
should be turned over to him, and again that it should be shipped on the
City of Memphis. In answer to this objection I have to say that although
a quantity of corn was turned over to him the other day, by Capt
Dunlap, at his request, he refused to receive it. Again; if the forage
should be shipped on the Memphis delay must follow as she will have
to discharge a considerable amount of freight at Paducah, and as a
Hospital boat will be otherwise liable to detention."—Copy, McClernand Papers, IHi.

1862, March 3.   Ill. AG Allen C. Fuller to USG. "Can you arm
two regiments if I send them to you"—Telegram received, DNA,
RG 393, Dept. of the Mo., Telegrams Received.

1862, March 5.   Capt. Simon M. Preston, St. Louis, to USG. "The
Maj Gen'l Com'd'g the Dept. directs that the requirements of para-
graphs III & IV, in Gen'l Orders No. 27 series 1861 from these Head
Quarters, as far as practicable be complied with by your command.
I send you by mail a few copies for distribution to officers not supplied."
—Copies, DLC-USG, V, 9, 88. On March 19, Capt. John A. Rawlins
wrote to Brig. Gen. John A. McClernand. "Maj. Gen'l U. S. Grant
Com'd'g instructs me to inform you that in pursuance of orders from
Head Quarters of the Dept. just received, the requirements of paragraphs III & IV in Gen'l Orders No. 27 series of 1861 as far as practicable must be complied with by your command, and also to send you
copies of said orders No. 27 which are herwith enclosed for distribution
to Officers not supplied; and further to call your attention to the pub-
lication of Gen'l Orders No. 46 current series of the Dept. by the
reading of the same at the Head of each regiment if it has not already
been done."—LS, McClernand Papers, IHi. General Orders No. 27,
Dept. of the Mo., concerned commissary regulations. General Orders

No. 46, Dept. of the Mo., Feb. 22, was issued "to impress upon all officers the importance of preserving good order and discipline among the troops as the armies of the West advance into Tennessee and other Southern States."—*O.R.*, I, viii, 563–64.

1862, MARCH 5.   C. C. Williamson, Fort Henry, to [USG]. "Statement in reference to Collision between steamers Champion and Belle Memphis."—DLC-USG, V, 10; DNA, RG 393, USG Register of Letters Received.

1862, MARCH 6.   Brig. Gen. John A. McClernand, Metal Landing, Tenn., to USG. "Enclose find charges & specifications prefered against Reader of Band 17th Regt Ills vols. I would suggest that a court martial be convened on board some steamer, and the case disposed of while on the passage up the river."—Copy, McClernand Papers, IHi.

1862, MARCH 6.   Brig. Gen. John A. McClernand to USG. "Notwithstanding the hindrance of falling snow, cold, and back-water my division will have been entirely embarked by 9½ oclock P. M.   Having no instructions to guide me hence I will await them. McAllister's Battery, which after having been received at Paducah was to have been sent to me by Genl Totten has not yet arrived. I trust you will order it to join me the moment it reaches Fort Henry. Good ammunition to replace the bad, now the only reliance for my Artillery, ought to be sent forward,   Forage also is wanted, which, however Capt Dunlap says will probably come up by morning. I would be pleased to see you personally a few minutes before I leave, which I suppose will not be before tomorrow"—Copy, McClernand Papers, IHi.

1862, MARCH 7.   Brig. Gen. William S. Ketchum, act. inspector gen., Dept. of the Mo., to USG. "Please direct the officer detailed to carry out Spl. Orders No. 211. from these Head Quarters, to make 5 muster out rolls. of the 14th Regt. Illinois Volunteers.—One for the Colonel—one for the Adjt. Genls. office, Washington—One for these Hd. Quarters and two for the Paymaster and direct him to charge all clothing drawn and not paid for; also any other other charge due the U. S. in dollars and cents."—Copies, DLC-USG, V, 4, 5, 7, 8, 88; DNA, RG 393, USG Hd. Qrs. Correspondence. On March 7, Capt. John C. Kelton issued Special Orders No. 211, Dept. of the Mo. "Major Genl. U S. Grant will detail an officer to muster out of service the Regimental Band of the 14th Ills. Vols.—"—Copy, *ibid.*, RG 393, Dept. of the Mo., Special Orders; DLC-USG, V, 83.

1862, MARCH 7. Special Orders No. 212, Dept. of the Mo. "It having been certified by Col. John A Logan 31st Regt. Ills. Infantry that Capt. Alexander S. Somerville commanding Co "K" of the said 31st Regt. Ills. Vols., on the 15th day of February 1862, in the Battle of Ft. Donelson in the face of the enemy did then and there exhibit personal fear and trepidation, leaving his command and lying down in a hollow out of danger, and the said certificate having been approved by Brig. Genl. John A. McClernand, and Major Genl. U. S. Grant, and there being no means of speedily trying and punishing said Capt. Somerville by a court martial, it is ordered, and directed that the said Capt. S. Somerville be mustered out of the service of the United States to date from the 15th day of February 1862, and further that this order be read at the head of the 31st Reg't. Ills. Infantry Volunteers.— Major Genl. Grant will see that this order is duly executed."—Copy, DLC-USG, V, 83. On March 14, Capt. John A. Rawlins issued Special Orders No. 24. "In pursuance of Special orders No 212 from Head Quarters Dept. of the Mo. dated St. Louis March 7th 1862 Col. Philip Fouke Com'd'g 30th Ills. infantry Vols. and U. S. forces Ft. Donelson Tenn. is herby detailed to muster out of service of the United States to date from 15th day of Feby. 1862 Capt. Alex. S. Somerville com'd'g Company "K" of the 31st Regt. of Ills. Vols. and further he will cause said Special Orders No 212 of the Dept. of the Mo. be read at the head of the said 31st Reg't. Illinois infantry Vol's"—Copies, *ibid.*, V, 15, 16, 82, 87, 89; DNA, RG 393, USG Special Orders.

1862, MARCH 7. Brig. Gen. John A. McClernand to USG. "One thousand haversacks & canteens are required for my command to enable me to comply with your order which directs the men to carry 3 days cooked rations. I request You to send this number of haversacks & canteens immediately to the Mouth of the Sandy, where my transports are moored. If there are none in the Quartermasters Department at Fort Henry, I would suggest to take them from such regiments as will stay at the Fort, until a new supply can be had."—Copies, McClernand Papers, IHi.

1862, MARCH 10. Brig. Gen. George W. Cullum to USG. "Our Hospitals are overflowing with sick and wounded. Many slight cases are sent down at great. expense & some suffering which can be treated in the Regimental Hospitals as well as here. None but severe cases should be sent to the rear."—Copies, DLC-USG, V, 4, 5, 7, 8, 88; DNA, RG 393, USG Hd. Qrs. Correspondence.

1862, MARCH 14. Brig. Gen. John A. McClernand, Camp Savannah, Tenn., to USG. "Allow me to congratulate you upon your reported restoration to the functions, ~~of your com~~ rank incident to your rank and command. I hope ~~to see you~~ soon to see you with us."—ADfS, McClernand Papers, IHi.

1862, MARCH 15. Maj. Gen. Charles F. Smith to Capt. John A. Rawlins. "I would be glad to have the General's directions in regard to ~~returning~~ sending back steamers. Genl. *McClernand's* division, as I have heretofore reported, occupies this place and its surroundings, hence I have been enabled to send back the transports of his command. Am I to disembark more troops? or keep them in hand for expeditions? I have now *Wallas's* division with its transportation at Crump's Landing, about 3½ miles up; *Hurlbut's* division with its transportation at Pittsburgh some 9 miles up—watching Genl. *Cheatem* and to prevent his moving against Genl *Sherman*; and *Sherman's* division with its transportation at *Cook's* landing still farther up (see my letter of yesterday). This is all apropos of keeping the transports with the troops. The gunboats are with *Sherman* and *Hurlbut*. I have not had time to hear from ~~Shem~~ *Sherman's* attempt; indeed he did not, I suppose, arrive ~~before~~ at his point of Landing before last night; and, as it rained hard all day yesterday and partly during the night I think he cannot make much progress during ~~the~~ to day. One other point in the matter of transportation occurs to me. There are no buildings in the town suitable for storing our supplies, hence they are kept afloat and the steamer remains as a matter of course."—ALS, DNA, RG 393, District of West Tenn., Letters Received.

1862, MARCH 18. Capt. John H. Hammond, asst. adjt. gen. to Brig. Gen. William T. Sherman, Pittsburg Landing, to Capt. John A. Rawlins. "The Division Surgeon having placed some 100 or more sick on board the Fanny Bullitt, I have permitted her to take them on to Savannah. There is neither house nor building of any kind, that can be used for a Hospital here. I hope to receive an order to establish floating Hospitals, but in the mean time, by the advice of the Surgeon, allow these to leave. Let me hope that it will meet with your approbation. The Order for debarkation came while Gen'l Sherman was absent with three Brigades, & no men left to move the effects of these Brigades. The landing too is small, with scarcely any chance to increase it. Therefore there is a great accumulation of Boats. Col McArthur has arrived and is now *cutting* a landing for himself. Gen'l Sherman will return this evening. I am obliged to transgress, and write myself in the meantime"—Copy, DNA, RG 94, Generals' Papers and Books, William T. Sherman, Letters Sent. At 4 P. M. of the same day, Sherman added a postscript. "Just back, have been half way to Corinth and to Purdy—all right—have just read this letter, and approve all but floating Hospitals. Regimental Surgeons can take care of all sick except chronic cases, which can always be sent down to Paducah   Magnificent plain for camping and drilling, and a military point of great strength. The enemy has felt us twice at great loss and demoralization—will report at length this evening   am now much worn out."—Copy, *ibid.* On the same day, John Riggin, Jr., wrote to Sherman. "You will use for Hospital purposes such boats as are now used for stores until permanent Hospital Boats are provided."—Copies, DLC-USG, V, 1, 2, 3, 86; DNA, RG 393, USG Letters Sent.

1862, MARCH 18.   Surgeon Henry S. Hewit to Capt. John A. Rawlins. "I have the honor to acknowledge a communication from Brig. General Sherman on the subject of the sick of his Division referred to me from Hd. Qrs. In reference to the subject I have th[e] honor to say that orders have been given to prepare accommodations in this town for 1000 sick and that all the available buildings are being converted into Hospitals. I beg leave to call your attention to the fact that there is great carelessness in sending off soldiers p[ur]porting to be sick from their re[gi]ments. and that many men who would recover in a few days with their regiments are hurried away or allowed to smuggle themselves on board the boats bringing sick—The Steamer City of Memphis is a floating hospital and will be due here tomorrow. A large requisition for medicines and hospital stores will be forwarded to St Louis to night—I deem it my duty to represent that severe and spreading sickness is impending and that urgent appeals should be made to the Head Quarters of this Dept. to provide for this inevitable burden."—ALS, DNA, RG 393, District of West Tenn., Letters Received.

Hewit enclosed an undated letter of W. R. Marsh, act. brigade surgeon, to Col. Jacob G. Lauman. "Orders having been recd. by the Capt of the White Cloud to put off all troops freight forth with, and the City of Memphis the Gen'l Hospital boat not having arrived it becomes necessary to make provision for the sick of the 7th Iowa. The same will doubtless soon be true of the whole brigade. Unable to find Division Surgeon who should provide for such contingencies I respect to suggest that you procure and order of the Gen'l. Comd., a portioning to this brigade one boat as a brigade hospital until further arrangements can be effected"—ALS, *ibid.* Lauman added an undated endorsement to Brig. Gen. William T. Sherman. "It is desired if it can be done that the above wish of the Brig Surgeon be carried into effect" —AES, *ibid.* On March 18, Sherman endorsed the letter. "I understand that Genl Smith has arrived and it is his duty to determine this question. My own opinion, after seeing the straggling sick that pass into Paducah, is that the sick men of different Regiments will receive better care & attention here along with their comrades at the Regimental Hospital tent, (or house easily built) than at the General Hospital at Paducah. I have therefore had all the sick of my Division provided for here."—AES, *ibid.* Also on March 18, Hewit endorsed the letter. "The application for a steamboat is disapproved   Genl Sherman's endorsement is a correct view of the subject—Respectfully referred to the Major Genl Commanding"—AES, *ibid.*

1862, MARCH 19.   Capt. Nathaniel H. McLean to USG. "Respectfully referred to Maj General Grant who will enquire into this accusation against Col Tuttle and report   This paper to be returned with said Report"—Copy, DLC-USG, V, 88. Written on a letter from H. L. Vasseur, vice consul of France, St. Louis, to Maj. Gen. Henry W. Halleck. "The undersigned Vice Consul of France at St Louis has the honor to transmit to you the following Claim which has been addressed to him by S Verlaque, french subject. Mr Verlaque (Sigismond) Tailor born at Salernes, Department of the Var, France, going from Memphis (Tennessee) to St Louis Mo. was arrested in the first days of February last at Commerce, Mo by order of, Col Tuttle Comdg 2nd Regt Iowa Vols, the papers and money which he has with him were seized, and when the next day he was allowed to proceed on his Journey, the money seized, amounting to the sum of about Ninety Dollars, could not be returned to him   all the efforts made by Mr Verlaque to regain possession of that sum have remained until now without result   In consequence the undersigned has the honor to request Major General Halleck to take if possible in consideration the demand of Mr Verlaque who is thus left without means ~~of~~ and in the impossibility to proceed on his Journey"—Copy, *ibid.*

1862, MARCH 20.   USG Special Orders No. 30. "O. H. Ross is herby appointed Special Mail Ag't. to take charge of, forward and receive all mails on the Tenn. River. He will appoint a place where all mails for the North will be received"—Copies, DLC-USG, V, 15, 16, 82, 87, 89; DNA, RG 393, USG Special Orders. See letter to Capt. Reuben B. Hatch, Dec. 23, 1861.

1862, [MARCH 21].   USG endorsement on a letter of Brig. Gen. Lewis Wallace to Secretary of War Edwin M. Stanton. "States that a letter was received from Hon H S Lane on 3rd of Feby stating that R E Bryant had been apptd Commissary. If he has not been apptd. asks that he may be and the request is endorsed by Genl Grant"—DNA, RG 107, Register of Letters Received. On April 5, Asst. Secretary of War Peter H. Watson wrote to Wallace that Capt. Robert E. Bryant already had been appointed.— Copy, *ibid.*, Letters Sent. On March 24, Wallace wrote to Stanton inquiring about the appointment of Capt. Charles W. Lyman as brigade q. m., and this letter was also endorsed by USG.—*Ibid.*, Register of Letters Received. On April 5, Watson wrote to Wallace that Lyman already had been appointed.—Copy, *ibid.*, Letters Received.

1862, MARCH 21.   Brig. Gen. John A. McClernand, Savannah, to USG. "On the 18th instant, I despatched Col L. F. Ross, Commanding the Third Brigade, upon an expedition in the direction of Wayesborough, for the purpose of clearing that section of country of Marauders, and destroying supplies collected for the rebel Army. The force assigned Col Ross for this expedition, comprised three regiments of infantry, Seven companies of Cavalry, and two twelve pounders howitzers from Taylors battery. The expedition proceeded on the 18th about two miles, encamping for the night on Steels Creek, near the plantations of Mr *Guold* and Mr *Carter*. On the morning of the 19th the force moved early over roads made heavy by rains during the night. A small town called 'Pin-Hook' was reached about noon, no enemy appearing. Learning that a mill some five miles north-east from 'Pin-Hook' and owned by a rebel named Martin, had been employed in Manufacturing Flour for the rebel army, Col Ross, proceeded and took possession of it and found some 150 Sacks of flour, with full evidence of its belonging to the enemy. He destroyed about 100 Sacks, distributing the remainder among the poor people of the neighborhood who had suffered from the lawless depredations of the public enemy. Col Ross, returned to Camp and reported about 10 o'clock yesterday Morning. He represents the country as hilly, and well settled and cultivated, especially in the Creek bottoms. He found the enemy to have left the country towards Columbia, probably crossing the Tennessee River at Florence. Evidence of loyal sentiment every where appeard, and the inhabitants were pursuing peaceably, their usual avocations. The expedition was conducted by Col Ross with his usual energy and judgment, and returned without molestation, and successful in its object."—LS, DNA, RG 393, District of West Tenn., Letters Received; ADf (dated March 20), McClernand Papers, IHi.

1862, MARCH 22. Capt. John A. Rawlins to Col. Michael K. Lawler. "I am instructed by Maj Genl U. S. Grant to say your leave of absence was granted to enable you to recover from Wounds recd in actions. All that is required of you is to report regularly every two weeks— your condition, and as soon as able report for duty with your Regt." —LS, Lawler Papers, ICarbS.

1862, MARCH 22. Brig. Gen. John A. McClernand to USG. "Under your order, an order was issued from these Head Quarters directing the *Surplus*. property in my command, to be delivered to Capt A. S. Norton Div. Qr Master, and by him to Capt A. S. Baxter Chief Qr Master of the Expedition. Capt Norton being about to accompany my command, reports to me that having recieved such property, he called to deliver the same to Capt Baxter—that (Capt Baxter being absent) he was informed by a Clerk that Capt B. declined to recieve ~~them~~; *without your order*. Capt Norton calls upon you to secure the aid of such order, if necessary, that he may be enabled to leave this post with his Division"—Copies, McClernand Papers, IHi.

1862, MARCH 22. Maj. Mason Brayman to Capt. John A. Rawlins. "Genl McClernand directs that Major Genl Grant be furnished a copy of letter of Col. I. N. Haynie, 48th Regt Ills. Vols. and to invoke the influence and authority of Genl Grant to induce a favorable respons[e] to the urgent and just appeal which is made. The condition of this Regiment is the condition of money others. Genl McClernand under this influence of similar representations and from his own knowledge of facts, brought the same matter to the notice of Maj. Genl Smith during his temporary command. Genl McClernand adds the remark that the men thus suffering finding their expectations with reference to the support of their families, and their own comfort while on exacting service, thus disappointed naturally conclude that their Goverment forgets them, and lose much of that fervour and ready disposition which induced their enlistment thus weakening the effeciency of the service. Genl McClernand would again request Major Genl Grant to make an effort (as he has once kindly done) to have the assignment of Major Cook to thise District of West Tenn with instructions to pay the troops now in this service and enduring these privations."—Copy, McClernand Papers, IHi.

1862, MARCH 25.   Col. T. Lyle Dickey, 4th Ill. Cav., to USG, sending "Statement of condition of the men under his command."—DLC-USG, V, 10; DNA, RG 393, USG Register of Letters Received.

1862, MARCH 26.   Maj. Gen. John A. McClernand to USG. "Painful and overwhelming domestic afflictions and almost of humanity itself, that one of ablest and best Brigade commanders should return home I allude to Col. Ross. If you should think proper to give him a temporary leave of absence arrangements will have to be made for a successor in the command of his Brigade, who will act until his return. I would recommend Col. Haynie, whose assignment for that purpose would require some exchanges of regiments, which will be explained by Col. Ross. Or if Col. Lawler returns before leave of absence should be granted to Col. Ross, he would a strong claim and would well answer" —Copy, McClernand Papers, IHi. Col. Leonard F. Ross, who had just received news of the death of his wife, left for Lewiston, Ill., on March 26.—"General Leonard F. Ross," *Iowa Historical Record*, IV, 4 (Oct., 1888), 173. During Ross' absence, Col. John S. Rearden commanded the 3rd Brigade, 1st Division.

1862, MARCH 30.   Special Orders No. 53, Dept. of the Miss. "Lieutenants Ludwick Felt and Wood Acting Signal Officers with the Six enlisted men under their charge will immediately proceed to the Dist of West Tennessee and report to Major Genl U S Grant to carry out such instructions as they may have received from the chief of their Corps The Quartermaster Dept will provide the necessary transportation"—Copy, DLC-USG, V, 83. On April 9, Capt. John A. Rawlins issued Special Orders No. 49. "Division Commanders will detail at once two 2nd Lieutenants from each Brigade and two enlisted men to each Officer to report to Lieut J. B. Ludwick on the Steamer Tigress As these officers and men are to recieve instructions in signaling, young men of inteligence who can learn rapidly will be selected." —DS, McClernand Papers, IHi; copies, DLC-USG, V, 15, 16, 82, 87, 89; DNA, RG 393, USG Special Orders.

1862, MARCH 31. Maj. Gen. John A. McClernand to USG. "that one steamer can conveniently debark troops at Pittsburg Landing, as soon as a boat is loaded here, order to proceed to her destination."— Register of Letters, McClernand Papers, IHi.

Index

All letters written by USG of which the text was available for use in this volume are indexed under the names of the recipients. The dates of these letters are included in the index as an indication of the existence of text. Abbreviations used in the index are explained on pp. xvi-xx. Individual regts. are indexed under the names of the states in which they originated.

paign, 183*n*, 195, 196*n*, 210*n*; occupies Nashville, 215*n*, 255*n*, 278, 279*n*, 280*n*, 281*n*, 282, 283*n*, 284, 286, 288*n*, 296, 298*n*, 307*n*, 415, 416*n*; sends troops to USG, 231*n*, 261*n*; promoted, 272*n*, 275*n*, 431*n*; USG confers with, 292, 293–94, 294*n*; letter to, Feb. 27, 1862, 293–94; requests troops at Nashville, 293–94, 296, 299 and *n*, 304–5, 306; returns troops to Clarksville, 305*n*, 318; in Tennessee River campaign, 319*n*, 361 and *n*, 367*n*, 392*n*, 393–94, 394*n*, 397, 423, 424, 428, 430*n*, 446*n*, 452*n*; telegram to, March 14, 1862, 361; letter to, March 19, 1862, 393–94; USG sends scouts to, 393–94, 394*n*, 396; USG comments on, 406; mentioned, 54, 141*n*, 154*n*, 205, 267, 341*n*, 343*n*, 441*n*, 448*n*

Buford, Napoleon B. (Ill. Vols.): letter to, Jan. 10, 1862, 29; commands Cairo, 29 and *n*, 76*n*; and Reuben B. Hatch's reports, 44*n*, 58; letter to, Jan. 14, 1862, 58; letter to, Jan. 31, 1862, 126; ordered to vacate buildings, 467; mentioned, 19*n*, 111*n*, 126*n*, 255*n*

Bulliss, Robert E. (Mo. Vols.): assigned to duty, 228*n*, 254; killed, 343*n*, 351, 351*n*–52*n*, 353*n*

Burgess, Thomas H. (Ill. Vols.), 92*n*

Burne, M. H. (of Cairo), 114*n*

Burnville, Tenn., 369*n*, 380*n*

Burrell, Orlando (Ill. Vols.), 468

*C*airo (gunboat), 246*n*, 262*n*, 279, 280*n*, 452*n*

Cairo, Ill.: forces sent to Ky. from, 7, 8, 11, 19, 19*n*–20*n*, 57*n*, 74; q.m. problems at, 22, 35, 36*n*, 37–38, 43*n*, 44 and *n*, 46–47, 47*n*, 52*n*, 55*n*, 58 and *n*, 79–80, 80*n*–84*n*, 97–98, 98*n*, 111*n*, 114*n*, 115*n*, 116*n*, 117*n*, 118*n*, 127*n*, 208*n*, 209, 210*n*; prisoners at, 25*n*, 87, 93, 140*n*, 162 and *n*, 170*n*, 221*n*, 226*n*, 233, 234*n*, 235 and *n*, 246, 248, 289*n*, 352*n*, 436*n*, 449–50, 450*n*, 459, 464; hospitals at, 25*n*, 231*n*, 235*n*, 260*n*, 261*n*, 283, 330, 403*n*, 442, 471, 473, 486–87; commander of, 29 and *n*, 100*n*, 118*n*, 129, 134–35, 173*n*, 231*n*, 450*n*; gunboats at, 49*n*–50*n*, 104*n*, 215*n*, 216*n*, 378; troops sent to, 53, 54*n*, 70*n*, 72*n*, 76, 85, 94, 133*n*, 138, 261*n*, 282*n*–83*n*, 471; USG returns to, 63, 74, 100*n*; steamboats at, 73, 85*n*, 111*n*, 114*n*, 115*n*, 125 and *n*, 127–28, 138, 205*n*, 294, 300*n*–301*n*, 340 and *n*, 342*n*, 359*n*, 463; forces leave for Fort Henry, 104*n*, 124, 131 and *n*, 132, 138, 149, 160*n*,

234; ammunition at, 126, 282*n*, 482; garrisoned, 132, 134 and *n*, 141, 142*n*, 143*n*, 289*n*, 297*n*, 303*n*; gunboats sent from, 182, 203, 328*n*–29*n*; mail service at, 204*n*, 205*n*, 227; bank, 212*n*; gunboats sent to, 260*n*, 262*n*, 278, 280*n*, 281*n*, 474; captured property sent to, 285*n*, 295, 325*n*, 330, 333, 354*n*, 421; administration at criticized, 287*n*–88*n*; Julia Dent Grant leaves, 292, 412; teams sent from, 302*n*–3*n*, 306; telegraph at, 320*n*, 464, 473; art. at sent to USG, 429, 431*n*; mentioned, 4*n*, 16*n*, 17*n*, 18*n*, 22, 28, 31*n*, 33*n*, 39*n*, 60, 61*n*, 78*n*, 88, 112*n*, 130, 142, 158*n*, 164*n*, 168*n*, 187, 211, 251, 266, 277*n*, 304, 307*n*, 326*n*, 331, 375, 405*n*, 406, 414, 415, 419*n*, 443, 462, 466, 470, 483

Calloway, Ky., 90*n*, 100*n*

Cameron, Simon (U.S. Secretary of War), 47*n*, 118*n*, 119*n*, 189*n*, 191*n*

Camp Beauregard, Ky.: threatened, 3, 4*n*, 11, 12; weakened, 51*n*; abandoned, 74, 75*n*, 247*n*

Campbell, Benjamin H. (of Galena), 116*n*

Campbell, Charles C. (Ill. Vols.), 65*n*

Campbell, Hugh (commission member), 355*n*

Camp Butler, Springfield, Ill., 77*n*

Camp Chase, Columbus, Ohio, 88*n*, 240*n*, 248*n*

Camp Dennison, Cincinnati, Ohio, 431*n*

Camp Dick Robinson, Garrard County, Ky., 280*n*

Camp Douglas, Chicago, Ill., 41, 84, 85*n*, 226*n*

Camp Jackson, St. Louis, Mo., 381*n*

Cape Girardeau, Mo.: steamboat returns to, 16*n*, 85*n*; cav. at, 33*n*, 94, 465, 473–74, 475; troops at, 64, 70 and *n*, 76 and *n*, 94, 122*n*, 161*n*, 289*n*; passports given at, 94 and *n*; command disputed at, 95, 95*n*–96*n*; prisoners at, 109, 109*n*–10*n*; ferry boat at, 114*n*, 462–63; letter to commanding officer, Feb. 6, 1862, 161*n*; telegram to commanding officer, Feb. 7, 1862, 161*n*; mentioned, 461, 463, 464, 468

Carbondale, Ill., 464

Carlin, William P. (Ill. Vols.), 130 and *n*, 131*n*

Carmichael, Eagleton (Ill. Vols.), 129, 253

Carondelet (gunboat): at Fort Henry, 160*n*; at Fort Donelson, 183*n*, 200, 201 and *n*, 202*n*–3*n*, 207*n*, 214*n*, 215*n*; sent to Nashville, 282; needed on Tennessee River, 361

Carpenter, Charles (scout): irregular services of, 16, 16*n*–17*n*; arrested, 153, 174